FOUNDATIONS OF GOVERNANCE:
MUNICIPAL GOVERNMENT IN CANADA'S PROVINCES

Municipalities are responsible for many essential services and have become vital agents for implementing provincial policies, including those dealing with the environment, emergency planning, economic development, and land use. In *Foundations of Governance*, experts from each of Canada's provinces come together to assess the extent to which municipal governments have the capacity to act autonomously, purposefully, and collaboratively in the intergovernmental arena.

Each chapter follows a common template in order to facilitate comparison and covers essential features such as institutional structures, municipal functions, demography, and municipal finances. Canada's municipalities function in diverse ways but have similar problems and, in this way, are illustrative of the importance of local democracy. *Foundations of Governance* shows that municipal governments require the legitimacy granted by a vibrant democracy in order to successfully negotiate and implement important collective choices about the futures of communities.

ANDREW SANCTON is a professor in the Department of Political Science at the University of Western Ontario.

ROBERT YOUNG is a professor in the Department of Political Science at the University of Western Ontario and Canada Research Chair in Multilevel Governance.

The Institute of Public Administration of Canada Series in Public Management and Governance

Editor: Patrice Dutil

This series is sponsored by the Institute of Public Administration of Canada as part of its commitment to encourage research on issues in Canadian public administration, public sector management, and public policy. It also seeks to foster wider knowledge and understanding among practitioners, academics, and the general public.

For a list of books published in the series, see page 545.

EDITED BY ANDREW SANCTON
AND ROBERT YOUNG

Foundations of Governance:

Municipal Government in Canada's Provinces

IPAC
The Institute of
Public Administration of Canada

IAPC
L'Institut d'administration
publique du Canada

UNIVERSITY OF TORONTO PRESS
Toronto   Buffalo   London

© University of Toronto Press Incorporated 2009
Toronto Buffalo London
www.utppublishing.com
Printed in Canada

ISBN 978-0-8020-9709-5 (cloth)
ISBN 978-0-8020-9650-0 (paper)

∞

Printed on acid-free paper

Library and Archives Canada Cataloguing in Publication

Foundations of governance : municipal government in Canada's provinces /
edited by Andrew Sancton and Robert Young.

(The Institute of Public Administration of Canada series in public manage-
ment and governance)
Includes bibliographical references and index.
ISBN 978-0-8020-9709-5 (bound)   ISBN 978-0-8020-9650-0 (pbk.)

1. Municipal government – Canada – Provinces.   2. Municipal government
– Canada.   I. Sancton, Andrew, 1948–   II. Young, Robert Andrew
III. Institute of Public Administration of Canada   IV. Series: Institute of
Public Administration of Canada series in public management and gover-
nance

JS1709.F69 2009   320.8'50971   C2009-901062-3

Canada School   École de la fonction
of Public Service   publique du Canada

Financial support from the Canada School of Public Service for this book is
gratefully acknowledged. The views expressed herein are not necessarily
those of the Canada School of Public Service or of the Government of Canada.

University of Toronto Press acknowledges the financial assistance to its
publishing program of the Canada Council for the Arts and the Ontario Arts
Council.

University of Toronto Press acknowledges the financial support for its
publishing activities of the Government of Canada through the
Book Publishing Industry Development Program (BPIDP).

Contents

Contributors

Serge Belley is professor at the National School of Public Administration (Quebec). His main areas of study and research concern municipal administration and the analysis of local and regional policies.

Laurence Bherer is assistant professor of political science at l'Université de Montréal. She researches public policy, urban politics, and democracy at the local level, and is co-editor of *Jeux d'échelle et transformation de l'État: le gouvernement des territoires au Québec et en France*.

Daniel Bourgeois is executive director of the Beaubassin Institute, an independent institute that conducts research on public policies. His research focuses on administrative decentralization, notably substate institutions like municipal councils, school boards and health authorities, and public services to minority groups. He is also an elected councillor for the city of Moncton.

Jeff Braun-Jackson is a former lecturer in the Political Science Department at Memorial University where he taught from 1995 to 2006. He has worked on provincial health-care reform and issues of regionalization in Newfoundland and Labrador, and is currently with the Ontario Professional Fire Fighters Association in Burlington, Ontario.

David M. Bulger is adjunct professor of political studies and philosophy at the University of Prince Edward Island.

David Cameron is professor emeritus in the Department of Political Science at Dalhousie University. He has written extensively on policy issues related to education and municipal government in Canada.

Tom Carter is the Canada Research Chair in Urban Change and Adaptation and professor of geography at the University of Winnipeg.

Guy Chiasson is a political scientist. He teaches local politics as well as regional development at the Université du Québec en Outaouais. His current research projects are on forest-policy renewal in Canada and urban governance in mid-sized cities.

Jean-Pierre Collin teaches urban studies at the Institut national de la recherche scientifique (INRS–Urbanisation, Culture et Société) in Montreal. He is the scientific director of the Villes-Régions-Monde network on urban and regional studies, and has recently edited, with Mélanie Robertson, *Governing Metropolises: Profiles of Issues and Depictions of Experiments in Four Continents.*

James Feehan is professor of economics at Memorial University of Newfoundland where he also serves as the joint director of the Institute of Social and Economic Research and the Smallwood Foundation for Newfoundland and Labrador Studies. His main research areas are public finance, the economics of public infrastructure, fiscal federalism, and the impact of natural-resource development.

Joseph Garcea is an associate professor of political studies at the University of Saskatchewan. He is co-editor of *Municipal Reform in Canada* and *Local Government Reform: A Comparative Analysis of Advanced Anglo-American Countries.*

Donald Gilchrist is an associate professor of economics and associate member in the School of Public Policy at the University of Saskatchewan.

Pierre Hamel is professor of sociology at the Université de Montréal and editor of the journal *Sociologie et sociétés.* His latest book is *Ville et débat public: Agir en démocratie.*

Pierre J. Hamel is a research professor at the Institut national de la recherche scientifique (INRS–Urbanisation, Culture et Société). He is interested in local public finance, ranging from local public-service management to local taxation, and has recently published *Public-Private Partnerships (P3s) and Municipalities: Beyond Principles, a Brief Overview of Practices.*

Edward C. LeSage, Jr is professor emeritus, Faculty of Extension, University of Alberta. Currently living in Salem, Oregon, where he pursues independent scholarship, he is co-editor of the recently published *Local Government Reform: A Comparative Analysis of Advanced Anglo-American Countries*.

Melville McMillan is a professor in the Department of Economics at the University of Alberta. His research and teaching interests are in public economics and, in particular, urban and local economics, fiscal federalism, and the demand for and supply of public goods and services. He has been a student of local government in Canada and internationally throughout his career.

Ron Penney is an adjunct professor with the Department of Political Science, Memorial University of Newfoundland. He is also chief commissioner (chief administrative officer) and city solicitor with the city of St John's.

Mathieu Rivard is the research coordinator at the Intergovernmental Committee on Urban and Regional Research (ICURR).

Andrew Sancton is a professor of political science and director of the Local Government Program at the University of Western Ontario. His latest book is *The Limits of Boundaries: Why City-regions Cannot Be Self-Governing*.

Jim Sentance is an associate professor and currently chair of the Department of Economics at the University of Prince Edward Island.

David Siegel is professor of political science at Brock University. He has written extensively in the fields of local government and public administration.

Patrick Smith is director of the Institute of Governance Studies and professor of political science at Simon Fraser University. He is also co-editor of the *Canadian Political Science Review*.

Kennedy Stewart is an assistant professor in Simon Fraser University's Graduate Public Policy Program and a research associate with the London School of Economics' Public Policy Group.

Frank Strain is professor of economics and the Dorothy and Edgar Davidson Chair in Canadian Studies at Mount Allison University in Sackville, New Brunswick.

Stephen Tomblin is a professor in the departments of Political Science and Medicine (Community Health) at Memorial University of Newfoundland. He has published widely on the issues of regional integration, economic development, and health restructuring.

Robert Young is a professor of political science at the University of Western Ontario, where he holds the Canada Research Chair in Multilevel Governance. He leads the Major Collaborative Research Initiative on multilevel governance and public policy in Canadian municipalities.

Preface

This book is a contribution to the study of local government in Canada and of the provincial-municipal systems that we believe are the foundations of governance in this country. We hope that it will be of interest and use to practitioners and that it will serve as a basic reference work and educational resource for students and scholars.

The use here of the term 'foundations' of governance is not meant to suggest that other Canadian governments are in some way built on municipal governments. The federal and provincial governments in Canada are constitutionally established whereas municipal governments and other local authorities fall squarely under provincial jurisdiction. But what is foundational across the country are the provincial-municipal systems of governance. On the one hand, municipalities deliver to citizens vital services such as policing, local roads, water supply, waste and sewage disposal, libraries, cultural facilities, and public transit. In the past, local authorities associated with municipalities also made significant decisions about important services – education, health, and social services – which have been gradually provincialized over the past several decades. But on the other hand, as provincial governments' activities have broadened in scope, municipal governments increasingly have come to serve as agents that implement provincial policy. They respond not only to their principal supervisory department within provincial governments but also to many other departments that regulate economic and social activity, in areas like land use, building standards, water quality, agriculture, the environment, emergency planning, and many others. This is why we think of local governments, in systemic partnership with the provinces, as foundational to governance in Canada.

While it stands alone as contribution to the literature, this collection forms part of a larger enterprise, a Major Collaborative Research Initiative (MCRI) funded by the Social Sciences and Humanities Research Council of Canada (SSHRC). The project title is 'Multilevel Governance and Public Policy in Canadian Municipalities.' It involves the coordinated efforts of over eighty researchers and a great many student research assistants. Our work has resulted in two other books. Edited by Robert Young and Christian Leuprecht, *Municipal-Federal-Provincial Relations in Canada* is a collection of diverse essays on multilevel governance involving municipalities, while *Spheres of Governance: Comparative Studies of Cities in Multilevel Governance Systems*, edited by Harvey Lazar and Christian Leuprecht, was intended to lay out some major structural alternatives to the Canadian system. The essays collected here in *Foundations of Governance* are overviews of the provincial-municipal systems, designed to orient further research into multilevel governance within the various provinces and in the major cities of Canada. A great deal more of this work will be forthcoming.

Careful readers will discern that most chapters were completed in mid-2008. Knowing that a volume such as this can never be completely up to date, we have resisted the temptation to make last-minute revisions to account for recent changes. We will be satisfied if the book better enables our readers to track such changes themselves.

For supporting a project of this magnitude, we are much indebted to SSHRC and its helpful officials. We also wish to thank the University of Western Ontario for some core support. For their interest in this book, we thank the Institute of Public Administration of Canada and the University of Toronto Press. Our own research was aided by Ajay Sharma at Western and Aldo Diaz at Statistics Canada, and some organizational help came from Ben Elling. Mario Levesque skilfully produced a comprehensive and useful index. We are grateful to our contributors for their perseverance. Our greatest debt is to Kelly McCarthy, the project manager of the MCRI. Not only did she support a complex network of researchers and maintain voluminous sets of files, but she also brought the manuscript to fruition by helping with editing and proofreading, finalizing all the financial data, and doing a formidable job with corrections and layout. Thank you Kelly.

FOUNDATIONS OF GOVERNANCE:
MUNICIPAL GOVERNMENT IN CANADA'S PROVINCES

Introduction

ANDREW SANCTON

This collection of essays is the most comprehensive attempt ever to describe and analyse the systems of municipal government in Canada's ten provinces.[1] It has been fraught with challenges, not the least of which are the huge differences in the populations of the provinces and the resulting variations in what their respective municipalities are expected to do. By assigning the writing of the essays to academic experts in each province, we gain the benefits that derive from detailed local knowledge. The disadvantage of this approach is that it is often hard for local authors to understand fully what is special or unique about their own systems in comparison with others. We have tried to mitigate this problem by developing a common template for all of the provincial essays, by meeting together on two separate occasions as our work proceeded, and by circulating drafts as we went along.

Our fundamental concern is to assess the extent to which municipal governments in Canada have the capacity to act autonomously, purposefully, and collaboratively in the intergovernmental arena. Conventional assessments in the past have focused on the fact that municipalities are 'creatures of the provinces.' Although constitutionally such a statement is obviously true and significant, we are less interested in formal, legal arrangements than we are with what municipal governments actually do, how they do it, and how they relate to other levels of government. These essays are primarily concerned with how municipalities relate to their respective provincial governments rather than to the federal government.

Authors were asked to discuss at least seven different factors within each province that we believe are crucial for understanding municipal capacity: 1) structures; 2) functions; 3) finances; 4) the nature of provincial oversight; 5) demography; 6) political culture; and 7) the ways in which various types of municipal interests are organized and articulated within the province. Each in turn will now briefly be introduced.

Structures

We need to know about municipal structures. At its core, this has to do with the size of municipalities. In theory, each province could have only a very few municipalities. Having, say, four municipalities in Ontario (north, east, southwest, and the Toronto city-region) would presumably mean that each of these 'municipalities' would have a huge budget and many staff with highly specialized skills. In these senses, they would have considerable capacity. But there is no prospect of such municipalities ever emerging, because everyone would acknowledge that municipalities of such size would be too big for almost all the functions that municipalities perform and it would be impossible for separate cities and towns to adopt policies to meet their own particular circumstances.[2]

In the past in Canada, there has been considerable commitment (in theory by 'experts' and in practice by governments in at least our larger provinces) to the notion that large city-regions are best governed by two tiers of municipal government, one for the larger region and another 'lower' tier in which there are a number of distinct municipalities to look after more local concerns.[3] With the exceptions of the regional municipalities of Waterloo, Niagara, Halton, Peel, York, and Durham (all of which have now been included by the Ontario government in the Toronto-centred 'Greater Golden Horseshoe'), Canada no longer has any two-tier systems of urban municipal government. A powerful case can be made that regional districts in British Columbia (especially as they relate to Vancouver and Victoria) are really two-tier urban systems, but the fact that the government of British Columbia has for forty years resisted the idea that regional districts are a distinct and formal level of government must at least be acknowledged, especially because such treatment might be an explanation of their longevity, if not their success. Since 2002, the Montreal and Quebec city-regions have both been covered by new municipal institutions known as 'metropolitan communities,' but they have very limited functional authority.

For good or ill, then, most of our urban areas are governed by a single tier of municipal government. How large these municipalities should be has been a topic of great debate in recent years in Canada and several of us have been on different sides.[4] Signs of the differing positions can be seen in the essays that follow. One point to note at this stage is that the central-city municipalities of Calgary, Ottawa, Edmonton, and Winnipeg (not to mention Toronto and Montreal), and even the suburban municipality of Mississauga, are all more populous than the city of Vancouver. Readers of our essays might wish to consider whether or not Vancouver gains or loses by having a central-city municipality that is relatively small for the size of its metropolitan region.

In the least populated areas of most provinces, there is no municipal government at all and, because of a desire to avoid property taxes as much as possible, the few residents of such areas generally have no desire for change. As Daniel Bourgeois and Frank Strain show in their essay, this is a serious problem in New Brunswick. Until the late 1960s, it was a serious problem in British Columbia as well, but the creation of regional districts has largely solved it. In most parts of populated rural Canada there is only one tier of municipal government. In Quebec there are two, the upper tier being 'municipal regional counties.' In the aftermath of municipal amalgamations in Ontario in the mid-and late 1990s, it is almost impossible to generalize about that province. In his essay on Ontario, David Siegel aptly states that 'a variety of forms were adopted, but it was clear that the large single-tier entity was the hallmark of this era.'

Functions

Our chapters on Ontario and Nova Scotia are of necessity more concerned with municipal functions than are the chapters for other provinces. This is because over the last two decades both provinces have been involved in a difficult process of rearranging functional responsibilities between the provincial and municipal levels. In both provinces, municipalities ended up with responsibility for a great many roads that had previously been under provincial jurisdiction. In Nova Scotia, municipalities lost responsibility for social services, while in Ontario municipal responsibility in this field was dramatically increased, leaving Ontario as the only Canadian province with substantial municipal responsibility for social services. In return, Ontario municipalities were given increased access to property-tax revenues since school boards no longer had the right to add their levy and the province increased its share of education funding. There has been much rhetoric in recent years about municipalities taking on increased responsibilities. Except in Ontario, there is very little evidence that this is the case.

For the other provinces, we decided that municipal functions were sufficiently similar that the volume's editors would be responsible for outlining common functions. The task of the authors of each provincial study would be to highlight in what respects their respective provinces differed from the norm.

Within all Canadian provinces, municipalities – both urban and rural – have at least some legal authority to act in relation to each of the following functions: fire protection; animal control; roads (but only in the cities of Charlotteown and Summerside in PEI); traffic control; solid-waste collection and disposal (but not in PEI); land-use planning and regulation; building regulation; economic development; tourism promotion; public libraries; parks and recreation; cultural facilities; licensing of businesses; emergency planning and preparedness; rural fences and drainage; regulation and/or provision of cemeteries; airports (though not airports formerly operated directly by the federal government); and weed control and regulation of cosmetic pesticides (although proposed provincial legislation in Ontario removes cosmetic pesticides from municipal jurisdiction).

The following are additional functions that are generally carried out by urban municipalities: public transit; regulation of taxis; water purification and distribution; sewage collection and treatment; downtown revitalization; and regulation of noise. Except in Newfoundland and Labrador, where it is a responsibility of the Royal Newfoundland Constabulary, urban municipalities are generally responsible for policing, although there are varying mechanisms in different provinces to insulate police from the direct control of municipal councils.[5] Some urban municipalities obtain their policing through contracts with the RCMP or with provincial police forces (Ontario and Quebec). The RCMP or provincial police forces generally provide policing in rural areas. Arrangements vary from province to province concerning the extent to which rural municipalities contribute to the cost. In Ontario, rural municipalities have paid the full cost since 1998.

Ontario, as noted, is the only province in which municipalities have the statutory responsibility to provide social services and contribute to their funding. In Alberta, municipal governments contribute to the funding of certain preventative social-service programs and of operating deficits incurred by the boards of residences for low-income senior citizens. Arrangements for municipal seniors' residences in Ontario are similar, except that they are operated directly by cities and upper-tier municipalities. Details are provided in the chapters on Ontario and Alberta.

In British Columbia, larger urban municipalities (especially the city of Vancouver) are engaged in social-planning functions mainly aimed at attracting funding from other levels of government, coordinating the work of non-profit agencies, and providing modest municipal subsidies to various kinds of social-service organizations, including community centres and non-profit child-care centres. In other provinces, there is even less municipal involvement in social services, ranging from none at all to minor expenditures for non-recreational social-service programs in community centres and for the staffing of social-planning groups.

Quebec and Ontario are the only provinces that have any financial responsibility for social housing. The city of Vancouver manages subsidized housing for seniors and people with disabilities but has no financial responsibility for these units. Even the management costs are paid by other levels of government. Regional districts in British Columbia manage rental units for low-income people but make no financial contribution.

Municipalities in Alberta and Ontario are responsible for providing land-ambulance services. The city of Winnipeg has a contractual arrangement with the regional health authority to provide ambulance services within its territory, but this appears not to be a municipal responsibility elsewhere in the province.

Property assessment is a provincial function in all provinces except Alberta, Manitoba, Ontario, and Quebec. In Ontario it is carried out everywhere by a municipally owned and financed corporation. In Newfoundland and Labrador, property assessment is a municipal function only in the city of St John's. Arrangements for property assessment in Saskatchewan are quite complex and are explained in our Saskatchewan essay. Municipalities are responsible for collecting their own property taxes, except in New Brunswick and PEI, where this is a provincial function.

The regulation of air quality is a municipal (regional district) responsibility in British Columbia. Public health is explicitly a municipal responsibility only in Ontario, where it is often carried out through regional or county public-health units. In Manitoba, municipalities have responsibility for the inspection of food-service establishments and for insect control.

Public utilities (other than water supply) are difficult to categorize. For example, electrical distribution in Ontario's urban areas is the responsibility of business corporations, most of which are still owned by municipalities. Some small Ontario municipalities own local telephone companies. The cities of Kitchener and Medicine Hat own their local natural-gas distribution systems. Two of Canada's major publicly traded utilities corporations, EPCOR and Telus, can trace their origins to being line departments of the city of Edmonton. Not surprisingly, they are still heavily involved in providing electricity, natural gas, and telecommunications infrastructure within the Edmonton region.

In many developed countries, municipal governments have direct responsibility for public education. This is nowhere the case in Canada, except that in Nova Scotia, as David Cameron explains in his essay, there are special provisions requiring the Halifax Regional Municipality to contribute municipal funds to the local school board. All of our authors have been asked to explain the extent to which local school boards are able themselves to draw on local resources by setting their own tax levy on local property. Only in Saskatchewan, Manitoba, and Quebec do school boards still have this authority.

Municipal Finance

Comparing municipal revenues and expenditures across provinces is not easy.[6] Researchers and practitioners in particular provinces generally make use of financial data collected by their respective provincial governments. Not surprisingly, the provincial data are collected in such a way as to reflect the particular features and functions of the municipalities in each province. The problem, of course, is that such data are not comparable across provinces. Fortunately, Statistics Canada does collect municipal financial data in a uniform manner for all the provinces. But such data often appear at odds with the provincial data. Another problem is that Statistics Canada produces different data sets relating to municipal revenues and expenditures and the choice of which one to use is not immediately obvious.

For our project, we need data that are comparable across provinces. As a result, we are not relying on the provincial data. The authors of the chapters in this book were asked not to use the provincially generated data unless they were essential to make a point about the special circumstances of their province. Some authors therefore had to work with data from Statistics Canada that were unfamiliar both to them and to the practitioners whom they interviewed and relied on for detailed information and for assessments about how well the system was working.

We are certainly not the first researchers to use municipal financial data from Statistics Canada's Financial Management System (FMS). But we are the first to explain and analyse some of the issues that they present. The initial challenge is to choose the most appropriate data set. The two choices are:[7]

1 Local Government Revenue and Expenditure (385–0003): This set includes financial data from local governments that are defined as 'municipal administrations; autonomous boards, commissions, and funds; and autonomous non-commercial, non-profit education institutions.' The reference to 'education institutions' means school boards.
2 Local General Government Revenue and Expenditure, Current and Capital Accounts (385–0024): This set is the same as the first except that it does not include financial data from school boards and it distinguishes between current and capital expenditures. The FMS documentation points out that federal and provincial governments treat capital outlays 'as expenditures at the time of purchase'[8] but that local governments normally do not. Because there is no definition of local government 'current' and 'capital' accounts in the FMS documentation, we must assume that the FMS distinction between capital and current simply reflects provincial and/or municipal usage.

Although FMS data relating to local government frequently appear in secondary sources, it is not always clear what data set is being used. We have decided to use the second set described above. The first was rejected because we are focusing on the activities of municipal governments and their associated boards and commissions; we are not studying the activities of school boards. In adopting the second set, we decided to present both operating and capital expenditures because, if we did not, it would appear that for many years in many jurisdictions (including for Canada as a whole), municipalities have been running deficits. In the real world, municipalities never budget for operating deficits and always distinguish between operating and capital expenditures. The format in which our data are presented is therefore as close as possible to the kind of financial reporting that municipalities actually use.

We also had to decide about what years to report. Easily available and consistent time series run from 1988 to 2007. We want to make use of the most recent reliable and available data, so we are reporting data for 2006. These data have been revised once. However, we are informed by Statistics Canada that the 2006 data will be revised again in 2009 and 2010. The latest available year (as of August 2008) for which data will not be further revised is 2004. We have therefore chosen to focus most of our analysis on 2004. To obtain some understanding of changes in revenues and expenditures over time, we compare 2004 with the situation ten years before, i.e., in 1995.

The first table in appendix 1 contains aggregate data for all of Canada. Subsequent tables use the same format to present the same data, but for each individual province. The table presenting the aggregate Canadian data will be described briefly below, in part because none of the provincial chapters will be focusing on the Canadian data and in part because such a description should help familiarize readers with the common format that we are using.

For 'Revenues,' the table aggregates both current and capital accounts. Capital-account revenue makes up only about 4 per cent of the total and includes such items as revenue from sales of capital goods and transfer payments from federal and provincial governments that are earmarked for capital projects. For some provinces, revenues from 'lot levies' were assigned to the capital account. For others – notably Ontario, by far the biggest generator of lot-levy revenue – there are no reported capital-fund revenues from lot levies. For our purposes, there was no advantage in making distinctions between operating- and capital-account revenue.

The most significant features of the 'Revenue' data are that the percentage of GDP absorbed by municipal revenues changed from 5.07 per cent in 1995 to 4.28 per cent in 2004 (and 4.44 per cent in 2006) and that, over the period 1995–2004, total municipal revenue increased by 34.43 per cent, not allowing for inflation. Per capita 'own-source revenue' (mainly revenues from property taxes and user charges) increased at a significantly faster rate (37.78 per cent), while per capita municipal revenue from provincial transfers declined by 21.46 per cent. Per capita municipal revenues from federal transfers increased by

19.91 per cent but their total amount in 2004 was still less than 10 per cent of total transfers. In financial terms, municipalities have clearly become more self-reliant over the past decade. Significant increases in federal transfers have not made up for cuts in provincial transfers.

For 'Expenditures,' we see that capital-account expenditures in 2004 made up about 22 per cent of the total. Over the previous ten years they had risen significantly more than operating expenditures (39.30 per cent vs. 33.03 per cent). For 'environment' and 'transportation and communication,' capital-account expenditures comprised about 40 per cent of total expenditures. At the same time, expenditures on debt charges (which appear as operating-account expenditures) have gone down by almost one-third over the period 1995–2004, a reflection presumably of both decreased interest rates and a greater tendency for municipalities to finance capital projects from accumulated capital reserves. Total per capita expenditures increased by 23.11 per cent between 1995 and 2004. Per capita expenditures on housing increased at a greater rate than those of any other expenditure category, but housing consumes less than 4 per cent of total municipal expenditures. Among the more costly operating items, expenditures on the 'environment' and on 'protection of persons and property' (the most costly category of all) have grown at a faster rate than total operating expenditures, while operating expenditures on 'transportation and communication' have grown at a rate below the overall rate of increase.

If we compare total revenues and total expenditures in 2004, we note that municipalities collectively spent more money in 2004 than they took in. As indicated earlier, the reason for this is that these totals include capital expenditures made in 2004. If we exclude such expenditures and compare operating expenditures ($43.2 billion, including $2.2 billion in debt charges) to total revenue ($55.3 billion), it looks like Canadian municipalities are in good financial shape. What these figures cannot tell us, however, is whether or not municipal capital expenditures are at a sufficiently high level to replace depreciating municipal infrastructure and to provide for new infrastructure in areas of fast growth.

Provincial Oversight

We all acknowledge that provincial legislatures can do whatever they want with municipalities. Their statutory authority in this field would appear to be virtually unlimited. But provincial ministries, including the ministries that deal explicitly with municipal affairs, can regulate and control municipalities only to the extent that they are authorized to do so by statute. While most provinces have some form of quasi-judicial body that acts as an appeal board for municipal land-use decisions, the authority of such boards varies dramatically from province to province. The Ontario Municipal Board (OMB) is famously the most powerful.[9] Even routine zoning decisions by the city of Toronto are appealed to the OMB and it is not unusual for the city council to be overruled. Despite their broad functional authority (and in some ways because of it), Ontario municipalities are probably subject to more provincial oversight than municipalities in any other province. In smaller provinces, municipalities are often subject not so much to provincial oversight as they are to direct provincial intervention in ways that simply are not contemplated elsewhere. The fact that provincial governments collect local property taxes in New Brunswick and Prince Edward Island is an example.

Our chapter on British Columbia suggests that the government of this province is usually content simply to leave municipalities alone. Such an approach has its attractions to those who generally favour municipal autonomy, but it can be frustrating to advocates of strong provincial action. In any event, Patrick J. Smith and Kennedy Stewart describe many ways in which the government of British Columbia takes action that is not always supported by its municipalities. Perhaps it is fair to suggest that municipalities in British Columbia are generally free (by Canadian standards at least) from provincial intervention with respect to their own structures and organization but that provincial involvement in, for example, local environmental and transportation issues remains frequent and important. Because it often has chosen to take a different course, British Columbia deserves more attention than it is usually given by observers of Canadian local government and urban policy making.

Demography

Our authors were asked to discuss demographic developments in their respective provinces because we all accept that systems of municipal government cannot be fully understood unless we know the demographic context. Generally speaking, however, readers will note that demographic differences within provinces seem far more important than differences among them. In all provinces, it is the largest city-regions that are growing fastest, while small towns that are distant from metropolitan centres and rural and northern areas face problems caused by slow growth or population decline. All of our authors make reference to these issues, none more dramatically than David Siegel, who suggests that we should think of the 'two solitudes' in Ontario: one is 'characterized by rapid population growth fuelled by increasing levels of cultural diversity'; the other is 'the rural and northern life of small towns and declining population.'

The accelerating growth of Canadian city-regions has been responsible for much of the current concern about urban governance and infrastructure. Municipal governments are arguably becoming more important as societies become more urbanized. Of necessity, urban municipal governments provide more services and spend more money per capita than do rural municipal governments. But demands for more provincial and federal involvement in urban affairs seem to grow along with the increases in urban population levels. One of the questions inherent in all of the essays that follow is the extent to which municipal governments really have become more important in urban areas in recent years. Readers will find evidence to support various possible answers. It would seem, however, that provincial governments are still the main policy makers with respect to major strategic urban infrastructure such as expressways, fixed-rail transit systems, and big investments in projects aimed at protecting the natural environment.

Political Culture and Elections

That there are huge differences in the political environment of the various Canadian provinces is no surprise. Readers will likely marvel at David Bulger's casual references to interviewing the premier of Prince Edward Island as part of the research leading to the writing of his chapter. It is no doubt easier to arrange such an interview than it is to interview the mayor of Calgary, let alone Toronto or Montreal. This volume does not provide comprehensive accounts of the political culture of each province, but it does attempt to provide at least a hint of the distinct flavour of municipal politics in each province and how this is influenced by the nature of provincial politics.

The most notable differences concerning politics and elections among the different provinces relate to political parties. The non-partisan tradition generally reigns supreme, but in Quebec and British

Columbia party names can be on municipal ballots, reflecting the fact that municipal political parties are of considerable importance in the major cities of both provinces. Why this has happened in these two provinces and not in other large provinces with large cities (Ontario and Alberta) is one of the great questions of Canadian urban politics. Anyone advocating a form of responsible party government at the local level needs to know the answer before proposing structural reforms aimed at bringing this about. Canada is unique among federations in having distinct systems of political parties at both the federal and provincial levels. In Montreal and Vancouver, voters have three levels of party systems to be concerned with. In neither city can it be claimed that a particular local party is merely a provincial or federal party going by another name.

Our essays also demonstrate that there is considerable variation in rules about the financing of municipal election campaigns. For example, we learn that in Alberta there are no spending limits and no limits on individual donations. The situation is similar in British Columbia, but disclosure rules apply even to campaigns of those seeking the nominations of recognized municipal parties. Quebec forbids donations from corporations and unions; both Quebec and Ontario have donation and spending limits.

There can be little doubt that the at-large elections in cities in British Columbia encourage the creation of slates and that such slates can easily evolve into more permanent party-like structures. But few outside British Columbia who favour party politics at the municipal level also favour at-large elections. Our chapter on British Columbia tells a quite different story about the politics of municipal government than is found in our other chapters.

Municipal Organizations

Municipalities are in the paradoxical position of being at the same time both governments and members of interest groups. Within their own communities they are governments. When mayors lobby on behalf of their own communities, they are acting like leaders of governments within multilevel systems. Indeed, much of their legitimacy in this process derives from the fact that they are directly elected by their voters. But most provinces contain hundreds of municipalities and on many issues they share common interests. So it makes a great deal of sense for them to establish municipal associations. To understand fully the municipal role in intergovernmental relations, we need to know how such associations are structured and how they work in each province.

Another distinct feature of municipal government is that municipal managers are much more likely to be functional specialists than they are at other levels. The head of the planning department is likely to be a certified land-use planner; the head of public works is usually a professional engineer; and the chief librarian is likely to have had graduate education in library science. Such specialization is so important at the municipal level that in many provinces there are functional organizations of managers from all or most of the municipalities. These organizations also often play an important role in the policy process, and they sometimes even advance positions that are not consistent with those of their municipal employers. Finally, of course, there are the unions. The country's biggest municipal union, the Canadian Union of Public Employees (CUPE), has strong interests in a wide range of municipal policy questions, especially privatization and contracting out.

The Three Northern Territories

This volume does not contain chapters on the systems of municipal government in Canada's three federal territories: Yukon, Northwest Territories, and Nunavut. According to the 2006 census, the combined population of the three territories was 121,000, less than that of Prince Edward Island, the least populous (136,000) of all the provinces. Collectively, the territories cover more than 3.5 million square kilometres, which is more than a third the area of Canada (9.0 million square kilometres) and more than twice the size of Quebec, the province with the largest territory (1.4 million square kilometres). But the uniqueness of the territories in relation to the provinces is not just about sparse population. Katherine Graham has recently explained how the municipal systems in the territories are significantly different from those in the provinces. She points to four important factors:

1. The populations of the municipalities within the territories are themselves very small. The three most populous municipalities according to the 2006 census are the territorial capitals: Whitehorse (20,641), Yellowknife (18,700), and Iqaluit (6,184).
2. The municipalities in the territories are all remarkably isolated from each other. Nunavut does not even have an intermunicipal road system.

3. Almost all the land in the territories is owned by the federal government, even within the municipalities. The process of land development is therefore quite different in the territories than in the provinces
and municipal revenues from property taxes are negligible.
4. Aboriginal land claims are increasingly influencing the evolution of
land regimes and municipal government in the territories to a much
greater extent than is found in any of the provinces.[10]

Municipalities in the north are unique, not just because they are small
and isolated but also because they are part of a rapidly evolving
process whereby the settlement of aboriginal land claims is changing
the entire nature of northern governance.

The Provincial Chapters

The order in which our provincial chapters are to be presented has the
potential to offend both our contributing authors and our readers.
However, provincial precedence for formal occasions is, fortunately
for us, an issue that has been resolved by the government of Canada.
In 'The Table of Precedence for Canada,'[11] provinces are listed in the
order in which they joined Confederation. The original four are ranked
by population, with Ontario coming first. We have decided to present
our provincial chapters in the same order so as simultaneously to hide
behind federal authority and benefit from the general principle that it
makes sense to read about older provinces before reading about newer
and ones.

Despite working from a common template, our authors have
approached their tasks in different ways. David Siegel's chapter on
Ontario focuses on how the province's municipalities are still recover-
ing from a period of tumultuous change that began soon after the
Harris government was elected in 1995 and that has recently seen new
legislation that significantly strengthens the legal authority of the city
of Toronto and subsequently that of all of the municipalities in the
province. Our chapter on Quebec, written collectively by many of its
major urban scholars, also emphasizes the dramatic impact on municipalities of centrally imposed legislative changes. But, whereas the city
of Toronto appears to be growing stronger, our Quebec authors rightly
question whether the city of Montreal – after experiencing amalgamation, political decentralization to boroughs, and the de-amalgamation
of fifteen former municipalities – is stronger now than it was before all
the changes were launched.

David M. Cameron's chapter on Nova Scotia takes up many of the same themes as Siegel, notably municipal amalgamation and functional realignment. He describes a system of school financing, especially in the Halifax Regional Municipality, that is genuinely unique in all of Canada. The chapter on New Brunswick by Daniel Bourgeois and Frank Strain is also unique in that it explores the effects of past linguistic tensions in the province and accounts for the fact that a significant number of the province's residents feel themselves fortunate to have escaped the jurisdiction of any municipality by living outside their boundaries in unincorporated areas.

Tom Carter's chapter on Manitoba naturally focuses on the dominance of the city of Winnipeg and the challenges for regional land-use planning caused by a faster rate of population growth in the municipalities surrounding the province's only large municipality. In contrast, Patrick J. Smith and Kennedy Stewart describe a municipal system in British Columbia that is infinitely more varied, in part because the provincial government has generally refrained from legislated institutional change.

The authors of our chapters on Prince Edward Island and Newfoundland and Labrador (which is the last of the provinces to be treated in this volume) are remarkably adept at pointing to the special characteristics of their respective island provinces. As already noted, David Bulger is able to present us with a pleasantly intimate portrait of Prince Edward Island, whose population is not much more than that of two of Toronto's forty-four municipal wards.

For Saskatchewan and Alberta, our authors provide rich descriptions and analyses of each municipal system. In each case the joint authors comprise both a political scientist (Joseph Garcea and Edward C. LeSage, Jr) and an economist (Donald Gilchrist and Melville L. McMillan), thereby ensuring that both political and financial issues are comprehensively explored. The Alberta chapter is especially detailed. We decided not to attempt to shorten it because it provides an indication of the complexities in municipal government that exist in virtually all of the provinces.

Conclusion

A collection of essays such as this invariably raises as many questions as it answers, especially given that authors have been deliberately encouraged to pursue the issues that they think are most important within their respective provinces. From reading the chapters that follow, some will likely conclude that many municipal shortcomings relate to size; that some municipalities are too small and that a very few might be too large. Other concerns will relate to finances. Should municipalities continue to be so reliant on the property tax? Should there be more funding in the form of provincial grants? For some, the focus will be on internal decision making. How can we expect municipalities to participate fully in the intergovernmental policy-making process when their (mostly) non-partisan decision-making structures are so different from the parliamentary norm and when their staffs are often so functionally specialized?

But the general picture that follows is one of significant change in the last few decades, change that has facilitated the emergence of Canadian municipal government as a full partner in many new forms of intergovernmental collaboration. It is relatively easy to think of ways in which more structural and financial changes could facilitate such collaboration. The real challenge is to do this while maintaining strong links between municipalities and the various territorial communities that they serve. Without such links, municipal government loses its essential purpose.

NOTES

1 The Canadian text on local government with the most thorough treatment of different provinces is C. Richard Tindal and Susan Nobes Tindal, *Local Government in Canada*, 7th ed. (Toronto: Nelson, 2009). For a recent treatment of legislated structural reforms in each of the Canadian provinces, see Joseph Garcea and Edward C. LeSage, Jr, eds., *Municipal Reform in Canada: Reconfiguration, Re-Empowerment, and Rebalancing* (Toronto: Oxford University Press, 2005).

2 For two classic articles on this general subject, see Robert A. Dahl, 'The City in the Future of Democracy,' *American Political Science Review*, 61, no. 4 (1967): 953–70; and Lisbet Hooghe and Gary Marks, 'Unraveling the Central State, but How? Types of Multi-level Governance,' *American Political Science Review*, 97, no. 2 (2003): 233–43.

3 For a survey, see Andrew Sancton, 'Signs of Life? The Transformation of Two-tier Metropolitan Government,' in Caroline Andrew, Katherine A. Graham, and Susan D. Phillips, eds., *Urban Affairs: Back on the Policy Agenda* (Montreal and Kingston: McGill-Queen's University Press, 2002), 178–98.

4 For an audio debate on the subject between Joseph Garcea and Andrew
   Sancton, see http://www.cbc.ca/thecurrent/2003/200311/20031106.html.
   See also Joseph Kushner and David Siegel, 'Are Services Delivered More
   Efficiently after Municipal Amalgamations?' and 'Citizen Satisfaction
   with Municipal Amalgamations,' *Canadian Public Administration*, 48
   (2005): 73–95 and 251–67.
5 Margaret E. Beare and Tonita Murray, eds., *Police and Government Rela-
   tions: Who's Calling the Shots* (Toronto: University of Toronto Press, 2007).
6 Harry M. Kitchen, *Municipal Revenue and Expenditure Issues in Canada*,
   Canadian Tax Paper no. 107 (Toronto: Canadian Tax Foundation, 2002);
   and Melville L. McMillan, 'Municipal Relations with the Federal and
   Provincial Governments: A Fiscal Perspective,' in Robert Young and
   Christian Leuprecht, eds., *Municipal-Federal-Provincial Relations in Canada*
   (Series: Canada: The State of the Federation, 2004) (Montreal and
   Kingston: McGill-Queen's University Press, 2006), 45–81.
7 Until 2008, there were three choices. Table 385–0004 has been terminated.
   It presented only the sum of the current and capital accounts that are pre-
   sented in Table 385–0024.
8 Statistics Canada, *Financial Management System (FMS)*, Catalogue no.
   68F0023XB, 2004, 46.
9 John G. Chipman, *A Law unto Itself: How the Ontario Municipal Board Has
   Developed and Applied Land Use Planning Policy* (Toronto: University of
   Toronto Press, 2002).
10 Katherine A.H. Graham, 'Municipal Reform in the Northern Territories:
   Now for Something Completely Different,' in Garcea and LeSage, Jr, eds.,
   Municipal Reform in Canada, 270–1.
11 http://www.canadianheritage.gc.ca/progs/cpsc-ccsp/pe/precedence
   _e.cfm#notes. See item 9.

1 Ontario

DAVID SIEGEL

The purpose of this chapter is to provide a general overview of the municipal system in Ontario with a particular emphasis on the way the system has changed recently in terms of the relationship of municipalities to the provincial government. I have argued elsewhere that municipal government in Ontario has been characterized by long periods of quietude punctuated by short periods of intense reorganization.[1] Specifically, I predicted that the years of rapid change in the latter part of the 1990s would be followed by a return to quietude. I was correct about the longer-term historical trend. I was wrong about what the future held.

The period of intense structural reorganization of the late 1990s has been followed by a period of intense intergovernmental activity during which Ontario municipalities generally, and Toronto specifically, are in the process of emerging from their position of 'hyper-fractionalized quasi-subordination'[2] (in J.S. Dupré's famous phrase) to be significant players on the national and even international stage. This awakening has come about because of a number of developing trends that will be discussed throughout this chapter.

Setting the Scene

Ontario is the most populous province in the country and its population is continuing to grow rapidly. This growth is occurring partly as a result of in-migration from other parts of Canada, but mostly because Ontario is the destination of more than half of the immigrants who enter Canada. Ontario hosts a huge number of head offices or chief Canadian offices of major companies. It has the highest gross domestic product in the country and the diverse nature of its economy makes it less susceptible to the boom-and-bust cycles found in the energy-rich provinces. Ontario clearly plays a key role in maintaining the economic health of Canada.

A significant part of Ontario's strong economic position is derived from the fact that it contains Canada's largest city – Toronto. In this era of globalization, there has been a great deal of discussion of the role that cities play as the main drivers of economic development. The extreme view is that the Westphalian nation-state has now outlived its importance and the keystones of global economic development from now on will be the global city-regions. Clearly, this is an arguable premise, but one does not have to embrace the entire argument to accept the idea that only a few major cities will be able to attract and retain highly qualified people and capital investment, both of which are exceedingly important for economic development and both of which are highly mobile in this global age.

Of Toronto's rivals, Vancouver is important both in the Cascadia region and as Canada's face on the ever more important Pacific Rim. Calgary and Edmonton have major roles in the energy sector. Montreal was historically Canada's largest and most important city and its leaders are clearly serious about regaining some of that status. However, there is little question that Toronto is Canada's premier global city-region.

Given the emerging importance of cities as economic drivers, it should not be surprising that much of the recent approach of the Ontario provincial government to municipalities has been predicated on reforming them, particularly Toronto and other cities in the Toronto-centred region, so that they will be able to be competitive on the world stage and fulfil their important economic and cultural roles.

This is a decided shift in the tone of municipal policy. Traditionally, Ontario has seen municipalities as vehicles for decentralized provincial service delivery. The main aim of provincial policy with regard to municipalities was to treat all municipalities in the same way and to ensure that they were kept under firm control but were viable enough to share the cost of provincial services and to act as the delivery agent of provincial policies across the province (quasi-subordination). The provincial government was responsible for broader issues related to the economic well-being of the entire province; the only role played by municipalities was to deliver services efficiently and keep property taxes low. Municipalities were not encouraged to think much about developing their own policies or making their own decisions.

This has changed recently with the recognition of the importance of large cities as the anchors of global city-regions and as the main drivers of economic development. Thus, the previous situation has been stood on its head. The old way was that the nation-state and its subnational units were the prime generators of wealth, and cities were the passive recipients of trickle-down development. The new way is that a few major global city-regions are the drivers of economic development and their national and subnational units are the bystander recipients of wealth generated by activities at the municipal level.

Because of Toronto's position in the national and world economies, this change has had a greater impact on Ontario than on other provinces, but it has been a difficult transition. The traditional culture of provincial-municipal relations has been based on treating all municipalities in the same manner – as subordinate entities created for the purpose of carrying out provincial policy. Globalization has forced Ontario to shift gears and to realize that Toronto and the Toronto-centred region is a special case, and that municipalities generally and Toronto specifically play an important role in furthering the economic development of the province. Thus, the Ontario government is in the process of shifting its municipal policy from a one-size-fits-all benevolent dictatorship to a more flexible partnership arrangement. As with all transitions, some parts of it move more smoothly than others, but it is clearly moving and has passed a point of no return. Toronto will have special status within Ontario and all Ontario municipalities are moving towards more autonomy.

One of the major problems that will be encountered in this transition is that there are really two and possibly even three Ontarios, and provincial policy with regard to municipalities will have to recognize the unique problems of these several Ontarios.

One Ontario is the Ontario of Toronto and several other relatively large cities. This is an environment of rapid growth fuelled by a strong manufacturing economy in transition towards a heavy emphasis on the financial and service sectors and by rapid increases in population resulting from significant movement from rural to urban areas within Canada and immigration from outside Canada, especially from Asia and the Caribbean. The major problems facing this Ontario are the usual ones of rapid growth. Where do we put the new people without giving in to urban sprawl? How do we integrate the new immigrants into Canadian society in a manner that balances respect for their native cultures and a need to create a Canadian culture? How do we build new infrastructure fast enough to keep pace with the rapid increase in population?

The other Ontario is the Ontario of small towns and rural areas. This is an Ontario of declining population as families become smaller, farms become larger and need fewer people to work them, and people move to the large cities. It is an economy that is still relatively prosperous in many places but is based on farming and small businesses, with some tourism in a few choice locations. It is a place of towns becoming smaller as highways make it easier for people to go to the big city to do their shopping. The major problem of this Ontario is retaining the current population or attracting enough new migrants to remain viable and maintaining the existing quality of public services as the number of residents and taxpayers declines.

Finally, there is a third Ontario in the north that looks in many ways like the second Ontario except that it has the added disadvantages of geography and climate. It has little chance of attracting major manufacturing or service industries to replace the dying resource-extraction industries and is losing population even more rapidly than the southern rural areas.

Thus, Ontario is rapidly developing into two solitudes. One solitude is characterized by rapid population and economic growth and by increasing levels of cultural diversity. The other solitude is the rural and northern life of small towns and declining population. Both of these solitudes are important, but they pose different problems for governing. One of the major challenges of Ontario municipal policy will be developing a policy that meets the needs of the two solitudes. Every province is facing this same problem to some extent. However, Ontario's situation is more extreme because it contains the largest and most diverse city in the country, and therefore it must deal with the greatest extremes.

This chapter will argue that, to date, Ontario has responded to this challenge in two ways. It has been moving to allow all municipalities more autonomy by providing them with broader legislative authority and more financial resources so that they can make their own policy decisions. The province is also taking steps to recognize the special status of Toronto to give it the tools to grow and develop as a global city-region. Together, these policies represent a major cultural shift in the provincial-municipal relationship. In the analysis that follows, I will discuss how this shift is occurring.

History and Structure of Municipal Institutions

The Legislative Regime

In the past, Ontario's approach to provincial-municipal relations was to establish one legislative regime that applied to all municipalities. The Municipal Act, which was passed in 1849 (styled the Baldwin Act after premier and reform politician Robert Baldwin) and amended frequently since, was based on the principle that municipalities could perform only those responsibilities for which they were delegated express authority by the provincial government – and in most cases the delegation was handled in a very detailed and proscribed manner.

Two major changes in the legislative regime have occurred recently which will have a significant impact on the future development of the municipal system. They both point in the direction of providing municipalities with more autonomy. The first affects all municipalities in the system; the second applies only to Toronto.

The first major change was a new Municipal Act that took effect on 1 January 2003.[3] This was based on earlier Alberta legislation and was designed to move away from the idea that all municipal functions had to be legislatively prescribed. It identified ten spheres of jurisdiction for municipalities and granted municipalities natural person powers. The new spheres of responsibility will be discussed in more detail later, but the concept of natural person powers means that municipalities are no longer bound by the concept of express authority and can generally perform whatever actions are necessary to function within the areas of jurisdiction identified. This legislation has provided municipalities with considerably more autonomy of action than they had under the previous Baldwin Act.

Municipalities have not exactly embraced this legislation.[4] In the first place, it is a major cultural change that municipalities have not yet learned to use. Municipalities had become comfortable with the idea of their role as creatures of the province with a relatively limited role in policy making. The fact that they would now have more autonomy means that they will have to make their own decisions, which requires them to approach their role in a more confident manner. It will take some time for municipalities to learn how to function in this fashion. Secondly, there have been some criticisms that the movement from detailed control to broader delegation has been more apparent than real. Critics have suggested that the legislation still provides the province with a great deal of power to issue restrictive regulations. Thus, the province could take back with one hand what it had seemingly delegated with the other.[5]

The second major change is the development of a new act for the city of Toronto which has the portentous title of Stronger City of Toronto for a Stronger Ontario Act[6] (referred to here as the City of Toronto Act) and which treats the largest city in the province in a special manner. This is the first time that the Ontario provincial government has accepted the idea that its largest city ought to have its own special governing regime.

The purpose of this modernized City of Toronto Act is to provide Toronto with comprehensive, enabling new powers that

- are commensurate with the city's size, needs, responsibilities, and capacity;
- recognize Toronto's importance as the economic engine of Ontario and Canada; and
- recognize that Toronto is a mature order of government capable of exercising its powers in a responsible and accountable fashion.[7]

The basic principle is that the new legislation 'should start from the premise that Toronto can exercise broad permissive governmental powers within its jurisdiction, subject only to specific exceptions in the provincial interest.' This gives the city of Toronto considerably more power than it previously had to legislate, raise revenue, and organize itself for service provision. This is groundbreaking both because of the process that saw the province and city jointly prepare the legislation and because of the highly permissive nature of the legislation itself.

Thus, it is clear that recent changes in the legislative regime under which municipalities in Ontario operate have conferred more autonomy on municipalities. The new Municipal Act that took effect in 2003 provided all municipalities with considerably more powers than they had previously. This was quickly followed by the new City of Toronto Act that extends that frontier even further. These initiatives manifest a new style of municipal-provincial relations. There seems to be a feeling of partnership now rather than the paternalistic approach that had been prevalent. This could be driven in part by the fact that two previous deputy ministers of municipal affairs had very long careers as senior municipal administrators before moving into their positions.

Virtually all previous deputies had come from within the provincial bureaucracy.

This current shift in the environment does not mean that the changes will be permanent. The province could backslide on its avowed cooperative agenda. The changes are also predicated on the idea that municipalities will be able to undergo a significant cultural transformation. Municipalities are accustomed to thinking of themselves as creatures of the province. They frequently complain of the paternalism inherent in that phrase, but in truth there is a certain comfort in being able to blame the province for problems. The new regime will require a cultural shift on the part of municipalities to take more responsibility for their actions and not lapse into the old habit of blaming someone else for what goes wrong. The stage has been set and the legislation is in place to allow municipalities more autonomy. It is now up to the province to live up to its commitments and up to municipalities to grow into their new role.

Municipal Structures

Municipal structures in Ontario have always been complex and inconsistent, and the level of inconsistency has increased in recent years. At the time of Confederation, all of southern Ontario had already been divided into counties, which were the upper-tier governments. Within the counties were towns (medium-size urban areas), villages (smaller urban areas), and townships (large rural areas). The counties were governed by an indirectly elected council composed of representatives who were elected to serve on the councils of the towns, villages, and townships.

County governments were never strong or dynamic units of governments, but they served their purpose fairly well. They tended to be farmer-dominated and focused on providing a basic level of services and minimizing taxes. Their main function was the provision of farm-to-market roads, but counties were also concerned with drainage, and some time later responsibility for social services and seniors' homes was added.

The large urban areas (cities and some of the larger towns) were separated from the counties. This means that, while the city or separated town was geographically within the county, there were no political links between them. The city or separated town was a one-tier unit of government which elected its own council with no representation or other formal ties to the county in which it was located. In practice, some administrative links developed. For example, most places had suburban road commissions which were a vehicle for shared decision making and funding for roads that ran between the county and separated city or town.

The idea that urban and rural interests were separated in this manner was seen as a good thing in the early years, because the two solitudes had largely different interests and concerns and there was no reason to combine them. However, over time, this separation came to be viewed as artificial and even problematic in some areas. Urban development began to jump the urban boundaries into rural areas. The motor car and better roads made the once formidable journey between urban and rural areas a simple everyday occurrence. The counties functioned very well as units of rural governance and they continue to operate reasonably well in predominantly rural areas of the province, but, where the urban-rural boundaries blurred, a new form of organization was needed.

The new model was metropolitan or regional government. Metropolitan Toronto was created in 1954 and a number of regional governments followed in the period 1969–74. The basic model for all these entities was the same although the details differed. The regional governments replaced the counties in areas that were perceived to be prime candidates for future urbanization, but generally followed county boundaries. Though they were two-tier governments like the counties, the regions included both the rural areas and the previously separated cities and towns. The idea was that the upper-tier region would have the planning and related powers necessary to preside over the conversion of this large rural area into an urban area.

In sum, the regions were different from the counties in that the regions included both rural and urban areas, and they exercised considerably more governing powers than the counties. However, there were some similarities between the counties and regions. They were both two-tier governments and the upper-tier representatives were usually indirectly elected as representatives of the lower tier, although over time direct election to regional council became more common. From the beginning of regional government, there was some question about whether this was just a transitional step towards complete amalgamation. Some regional governments still exist, but others have been transformed into single-tier governments.

The next round of changes occurred in the mid-1990s when Mike

Harris's Conservative Party came to power on the wave of the Common Sense Revolution. The Harris government felt that service delivery and accountability would be improved if municipalities were consolidated into larger units.[8] This was highly contentious both among academics who argued that the presumed improvements would not occur[9] and among local residents who resisted losing their local municipality.[10]

However, the government forged ahead and, in the period from 1996 to 2000, the number of municipal units in Ontario was cut by almost half, from 850 to 445. Some of the changes were fairly unremarkable in the grand scheme of things. For example, Elgin County went from fourteen municipalities to seven, and some responsibilities were shifted between the counties and the lower tier. But some changes were much more extensive. While a variety of forms were adopted, it was clear that the large single-tier entity was the hallmark of this era just as two-tier regional governments had been the hallmark of earlier years. Single-tier structures were implemented in a number of smaller areas, but the highest-profile changes were in three of the largest cities in the province – Toronto, Ottawa, and Hamilton. In all three cases, two-tier regional or metropolitan governments were replaced by single-tier cities. Most of these single-tier governments cover large areas encompassing a central urban core (or several urban centres) and significant suburban and rural areas. Most of the new municipalities have significant room for expansion and the planning powers to control how that expansion will occur.

Yet even the creation of the 2.2-million-person megacity of Toronto did not solve the 'Toronto problem.' The real extent of the Toronto-centred region is somewhat unclear but it certainly extends beyond the borders of even the enlarged megacity. The usual method of handling this type of spillover problem is to create one or several supra-regional special-purpose bodies in such areas as transportation or land-use planning. After the establishment of the megacity, an organization called the Greater Toronto Services Board was created to coordinate some services in the area around Toronto.[11] The tensions generated within the board led to its elimination after a very short period. Since then, coordination has been handled by a series of ad hoc arrangements. For example, a Greater Toronto Transit Authority was established in 2006. Expenditures on social services are pooled for Toronto and the surrounding regions in recognition of the fact that many people needing social services come to the city of Toronto from the outer suburbs. The effect of this is to redistribute funds from the suburban municipalities to the city of Toronto. This is an obvious irritant for the suburban municipalities,[12] but, to the city of Toronto, the arrangement is equitable because it sees itself as the catchment area for many of the social problems exported by the suburbs.

The issue of coordination of policy making and service delivery in the broad greater Toronto area is an issue that must be handled better than it currently is. The creation of the megacity integrated government within the core area but did nothing to improve integration in the broader region.

Another change in governance that has occurred has been the gradual elimination of many special-purpose bodies and the transfer of their responsibilities to municipalities. For example, planning boards and water and sewer commissions have been eliminated as separate entities and their duties moved into the municipal administration proper. In northern Ontario and in the counties and separated cities, public-health services and regulations are the responsibility of intermunicipal special-purpose bodies known as health units. Library boards and transit commissions still operate in many municipalities.

There are two especially important special-purpose bodies that remain and that require some discussion. Every municipality that is responsible for providing policing must have a police services board to supervise policing within its boundaries. It can do this by establishing its own police service or by contracting with the Ontario Provincial Police. The number of members on the police services board is a function of the size of municipality, but it always consists of an odd number of people, the majority of whom are appointed by the municipal council and the minority by the provincial government. The board is completely independent of council to ensure that there can be no political involvement in day-to-day policing activities. The need for this independence is well understood and gives rise to no difficulty with council. However, the police services board has the right to requisition from the municipality whatever funds it needs to operate.[13] This intrusion into council's financial role provokes a great deal of tension.

Boards of Education are even more autonomous from council. Boards are governed by trustees who are elected at the same time as municipal councillors, but there are few other connections between the two bodies. The system of school board funding was changed quite radically by the Harris government. Currently, the ministry uses a formula to determine the total 'Grants for Student Needs.'[14] This grant is then provided in two ways. The province establishes tax rates for education which are used throughout the province. Each local municipality applies these rates to all residential and commercial properties and remits the proceeds to the school board. The province then provides the difference between the total grant and the amount derived from the property tax in the form of a transfer payment.

In summary, there have been huge changes in municipal structures in the last few years. Mostly this has consisted of the creation of larger, usually single-tier, municipalities. Municipal councillors generally resisted these changes, but most councillors and staff in restructured municipalities have now accepted the inevitable and the new municipalities are functioning as well as the previous ones.

It can be argued that the revisions in the municipal system have made the new municipalities stronger than their predecessors and given them more tools to exercise the autonomy provided them under the changes in the Municipal Act mentioned earlier. Since the new municipalities are likely to be larger single-tier entities, the mayor speaks for a larger number of people and can do so without fear of contradiction by other mayors or officials of other municipalities. Previously, seven heads of council spoke for Toronto and they seldom spoke with one voice. Mayor David Miller of Toronto has clearly done a good job of speaking forcefully for his new megacity and mayors in other jurisdictions will likely follow his lead.

The new municipalities cover larger areas, thus improving fiscal equity across the entire area and improving the ability to deliver certain services such as land-use planning, public transit, streets and roads, and economic development. Hardly anyone believes that the new system saves money as was hoped, but the larger municipalities have larger budgets and are therefore able to hire more highly qualified professional people. Surveys in some municipalities, though, have indicated that citizens have seen no change in the quality of service delivery.[15]

In short, these new municipalities are better positioned to exercise the greater amount of autonomy that they have been given by the new legislation discussed earlier in this section. Toronto particularly will be able to increase its status significantly as a result of its new powers and the enhanced status of its mayor.

Functions

The functions that Ontario municipalities are charged with carrying out have changed over time in tandem with many of the structural changes discussed above. In the early years, the real stuff of municipal government was animal control, disputes over fences, and building local roads. The modern municipality has significantly more powers and those powers have expanded steadily over time, but one of the most significant changes occurred during the Common Sense Revolution. The Conservative government appointed the 'Who Does What' task force, chaired by former Toronto mayor David Crombie, to review the then-existing allocation of functions between the province and municipalities and to recommend how responsibilities could be allocated in a more rational fashion.[16]

The province did not accept all the task force recommendations, but it did undertake a major reallocation of responsibilities in a program called Local Services Realignment (LSR) by the province[17] and 'downloading' by municipalities. This was probably the greatest single realignment of powers in the history of the municipal system.[18] The municipal epithet of downloading is certainly apt in that a great number of powers were moved from the province to municipalities. From the provincial perspective, there was also a significant shift in finances at the same time that will be discussed in more detail later. In the early stages of the exercise, the province used the phrase 'revenue-neutral' a great deal to describe the unfolding process. Municipalities objected that this phrase was simply not correct; more responsibilities than revenues were being shifted to them. Eventually the phrase fell into disuse, except as an ironic epithet.

There is still considerable dispute about the extent of financial obligations imposed on municipalities. So many changes occurred at the same time that this dispute will never be settled in a definitive fashion. However, there is no question that both responsibilities for many functions and financial arrangements were shifted considerably. This will be discussed in more detail later in the section on finances.

The shifting of functions was accompanied by another major change in the provincial-municipal relationship which came in the form of the new Municipal Act effective 1 January 2003.[19] This provided municipalities with natural person powers and defined ten spheres of responsibilities (see Table 1 below) in which municipalities would have considerable authority to act.

This simple list of spheres of jurisdiction does not tell the entire story because there is still some level of involvement of other governments in many of these functions. In the complex federal system that Canada has become, it is rare that any level of government has autonomy to

Table 1
Spheres of jurisdiction, 2003 Municipal Act[20]

---

1 Highways
2 Transportation systems, other than highways
3 Waste management
4 Public utilities
5 Culture, parks, recreation, and heritage
6 Drainage and flood control, except storm sewers
7 Structures, including fences and signs
8 Parking, except on highways
9 Animals
10 Economic-development services

---

operate freely without regard to other governments. With regard to municipal functions, the major difference between Ontario and other provinces is that Ontario municipalities still play a significant role in the areas of social services and public health. At one time, social services were primarily the responsibility of local governments, religious groups, and voluntary associations in all provinces, but gradually all provinces except Ontario took over full responsibility for social services and public health. The prime reasons for the shift to the provincial level were the high cost of providing the service and the need for uniformity in administration across the province.

Much of the cost of public-health services is borne through significant grants from the province. Yet, even so, social services have a major impact on the budget of Ontario municipalities. Interprovincial comparisons of per capita municipal expenditure always show Ontario municipalities as one of the biggest spenders in the country because they have responsibility for social assistance. The volatility of social-assistance costs exacerbates the problem because these costs increase when there are significant unemployment problems in an area which also results in tax-collection problems. Thus, municipalities suffer a double pressure – increased social-service expenditure at a time when property-tax collections are difficult.

Responsibility for social services has not shifted to the province in spite of several reports advocating this shift[21] because of a budgetary impasse. There is a great deal of money at stake here because Ontario municipalities have always provided a significant amount of the funds for social assistance. The provincial government simply does not have the funds necessary to take over complete funding of the services.

Also, a provincial takeover of funding responsibility would provide a huge windfall to some municipalities. The only way that the province could assume responsibility for paying for social services would be if some other shift occurred at the same time such as municipalities taking over some provincial spending responsibility. That would raise such difficulty that it is not likely to happen soon.

Local Services Realignment involved a number of shifts of responsibilities between municipalities and the province. Yet it seems clear that municipalities ended up with more responsibilities than they had before. The method of delegation through the concept of spheres of responsibility in the new Municipal Act also gives municipalities considerable flexibility in how to carry out their responsibilities. Municipalities have initially reacted negatively to these changes because they feel that they have been the victim of downloading in that additional functions have been imposed on them without accompanying financial changes. Discussion of the financial regime will have to wait for a later section, but it is evident that municipalities now have additional responsibilities. Though municipalities have focused on the financial consequences of the new responsibilities, these responsibilities provide municipalities with considerably more status in that they are delivering more services and they have more autonomy in how they will deliver those services.

Electoral Rules

Ontario's municipal electoral regime is set out in the Municipal Elections Act.[22] From 1982 until 2003, municipal elections were held every three years. Beginning with the 2006 elections, municipal politicians have been elected for four-year terms. The second Monday in November was chosen as the election date because it allows a significant campaign period after the summer, and because of its proximity to the beginning of the municipal fiscal year on 1 January. The downside of this date is that it is frequently plagued by bad weather. The council elected in November formally takes office at the first scheduled meeting in December.

In all lower-tier and single-tier municipalities the mayor is elected at-large. The system varies in upper tiers. In all counties and some regions, the head of council (warden in a county and chair in a region) is elected by councillors, but a few regions have direct election of the chair.

The method of election of councillors can be by ward or at-large or some combination of the two. There are single-member wards and multiple-member wards. In the same municipality, there can be large wards with several members and smaller wards with only one member. There are a small number of municipalities that elect some members at-large and some by ward. In two-tier systems, there are some lower-tier municipalities that elect some members by ward and some members who serve on both the upper and lower tier at-large. If this sounds confusing to the casual reader, it can also be confusing to residents. Municipal elections can produce very long ballots when there are elections for municipal council and several school boards (public, Catholic, English, French) at the same time.

The decision about method of election including ward boundaries is made by the local council, but that decision is subject to appeal to the Ontario Municipal Board (OMB). The role of the OMB will be discussed in more detail in a later section.

In order to vote in the municipal election, one must be at least eighteen years old, a Canadian citizen, and either reside in or own property in the municipality. The requirements to hold office are the same except that judges,[23] MPs, and MPPs[24] are prohibited from holding municipal office. An employee of the municipality is allowed to run for office if he or she takes an unpaid leave of absence during the campaign and resigns from municipal employment if elected.[25]

Ontario has experienced the same problem as other jurisdictions with regard to low voter turnout at municipal elections. No central registry of province-wide figures is maintained, but a turnout of 30 per cent seems to be the norm, with hardly any municipalities exceeding 50 per cent.

Ontario has had fairly strict electoral financing laws for about twenty years.[26] The law was originally passed as a reaction to serious concerns about the role some land developers were playing in elections in the Toronto area. The legislation has not ended allegations of inappropriate behaviour, but it has made the process more transparent.

The law prohibits anyone from raising or spending money on a political campaign until they have been formally nominated for office. The nomination period opens on the first working day of January in an election year. Contributions are allowed from individuals, corporations, and unions. The maximum contribution from any individual or group of related corporations is $750. There is also a maximum expenditure that candidates can make which is calculated on the basis of the number of electors in the candidate's area. The candidate is required to file a statement of revenue (listing all contributors who provided more than $100) and expenses. This list is always eagerly awaited by journalists and its highlights are published in local papers.

As one would expect, there are sometimes allegations that candidates have violated the rules, but there is fairly general satisfaction with the existing legislation and a feeling that it has made the process more transparent and cleaned up some of the worst cases of inappropriate behaviour.

Local political parties have never played a significant role in Ontario municipal elections. The Liberal Party fielded a candidate in the 1969 Toronto mayoralty election and was embarrassed by its inability to win.[27] This event is frequently cited as a lesson to all national parties that the gains in obtaining local office are not as great as the downside embarrassment of losing. Better to stay out altogether.

In fact, the political culture of Ontario attaches something of a stigma to any form of party involvement in local politics. Candidates are quick to deny allegations that their municipal campaign is supported by a party. This seems to be a hangover from the turn-of-the-century reform movement of one hundred years ago, when it was commonly felt that there was something unseemly about parties. It is better in local elections that each candidate speak for her or himself.

However, there have been examples of somewhat weak caucuses or coalitions of council members forming after they have been elected. This has been seen several times in Toronto and less often in Hamilton, Oshawa, and other cities. It has happened most frequently among councillors on the left of the political spectrum, so these groups are frequently dubbed as 'NDP' by the media, although they usually do not have formal links to the New Democratic Party. Members of the so-called caucuses are usually lukewarm in accepting the label. On the one hand, the existence of the caucus gives them a certain amount of power around the council table – if the coalition hangs together, which it sometimes does not. On the other hand, they are all aware of the stigma mentioned above. In Toronto, the NDP does seem to have some sway in nominating candidates, and candidates sometimes indicate their partisan allegiance to the other national or provincial parties by subtle signals such as the colour of their election signs, but the involvement of national or provincial parties in local elections in Ontario is quite limited.

While candidates generally eschew political labels and deny active, overt party involvement, councillors are political animals and will frequently be members of national or provincial parties. During election campaigns, fellow party members can provide a good core of supporters who are familiar with the electoral process. However, candidates are usually careful to involve people from more than one party to escape the charge that party politics is at work.

Once elected, councillors will generally check their party loyalties at the door when they enter the council chamber. There is some concern that the intrusion of partisan politics at the local level will complicate the municipality's relationship with other levels of government. For example, a previous mayor of Niagara Falls, who was a known Liberal, criticized the Harris government in a partisan manner and was chastised locally because of concern that his actions would hurt the city. The current mayor of Niagara Falls, who has run unsuccessfully for provincial office under the Conservative banner, has not criticized the current Liberal government in the same way.

The political culture of Ontario does not lead to strong participation in local government. Voter turnouts, as noted, are low. The general interest in the workings of local government, beyond concerns about property-tax increases and scandals, is quite limited. The province, some municipalities, and some good-government interest groups have lamented this problem and pondered what can be done about it, but no satisfactory approach has been found. The political culture of Ontario orients Ontarians much more towards the federal government than either the provincial or municipal levels.

There is no systematic census of the demographic characteristics of municipal politicians, but observers would probably agree on a broad general outline. Until the last twenty or thirty years, most councils resembled classic old boys' clubs – predominantly white, middle- to upper-class businessmen and farmers. In the last few years, the door has gradually been opened to more women and visible minorities. At least one female mayor has won in many of Ontario's large- and medium-size cities, such as Toronto, Ottawa, London, Windsor, Oakville, and Vaughan, and of course there is the indomitable Hazel McCallion in Mississauga. A 1997 article noted that there had been a slow but steady increase in the percentage of women on councils in Ontario over the 1982–94 period.[28] More recent systematic data does not seem to be available.

Provincial Government Oversight

Provincial government oversight in Ontario is quite similar to the regime in other provinces. There are two main provincial bodies involved in oversight. One is a traditional department – the Ministry of Municipal Affairs and Housing – and the other is a quasi-autonomous, quasi-judicial body – the Ontario Municipal Board. In addition, virtually every other provincial ministry has some involvement with municipal governments.

Ministry of Municipal Affairs and Housing

The Ministry of Municipal Affairs and Housing is a cabinet-level portfolio, but it is usually viewed as a relatively junior appointment – a reflection of the importance generally assigned to the role of municipalities. The portfolio is customarily the first one held by a new cabinet minister, and traditionally this minister does not come from Toronto, though there have been some recent exceptions. This latter tradition probably derives from Ontario's historical focus on rural areas and a concern that Toronto not receive any sort of special treatment.

According to the Ministry of Municipal Affairs and Housing Act:

(1) The Minister is responsible for the policies and programs of the Government of Ontario in relation to,
(a) municipal affairs, including the co-ordination of programs of financial assistance to municipalities;
(b) community planning, community development, maintenance and improvement of the built environment and land development; and
(c) housing and related matters.[29]

In practice, the ministry has an ambivalent relationship with municipalities – somewhat reflective of how municipalities feel about the ministry. One of the ministry's prime roles is to represent the interests of municipalities in cabinet and ensure that municipalities have the legislative powers and financial and other resources needed to carry out their mandate. However, the ministry also has a regulatory relationship with municipalities in that it must ensure that they are operating properly. Obviously, this latter role can produce significant resistance to ministry control on the part of municipal councillors who see themselves as having a strong mandate from their electorate to govern their municipality.

The ministry is responsible for all municipal legislation, which means that it is responsible for the overall structure and organization of municipalities as well as municipal-election rules, conflict-of-interest legislation, and all other aspects of the legislative framework within which municipalities operate.

The ministry has some fairly draconian powers, but the most draconian are seldom used. It has the power to take over the operation of a municipality and suspend all local authority. This is done only in very extreme circumstances, usually when a municipality has experienced the closure of a major industry and, being unable to collect property taxes, has no local sources of revenue. The ministry then provides funding to the municipality and takes over complete operation of municipal services. The ministry would like to do this for only a limited period of time while the municipality puts itself on a better footing, but sometimes its control can go on for a substantial period. There are seldom more than one or two municipalities operating under this form of ministry control at any time.

The ministry is also responsible for municipal organization. In the 1990s the ministry took the lead in pushing for the restructuring and amalgamation of municipalities described earlier. This created significant tensions between the ministry and municipalities when municipalities resisted the changes that were being imposed. The ministry is no longer pushing for amalgamations, but it remains the major contact point for municipalities wanting to restructure.

The ministry provides an unconditional grant to municipalities. The unconditional grant has operated on a somewhat ad hoc basis since the advent of Local Services Realignment. Its implicit purpose has been to offset perceived inequities of LSR to individual municipalities. It has been controversial, however, because it is very difficult to devise a comprehensive formula-based system that is responsive to the needs of the wide diversity of municipalities in Ontario while limiting total outlays to a reasonable amount.

The ministry operates a number of field offices across the province. People in these offices serve as a two-way conduit to carry the ministry message to municipal councillors and staff and to provide feedback to head office about the concerns of municipalities. These field offices try to maintain an ongoing relationship with municipalities in their area. They organize seminars to advise councillors and staff about the impact of changes in legislation and regulations. They also respond to requests for advice or assistance from individual municipalities. A significant amount of time of the people in these offices is spent responding to public questions or complaints about municipal actions or lack of action.

Ontario Municipal Board

The Ontario Municipal Board is a quasi-autonomous, quasi-judicial body. Its main role is to hear appeals from municipal decisions in the areas of planning and electoral systems. The OMB also approves all long-term borrowing by municipalities. In the words of a recent OMB annual report: 'The Ontario Municipal Board (OMB) is an independent adjudicative tribunal established under statute by the Province of Ontario. The Board hears appeals and applications on a wide range of municipal and land-related matters including official plans, zoning by-laws, subdivision plans, consents, and minor variances, land compensation, development charges, ward boundaries, and aggregate resources.'[30]

The board is quasi-autonomous because it reports to the attorney general on an arm's length basis and its members are appointed for three-year periods. The board members are usually people in the latter stages of their careers who have served as municipal politicians or staff or who have related experience. There is criticism that some appointments have a political motivation, but most members of the board bring a significant amount of experience and credibility to their position. While being of the correct political stripe has never hurt anyone's chances of being appointed to the board, appointees generally have a significant amount of credibility in the municipal system.

There are typically thirty to forty members of the board, but most hearings are conducted by a single member, with larger matters having two or three members presiding. The hearings are conducted in the affected community, usually in the council chamber, hotel meeting room, Legion hall, or similar venue. In hearings, board members must behave in a judicial manner and hearings generally have most of the trappings of a formal judicial proceeding. Members are also aware, however, that they are frequently dealing with concerned citizens who have limited experience in judicial manners, so they will sometimes provide assistance to citizens about how to conduct themselves in a hearing.[31] Thus, the conduct of the hearings can fluctuate between rigid judicialism and more informal proceedings with the presiding member offering advice to applicants.

The bulk of the board's work concerns planning matters. Virtually any planning-related decision taken by a municipality can be appealed to the board – adoption or amendment of an official plan, adoption or amendment of a zoning by-law, subdivision approval, condominium approval, and so forth. Both municipal decisions and non-decisions can be appealed to the board. For example, if a proponent requests that a council change an existing provision in the official plan or a zoning by-law and council refuses to do so, then the proponent can appeal council's non-decision in the same manner that a decision of council can be appealed.

The OMB has a reputation for being fair and even-handed. There has never been a scandal involving inappropriate actions of an OMB member. However, municipalities generally dislike the oversight of the OMB in municipal decisions. As a matter of principle, elected councillors who represent the local community resent having their decisions second-guessed by a group of outsiders coming into town for a few days. Municipalities are also bothered by the huge cost that can frequently accompany a board hearing. The objection of even one citizen can trigger a formal hearing and the municipality must take it seriously because the board has the authority to side with that one citizen against the decision of council.

In the past, the board has also been plagued by a lengthy backlog of cases delaying the decision process considerably. This currently seems to be under control, but it has been a recurring problem.

A major irritant currently is the sense that the board usually decides in favour of proponents who want a change in the official plan or a zoning by-law to undertake new development, regardless of the municipality's position.[32] The entire planning process is essentially a clash between the rights of a landowner who wants to assert property rights and the collective rights of community members who want to exercise some collective control over how their community will develop. There is a sense that the onus is on the community to prove why its collective rights should supersede those of a landowner who wants to use her or his land in a particular way.[33] The proponent does not always win, but the onus placed on the municipality to prove its case puts it in a difficult situation. The ability of individual developers to appeal to the OMB also can make it difficult for a municipality to maintain uniform development standards.

In many cases, municipalities try to avoid a hearing by negotiating with a proponent, but they feel that they are negotiating from a position of weakness. With the proponent likely to be successful in a hearing, the municipality strives to win some minor concessions to avoid expensive proceedings where it believes that it will ultimately lose anyway.

The OMB also hears appeals from decisions (or non-decisions) of councils about changes in the electoral system – moving from ward to at-large elections (or vice-versa) or changing ward boundaries. These frequently originate from local business or residents' groups that want a change in the status quo. As in the case of planning, residents can appeal either a decision by council or the refusal of a council to act on a request for change.

As a quasi-judicial agency, the OMB is not bound by precedent. Groups affected by these electoral decisions have found it somewhat difficult to find a consistent stream of reasoning in the fairly limited number of decisions the board has rendered on electoral matters.[34] To the extent that there is any consistency, there seems to be considerable respect for the decisions of council as the elected body for the municipality. This is disconcerting to citizens' groups because they feel that councillors are unlikely to change the rules that got them elected,[35] so the groups' only hope for change is an appeal body such as the OMB. It is also ironic that the board, which is reluctant to override council decisions about electoral matters because they are made by a duly elected council, seems to have less compunction about overturning planning decisions made by the same elected council.

The OMB has incited considerable controversy over the years. Municipal councils are generally upset at the idea of having their decisions subject to review, although there is frequently a minority of councillors who welcome a second pass at the decision. Developers generally like the idea that they get a second shot at a decision, and in the sort of legal forum in which most developers feel comfortable. However, appearing before the board is expensive and developers are not always successful. Residents' groups see the board as a second chance to overturn an undesirable council decision, but they frequently do not like the board's decisions. The OMB is a venerable old institution. Like many other venerable old institutions, it is frequently subject to attack, yet there is also a sense that it serves a real purpose and so, while it has been subject to periodic change, it is unlikely that it will be the subject of radical overhaul.

Other Ministries

Virtually every ministry of the provincial government in addition to the Ministry of Municipal Affairs and Housing has some dealings with municipalities related to the ministry's interest in certain functional areas. For example, the provincial Ministry of Transportation works with municipalities to ensure that connections between the provincial highway system and the local road system work properly and also that local roads are maintained to an appropriate standard. The provincial ministries have several leverage points.

The strongest is the use of conditional grants. Ontario municipalities traditionally received a fairly large portion of their budgets through conditional grants from provincial ministries. The conditional aspect of the grant usually required that the money be spent on a particular function such as roads, but the conditions were often much more detailed, for example, specifying that only roads built to a particular standard could qualify for provincial matching funds. Since municipalities are highly dependent on provincial funding, these transfers provided significant leverage that allowed ministries to exercise detailed control over municipal activities. As will be discussed below, many of these conditional grants have now been eliminated. This has considerably reduced the leverage that ministries have with municipalities.

Provincial ministries can also impose certain requirements on the way municipalities deliver services even though the province provides no funding. These are sometimes called 'unfunded mandates.' The municipality must deliver services to a provincial standard even though the province is not providing any provincial support for the service. This power sounds draconian, but it gives municipalities more flexibility than might be apparent at first. These rules are a fairly blunt instrument wielded by the province. With a conditional grant, the province could cut the grant of a misbehaving municipality. With this blunter instrument, the province's recourse against an uncooperative municipality is less clear. The province could demand that delivery of the service be modified in some way to conform to provincial standards, but, if the municipality's residents are satisfied with the existing mode of service delivery, what can the province do?

Rather than impose rigid requirements, provincial ministries can work with staff at the municipality to set suggested ideal standards. In this case, professionals at the provincial level can work with professionals at the local level to adopt certain suggested standards such as number of library books per capita that will become an agreed standard.

These provincial ministries formerly had a great deal of power over municipal activity wielded through conditional grants and through a general atmosphere of paternalism that was enhanced by a disparity of expertise: municipal staff members were frequently less knowledgeable and less professional than provincial public servants and so had to rely on provincial people for advice. Over time, much of this atmosphere has changed. The demise of conditional grants has weakened ministry control over municipalities. The professionalization of municipal staff has lessened their reliance on provincial public servants. Generally speaking, there is still a cordial relationship between provincial and municipal people at the working level, but it is now more likely to be based on a partnership than on paternalism.

Land-use Planning

The above sections discussed the main institutions of provincial oversight. Any discussion of provincial oversight must also discuss the land-use planning process which spans several of the structures discussed earlier. Land-use planning was mentioned in the discussion of the Ontario Municipal Board, but the full nature of provincial control over land-use planning decisions is much more complex.

Official plans are prepared by municipalities, but municipalities must prepare or amend plans with a clear eye on how a number of provincial agencies will view such documents. Land-use planning is a good example of a policy field that requires a significant level of municipal-provincial cooperation. A municipality's official plan literally applies only within the municipality, but the consequences of that official plan can extend far beyond the municipality's boundaries. Traffic patterns within one municipality can have a major impact on adjacent municipalities. The way one municipality handles environmental issues can have extremely far-reaching consequences. Thus, what might seem to be a municipal decision could have an impact on large areas of the province. This creates a legitimate provincial interest in some aspects of a municipal plan.

When the municipality prepares (or amends) its official plan, it must ensure that this plan is consistent with[36] a series of Provincial Policy Statements in areas such as brownfields, housing, water, and agriculture.[37] These are classic examples of fields where decisions made within one municipality can have extensive externalities.

One of the most far-reaching and contentious provincial policies is the new greenbelt policy.[38] This has been supplemented by a later policy statement called *Places to Grow: Better Choices. Brighter Futures*[39] which is also titled 'Growth Plan for the Greater Golden Horseshoe.' In these two related documents the province has defined an area in southern Ontario just beyond areas of existing development where new development will not be allowed. These greenbelt areas will be reserved for agriculture, parks, environmental reserves, or similar uses. The purpose of the policy is to discourage urban sprawl and encourage denser development on existing urban land. Of course, an important consequence is that the policy will limit the ability of some municipalities to grow while directing growth to other municipalities. The province has been quite resolute in standing behind its legislation in the face of considerable opposition from certain municipalities and landowners. Time will tell if the province will stay the course.

The general thrust of this chapter is that municipal autonomy has been increasing. Greenbelt policy is an exception.[40] The reasons for this were described earlier. It is very difficult for any one municipality to stand resolute against urban sprawl, and so some kinds of regulations need to be imposed from above.

As mentioned, the municipality prepares its plan or amendments ensuring consistency with these provincial policies. Then the plan (or amendments) must be sent to the Ministry of Municipal Affairs and Housing. The ministry reviews the plan to ensure consistency with Provincial Policy Statements and sends it to a number of other ministries for comment. The Ministry of Transportation will be concerned about the impact of the proposal on the highway system. The Ministry of the Environment will be concerned about drainage and related environmental issues. Many ministries will have some interest in the official plan. After what seems like a huge amount of time from the perspective of the plan's drafters, these ministries provide their comments to the municipality, which frequently feels frustrated by the whole process. It is very difficult to prepare an official plan – a huge number of conflicting interests must be weighed and compromise obtained – and so municipalities find it irksome to have to respond to a ministry that has a uni-dimensional perspective on a very complex issue. Further, the process can become a long, repetitive one in which the municipality must amend the proposal to satisfy concerns of several

provincial ministries without moving so far away from the initial proposal that it alienates its own citizens.

However, the process is still not complete even after this difficult
exercise. As indicated earlier, citizens or proponents can appeal any
municipal planning decision (or refusal of a municipality to make a
decision) to the Ontario Municipal Board. An appeal by only one
citizen can trigger a process that will delay a decision for an extended
period and cost the municipality a significant amount of money and,
equally important, time. Even if the appeal seems vexatious or trivial,
the municipality cannot take it too lightly because losing an appeal at
the OMB can have serious consequences.

The land-use planning process is one of the most complex, and frequently time-consuming, processes for a municipality. Dealing with
the province around these issues can be very frustrating for a municipality that values its autonomy and needs a certain outcome from a
planning decision to further its economic development. Yet this is an
area where some level of provincial involvement seems warranted to
control potential negative externalities.

This section has discussed a number of institutions of provincial
oversight and the issues around those institutions. The constitutional-
legislative framework is quite clear – provincial governments have
complete control over their municipalities. This control can be exercised in some draconian ways such as taking over the complete operation of a municipality. But, in practice, municipalities are becoming
quite sophisticated and the level of real control that the province can
wield is sometimes more limited than it appears. A part of the balancing of provincial oversight comes in the form of the power of collective
action by municipalities.

Municipal Associations

This collective action goes on at several levels and in numerous ways.
The Association of Municipalities of Ontario (AMO) is a classic pinnacle association. 'The mandate of the organization is to support and
enhance strong and effective municipal government in Ontario. It promotes the value of the municipal level of government as a vital and
essential component of Ontario and Canada's political system.'[41]
AMO engages in the usual activities undertaken by most interest
groups. It lobbies the government on behalf of its members and negotiates with the government about legislation, finances, and other

matters of concern to its members. It has a publication program to disseminate information to governments, its members, and other interested parties. It also operates Local Authority Services (LAS), which provides certain services to municipalities.

Ontario is somewhat unusual in that there is only one municipal association with a mandate to represent all municipalities. In most other provinces, there are several associations representing different groups of municipalities (urban, rural, cities, villages). The strength of these specialized associations is that they are quite homogeneous; their weakness is that no one association speaks for all municipalities. Ontario's municipalities have chosen to go in the other direction. AMO's strength is that it has a mandate to speak for all municipalities; its weakness is that it must attempt to represent the interests of a large and very diverse group of municipalities under one roof. The association deals with this diversity by having caucuses representing several different types of municipalities such as counties, large urban, northern, regional and single tier, rural, and small urban. These groups have their own structures within AMO and even hold separate conferences geared to their specialized memberships.

AMO's highest-profile and most important activity is as a lobbying organization. A major coup for the association was the negotiation of a Memorandum of Understanding (MOU) with the province in 2004 in which the province agreed to consult with the municipal sector (generally through AMO) before it made changes that affect municipalities. This is very important to municipalities because it guarantees that they will have advance notice of any significant changes affecting them and that they will have an opportunity to make their views known to the government before it acts. Of course, the MOU is not as large a concession as it might at first appear. One section of the agreement says that 'the purpose of consultation with AMO is to ensure that municipal and provincial interests are identified and understood.' The next section makes it clear that the consultations will 'not affect the ability of Ontario to set its own priorities and make decisions.'[42] While not perfect, the MOU is seen as an important step forward in the municipal-provincial relationship because it recognizes the right of municipalities to be informed of pending changes and ensures that the province is aware of the impact of these changes on the municipal sector.

Much of AMO's work is done through a myriad of committees that illustrate the range of municipal concerns. The association has committees dealing with such diverse topics as affordable housing, biosolids, community and social services, fire services, line fences, and public health. These committees act as two-way conduits to gather information from AMO members to pass along to the province and to ensure that municipalities are aware of pending provincial actions. The committees frequently engage in extended negotiations with the relevant provincial ministry about changes in legislation or regulations. Thus, these committees provide a valuable service to the municipal sector by ensuring that its interests are represented whenever the province is considering changes in the legislative regime.

A major focal point of AMO's activity is the annual conference which attracts huge numbers of people. The minister of municipal affairs always speaks at the conference and there are usually several other cabinet ministers present, sometimes including the premier. In 2005 the federal minister of finance spoke to the conference about the New Deal for Communities. The conference also serves as an opportunity to disseminate information about the latest trends in the municipal sector. One of its most important symbolic activities is the passing of resolutions generally directed at advising federal and provincial governments about the feelings of the municipal sector on certain issues. Obviously, the resolutions are not binding, but they are important in making the views of the municipal sector known and setting the agenda for future discussions.

Local Authority Services is a separate corporation created by AMO to provide common services to municipalities. Currently it offers a method of pooling excess funds of municipalities and investing them at preferential rates. It also arranges for bulk purchasing of long-distance telephone services and natural gas at a reduced cost. These are services that individual municipalities can choose to use or not, but they have generated significant savings for the municipal sector.

AMO is a very well-respected organization that plays an important role on the municipal scene. However, like all interest groups, it has its high and low points. As a pinnacle organization, its mandate is to represent all 445 municipalities in Ontario. It is very difficult for AMO to satisfy the interests of such a large and diverse array of municipalities. The association's credibility comes from the fact that it currently represents 400 of the 445 municipalities in Ontario. Unfortunately for AMO, one of the municipalities that it does not represent is the city of Toronto. Toronto has always been a bit uneasy about the ability of the AMO to represent its interests. This uneasiness blew up over the signing of the Memorandum of Understanding[43] mentioned above, and Toronto has opted to withdraw from AMO and look after its own interests. Toronto's position is that it is large enough and important enough that it should have its own seat at the table rather than having its interests mediated through an organization that it sees as being dominated by smaller municipalities.[44] Attempts are being made to patch this rift, but, as long as it exists, the absence of the largest city in the province clearly weakens AMO's status to some extent; nevertheless, the association still represents almost 90 per cent of the municipalities in the province and so its position is secure.

Ontario also has a number of associations representing municipal staff members such as the Association of Municipal Managers, Clerks and Treasurers of Ontario, the Municipal Finance Officers' Association of Ontario, the Municipal Engineers Association, and the Ontario Municipal Administrators' Association. These associations perform many of the same functions as AMO or any other interest or professional group, except that they are obviously smaller and more specialized. Staff members can be involved in AMO, and many of them are, but many of them feel more comfortable in an association directly related to their functional responsibilities within the municipality. Most of these organizations have been in existence for an extended period and have a very high status among their members and among the provincial ministries with which they deal.

The Ontario Municipal Management Institute is an organization for managers that cross-cuts all the other managers' associations. It provides training programs, but its major activity is accreditation of its members. Any manager is eligible to join and, by pursuing a customized training and development program, can progress through the several ranks to become a fully accredited certified municipal manager.

There is no question that the presence of an agency for collective action like AMO improves the position of municipalities vis-à-vis the province. Of course, the province still possesses the ultimate constitutional authority to control municipalities. However, the presence and strength of AMO provide municipalities with a significant amount of countervailing power. The province must listen to an organization with the size and status of AMO and cannot dismiss its concerns lightly. The negotiation of the Memorandum of Understanding is clear evidence of the status of AMO. The MOU is not a panacea to solve all the problems of municipal-provincial relations, but it is plainly a step in the right direction. While the tension between AMO and the city of Toronto is unfortunate, AMO will always have the same challenge that any interest group has in accommodating the interests of the diverse array of organizations that it has a mandate to represent. However, it has made significant progress in the last few years, and there is no question that it adds to the relative power that municipalities have begun to wield.

Finance

The purpose of this section is to review the financial position of Ontario municipalities and to determine how that position has changed in recent years. Ultimately, the section will address the important issue of fiscal sustainability. Is the current fiscal regime adequate to allow Ontario municipalities to meet all their service-delivery responsibilities on a long-term basis?

An important caveat in this analysis is that the figures below represent data for the entire Ontario municipal system. There are currently 445 municipalities in Ontario; each of them will be affected in a different way by the trends discussed here. This section contains many general statements; those statements are accurate for the system (the 445 municipalities in total), but they do not reflect accurately the position of every individual municipality.

Figure 1 illustrates the trends in revenue and expenditure in Ontario municipal governments for the period 1988 to 2006.[45] (For a more detailed breakdown, see the data in the appendix.) The figures are per capita so that they control for changes in population and in constant dollars, to remove the effect of inflation. Therefore, these are real changes in revenue and expenditure arising from basic changes in the size and scope of local government beyond the impact of increasing population and inflation.

One obvious observation is that the revenue and expenditure lines parallel one another quite closely. This should not be surprising since municipalities are not allowed to operate at a deficit. The fact that municipalities can borrow funds for capital purposes explains the small deficits in some years. The first part of the period demonstrates remarkable stability followed by a short, small dip, then there is a significant increase in both revenue and expenditure in 1998 followed by a continuing steady climb. This illustrates real growth in the size of local government over the latter period because the impact of both

Figure 1: Ontario municipal revenue and expenditure,
per capita constant dollars

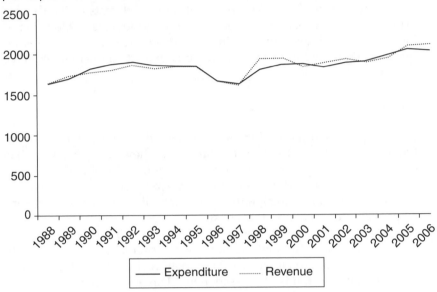

population growth and inflation has been removed, and it reflects the downloading that occurred during the years of the Harris govern-ment's Common Sense Revolution. While the Harris government came to power in 1995, it took some time for all the changes to be reflected in increasing municipal expenditure. This figure indicates that the size and scope of the municipal sector has increased signifi-cantly as a result of Local Services Realignment during the Common Sense Revolution.

Municipal Revenue

Figure 2 illustrates the relative importance of municipalities' three major revenue sources – property and related taxes, transfers from other levels of government (mostly the provincial government), and user charges such as sewer and water rates and swimming pool and arena charges. It shows the trend in each of these three items as a per-centage of total municipal revenue.

Figure 2: Ontario municipal revenue sources as a percentage
of total municipal revenue

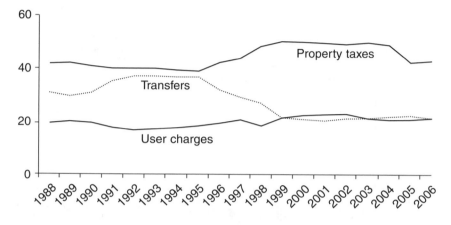

This figure is similar to Figure 1 in that it illustrates a fairly stable situation in the early 1990s, followed by some significant changes at the time of the Common Sense Revolution. One of the goals of the Harris government was to increase the self-reliance of municipalities by reducing their dependence on provincial transfer payments. This reflected the government's intention to reduce provincial expenditure, but it also arose from a desire to decrease provincial-municipal entanglement and increase the direct accountability of municipalities to their electorates. The idea was that municipalities should be spending their own funds rather than relying on conditional grants from other governments. The figure indicates that there was a significant reduction in transfer payments matched by an increase in own-source revenue, mostly in the form of the property tax but user charges and other revenue increased during the period as well.

Predictably, municipalities voiced great concern about the loss of provincial transfer payments, but the province made another major shift at the same time which cushioned the impact of the loss of transfers. Municipalities have always shared the property tax with school boards. Municipalities and school boards each levied their own property tax independent of one another, but one consolidated tax bill covering both levies was sent out by the municipality. In spite of the best efforts of municipalities, most taxpayers had only a vague under-

Figure 3: Distribution of the property tax

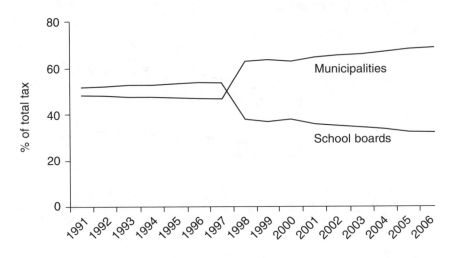

standing of the separate components of the tax bill; for most taxpayers, they saw the entire tax bill (which came from city hall) as one lump sum. While this poor understanding on the part of taxpayers was undesirable, it became convenient when the province wanted to real-locate the property tax. The province provided school boards more transfer payments but required them to reduce their reliance on the property tax. In fact, school boards no longer had the authority to set their own rate of taxation. The provincial government sets a uniform residential rate across the province. Municipalities were then able to occupy the tax room vacated by school boards in a shift that had no effect on the bottom line of the average taxpayer. The province was never totally clear about the purpose of this shift, but several observers have speculated that it arose from a desire to have greater control over the primary and secondary education sector.[46]

Figure 3 illustrates the impact of this change.[47] In the early 1990s, more than half of the total property-tax levy went to school boards. This changed abruptly in 1998 when the ability of school boards to rely on the property tax was reduced and municipalities stepped in to occupy the tax room vacated by school boards.

This could be considered just an accounting sleight of hand in which funds were moved around but everyone's bottom line was left pretty much the same. However, the shift had a significant impact on municipalities, which were now receiving more of their funding in the form of own-source revenue, specifically the property tax, and less in the form of conditional funding through provincial transfers. The significance of the change is that municipalities have complete control over how they spend own-source revenue, whereas conditional grants were always tied to provincial priorities in some way.

Municipalities have resisted a greater reliance on the property tax because it is always easier to spend someone else's money, but this shift means that municipalities will now have more autonomy and more control over how they can spend funds. As municipalities realize that they now have more own-source revenue free of the restrictions imposed by conditional transfer payments, and are free to do whatever they want with it, they will realize that they can make decisions about programs without always looking over their shoulder at what the province wants. Over the last thirty years, provincial governments have experienced this autonomy as many federal grant programs have moved from detailed conditional grants to unconditional grants or grants with only loose conditions. It seems that municipal governments are about to begin to experience the same freedom vis-à-vis the provincial government. It will take some time for municipalities to understand how much autonomy they have and to begin to test its limits, but it will happen at the provincial-municipal level in the same manner that it happened at the federal-provincial level.

Local taxpayers are not very concerned about the split of property tax between the municipality and the school board. Their main concern is the general perception that property taxes keep climbing higher and higher with no end in sight. Figure 4 provides an interesting perspective on that conventional wisdom.

The solid line represents total property and related taxes levied (municipal and school board) on a per capita constant dollar basis. This shows the real change in property tax after eliminating the impact of growth in population and inflation. The dashed line shows total property as a percentage of personal disposable income. This relates total property tax to the ability of residents to pay the tax as measured by their after-tax income.[48]

Not surprisingly, the two lines tell a similar story. The slope of the per capita constant dollar line indicates that the level of the property tax has increased at a rate less than inflation, although it has plateaued or even increased slightly in recent years. The trend of property tax as

Figure 4: Trend in total property tax, 1991–2006

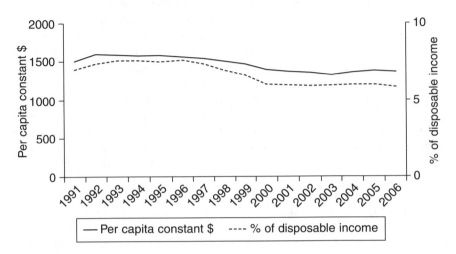

a percentage of disposable income indicates that the property tax has been increasing more slowly than the level of personal incomes. This suggests that, while the absolute amount of the property tax has been increasing, it has been increasing at a lower rate than the average person's ability to pay as measured by personal income. Thus, in real terms the relative burden of the property tax in Ontario has actually been declining. This conclusion is also supported by Harry Kitchen's finding on the national level that, in the 1970–2000 period, municipal property taxes as a percentage of gross domestic product increased more slowly than provincial income taxes and provincial consumption taxes.[49] There is frequently a great deal of rhetoric about the level of property tax approaching some unbearable limit or about the property tax being inadequate to fund municipal responsibilities. However, the information presented here indicates that, far from reaching some limit, property taxes have actually been declining based on the ability to pay.

There are several reasons why these findings do not square with the conventional wisdom that holds that property taxes are always increasing. The conventional wisdom is correct in that each year's tax bill is usually greater than the previous year's. Much of the increase, however, reflects inflation, which also affects personal incomes. Residents know that their tax bill has increased, but they forget that their income has usually increased also. When inflation is removed, as it is in the solid line in Figure 4, much of the apparent increase disappears. And, when property tax is related to personal income, as it is in the dotted line in Figure 4, the entire increase disappears. This could explain why retired people and others on fixed incomes are the most vociferous complainants about increases in the property tax; employed people are receiving salary increases roughly in line with the increase in the property tax and so are less disturbed.

Another reason why this does not square with the conventional wisdom is that Figure 4 does not take into account distribution of the property tax. Both lines reflect the total property tax (commercial, industrial, and residential) collected. However, in the wake of concerns about reassessment discussed above, the provincial government has imposed limits on the increases in taxes on commercial and industrial properties, meaning that residential properties are bearing a significant portion of any increases in the overall property tax.[50] Thus, even though total taxes have been declining, the portion borne by residential ratepayers may have been increasing. The data are not available to test whether this is in fact the case.

The assessment system has been a significant problem in Ontario. Because it was allowed to become very out of date, by the mid-1990s some municipalities had not seen reassessments in fifty years. This caused huge inequities among similar properties. Then, when catch-up reassessments were done, the predictable result was large shifts in the property-tax burden – correcting the long-standing inequities. This became such a political problem that the province stepped in to cushion the impact of the change on certain property owners, particularly commercial and industrial ones. The consequence was another round of distortions which have placed a heavy burden on residential taxpayers.[51] It had become a very complicated and highly charged situation.

Another form of redistribution occurred in some amalgamated municipalities where a conscious decision to equalize taxes between core urban areas and suburbs usually increased the portion of taxes borne by suburban dwellers. Thus, these suburban dwellers might be quite right in their feeling that their property tax has been increasing in real terms. The total numbers shown in the Figure 4 are accurate, but the totals could mask significant distributional changes.

As indicated in Figure 2, provincial transfers are a declining source of revenue for municipalities, but still constitute about 20 per cent of total revenue. In the early 1990s, most of these transfers were conditional and were provided through almost every provincial ministry. As a part of Local Services Realignment, most of these conditional transfers were phased out or rolled into one larger unconditional grant administered through the Ministry of Municipal Affairs and Housing.

Some of these grants had an equalization element, but it was difficult to find a sound basis for equalization. The obvious one would seem to be assessment for property-tax purposes; this was the basis of a municipality's largest source of revenue. Thus, municipalities with a lower than average property-tax assessment base would receive added funding through equalized grants. However, the Ontario assessment system was in such a sorry state that there was little confidence in the values that it generated. Therefore, equalization was used to some extent, but not heavily. One element of equalization was that several grants provided more funds to northern municipalities in recognition of the fact that it cost considerably more to purchase goods and services in remote northern locations. The new unconditional grant being developed by the ministry will likely have an equalization element in it, but working out its exact nature is one of the contentious points in the current discussions.

The one element that ran through all of these ideas was the principle that more funding should go to financially weak (however that would be defined) municipalities. Thomas J. Courchene has recently presented a proposal that would stand this logic on its head.[52] His argument is that Toronto constitutes an important global city-region and that it is in the interest of both the national and provincial governments to ensure that Toronto is in a proper position to take its place on the highly competitive world scene. This might require providing preferential funding to Toronto even though it is one of the wealthiest areas in the province. The idea of providing extra funding to a wealthy area rather than a poor one flies in the face of the usual Canadian way of doing things. However, it is an issue that the province will have to come to grips with. Will Toronto have special status financially in the same way that it has its own legislation? This is a political minefield in other parts of the province, but it is something that would considerably enhance the status of Toronto as an international city.

User charges are the third major source of municipal revenue. Most user charges in Ontario municipalities relate to water and sewers, services that are required by provincial legislation to be self-funding. In order to meet the self-funding requirement, these charges have been increasing rapidly in some jurisdictions, which has attracted significant opposition. Other types of charges also raise difficult political issues. Charges to use recreational facilities will pit councillors against one of the most highly organized local associations – recreation groups. Councillors are also aware that many user charges will fall disproportionately on low-income families. In sum, user charges are an important revenue source that municipalities should be looking at carefully, but there are clearly political concerns that limit the amount of money that can be raised from them.

Municipal Expenditure

The expenditure side of the budget did not experience the same radical shifts as the revenue side during the Common Sense Revolution, but Figure 5 illustrates some interesting trends. This figure shows gross expenditures, which means that these are the total expenditures of the municipalities, including conditional transfer payments. Ontario is the only province that still requires its municipalities to make a major contribution to social-service expenditures and the figure indicates that this has been a significant burden for them. Furthermore, data contained in the appendix demonstrate that in 2004 Ontario accounted for more than 95 per cent of all Canadian municipal expenditures on social services.

One of the major complaints of municipalities is not just the magnitude of these expenditures but their volatility, which is demonstrated well in Figure 5. The portion of municipal expenditure devoted to social services ballooned in the early 1990s because of poor economic conditions. Social-assistance expenditures have been declining in recent years when the economy has been fairly strong, but, if the economy suffers a downturn, as it is at the time of writing, municipalities will be forced to spend more on social assistance and reduce expenditure elsewhere.

Everyone involved in the system (even provincial public servants in private conversations) recognizes that this is a problem and that social-assistance expenditure needs to be moved to the provincial level. But established budget patterns make such a shift difficult. As noted earlier, this is a huge expenditure and there is currently not sufficient funding in the provincial budget to cover it. As well, relieving municipalities of this expenditure would provide them with a significant windfall that the province is not willing to provide. The only solution

Figure 5: Ontario municipal expenditure as a percentage of total expenditure

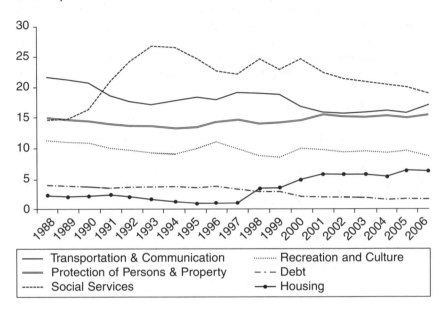

is a transfer of several expenditure responsibilities and/or revenue sources in such a manner that the books would balance, comparable to what was done during the LSR exercise. However, there seems to be no such obvious shift available now. Therefore, the status quo is likely to continue even though all participants recognize its deficiencies.

The next expenditure category is transportation and communication, which is basically roads although some of the most urbanized municipalities spend significant amounts on public transit. This was a major expenditure at the beginning of the period under review but has been declining steadily. The next category, protection of persons and property, is almost entirely fire and police. This expenditure has been fairly stable, although it has been increasing slightly as a percentage of total expenditure in the last few years. It looks as though it is poised to become the second largest object of expenditure if this upward trend continues. Expenditure on recreation and culture has fluctuated slightly within a fairly narrow band. Housing provides a good example of a service that was downloaded to municipalities during

Figure 6: Ontario municipal debt burden and reserves,
per capita constant dollars

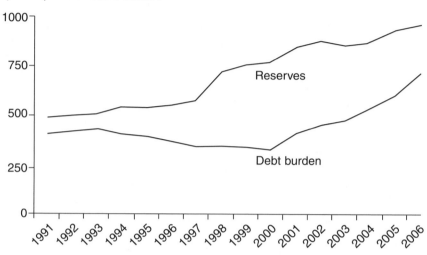

the Common Sense Revolution. As the trend indicates, municipalities have always had some obligation for housing, but it increased signifi-cantly in the late 1990s. Data in the appendix show that in 2004 Ontario accounted for about 75 per cent of total Canadian municipal spending on housing.

The level of expenditure on debt charges (annual interest and retire-ment of principal) is very interesting. In 2004 debt charges made up 1.9 per cent of total Ontario municipal expenditure. Between 1995 and 2004, spending on debt charges declined by 30.0 per cent. Figures for 2006 suggest that expenditures on debt charges are on the rise again, but such expenditures remain significantly below the Canadian per capita average. Local governments in Ontario seem to be considerably more financially conservative and fiscally responsible than other Canadian governments. With only about 2 per cent of total expendi-ture going to debt charges, Ontario municipalities have some room to increase borrowing if they choose to do so.

Figure 6 illustrates the trend in municipal debt burden on a per capita constant dollar basis.[53] It indicates that debt burden was actu-ally declining through the 1990s but has increased fairly significantly in the last few years. This could be seen as undesirable, but, as discussed in the previous paragraph, Ontario municipalities are beginning from a very secure financial position.

It might seem surprising that the level of debt burden is increasing when Figure 5 indicated that debt charges are declining. There are two explanations for this anomaly. First, the increase in debt burden has developed only in the last few years, so municipalities are not yet seeing its full impact on their operating budgets. Secondly, municipalities (and other debtors) are currently benefiting from historically low interest rates. Paradoxically, municipalities could benefit from paying off old, high-interest-rate debt and incurring additional new low-interest-rate debt.

The same figure shows the trend in the level of municipal reserves on a per capita constant dollar basis. Reserves are funds that the municipality has set aside for some future purpose. These can be unrestricted in that the council may decide to build up a fund for some future purpose such as construction of a new municipal building. Or they can be restricted, such as funds collected in development charges which can be used only to finance the provision of services in new subdivisions. The presence of increasing reserves is a sign of financial health. The fact that reserves have been growing fairly rapidly in the last few years augurs well for municipalities.

The two lines of the figure seem to be sending a contradictory message. Debt burden is increasing, which could cause financial concern. At the same time, the level of reserves is increasing, which is a sign of financial health. Reserves cannot be viewed as a direct offset of debt, nor can they be viewed as a way of dealing with the infrastructure deficit. A significant portion of municipal reserves is earmarked for specific purposes – generally providing services in new developments. These funds cannot be used either to liquidate debt or to deal with the infrastructure deficit which is typically found in older sections of the city. However, a strong reserve position is still a sign of financial health in that reserves are an asset that the municipality can use to offset certain types of future expenditures.

On balance, this figure paints a positive picture of the current municipal situation in Ontario. Viewed in isolation, the increasing debt burden would raise mild concern, although the fact that Figure 5 indicates that debt charges as a percentage of total expenditure are well under control would mitigate that concern considerably. The high and rising level of reserves reduces potential concern about increasing debt burden. However, these trends need to be watched with caution. If the level of debt burden continues to increase, it could be a cause for worry at some future time.

Fiscal Sustainability

After this extensive review of finances, the most important question has to do with fiscal sustainability.[54] Do Ontario municipalities have access to adequate sources of revenue to allow them to carry out their responsibility over the long term? The answer to the question is mixed. One way in which it is mixed relates to the caveat mentioned at the beginning of this section. The data presented above relate to the entire municipal system; every individual municipality in the system will be affected somewhat differently. That said, there are some broad conclusions that can be drawn about the system as a whole.

At first blush, Ontario municipalities seem to be in a very sound financial position. Figure 1 indicates that expenditures have been increasing significantly but that revenues have kept pace with the increasing expenditure. Figure 2 indicates that the sources of municipal revenue have shifted. Municipalities are receiving less funding in the form of transfer payments but more funding through the property tax because municipalities have occupied some property-tax room formerly occupied by school boards. This is actually a beneficial shift for municipalities because it increases their autonomy as they become less reliant on tied conditional grants and more reliant on own-source revenue.

There is a general feeling in Ontario that the status quo produces a satisfactory level of services. Streets are generally paved as needed; water and sewer systems work well; people are usually able to access the social services they need, though sometimes with difficulty. The infrastructure deficit is looming, but, currently, most Ontario residents are reasonably satisfied with the level of services they receive.

Figure 4 indicates that municipalities have been able to generate adequate levels of property tax without major real increases in the property-tax burden. Municipal property taxes have actually increased at a rate less than both taxpayers' ability to pay and provincial taxes. Finally, Figure 6 indicates that municipalities have been able to accomplish this with a modest increase in the debt burden which was actually exceeded by the increase in reserves. Melville McMillan's comment about Canadian municipalities generally seems to apply well to Ontario: 'The data examined [in his paper] suggest that many of the claims of municipal crisis and incapacity may be overstated. For the most part, municipalities appear to have coped well through rather difficult times.'[55] This makes the picture seem rosy, but there are some clouds on the horizon.

All of this has occurred at a time when the Ontario economy has been expanding in a moderate but steady fashion – fast enough to produce a reasonable number of new jobs, but not so fast as to generate inflation. This has had a buoyant effect on the property tax and has caused a relative reduction in the amount that Ontario municipalities must spend on social services (Figure 5). How much longer will this last? Municipalities have also benefited from historically low interest rates that have allowed them to carry debt in a relatively easy fashion. How much longer will this last?

There are also some issues on the expenditure side. In spite of the recent increase in expenditure, there are still concerns about infrastructure. Are Ontario municipalities spending enough on maintaining and updating their infrastructure? Or will years of deferred maintenance lead to a serious crisis that will require major expenditures? The best method of dealing with the infrastructure deficit is to develop a plan which allocates a certain amount of expenditure each year so that the problem never deteriorates to crisis proportions. Currently, most municipalities are able to meet their current expenditure requirements but are falling further behind on the infrastructure deficit. This can continue for a limited period, but ultimately it will cause serious problems.

Finally, the most serious problem could arise from the idea that the current situation is generally characterized as satisfactory. Satisfactory has a double meaning. On the one hand, it means that there are no serious deficiencies. On the other hand, 'satisfactory' means something that is short of excellent or outstanding. Our existing cities work in a satisfactory manner, but is satisfactory good enough? This chapter has raised the importance of Toronto and other Ontario cities in a globalizing world. Is it enough that these cities are satisfactory? Or do we need to follow Courchene's advice and pump additional money into Toronto and other large cities to ensure that they can be competitive with other world-class cities? If we do accord privileged treatment to Toronto, then what do we do about the other smaller and declining rural areas that have their own set of problems?

Conclusion

This chapter began with the premise that Ontario municipalities are moving from their previous state of hyper-fractionalized quasi-subordination towards a position where they will exercise more autonomy and begin to take on their rightful role as a full-fledged order of government, not equal to the federal and provincial orders but of a sufficient status that they will be able to make their own decisions and behave like true governing institutions and not simply vehicles for the delivery of provincial services.

In the last decade, municipalities in Ontario have developed the ability to exercise more autonomy. There is a new Municipal Act in place that confers natural person powers on municipalities and provides them with spheres of jurisdiction rather than the previous narrow and legalistic approach. The jury is still out on exactly how much more autonomy this conveys. A certain amount will depend on how much autonomy municipalities are willing to exercise (more on that later), but it is clear that the Ontario government has opened up the municipal legislation and shown itself willing to adopt a different philosophy with regard to municipal-provincial relations. It is unlikely that there can be an about-face from this change. How rapidly the change will proceed is partly a function of how municipalities respond to it.

To complement the legislative autonomy conveyed in the new Municipal Act, municipalities have also seen a shift in their revenue sources from a major reliance on conditional grants to a greater reliance on the property tax and other forms of own-source revenue. This change was initially greeted with outrage from the municipalities because the previous system of spending someone else's money was very attractive, but over time municipalities will come to understand that the shift means that they are now receiving approximately the same amount of money they received before, but with fewer strings attached. Currently, municipalities still feel restricted by some remaining provincial conditions on service delivery. However, these restrictions are no longer backed with conditional grants. Municipalities will soon discover that purported conditions of this sort that are not backed by conditional grants are hollow. Provincial governments discovered this very quickly vis-à-vis the federal government and it will not take municipalities long to recognize how their position has changed vis-à-vis the provincial government. A major difficulty that remains for Ontario municipalities is Ontario's anomalous situation with regard to social services. As mentioned earlier, the high cost and volatile nature of social-service expenditure pose significant problems for Ontario municipalities.

Some municipalities will also benefit from another change that was initially greeted with outrage. The full impact of the amalgamations is not yet clear. It does seem that none of the predicted savings have materialized. However, larger and more unified units of government have been created. On the political stage, the mayors of these large single-tier cities have an undivided mandate from a large number of electors. The mayor of Toronto is elected by 2.2 million people. No other politician in this country can make that statement. And the mayor of Toronto no longer shares that mandate with other mayors and a metropolitan chair. The mayors of these new, larger municipalities will have considerable power coming from their personal status and the size of the geographic area that they represent.

Critics of amalgamation argued that the increased size of municipalities would make them unwieldy. Yet their increased size also increases fiscal equity across the entire metropolitan area and provides the larger municipality with more scope for the provision of such services as transportation, land-use planning, and economic development. The hyper-fractionalized nature of municipalities was particularly problematic in policy fields like land-use planning. Amalgamations have created larger entities that have control over much larger areas.

The move towards autonomy will be assisted by the fact that Ontario municipalities are in relatively good financial position. The data make it clear that property taxes, measured in real relative terms, have not been increasing. There is a serious political problem in getting this message across to the average taxpayer, but it is true nonetheless. Ontario municipalities are also in a good position with regard to debt and reserves. The debt burden has been increasing but is at manageable levels. The level of reserves has also been increasing, which suggests that Ontario municipalities should be in a good position to fund the construction of infrastructure in newly developing areas.

There is a downside to the increasing autonomy. In a further parallel of the federal-provincial relationship, the provincial government will see its ability to require municipal actions and ensure uniformity across all municipalities diminished. As noted, the province has the tools to reduce this level of autonomy. It will be interesting to see how the competing pressures for autonomy and uniformity play out over time.

However, there are some problems lurking on the road to autonomy regardless of provincial actions. As mentioned earlier, Ontario municipalities seem to be in good shape financially, but they have arrived at this position, in part, by economizing on infrastructure expenditure. As with other provinces, Ontario municipalities must confront a major hidden infrastructure deficit. The expected infusion of federal and provincial gas-tax funds will certainly help, but there is some question whether these funds will be adequate and how long they will continue to flow.

A more fundamental issue is how Ontario municipalities will react to these movements towards autonomy. Municipalities are legally and constitutionally creatures of the province. Municipal councillors sometimes take umbrage at this language, but there is also a certain comfort in it. When money is tight or things go wrong, it is convenient to blame the province. This has created a culture of comfortable subordination. Municipalities now have the tools to become more autonomous and make their own decisions. Will they use that autonomy to become a real order of government? Or will they stay locked into comfortable subordination?[56] Changes in culture take significant time and effort to accomplish. Time will tell what course the municipal sector chooses.

Another major issue that will need resolution is the position of Toronto. By any definition, Toronto is a major world city and the anchor of a global city-region. The normal culture in Ontario has been that all municipalities are treated the same. If any favouritism is shown, it is generally shown on the basis of need such as the special grant for northern municipalities. Will Ontario be able to move away from this way of thinking to favour its largest and, by many measures, wealthiest city? The passage of the new City of Toronto Act is a decided step in that direction. The next step could be the establishment of a new funding regime. This is much more difficult. Toronto can have its own legislation with no impact on other municipalities. Money that flows to Toronto, however, is money that does not flow to other cities. This will be more contentious.

In sum, the Ontario municipal system is currently working quite well. It has absorbed a number of changes in the last few years and is on the verge of a major cultural shift as a result of those changes. Yet there are some problems lurking in the form of the infrastructure deficit and also in terms of deciding how to deal with the special needs of the city of Toronto. The future of the municipal system and of the province will be determined by how well these structural and cultural shifts are handled over the next few years.

NOTES

1 David Siegel, 'Municipal Reform in Ontario: Revolutionary Evolution,' in Joseph Garcea and Edward C. LeSage, Jr, eds., *Municipal Reform in*

Canada: Reconfiguration, Re-Empowerment, and Rebalancing (Don Mills, Ont.: Oxford University Press, 2005), 127–48.

2 J.S. Dupré, *Intergovernmental Finance in Ontario: A Provincial-Local Perspective* (Toronto: Queen's Printer, n.d.), 5.

3 Municipal Act, 2001, S.O. 2001, c. 25.

4 George Rust-D'Eye, 'One Year Later: Ontario's New Municipal Act,' *Municipal World* (April 2004), 25–6.

5 David Tang, Michael Kovacevic, and Rod Seyffert, 'Ontario's New Municipal Act: An Overview,' *Municipal World* (March 2002), 19–22.

6 S.O. 2006, c. 11. The city of Toronto had had its own act for many years, but this amounted to some minor embellishments of the Municipal Act which applied only to Toronto. The new act includes a number of provisions that apply only to the city of Toronto.

7 http://www.toronto.ontario.ca/English/Subpage.html (accessed 23 August 2005).

8 Ontario, Ministry of Municipal Affairs and Housing, *A Guide to Municipal Restructuring* (August 1996).

9 Robert L. Bish, 'Local Government Amalgamations: Discredited Nineteenth-Century Ideals Alive in the Twenty-First,' *C.D. Howe Institute Commentary*, no. 150 (March 2001); Andrew Sancton, 'Reducing Costs by Consolidating Municipalities: New Brunswick, Nova Scotia and Ontario,' *Canadian Public Administration*, vol. 39, no. 3 (1996): 267–89; C. Richard Tindal, 'Municipal Restructuring: The Myth and the Reality,' *Municipal World*, vol. 106, no. 3 (1996): 3–7; Richard Tindal, 'Sex, Lies and Amalgamations,' *Municipal World*, vol. 107, no. 2 (1997): 6.

10 The Toronto story is told in: Martin Horak, 'The Power of Local Identity: C4LD and the Anti-Amalgamation Mobilization in Toronto,' Research Paper no. 145 (Toronto: Centre for Urban and Community Studies, University of Toronto, 1999). The story of three other municipalities is told in Thomas R. Hollick and David Siegel, *Evolution, Revolution, Amalgamation: Restructuring in Three Ontario Municipalities* (London, Ont.: Department of Political Science, University of Western Ontario, 2000).

11 Andrew Sancton, 'Differing Approaches to Municipal Restructuring in Montreal and Toronto: From the Pichette Report to the Greater Toronto Services Board,' *Canadian Journal of Regional Science*, vol. 22, nos. 1, 2 (1999): 187–99.

12 Region of Peel, 'Greater Toronto Area (GTA) Pooling: 2002 Current Budget,' www.region.peel.on.ca/finance/2002-business-plan/pdfs/region-financed6.pdf (accessed 2 September 2005).

13 There is a right to appeal the amount requisitioned to a provincial body. The appeal route is seldom used and is even less seldom successful.

14 This system is described and illustrated very well in a financial report prepared by the Thames Valley District School Board: http://www.tvdsb.on.ca/budget/pdf/2005-06revenues.pdf (accessed 21 June 2006). See also Enid Slack and Richard M. Bird, 'The Fiscal Sustainability of the Greater Toronto Area,' ITP Paper 0405 (Toronto: Joseph L. Rotman School of Management, 2004), 35–6.

15 Joseph Kushner and David Siegel, 'Citizen Satisfaction with Municipal Amalgamations,' *Canadian Public Administration*, vol. 48, no. 1 (2005): 73–95.

16 Katherine A. Graham and Susan D. Phillips, '"Who Does What" in Ontario: The Process of Provincial-Municipal Disentanglement,' *Canadian Public Administration*, vol. 41, no. 2 (1998): 175–209; Peter Meyboom and Dana Richardson, 'Changing Who-Does-What in Ontario: Ontario's Approach towards Municipal Empowerment – Process, Results and Lessons Learned,' paper presented at conference of the International Institute of Administrative Sciences, Quebec City, 14–17 July 1997.

17 Ontario and Association of Municipalities of Ontario, *Local Services Realignment: A User's Guide* (Toronto: Queen's Printer for Ontario, 1999).

18 These changes are summarized in more detail in Siegel, 'Municipal Reform in Ontario,' 136–7.

19 Municipal Act, 2001, S.O. 2001, c. 25.

20 Municipal Act, 2001, S.O. 2001, c. 25, s. 11.

21 *Report of the Provincial-Municipal Grants Reform Committee: Volume I* (1977), chapter 8; Meyboom and Richardson, 'Changing Who-Does-What in Ontario.'

22 S.O. 1996, c. 32. Before each municipal election, the Ministry of Municipal Affairs and Housing prepares a very useful guide: 'Candidate's Guide-2003 Municipal Elections.'

23 S.O. 2001, c. 25, s. 258.

24 S.O. 1996, c. 32, s. 29.

25 S.O. 1996, c. 32, s. 30.

26 S.O. 1996, c. 32, ss. 66–82.

27 Stephen Clarkson, *City Lib: Parties and Reform* (Toronto: Hakkert, 1972).

28 Joseph Kushner, David Siegel, and Hannah Stanwick, 'Ontario Municipal Elections: Voting Trends and Determinants of Electoral Success in a Canadian Province,' *Canadian Journal of Political Science*, vol. 30, no. 3 (1997): 548–9.

29 R.S.O. 1990, c. M.30, s. 4.

30 Ontario Municipal Board and Board of Negotiation – Annual Report 2003–2004, 6.

31 The board distributes several user-friendly publications geared to assist-

ing non-lawyers who want to appeal to it: 'Your Guide to Ontario Municipal Board Hearings' (Toronto: Queen's Printer for Ontario, 2004); 'You May Want to Make an Appeal to the Ontario Municipal Board' (Toronto: Queen's Printer for Ontario, 2004).

32 David Caplan, 'The OMB Is Broken: Here's How to Fix It,' *Municipal World* (January 2003), 11–12. For a contrary view, see Ian Rowe, 'It's Time to Stop Unfair Criticism of the OMB,' *Municipal World* (July 2004), 25–8, 53.

33 John G. Chipman, *A Law unto Itself: How the Ontario Municipal Board Has Developed and Applied Land Use Planning Policy* (Toronto: Institute of Public Administration of Canada and University of Toronto Press, 2002).

34 Larry Savage, 'Mixed Signals: The OMB and Municipal Electoral Systems,' *Municipal World* (September 2003), 15–20, 40.

35 Robert Williams, 'Democratic Renewal: Time to Start Taking Municipal Elections More Seriously,' *Municipal World* (March 2005), 31–3, 44.

36 Planning Act, R.S.O. 1990, c. P.13, s. 3 (5).

37 http://www.mah.gov.on.ca/userfiles/HTML/nts_1_17433_1.html (accessed 2 September 2005).

38 Rodney Northey, 'Ontario's Greenbelt Act,' *Municipal World* (July 2005), 13–16; Bob Lehman, 'Ontario's Growth Plan for the Golden Horseshoe: A Plan for all Plans,' *Municipal World* (July 2005), 21–5.

39 Ontario, Ministry of Public Infrastructure Renewal, *Places to Grow: Better Choices. Brighter Futures* (Ministry of Public Infrastructure Renewal, 2006).

40 Shari Elliott and Marshall Green, '*Greenbelt Act* Signals Further Erosion in Local Autonomy,' *Municipal World* (July 2005), 17–18.

41 http://www.amo.on.ca/Content/NavigationMenu/AboutAMO/Aboutus/default.htm (accessed 24 August 2005).

42 Ontario and the Association of Municipalities of Ontario, Memorandum of Understanding, Schedule C, ss. 1.4, 1.5, http://www.mah.gov.on.ca/Page5022.aspx.

43 Katherine Harding, 'Miller Says Secret Pact Is a Threat to New Deal among Governments,' *Globe and Mail*, 21 August 2004.

44 Ontario Examines Alberta Model, www.munimall.net/articles/05/050203sewell.nclk (accessed 10 February 2005).

45 Unless otherwise noted, all data in this section come from Statistics Canada, CANSIM II, tables 3850004 and 3850024.

46 John Ibbitson, *Promised Land: Inside the Mike Harris Revolution* (Scarborough, Ont.: Prentice Hall Canada, 1997); Graham and Phillips, '"Who Does What" in Ontario.'

47 The property-tax data in figures 3 and 4 are from the Financial Informa-

tion Returns provided by municipalities to the Ontario Ministry of Municipal Affairs and Housing. Supplied directly to the author by the ministry for years 1991 to 2000 and available at www.oraweb.mah.gov.on.ca/fir/welcome.htm (accessed 12 April 2008) for the more recent years.

48 Personal disposal income data are from CANSIM II, table 3840013.

49 Harry M. Kitchen, *Municipal Revenue and Expenditure Issues in Canada* (Toronto: Canadian Tax Foundation, 2002), 334.

50 Enid Slack, 'Property Tax Reform in Ontario: What Have We Learned?' *Canadian Tax Journal*, vol. 50, no. 2 (2002): 582–3.

51 John Barber, 'Sir David versus the Killer Bunnies,' *Globe and Mail*, 24 June 2006.

52 Thomas J. Courchene, 'Citistates and the State of Cities: Political-Economy and Fiscal-Federalism Dimensions,' IRPP Working Paper Series no. 2005–03 (Montreal: Institute for Research on Public Policy, 2005).

53 The data in this figure is from the Financial Information Returns provided by municipalities to the Ontario Ministry of Municipal Affairs and Housing. Supplied directly to the author by the ministry for years 1991 to 2000 and available at www.oraweb.mah.gov.on.ca/fir/welcome.htm (accessed 12 April 2008) for the more recent years.

54 An excellent discussion of the issue of fiscal sustainability is found in Kitchen, *Municipal Revenue*, chapter 13.

55 Melville McMillan, 'Municipal Relations with the Federal and Provincial Governments,' in Robert Young and Christian Leuprecht, eds., *Municipal-Federal-Provincial Relations in Canada* (Series: Canada: The State of the Federation, 2004) (Montreal and Kingston: McGill-Queen's University Press, 2006), 65.

56 David Siegel and C. Richard Tindal, 'Changing the Municipal Culture: From Comfortable Subordination to Assertive Maturity – Part I,' *Municipal World* (March 2006), 37–40; 'Changing the Municipal Culture: From Comfortable Subordination to Assertive Maturity – Part II,' *Municipal World* (April 2006), 13–17.

2 Quebec

SERGE BELLEY, LAURENCE BHERER, GUY CHIASSON,
JEAN-PIERRE COLLIN, PIERRE HAMEL, PIERRE J. HAMEL,
AND MATHIEU RIVARD WITH THE COLLABORATION OF
JULIE ARCHAMBAULT

The objective of this chapter is to shed light on how the municipal system works in Quebec.[1] We begin in the 1960s when, as was true of other components of the state during the Quiet Revolution, the municipal system came under pressure to modernize its management structure and practices. This pressure did not lift in the following decades but it took different forms. Added to this was the fact that the provincial government had to face both a 'political crisis' against the backdrop of a 'perceived crisis' in public finances – rightly or wrongly defined as such by some – and increasing globalization trends. In this context, the task at hand for local powers was to establish new alliances on governance issues with private-sector stakeholders as well as stakeholders in the public sector. In short, it seems that the Quebec municipal system has been under constant pressure since the 1960s and has more or less resisted repeated demands from the government to undertake an in-depth review of its structures, management mechanisms, priorities, and fundamental values. This resistance was overcome on occasion, however, thereby transforming the balance of power between provincial and local government.

Today, the actors in the municipal field are a far cry from the traditional elites that were closely linked to the former 'État duplessiste.'[2] Thanks to the many successive reforms since the 1960s – though a number of them were far from successful – the municipal system has gone through a series of major transformations that have changed its general form and operating process. Yet, though traditional elites were strongly challenged on several occasions, we did not witness, as was the case in other sectors, a radical changing of the guard. Overall, the municipal world remains a conservative environment aimed at perpetuating the status quo.

These introductory remarks should not be construed as passing judgment on the municipal system or on the part that it plays in the economic, social, and political management of today's Quebec. Instead, they draw the reader's attention to the complex reality of institutional change. Given the cultural and ideological constraints facing the municipal environment, in addition to economic and social constraints, and the resources at its disposal, its orientations have tended to be conservative. Furthermore, the nature of its political leadership is also involved.

Certain normative elements are mixed here with descriptive and analytical aspects. This is, to a degree, inevitable, for where governance is concerned, organizational principles are based on axiological choices. There is never only one way of doing things. In the end, everything is a matter of choices made by a society, even if such choices remain characterized both by certain constraints imposed by the context and by available resources that necessarily limit potential actions.

The Evolution of the Quebec Municipal System

Our purpose here is not to offer a complete review of the history of the Quebec municipal system. Nonetheless, we should note that this system has its roots in the British desire to better control the territory and to resort, for this purpose, to decentralized authorities pursuant to Lord Durham's recommendations. In Durham's opinion, creating these authorities would facilitate the implementation of governmental plans in addition to improving public administration. Finally, we should remember that Durham's recommendations aimed at finding a solution to the causes of the 1837–8 rebellions.

By setting up municipalities, the anglophone bourgeoisie was, at the same time, making an alliance with the clergy. By being 'subservient' to the power of the clergy, municipalities could be agents for the control of populations and territories. They embodied a compromise between civil power and the clergy and, moreover, became a means to neutralize the aspirations of the 'bourgeois and anti-clerical' elite.

In 1870 the government adopted the Municipal Code to govern both rural and urban municipalities, thereby confirming the 'two-level municipal management system' established fifteen years previously. It was only in 1903 that the Quebec legislature adopted the Cities and Towns Act, which established for the first time a clear demarcation between the urban and the rural. Then came the creation of the ministère des Affaires municipales in 1918. Its mandate was not only to 'keep an eye' on municipalities' operations but also to help them adapt to urban transformations. However, its approach was more suitable to a rural environment than to an urban one. In fact, urban reality was, for a long time, somewhat of a mystery to officials in this ministry. Over the years, these officials had little success in providing the appropriate tools for large urban agglomerations because they assessed their problems in light of the municipal system as a whole and, at times, in light of issues that were particular to rural municipalities: 'After more than a hundred years of municipal life, this ministry ... still had a rather "rural" outlook.'[3]

When the Quiet Revolution got under way at the beginning of the 1960s, its promoters believed that the modernization of Quebec society could be accomplished only through the modernization of its institutions, starting with government itself. Many drew attention to both economic inequalities among municipalities and the major issues facing them: financial crises, problems in providing efficient and modern services, and problems in both industrial and regional planning.[4]

In 1961 there were 1,748 municipalities across Quebec's territory, falling under several categories: cities (50), towns (171), counties (74), villages (333), parishes (558), townships (13), and non-designated entities (371). Given their large number and the small populations they serviced, most municipalities necessarily had few resources and powers, whether for the provision of local services or for planning or economic-development activities. The solution that seemed most feasible stemmed from an assessment made by the technocrats: 'Municipalities must regroup in a rational fashion in order to form growth and service centers.'[5]

Pierre Laporte, then minister of municipal affairs, started his campaign for support among elected municipal officials during the summer of 1964. He pushed a law through the legislature pertaining to voluntary mergers of municipalities – Bill 13 – that allowed some mergers the very next year. But the only large-scale amalgamation that the government accomplished was, in the end, the merger of the fourteen municipalities on Île-Jésus, following the Sylvestre Commission's recommendations. This merger created Laval, which became the second-largest municipality in Quebec (until it lost its ranking to Quebec City following the mergers and de-mergers around 2000).

The rise to power of the Union Nationale in 1966 meant a change of position on the part of the government with regard to regionalization and mergers. The level of opposition was duly noted and the decision was made to jettison Laporte's plan, at least temporarily. But the problems did not disappear so easily, given that Quebec municipalities were struggling to meet the needs and social demands of post-war industrial society. This is why the government adopted a new analytical and restructuring approach to the entire municipal system – the Renouveau municipal et urbain (REMUR) project – which aimed at in-depth transformation. While another change of government led to the project being abandoned, this did not keep the state from addressing the problems of managing and planning large urban agglomerations: two urban communities (Montreal and Quebec) and one regional community (Outaouais) were created. It is worth noting that the municipalities regrouped within these authorities managed 'close to 70% of all municipal expenditures in Quebec.'[6]

In the case of Montreal at the end of the 1960s, the government launched a reform of the planning and management of municipal services, as well as of the territory, partly to resolve the issue of financing the city's services, in particular police services. This reform was based on principles of cost reduction, efficiency, and distributive justice. In subsequent years, municipalities were the subject of a number of reform projects that fell short of thorough change. Furthermore, these partial reforms did not reverse 'the trend of central administrations invading local jurisdictions.'[7] This trend was confirmed with Bill 125, adopted by the Parti Québécois (PQ) government in 1979. Under the guise of 'decentralization,' Bill 125 enabled the government to establish very clear-cut controls over the municipal system and, at the same time, to proceed with the modernization that promoters of the Quiet Revolution had unsuccessfully tried to implement.

Basically, the bill created regional county municipalities (RCMs). The RCM councils are composed of the mayors of the urban and rural municipalities located on their territory. Each is chaired by a warden who is 'chosen among the mayors, for a four-year mandate, by a two-thirds majority of the county council members.'[8] In the beginning, RCMs had three types of powers:

1 land-use and urban planning (the RCMs and the municipalities of which they are composed must prepare a development plan, along with master plans that are in accordance with the development plan);

2 the powers of a county corporation relating to roads, bridges and waterways, registry offices, and real estate assessment; and
3 the signature of agreements on various matters between cities and towns in their territory (real estate assessment, collection of real estate transfer taxes, and domestic waste management).

By requiring that RCMs prepare development plans and that their municipalities prepare conforming master plans – all this within a pre-established process and constrained deadlines – the government was strengthening its control over municipalities. In addition, the act introduced a new type of relationship between rural and urban municipalities, thereby eliminating the old county councils system.

During the Quebec-Municipalities Conference held in 1978, prior to the adoption of Bill 125, the government had announced three priority fields of action: the taxation system, municipal democracy, and a decentralization policy. As we will see in the following sections, while there were some modifications made to the financing and the governance of municipalities, the decentralization policy never materialized.

Main Characteristics of the Municipal System

The most recent changes to municipal-system operations were clearly foreshadowed in a white paper on municipal reorganization that was tabled in the National Assembly in April 1999 by the minister of state for municipal and metropolitan affairs and published the following year under the title *La réorganisation municipale: changer les façons de faire, pour mieux servir les citoyens.*[9] It was a political process that proposed, once again, to review the municipal system from an organizational, fiscal, and legal standpoint.

The main objectives were to examine how municipal institutions were configured and operated, with the stated aim of increasing their autonomy and management capacity based on an analysis of contemporary urban reality. The goal, above all, was the 'strengthening of urban centres across Quebec.'[10] In fact, the government was proposing to improve municipal-management performance through the merger of local municipalities and the strengthening of urban agglomerations and RCMs. This is what led the then minister of state for municipal and metropolitan affairs to insist on three major elements: 'the strengthening of rural communities, the strengthening of urban centres and the organization of urban and rural connections.'[11]

The government of Quebec developed a three-point strategy to consolidate the core communities. The first phase pertained to villages/parishes and small municipalities located in agglomerations of less than 10,000 residents. The goal was to group these municipalities together as much as possible by calling on the goodwill of local political actors. The second phase involved agglomerations of more than 10,000 residents, that is, 263 municipalities across Quebec. The third phase affected small local communities – 700 in total – located far from large urban centres and forming a single municipality. While the first phase was quickly implemented, 'the strategy as a whole was temporarily put on the back burner because of the absolute priority given to the zero deficit goal'[12] by the provincial government, thereby decreasing the resources initially allocated to facilitate municipal mergers.

Following the publication of the white paper on municipal reorganization, the government passed a series of bills and draft regulations aimed at improving local governance.[13] The government developed two complementary orientations to reach this goal: the grouping together of municipalities through mergers and the strengthening of urban agglomerations and RCMs. The government's gamble was that decreasing the number of municipalities within the territory would:

1 produce a more equitable sharing of the fiscal burden among taxpayers;
2 improve the performance of municipal management; and
3 support municipalities in more efficiently facing urban planning and development challenges.

Such concerns had existed since the 1960s. Furthermore, they are not very different from those recently expressed in Ontario. In Ontario, whose population is one-and-a-half times the size of Quebec's, the number of municipalities decreased from 851 in July 1996 to 447 in January 2001.[14]

Despite the government's repeated efforts since the early 1960s to decrease the number of municipalities, as of March 2000, there were still slightly more than 1,300 municipalities in Quebec. However, in 2001, this number decreased rapidly, in part because of initiatives taken by some municipalities but more importantly because of laws forcing municipalities to amalgamate: 213 municipalities (or portions of them) were amalgamated into 42 new municipalities, lowering the overall total to slightly over 1,100.

Table 1
Results of municipal reorganization in Quebec[15]

- 1,139 local municipalities
- Nine cities with more than 100,000 inhabitants (Montreal, Quebec, Longueuil, Laval, Gatineau, Saguenay, Sherbrooke, Lévis, and Trois-Rivières)
- Medium-sized cities in almost all regions
- Creation of three categories of RCMs (86 in total)
  - rural
  - mixed (urban and rural)
  - on metropolitan communities' territory
  (in addition to 14 cities exercising RCM powers)
- Creation of two metropolitan communities (Montreal and Quebec)
- Creation of 11 agglomerations

This picture changed again slightly with the de-mergers that occurred in 2003 following the Liberal Party's rise to power: 31 of 213 amalgamated municipalities chose to be reconstituted and the total number of Quebec municipalities increased to 1,139 as of 1 January 2006. Nevertheless, the trend towards consolidation remained intact.

Table 1 summarizes the result of recent structural changes. In 2006 there were 1,139 municipalities, including 14 cities vested with the powers of an RCM; the remaining 1,125 were grouped within 86 RCMs. This reform resulted in a network of nine cities with more than 100,000 inhabitants that accounted for 47 per cent of Quebec's population. Rural Quebec was hardly affected by this operation. In the future, some believe, smaller communities will go through a process of progressive integration into RCMs rather than formal mergers.[16]

A working group led by two mayors, Francine Ruest-Jutras (Drummondville) and Roger Nicolet (Austin), made recommendations regarding the operations of those RCMs that are both rural and urban.[17] These recommendations led to changes in the decision-making structures of RCMs. One of the main recommendations aimed at diminishing the central city's influence on the decisions of this type of RCM. Around the same time, the government introduced the possibility of electing a warden by universal suffrage. In a first phase, this reform was applied to rural RCMs. It was then extended in 2002 to all RCMs with the exception of those located in whole or in part on the territory of the Communauté métropolitaine de Montréal (CMM).[18] Adopted in December 2002, the Act to Amend Various Legislative Provisions concerning Regional County Municipalities (Bill 77) also gave

RCMs located outside the CMM new powers for municipal waterway management, land-use planning, social housing, and regional parks. RCMs were also given the opportunity to designate facilities, infrastructures, services, and activities of a supra-local character and to establish financing and management procedures akin to the powers vested in metropolitan communities.[19] Furthermore, following the same logic, the government decided to strengthen RCMs indirectly, starting in 2003, by using them as a basis to develop local health and social-services networks (LSNs). The same scenario is used for administrative regions, for instance, in the case of health and social-services agencies whose territory mirrors RCM boundaries.

A brand new creation, the urban agglomeration councils, contributes to the government's efforts to foster consolidation, despite the fact that some municipalities have opted for de-mergers. Indeed, in order to preserve an organic bond between the central city and the municipalities that chose to be reconstituted, the government added urban agglomeration councils to an already busy political landscape. In Montreal, Quebec City, and Longueil in particular, and elsewhere where municipalities de-merged, like Mont-Tremblant (eleven agglomerations altogether), urban agglomeration councils are vested with an important component of the powers that were formerly exercised by local municipalities. As such, they manage a substantial part of the budget. In Montreal, for example, the agglomeration council manages more than a third of 'municipal' expenditures; in a way, it took on the responsibilities of the defunct Montréal Urban Community (MUC), which disappeared with the merger of all the autonomous municipalities of which it was composed. The MUC's responsibilities included public transportation, police services, water purification, regional parks, air-pollution control, and food inspection. In addition to these activities, the agglomeration council is responsible for fire-prevention services, which were a function of local municipalities.

How agglomeration councils operate is the subject of ongoing criticism. This is especially the case in Longueil, but it is true in Montreal as well. These criticisms come from 'related' municipalities, that is, those that chose to de-merge but that are nevertheless compelled to cooperate. Criticisms focus on the decisive power of the central city which, with the exception of Longueil, has more than half of the agglomeration's population in its territory and automatically gets more than half of the voting rights on the agglomeration council. The government of Quebec is forever trying to deal with what has become a veritable hornet's nest, by trying to keep the agglomerations operational while at the same time meeting the aspirations for greater autonomy of the 'related' municipalities. The last attempt in this regard would be the possible creation of a 'secretariat' associated with the agglomeration council in Montreal, in which related municipalities would be in the majority and through which they could ask the central city's public servants to carry out studies on subjects that they deem important. Already, the central city has expressed its concern that this new mechanism might enable related municipalities to jam the agglomeration council's operations, while the related municipalities are stressing that this proposed secretariat is far from meeting their demands for more autonomy.

Also going in the direction of greater coordination among local municipalities is the development, at the regional level, of structures for cooperation, planning, and intervention in the case of the Quebec City and Montreal agglomerations. For example, the CMM covers the whole census metropolitan area (CMA) as delimited by Statistics Canada during the 1996 census.[20] Without abolishing the RCMs or the other structures already in place in the administrative regions (five altogether in the case of Montreal), the new authority is vested with powers in different areas. It was given the role and the power to plan or coordinate interventions for the whole region – for example, with respect to transportation infrastructure, the management of regional equipment, and international promotion – though some of these interventions are to be shared with the new 'Ville de Montréal.'

Where land-use planning is concerned, the CMM has the mandate of preparing 'a metropolitan development plan.' In this matter, its approach involves setting out 'a strategic vision of economic, social and environmental development to facilitate the coherent exercise of the Community's jurisdiction.'[21] The CMM has the additional responsibility of fostering economic development involving 'any promotion of its territory to stimulate and attract economic growth and diversification.'[22]

Conversely, the establishment of boroughs ('arroundissements') in Montreal was a step towards renewed fragmentation. Boroughs had already been in existence in Montreal for a number of years but with very limited advisory powers; in fact, as discussed below, they had even fewer powers than the neighbourhood councils in Quebec City. As a result of the mergers of 2001–2, formerly autonomous municipalities were converted into boroughs in Montreal and also in a few other cities (Quebec, Longueuil, Saguenay, Sherbrooke, Lévis, Grenville-sur-la-Rouge, and Métis-sur-Mer). The city of Montreal in particular had to deal with discontent in these new boroughs, and the strategy it adopted was to give them back some room to manoeuvre, by extending the range of responsibilities devolved upon all the boroughs. What the new boroughs formed from the formerly amalgamated municipalities perceived as too little power appeared, on the contrary, to be a golden opportunity to the old boroughs, which discovered new possibilities for action resulting from this autonomy. We know how the story ended: these concessions were not enough to satisfy fifteen municipalities, which regained a good portion of their autonomy through de-amalgamation, while a large part of their former powers was cut, only to be vested in the agglomeration council. But the new autonomy given to Montreal's nineteen boroughs is underestimated. Indeed, a borough even has the power to levy a tax for itself (and five of them exercised this power in 2006). Finally, some may say that, between the agglomeration and the boroughs, it is Montreal that has all but disappeared. Indeed, of its total budget of $3.9 billion for 2006, $2 billion was allocated for agglomeration services and is managed by the agglomeration council, while $1.9 billion was allocated for local services. But, out of this $1.9 billion, close to $850 million is managed by the boroughs for 'proximity' services, leaving city council with the power of managing $1.1 billion for 'central and corporate' services. Another viewpoint is that, in reality, the city council almost entirely controls the agglomeration council and its budget.

Quebec is divided into seventeen administrative regions, and the Montreal metropolitan community's territory is fragmented. It is split among the five administrative regions located in the extreme southwest of the province – regions 06 (the Montreal agglomeration) and 13 (Laval) and part of the territories of regions 14 (Lanaudière), 15 (Laurentians), and 16 (Montérégie). Furthermore, the CMM's territory cuts across, in whole or in part, the territories of ten RCMs, two municipalities vested with the powers of an RCM (Laval and Mirabel), and two agglomerations also vested with the powers of an RCM (Longueuil and Montreal). So, in addition to the Montreal and Longueuil agglomerations, the CMM extends to: Beauharnois-Salaberry; Deux-Montagnes; Lajemmerais; L'Assomption; La Vallée-du-Richelieu; Les Moulins; Laval; Mirabel; Roussillon; Rouville; Thérèse-De Blainville; and Vaudreuil-Soulanges. At the local level, the CMM's territory regroups 82 local municipalities and 3.5 million inhabitants.

In the heart of the CMM, the territory officially called the 'Montreal agglomeration' corresponds to the former Montreal Urban Community; it therefore comprises the island of Montreal and Île-Bizard (in the northwest). The agglomeration includes fifteen 'reconstituted' or 'related' municipalities in addition to the city of Montreal (1.6 million inhabitants); the latter is in turn divided into nineteen boroughs.

Governance and Territorial Issues

The recent reform of the Quebec municipal system introduced a series of changes in the local planning and management process: for example, the new modes of interaction now prevailing between rural and urban RCMs. But, above all, the regrouping of municipalities resulting from mergers and, later on, from demergers has introduced new requirements for intermunicipal coordination. By creating larger urban agglomerations, the government intended to improve management, efficiency, and economies of scale but also to achieve more fairness with respect to both citizens' tax burden and access to services. The same goals were pursued with the establishment of bodies responsible for consultations, decisions, and interventions at the metropolitan level. The creation of boroughs in the large agglomerations of Montreal and Quebec City, thereby decentralizing management and fostering proximity services more in tune with the population, is also part of this approach.[23]

In a way, these many changes aimed to modernize municipal and urban management. Accordingly, the reformers were to a large extent following the lead of the Quiet Revolution technocrats who, after overcoming many obstacles, succeeded, through Bill 125, in replacing the old county councils with RCMs and bringing about certain changes in the local elites by the same token.

However, the last wave of municipal reorganization took place in a very different context. Constraints on local, urban, and regional planning are less the result of bygone days than of pressures stemming from economic transformations on a global scale. In this context, municipalities and urban environments are called to play a dynamic role, not only in ensuring the quality of public services supplied to companies and populations in their territories but also with respect to social integration and local democracy.

Municipalities' Jurisdictional Spheres

According to section 92 of the Constitution Act 1867, municipalities are a provincial field of jurisdiction. This means, as it is often said, that municipalities are 'provincial creatures.' Thus, from a legal and constitutional standpoint, the existence, powers, and structure of municipalities depend entirely on provinces' goodwill, given that the constitution does not give any exclusive powers to local governments. Of course, in practice, municipalities sometimes exceed their legal mandate to exercise de facto powers that the provinces did not explicitly delegate to them. However, understanding municipal fields of jurisdiction in Quebec involves considering the fundamental fact of the province's legal power to determine municipal jurisdictions.

A whole range of provincial laws determine how power is shared between Quebec and its municipalities and impose strict (though variable) controls. These laws differ in nature. First, there are those that strictly concern the municipal world: the Municipal Code, which mostly addresses rural municipalities, and the Cities and Towns Act for more urban municipalities. Some of these laws are more 'territorialized' because they determine the powers that are specific to one or more municipalities in particular (the charters that determine the powers of large cities, the laws on metropolitan communities, and so on). Through legislation adopted by Quebec's National Assembly, municipalities are vested with certain powers. They may not exceed these powers. Furthermore, they may not delegate them to other authorities without legislation allowing it. The administration of the municipality is also governed by regulations that are clearly outlined in the legislation. Elected officials are obliged to abide by those rules, contrary to private enterprise, which may set its own rules according to management principles that they deem appropriate.[24]

As well, there are also 'sectoral' laws whose main subject is not municipal governance but sectors of activity (the environment, transportation, rural development, and others) that interact with municipalities. These laws are significant for the municipal system in that they determine and provide a framework for certain municipal responsibilities within these sectors of activity (for instance, the preservation of historical monuments under the Cultural Property Act). Table 2 provides additional information about how powers (or responsibilities) are shared between municipalities, boroughs, agglomeration councils, RCMs, metropolitan communities, and the government of Quebec.

As mentioned in the previous section, the establishment of agglomeration councils in January 2006, particularly in Montreal and Quebec City, means that these metropolitan areas are governed by a number of decision-making levels: the boroughs, the cities, the RCMs, the agglomeration councils, and the metropolitan communities. This is not counting the 'regional' level (administrative regions) under the governance of the regional conferences of elected officials mandated by the government of Quebec to manage the funds allocated for regional development. The coexistence of these many levels makes for complex local governance as well a fragmentation of powers among numerous actors within the local public sector. The following examples illustrate this fragmentation.

In public transportation, agglomeration councils or the municipalities and the RCMs share a management role, while the metropolitan communities are responsible for the coordination and planning for the entire 'city-region' and, in addition, contribute to the financing along with the government of Quebec. In the case of Montreal, there is also the Agence métropolitaine de transport (AMT), which is run by a local board of directors and whose mandate covers the entire Montreal region but with no accountability to the elected officials who are directly concerned. Instead, the AMT answers first to the ministère des Affaires municipales et de la Métropole and then to the ministère des Transports.

Social housing concerns all levels of local governance, whether for the implementation and management of programs (borough councils, RCMs, and municipalities) or for their financing (municipalities, agglomeration councils, RCMs, and metropolitan communities).

For the environment, very few responsibilities are entirely in the hands of local municipalities. Even water purification and distribution as well as waste management, which were municipal responsibilities well before the modernization of the supra-local level in the 1970s, have been redefined to make room for new contributors. In the case of water purification, the metropolitan communities are responsible for controlling waste-water dumping and regulating water-purification facilities. Only the responsibility for underground sewer mains was left untouched, and even then, only in the absence of an agglomeration council; otherwise, the council is responsible for collector mains while the municipalities are responsible for 'local' mains.

Where waterway management is concerned, local municipalities (outside the agglomeration) are responsible for municipal waterways within the municipality's limits, while the RCMs are responsible for 'regional' waterways. The sharing of responsibilities is murkier and more divided in the case of waste management, where boroughs and municipalities (or agglomeration councils) share the responsibility for garbage collection while agglomeration councils and RCMs (an option in their case) are jointly responsible for implementing the waste-management plan at their respective levels. The scenario is the same for parks, green spaces, and land-use planning, an area of jurisdiction associated with the creation of RCMs towards the end of the 1970s. Where land use and urban planning are concerned, all five levels have significant powers, whether it is boroughs developing zoning by-laws and holding public consultations, municipalities and agglomeration councils establishing master plans, or RCMs and metropolitan communities making development plans.

The sports and leisure sector as well as cultural amenities are the subject of complex governance. In both cases, local facilities fall under the responsibility of the municipalities and their boroughs, while the 'wider-range' facilities fall under the responsibility of either the agglomeration councils or the RCMs. The Montreal and Quebec City agglomeration councils must set up an arts council to support arts organizations in their region while this responsibility is optional for other large cities (Gatineau, Sherbrooke, Saguenay, and so on). Financial support to organizations promoting physical or cultural activity is the responsibility of both local municipalities and RCMs, while municipalities and metropolitan communities contribute to the financing of regional facilities.

The legislative structure that defines municipal powers goes well beyond municipal laws (the Municipal Code and the Cities and Towns Act) to include a number of sectoral laws as well as certain laws pertaining to specific municipal territories. The issue of powers is also a complex one because of the multiplication of levels of governance in local and regional territories. With five levels of local governance coexisting in the Montreal and Quebec City agglomerations, large areas of public intervention are fragmented among multiple actors. Moreover, the delineation of responsibilities among these various entities is not always clear. It is increasingly difficult to understand municipal powers unless we consider the interlocking of levels of government.

Table 2
The sharing of powers

Powers	Borough	Municipality	Agglomeration Council (AC)	Regional County Municipality (RCM)	Metropolitan Community (MC)	Government of Quebec
Police		Yes (if no AC)	Yes			Sûreté du Québec, Sécurité publique
Fire prevention	Advises on the development of the fire-risk coverage plan	Yes (if no AC)	Yes, fire-risk coverage plan	Fire-risk coverage plan		
Animal control		Yes				
Roads, road maintenance, traffic and parking	Local roads (snow removal and public works)	Roads, road maintenance, traffic and local parking, bicycle paths	Roads and traffic management at AC territory level	Local roads management (optional)	Metropolitan arterial road network network	Provincial road network
Public transportation		Management, fare system: Yes (if no AC)	Management, operations	Management (optional)	Coordination, planning, and contribution to financing (in Montreal: power shared with the AMT)	Contribution to financing (especially for capital expenditures, Metro, rolling stock, buses)

Table 2 (*continued*)

Powers	Borough	Municipality	Agglomeration Council (AC)	Regional County Municipality (RCM)	Metropolitan Community (MC)	Government of Quebec
Water purification and distribution		Yes (if no AC)	Yes		Regulate or prohibit waste-water dumping, regulations on water-treatment equipment (not in force in Montreal)	Provincial policy on water; contribution to capital-expenditures financing
Sewers		Yes (if no AC)	Yes			
Land-use planning	Urban planning by-laws including zoning, subdivisions and layout, public consultations on urban planning	Master plan (if no AC), zoning bylaw	Master plan	Development plan outside the MC and, until 2005, for the RCMs included in the MCs	Development plans (starting in 2005 for the CMM and 2006 for the CMQ)	Major orientations (general framework)
Buildings and housing	Variance on the ban to convert a building to a condominium, implementation of city's programs	By-laws and permit delivery, program development, powers of the Régie du bâtiment (optional)		Establishment of a regional office for housing (optional)		Provincial norms

Table 2 (*continued*)

Powers	Borough	Municipality	Agglomeration Council (AC)	Regional County Municipality (RCM)	Metropolitan Community (MC)	Government of Quebec
Economic development	Financial support to local economic development, social and community development organizations	Support for business, industrial parks, and international promotion of their territory (if not in MC)	Support for business, planning, territory's promotion, local development centres (CLD), congress centres, some ports, airports, industrial parks	Technical and financial support for business (optional), CLDs financing and operations, strategic-vision and development-plan preparation (optional and if not in MC), local investment fund (optional)	Economic development, planning, coordination, international promotion (in Montréal, power delegated to Montréal international)	Support for businesses, planning, specific programs
Urban revitalization		Yes				Financial support
Tourism promotion		Yes	Yes			Yes
Public libraries		Yes				
Parks and green spaces	Local parks	Local parks and green spaces	Local parks (municipal)	Establishment and management of regional parks (optional)	Green and blue spaces	Quebec's national parks

Table 2 (continued)

Powers	Borough	Municipality	Agglomeration Council (AC)	Regional County Municipality (RCM)	Metropolitan Community (MC)	Government of Quebec
Watercourses		Municipal watercourses (if no AC)	Municipal watercourses	Regional watercourses with a right to withdraw for municipalities (if not in MC), rural RCMs also manage local watercourses		
Sports and leisure	Local leisure facilities and activities, local parks	Local facilities, support to organizations, contribution to the financing of metropolitan equipment located on its territory	Agglomeration facilities	Supra-local facilities (optional and if not in MC), financial support of sports organizations and clubs (optional)	Contribution to the financing of metropolitan facilities	Contribution to the financing of metropolitan facilities
Cultural facilities and activities	Local facilities and activities	Local facilities and activities, contribution to metropolitan facilities financing	Agglomeration facilities (and activities), and arts council	Supra-local facilities (optional and if not in MC), financial support for cultural-activities promotion and organizations (optional)	Contribution to the financing of metropolitan facilities, artistic and cultural development (Montreal), financial support and promotion	Supra-local facilities and services, contribution to metropolitan facilities financing

Table 2 (continued)

Powers	Borough	Municipality	Agglomeration Council (AC)	Regional County Municipality (RCM)	Metropolitan Community (MC)	Government of Quebec
Emergency services		Yes (if no AC)	Yes, '911' emergency service, emergency-preparedness plan			Provincial level planning
Daycare		May exercise the powers delegated by the minister				
Fences		Regulation				
Social housing	Manage city programs (Montreal)	Contribution to financing	Yes	Management (optional), contribution to financing (optional)	Contribution to financing	Contribution to financing
Assistance to the homeless		Yes (if no AC)	Yes			
Real estate assessment		Yes (if no AC)	Yes	Yes[25]	Program for the sharing of growth in the property-tax base	
Waste management	Waste collection	Waste collection and disposal (if no AC)	Disposal and recycling, management-plan implementation	Management-plan development (outside MC), waste management (optional)	Development of a metropolitan waste-management plan	Quebec policy on waste management

Table 2 (*continued*)

Powers	Borough	Municipality	Agglomeration Council (AC)	Regional County Municipality (RCM)	Metropolitan Community (MC)	Government of Quebec
Municipal Court		Yes (if no AC)	Yes			
Environment and sustainable development		Quebec City: limited regulation powers; Montreal: frequent interventions, pesticides for instance				Regulate or prohibit pollution emission (not in force in Montreal)
Unorganized Territories				Yes		
Other	Enforcement of regulation on nuisances and pesticides	Montreal manages income-security services (agreement with the government of Quebec)	All other powers that had been attributed to the organization from which the city took over (RCM or Urban Community)	All other powers delegated by local municipalities (optional) and by the government (optional with right to withdraw for local municipalities)	Powers delegated by the government (none to date)	
Sources of financing – Autonomy						
Taxation	Indirectly: additional rate to municipal taxes, providing city council agrees.	Yes (property taxes and real estate transfer taxes)	Yes (property-tax base)	No	No	Yes (all fiscal areas)
Fee fixing	Yes	Yes	Yes	Yes (optional)	Yes (optional)	Yes

Local Public Finances

To describe local public finances briefly, one must essentially divide municipal expenditures into four major blocks:

1 transportation (roads and public transit);
2 prevention (fire and police services);
3 the environment (water and waste); and
4 leisure and culture.

Unlike some other parts of Canada, Quebec municipalities have very few responsibilities in the education and health sectors: the government of Quebec exercises most of the powers in these areas through networks (mostly school boards and 'Cegeps' in the former, and health and social-services centres in the latter) which it almost entirely finances and closely controls.[26]

The situation is even simpler in terms of financing. Quebec municipalities receive very little in terms of transfer payments from governments and their main source of revenue is property taxes. In addition, contrary to practices elsewhere in North America, municipal capital investments are rarely paid outright (with money saved for his purpose over the years) but are instead financed through loans generally amortized over twenty years.

There is not space here to describe in detail how the financial reform that took place towards the end of the 1970s defines the channels of power in local public finances. The objective at the time was to strengthen municipalities' fiscal autonomy and also local responsibility for providing services. Essentially, municipalities were allowed to increase property taxes, which were already their main source of revenue. To make it easier for them, school boards were withdrawn almost entirely from this tax base, allowing municipalities to occupy the 'vacated space.' In return, the government naturally increased transfer payments to school boards while, at the same time, cutting back on transfer payments to municipalities. Thus, municipalities' own-source revenue was increased, reaching 95 per cent of their total revenue after the reform, compared to 76 per cent before. (This percentage can be misleading, however: if all municipal agencies are included, that is, if consolidated municipal revenue is considered in the calculation, 'autonomous revenue in 1982, in fact, accounted for less, i.e. a ratio of 85.4%.'[27])

All things considered, the reform accomplished what it was meant to accomplish, given that autonomous revenue in 2004 accounted for 87 per cent of municipalities' total revenue, with property taxes alone accounting for two-thirds of this total, while the transfer payments that made up the difference were greatly decreased. This is particularly true for unconditional transfer payments, which account for only 3 per cent of municipal revenue (see Table 3).[28]

Table 3 makes it appear that transfer payments (conditional and unconditional) weigh lightly in the composition of municipal revenue and that this is one of the major differences between Quebec and the rest of Canada (ROC): total transfer payments were 13 per cent in the former versus 16 per cent in the latter.[29] But this interpretation is partly wrong because the weight of transfer payments in municipal budgets in the ROC can be explained to a large extent through two atypical cases. First and foremost is the case of the government of Ontario, which makes substantial transfer payments to municipalities, given their extensive responsibilities for health services and even greater responsibilities for front-line social services (that is, about 25 per cent of municipal budgets in Ontario). Second is Nova Scotia, which is similar to some extent, but with respect to education. In fact, if the transfer payments that are particular to Ontario and Nova Scotia are set aside, transfer payments in municipal budgets in Quebec account for a ratio equivalent to (and perhaps even higher than) those in the ROC.

Another differentiating factor, less remarkable but somewhat more important, is the weight of revenue generated from sources other than taxes in municipal budgets. Municipalities in the ROC generate more revenue by selling goods and services (water, electricity, and others) and through investments; if we look more closely, with the benefit of more details than the data presented in Table 3, we would see that more consistent investment revenue clearly makes the difference.[30]

In Quebec, own-source revenues other than property taxes and revenue generated through the sale of goods and services are not generally the result of a true rate-fixing mechanism. The ministère des Affaires municipales et des Régions persists in designating taxes other than property taxes as 'fiscal fees' though in reality they are actually 'user fees.' In other words, these taxes, in some municipalities, are used to impose certain charges (for drinking water, waste-water treatment, or other services) on the basis of parameters other than a property assessment (which is a fixed tax per household, on the basis of a

Table 3
Revenue and expenditures of general local administrations, Quebec and ROC, 2004[31]

Revenue		Quebec		ROC	
			Per capita		ROC – Quebec Per capita[31]
		%	$	%	$
Own-source revenue					
Property taxes		50	746	41	-1
Other property-related taxes		15	217	8	-70
Other taxes		0	7	2	24
	Total taxes	65	970	51	-47
Sales of goods and services		18	263	24	163
Other own-source revenue		4	57	7	72
Transfer payments					
Conditional transfer payments from the province		10	152	13	83
Unconditional transfer payments from the province		3	42	3	13
Total transfer payments from the province		13	194	16	96
Conditional transfer payments from the federal govt.		0	2	2	27
Total transfer payments		13	196	18	123
Total own-source revenue		87	1 290	82	188
Total revenue		100	1 4860	100	310
Total revenue ($M)		11247		44,049	

Expenditures	Quebec		ROC	
		Per capita		ROC – Quebec Per capita[32]
	%	$	%	$
General public administration services	13	195	10	-16
Person and property protection	17	267	16	27
Transport and communications	23	359	18	-23
Health	0	1	3	59
Social services	1	14	13	217
Education	0	2	0	8
Resources conservation and industrial development	3	48	2	-16
Environment	16	251	16	39
Recreation and culture	13	202	12	12
Housing	3	51	4	15
Regional planning and development	3	42	2	-14
Debt servicing	7	110	3	-51
Other expenditures	0		0	0
Surplus or deficit	-4	-55	0	57
Total expenditures	100	1 541	100	253
Total expenditures ($M)	11,647		44,002	

lot's area or frontage or otherwise). Added to this is revenue generated through transit fares. Public transportation agencies' revenue (collected from users) accounts for most of the revenue generated by the sales of goods and services and of own-source revenue other than taxes. Otherwise, true revenue from the sale of goods and services is low because metering water usage remains a very limited practice and the number of municipal 'public utilities' is almost insignificant.[33] Towards the end of the nineteenth century, a number of municipalities in Quebec, as was the case elsewhere, had established government control over the local 'Water & Power' and eighty municipalities and cooperatives operated electricity-distribution services. But most of the municipalities decided to sell to Hydro-Québec in 1963 when electricity was nationalized or in the years that followed;[34] only nine municipalities and one cooperative in Quebec still (happily) supply power on a retail basis: Alma, Amos, Baie-Comeau, Coaticook, Joliette, Jonquière (Ville de Saguenay), Magog, Sherbrooke, Westmount, and the Coopérative régionale d'électricité de Saint-Jean-Baptiste de Rouville.

Overall, Table 3 shows that per capita revenue of municipalities in the ROC is greater than that of their Quebec counterparts (+ $310 per capita). However, the higher transfer payments (+ $123 on average) to municipalities in the ROC do not compensate for their greater financial responsibility for health (+ $59) and social services (+ $217 mostly in Ontario) and in education services (+ $8 on average, Nova Scotia in particular). But, clearly, the higher revenue under the headings of goods and services sales (+ $163) and 'other own-source' revenue (+ $72) more than adequately compensates for slightly lower property-tax revenue (- $1).

Furthermore, the crown does not pay taxes – a well-known fact – and higher-level governments pay grants 'in lieu of taxes' or, more precisely, compensation as a substitute for taxes. The federal government pays compensation that is more or less (in fact, almost systematically less)[35] equivalent to the non-residential property tax. The government of Quebec, for its part, pays full and complete compensation for those buildings that specifically house government offices; but the story is different when it comes to properties used by the health, education, and social-services systems. Depending on the highs and the lows of its budgetary situation, the government, which has never paid 100 per cent compensation for the taxes on these properties, increases and decreases these compensation rates, each time having an unquestionably 'good' excuse for doing so, since, as the saying goes, 'might makes right.'[36] 'In 1980... the Government of Quebec had set its compensation ratios at 100% for its offices ... at 80% for properties used for the health and higher education system, and at 40% for elementary and secondary schools. In 1983, the compensation ratio for schools was increased from 40% to 50% but there were no subsequent increases. On the contrary, in 1992, the school ratio was lowered from 50% to 25% for budgetary reasons and with the added argument that the schools were part of the local heritage assets.'[37]

Another revenue source is worth mentioning, for, despite its insignificant appearance, it is, in fact, very atypical. Real estate transfer taxes (better known as the 'welcome tax') are collected from the buyer of a property. It is therefore a true consumption tax, being generated by a purchase[38] – a percentage is applied on the value of a purchased good – and it is thus the only tax of its kind remaining in the municipal quiver; despite the stream of reforms, municipalities have remained confined to property-related taxes, except for this one exception. Quebec municipalities do not collect consumption or income taxes, although this has not always been the case.[39]

It would seem that the major new element in municipal revenue is the increasing importance of school-property taxes. In rural sectors where municipalities offer few services and therefore collect few taxes, school taxes are almost as high as municipal taxes. In fact, it seems that the government might be tempted to curtail its financing of school boards by forcing them to increase school-property taxes up to the maximum ceiling possible (or perhaps even abolish its financing, leaving school boards free to raise their tax rates to levels that they consider sufficient to meet their needs). For a long time now, the government has stated that property-based taxation is insufficiently exploited and that municipalities, rather than complain about a resource shortage, particularly for infrastructure rehabilitation, should have the courage to increase taxes. The provincial government might even be tempted to step into this 'underexploited' area by itself taxing property alongside municipalities and school boards. It could also abolish school taxes in order to collect a province-wide property tax that would be, formally or not, dedicated to the school system.

Since 2001, Quebec municipalities have been able to establish five categories of properties to which slightly different taxation rates can be applied.[40] It is also noteworthy that the taxation system in Quebec provides for a partial reimbursement of property taxes to agriculture and forestry producers. Since 1979, it also includes a property-tax reimbursement program[41] (which, as years went by, became accessible only to very low-income households); this tax credit introduces a dose of proportional taxation into a system which would otherwise be clearly regressive for average-income taxpayers. But, given that property taxation is an inevitable reality (no havens, no loopholes), it is, overall, more progressive than is generally believed, for the wealthiest households are required to make a contribution that is often more commensurate with their financial means.[42] Finally, property assessment in Quebec has reached a high degree of sophistication. Indeed, contrary to what often takes place elsewhere, the assessment roll, which is the basis of property taxation, is a fairly close reflection of the actual market value of properties.

In terms of expenditures, we can limit our comments to three other elements. First, it is fascinating to see the extent to which municipal expenditures are 'predictable' when one knows the size, and especially the type, of a municipality: industrial or rural, residential, or with a strong commercial or other character. The analysis of what composes a municipality's property-tax base allows one to infer, almost mechanically, the volume and the kind of expenditures it makes.[43] The room to manoeuvre for elected officials therefore appears to be very slim and one may wonder why municipal autonomy, both in spending and financing, should be cause for celebration when, in reality, it means ending up doing what every similar municipality is doing. Of course, it is all in how things are done and, clearly, great municipal politicians do things differently or even, at times, do different things (or at least they appear to do so). Given the restrictive playing field, they deserve all the more credit.

Furthermore, Quebecers witness the same scenario found in all industrialized countries: upper-level governments are downloading some of their responsibilities onto municipalities (directly, or indirectly by establishing new standards) without providing them with the necessary resources to cover these new expenditures. Sometimes, the proposal appears appealing enough for municipalities to acquiesce without complaint, though they soon realize that the gift comes with a number of constraining obligations. Since 1993, this has been the case with the maintenance of secondary roads or of collector roads in rural sectors. Compensated by the ministère des Transport with a pre-determined amount, municipalities take care of snow removal without problems but then progressively discover the full extent of the tasks involved in road maintenance (especially given the poor maintenance sometimes done by the ministry during the years preceding the transfer of the responsibility).[44] Hence some municipalities start to cut corners and to defer sine die work that appears unimportant (such as culvert maintenance), thereby risking an acceleration of the infrastructure's degradation.

In their quest for new financial means from higher-level governments, Quebec and Canadian cities have made infrastructure their key issue. Probably because they did not think they were in a position to ask legitimately for money to support their operating expenditures, the issue of the lack of investment in infrastructure came to the forefront, at least in political discourse. Sometimes, a relaunch of the jointly financed Canada-Quebec infrastructure program is called for, and sometimes ad hoc transfer payments are requested, which cities will then ask to be made permanent. Hence, municipalities recently started to receive a portion of the gasoline-excise tax and they are also now exempted from the Goods and Services Tax (GST); in Montreal, these sums of money, which will be used to support municipal investments in all infrastructure rehabilitation (roads, public transportation, and so on) are clearly lower than those invested in water purification and distribution alone.[45] Therefore, this is not a 'gold mine' by any means, but municipalities generally make a habit of not refusing anything offered to them. On even rarer occasions, some Quebec municipalities will, reluctantly, take on the cause championed by the Federation of Canadian Municipalities (FCM), which claims – and it's a good argument – that the real fiscal imbalance is not the one that most Quebecers tend to think about (the federal-provincial one) but is rather the one that concerns municipalities.[46] And yet it is clear that Quebec municipalities cannot play this card in the same way that their ROC counterparts would.

By doing what ought to be done and what they should have always done, some municipalities perhaps show that the need for a new way of sharing resources may not be as pressing as is generally perceived. For example, in 2004, the city of Montreal decided to progressively make up for the lack of resources for water-related infrastructure rehabilitation with a very modest annual increase of property taxes; by 2013, the city expects to reach an adequate 'cruising speed' in terms of its investments.[47] The turnaround is under way and results are already tangible, to the extent that the issue of infrastructure financing may resolve itself, at least in the case of water-related infrastructures.

Governmental Controls

Although they have numerous powers and are to a large extent financially autonomous, Quebec municipalities are the subject of a range of controls by the provincial government. Whether for the environment, land-use planning, emergency services, or territorial development, public organizations (including ministries with jurisdictions in different areas) control local authorities in the initiation, development, and implementation of policies. In reality, it is the ministère des Affaires municipales, du Sport et des Loisirs (MASL), which in February 2005 became the ministère des Affaires municipales et des Régions (MAMR), that implements the majority of control measures provided in provincial statutes. However, if the law requires it, other ministries or public organizations may intervene and control municipalities' activities.

Governmental agencies are responsible for the application of Quebec statutes and this involves countless controls; strictly considering the major ones, we count twenty-four that concern municipal affairs. Governmental controls may be grouped into two categories: controls that are common to several statutes and specific controls stemming from each statute.

The first type of control concerns municipalities' obligation to submit periodically various information to the MAMR, on pre-determined dates – for example, the assessment roll (An Act respecting Municipal Taxation, s. 71); the annual activity report of the police department (Police Act, s. 264); and information regarding the origin, nature, characteristics, quantities, destination, and elimination methods of waste that a municipality collects, turns over to a third party, or takes charge of (Environment Quality Act, s. 68.1). Municipalities must also, in many cases, and according to the demands of the MAMR and other ministries, prepare certain documents generally related to the planning and management of different areas in municipal administration. For example, there is the requirement to adopt a master plan conforming to the development plan (Act respecting Land-use Planning and Development, s. 82).

Probably, one the most important control mechanisms is the requirement for each municipality, in several fields, to obtain the consent of the ministry concerned prior to implementing a decision, a rule, or a by-law. Here are a few examples:

- municipalities may not 'establish waterworks, a water supply intake or water purification appliances or carry out work respecting sewers or the installation of devices for the treatment of waste water' before submitting a plan to the ministry (Environment Quality Act, s. 32);
- they must also obtain authorization before establishing air-pollution monitoring stations or alert systems for air pollution (Environment Quality Act, s. 47);
- they may not borrow to make up a deficit (Act respecting Municipal Debts and Loans, s. 3);
- they may not borrow on foreign money markets without ministerial authorization (Act respecting Municipal Debts and Loans, s.15);
- they may not divide their territory into a number of electoral districts that is smaller than the minimum number or greater than the maximum number (Act respecting Elections and Referendums in Municipalities, s. 10); and
- 'every by-law ordering a loan shall be submitted to the qualified voters and to the Minister of Municipal Affairs and Regions for approval' (Cities and Towns Act, s. 556).

It is also important to specify that, according to section 365 of the Cities and Towns Act, municipal councils may not repeal a by-law that requires ministerial approval without following the same prescribed process (that is, an approval). However, a council may immediately amend a by-law requiring approval from the government, provided that the amendment does not increase the charges upon taxpayers or change the goal of the by-law. The minister may then approve the by-law so amended.

In principle, Quebec municipalities enjoy a great degree of financial and political autonomy to manage their territory. However, this latitude has its limits in a number of areas of activity. Indeed, the management of municipal affairs must follow a series of regulations and processes that are defined by law. The most common among these are requirements to submit information to various ministries and to obtain the approval of the minister concerned prior to implementing a rule or a by-law. The first is the less restrictive, given that it simply involves a municipal clerk providing information, such as the assessment-roll summary, the name of the city council members following an election, the police department internal regulations, or 'all information concerning the execution of the municipal law, and all other information which he may be able to give with the concurrence of the council' (Cities and Towns Act, s.55).

The requirement of ministerial approval is the most common and the most restrictive. It is also the requirement that appears to have the greatest impact on the management process, given that towns and villages are delayed in the implementation of their by-laws in addition to being obligated, in many cases, to amend them according to the minister's requirements. Therefore, municipalities are not 'masters in their own house' where many of their powers are concerned.

The law is more restrictive in the case of emergency services and the environment to the extent that it gives the minister the right to take certain initiatives, such as asking for environmental-impact studies or imposing severe sanctions. However, these powers may not be used unless all conditions that are established in the law are met. Furthermore, the minister has the right to rule by order-in-council with respect to the organization of new municipalities. This is fairly restrictive, given that central cities and former municipalities must follow the minister's decision in case of a disagreement.

One of the main tools for controlling municipalities is the Commission municipale du Québec. It was originally established in 1932 to oversee and control the finances of municipalities and school boards at a time when school boards were dealing with serious financial problems. Over time, its mandate significantly evolved and judicial powers were added to its administrative responsibilities. Table 4 summarizes the powers given to the commission.

A recent bill proposed the abolition of the Commission municipale but it appears that this has been put on the backburner indefinitely. The bill would have distributed the commission's powers between the ministère des Affaires municipales et des Régions, the Tribunal administratif du Québec, the Commission des normes du travail, and the Chief Electoral Officer of Quebec (CEOQ).[48]

Far from getting lighter, governmental controls are actually becoming more restrictive, going into much more detail than before. This is the case, for example, with infrastructure rehabilitation, for which the government offers support to municipalities in many ways through various programs. It will no longer be enough to submit a report in the pre-determined format to the department concerned, for the ministry no longer authorizes municipalities to decide the order in which work will be done according to their needs. Prioritization of the work must

Table 4
The responsibilities of the Commission municipale du Québec[49]

Administrative powers	Judicial powers
Temporary administration of municipalities whose councils are unable to hold session	Arbitration of disagreements between municipalities
Approval of certain municipal by-laws	Notice of compliance concerning urban and land-use planning documents
Registrar of urban and land-use planning documents	Setting up rates for water and sewage services, fees for the use of underground mains and other public services (waste collection, facility usage, etc.)
Preparation of the list of supra-local facilities (as required by the minister)	Decisions on tax exemptions for certain organizations
Nomination of directors of elections (exceptional cases)	Discharge of directors of elections
Conduct studies on possible municipal re-organizations (as required by the minister or the municipalities)	Rescinding the mandate of elected officials unable to attend city council
Analysis of the process of public calls for tenders by municipalities (as required by the minister)	Determining who is responsible for road maintenance
State supervision of municipalities	Inquiries and orders to execute certain intermunicipal works
Inquiries (as required by the minister)	

now be done according to a precise course, detailed step by step in a guide.[50] This is how the ministry's website explains the requirement: 'This guide helps you to prepare an intervention plan in order to determine the priorities with respect to replacing water and sewer mains. Please note that this plan is mandatory for all main replacement projects submitted as part of the FIMR program [Fonds sur l'infrastructure municipale rurale].'[51] The guide explains, among other things, how to weigh the importance of the water main – for example, whether it services a hospital versus how badly deteriorated it is. Hence, it is no longer enough for ministry officials to ensure that the subsidies are indeed used for infrastructure rehabilitation; they must also know whether, in their opinion and according to their own criteria, these investments are made for the most important, urgent, or fundamental public works.

Table 5
Breakdown of municipalities by population range, Quebec, 2006[52]

Number of inhabitants	Number of municipalities	Population %
Less than 2,000	753	8.6
From 2,000 to 9,999	294	15.3
From 10,001 to 49,999	74	21.1
From 50,000 to 99,999	9	8.1
100,000 and more	9	46.9
Total	1,139	100
		N = 7.5 M

The approach advocated in the guide is mandatory for projects submitted for funding under the FIMR but it is also highly recommended for all other types of applications: 'This guide provides minimal guidelines for the preparation of the intervention plan; it should *not necessarily* be substituted for processes already in use by municipalities or consultants.'[53] The ministry decides whether or not to support projects submitted by municipalities, and all those that apply for this support are perfectly free to adopt the approaches that are favoured by the decision makers.

The Demographic Dynamic

Quebec's territory is vast but the habitable areas are limited: the core of the Quebec population is concentrated around the St Lawrence River, particularly in the southernmost part of the territory. The province has a population of 7.5 million people. Just under half (3.5 million) live in the municipalities that make up the Montreal metropolitan community in the south and almost 10 per cent (710,000) live in the Quebec metropolitan community, a mere 250 kilometres northeast of Montreal. These two agglomerations make up 56 per cent of the total population.

Quebec has only nine municipalities of more than 100,000 inhabitants, with 1.6 million inhabitants in Montreal alone; together, these nine largest municipalities account for almost half of the population.

With the exception of Saguenay, all these municipalities are located in a relatively small triangle in southwestern Quebec. The seven northern regions of Quebec are experiencing constant demographic decreases,

Table 6
The eighteen largest cities in Quebec[54]

Municipalities	Population in thousands
Dollard-Des Ormeaux	51
Saint-Hyacinthe	51
Shawinigan	52
Saint-Jérôme	64
Drummondville	67
Brossard	70
Repentigny	75
Saint-Jean-sur-Richelieu	85
Terrebonne	89
Trois-Rivières	126
Lévis	127
Saguenay	146
Sherbrooke	146
Longueuil	231
Gatineau	244
Laval	365
Quebec	493
Montreal	1,638

while three central regions are seeing slight increases. Seven of the seventeen regions – those in the south – are experiencing growth.

Despite government efforts to regionalize immigration and encourage settlement throughout the territory, immigrants tend to concentrate in the Montreal region, with the most recent arrivals settling in that region's heart, in the centre of the island of Montreal.

Associations and Local Public Politics

This section presents the primary political and professional associations active in the municipal sector of Quebec, as well as employers and labour organizations that occasionally intervene in debates concerning the adoption or modification of laws and municipal programs.

Political Associations

Two associations of municipalities are recognized by the government as legitimate representatives in municipal matters, both holding equal status for all intents and purposes; as officially recognized representatives, they are almost always invited to participate in all consultation processes, whether formal (as in parliamentary committees) or informal.

THE UNION DES MUNICIPALITÉS DU QUÉBEC (UMQ)
'With its 230 members accounting for more than six million citizens and managing more than 90% of municipal budgets, the *Union des municipalités du Québec* represents the municipal world in all its diversity. Covering almost 75% of the municipalized territory in Quebec, its weight and legitimacy allows it to intervene in the public discourse in the name of more than 80% of the Quebec population.'[55] In practice, the UMQ brings together those urban municipalities that fall under the purview of the Cities and Towns Act or that have a specific charter.

The UMQ has organized regional, as well as sectoral, caucuses to bring together municipalities of similar types. In fact, the UMQ has great difficulty in maintaining cohesion within its ranks and finding ways for different categories of municipalities to cohere; thus, the largest among them disaffiliate themselves fairly regularly, only to rejoin the ranks until the next squabble.

LA FÉDÉRATION QUÉBÉCOISE DES MUNICIPALITÉS (FQM)
If the UMQ is the small club of large municipalities, the FQM is the large association of the smallest. Active in 85 per cent of the Quebec territory, especially in rural areas but also in urban and peri-urban ones, the Fédération québécoise des municipalités represents more than 900 municipalities, and essentially all of the RCMs. This federation, created sixty years ago, has always played the role of spokesperson for the regions.

The FQM has a board of directors representative of its members. It is made up of thirty-eight mayors elected by mayors of member municipalities of their region, one representative of bilingual municipalities, one representative of municipalities with more than 10,000 inhabitants, one representative of municipalities included in the Communauté métropolitaine de Montréal, and one representative of those included in the territory of the Communauté métropolitaine de Québec.

Professional Associations

LA CORPORATION DES OFFICIERS MUNICIPAUX AGRÉÉS DU QUÉBEC (COMAQ)
Proud of its status as a professional corporation established in 1968 by the National Assembly through a private bill, the Corporation des officiers municipaux agréés du Québec today brings together more

than 550 managers who are active in more than 250 municipalities, affecting almost 85 per cent of the Quebec population.

Any manager in a municipal position related to the general, legal, or financial administration may join the COMAQ. The corporation is regularly convened by the government to participate during public consultations; as well, COMAQ is often closely involved with the Ministère des Affaires municipales to develop guidelines for municipalities.

L'ASSOCIATION DES DIRECTEURS GÉNÉRAUX DES MUNICIPALITÉS DU QUÉBEC (ADGMQ)

The mission of the Association des directeurs généraux des municipalités du Québec is to promote and develop the professional interests of its members and ensure effective representation before government and municipal authorities.[56] It brings together some 190 members throughout Quebec.

Employers and Labour Organizations

LE CONSEIL DU PATRONAT DU QUÉBEC (CPQ)

Le Conseil du patronat du Québec[57] is a non-profit association that represents the employers of more than 70 per cent of the total Quebec labour force, giving it an influential voice at every stage of the development and implementation of bills, regulations, and government policies having a fundamental impact on the business world. The CPQ brings together most sector-based employers' associations in Quebec as well as 300 of the province's largest companies.

The CPQ intervenes in a way that is as aggressive as it is predictable to strengthen the private sector in the provision of local public works services.

L'UNION DES PRODUCTEURS AGRICOLES (UPA)

The Union des producteurs agricoles[58] is an organization bringing together Quebec's agricultural and forestry producers. A unique phenomenon, the UPA holds a de facto monopoly on the sector as a whole; anything affecting the rural world in general, and agricultural issues in particular, will inevitably attract the attention of the UPA.

The UPA and the municipalities engage in 'animated' discussions on many issues, including the necessity of balancing the development of communities with the protection of agricultural land, supported by a law to contain urban sprawl. In addition, the UPA is at the centre of debates on – depending on one's perspective – the 'right to produce' or the nuisances associated with certain kinds of production, notably hog production. Whether they wish to or not, most RCMs and local municipalities in rural areas therefore work constantly with the UPA on a range of subjects affecting, directly or indirectly, the occupation of the territory.

FÉDÉRATION DES TRAVAILLEURS DU QUÉBEC (FTQ)

Boasting more than half a million members, the Fédération des travailleurs et travailleuses du Québec is affiliated with the Canadian Labour Congress (CLC). It brings together, on a voluntary basis, most of the unions affiliated with the CLC that exist in Quebec. Heir to the North American trade-union tradition, the FTQ, like the CLC, was born as a result of the merging of the two major American labour unions, the AFL and the CIO.

The FTQ includes most Quebec members of the 40 'international' (North American) unions, Canadian unions (with CUPE – the Canadian Union of Public Employees – alone accounting for almost 100,000 Quebec members), and Quebec unions.

The FTQ claims to be the leading central labour body in Quebec and this is still likely true in terms of workforce. We should note, however, that the FTQ is not the peak umbrella organization, since practically all its affiliates are ultimately connected to Canadian or 'international' structures. Bearing this in mind, the FTQ is probably on equal footing with the Confédération des syndicats nationaux (CSN) in that the latter's affiliates do not answer to any higher authority, while its membership has increased significantly in recent years. In other words, the total amount of union dues paid to the CSN is equal to, if not greater than, the contributions collected by the FTQ.

CONFÉDÉRATION DES SYNDICATS NATIONAUX (CSN)

Now approaching the milestone of 300,000 members, the CSN is an offshoot of the Confédération des travailleurs catholiques canadiens; in terms of workforce, it probably constitutes the second-largest grouping of municipal employees.

CANADIAN UNION OF PUBLIC EMPLOYEES (CUPE)

Affiliated with the FTQ, the Canadian Union of Public Employees is the largest union in Canada. With more than half a million members across Canada, it represents workers in the fields of health, education, municipalities, libraries, universities, social services, public services, transportation, emergency services, air transportation, and communications. It likely has the greatest number of municipal employees in Quebec.[59] In municipalities, CUPE is probably the union that invests the most in combating, often victoriously, movements towards privatization, outsourcing, contracting out, and other public-private partnerships (PPPs).

The Evolution of Relations between the Government and the Various Actors in the Municipal World. Since the early 1980s, the mounting tension between the associations of elected municipal officials and the government of Quebec can be largely attributed to the deterioration in federal and provincial public finances and the attempts to redress the situation undertaken by these governments.[60]

Infighting within the municipal political associations themselves provoked some of the tensions observed in provincial-municipal relations. The 2000 territorial reform, which resulted from repeated demands by the big cities (essentially the central cities in the metropolitan regions) for a streamlining of structures and local fiscal reform, effectively placed the mayors of these cities and those in the suburbs at loggerheads within the UMQ. Similarly, the policy to reduce the number of very small municipalities and the government project to decentralize new responsibilities towards local authorities also created disagreements within the FQM. Such internal tensions were the origin of the modifications brought to the decisional and consultative structures of these associations at the beginning of the 2000s. These modifications became all the more urgent given the significance of members' annual contributions to the associations and the fact that membership is voluntary.

The municipal political associations, the UMQ and the FQM, remain the principal interlocutors and spokespersons for elected municipal officials before the government of Quebec. The government recognizes the importance of their role and instituted several years ago a formal mechanism for consultation and exchanges (Table Québec-municipalités) in which these associations are officially represented and where projects and policies of interest to the municipal world are discussed. An examination of the latest legislative reforms affecting municipalities shows, however, that many other groups may also express an opinion and attempt to influence government decisions. This is notably the case for the primary employers and labour organizations that are quick to take a position when the interests of their members are concerned.

Political Life and Elections in Municipalities

As elsewhere in Canada, Quebec municipalities hold a vision of their function that is more administrative than political. According to Richard C. and Susan N. Tindal, this ambiguous political status is not unlike the two models that exist within the Canadian municipal system: 1) the municipality is a political authority that represents the local community, its main function being the production of local public goods; 2) the municipality functions as a property-related services-production company inspired primarily by private-enterprise strategies.[61] In Quebec, two reforms adopted at the beginning of the 1970s have diminished the influence of the apolitical model. On the one hand, municipal political parties have been recognized since 1977, which remains an incongruity on the Canadian landscape. On the other hand, a series of measures initiated by the government or by certain municipalities have allowed the political scene to be opened to citizens through the implementation of participatory measures. One may rightly wonder if, thirty years later, these two reforms have contributed to the decline of municipal apoliticism in Quebec.

Political Representation

MUNICIPAL POLITICAL PARTIES
In Canada, while there is a general consensus on the need for political parties, their relevance at the municipal level is frequently contested. Quebec is the exception,[62] since the Castonguay report of 1976 (whose goal was to outline the state of municipal affairs) and the 1978 Quebec-Municipalities Conference, which recognized municipal political parties as essential to voter turnout and a healthy local democracy.[63] The Act concerning the 1978 Elections in Certain Municipalities Modifying the Cities and Towns Act then confirmed the contribution partisan organizations make at the municipal level.

To be recognized, a municipal political party must make a request for authorization to the Chief Electoral Officer of Quebec. Previously, to be authorized: 1) a municipal political party had to commit to running a candidate for at least one-third of the offices in all future general elections; and 2) its candidates for the offices of mayor or city councillor had to demonstrate a certain level of popular support by collecting a number of signatures, determined according to the size of the municipality, in a minimum number of electoral districts.[64] These requirements were reduced considerably in 2005: 1) the criterion for the number of candidates was eliminated; and 2) the number of signatures to be collected was reduced while the requirement concerning the number of electoral districts was withdrawn.[65] These new provisions allowed for the creation of a new political actor on the municipal stage, one that has been particularly present in recent Montreal elections: the borough political party.

The CEOQ's intervention also meant that the financing of municipal political activities falls within the framework of the same principles that prevail at the provincial level. The Act respecting Elections and Referendums in Municipalities effectively prescribes that political financing be based on the possibility of equitable financing, allowing for fair competition between partisan organizations. To this end, parties' authorized revenue is limited to popular financing, complemented by partial state support. Thus, the right to contribute to political parties or to finance independent candidates is reserved for voters. Contributions coming from corporate entities are prohibited.

The size of municipalities constitutes the first discriminatory element in the new provisions about political financing: 'At the very beginning, they only applied to municipalities of 100,000 inhabitants or more having elections in 1978, that is, Montréal and Longueuil, and were optional in those with 20,000 inhabitants or more. In 1979, legislators made them applicable in the 13 municipalities of 20,000 inhabitants or more without exception.'[66] In 1998 the application was broadened once again. Municipalities of 10,000 inhabitants or more were now subject to the rules on financing and the control of electoral spending, increasing the number of targeted municipalities from 61 to 125 and the number of people affected from 4.1 million to 5 million. Finally, in 1999 the provisions were also applied to municipalities of 5,000 inhabitants or more, bringing the number of municipalities to 203 and people affected to 6 million. With the mergers, this number of municipalities decreased to 146 in 2002, without modification of the criteria subject to the law.[67] In 2005 the CEOQ proposed extending the rules for political financing to municipalities of less than 5,000 inhabitants, while simplifying certain obligations. This proposal, however, was not acted on by the government.

Since this recognition, the municipal political parties have become a political reality of municipal democracy. Municipal reorganization reinforced this phenomenon:[68] an analysis of authorizations made by the CEOQ highlights the fact that the number of political parties is clearly growing. Whereas in the 1980s and 1990s, the number of authorizations issued varied from one to thirteen per year, this number climbed to between seven and twenty-six after 2000. These observations suggest that the municipal scene is becoming increasingly politicized.

However, a more thorough analysis qualifies this picture considerably. A study of recognized municipal political parties in Quebec in 2003 by Jean-Pierre Collin and Mélanie Robertson[69] shows that, in practice, the ideology of non-partisanship dominates the municipal scene, and what we call political parties are, in fact, political teams that are assembled and dismantled with the coming and going of elections or specific issues between elections. What is more, many of these coalitions claim to have a non-partisan orientation. In fact, in small- and medium-sized municipalities, electoral teams are preferred to partisan organizations, while in the large municipalities political parties are characterized by great instability. Their degree of organization remains weak compared to partisan organizations at higher levels of government and many of these coalitions claim to have a non-partisan approach to municipal political life. In addition, the recognition of municipal political parties did not mean the end of independent elected officials, a phenomenon that remains unusual at other political levels.

Despite the instability of municipal political parties, the exceptional longevity of one municipal political party is worth noting: the Rassemblement populaire de Québec (RPQ), which became the Renouveau municipal de Québec (RMQ) in 2001, effectively remaining a 'strange animal' in that it has existed since 1977. Directed by Jean-Paul L'Allier between 1989 and 2005, the RMQ also differs in its ideological orientation. With its Montreal counterpart, the Regroupement des citoyens de Montréal (RCM)[70] (1974–2001), it is one of the exclusively municipal political parties that is openly progressive and defends a more politicized concept of municipal affairs.

Thus, despite the presence of political parties, one wonders whether the municipal political model of Quebec differs much from its Canadian counterparts. Indeed, other than the RMQ, there exist few local political parties with an internal and organized political life.

Voter Turnout

Few analyses in the field of electoral studies examine municipal voting in Quebec. Generally, voter turnout remains weak (calculating only mayoral elections where there was political competition).[71] It varied between 49 per cent and 56 per cent between 1996 and 2002, all municipality sizes combined. Voter turnout decreases as the size of the municipality increases. In the smallest municipalities (less than 2,000 inhabitants), the rate of electoral participation is 64 per cent, while in the largest municipalities (more than 100,000 inhabitants) the rate is 50 per cent. As well, voter turnout is weaker in urban areas: citizens of a municipality located in a census metropolitan area cast fewer ballots than those in similarly sized municipalities in more rural areas. Voter turnout tends to be similar in large municipalities, while in small municipalities the differences are more striking. This explains why, between 1996 and 2002, voter turnout fluctuated between 16 per cent and 96 per cent. Another important variable is the number of uncontested elections. The smaller the size of the municipality, the higher the rate of elections by acclamation; indeed, between 1996 and 2002, 59 per cent of mayors were elected unopposed.[72] A more detailed examination of uncontested elections shows that, in most cases, they were re-elections. Note that, with the emergence of a partisan system, the phenomenon of acclamation tends to diminish in large cities like Montreal, where it no longer exists. However, we still find it – quite often, in fact – in the cities in the centre and west of the island of Montreal[73] and elsewhere in the metropolitan region.[74]

Thus, the rate of voter turnout in municipalities, all sizes combined, is generally low while citizens of small rural municipalities often do not have the opportunity to vote because of a lack of opposition. To give municipal elections greater visibility, the provincial government decided that, starting in 2005, not only will all municipal elections be held on the same day, but they will be held in the same year as well. This new practice, however, does not yet seem effective since the rate of voter turnout hit a new low in 2005, with an average of 45 per cent. This confirms the weak level of interest attracted by the municipal level of government, which is torn between an administrative and a politicized model. Municipal issues do not seem to be the subject of debate on the values underpinning conceptions of the common good.

One may question if the weakness in voter turnout is due to the tradition of equating the municipality with a democracy of property owners.[75] Until the 1960s, property owners were recognized as the primary constituents at the municipal level. It was not until 1968 that the weight of the constituency of property owners was reduced with the adoption of universal suffrage for Montreal and Quebec municipalities as a whole. Starting then, property owners could no longer vote in each ward in which they owned properties. A constituent could vote in one capacity only – as a resident, a property owner, or a tenant at a place of business. However, though a voter has only one voting right per municipality, property owners can vote in all municipalities where they own properties. The same logic applies to the tenant at a place of business. This practice may seem surprising, but it is based on an inescapable reality of municipalities. The aphorism 'No taxation without representation' takes on unexpected meaning here. Given the importance of property taxes for municipalities, property owners and occupants of business establishments become stakeholders and voters too important to ignore. Municipal citizenship is consequently broadened (or restricted) with the title of property.

Municipal 'Parliamentarism'

While the Quebec municipal system remains strongly marked by a non-partisan approach focused on the management of local issues, the political structures reflect a will to keep municipalities in the fold of representative politics. The legacy of the parliamentary system is notable here, especially in medium-sized and large cities.[76] First, the division of powers between the legislative and executive branches is practised. The mayor does not lead the meetings of the town council (except in the smallest municipalities). Instead, a president is chosen from among the members of the majority, while the mayor remains seated with his or her municipal councillors, without distinction in the staging of legislative power.[77] The separation between the executive and the legislative branches means that members of the executive committee (the 'cabinet' of the city)[78] sit within the assembly, that is, without a preferential place, as is the case in France, for example.

The influence of the parliamentary model also allows for the nomination of an opposition leader. This person is the leader of the largest opposition group on council. At the discretion of the team in power, elected opposition officials are also invited to participate in standing and special committees for the city. It is in the majority's best interest to integrate the opposition to create new alliances or, at least, to establish a collaborative work atmosphere. Indeed, the precariousness of municipal political groups leaves the door open to repeated political power plays. The majority can hope that municipal councillors will change teams, thus reinforcing the majority, and vice versa. As well, since 1984, as part of the recognition of political parties, the cities of Montreal, Quebec, and Laval must provide sufficient resources to allow the opposition to do its work (information, work space, clerical services, research fees, and so on). One-fifteenth of a per cent of the total budget for the city is reserved for research and clerical costs for the parties. This budget is broken down, with 51 per cent going to the majority party, 10 per cent to the main opposition party, 5 per cent to the other parties, and 34 per cent to elected representatives of the opposition. Since 2002, these measures have been extended to apply to all municipalities of more than 50,000 inhabitants.

In a slight departure from the parliamentary model, the mayor is elected directly. One of the original features of municipal electoral rules lies in the double vote: a first vote for the office of mayor and a second vote for the office of municipal councillor of the district in which the voter resides. This provision has two fundamental repercussions for the Quebec municipal system, one more definite and one subject to the changing political climate. First, the direct election gives the mayor guaranteed political visibility. The listing of the candidates' names on the ballot and the media strategy centred on the image of the mayor ensure that the winner will have a certain level of recognition among constituents interested in municipal issues, while the candidates for the office of municipal councillor have less conspicuous role in the electoral campaign. Secondly, the mayoral candidate for a political team can be elected without having the majority of city councillors of his or her group in the municipal council. In a situation where the mayor is 'in a minority,' the game of reforming alliances becomes an important dynamic within the municipal council. The mayor's faction will seek to divide the opposition or to bring municipal councillors into its camp. The weakness of partisan divisions and ideologies allows for this sort of rearrangement. In such a context, the opposition obtains a neutralizing power and has significant strength in negotiation.

Participatory Democracy

In the early 1970s, a series of laws regarding the democratization of municipalities was adopted.[79] Since then, these principles have seen little change. Admittedly, municipal reorganization in 2001 offered an occasion for some revision of the electoral process but participation in the periods between elections was not an area of great concern. Instead, legislators tried to standardize the cities' powers in terms of participatory democracy by bringing Quebec and Montreal back to 'normality,' while sanctioning some of the experiments that these two cities had developed over the preceding fifteen years.

Generally speaking, Quebec municipalities have the power to consult their citizens in all areas of jurisdiction granted to them.[80] The law leaves the form of these initiatives in participation to the discretion of the municipalities. Only the power to create advisory committees is explicitly mentioned. In practice, the method of participation may take several forms: an information session, a public hearing, a referendum, an advisory committee, and others.

In addition to the general provisions, Quebec legislators provided that consultation would be required on specific subjects. First, during public meetings of the municipal council, the question period reserved for citizens is mandatory. It is the occasion to bring up themes that are not on the meeting agenda and to challenge representatives. Through this provision, a certain level of accountability is imposed.

The consultation requirement also touches the field of urban planning and municipal finances. Municipal authorities must submit for public approval any master plan, modification of same, or zoning laws as well as all borrowing by-laws.[81] Here again, the weight of history marks the democratic organization of Quebec municipalities. Besides the fact that the provincial government exercises a tight control of municipal finances, it is also in the interest of property owners and merchants to keep a close eye on the city's debt load. For its part, the referendum on urban planning is part of the government's wish to give citizens back their place in decisions affecting their living environment.[82] However, few issues make it to the referendum stage because authorities will usually prefer to abandon a project if opposition seems too intense.

A third provision in Quebec law more specifically addresses how participation in municipal life is exercised. A referendum is also prescribed by the Act respecting Municipal Territorial Organization in the case of municipal reorganizations. After having completed negotiations between municipalities, elected officials must begin a process of public consultation. If they deem it necessary, local officials may hold a referendum to obtain the public's opinion on the possibility of merging. Moreover, the minister of municipal affairs may also impose a referendum if he or she feels that the public is resistant to the proposed change or that there were breaches in local democratic processes. This legislative provision was not applied, however, during municipal reorganizations between 2000 and 2002. The succeeding government gave citizens an opportunity to vote on the issue in a referendum, but according to new rules established in Bill 9.[83]

Quebec legislators provided for a final measure in the participatory process. Municipalities are encouraged to form urban planning advisory committees, composed of citizens and at least one elected official. This committee generally has the power to do studies and make recommendations. The municipality may call upon this committee for advice about any issue related to urban planning. For minor variations in zoning and the production of many urban planning documents, the advisory committee's input is mandatory; without it, the decision-making process will be nullified. Unfortunately, few studies shed light on the quality of this device. The low levels of participation (at most five to eight people) and the absence of public meetings cast a shadow of doubt on the democratic benefits of the urban planning advisory committee.

When reviewing the mechanisms of participation provided for under Quebec law, one should not overlook a reality that is entirely characteristic of the Quebec municipal system. Until recently, the rules for participation in issues of urban planning and borrowing by-laws did not affect one-sixth of Quebec's population. Indeed, before the 2002 municipal reorganization, the cities of Quebec and Montreal were not subject to the provisions of the Act respecting Land Use Planning and Development. Similarly, the referendum on borrowing by-laws was not integrated into the charters of the two cities. But, since the municipal reorganization, the cities of Quebec and Montreal have been subject to conditions similar to those in the aforementioned act. The two cities may also, therefore, need to hold referendums.

The ban on referendums did not, however, prevent Montreal and Quebec from developing policies on citizen participation. Seeking to fulfil principles enacted in the Act respecting Land Use Planning and Development, the two cities implemented original and varied consultation mechanisms in the early 1980s: neighbourhood councils, standing committees, public hearings, ad hoc working groups, and so on. In this respect, the politics of the city of Quebec are more progressive than those of Montreal, and have been so for some time.

Neighbourhood councils have existed in Quebec City since 1993. In the new Ville de Québec, this advanced experiment in participatory democracy, surely one of the most robust public consultation policies around, was extended as a result of the intervention of legislators who made the adoption of a policy on public consultations and district councils mandatory, leaving it to municipal authorities to define the conditions and procedures.[84] A legislative requirement about participation exists in Montreal as well, but it concerns the establishment of an Office de la consultation publique. In addition, because of significant decentralization towards the boroughs, certain experiments in participation have been undertaken.[85] The city also adopted an innovative tool, the Charter of Rights and Responsibilities, which defines the nature of urban rights and gives significant weight to citizen participation. Article 16 of the charter provides for the mandatory definition, before 2010, of 'the right of citizens' initiatives regarding public consultations.' Though this democratic experimentation is laudable, the effect of its various initiatives remains difficult to evaluate. While the introduction of participation measures does not seem to have stimulated voter turnout, it still appears that the Montreal and Quebec experiments demonstrate a greater commitment on the part of citizens to the process of municipal decision making, the result in particular of an interestingly systematic recourse to public consultations.

New Tendencies in the Municipal World

The City Contract

At the time of its signing, the City Contract of Montreal undoubtedly seemed to be one of the most innovative reforms of the last few years. As far as the ministry was concerned, city contracts were to apply to the eight other big cities in the province of Quebec and eventually to the CMM,[86] but, owing to a lack of time and a lack of interest on the part of the Liberal government that came to power in April 2003, only Montreal really benefited from this measure. The City Contract for Montreal was signed by the municipal authorities and the Parti Québécois government on 30 January 2003. (A contract with Quebec City was also signed shortly before the April 2003 election, but it was never implemented, the new government having decided not to respect the agreement. The city of Longueuil was also supposed to sign a contract with the ministère des Affaires municipales, but this step never materialized.)

The City Contract is described as 'an innovative and structuring tool that redefines, extends and modernizes the long-established partnership between the Government of Quebec and Ville de Montréal.'[87] Established shortly after the creation of performance contracts for hospital and university centres, and inspired by various French mechanisms of contractualization, the step of creating City Contracts aimed to 'loosen government control and transfer the administration of certain programs to municipalities.'[88]

For the first time, the various agreements between ten ministries of the Quebec government and the city of Montreal were brought together in one document that specified the objectives to be met by the signatories. These objectives were presented in the document in their original context, followed by precise commitments made by the partners concerned. The series of measures included in the City Contract of Montreal represent $1.4 billion, with $587 million in new money. Considering the constrained financial situation of municipalities, and particularly that of the province's big cities, the money that it represented for Montreal was all the more interesting.

Beyond the written commitments and the promise of greater management autonomy for the city, the mayor and elected officials were almost certainly seduced by the amount of funding at stake, given that city finances were already stretched to the limit. According to Gérard Divay and Anne-Marie Séguin, the primary objective of the City Contract is to mitigate the financial problems resulting mainly from the inadequate contributions to pension plans and the chronic underfunding of infrastructure.[89]

Some years have passed now and we can observe that the City Contract project has had its share of failures, partially due to the absence of political will on the part of the provincial government. In fact, the Liberal government has never wanted to make a meaningful commitment to the big cities, especially Montreal. In the context of the demergers or 'dismemberments' of cities created through the 2000 reform, the moment was perhaps poorly chosen for implementing a new way of conceiving relationships between big cities and the provincial government. The continuing uncertainty surrounding the City Contract since the change of government and the disregard for certain clauses prevent a complete evaluation of the experiment. In fact, what creates confusion regarding the City Contract is the term 'contract' itself. The form of the City Contract, as it is presented in Quebec and in France, is more an integrated agreement than a true contract. The power relationship between the signatories and the absence of real incentives or restraining mechanisms result in a situation where there are few consequences for disregarding commitments, especially for the government.[90] Montreal in particular is seeking ways to include, in a direct way, the federal government in a similar formula.[91]

Resorting to Orders-in-Council

In the reform movements of recent years, that which distinguishes the Parti Québécois (2000–3) from the Liberals (2003–) is the fact that the former focused mainly on structures. The PQ government did not have time before the 2003 election to complete its reorganization through decentralization and the reallocation of certain powers. As well, the characteristic feature of the period from 2000 to 2003 is the way in which reforms were put into place. The government at the time decided to use a profusion of orders-in-council to pass various aspects of the reform: 'The use of Orders-in-Council, which had been conceived as an exceptional measure, had become commonplace at every stage of reform. Introduced with the first legislation of 2000, resorting to Orders-in-Council continued despite the change of government and touched fundamental aspects of the reform.'[92] The principal effect of this approach was to withdraw the making of all important decisions from public debate. The practice was maintained during the first few months of the Liberal government.

The 2003 Reforms: A Change of Approach

The arrival to power of the new Liberal government in 2003 had a considerable effect on the municipal world in Quebec, partly because the government was questioning the reforms of the previous government, and partly because it had also decided to reform certain structures and create others. The Liberal government distinguished itself from the previous government on two key points. First, despite the reorganization and creation of certain structures, the Liberals concentrated mainly on programs and the legislative framework of local and regional institutions. The second and remarkable departure from the previous government is the regional character of its actions: the regions became the transmission channel of interventions, at the expense of municipalities, RCMs, and metropolitan communities.

The Liberal Party program in the lead-up to the 2003 election included a series of orientations to develop the regions of Quebec, such as 'decentralizing the decision-making powers and simplifying procedural structures ... and elaborating policies favouring demographic growth and territorial occupancy.'[93] The regions to which the Liberal Party's document is referring are mainly resource regions located on the periphery of major centres. However, in the context of Quebec, the administrative regions do not have true powers. They are, above all, territorial delimitations upon which the Quebec government's policies are articulated. But the administrative regions are also the headquarters of consultation bodies, the conseils régionaux en environnement (CRE), the conseils de la culture (CRC), and, until 2003, the conseils régionaux de développement (CRD). In fields such as health and social services, the administrative regions also served as functional territories for organizations like the regional directorates of health and social services.

The ministère des régions and the ministère des affaires municipals: Recent Changes

Following an electoral campaign that was run in part under the theme of regional development, the Liberal government showed a definite bias towards the regions, one that was demonstrated by the first configuration of the cabinet: the ministère des Régions was incorporated into the main economic ministry, the ministère du Développement économique et régional et Recherche.[94] This bias towards the regions as the engine for economic interventions had consequences for municipal affairs, in terms both of policy coordination and of programs. Thus, the regions became, to some extent, the preferred vehicle of economic-policy development of the Charest government.

However, after less than two years in power, the government's poor performance and the level of dissatisfaction with its policies reached new heights and forced the premier to readjust his position. He undertook a cabinet shuffle, which was not without effect on the municipal world. In fact, many observers, including the Organization for Economic Co-operation and Development (OECD) in a study of Montreal published in 2004, pointed to the problems of jurisdictional entanglements due, in part, to the fact that municipal and regional affairs fell under the responsibility of two different ministries, thus complicating the coordination and the coherence of the government's policies.[95] The February 2005 reshuffle meant that, for the first time since 1995, these two entities were now reunited within the new ministère des Affaires municipales et des Régions. Time will tell if this decision will improve the cohesion of various departments' actions, particularly in the region of Montreal where no fewer than five administrative regions are included in or overlap the territory of the CMM which, like other municipal organizations, is part of the world of municipal affairs.

THE REGIONAL CONFERENCE OF ELECTED OFFICERS

To implement its regional-development goals, the government replaced the conseils régionaux de développement – consultation organizations that were bringing together the dynamic forces in the regions – with the Regional Conferences of Elected Officials (conférences régionales des élus or CRÉ). One of the main differences between the two structures is the predominant role given to local elected officials. Unlike the CRDs, the CRÉs are led by a board of directors composed primarily of mayors of municipalities of 5,000 inhabitants or more and of wardens of regional county municipalities.[96] Previously, the composition of the CRDs was more flexible and the list of stakeholders varied from one region to another. This transformation of the primary structure of regional consultation was the subject of much criticism. For example, for Bernard Jouve, 'the regionalization undertaken by the provincial government for the benefit of local elected officials carries the risk of autocratic and technocratic drifts. It especially goes against what made Quebec governance so original: the establishment of partnership structures in which the civil society, through its representatives, actively participated in public affairs.'[97]

In addition to a mandate to produce a five-year plan for the development of the region (a responsibility the CRDs had as well), the new law gave the CRÉs a larger role – to evaluate local and regional planning and development organizations. The CRÉs are also invited to present recommendations to the government on the future of these organizations.[98] As well, the legislation allows the minister the possibility of assigning any other mandate to the CRÉs.[99] In some cases, the mandates given are similar to those already assigned to existing organizations. For example, the metropolitan communities have planning powers in many realms of their territory. This is, indeed, one of the problems with the superimposition of reforms in recent years, where there is difficulty using the resources already in place and a preference to add new structures. At the end of the day, the problem of jurisdictional entanglements continues to grow.

A 'NEW' CONCEPT OF THE ROLE OF THE STATE

The Liberal Party's rise to power also marked a break with the way of conceiving the role of the state, compared to the previous government. Definitely less interventionist, the Liberal Party sought to re-examine certain activities of the state to improve efficiency and to evaluate the relevance of certain organizations' mandates and structures, reducing their number if necessary.[100] In addition, from the beginning, the government showed a clear leaning towards public-private partnerships, the famous PPPs. An agency for the promotion of PPPs was established within the highly influential Conseil du trésor, and a division of the ministère des Transports was also considering the possibilities of partnerships in roadwork projects; however, despite this marked interest, PPP projects were long in materializing and only two have been started to date – the new concert hall for the Montreal Symphony Orchestra and the extension of Highway 25, north of Montreal.

The legal framework in which Quebec municipalities have evolved has been modified considerably by the introduction of several significant bills that directly affect the municipalities. The primary legislative measures presented by the current government that affect the municipal world are:

- Bill 60 (Act respecting the Société de financement des Infrastructures locales [SOFIL] du Québec and Amending the Highway Safety Act);
- Bill 61 (Act respecting the Agence des partenariats public-privé du Québec);
- Bill 62 (Municipal Powers Act); and
- Bill 76 (Act to repeal the Act respecting the Commission municipale and to Amend Various Legislative Provisions).[101]

The Société de financement des infrastructures locales du Québec is a new body that serves, as its name suggests, to finance infrastructure projects for municipal organizations. However, the unique characteristic of this corporation is that it will change the methods of allocating funds under infrastructure-financing programs involving the federal government. In fact, the act stipulates that the government may henceforth determine the 'forms and conditions' of payments of financial resources to municipal organizations.[102]

The second bill to be adopted concerning infrastructure is the one that established the Agence des partenariats public-privé du Québec. Undoubtedly, this bill is the one that has raised the greatest public outcry, particularly from central labour bodies which, for obvious reasons, do not look favourably on this new orientation. The agency in question has as its principal function the promotion of PPPs, under the direct responsibility of the president of the Treasury Board.[103]

Recently, municipalities have been authorized to grant long-term contracts (up to twenty-five years). This breaks with a long tradition whereby the ministère des Affaires municipales imposed caution by preventing the municipalities from entering into long-term commitments of any kind, either for a contract with a company or for a collective agreement, except with explicit ministerial authorization. Now they are allowed to grant contracts which include the management and the delivery of services, as well as their financing. Water is at the centre of the new experiment, but this first step regarding water will serve as an example for what follows. Starting in January 2006, the reconstituted cities of Westmount and Côte-Saint-Luc entered into a contract with a private firm for the management of water-supply networks involving a diagnosis of the state of these networks: the original two-year contract was supposed to be a prelude to a longer-term agreement, which could have taken the form of a PPP.[104] But the municipal council of Westmount, not known for its leftist tendencies, decided not to renew the contract. We do not know what Côte-Saint-Luc's decision will be, but one thing is certain: the enthusiasm for PPPs does not seem to have won over the municipalities, at least for the time being.

For some observers, municipalities are 'at the heart of the re-engineering or the modernization of the State.'[105] It should be expected that the municipalities or regional authorities will be given new functions. Judging from the documents presented as part of negotiations on the new fiscal pact, the government seemed decided on using the creation of regional authorities, especially CRÉs, to shed certain responsibilities.[106] But, generally, the promise of reducing the number of organizations and state structures was not fulfilled in the municipal world. In fact, the reverse actually occurred, since the government created new ones instead. Finally, Quebec municipalities have new powers of economic development since the adoption of Bill 21 in June

2006. They may now set up tax-credit programs as an incentive for businesses to establish themselves in their territories, or to expand or modernize their facilities. Direct assistance for businesses in difficulty is now also possible. The new legislation contains specific provisions to avoid having businesses move from one municipality to another.

Governance and Intergovernmental Relations

Constitutionally, Quebec municipalities are under the exclusive (and jealous) control of the government of Quebec. For over thirty years, successive teams of Liberals and *Péquistes* have adopted and maintained the same policy in this respect: the Quebec government severely limits direct ties between the municipalities and federal government departments through the (almost) rigorous application of the Act respecting the Ministère du Conseil executif.[107]

Despite its overzealous defence of the 'exclusive preserve' that constitutes the municipal world, the government of Quebec regularly makes reasonable accommodations with the federal government. Thus, when the federal government grants subsidies in a field affecting municipal powers, arrangements are made so that the government of Quebec may apply its own standards, adapted to its own goals, with the federal government not really having much to say about it. Frequently, things move quickly, but it often happens that an agreement is reached only after months of quarrelling on the subject of respecting each side's jurisdiction. Typically, the federal government ends up agreeing to pay out 'Quebec's share' in an envelope deposited in a 'mailbox.'

An example of such a 'mailbox' is SOFIL,[108] the recently created ad hoc organization that serves essentially as a 'decontamination airlock' or acclimatization tool for the transfer of funds from the federal government to the municipalities, no strings attached, and without the federal standards that would normally come with the package. This has been the practice since (at least) the very first jointly funded infrastructure program (the Canada-Quebec Infrastructure Works Program, launched in 1994), when the minister of municipal affairs at the time, Claude Ryan, piloted his ship alone, without fear or reproach, directing each stage of the program's implementation from the major orientations right down to the meticulous examination of each decision.[109]

The infrastructure issue has become a strategic one over the course of recent years and each level of government tries to benefit. For the municipalities, particularly the big cities, infrastructure is the ultimate battle-standard for demanding the diversification of financial and fiscal resources. The municipalities, using recently published works and studies, claim that their difficult financial situation in the 1990s forced them to delay investments in infrastructure. It is worth remembering that the municipalities cannot have a deficit and so, to reduce their expenses, many of them have postponed investments in infrastructure.

A more vigorous examination of the workings of SOFIL will eventually allow us to shed light on the collaboration practices between higher-level governments and the municipalities, at least on the issue of infrastructure.

Conclusion

Municipalities in Quebec were instituted in the middle of the 1800s, and the first century of their existence saw no fundamental alterations to the original operation of the system. Since the 1960s, however, municipalities have been the target of provincial government technocrats with dreams of 'modernizing' them. Reform plans have proliferated, and, while most have remained dead letters, some have been implemented in the end.

Certainly, constant provincial pressure has led slowly but surely to a decrease in the number of municipalities, with a sharp acceleration of the pace of amalgamations occurring around 2000. Now we find one-third fewer municipalities than in 1961. It remains true, though, that in proportion to its population Quebec still has four times as many municipalities as Ontario does.

Confronted by reform initiatives, the municipalities put up such a determined resistance that it was not until the end of the 1970s that the Regional County Municipalities were created, outside the largest urban centres. Rather than reforming the municipalities themselves, the RCMs were designed to allow coordinated local action while introducing a modicum of long-term planning. Urban Quebec received a quicker and more substantial dose of reform, ten years before the RCMs were created, when the major agglomerations were crowned with Urban Communities charged with important services – police, public transit, and sewage treatment. Then, in 2000, the provincial government amalgamated large numbers of municipalities in the metropolitan areas. Despite some 'défusions' that took place three years later, the urban agglomerations are still governed by a small number of autonomous municipalities, or by a single one. In Montreal, however, while one big city was created, this centripetal movement was offset to some extent by the simultaneous creation of boroughs that possess a budgetary autonomy that is limited but nevertheless genuine.

Paradoxically, the structural reforms that were meant to strengthen at least the larger municipalities were not accompanied by a real devolution of powers; nor was greater autonomy granted by the province. Despite this, there is a sense in which municipalities have indeed become more autonomous, on the financial front and in principle, because provincial-municipal transfers have been substantially reduced. So local administrations have been left to their own devices – they have complete freedom to raise highly visible property taxes or to raise equally painful user fees. In general, though, the last few decades have brought not more municipal autonomy but rather the reinforcement of provincial control. This is evident in the evolution of shared-cost programs. The Quebec government now offers very specific grants, more targeted, with precise standards, and with project-evaluation criteria and methodologies that must be followed to the letter in order to maximize the chances of securing the funding.

During this turbulent period we have witnessed the rise and development of municipal political parties. Of course, the parties are sometimes nothing but labels attached to heterogeneous lists of candidates who have little in common politically, but sometimes they are genuine parties. In Montreal, notably, and even more in Quebec City, they are autonomous and quite independent of the parties represented in the National Assembly and the Canadian Parliament, and they have the apparatus of any proper political party – more or less detailed platforms, patiently assembled by the activists, financing that respects the electoral laws, and permanent organizations complete with committee structures and other organs.

It remains true in the end that Quebec municipalities have not experienced a real increase in their powers over the past years. This is despite the wishes and recommendations of many actors, including the recent National Commission on Local Finances and Taxation – the Bédard Commission. Quebec municipalities have neither the institutional depth nor the fiscal and political power that characterize many of their counterparts in the advanced industrial countries.

NOTES

1 Translator's note: Most organizations (public, quasi-public, and private) in Quebec operate in French exclusively and do not have an official English translation of their corporate designation. The following lexicon provides unofficial translations of these names and titles for the benefit of readers who are less familiar with French. Though the official names of the city of Montreal and Quebec City are Ville de Montréal and Ville de Québec as per their new charters, we have used their former designations in English to make for easier reading, given that they are frequently referred to in the chapter.

Agence métropolitaine de transport (AMT)	Metropolitan Public Transportation Agency
Association des directeurs généraux des municipalités du Québec (ADGMQ)	Association of Municipal Directors General of Quebec
Agence des partenariats public-privé	Public-Private Partnership Agency
Bureau de l'aménagement de l'Est du Québec (BAEQ)	Eastern Quebec Planning Bureau
CÉGEP (Collège d'enseignement général et professionnel)	Post-secondary general and professional college (similar to community colleges)
Centrale des syndicats du Québec (CSQ)	Quebec Labour Congress
CMM	Montreal Metropolitan Community
CMQ	Quebec City Metropolitan Community
Commission des normes du travail	Labour Standards Board
Commission municipale du Québec	Quebec Municipal Commission
Communauté métropolitaine de Montréal (CMM)	Montreal Metropolitan Community
Communauté métropolitaine de Québec (CMQ)	Quebec City Metropolitan Community
Confédération des syndicats nationaux (CSN)	Confederation of National Trade Unions
Confédération des travailleurs catholiques canadiens	Confederation of Catholic Canadian Workers

Conseil d'orientation économique du Québec (COEQ)	Quebec Economic Advisory Council
Conseil du patronat du Québec	Quebec Employers' Council
Conseil du Trésor	Treasury Board
Conseils régionaux de développement (CRD)	Regional Councils for Development
Conseils régionaux de la culture (CRC)	Regional Councils for Culture
Conseils régionaux en environnement (CRE)	Regional Councils for the Environment
Corporation des officiers municipaux du Québec (COMAQ)	Corporation of Chartered Municipal Officers of Quebec
CRÉ (Conférence régionale des élus de Montréal)	Regional Conferences of Elected Officers
Fédération des travailleurs du Québec (FTQ)	Quebec Federation of Labour
Fédération québécoise des municipalités (FQM)	Federation of Quebec Municipalities
Fonds sur l'infrastructure municipale rurale	Municipal Rural Infrastructure Fund (joint program)
Ministère des Affaires municipales	Ministry of Municipal Affairs
Ministère des Affaires municipales et de la Métropole	Ministry of Municipal and Metropolitan Affairs
Ministère des Affaires municipales et des Régions	Ministry of Municipal and Regional Affairs
Ministère des Affaires municipales du Sport et des Loisirs	Ministry of Municipal Affairs, Sports and Leisure
Ministère des transports	Ministry of Transport
Ministère des Régions	Ministry for Regional Affairs
Ministère du Conseil exécutif	Executive Council Ministry
Ministère du Développement économique, de l'Innovation et de l'Exportation	Ministry of Economic Development, Innovation and Trade
Ministère du Développement économique et Régional et Recherche	Ministry of Economic Development, Regional Affairs and Research
Office de la consultation publique	Public Consultation Office

Renouveau municipal et urbain (REMUR)	Municipal and Urban Renewal Project
ROC	Rest of Canada
Société de financement des infra-structures locales du Québec (SOFIL)	Local Infrastructure Finance Company of Quebec
Table Quebec-municipalités	Quebec-Municipalities Round-Table
Tribunal administratif du Québec	Administrative Tribunal of Quebec
Union des municipalités du Québec (UMQ)	Union of Quebec municipalities
Union des Producteurs agricoles (UPA)	Union of Agricultural Producers

2 Rita Bissonnette, 'La régionalisation municipale au Québec (1960–1980): visées technocratiques et résistances locales,' Thèse de maîtrise, Études supérieures, Université d'Ottawa, 1982.

3 Ibid., 22. Note that this quotation is a translation into English of French text. The same applies to all other quotations from French-language works, statutes, and documents included in this chapter.

4 Jean Meynaud and Jacques Léveillée, *La régionalisation municipale au Québec* (Montreal: Nouvelles Frontières, 1973).

5 Ibid., 41. This decision was taking place within a context characterized by a regionalization approach that was supported both by the planning vision of the Conseil d'orientation économique du Québec (COEQ) and by the views developed by the Bureau de l'aménagement de l'Est du Québec (BAEQ) in terms of regional issues. In retrospect, we can look at this regionalization from the perspective of a process of territorialization of public activity whose purpose was to modernize Quebec, starting with the definition and establishment of planning, regulation, and intervention structures. Richard Morin, *La régionalisation au Québec, Les mécanismes de développement et de gestion des territoires régionaux – 1960–2006* (Montreal: Saint-Martin, 2006).

6 Meynaud and Léveillée, *La régionalisation municipale*, 106.

7 Gérard Divay and Jacques Léveillée (with the collaboration of B. McCann), *La réforme municipale et l'État québécois*, Études et Documents no. 27 (Montreal: INRS-Urbanisation, 1981), 43.

8 Bissonnette, 'La régionalisation municipale,' 237.
9 Government of Quebec, *La réorganisation municipal: Changer les façons de faire, pour mieux servir les citoyens* (2000).
10 Ibid., ix.
11 André Boisclair, '2002: le nouveau visage du Québec,' *Municipalité*, 33, no. 1 (2002): 18.
12 Jean-Pierre Collin , 'Le milieu rural et les MRC en attente de réforme,' in Roch Côté, ed., *Québec 2002: Annuaire politique, social, économique et culturel* (Montreal: Fides, 2001), 235.
13 Ministère des Affaires municipales et de la Métropole, *Les enjeux en matière de gouvernance et les initiatives provinciales*, Document de travail, Rencontre provinciale-territoriale 2001 des ministres responsables des administrations locales (2002), 28.
14 Jean-Pierre Collin and Jacques Léveillée, in collaboration with Mathieu Rivard and Mélanie Robertson, *L'organisation municipale au Canada: un régime à géométrie variable, entre tradition et transformation* (Montreal: Groupe de recherche sur l'innovation municipale, 2003), 5.
15 Government of Quebec, ministere des Affaires municipales et Régions, *Quebec Municipal Organization*, December 2006.
16 Pierre J. Hamel et al., 'Le futur moins que parfait des très petites collectivités: recomposition territoriale dans l'arrière-pays québécois,' in Laurence Bherer et al., eds., *Jeux d'échelle et transformation de l'État: le gouvernement des territoires au Québec et en France* (Quebec: Presses de l'Université Laval, 2005), 177–201.
17 That is, an RCM that includes a city or an urban agglomeration of at least 10,000 inhabitants with a number of rural municipalities located in its outskirts.
18 Government of Quebec, Ministère des Affaires municipales du Sport et du Loisir (MAMSL), *La municipalité régionale de comté: Compétences et responsabilités* (2004), 25.
19 This power is optional in the case of Quebec City's metropolitan community and has yet to be exercised. In the case of Montreal, four facilities are financed at the metropolitan level.
20 As was the case for Montreal's metropolitan community, Quebec City's metropolitan community started its operations on 1 January 2002. See Government of Quebec, Bill 170, An Act to Reform the Municipal Territorial Organization of the Metropolitan Regions of Montréal, Quebec and the Outaouais, Quebec, assented to 20 December 2000.
21 Bill 134, An Act respecting the Communauté métropolitaine de Montréal, Quebec, assented to 15 June 2000, s. 127.

22 Ibid., s.151.

23 Mathieu Rivard et al., 'Les nouvelles tendances dans le domaine munici-
    pal au Québec: Changer et … rechanger les façons de faire pour mieux
    servir les citoyens.' Speech delivered at the symposium Les municipalités
    au Québec et au Canada: d'administration locale à véritable ordre de
    gouvernement, part of the convention of the Association francophone
    pour le savoir (ACFAS), Saguenay, May 2005, http://www.vrm.ca/
    documents/ACFAS2005Quebec.pdf (accessed 8 March 2007).

24 MAMSL, *Mairesse ou maire, conseillère ou conseiller… Pourquoi pas vous?*
    (2002).

25 With the exception of the fifty-one rural RCMs that exercise this power
    across their territory, RCMs exercise it for those municipalities that are
    governed by the Municipal Code.

26 As a consequence, Quebec's municipalities do not carry much financial
    weight. Their per capita expenditures are 15 per cent lower than the
    average expenditures of municipalities in the rest of Canada and less
    than half of the expenditures of their European counterparts; that is,
    $1,512 per capita in Quebec in 2004, compared to 2,300 euros per capita
    (about $3,280 CAD at the current rate) on average for the twenty-five
    countries in the European Union. In Sweden alone, 44 per cent of all
    public expenditures move through municipalities and per capita 'munici-
    pal' expenditures were 6,980 euros in 2001. We should also mention that,
    in the two largest Swedish cities, two-thirds of local public expenditures
    move through the boroughs! Micheline Falzon et al., *Les finances locales
    dans les vingt-cinq pays de l'Union européenne. Local finance in the twenty-five
    countries of the European Union* (Paris: Dexia, 2004), 55.

27 Commission nationale sur les finances et la fiscalité locales, *Pacte 2000,
    rapport de la Commission nationale sur les finances et la fiscalité
    locales*(Quebec: Government of Quebec, 1999), 27.

28 Prior to this, most of the substantial unconditional transfer payments
    consisted of a 'rebate' on the sales tax. In 1965 Quebec had ousted munic-
    ipalities from the field of consumption taxes and, in compensation,
    repaid them the equivalent of a third of the Provincial Sales Tax (PST)
    (based on a somewhat distorted formula by which it became more prof-
    itable for a municipality to attract businesses on its territory rather than
    new homes). Pierre J. Hamel, 'Le "Pacte fiscal" entre le gouvernement du
    Québec et les municipalités: la raison du plus fort est toujours la
    meilleure,' *Organisations et territoires*, vol. 11, no. 3 (2002): 33.

29 The relatively few federal transfer payments to Quebec's municipalities
    can likely be explained by the Quebec law that limits direct dealings

between the federal government and municipalities and that more or less makes it mandatory for federal funds to be transmitted through a mechanism controlled by Quebec ministries. See below.

30 A number of municipalities in Ontario distribute electricity (and sometimes gas), and income revenue in Alberta and British Columbia is considerable. There was a time when Edmonton had the largest per capita municipal budget, given that, in addition to conventional municipal services, it also supplied electricity and gas as well as telephone services (sold in 1995 to a company that became Telus). Still today, 18 per cent of total revenue that goes towards Edmonton's operating budget comes from the return on the city's investments – 13 per cent alone from EPCOR (water, gas and electricity) – and another 22 per cent comes from user fees, fines, and permits, while property taxes account for 50 per cent of municipal revenue compared to 67 per cent for the average Quebec municipality. City of Edmonton, *Approved 2006 Budget Summary* (2006), 25.

31 Statistics Canada, CANSIM II, 385–0004.

32 The last column in Table 3 – 'ROC – Quebec per capita $' – shows the difference between per capita revenue and expenditures of municipalities in the ROC and in Quebec. For instance, on the first line, note that municipalities in the ROC collect $7 less in property taxes than their Quebec counterparts.

33 Water taxation is gaining ground for non-residential users, in Montreal in particular, but water meters will likely remain a rarity in homes in Quebec. In fact, most municipalities evaluating the opportunity of installing water meters give up on the idea and some that have functional meters have stopped using them, as was recently the case in Sherbrooke and Lévis. Élisabeth Fleury, 'Lévis abandonne les compteurs d'eau pour les résidences,' *Le Soleil*, 18 November 2006, 19. A number of reasons lie behind these decisions. First, residential meters are remarkably inefficient; their purchase, installation, and management costs are disproportionate. Francis Lebuis and Jean-Claude Lauret, *Parc de compteurs d'eau et coûts d'investissement pour l'utilisation de compteurs d'eau à la Ville de Montréal*, as part of a mandate given by the city of Montreal to PricewaterhouseCoopers and entitled *Stratégie et structure financières pour la gestion publique de l'eau sur le territoire de la Ville de Montréal* (Montreal: Gaz Métro, 2003). In the end, water meters' iniquity and their unforeseeable impact make them particularly inefficient. Pierre J. Hamel, 'Les compteurs d'eau résidentiels: une mauvaise idée,' *Bulletin de la Ligue des droits et libertés*, vol. 49, no. 1 (2006): 22–3.

34 AREQ (2005), *Historique* , http://www.areq.org/historique.htm (accessed 8 March 2007).
35 Commission nationale sur les finances et la fiscalité locales, 15.
36 'la raison du plus fort est toujours la meilleure': Jean de La Fontaine (1668), 'Le Loup et l'agneau,' *Fables*, livre no. 1, fable no.10.
37 Commission nationale sur les finances et la fiscalité locales, 122.
38 It is not a property tax, which is a tax on capital (or on a patrimony), given that it is not generated by the possession of a property; neither it is an income tax, given that it is not generated by earning a revenue (from a property or otherwise).
39 Jean-Pierre Collin, 'Les stratégies fiscales municipales et la gestion de l'agglomération urbaine: le cas de la Ville de Montréal entre 1910 et 1965,' *Urban History Review / Revue d'histoire urbaine*, vol. 23, no. 1 (1994): 19–31; Hamel, 'Le "Pacte fiscal,"' 33.
40 Ministère des Affaires municipales et de la Métropole (2006), *Taxation – Variété de taux de la taxe foncière générale*, http://www.mamr.gouv.qc.ca/finances/fina_fisc_taxa.asp.
41 Government of Quebec, *Budget 1979–1980, Renseignements supplémentaires, Réforme de la fiscalité municipale* (Quebec: Ministère des Finances et Ministère des Affaires municipales, 1979).
42 Pierre J. Hamel, '"Deffence et illustration" de l'impôt foncier assis sur la valeur marchande,' in Richard Morin et al., eds., *Gestion locale et nouvelles problématiques urbaines au tournant des années 1990*, coll. Études urbaines (Montreal: Département d'études urbaines et touristiques, Université du Québec à Montréal), 37–45. The title is, of course, a nod to Joachim du Bellay's pamphlet, published in 1549 and entitled 'Deence et illutration de la langue française.'
43 Jean-Pierre Collin and Pierre J. Hamel, 'Les contraintes structurelles des finances publiques locales: les budgets municipaux dans la région de Montréal, en 1991,' *Recherches sociographiques*, vol. 34, no. 3 (1993): 439–67.
44 The situation has become so untenable that the ministry has agreed to reopen the file, to increase its transfer payments (Voirie locale et ponts: le MTQ a entendu la FQM et mettra à jour les programmes [Quebec, 16 November 2006], http://www.fqm.ca/content/view/260/30/) and to go as far as taking over some of the infrastructure (Bruno Bisson, 'Ponts municipaux: des besoins de 370 millions en cinq ans. Plus de la moitié des ponts sont déficients, selon le Ministère' [*La Presse*, 17 November 2006]).
45 By adding the transfer of a portion of the gasoline-excise tax and the GST exemption, the city of Montreal will receive annually an amount likely

between $40 million and $60 million Though this amount is not astronomical, at least it is something, even if it is, in reality, very little. Indeed, when included in a $3.9-billion annual budget, these millions coming from the federal government are equivalent to barely more than 0.01 per cent of this budget – in other words, a little more than one hundredth of 1 per cent of the city's budget. This is much less than what Montreal itself transfers to the Water Fund that it set up in 2004. The transferred money is raised through a special tax whose rate (and returns) increases every year: following an initial level of $25 million in 2004, the transfer increased by $20 million each year to the point where the annual transfer reached $85 million in 2007; it is anticipated that the annual transfers to the Water Fund will reach a plateau of a least $200 million by 2013.

46 Federation of Canadian Municipalities, *Édifier des fondations solides pour notre prospérité. Rétablir l'équilibre fiscal. Building Prosperity from the Ground: Restoring Municipal Fiscal Balance* (2006).
47 Ville de Montréal, 'Water Fund,' *2006 Budget*, 87–92.
48 Government of Quebec, Bill 76, An Act to Repeal the Act respecting the Commission municipale and to Amend Various Legislative Provisions, http://www.assnat.qc.ca/eng/37legislature2/Projets-loi/Publics/04-f076.htm (accessed 17 August 2006).
49 Commission municipale du Québec, http://www.cmq.gouv.qc.ca/responsab.htm.
50 Ministère des Affaires municipales et des Régions, *Guide d'élaboration d'un plan d'intervention pour le renouvellement des conduites d'eau potable et d'égout* (Quebec: Government of Quebec, 2005).
51 Ministère des Affaires municipales et des Régions, *Infrastructures – Documentation et liens 2006*, http://www.mamr.gouv.qc.ca/infrastructures/infr_docu.asp.
52 Ministère des Affaires municipales et de la Métropole. Data compiled according to the official population for 2006 in the December 2005 order-in-council, http://www.mamr.gouv.qc.ca/publications/organisation/org_mun_qc_ang.pdf.
53 *Guide d'élaboration d'un plan d'intervention pour le renouvellement des conduites d'eau potable et d'égout*, 2. Emphasis added.
54 Ibid.
55 Union des municipalités du Québec, 'L'UMQ prend position: L'Union des municipalités du Quebec se prononce en faveur du maintien de l'intégrité territoriale des nouvelles villes,' *Quoi de neuf?* 2003, http://www.umq.qc.ca/afficher_nouvelle.asp?ID=7602.

56 L'Association des directeurs généraux municipaux du Québec (ADGMQ), 2006, http://www.adgmq.qc.ca/.

57 Conseil du patronat du Québec, 2006, http://www.cpq.qc.ca/.

58 Union des producteurs agricoles, *Qui sommes-nous?* 2006, http://www.upa.qc.ca/fra/qui_sommes_nous/mission_valeurs.asp.

59 Canadian Union of Public Employees, *Au sujet du SCFP*, 2006, http://www.scfp.ca/ausujetduscfp.

60 On this point see Serge Belley, 'La recomposition des territoires locaux au Québec: regards sur les acteurs, les relations intergouvernementales et les politiques depuis 1990,' in Laurence Bherer et al., eds., *Jeux d'échelle et transformation de l'État : Le gouvernement des territoires au Québec et en France* (Quebec: PUL, 2005), 203–30.

61 Collin and Léveillée, *L'organisation municipale au Canada: Un régime à géométrie variable, entre tradition et transformation*, 4; and Richard C. Tindal and Susan N. Tindal, *Local Government in Canada* (Toronto: Nelson Thomson Learning, 2000), 13.

62 Louise Quesnel, 'La démocratie urbaine dans les villes canadiennes,' in Vincent Hoffmann-Marinot and Oscar W. Gabriel, eds., *Démocraties urbaines* (Paris: L'Harmattan, 2000), 291–348.

63 Alain Baccigalupo and Luc Rhéaume, *Les administrations municipales québécoises, des origines à nos jours: anthologie administrative* (Montreal: Agence d'Arc, 1984), 945, 970.

64 F. Bordeleau, *Le financement politique et le contrôle des dépenses électorales au Québec – D'hier à aujourd'hui*, Collection Études Électorales (Sainte-Foy: Chief Electoral Officer of Quebec, 2003), 25.

65 Government of Quebec, Bill 111, An Act to Amend Various Legislative Provisions concerning Municipal Affairs, s. 99. A political party that does not present candidates may apply to be a private intervener providing it does not make expenditures in relation to the electoral campaign.

66 Bordeleau, *Le financement politique*, 23.

67 Ibid., 24.

68 Serge Belley, 'Forces et faiblesses des acteurs de la nouvelle scène municipale,' *Télescope*, vol. 10, no. 2 (2003).

69 Jean-Pierre Collin and Mélanie Robertson, 'Metropolitan Change and Related Political Behavior in a Canadian Metropolis.' Working Paper presented at the meeting of the International Metropolitan Observatory, Université de Bordeaux, 9–10 January 2004, http://www.vrm.ca/documents/IMO_WorkingPaperno1.pdf.

70 Though the RCM also had a long political life, it was not in power for as long as the RPQ, which, with Jean-Paul L'Allier at its head, remained in

office from 1989 to 2005. In addition, after its defeat in 1994, the RCM was in a political-survival mode for a number of years.

71 Patrick Champagne and Renaud Patry, 'La participation électorale dans les municipalités québécoises,' *Muni-Stat*, vol. 1, no. 1 (2004): 1–5.

72 Ibid.

73 For instance, Westmount and Baie d'Urfé.

74 For instance, Terrebonne and Boucherville as well as some city councillor seats in the city of Laval.

75 Quesnel, 'La démocratie urbaine.'

76 Ibid.

77 In smaller municipalities, the mayor presides over the assembly. The absences of a party system and of territorial representation oblige a departure from the British model. The need for a 'neutral' president, to arbitrate the various forces in the municipal council, is less imperative given that, most of the time, elected officials work together on the basis of an apolitical consensus. Furthermore, because councillors in smaller communities are elected on the basis of a seat number rather than for an electoral district, the municipality speaks with a single voice. Hence, during public meetings, a small municipality's mayor has a greater visibility than the mayor in a city. Small municipalities in Quebec present many other differences from cities where the status of elected officials is concerned. However, for present purposes, we will limit ourselves to describing the situation in the cities unless otherwise mentioned.

78 Only executive committees that are established in a municipal charter have true decisional powers. This is the case in Montreal, Quebec City, Laval, Longueuil, and others. In other municipalities, decisions are not effective if they are not adopted by the municipal council.

79 The legislative provisions with respect to public consultation are found in the following statutes: 1) the Municipal Code and the Cities and Towns Act establish general rules for rural and urban municipalities; 2) the Act respecting Land Use Planning and Development creates obligations and opportunities for public consultations with respect to land use and urban planning and zoning; 3) the Act respecting Elections and Referendums in Municipalities concerns the public-consultation process; and 4) the Act respecting Municipal Territorial Organization dictates public-consultation mechanisms when municipalities are to be merged.

80 This section is based on Louise Quesnel, *La consultation des citoyens comme outil de la démocratie locale* (Toronto: Les Presses du CIRUR, 2000); Ministère des Affaires municipales, *La prise de décision en urbanisme* (Quebec: Les publications du Québec, 1995).

81 The cities of Montreal and Quebec were not subject to this obligation until 2002.

82 Though this provision was made available to all citizens in 1978, referendums on zoning changes existed since 1956 but only property owners in the affected sector were entitled to vote. Prior to that date, the system favoured major landowners, given that approval required not only a numerical majority but also a majority representing land value. See Marie-Odile Trépanier, 'Formes traditionnelles et réforme récente du droit de l'urbanisme au Québec: changement de fond ou changement de formes,' in Jacques Léveillée, ed., *L'aménagement du territoire au Québec : Du rêve au compromis* (Montreal: Nouvelle optique, 1982), 11–42.

83 An Act respecting the Consultation of Citizens with respect to the Territorial Reorganization of Certain Municipalities, http://www2.publications duquebec.gouv.qc.ca/dynamicSearch/telecharge.php?type=5&fi le=2003C14A.PDF.

84 Laurence Bherer, 'Le cheminement du projet de conseil de quartier à Québec (1965–2003): Un outil pour contrer l'apolitisme municipal?' *Politiques et sociétés*, vol. 25, no. 1 (2006): 31–56; Laurence Bherer, 'Les promesses ambiguës de la démocratie participative,' *Éthique publique*, vol. 7, no. 1 (2005): 82–90.

85 Laurence Bherer and Luc Rabouin, 'Budget participatif et démocratie locale: l'exemple du Plateau,' in M. Venne and M. Fahmy, eds., *L'annuaire du Québec 2007* (Montreal: Fides, 2007), 306–12.

86 André Boisclair, '2002: le nouveau visage du Québec,' *Municipalité*, vol. 33, no. 1 (2002): A3.

87 *Contrat de ville, City contract Montréal*, 2003, 8.

88 Boisclair, '2002: le nouveau visage,'C9.

89 Anne-Marie Séguin and Gérard Divay, 'Le contrat de ville de Montréal et la lutte à l'exclusion,' in Michel Venne, ed., *L'annuaire du Québec 2004* (Montreal: Fides, 2004), 832.

90 OECD, *Territorial Reviews Montréal*, 132, http://www.oecd.org/dataoecd/35/11/26010229.pdf, http://www.oecd.org/dataoecd/27/38/27561736.pdf.

91 *Déclaration du GV 22, BC22 Declaration*, 2004, http://cmm.qc.ca/bc22/documents/pdf/declaration_ang_signee.pdf.

92 Jean-Pierre Collin and Mariona Tomàs, *Building Metropolitan Governance Capacity: The Case of Montreal: A Three-tier Model between Innovation and Confusion* (Montreal, 2005), 21.

93 Parti libéral du Québec (PLQ), *Faire confiance aux régions: Priorités d'action*

politiques pour des emplois et des services en région. Discussion paper (Montreal, 2003), 10.

94 The name of the ministry was at first ministère du Développement économique et régional and was changed to ministère du Développement économique et régional et Recherche, and later on to ministère du Développement économique, de l'Innovation et de l'Exportation.

95 OECD, *Territorial Reviews.*

96 Act respecting the Ministère du Développement économique et régional et de la Recherche, Bill 34, assented to on 1 April 2004, http://www2.publicationsduquebec.gouv.qc.ca/dynamicSearch/telecha rge.php?type=5&fi le=2003C29A.PDF.

97 Bernard Jouve, 'L'imputabilité politique en question. La régionalisation du gouvernement Charest au profit des élus locaux comporte des risques de dérives autocratiques,' *Le Devoir*, 27 April 2004, A7.

98 Communauté métropolitaine de Montréal (CMM) and Caucus d'affinité de la Métropole de l'UMQ, *Mémoire sur le projet de loi 34 relatif à la création des conférences régionales des élus. Pour une Communauté métropolitaine de Montréal compétitive* (Montreal, 2003), P4.

99 Loi sur le ministère du Développement économique et régional et de la Recherche, art. 99.

100 Marie-Claude Prémont, 'La réingénierie québécoise version municipale,' *Flux, Cahiers scientifiques internationaux réseaux et territoires*, no. 60/61 (2005): 69–82.

101 Contrary to the first three bills, Bill 76 has not yet been adopted.

102 Section 5 of the act provides that the government may grant any other financial assistance in the form and on the conditions that may be determined by regulation.

103 Municipalities, however, were shielded from the application of the law by the government.

104 Round-table forum: 'La gestion de l'eau: quel rôle pour l'entreprise privée?' http://www.vrm.ca/Gestion_Eau.asp; Ève Gauthier, 'La démocratie soluble dans l'eau privatisée,' *Alternatives, le journal*, vol. 12, no. 6 (2006): 5.

105 Marie-Claude Prémont, 'Le sens de l'événement: la réingénierie québécoise version municipale,' *Flux : cahiers scientifiques internationaux réseaux et territoires*, no. 61/62 (2005): 69–82.

106 But, since the signing of the agreement, nothing has changed where the sharing of responsibilities is concerned: MAMSL et ministère des Finances du Québec, *Repenser les relations avec les municipalités* (Quebec: Government of Quebec, 2004).

107 http://www2.publicationsduquebec.gouv.qc.ca/dynamicSearch/
telecharge.php?type=2 &file=%2F%2FM_30%2FM30_A.htm.

108 Ministère des Affaires municipales et des Régions, *Guide relatif aux
modalités révisées de transfert aux municipalités du Québec d'une partie des
revenus de la taxe fédérale d'accise sur l'essence et de la contribution du gouvernement du Québec pour leurs infrastructures d'eau potable, d'eaux usées et
de voirie locale*, 2006, http://www.mamr.gouv.qc.ca/publications/
infrastructures/guide_transfert_taxe_essence.p df;
http://www.infrastructure.gc.ca/alt_formats/pdf/REV-gt-
guide_can_qc_e.pdf.

109 The September 1994 election placed the Parti Québécois in power just
after numerous decisions had been made and the program was 'starting
its engines.' The new *Péquiste* minister re-examined his predecessor's
decisions and finally concluded that he could not see anything wrong
with what had been done.

3 Nova Scotia

DAVID M. CAMERON WITH PAUL A.R. HOBSON

The basic structure of municipal government in Nova Scotia has, with a few notable exceptions, changed remarkably little over the past century and a quarter. The foundation of the municipal system is the county, of which there are eighteen. Three of these are now incorporated as 'regional' municipalities, containing both urban and rural communities in single-tier municipal units.[1] Of the remaining fifteen counties, nine are incorporated as municipal units covering the entire county, while six are divided into two municipal districts each.[2] In Nova Scotia parlance, these rural municipalities are simply referred to as the municipalities. In municipal circles, they are the 'rurals' (as distinct from the towns and 'regionals'). There are twenty-seven incorporated towns.[3] The significant feature of the towns is that they are completely separated from the county or district within which they are physically situated. There are no longer any cities in Nova Scotia, since Halifax, Dartmouth, and Sydney have all been consolidated into regional units.

Another twenty-two communities have been incorporated as villages. A village has limited powers of self-government, as set out in provincial legislation. Villages are distinguished from towns principally by the fact that they continue as constituent units within their respective rural municipality.[4] Finally, also within the rural municipalities are local service commissions, incorporated and operating under provincial legislation, providing services such as street lighting and fire protection. Village commissions and service commissions are authorized to levy taxes in addition to those levied by the host municipality.

To put this description into perspective, the regional municipalities contain 53 per cent of the provincial population, 50 per cent of the dwelling units, 20 per cent of the province's land area, and 55 per cent of the property assessments. The towns contain 12 per cent of the population, 12 per cent of the dwelling units, 1 per cent of the land area, and 12 per cent of the assessments. The rural municipalities contain 35 per cent of the population, 37 per cent of the dwelling units, 80 per cent of the land area, and 33 per cent of the assessments.

Relations between municipalities and the provincial government are managed through a myriad of provincial departments but are coordinated through the Department of Service Nova Scotia and Municipal Relations. In 1999 a host of separate pieces of legislation were consolidated into the omnibus Municipal Government Act.[5] It, along with the Municipal Grants Act, now defines the roles and powers of municipalities in the province.

Mention should also be made of First Nations governments. There are thirteen First Nations communities in the province, with a combined population in excess of 12,000.[6] The principal relationship of First Nations communities is with the federal government, but the province recently established an Office of Aboriginal Affairs to coordinate relations on a tripartite basis.

Historical Overview

Before 1776, what rudimentary local administration existed was provided through what has come to be known as the Virginia model: courts of general sessions with justices of the peace appointed by the governor and his council, along with grand juries drawn by lot from among local property owners and serving in a largely advisory capacity. It was a minimal system at best, but it sufficed to regulate the peace and attend to such public works as colonial circumstances required. It also served to keep at bay any move by local inhabitants to establish local self-government along the New England model.

False Starts and Early Beginnings

An elected assembly was established for Nova Scotia in 1758, the first in what would later become Canada. Townships were also recognized, but only for purposes of electing representatives to the provincial assembly.

As a result of the American Revolution, Nova Scotia and Quebec[7] were inundated with United Empire Loyalists,[8] many of whom brought with them experience with more democratic traditions of local government. While there was some support for local self-government, provincial colonial authorities staunchly resisted such manifestations of local democracy.

In 1848 Nova Scotia became the first British colony to adopt the system we now know as responsible government. And, in a strange juxtaposition of cause and effect, the granting of responsible government seems to have taken whatever wind remained in the sails of municipal democracy. It was as though Nova Scotians could handle only so much democracy, and, having achieved it at the provincial level, people lost interest in securing it at the local level as well. Halifax was something of an exception. Here, municipal incorporation had long been sought by many of its leading business and other leaders and had finally been granted in 1841. The province did pass permissive legislation in 1855, allowing for local townships to incorporate. But only one community, Yarmouth, took up the opportunity and was incorporated in 1857. It proved to be so unpopular that the corporation was dissolved a year later.

The roots of the current system of municipal government in Nova Scotia were clearly planted in 1867 amidst the events surrounding Confederation. It was not, however, because Nova Scotians had suddenly embraced local democracy. The fact of the matter was that elected local governments were forced upon the people in a dramatic instance of what we would now characterize as 'downloading.'

The Fathers of Confederation, having decided to transfer virtually all known tax revenues to the federal government, then had to agree on a system of subsidies to the provinces. But the Canadas had systems of local government, with municipal taxation of real and personal property, while Nova Scotia and New Brunswick did not, except for Saint John and Halifax. Consequently, the per capita revenue needs of the several provinces were dramatically different.[9]

In the end, Charles Tupper, for Nova Scotia, solved the problem. Nova Scotia would simply get by on what Ontario and Quebec required, with or without municipal institutions and the associated access to direct taxation. On the other hand, Leonard Tilley held out for better terms for New Brunswick and received a slightly better deal. Not surprisingly, perhaps, Nova Scotians were not impressed with what Joseph Howe was wont to call 'the botheration scheme,' and returned almost complete slates of anti-confederates in the ensuing federal and provincial elections.

The upshot was that Nova Scotia found itself in a financial strait-jacket, a straitjacket that was made all the tighter by the economic recession that gripped the new country in the latter 1870s. A new Conservative provincial government, elected in 1878, confronted the situation with a total surprise: it introduced the 1879 County Incorporation Act, which simply forced the municipal incorporation of the province's existing counties. In actual fact, only twelve of the eighteen counties were incorporated as such. The remaining six were divided into two municipal districts each, yielding a total of twenty-four municipalities. The intent was perfectly clear: the new municipalities were given the power to levy a property tax and were now required to look after roads and bridges (the province meanwhile, slashed its spending on those items).

One further element was necessary to complete the municipal system. After Halifax, a number of the urban centres sought and were granted incorporation by special acts. At least eight towns were incorporated in this fashion between 1873 and 1886. So, in 1888, the government introduced the Towns Incorporation Act, which regularized the procedure and standardized the legislation. It also confirmed the practice of separating the towns from their surrounding rural areas, a practice virtually unique in Canada. The incorporation of cities, which in addition to Halifax came to include Dartmouth and Sydney, continued until 1999 and was accomplished through separate acts.

On the Road to Reform: The Graham Commission Report

The basic structure of municipal government in Nova Scotia, as established by the County Incorporation Act of 1879 and the Towns Incorporation Act of 1888, remained essentially unchanged for over a century. A few additional towns were added after 1888, bringing the total number to thirty-eight by 1923. After that point, the practice of creating new towns was essentially abandoned, with the future exception of Bedford, which was incorporated as a town in 1980 (Bedford happened to be the home of the then premier of the province). Instead of additional towns, small urban centres were subsequently incorporated as villages or as local service commissions. Unlike towns, these bodies remain part of the rural municipality within which they are physically situated. They levy additional tax rates to pay for specific local services not available in the rest of the rural municipality.

A couple of developments are worthy of note at this point. One was the formation, in 1906, of the Union of Nova Scotia Municipalities (UNSM), a body that now represents all municipalities in the province. The union has become a quite powerful lobby in provincial politics, although it has often found it easier to oppose change than to agree on positive alternatives.

An example of this occurred in 1947 when the province convened the first ever provincial-municipal conference to review the structure of municipal government and provincial-municipal finance. Municipal representatives were unable to agree on virtually anything, except the need for more money, and so the province commissioned an independent review, to be undertaken by Donald Rowat of Dalhousie University.

Rowat concluded that Nova Scotia's municipal units were simply too small to respond effectively and efficiently to the demands emerging in the post-war era, especially in relation to health and social welfare, the administration of justice, education, and planning. He proposed the addition of nine upper-tier or regional governments to take on these responsibilities.[10] To make regional government work, Rowat argued that a system of standardized property assessments should be instituted, which should then support provincial equalization grants to the new regional municipalities.

No action was taken on Rowat's proposals, and Nova Scotia passed through the post-war growth of government with its municipalities unreformed and seemingly unreformable. Continued growth in the Halifax area did prompt a series of boundary adjustments affecting both Halifax and Dartmouth, as well as the incorporation of Bedford as a town. Indeed, the greater Halifax area seemed to be moving haltingly, if inexorably, towards some form of metropolitan government. Several studies were commissioned, but the only concrete action was the establishment of a Metropolitan Authority, initially to operate a jail for Halifax, Dartmouth, and Halifax County (and later Bedford). Over time, its jurisdiction was expanded to include a regional transit system and a sanitary landfill.

When a new Liberal government, with Gerald Regan as premier, was elected in October 1970, it established yet another study, the far-ranging, three-person Royal Commission on Education, Public Services and Provincial-Municipal Relations, chaired by Dr John Graham, a Dalhousie professor of economics. Thirty-eight months later, the commission released its massive report. Among its many recommendations, some of them set forth in excruciating detail, three lie at the heart of what would have constituted a virtual revolution in municipal government and provincial-municipal relations in Nova Scotia.

The commission's first recommendation was to draw a sharp, if arbitrary, line between what it considered to be local and general services, the latter to be the responsibility of the provincial government. These included education, public health and hospitals, public welfare, the administration of justice, and civil defence. A number of support services, integral to the taxing authority of municipalities, were also recommended to be assumed by the province. These included responsibility for property assessment, tax collection (including local improvement taxes), capital borrowing, and the administration of pension plans for municipal employees.

The second recommendation seemed oddly juxtaposed against the first. Having proposed that municipalities be stripped of virtually all of their 'general' and support services, the commission turned around and recommended that municipal boundaries should be considerably enlarged. The existing twenty-four rural municipalities would be reduced in number by more than half, to eleven renamed counties (three of the proposed counties, Halifax, Cape Breton, and Pictou, were to be designated 'metropolitan' counties). These eleven counties were to be one-tier municipalities, with responsibility for all of the local services assigned to that level of government. Yet existing towns and village commissions were to be retained as municipal units, with elected councils but no independent service responsibilities. On the one hand, they were to be purely advisory, acting like area-interest groups, to keep the county council aware of their particular needs. On the other hand, they might take on responsibility for delivering some services, either under contract with the county council or at their own expense (but with the approval of the county). The commission also recommended that 'community associations' be formed when so requested by local community groups, their purpose being to bring local concerns to the attention of the regional council.

The third recommendation was then to align provincial and municipal revenue sources with the proposed transformation of service and expenditure responsibilities. This, in turn, came in two parts: the realignment of taxing powers and the redesign of provincial grants to municipalities.

The proposed rearrangement of service responsibilities was estimated to cost the province an additional $80.6 million. The bulk of this would be paid for through the transfer to the province of the taxation of non-residential (that is, commercial and industrial) property.[11] The rationale was that taxes on non-residential property are generally shifted outside the municipality in which the property is located (they become a cost of doing business and are embodied in the price of the goods or services) and are therefore best captured by the province and used for the benefit of the whole province.

The proposed change in provincial grants was perhaps the most important feature of the entire package. The commission recommended scrapping virtually the whole hodgepodge assortment of existing grants and substituting a comprehensive equalization grant, modelled on the federal-provincial revenue-equalization formula. Under this proposal, each municipality (county) would be assured of access, through a combination of its own taxes and the provincial equalization grant, to at least the average per capita revenue available to the three wealthiest municipalities. Because Halifax had a per capita tax base well above any of the others, it was to be excluded from the formula. It would not be eligible for equalization, and it would not contribute to raising the equalization entitlements of the other municipalities.[12]

The commission's report elicited strong opposition, especially the proposed consolidation of municipal units. The legislative committee struck to review the document was unable to reach consensus and issued no report of its own. Some of the recommendations were implemented over the next few years, but on a piecemeal basis. The issues raised, however, did whet some appetites. It seemed that something, perhaps something less comprehensive, did need to be done.

The Twin Pillars of Change:
Service Exchange and Consolidation

Eighteen years later, and after two changes in government, the Conservative premier, Donald Cameron, decided to revisit the issue of municipal reform, establishing a task force of departmental and municipal officials with two explicit priorities for change: 'reallocation of responsibility for financing and delivery of services, with structure and boundary changes to follow if necessary.'[13]

Reporting in April 1992, the task force set forth a proposed rationalization of responsibilities, drawing a sharp line between what was to be assigned to the province and to the municipalities. The proposed service exchange would see police services, except highway patrols, become a wholly municipal responsibility, along with roads, other than arterial and collector highways. Conversely, responsibility for social services, public health, and the administration of justice would be assumed by the province. To complete the picture, all remaining shared-cost programs would be terminated, while the existing equal- ization scheme would be revised to take account of the increased costs to rural municipalities associated with the assumption of responsibil- ity for roads and policing. It seemed that the spirit, at least, of Graham's royal commission report would finally see the light of day. The notable exception was that education, by far the most expensive of the services Graham had recommended be transferred wholly to the province, was not part of this exchange.

The proposed service exchange was mightily affected by the provin- cial government's insistence that the net results be 'revenue neutral.' To ensure this, changes in funding arrangements were proposed that were designed to negate the fiscal benefits of some $13 million that municipalities would have gained from the transfer of spending responsibilities to the province. While the government announced that the recommended service exchange would proceed, beginning in 1995, the scale of the exchange was significantly reduced, particularly in relation to social assistance, homes for special care, and roads. In the latter case, rural municipalities would now assume responsibility only for the maintenance of so-called 'Class J' roads, servicing subdivisions. The cost of services to be transferred to the province was cut almost in half, from the original proposal of $96 million to the actual transfer of $53 million.

Ironically, while the aggregate impact of the service exchange was indeed revenue neutral, this was not the case for individual munici- palities. As Igor Vojnovic observed, despite provincial statements to the contrary, the impact was decidedly regressive: 'While the Province of Nova Scotia argued in its 1993 discussion paper that one of the aims of the service exchange was to alleviate the fiscal pressures of the financially weak municipalities, it was the fiscally weakest grouping that faced the most significant fiscal burdens after the exchange.'[14]

Even more dramatic was the impact of the exchange for the two urban areas that were about to be consolidated, Halifax and industrial Cape Breton, slated to become the Halifax Regional Municipality (HRM) and the Cape Breton Regional Municipality (CBRM). Again citing Igor Vojnovic, the four municipalities that would form the HRM collectively posted, as a result of the exchange, a net gain in revenues over expenditures of $8.5 million. The eight municipalities that would comprise the CBRM, all of which were fiscally challenged, would face a deficit of $4.9 million.[15]

The task force favoured a 'unitary' or one-tier government for each of the eighteen counties in the province, with individual boundary adjustments as circumstances might warrant. It recognized, however, that no comprehensive reform was possible 'so long as urban units pay for police and roads while rural units do not.'[16] Instead, it identified five counties, which it considered to be 'the critical areas,' containing most of the province's urban population, and which should be addressed first. The five counties were Cape Breton, Halifax, Pictou, Colchester, and Kings.

Premier Cameron accepted the task force recommendations for Halifax and Cape Breton and appointed commissions to work out the details of implementation. Pictou, Colchester, and Kings counties would be left for later, but the government was defeated before further action could be taken. To the surprise of many, the new Liberal premier, John Savage, reversed his earlier opposition to amalgamation and moved quickly to appoint implementation commissioners, first for Cape Breton and shortly thereafter for Halifax. The amalgamation of the eight municipalities in industrial Cape Breton came into effect on 1 August 1995.[17] The commissioner had estimated that amalgamation would yield annual savings of some $6.5 million. In the first year of operation, the consolidated municipality faced a deficit of $15 million.[18] The consolidation of Halifax, Dartmouth, Bedford, and Halifax County came into effect almost a year later, on 1 April 1996.

There has been much speculation as to the reasons for the Halifax amalgamation (the reason for merging the Cape Breton municipalities was obvious: several of them were virtually bankrupt, dependent on special grants from the province). Andrew Sancton argues that it was a case of autonomous state action, possible because there was neither organized support nor opposition.[19] There was also a very practical reason. The net effect of the rationalization of service responsibilities would favour Halifax, Dartmouth, and Bedford but disadvantage Halifax County. Amalgamation would mask this.

There is one other feature of the Halifax amalgamation that warrants mention. As recommended by the implementation commissioner, provincial legislation provided for the establishment of community councils. Each community council must contain at least three regional councillors. They have limited authority to make recommendations on budgetary priorities as well as to make certain decisions on land-use planning. They have no independent taxing powers.

A third consolidation also occurred in Nova Scotia, taking effect on the same date as the establishment of the HRM. The amalgamation of the town of Liverpool with the surrounding Queens County, to form the Queens Regional Municipality, was a consolidation of a quite different nature. For one thing, it was entirely voluntary. There was no provincially appointed commissioner and, consequently, no exaggerated claims of anticipated savings. And, as with Cape Breton, but unlike Halifax, there were no community councils.

Service Exchange: The Continuing Saga

Municipal amalgamations in Cape Breton, Halifax, and Queens seem to have satisfied the provincial government's appetite for forced consolidation, at least temporarily. Not so with service exchange. The upshot of the 1995 changes was to open new demands for further adjustments as the longer-term effects began to be felt in different parts of the province.

The first initiative came within months of the 1995 exchange. The most significant feature of this change was to relieve the CBRM of some $3.4 million in expenditure responsibilities for social services. The HRM and Queens, the other two regional municipalities, also benefited financially from this transfer, but not nearly to the same extent ($2.8 million and $200,000, respectively).

Pressure continued for further adjustments, spearheaded by the Union of Nova Scotia Municipalities. By 1997, agreement had been reached to undertake a joint review of the respective roles and responsibilities of the provincial and municipal governments. The list of immediate issues included the funding of social services, the maintenance and repair of bridges, and mandatory municipal contributions to the financing of education. The list was subsequently expanded to include the full funding of equalization.

The first step in this initiative was the signing, in April 1998, of a memorandum of understanding (MOU) between the provincial minister and the president of the UNSM. It established that responsibility for maintenance and repair of bridges, previously covered under a shared-cost arrangement between the province and municipalities, would now be the sole responsibility of the province. It also provided for a phased reduction in municipal contributions to social services, over a five-year period. Finally, it restored funding of the equalization grant, which had been reduced as the result of the expected levelling consequences of the service-exchange program. Education was not addressed. But, most important, the MOU promised a longer-term 'comprehensive review of provincial and municipal roles and responsibilities, to commence in 1998.'[20]

The Roles and Responsibilities review was to proceed in three phases. Phase one, identifying outstanding issues, was completed by the end of 1998. Phase two, examining more closely the issues identified in phase one, was finished by early 2000. By then, the Liberal government, now headed by Russell MacLennan, who had replaced John Savage following the latter's resignation, had been defeated at the polls. The new Conservative premier, John Hamm, was elected with a majority government in July 1999. Phase three of this exercise, with recommendations, was completed by the spring of 2001 and involved a further proposed exchange of responsibilities. On the one hand, some $21.9 million in expenditures would be assumed by the province. These expenditures were associated with public housing, correction services, and an increase in provincial grants in respect of property taxes for university residences. In return, the municipalities would internalize the cost of equalization, effectively removing it from the provincial budget.

One issue has come to dominate attempts to rationalize municipal government in Nova Scotia. That issue is roads, which has been at the centre of provincial-municipal relations since 1879. The fact of the matter is that so long as towns (and regional municipalities) have responsibility for local roads, and rural municipalities do not, no overall restructuring is possible. At the same time, so long as no equitable formula can be found that would recognize the varying costs of maintaining existing roads, many of them built by previous provincial governments, rural municipalities will continue to resist assuming responsibility for their local roads. The upshot is that, in all municipal accounting and in provincial-municipal finance, towns and rural municipalities must always be kept in separate accounts.

The Municipal Government Act and Provincial-Municipal Relations

Nova Scotia's Municipal Government Act, passed in 1998 and coming into effect on 1 April 1999, attempted to bring the governance of municipalities in the province more in line with a trend in municipal governance and provincial-municipal relations generally in Canada. Indeed, the subtitle of the act, 'Progressive Powers for Municipalities,' provides a clear signal of this intention. The stated purpose of the act provides further specificity, indicating that it is intended to give municipalities a general power to govern, 'to give broad authority to councils ... and to respect their right to govern municipalities in whatever ways the councils consider appropriate within the jurisdiction given to them.' With that single limitation, confining municipal authority to delegated jurisdiction, they are to be free to 'provide good government,' to 'provide services, facilities and other things that, in the opinion of the council, are necessary or desirable for all or part of the municipality,' and to 'develop and maintain safe and viable communities.'[21]

Specific Legislative Powers

So much for good intentions. When it comes to the fine print, the legislation is not quite as progressive as the above quotations might suggest, although the language is still couched in permissive terms. Thus, a council 'may' make policies setting the fees to be charged for licences, inspections, permits, and the impoundment of animals, as well as the rate of interest to be charged on overdue taxes or other charges. It may also regulate the use of solid-waste management facilities and set fees to be charged. Municipalities may also acquire, sell, or lease property, but property sold or leased must be at market value unless it is for a non-profit organization or is approved by a two-thirds majority of council members (and if the property is valued at more than $10,000 the council must first hold a public hearing).

Nova Scotia's municipalities are granted a number of specific powers, although the list is far from exhaustive, and it is not indicated why these specific powers are singled out for specific authorization. The significance of this will be discussed later when we examine the power to spend money. The specific powers authorized by the Municipal Government Act may be summarized under the following headings:

(a) Expropriation: municipalities may expropriate property, but only for purposes for which it may spend money (this is a critical point that will be discussed further below), but no municipality may expropriate the property of another municipality. Municipalities are bound by the provincial Expropriation Act.

(b) Plebiscites: municipalities may instruct the municipal clerk to conduct a plebiscite applicable in the whole or a part of the municipality, and, where such a plebiscite is directed, it must be conducted in conformity with the Municipal Elections Act.

(c) Police Services: a municipality may provide police services but in so doing is subject to the provisions of the Police Act, and, once established, the police service comes under the authority of a board of police commissioners. Furthermore, a council may contract with the RCMP, the minister of justice, or another municipality for the provision of police services.

(d) Public Transportation: a municipality may provide public transportation, either by owning and operating the service itself, by subsidizing a private operator, or by a combination of the two.

(e) Area Improvement and Promotion: municipalities may take a variety of actions designed to promote the municipality, including beautification of property, either municipally or privately owned, promotion of business districts, and establishment and maintenance of parking facilities. They may also set and collect area rates applicable where such improvements apply.

(f) Business and Industrial Development: municipalities may engage in business and industrial promotion, including advertising and grants to other bodies engaged in such promotion activities, but they are specifically prohibited from granting tax concessions or other forms of financial assistance to businesses or industries.

(g) Regional Libraries: a municipality may enter into an agreement with other municipalities for the provision and operation of a regional library, as provided under the provincial Libraries Act.

(h) Highways and Housing Agreements: finally, municipalities may enter into agreements related to highway construction or improvement pursuant to the Public Highways Act, and may enter into agreements with Canada Mortgage and Housing Corporation.

While these seem reminiscent of the traditional approach to provincial legislation for municipalities, wherein a municipality was authorized to do only what was specifically authorized in provincial legislation, it must be remembered that the above list is far from exhaustive, and is obviously designed, at least for the most part, to remove any uncertainty regarding municipal powers under provincial legislation directed specifically to other applications (police, libraries, transit systems, and so on). That changes, however, when we come to the question of municipal expenditures. Here we encounter a profound paradox. The broad sweep of municipal authority promised in the preamble to the act is effectively repudiated in the assignment of spending authority. Municipalities may do 'whatever the councils consider appropriate' but they may spend money only on things specifically authorized by the province.

The Spending Power of Municipalities

The list of approved objects of expenditure is long (forty-nine items) but also exhaustive. According to the Municipal Government Act, councils may spend money on the following items:

- election and plebiscite expenses
- repayment of borrowed money
- emergency-response systems
- fire departments
- school-crossing guards
- recreational programs
- economic development
- public transportation
- solid-waste management
- approved travel expenses
- assessments on municipal utilities
- public libraries
- furnishings and equipment
- streets, sidewalks, etc.
- underground utilities
- pounds
- recreational facilities
- public markets
- property held in trust
- water systems
- industrial parks
- parking lots and structures
- wharves and public landings
- contributions to hospitals
- insurance premiums
- police services
- snow and ice removal
- training of volunteer fire-fighters
- emergency measures
- promotion of business and tourism
- lighting
- flood prevention
- salaries of councillors and staff
- pension contributions
- UNSM and other professional fees
- property for municipal purposes
- acquisition of equipment
- private roads approved by council
- distribution of utilities
- fire-alarm systems
- other authorized expenditures
- certain clubs or charities
- waste- and storm-water systems
- buildings for medical use
- landing strips and airports

- public grounds, community centres, etc.
- ponds, reservoirs, etc. for fire prevention

- agreements with other agencies

Provincial Oversight

As just indicated, despite some movement towards granting munici-palities a general power to govern, the province of Nova Scotia retains quite firm control over the operation of its municipalities. The province often uses its outright legislative superiority to mandate stan-dards in areas such as policing and water purification. The province also has other instruments at its disposal. Perhaps most important is the provincial department itself, currently styled Service Nova Scotia and Municipal Relations. This department combines a wide range of regulatory responsibilities of the province as well as relations with its municipalities. Reflecting current jargon, it describes itself as provid-ing a single window for a wide range of government services to the public and to municipalities. It has three operational units, one han-dling provincial property assessments, another provincial regulatory 'services,' and a third municipal relations.

A potentially significant event took place in September 2005, with the signing of an MOU between the minister, on behalf of the province, and the Union of Nova Scotia Municipalities, on behalf of all munici-palities in the province. The memorandum declared the province and its municipalities to be both 'orders of government' serving the same taxpayer, and pledged them to work cooperatively under a set of guiding principles. These principles committed each party to respect the jurisdiction of the other, to consult in a timely fashion, and to seek to resolve differences through dialogue and discussion.[22]

An indication that all is not quite as smooth in provincial-municipal relations as this MOU might suggest is provided in the recent decision by the UNSM to undertake its own study of fiscal relations, under the title 'Fair and Equitable Funding.' The study was a direct result of municipal frustration with the outcome of recent attempts at negotiat-ing a new fiscal and jurisdictional relationship under the rubric of 'service exchange.' A group of consultants was contracted, and they reported in April 2005 that a number of anomalies remained in both the service responsibilities assigned to municipalities (especially in relation to education, corrections, public housing, and roads) and the system of provincial grants (especially the equalization grant and the treatment of taxes levied against Nova Scotia Power Inc. [NSPI]). They also identified some serious anomalies in the relative treatment of municipalities, with the Cape Breton Regional Municipality especially hard hit.[23]

In addition to Service Nova Scotia and Municipal Relations, two other provincial agencies play a major and direct role in regulating municipal activities. One of these is the omnibus, quasi-judicial body known as the Nova Scotia Utility and Review Board (NSURB). It was established in 1992 and assumed the responsibilities of a number of boards and commissions, including the Nova Scotia Municipal Board. Several additional responsibilities have been added subsequently. Among its many duties and responsibilities, it adjudicates appeals from Regional Assessment Appeal Courts, sets the rates charged by the Halifax-Dartmouth Bridge Commission, determines the value of expropriated property when the parties cannot agree, determines the number and boundaries of municipal and school board electoral constituencies, and rules on appeals of land-use by-laws, rezoning, and development agreements as well as refusals to issue development permits or approve subdivision plans.[24]

Another significant provincial agency is the Municipal Finance Corporation. It was established in 1979 and provides provincially guaranteed short- and long-term financing to municipalities, school boards, and health authorities for capital projects. It offers interest at the provincial rate, plus an administrative premium. An interesting feature of the corporation is that, by law, 40 per cent of its directors must be recommended by the UNSM. There are currently five directors, two of whom are UNSM nominees.[25]

Municipal Revenues

The general picture of municipal revenues is set out in the appendix, along with comparable data for Canada as a whole. Some interesting observations emerge from this comparison. On a per capita basis in 2004, Nova Scotia municipalities had access from all sources to almost 28 per cent less revenue than the national average ($1,243.73 compared to $1,723.19). This partially reflects the municipal consequences of the province's have-not status, but it also reflects the reduced municipal-expenditure responsibilities attendant upon the service-exchange program. Interestingly, Nova Scotia's municipalities raised almost the national average in property-related taxes (just 7.45 per cent less, $689.86 per capita compared with $745.14). This is partly a reflection of the mandatory education levy which municipalities are required to raise on behalf of school boards. It also reflects the relatively lower dependence on non-property-tax revenues. In that case, Nova Scotia was well below the national average in 2004 ($8.46 compared to $25.42 per capita). Similarly, Nova Scotia municipalities raised considerably less revenue from sales of goods and services than did Canadian municipalities generally ($226.77 per capita compared with $387.45). Other own-source revenue actually declined over the past decade. Nova Scotia municipalities raised fully 93.2 per cent of their total revenues from their own sources, 71.6 per cent of it from property and property-related taxes. Nova Scotia municipalities' reliance on their own-source revenues is the highest in Canada. By way of contrast, municipalities across Canada in 2004 raised, on average, 83.1 per cent of their revenues from their own sources, and just 52.7 per cent from property and property-related taxes.

The effect of the service-exchange exercise can be seen clearly in the revenue data. Nova Scotia municipalities received only $70.90 per capita in provincial transfers in 2004. This compares with $266.95 for Canada as a whole. Moreover, while the Canadian figure declined by just under 22 per cent between 1995 and 2004, the figure for Nova Scotia dropped by 76 per cent in the same period.

Several features of the revenue structure of Nova Scotia municipalities warrant additional comment, beginning with the property tax itself.

Property Taxes

The assessment of property in Nova Scotia is the responsibility of the provincial government, operating through the department known as Service Nova Scotia and Municipal Relations. A new arms-length agency, the Property Valuation Services Corporation (PVSC), assumed responsibility for valuing individual properties as of 1 April 2008. However, the cost of the assessment function has, since 2001, been charged to the appropriate municipality. Prior to 1995, the province adjusted individual assessments every three years. Since 1995 this has been done annually.

Nova Scotia municipalities are authorized to levy a residential tax rate against the assessed value of taxable residential property and resource property. They can also levy a commercial tax rate against the assessed value of taxable commercial property and, in addition, against the separate business-occupancy assessment. As well, municipalities can set separate commercial and residential tax rates for the areas of the municipality determined to be rural areas and receiving a rural level of services, suburban areas receiving a suburban level of services, and urban areas receiving an urban level of services. Municipalities may also set a minimum tax per dwelling unit and the minimum tax may be set at different levels for different areas of the municipality.

Municipalities can set area rates in respect of expenditures in a defined area, or for the benefit of that specific area. In lieu of levying an area rate, municipalities can levy a uniform charge on each taxable property assessment or dwelling unit, in the specified area.

Recreational property is subject to a levy, known as the recreational property tax, equal to a fixed amount per acre, or part of an acre, for all of the land assessed as recreational property. Farm property is exempt from taxation. In lieu of taxes, the municipality in which the farm property is situated is paid a grant equal to a fixed amount per acre. This grant is to be increased in each fiscal year by the same percentage increase as the Consumer Price Index (CPI). Land used for forestry purposes is subject to the forest property tax, set at twenty-five cents per acre, if the forest property is classified as resource property; and forty cents per acre, if the forest property is classified as commercial property. In addition, where an area, village, or commission rate is levied for fire protection, the owner of the forest property is liable to pay an additional annual tax not exceeding one cent per acre.

Municipalities may levy a fire-protection rate against the value of all assessable property and business-occupancy assessment in the area served by a water system in the municipality in order to recover that part of the cost of the water system that is attributable to fire protection.

Capping Property Assessments

Some properties in Nova Scotia, especially those with ocean frontage on the south shore of the province (Chester, Lunenburg, Mahone Bay, Shelburne, and Queens especially), began experiencing above-average increases in property assessments, largely as the result of spiralling property sale values often associated with overseas purchases. In order to protect provincial residents against dramatic increases in their property assessments, the province moved in 2004 to limit year-over-year increases in individual assessments, beginning in 2005. Known as the Cap Assessment Program (CAP), the scheme required property owners to apply to have their assessment 'capped.' The CAP program limited residential or vacant resource property assessments for qualified applicants to a maximum increase of 10 per cent in any one year.

In 2006 the Liberal Party, the smallest of the three parties represented in the provincial Legislative Assembly, introduced a bill to expand the program significantly. With only a minority in the legislature, the governing Conservatives accepted the motion, and were joined by the New Democratic Party to make the vote unanimous.

The revised CAP scheme made two dramatic changes, both to take effect from the 2008–9 fiscal year. First, residents no longer need to apply; the limit on assessment increases will now be automatic. Second, the cap on assessment increases is reduced from 10 per cent to the current CPI.

The new scheme has received mixed reviews. Writing in the Halifax *Chronicle Herald*, the provincial newspaper, Marilla Stevenson praised the change on the grounds that it will end the virtually automatic annual increases in property taxes in many municipalities occasioned by increased assessments.[26] On the other hand, the Union of Nova Scotia Municipalities strongly opposes the change. It commissioned a study by the Deloitte & Touche consulting group which pointed out the likely inequities that will arise from capping some assessments and not others, and therefore shifting the tax burden onto those with 'uncapped' assessments.[27] Only properties that continue in the hands of the same owners are capped; once a property is sold the assessment reverts to full market value and the cap is then applied anew. Moreover, the cap does not apply to apartment buildings. The UNSM then passed a resolution, unanimously, calling for a return to the previous 10 per cent limit and proposing the introduction of a means-tested assessment cap.[28]

Taxes on Business Property

Until it was phased out, beginning in 2006 and to be completed by 2010, municipalities could levy a business-occupancy tax. This was essentially a second property tax, levied against the occupant of a business and calculated as a percentage of the assessed value of the property. In the case of owner-occupied businesses, the owner paid both taxes.

In addition, two businesses are treated separately by the province. Taxation of Aliant telecommunications company property (buildings) is paid directly to the province. Aliant also makes payments to each municipality based on 4 per cent of revenues derived from local service supplied in each municipality. Taxation of Nova Scotia Power property (buildings) is also paid to the province. Additionally, the NSPI makes a payment in lieu of taxes, through the province, to municipalities (see below). Property taxes paid by Imperial Oil for its refinery in Dartmouth (HRM) are capped by the province.

Exemptions from Property Assessment

Municipalities may provide tax exemptions for low-income taxpayers and may provide for tax deferral. The Assessment Act lists properties that are exempt, including churches, cemeteries, schools, jails, courthouses, public lands, municipal lands, Legions and property of the Army, Navy and Air Force Veterans, and property used for Boy Scouts and Girl Guides. All property of not-for-profit and charitable organizations is taxable. Municipalities may, however, enact by-laws to provide complete or partial tax exemptions for such properties where they are used for the public benefit. Municipalities may also grant a property-tax exemption, sometimes known as the widow's and orphan's exemption, for anyone whose income is below an amount set by the municipality.

Deed Transfer Tax

Section 102 of the Municipal Government Act permits municipalities to levy a deed transfer tax as a percentage of the sale price of a property. Where a municipality levies a deed transfer tax, it applies every time a property is sold. Municipalities are free to set the rate of the deed transfer tax, provided that rate does not exceed 1.5 per cent of the value of the property sold. Not all municipalities actually levy this tax.

The NSPI Levy

The NSPI levy is used to finance a portion of the equalization grant ($11.05 million), as well as the HST (Harmonized Sales Tax) Offset ($6 million) and grants in lieu paid to municipalities ($13.95 million). During 2002–3, it was announced that the NSPI would pay $26.4 million to the municipalities, an increase of $10.7 million over the previous year. Of the increase, $8.25 million was to be used to fund an increase in the equalization grant pool, with the balance to be paid out as grants in lieu of taxes. In 2003–4 the payment rose to $31 million, an increase of $4.6 million over the previous year. A portion of the increase was used to finance a further increase to the municipal equalization program ($2.8 million), and the balance was paid out as additional grants in lieu of taxes ($1.8 million). The HST Offset is distributed in accordance with each municipality's HST liabilities. Grants in lieu are distributed in accordance with each municipality's share of the total NSPI assessment. Of the additional $1.8 million to be paid to municipalities with major NSPI properties, Cape Breton Regional Municipality was to receive $704,000, Queens $455,000, Trenton $267,000, and Annapolis Royal $200,000. The remainder was to be split among the municipalities of Annapolis County, Digby County, and Yarmouth County and the towns of Antigonish, Canso, Kentville, and Mahone Bay.

Provincial-Municipal Equalization

Nova Scotia's equalization grant dates from 1980, when it was introduced as part of a general operating grant. As one component of the Roles and Responsibilities exercise, a general revision of the program was contemplated, with the objective of moving to full equalization.

Then came the political problem. Consistent with the province's long-standing commitment to revenue neutrality, and in sharp contrast to its own treatment under the federal-provincial equalization scheme, the provincial-municipal formula was to be self-financing. That is, wealthier municipalities would pay into an equalization fund and poorer municipalities would draw from it.

At that point, the major potential contributor, the HRM, raised serious concerns over the estimated cost to the municipality. A counter-proposal was made, whereby the HRM offered to assume additional responsibilities currently borne by the province rather than give up property-tax revenues.[29] The UNSM then developed a proposal (supported by the HRM council) to use revenue from municipal deed transfer taxes to fund the equalization program, rather than using the general property tax. The main problem with this proposal was that not all municipalities actually levied a deed transfer tax, and those that did used different rates, so that transition to a uniform levy would be problematic (but certainly not impossible).

In any event, the province rejected both proposals and also backed away from its own scheme. In its April 2003 budget, the province announced that it would use revenue from an increase in provincial property taxes paid by Nova Scotia Power, under a special deal with the province dating back to the privatization of the corporation, to finance the equalization program.

This deal raised the ire of the Cape Breton Regional Municipality in particular, since it is home to about half of Nova Scotia Power's facilities. Nova Scotia Power, although privatized a decade ago, still does not pay property taxes to the municipalities in which its facilities are located, but pays a special, negotiated, levy to the province. The province now pays a portion of the proceeds of this levy to municipalities that qualify for equalization.

The accumulated frustration that has attended the lengthy search for a new deal that would better align provincial and municipal expenditure responsibilities with revenue-raising capacities led in due course to the decision by the UNSM to launch its own investigation. The purpose this time would be to arrive at a principled basis for the allocation of municipal responsibilities that might then provide a framework for subsequent negotiations with the province.

The current equalization grant is based on a measure of local expenditure need and local revenue base.[30] Municipalities are grouped into one of two classes. Class I includes regional municipalities and towns. Class II includes county and district municipalities. Expenditure need is measured by standard expenditure per dwelling unit by class of municipality for basic services multiplied by the number of dwelling units.[31]

The standard expenditure per dwelling unit for each class of property is calculated as the average operating-expenditure estimates per dwelling unit for each class. This standard is based on the estimated operating cost of providing the following services – police protection, fire protection, other protective inspections, transportation services excluding public transit, and 50 per cent of garbage collection and disposal and storm sewage collection and disposal, excluding sanitary sewerage. The remaining municipal expenditures, such as spending on recreation and culture, fiscal services including the provincially mandated education levy, and debt service, are excluded. The separation of these services into two components was designed to equalize for services that are essentially non-discretionary and necessary for a functioning municipality.

The revenue base is calculated by taking uniform assessment per dwelling unit and multiplying it by a standard tax rate and then by the number of units. The standard tax rate for each class equals the total standard expenditures for all municipalities within the class divided by the total uniform assessment for the same municipalities within each class.

As part of the service-exchange exercise, funding for the equalization grant was significantly reduced in the attempt to preserve fiscal neutrality. The equalization-grant pool has been gradually restored since that time. It was topped up by $8.25 million in 2002–3 along with changes to the equalization program itself. It was further topped up by $2.8 million in 2004–5. Both of these increases were funded out of increased payments from the NSPI to the province.

Finally, some rural municipalities were eligible for additional equalization payments following the 2002–3 reforms to ensure that their grant was not reduced. These payments were also financed through the NSPI levy.[32]

The HST Offset

The HST Offset provides another source of unconditional transfer from the provincial government to the municipalities. Prior to Nova Scotia signing on to the Harmonized Sales Tax (HST) Agreement with the federal government, the municipalities were exempt from paying the provincial sales tax. Also, through rebates, the municipalities received partial exemption from the federal Goods and Services Tax (GST) and were exempt from paying sales taxes on automobiles, trucks, and heavy equipment. Since municipalities were expected to pay the HST on all purchases, it was estimated that the additional cost would amount to somewhere between $6 million and $11 million.

At the same time, the NSPI was expected to benefit from input tax credits through the new HST. The UNSM had long taken the position that the NSPI was not paying appropriate levels of payments in lieu of taxes. These two factors, combined with the fact that municipalities were to see cost increases from the HST, prompted the creation of the HST Offset Program. The program was to increase NSPI payments in lieu of taxes over an eight-year period in $2-million increments to a maximum of $10 million annually. This was to be distributed to Nova

Scotia municipalities on the basis of HST costs, to offset the impact of the new harmonized tax. The $10-million goal was never reached, ending at $6 million in 2002–3.

The Foundation Grant and Top-Up Grants

Following restructuring of the equalization program in 2001, a Foundation Grant program was introduced under which each town was eligible for a $50,000 annual grant. In addition, top-up grants were introduced to ensure that any rural municipality that would face a reduction in its equalization grant following restructuring would be compensated accordingly. Both the Foundation Grant and the Top-Up Grant were to be funded out of the equalization grant pool.

Grants in Lieu of Taxes[33]

Grants in lieu of taxes are payable in respect of provincial property and provincially occupied federal property and are set equal to the full taxes that would be payable in respect of the property and business-occupancy assessment if it were not exempt from taxation.

The grant payable in respect of property of supported institutions, such as university residences, is set equal to 40 per cent of the full taxes that would be payable in respect of the property and business-occupancy assessment if it were not exempt from taxation. The 2005 provincial budget raised this amount to 50 per cent.

The balance of the NSPI levy (after deductions used to finance the municipal equalization program, and the HST Offset) was to be paid out as a grant in lieu of taxes. That a portion of the NSPI levy is used to finance municipal equalization is somewhat problematic. This means that, in part, the funding of equalization is distributed in proportion to shares in NSPI assessments. Moreover, that a portion of the NSPI levy is used to finance the HST Offset means that municipalities contribute to the cost of the HST Offset in proportion to shares in NSPI assessments. This is particularly irksome to municipalities with relatively large NSPI assessments, such as the Cape Breton Regional Municipality.

Expenditures

Data on municipal expenditures in Nova Scotia, as well as comparative data for Canada, are set out in the appendix. Again, a few observations regarding the picture captured by these data are appropriate. As would be expected, given the relatively lower municipal revenues, expenditures in 2004 fell well below the national average as well ($1,220.13 per capita compared to $1,734.67, a difference of $514.54 or 29.6 per cent). And, once again, the effect of service exchange is apparent in the relatively low expenditures on health ($1.69 per capita compared to a national average of $45.96), social services ($10.24 compared to $180.04), and housing ($2.70 compared to $62.62). Most other categories are within the expected range, given the overall lower level of funds available, although it is interesting to note that spending on recreation and culture is below the national average.

Expenditures on general government services in 2004 were modestly lower than the national average, at $160.19 per capita compared to $182.43. One factor that might account for this is the compensation paid to municipal councillors. For towns and rural municipalities in Nova Scotia, remuneration of councillors and mayors (or wardens, as some heads of Nova Scotia rural municipalities are still known) is relatively modest.

Councillors in towns, for example, receive stipends of less than $4,000 (Trenton and Annapolis Royal) to over $18,000 (New Glasgow), while the mayors receive from just over $6,000 to $26,600 (New Glasgow). In rural municipalities, councillors' remuneration ranges from $10,000 (St Mary's) to just over $20,000 (Yarmouth), while mayors or wardens receive from $17,000 (St Mary's) to $40,000 (Pictou). For the two regional municipalities, councillors in the CBRM receive $32,440 while those in the HRM receive $54,425. The mayor of the CBRM is paid $89,783, while the mayor of the HRM is paid $127,000. In all but the HRM, one-third of the salary is a tax-free allowance.[34]

School Boards and Education Finance

Perhaps the most outstanding discrepancy between Nova Scotia and the rest of Canada concerns education. On a per capita basis in 2004, Nova Scotia municipalities spent $182.65 on education, while the average for the country was $6.54. In Nova Scotia, municipalities levy a provincially mandated property tax on behalf of local school boards. These levies are subject to equalization through the (limited) provincial-municipal equalization program.

The provincially mandated education levy is calculated as the value of the provincially set education rate times the previous year's uniform assessment. For 2004–5, the education rate was set at $0.351 per $100 of uniform assessment. Given rising assessments across the province over the past years, even a constant mandatory education rate has resulted in increasing education contributions from the province's municipalities. This amount is paid to the relevant school board. In addition, municipalities may provide supplementary funding to school boards.

Municipalities in Halifax, Cape Breton, and Queens County were not the only local governments to be consolidated at the hands of the provincial government in Nova Scotia. A more comprehensive consolidation of school boards actually preceded the limited municipal project. School board consolidation took place in two stages. The first occurred in 1981 when the then eighty-five boards were reduced in number to twenty-two. This was followed in 1996 by a further reduction to six regional boards, plus a province-wide French-language system, the Conseil scolaire acadien provincial. Four years later, the province created a somewhat anomalous situation in the southernmost part of the province. The Southwest Regional Board, comprising schools in the former districts of Digby, Shelburne, Lunenburg, Claire-Argyle, Yarmouth, and Queens, was split in two for educational purposes, while the regional board continued as a single unit for buildings, finance, and transportation. The arrangement was initially characterized as a pilot project, but in 2004 the split was made permanent and the joint regional board dissolved.

Financial difficulties led to a restructuring of a somewhat different kind for the Strait Regional Board, serving Inverness, Richmond, Antigonish, and Guysborough counties. Here, the board was not split but the business end of the board's operations was taken over by a chief executive officer reporting directly to the minister, leaving the elected board responsible for educational matters only.

Problems within the Halifax Regional School Board (HRSB) were not financial but political. Things became so bad between board members that in December 2006 the minister of education took the dramatic step of dismissing the entire board and appointing a recently retired provincial civil servant, Howard Windsor, as a one-person school board. New elections were scheduled for 18 October 2008, at the same time as the next scheduled municipal and school board elections, which operate on a four-year cycle.

Nova Scotia's Education Act contains an important provision with respect to financing public elementary and secondary education. The origins of this arrangement date back to the 1954 Pottier royal commission report which recommended the introduction of a so-called 'foundation plan' of education finance, under which a minimum standard of service was prescribed by the province, to be financed through a combination of provincial grants and mandatory municipal levies. The latter are based on a uniform levy on equalized property assessments, as determined by the province.[35] The critical feature of this scheme is the fact that the prescribed standard of service is the minimum, often referred to as the core program, to be raised through a uniform and compulsory property tax, known as the Mandated Education Tax (MET), collected by municipalities and equalized up to the foundation level by the province out of its general revenues.

The HRM and Supplementary Funding

Significantly, the Education Act has always permitted school boards to request, and municipalities to provide, additional funds over and above the foundation level of support. This is where the issue becomes more complex. Prior to the consolidation of school boards in 1996, the three school boards within the geographic boundaries of Halifax County (Halifax city, Dartmouth, and Halifax County-Bedford) were both distinct school districts and municipalities and therefore the school boards could request supplementary funds from their respective municipalities, over and above the provincially prescribed foundation level. Both Halifax city and Dartmouth did that, albeit at different levels. Halifax County did not provide this supplementary funding across the whole municipality, but did allow additional area rates, sometimes referred to as 'school trustee levies,' to support specific projects in specific schools.[36] No other municipalities in the province provide supplementary funding for their school boards.

What would happen under the new Halifax Regional Municipality and its sister but now independent and separately elected Halifax Regional School Board? In his report setting out an implementation plan for the new municipality, William Hayward acknowledged that 'supplementary funding for the three school boards in Halifax County could become a significant problem for a unitary government.' And he went on to state that 'immediate elimination of supplementary funding would throw the district boards into disarray.'[37] His proposed solution was to continue providing supplementary funding to the separate parts of the proposed regional municipality, financed out of differential, or 'area,' rates for a transitional period of ten years, but after that to make any continuing supplementary funding uniform across the municipality and paid for through a uniform tax levy.

The province did not fully accept Hayward's recommendation. Under the Halifax Regional Municipality Act, now part of the Municipal Government Act, the Halifax Regional Municipality was required to raise from the taxpayers of two of the former municipalities, Halifax and Dartmouth respectively, at least the amounts raised through supplementary funding in the 1995 fiscal year. These monies were then to be paid over to the HRSB to be used for additional educational programs or services, only in the schools of the two former municipalities but otherwise as the HRSB determined. The HRM council could reduce the amounts but not by more than 10 per cent per year (unless a larger decrease was agreed to by the HRSB). Supplementary funding across the former county and Bedford, which had been abolished with amalgamation, was reintroduced in 2000–1 through the mechanism of an area rate and therefore was not protected by the 10 per cent limitation.

This created the rather anomalous situation in which some parts of a single municipality pay higher taxes for education and receive additional educational services as compared with other parts of the same municipality. The overall situation is summarized in Table 1.

The HRM council did actually decrease its supplementary funding by 4.7 per cent in the first year after amalgamation. Thereafter it was frozen, resulting in a gradual deterioration as the funds fell behind inflation. The issue simmered, however, as council members grew increasingly frustrated by the suspicion that supplementary funding was being diverted to other purposes, treated as general revenue by the school board, while board members were upset by what they perceived to be an inequitable situation and generally favoured a move to a uniform tax rate across the municipality.

Pressure from parents, especially in the two former cities, has been strong enough to maintain supplementary funding, while taxpayer resistance, and opposition from councillors, has prevented expansion of the system to bring all parts of the municipality into a uniform regime. A number of attempts were made to resolve the impasse, but without success, until the dismissal of the elected school board provided a unique opportunity to work out a compromise.

Staff members of both the school board and municipality were able to hammer out a draft agreement in 2007 which was then ratified by

Table 1
Supplementary funding in the HRM, 2004–5[38]

	Halifax	Dartmouth	County/Bedford
Tax Rate[39]	9.8¢	8.1¢	3.7¢
Assessment	$12.5 billion	$6.5 billion	$9.0 billion
Supplementary funding	$12.3 million	$5.2 million	$3.3 million
Funded FTE positions	213.7	88.2	62.0
Enrolment	12,978	9,064	33,615
Sup. funding per student	$947	$578	$98

the full council and the one-person board and given authorization by the province in 2008. Under this agreement, supplementary funding will continue but will be brought to a uniform level across the entire municipality, with the same tax rate. To get to that outcome, the school board agreed to a cut in the level of supplementary funding according to a four-year phased schedule that will reduce the total from $20.4 million to $19 million by 2010–11. A key provision of the agreement is contained in the following: 'HRSB commits to maintaining the current level of supplementary education funds spent on arts and music programs in Halifax and Dartmouth with a goal of enhancing these programs over the next four years in the Bedford/County area.'[40]

Most municipal officials in Nova Scotia are strongly opposed to supplementary funding. They see it as a device by which the province escapes its responsibility for fully funding education. By permitting the wealthiest municipality in the province, with over a third of the total enrolment, to augment the core provincial program, the province is relieved of what should be its responsibility to all students in the province. Others see it simply as an issue of equity: that similarly situated individuals should receive similar services at a similar cost throughout the province. There are defenders of supplementary funding, of course, who see it as an expression of community choice; if residents of some communities are prepared to tax themselves at a higher level in order to obtain benefits for their children, why should they be denied that opportunity?

Demography

Nova Scotia's population has changed very little over the past decade, hovering around a 2001 total of 900,000. This stability, however, masks significant change within the province. There are really three Nova Scotias: Cape Breton, greater Halifax and environs, and the rural mainland. Interestingly, these three parts of the province are characterized by distinct voting behaviours, with the Liberals concentrated in Cape Breton, the NDP in greater Halifax, and the Progressive Conservatives in the rural mainland.

Perhaps the most striking feature of the province's demography is the extent to which it varies across these three regions. The rural mainland is in decline, losing population gradually but relentlessly. Cape Breton is also in decline, having lost a significant portion of its industrial base (coal mining and steel production), but it continues to be a vibrant cultural community. Greater Halifax is a boom city, growing rapidly in population and economic activity. These regional variations have an obvious and immediate impact on municipal government. Not only the HRM but also the adjacent towns have rising assessments and political outlooks shaped by growth. The rural municipalities and many of the small towns, not to mention the municipalities of Cape Breton, are often faced with all the problems of stagnation and decline.

English is the dominant language in Nova Scotia, with 93.2 per cent of the population claiming English as their mother tongue. French follows at 3.8 per cent while all other linguistic groups account for the remaining 3 per cent. Interestingly, when measured by ethnic origin rather than mother tongue, French is much more prominent, at 17 per cent. This, of course, means that a large proportion of Nova Scotians who still claim a francophone heritage no longer speak the French language. Another striking characteristic of the demography of Nova Scotia is the paucity of immigrants. Only 4 per cent of Nova Scotians were born outside Canada, compared to the national average of 18 per cent. Attracting a larger number of immigrants (and persuading them to stay once here) has become a major priority of federal and provincial policy makers.

Nonetheless, the Acadian population has retained one important advantage. It is relatively concentrated in a few communities in Cape Breton and southwestern mainland Nova Scotia and, consequently, has been able to retain its cultural distinctiveness. As a result, it continues to exercise a political influence disproportionate to its numbers.

There are two visible minority groups in the province, aboriginals or First Nations people, and blacks, mostly African Nova Scotians. According to the 2001 census, 28,500 Nova Scotians (3.2 per cent of the population) claimed 'North American Indian' as their ethnic origin, while 19,670 (2.2 per cent of the population) defined themselves as

'Nova Scotia Blacks.' Both groups tend to live in relatively small and isolated communities, First Nations people as the legacy of federal government policy and blacks as the result of discrimination by the mainstream population. A particularly sorry episode in black history was the forced destruction of 'Africville' between 1964 and 1970, and the relocation of its residents from their community to public-housing units.[41]

Political Culture

The rural municipalities in Nova Scotia constitute a powerful political lobby. Currently, they command the attention of the governing Progressive Conservative Party, whose political strength resides in the rural mainland. By the same token, there is the perception outside the HRM that it receives a disproportionate share of the government's attention and resources. Ironically, officials within the HRM often take the view that the municipality does not really benefit from provincial attention. For example, the recent capping of the property assessment of the refinery in Dartmouth owned and operated by Imperial Oil has particularly irked HRM's current mayor, Peter Kelly. These kinds of grievances, however, do not appear to be very significant in the minds of the population at large. That population, enjoying a robust economy, seems generally content with things as they are.

The CBRM has its issues, too. Currently, the CBRM is engaged in a court case against the provincial government, arguing that it is not receiving its fair share of provincial revenues. It argues, for example, that net transfers to the region fall well short of the region's contribution to generating equalization entitlements flowing to the provincial treasury from Ottawa. The treatment of the NSPI levy adds to the region's sense of neglect.

An important feature of the political culture of Nova Scotia is the tradition of cooperation among the province's municipalities, especially those with similar characteristics. There is, for example, considerable cooperation between the HRM and CBRM within the regional caucus of the UNSM. Similarly, there is a significant degree of solidarity within the towns and rural caucuses.

The conservative culture of the province can also be seen in the general distaste for further municipal amalgamations. 'Unfinished business' in that area would certainly include the Annapolis valley and the area around Stellarton and New Glasgow, but no one seems anxious to initiate change. Also, the province appears to have no appetite for forcing an amalgamation of the towns of Mulgrave and Canso with the wealthier municipality of the County of Guysborough. Canso, despite virtual bankruptcy, recently voted to maintain its status as a town.

Municipal politicians appear to be ahead of their constituents when it comes to issues of local governance. The rural caucus, for example, has promoted the notion of municipal amalgamation in Guysborough County. Similarly, in Cumberland County, where there are five municipal governments (as well as two villages) for a population of just under 53,000, the rural caucus has advocated some rationalization. The outcome of a recent plebiscite in Antigonish County only added to this confusion. This issue dates back to 2001 when the town of Antigonish applied to the NSURB to annex some 2,000 hectares of county land. The county's response was to apply immediately for amalgamation of the two municipalities. The matter was finally put to a non-binding referendum vote, the outcome of which settled nothing. People in the county voted 84 per cent in favour of amalgamation; people in the town voted 74 per cent against.[42] The issue remains with the NSURB to resolve.

With regard to service exchange, the government shows little interest in moving forward. Issues like roads in the rural municipalities and responsibility for education funding, while they may vex municipal politicians, appear to be very much on the backburner as far as the provincial government and the general public are concerned.

Finally, an important feature of the political culture of local government in the province, as elsewhere, is the lingering significance of property ownership. This, of course, has its roots in the past limitations of the municipal franchise, but it finds its current expression in a widespread perception that those who own property have a greater stake in municipal government than those who do not. The link between this and the generally low voter turnout is an important but untested question. Closely allied to that question is a general ambivalence about the proper role of municipalities and municipal government in the provincial scheme of things. The question can be simplified to this: Are municipalities essentially administrative units carrying out largely mundane, if important, service functions, or are they also political institutions seeking to chart the future shape and style of human communities? The answer comes in different forms, but with generally the same effect. The common attempt to separate services to people (provincial and federal) from services to property (municipal) is a familiar answer to the same question. So too is the long-standing penchant of municipal politicians, led forcibly by the UNSM, to offload to the province responsibilities that are seen as not directed related to property or, as is often argued, responsibilities that are seen as political in nature (education, social welfare, and so on).

In short, Nova Scotia's political culture, at least so far as local governance is concerned, remains, as it always has been, marked by a sturdy streak of conservatism. Change can occur, but it generally occurs when, as Andrew Sancton observed about the consolidation of metro Halifax, there is little political cost attached. A conservative culture has its strengths, particularly in the stability it affords to those who are well served by existing arrangements. But it also has costs, especially for those seemingly destined to remain disadvantaged by existing arrangements.

Organizations

There is no question about the importance of one organization in the municipal scheme of things. That organization is the Union of Nova Scotia Municipalities. It was established in 1906 during a meeting of the then Union of Canadian Municipalities (now the Federation of Canadian Municipalities) held in Halifax. By the end of its first year, it had twelve members. As discussed earlier, the UNSM has not always commanded the close attention of the provincial government, but in recent years it has come to be recognized as the official voice of the collective interests of municipalities, and its membership has grown to include all fifty-five municipal units. This, of course, means that it must find a single, collective voice, not always a simple task.

One means the UNSM employs to articulate the different interests of its member municipalities is the use of caucuses. Many issues are initially addressed in these three constituent groups, the 'regionals' (HRM and CBRM), the 'towns,' and the 'rurals.' It is interesting that Queens, while officially a region, sits as part of the rural caucus.

A potentially significant milestone in the role of the UNSM was the signing, in September 2005, of a memorandum of understanding between the province and the UNSM. It recognized municipalities as an 'order of government' but gave no definition of what that might mean. It also recognized the UNSM as 'the single, unified voice of municipalities in Nova Scotia.'[43] Significantly, it described the MOU as a statement of intentions and not as a contract in the legal sense. It then committed the parties to regular and ongoing consultation, to respect each other's areas of jurisdiction, and to seek to resolve differences through dialogue and discussion.

The UNSM plays three distinct roles in representing municipal interests. First, it acts as a clearing house of information, keeping municipalities informed of developments, including best practices, in other municipalities, the province, and the federal government. Second, it represents the municipalities, collectively, in discussions and negotiations with both the federal and provincial governments. And, third, it undertakes both research and public information, with the purpose of improving municipal governance and increasing public awareness of municipal affairs. It has had considerable success in its advocacy and representational functions. A couple of recent examples would include negotiating the federal-provincial HST rebate and the distribution of the federal gas-tax revenues.

Another organization of note, albeit one of more recent vintage, is the Association of Municipal Administrators (AMA). It grew out of the Dalhousie University four-year (part-time) certificate in municipal administration, and was established in 1969 when the first twenty-six graduates of that program decided to form a continuing organization. It now operates as a companion organization to the UNSM and shares office and staffing with it. The AMA has placed a high priority on the professional development of municipal administrators, particularly at the senior level, including the growing recognition of the office of chief administrative officer, or CAO. It has some two hundred members.

In this regard, it is worth noting the establishment of a municipal internship program under the auspices of the provincial department. The program was established in 2005 and was recently extended. It is designed to attract recent post-secondary graduates to municipal administration. The province subsidizes a municipality prepared to hire an intern, up to $25,000 or 50 per cent of the cost of training and supporting an individual intern.

Finally, the Institute of Public Administration of Canada (IPAC), a national organization of public servants and academics with provincial chapters, has a strong municipal focus and a significant presence in Nova Scotia. Other provincial associations also address local and municipal issues.

The Political Dimension

Municipal elections in Nova Scotia are now held every four years (prior to 1982 they were held every three years), on the third Saturday in October. All persons are eligible to vote if they are at least eighteen years of age, hold Canadian citizenship, and have lived in the municipality for at least three months. However, unmarried students may vote in their home constituency regardless of how long since they last lived there. Elections for school boards are held at the same time as municipal elections. There may also be plebiscite or referendum questions if agreed to by council. An unusual variation on that provision occurred in 2004 when the *provincial* government ordered a question regarding Sunday shopping to be placed on all *municipal* ballots. Some councillors objected on the grounds that voters might be confused as to who was responsible for the question. Despite that, the plebiscite did result in a higher than normal voter turnout, at 47 per cent. The option of more open Sunday shopping was defeated by a narrow margin (52 per cent to 48 per cent), which seemed to confirm Nova Scotia's unique status as the only Canadian province to ban virtually all Sunday shopping. That was not to last, however. In 2006 the Supreme Court of Nova Scotia threw out the ban. Four days later, the premier announced that stores would be allowed to remain open seven days a week, with the sole exception of Remembrance Day.

Municipal and school board boundaries are set by the NSURB. It has set a standard by which the number of electors must be within +/- 10% of equality, although in clearly demonstrable anomalous cases the board may permit variances of up to +/- 25%.

There are no political parties recognized in municipal elections, and no apparent interest in any quarter in changing this tradition. This does not mean that the political affiliation of candidates is unknown. Successful candidates in municipal elections sometimes run provincially but there is no tradition of treating municipal (or school board) elections as a stepping stone to higher office, and there are notable examples of movement in both directions.

There are no limits on the amount of money a candidate may spend on an election, nor on how much an individual or association may contribute. However, candidates are required to record the names and addresses of all contributors within sixty days of the election, and this information is made public. Anonymous gifts are not permitted.

Unfortunately, no data are available on voter turnout in Nova Scotia, although it is known to follow the national pattern of falling well below federal and provincial results, which themselves have been falling in recent years. Voter turnout is not currently reported in the 'municipal indicators' project of the provincial government but it has now been added and presumably will appear in future reports. This was one of the recommendations contained in the 2005 report of the Women in Local Government Project initiated by the UNSM and co-sponsored by the Nova Scotia Advisory Council on the Status of Women and the YWCA, with financial and staff support provided by the province.

That report opened by observing that only 21.7 per cent of municipal councillors in the province are women, the third-lowest proportion in Canada, while only four of the fifty-five mayors or wardens are women. A mere 14.5 per cent of CAOs are women, compared to a national average of 50 per cent. On this score, Nova Scotia had the lowest percentage of women CAOs of all the provinces. The report attributed the low rate of participation by women to a variety of factors, including a lack of awareness of the importance of local government, a lack of understanding of the gendered nature of public institutions generally, and a variety of socio-economic factors. It observed that 'Nova Scotia lags behind the rest of Canada and much of the world for women's participation in local government.'[44]

Some Outstanding Issues

Halifax: The Challenge of Consolidation

Much has been written about the advantages and disadvantages of municipal consolidation. The central question is often whether consolidation actually results in reduced or increased unit costs, and whether there is an increased or decreased sense of community within the enlarged municipality. The Halifax Regional Municipality provides some interesting insights into this ongoing debate. Its experiment with community councils provides something of a test case of attempts to combine a large municipal unit with more localized vehicles for the articulation of community interests.

The case of the HRM also sheds light on the dynamics of how a newly enlarged municipality goes about building a greater sense of community cohesion. The experience has been both positive and negative. On the negative side, the story of the Halifax Regional School Board and supplementary funding demonstrates how institutional arrangements of an intergovernmental nature can create serious barriers to functional integration. Meanwhile, the HRM itself has made considerable progress in finding institutional means to bridge gaps that represent the legacy of years of separate existence. There are many areas in which this progress could be examined, including the current efforts at both comprehensive and area-based land-use and community planning. A particularly revealing context is provided by the budgetary process and the manner in which competing demands for resources are reconciled in the relatively open process of council government.

One of the first issues that had to be addressed in the HRM, following the consolidation of four municipal corporations, was how to resolve the issue of setting the tax rate in a situation where levels of services vary widely in different parts of the now consolidated municipality. The second question then became how to move towards a more uniform standard of services across the whole municipality. Each of these questions deserves separate attention.

Central to the question of tax rates was the dependence of Nova Scotia municipalities on the property tax, and the relationship between property values and taxes. Two schools of thought quickly emerged on this issue. One, generally associated with urban interests, sees property values, and therefore assessments,[45] as essentially capturing differences in service levels. For example, properties in an area without sidewalks or snow ploughing will tend to be assessed at lower rates than properties in an otherwise comparable area that enjoys both these services. The lower assessments will translate into lower taxes, compensating for the lower level of services. Accordingly, in this view, property tax *rates* should be uniform across the municipality since differences in service levels have already been captured by differences in property values and assessments.

The competing view, advanced most frequently by those espousing rural and suburban interests, argues that property values and assessments are not nearly so sensitive to specific service levels and therefore imposing a uniform tax rate on all properties would result in serious inequities for those who would be forced to pay for services they do not receive.

The clash of views and interests occupied a good deal of council and staff time, until a compromise position was finally agreed to. Under the provincial Municipal Government Act, municipalities may set tax rates at three levels, based on the services provided: urban, suburban, and rural. This was the route the HRM chose to follow and, as a result, taxpayers in the HRM pay one of three general tax rates depending on whether their property is designated urban, suburban, or rural. Residents in rural areas who receive specific suburban or urban services pay for them through separate 'area rates' applicable to that area alone. Similarly, residents of suburban areas who receive urban services also pay additional area rates.

Rural services included in the general rural tax rate include police, solid-waste collection and disposal, recreation, sports fields and playgrounds, planning, libraries, and general administration. Services that are included in suburban and urban general rates but would be paid through a separate area rate if provided in rural areas include fire suppression, street lighting, crosswalk guards, and recreation in addition to that included in the rural general rate. Services that are included in the urban rate alone include transit and sidewalks. Water and sewer services, where provided, are paid for through separate pollution-control and water charges collected through a water bill administered by the Halifax Regional Water Commission.

Meanwhile, efforts are under way within the HRM to further regularize and standardize services and tax rates throughout the municipality. In 1997–8 a Tax Structure Committee was established by council, reporting in December 2002. It proposed that the services categorized as general, and therefore paid for throughout the HRM, be expanded to encompass fire protection, including volunteer fire departments, street lighting, cost-sharing of recreational facilities, and the HRM call centre. Plans were also approved in the 2005 budget to extend snow ploughing to all parts of peninsula Halifax, something that many property owners had previously been required to arrange for themselves.

Tax Reform Committee of the HRM

The provincial decision to reduce the cap on assessments for some properties provided the main impetus for the establishment by the HRM council of its Tax Reform Committee in January 2007. The committee, composed of six councillors (two urban, two suburban, and two rural) and seven private citizens, undertook a fundamental re-examination of the entire property-tax system and reached the conclusion that the tax is unfair and inefficient, satisfying neither the principle of ability to pay nor that of benefits received. It took particular aim at the provincially imposed cap on assessment increases, especially the provision by which properties that are sold revert back to full market valuation (at which point the cap on assessment increases begins anew, but at the new, higher, level).

The committee argued that no tinkering can significantly improve the property tax and that a new approach is required. Its recommendation was to move to a tax system based squarely on the principle of benefits received. Municipal taxes should not be based on the value of individual properties but rather on the services actually provided. Services that primarily benefit individuals should be paid for through user charges or fees. Services that primarily benefit a local community should be financed by means of a local tax rate, based on four defined zones within the municipality. And, finally, services that benefit the entire regional municipality should be financed through a general tax rate applicable throughout the region but charged to all residents irrespective of the value of the property they might own or rent (here the committee offered the suggestion that, if the province were to allow a municipal income tax, then these 'regional' services should be paid for by means of such a tax).

Two exceptions were proposed, in which cases taxes would continue to be based on property assessments. One exception would apply in the case of provincially mandated services, such as education. The second exception would apply to taxes on commercial properties, including the business-occupancy tax.

People in different parts of the municipality, where different services are provided, would pay different rates of tax. In deference to the principle of ability to pay, low-income families would receive a rebate, partially based on the size of the family. Finally, the committee proposed that the deed-transfer tax be phased out.[46]

The proposed tax reform was submitted to council in March 2008. At the time of writing, no discussion has taken place and no decision made. In any case, the committee did not propose that its recommendations be adopted by council. Rather, it proposed that the plan be submitted for public consultation. Nevertheless, the proposed changes would represent a radical change for municipal finance, with implications not just in Halifax or Nova Scotia but in Canada generally. It will be worth watching to see if it does bear fruit in the coming months and years.

Community Councils

As indicated earlier, one of the unique features of the legislation establishing the Halifax Regional Municipality was the provision for the establishment of community councils within the municipality. No such councils are provided for in either of the other two regional municipalities, Cape Breton or Queens.

The idea of community councils can be traced back to the establishment of area rates and ratepayers associations within Halifax County. It was an idea that was strongly endorsed by the Graham Commission in its 1974 report. It has often been advocated as a way of reconciling the perceived need for both larger municipal units with the maintenance of more local attachments. The ill-fated Winnipeg 'Unicity' experiment provided one of the most comprehensive rationales for the idea of community councils.[47]

The legislation providing for community councils within the HRM is permissive and was strongly opposed initially by some councillors. There are currently six community councils in the HRM. Each consists of the councillors representing constituencies that are geographically contiguous and are identifiable as constituting more or less distinct parts of the regional municipality. Peninsula Halifax, the original city, makes up one community council, as does much of the former city of Dartmouth. The eastern and western extremities of the HRM are similarly represented in their respective councils, as are the suburban and mixed rural-suburban areas adjoining peninsula Halifax. The councils vary considerably in size, with the urban councils containing larger numbers of councillors. The largest is Harbour East (Dartmouth) with six councillors. Chebucto (mainland Halifax) has five, while Peninsula (old, or peninsula, Halifax) has four. The remaining three communities (Marine Drive Valley and Canal, North West, and Western Region) have three councillors each.

The community councils are advisory to the municipal council. Their powers are limited to monitoring the provision of services within their respective communities, and making recommendations as a result. In this, the scope of their purview is quite broad. They may make recommendations to the municipal council 'respecting any matter intended to improve conditions in the community.'[48]

Community councils do play what appears to be an important formal advisory role in the planning process under way in the HRM. They also have control over the expenditure of an allowance of $25,000 per district known as the 'Building Communities Fund,' which is provided annually by the council. There is also an allotment of $40,000 per district for capital improvements. Most of this money goes for recreation projects.

The record of community councils to this point is at best mixed. They are not 'community' councils in the normal meaning of that term. Rather, they are subcommittees of council, representing areas distinguished more by geography and previous municipal status than by socio-political identification. At best, perhaps, these community councils offer area-based councillors the opportunity to press certain issues of local concern that might not be so easily advanced in a full council meeting.

A Detour on Roads

Roads were the stumbling block of the service-exchange initiative: rural municipalities were not prepared to take on such a responsibility. As part of the Roles and Responsibilities review, the idea of 'urban core areas' was introduced. Urban core areas were 'areas which are built up and developed … [that] tend to have dense development and often curbs and sidewalks as well as municipal services such as sewer and water, regardless of whether or not they are contained inside rural or regional municipalities … [that] function as towns, have significant tax bases per kilometer of road and often have Works Departments.'[49]

In other words, the idea was to separate out the urbanized areas of the rural municipalities. What this meant was that communities with comparable urban density in terms of dwelling units (minimum 250 dwelling units per square mile) situated adjacent to a city or a town or separate but with urban character (provision of water and sewer and other urban facilities) would be comparable to towns in terms of their expenditure responsibilities.

Also, a clear delineation of responsibilities was proposed, in which controlled access, high-speed roadways, and arterial and collector roads in rural areas would be owned and operated by the province (except in urban core areas where such roads would be operated by the municipality but with appropriate cost-sharing provisions) while local roads (those that have land access as their primary function) should be owned and operated by the municipality, including those in urban core areas of rural municipalities.

From the perspective of the cities and towns, which already owned their roads, this came down to the matter of defining appropriate cost-sharing arrangements. From the perspective of rural municipalities, the distinction between roads that are local and those that are arterial or collectors was important, as was concern over the cost implications of assuming full responsibility for roads. The ultimate decision was that rural municipalities would assume ownership only of 'Class J' roads. The elimination of cost-sharing arrangements for roads with the province resulted in cities and towns being forced to assume an additional fiscal burden, while this was not so for the rural municipalities. Moreover, the higher tax costs for urban municipalities would promote urban growth (that is, sprawl) in the rural municipalities.

Treating urban core areas in rural municipalities on an equal footing with urban municipalities would eliminate this source of unfairness. In addition, fairness dictates that appropriate cost-sharing arrangements in respect of arterial and collector roads be reinstated.

Having urban core areas in rural municipalities assume full responsibility for roads on par with urban municipalities would have implications for equalization. The increased expenditures would be reflected in municipal equalization entitlements. Provision would have to be made to ensure that such additional entitlements are reflected in the budgets pertaining to the urban core areas. Alternatively, and perhaps more appropriately, urban core areas could be treated like towns for purposes of equalization calculations, much as the rural areas of the regional municipalities were treated as rurals prior to 2002. Again, provision would have to be made to ensure that such additional entitlements are reflected in the budgets pertaining to the urban core areas.

Whither Multilevel Governance in Nova Scotia

The provincial government has taken some steps to improve municipal government and provincial-municipal relations in Nova Scotia, but in each case progress is marked by questions about how much has really changed. The consolidation of municipalities in Cape Breton certainly solved, or at least managed, a long-standing problem of so many small, virtually bankrupt towns in the area. The parallel consolidation in Halifax County had no such compelling impetus, and remains a contested accomplishment. The case of Queens is different and has had quite different results. This was a consolidation requested by the municipalities concerned, and it has proceeded with little opposition or rancour. In this regard, there remains much unfinished business. Many of the towns are losing population and their tax base, yet their fierce determination to remain independent of their surrounding county leaves them with no obvious remedy, except to appeal for greater provincial assistance. Meanwhile, the separate treatment of roads in towns and rural municipalities makes consolidation financially problematic. At the same time, some villages are growing and prosperous, but without the assumed benefit of independent municipal status. A general sorting out of municipal jurisdictions remains both as critical and as difficult as ever.

The service-exchange exercise has succeeded in bringing municipal responsibilities much more closely in line with their own-source revenues, but the province's insistence on revenue neutrality (that is, that the exchange not cost the province any money) has left some unfinished business here as well. The case of education and supplementary funding is perhaps the most outstanding example. There is also clear evidence of unfairness in the treatment of some municipalities in the province, a situation that cries out for a more robust program of fiscal equalization.

The phasing out of the business-occupancy tax was certainly a step in the right direction, since it was tantamount to double taxation. But, at the same time, the provincial government has an unenviable record of interfering with municipal taxation whenever it serves a political purpose. The tax treatment of specific corporations, like Aliant, Nova Scotia Power, and Imperial Oil, has created some serious inequities for the municipalities affected. Add to this the dubious decision to limit assessment increases beyond the cost of living for some taxpayers. Over time this is bound to create a legacy of unfairness in the incidence of property taxation, especially among taxpayers in certain municipalities.

The recent revival of federal interest in municipal issues, with support for infrastructure projects and the gasoline and diesel fuel rebate, has been managed remarkably smoothly, and here considerable praise is due the UNSM and its successful efforts at facilitating intergovernmental accommodation. But even here, there are fears that the province may undercut what the municipalities and federal government might have accomplished. The HST Offset is the classic case in point.

And then there is the new Municipal Government Act. It is full of progressive allusions, suggesting a new approach to municipal governance. The recently signed memorandum of understanding between the province and the UNSM, with its affirmation that municipalities represent an order of government, seemed to confirm this new recognition of municipalities as more that mere creatures of the province. And yet the act was careful to circumscribe the spending authority of municipalities and to avoid any possibility that the new recognition accorded municipalities might have any legal standing. Still, it is hard to avoid the conclusion that something has changed. What the exact nature and extent of that change will turn out to be remains unclear. But what is clear is that municipalities have been given a broader brush with which to paint.

It is what the future picture of municipal government in Nova Scotia will look like that remains obscure. And perhaps what is even more important is not the precise picture of the future but the answer to a more basic question: What are municipalities ultimately for? It will be a hollow victory if municipalities are granted a general power to govern inconsequential matters.

NOTES

1 The three regional municipalities are Halifax (HRM), Cape Breton (CBRM), and Queens County (RQC).
2 The nine county municipalities are Annapolis, Antigonish, Colchester, Cumberland, Inverness, Kings, Pictou, Richmond, and Victoria. The six counties containing two municipal districts each are Digby (Digby and Clare), Guysborough (Guysborough and St Mary's), Hants (East and West Hants), Lunenburg (Chester and Lunenburg), Shelburne (Barrington and Shelburne), and Yarmouth (Argyle and Yarmouth).
3 The towns in Nova Scotia are Annapolis Royal, Bridgetown, and Middleton (Annapolis Co.), Antigonish (Antigonish Co.), Stewiacke and Truro (Colchester Co.), Digby (Digby Co.), Canso and Mulgrave (Guysborough Co.), Hantsport and Windsor (Hants Co.), Port Hawkesbury (Inverness Co.), Berwick, Kentville, and Wolfville (Kings Co.), Bridgewater, Lunenburg, and Mahone Bay (Lunenburg Co.), New Glasbow, Pictou, Trenton, Stellerton, and Westville (Pictou Co.), Clark's Harbour, Lockeport, and Shelburne (Shelburne Co.), and Yarmouth (Yarmouth Co.).
4 The villages are Lawrencetown (Annapolis Co.), Havre Boucher (Antigonish Co.), Bible Hill and Tatamagouche (Colchester Co.), Pugwash and River Hebert (Cumberland Co.), Freeport, Tiverton, Westport, and Weymouth (District of Digby), Dover (District of Guysborough), Aylesford,

Canning, Greenwood, Kingston, New Minas, Port Williams, and Corn-
wallis Square (Kings Co.), Chester (District of Chester), Hebville (District
of Lunenburg), St Peter's (Richmond Co.), and Baddeck (Victoria Co.).

5 Nova Scotia, Municipal Government Act, c. 18, Statutes of Nova Scotia,
1998. This act consolidated and revised what had previously been separate acts, namely: the Municipal Act, the Towns Act, the Halifax Regional
Municipality Act, the Cape Breton Regional Municipality Act, the Region
of Queens Municipality Act, the Municipal Affairs Act, the Municipal
Boundaries and Representation Act, the Deed Transfer Act, the tax-collection provisions of the Assessment Act, the Planning Act, and the Village
Services Act.

6 The First Nations of Nova Scotia are: Acadia, Annapolis Valley, Bear
River, Chapel Island, Eskasoni, Glooscap, Membertou, Millbrook,
Paq'tnkek, Pictou Landing, Shubenacadie, Wagmatcook, and Waycobah.

7 At the time of the American Revolution, four colonies remained loyal to
Britain: Quebec, Nova Scotia, Prince Edward Island, and Newfoundland.
In 1784, as the result of a massive influx of United Empire Loyalists, New
Brunswick and Cape Breton Island were separated from Nova Scotia as
distinct colonies, although Cape Breton would be rejoined in 1820.
Quebec, in 1784, was also split into two colonies, Upper and Lower
Canada.

8 Nova Scotia received between 30,000 and 35,000 Loyalists, more than
tripling the existing population, much of which also consisted of people
who had arrived earlier from the Thirteen Colonies to the south.

9 According to Alexander Galt, one of the Canadian representatives, the
Canadas together would need a subsidy of 38 cents per capita, while
New Brunswick and Nova Scotia would need $1.33 and $1.70 respec-
tively. Cited in Canada, *Report of the Royal Commission on Dominion-
Provincial Relations*, Book I, 45.

10 Donald C. Rowat, *The Reorganization of Provincial-Municipal Relations in
Nova Scotia* (Halifax: Institute of Public Affairs, Dalhousie University,
1949).

11 It was recommended that a split tax rate be used, $2 per $100 of the
assessed value of farm, forest, and fishing property, and $4 per $100 of
the assessed value of all other property.

12 The commission actually proposed that there be two equalization formulae, one for the counties and another for the cities and towns, both based
on the same principles.

13 Nova Scotia, Task Force on Local Government, *Report to the Government of
Nova Scotia* (April 1992), 6.

14 Igor Vojnovic, 'The Fiscal Distribution of the Provincial-Municipal Service Exchange in Nova Scotia,' *Canadian Public Administration*, vol. 42, no. 4 (1999): 529.

15 Ibid., 530.

16 Task Force, *Report*, 25.

17 The eight municipalities were: Glace Bay, Louisbourg, Dominion, Sydney, New Waterford, Sydney Mines, North Sydney, and Cape Breton County.

18 C. Richard Tindal and Susan Nobes Tindal, *Local Government in Canada*, 6th ed. (Scarborough, Ont.: Thompson/Nelson, 2004), 134.

19 Andrew Sancton, 'Why Municipal Amalgamation: Halifax, Toronto, Montreal,' in Robert Young and Christian Leuprecht, eds., *Municipal-Federal-Provincial Relations in Canada* (Series: Canada: The State of the Federation, 2004) (Montreal and Kingston: McGill-Queen's University Press, 2006), 12.

20 Nova Scotia, *Memorandum of Understanding respecting Short Term Policy Initiatives and Comprehensive Review of Roles and Responsibilities*, 7 April 1998.

21 Nova Scotia, Municipal Government Act, s. 2.

22 *Memorandum of Understanding (MOU) between the Union of Nova Scotia Municipalities (UNSM) and the Province of Nova Scotia*, 15 September 2005.

23 David Cameron, Paul Hobson, and Wade Locke, 'A Question of Balance – An Assessment of the State of Local Government in Nova Scotia.' Discussion paper prepared for the Union of Nova Scotia Municipalities as part of its Fair and Equitable Funding Project, April 2005.

24 Nova Scotia Utility and Review Board, http://www.nsuarb.ca/about/index.html (accessed 10 June 2006).

25 Municipal Finance Corporation, http://www.gov.ns.ca/nsmfc/ (accessed 10 June 2006).

26 Marilla Stephenson, 'New Rules for Assessing Those Tax Bill Hikes,' Halifax *Chronicle Herald*, 29 January 2008.

27 Deloitte & Touche, *CAP Program Analysis – Union of Nova Scotia Municipalities*, February 2007.

28 Union of Nova Scotia Municipalities, 'Mayors and Wardens Vote Unanimously on Property CAP Assessment Program Resolution,' 12 March 2007, http://www.unsm.ca/Cap_Assessment_Release_%20March%2012.pdf.

29 Halifax *Mail Star*, 22 March 2001, 1.

30 For details, see the Municipal Grants Act.

31 Previously there were four classes: regional municipalities, large towns, small towns, and rural municipalities. The rural areas of regional munici-

palities were treated as rural municipalities for purposes of calculating grant entitlements.

32 The practice of 'red circling' certain municipalities is now to be phased out.

33 Nova Scotia, Municipal Grants Act. We note that, while the act refers to 'Grants in Lieu,' the municipalities prefer the term 'Payments in Lieu.'

34 Union of Nova Scotia Municipalities, *Remuneration and Benefits Survey for UNSM Officials – 2006.*

35 When Judge Pottier initially proposed this scheme, he had to devise a means by which he could translate widely varying ratios of assessed property values to a standard that was uniform across the province. He did this by sampling individual properties and personally constructing a table of full-value equivalents.

36 These area rates applied to residents of areas within a municipality, corresponding to school-attendance areas. These had formerly been governed by school trustees, giving rise to the term 'school trustee levies.'

37 C. William Hayward, *Interim Report of the Municipal Reform Commissioner, Halifax Metropolitan Area* (Halifax: Department of Municipal Affairs, 1993), 28.

38 Halifax Regional School Board, *Supplementary Fund Business Plan & Budget, 2005–2006.*

39 Municipal tax rates in Nova Scotia are expressed as so many cents per one hundred dollars of assessment. This is the same as a mill rate, but that term is not used in this province.

40 Halifax Regional School Board, *Supplementary Education Funding*, 4 April 2007, 4.

41 Donald H.J. Clairmont and Dennis W. Magill, *Africville: The Life and Death of a Canadian Black Community* (Toronto: Canadian Scholars Press, 1999).

42 Halifax *Chronicle Herald*, 'Town No, County Yes,' 19 June 2006.

43 Nova Scotia, *Memorandum of Understanding between the Union of Nova Scotia Municipalities and the Province of Nova Scotia* (Halifax: 15 September 2005).

44 Nova Scotia, Women in Local Government Project, *Untapped Resources: Women and Municipal Government in Nova Scotia* (Halifax: UNSM, NSACSW, YWCA, SNSMR, 2005), 33.

45 Nova Scotia has for years had a province-wide system of standardized assessments, administered by the province. It can therefore be reasonably assumed that municipal assessments generally reflect actual variations in property values.

46 Halifax Regional Municipality, Tax Reform Committee, *Creating a Modern Property Tax System for Halifax*, 18 March 2008.
47 Lloyd Axworthy and Jim Cassidy, *Unicity: The Transition* (Winnipeg: Institute of Urban Studies, 1974).
48 Nova Scotia, Municipal Government Act, Part IV, s. 73.
49 Nova Scotia, *Municipal-Provincial Roles and Responsibilities Review: Roads Ownership, Maintenance and Improvements, Version 1.1* (Halifax: November 1999).

4 New Brunswick

DANIEL BOURGEOIS AND FRANK STRAIN

'There are too many governments in New Brunswick.'
    – Frank McKenna, premier of New Brunswick, 1995[1]

The number, size, and functions of municipalities have had a significant impact on how New Brunswick has been governed. These issues
motivated the provincial government, in 1962, to establish the (Byrne)
Royal Commission on Municipal Finance and Taxation. The commission went way beyond its initial mandate and recommended, in 1963,
that the province overhaul its entire apparatus by centralizing 'services to people' in provincial institutions, eliminating county councils,
and decentralizing 'services to properties' in municipalities that would
henceforth fall under closer scrutiny and tighter controls by the
province. The provincial government agreed, arguing that this would
provide standardized services to all New Brunswickers, whether they
lived in rural or urban, richer or poorer, or francophone or anglophone
areas. The initiative was called the Equal Opportunities Program
(EOP) of 1966–7.

Since 1966, however, municipal councils have been forced to deal
with (or have decided to tackle on their own volition) a greater number of increasingly complex issues in spite of strict provincial reins,
and regional problems have sprouted with minimal, reactive, incremental, and disjointed institutional capacity to resolve spillovers and
problems with 'free riders.'[2] Issues concerning the number, size, and
functions of municipalities have thus come full circle and are increasing tensions between many provincial and municipal institutions. This
is in great part because the province dealt with these issues superfi-
cially in 1966, putting province-wide 'services to people' ahead of local

'services to properties' in the quest for equal opportunities. One could thus argue that the province only partly resolved the problems facing municipalities in 1966. But tensions also exist because the provincial government has for forty years shied away from any significant alteration to its municipal governance, in spite of significant changes in municipal functional and financial responsibilities, because it fears tampering with the EOP or, more precisely, because it fears the public perception that it wants to do so. This is ironic because a royal commission established to resolve municipal inequities in fact resolved everything but (as did the ensuing government policies). Indeed, as our research shows, significant inequities persist between municipalities forty years after the EOP was put in place, thus putting into question its egalitarian principles.

Our research thus suggests that the EOP and the Byrne report have become political sacred cows blocking all significant municipal reforms in New Brunswick. Ideological blinders explain why many actors working in the municipal field in New Brunswick express satisfaction with the present system and admiration for the EOP yet at the same time request significant changes that could jeopardize its egalitarian principles. They are aware that New Brunswick's municipal governance contains several serious flaws and propose radical ideas to resolve them, but they immediately add that such ideas should be implemented only if they do not 'go against Byrne.'

Our research identifies these flaws, ideas, and limits. Explaining why, conventional wisdom notwithstanding, significant municipal reforms are not anathema to the Byrne report, we argue for an exhaustive study of municipal governance and issues in New Brunswick. In short, it is our view that what is needed is a second royal commission.

This chapter contains four sections. The first presents an outline of the Byrne report and the EOP. The second overviews municipal governance in present-day New Brunswick. The third delves into the financial structure of municipal governance in the province. The last section analyses the data collected[3] and presents arguments in favour of a significant municipal reform.

The Byrne Royal Commission and the Equal Opportunities Program[4]

Forty-five years ago, the structure of local government in New Brunswick was highly decentralized, with a patchwork of six incorporated cities, 21 incorporated towns, one incorporated village, 15 counties, 70 Local Improvement Districts, 12 local commissions, and 422 school boards. All had revenue-raising responsibilities. This amounted to one local government with powers of taxation per 1,093 New Brunswickers. On the expenditure side, local authorities had de facto responsibility for education, health, welfare and social services, a variety of legal services, local roads, water and sewers, and a significant proportion of culture and recreation. Tax bases were numerous, including poll taxes, and were defined and collected locally.

Three serious problems had emerged in the governance structure which had evolved in New Brunswick since counties were established in 1784. First, public demands for welfare-state activities had increased dramatically after the Second World War but the property-tax base, the main source of local revenues, had not. Many of the local governments could not financially cope with the increased demands. Secondly, disparities in property values across regions left some local governments unable to provide services demanded, thereby creating large disparities in service provision between counties and municipalities. Thirdly, expansion of public services increased the complexity of governance and many local leaders and administrators lacked the skills and training to cope. The small size of most municipalities made it impossible to obtain the critical mass necessary to achieve the administrative specialization required to meet effectively their increasing administrative responsibilities. To complicate matters, the inequities reinforced ethnic and geographic cleavages. The rich, anglophone, and urban counties and municipalities (there was a strong correlation between the three) in the southern and western half of the province could afford more and better education, health, justice, social, and municipal services than could the poorer, rural francophone counties in the northern and eastern half. Regional and municipal inequities were so significant that they warranted a royal commission.

The Royal Commission on Finance and Municipal Taxation concluded that inequities were systematic and that only an overhaul of the entire provincial apparatus could resolve them. Consequently, it recommended the elimination of county councils, the reduction of the role of municipalities to 'services to properties' (water, sewer, streets, and so on), and the centralization of the provision of 'services to people' (mainly health, education, justice, and welfare) – along with the collection of taxes – under the control of provincial technocratic commissions. The province agreed with the commission's conclusions in its *White Paper on the Responsibilities of Government*, published in

1965, but, instead of independent provincial commissions, it central-ized local responsibilities in its own departments, thereby ignoring the acerbic critique of elected officials found throughout the Byrne report.[5]

Administrative competence was indeed the critical factor in the rec-ommendation to centralize. The commission believed that provincial institutions were in a better position than local bodies to hire skilled administrators and to reap potential gains from a division of labour within the public service, and that politics should be removed from the allocation of public services by handing the responsibility over to spe-cialized technocrats. The need for administrative competence also explains the recommendation to replace county councils in rural areas with Local Service Districts (LSDs) because these were not a form of local government with elected representatives choosing tax and expenditure policies appropriate to the district. Instead, the tax and expenditure policies in the LSD were to be (and are) determined by the minister and his or her officials. Gains from improvements in admin-istrative competence (which must be small relative to income) were considered more important than any reductions in responsiveness to local preferences.

The EOP led to major legislative and administrative reforms, includ-ing a new Municipalities Act in 1966. The overarching objective was to guarantee that all citizens, irrespective of wealth, language, and resi-dence, had the right to the same provincial benefits and services. By assuming responsibility for education, health, justice, and welfare services, the provincial government solved two problems. First, be-cause it had access to a variety of revenue sources, including revenue sources more sensitive to growth in income than the property-tax base, the government was in a better position than local institutions to finance expansion of the welfare state. Secondly, because it now con-trolled expenditures, it could ensure that all New Brunswickers had access to relatively equal levels of 'soft' services in a horizontally equi-table way.

The primary mechanisms for implementing the EOP were the cen-tralization of responsibilities and taxation and the introduction of an equalization grant for municipalities. Centralization of welfare-state services alone would have achieved the type of equality of opportu-nity most people have in mind when they use the term. But, given the simultaneous introduction of equalization, it is clear that the equity goal being pursued went beyond equality of opportunity to include horizontal equity where citizens have access to comparable standards for all public services at reasonably comparable tax rates.

The EOP has been judged a major success on most fronts by most analysts, but some have questioned the government's selective use of the Byrne recommendations and the popular ignorance of its contents, thereby creating a political ideology that blocks significant changes.[6] More important, they argue, the measures taken did not solve the problems for which the Byrne commission was established. Inequities in health, education, justice, and welfare services have been virtually eliminated since 1967, but municipal inequities remain and, as our data suggest, will probably increase in the future. The EOP successfully standardized 'soft' services, but it failed to establish financial and functional equity between municipalities for 'hard' services. The province increasingly standardized local services (notably, land-use planning and police services), but it also reduced the equalization grants, thus enabling wealthier municipalities to cope with provincial downloading and increased costs while poorer municipalities, notably those in the northern half of the province, are increasingly unable to do so. Recent efforts to reduce municipal inequities have been downplayed because, ironically, they are perceived as a threat to the Byrne report and the EOP. The fear is that more negative consequences than positive ones could result from these reforms. Yet an increasing number of people are advocating significant changes to the province's municipal governance.

Overview of Municipal Governance

This second section outlines the basic components of municipal governance in New Brunswick. It presents the structure, functions, political dimensions, and demographic profile of municipalities, as well as the provincial government's oversight of local-service allocation, the municipal organizations involved in local governance, and the general political culture within the province as it pertains to municipal governance. Recent trends are identified for each component.

Structure

In spite of a massive EOP centralization effort in the 1960s, some five hundred local institutions, including fourteen regional school boards and eight health authorities, provide local public services sanctioned

by the province. They fall under four types: municipalities, local services districts, rural communities, and regional agencies, boards, and
commissions (ABCs).

The 102 municipal corporations serve 63 per cent of the 730,000 citizens, cover 20 per cent of the province, and are governed by 632
elected councillors (including mayors). The 268 unincorporated LSDs[7]
serve 37 per cent of the citizens, cover 80 per cent of the province, and
are governed by the minister of local government, with advice provided by 810 to 1,350 elected LSD advisory council members.[8] Rural
communities are a novel institution established by the province to
enable contiguous rural LSDs to gradually acquire the responsibility to
allocate local services or to share common services or amalgamate.
Thus far, two rural communities have been established, but feasibility
studies are under way in numerous other rural areas. Finally, New
Brunswickers receive services from fifteen community economic-
development agencies, twelve solid-waste commissions, and twelve
land-use planning commissions, as well numerous ad hoc regional
commissions responsible for police services, waste water, airports,
libraries, public transit, emergency planning, pest control, and so on.
Ten regional commissions serve the three municipalities of the Greater
Moncton area alone. In addition, a multitude of local services are provided on a regional basis through agreements rather than joint institutions. For instance, most LSDs buy fire services from a neighbouring
municipality without creating a regional fire department.

Municipalities are the core local institution, as all agree they should
remain. Having more authority and autonomy than LSDs and ABCs,
they are perceived as a 'level of government'[9] almost on a par with the
federal and provincial governments, even if amalgamations in the
mid-1990s eliminated the 'myth of local democracy.'[10] Not only do
they have the legal authority to collect significant revenues, especially
in the form of property taxes, something forbidden to school boards
and regional health authorities, but they also have the power to regulate numerous significant issues, usually through by-laws concerning,
among other things, construction, land use, and tax rates. LSDs and
ABCs do not have such authority.

The minister takes decisions on behalf of the LSDs. Most of them
have elected advisory committees, but their members are restricted to
an advisory role reporting to the provincial government on matters of
local-service provision. Public meetings can also be held to vote on the
establishment or discontinuance of services and any related tax-rate

changes, but the final decision on whether a service is established or rescinded rests with the provincial cabinet on the recommendation of the minister. Finally, while municipalities fund and govern most of the regional commissions, the LSDs do not wield significant power in these bodies even though they fund and delegate representatives to regional ABCs.

New Brunswickers living in the 268 unincorporated LSDs are governed by the minister of local government. Three broad types of services are provided by the province to LSD residents: mandatory services (policing, roads, and dog control), services designated in legislation (land-use planning, solid-waste collection and disposal, and property assessment), and elective services (such as fire protection, recreation, community services, and street lighting). Elective services are provided to LSDs only if residents accept through referenda to pay for the services through an increase in the property-tax rate sufficient to cover the costs, and if the provincial cabinet approves.

All 102 municipal body corporates – 8 cities, 26 towns, and 68 villages – are equal under the Municipalities Act, in spite of vast differences in terms of wealth and population. All of them, for example, must provide police services and operate free of deficits. All qualify for provincial unconditional grants in order to ensure that those with smaller tax bases can provide basic local services at a reasonable rate. And all municipalities are governed by the same provincial statutes regulating elections, debentures, borrowing, land-use planning, heritage preservation, easements, and the like. Nevertheless, the eight cities provide more services and borrow more funds and more easily, for instance, than do smaller municipalities. Thus, in spite of the EOP centralization of functions and standardization of services, there are significant differences between municipalities in the quantity and quality of local services. Each municipality is relatively free to provide all services its elected council deems fit, providing it can afford them. Those that can afford more provide more.

Equity between municipalities thus exists in principle only. The ability to pay explains the significance in inequities, but other factors also play a role. Some municipalities intervene in more functions for political reasons. Dieppe, for instance, has established its own economic-development corporation in addition to the regional economic-development agency, is seeking its own water supply in spite of an existing regional water supply, and wants its own urban-planning commission irrespective of the existing regional land-use body.[11] Such actions seem a consequence of the regional void left by the Byrne report and the EOP reforms, as well as provincial recalcitrance in filling the void and in resolving municipal inequities.

Functions

The Municipalities Act leaves remarkable scope for municipal-service provision. It describes municipal services as

> any service deemed by the council to be expedient for the peace, order, and good government of the municipality, and for promoting the health, safety, and welfare of the inhabitants of the municipality including, without restricting the generality of the foregoing, the following: (a) drainage; (b) fire protection; (c) garbage and refuse collection and disposal; (d) sewerage; (e) sidewalks; (f) roads and streets; (g) regulation of traffic; (h) street lighting; (i) water; (j) parks; (k) community services; (l) tourist promotion and development; (m) industrial development and promotion; (n) urban redevelopment and urban renewal; (o) housing; (p) land assembly; (q) recreational and sports facilities and programs; (r) first aid and ambulance services; and (s) the sale of gas and the provision of customer services as defined in the Gas Distribution Act, 1999.[12]

The only function imposed by the Municipalities Act on municipalities is policing. Additional mandates for planning (the creation of a municipal plan[13] and associated by-laws) and dog control are specified in regulations and other acts, but the vast majority of municipalities also provide fire protection and many services to properties ('hard services'), like streets and sidewalks, water, sewage, solid-waste collection, and parks and recreation. In general, the larger the municipality, the more services they provide. Cities also provide public transit, building inspection, animal control, traffic and parking control, libraries, and taxi permits. They are also more likely to be involved in tourism promotion, downtown revitalization, and cultural facilities such as museums, concert halls, and art galleries. Again, size and wealth are critical factors. Some towns, notably Riverview and Rothesay, are bigger than most cities, but they do not intervene in as many functions or as intently as cities because, as bedroom communities to contiguous cities, they have little desire to increase and expand services.

In New Brunswick, as stated earlier, provincial institutions provide most services to people or 'soft services.' Municipalities are no longer involved in education, health, justice, job training, social services, or seniors' housing. Also, the province assesses properties and collects property taxes. Moreover, regional ABCs provide many of the key local services – solid-waste disposal, economic development, and emergency measures. In many municipalities, some services are offered by non-governmental voluntary organizations, with some grant support from the province and municipalities. As a consequence, there is a significant variation in the nature and scope of activities across municipalities. Further, variation in levels of service provision results in variation in tax rates since municipalities can choose their own tax rate based on the cost of the services they choose to supply and this rate is applied to the property-tax base assessed by the province.

Changes in municipal functions since the introduction of the EOP have been relatively minor. Total expenditures (per capita and adjusted for inflation) during the 1988–2005 period have grown at an average rate of about 1.5 per cent per year. Protection of persons and property, which includes policing and fire protection, declined in relative importance as did expenditures on recreation and culture. On the other hand, expenditures on environmental protection generally (water and solid-waste disposal in particular) and expenditures on land-use planning grew in relative importance. This undoubtedly reflects public demands for environmental protection and, given that these demands can be expected to grow in the future, points to an important issue for multilevel governance structures. Community development and tourism also saw significant increases. This may be a cause for concern since competition among municipalities may not generate net new business within the province but instead result in a transfer of wealth from locals to tourists and footloose businesses.

Salaries and benefits of staff represent most of the expenditures. Thus, although municipalities are responsible for 'hard services,' human resources associated with these services, notably police, fire, and public works, account for more than one-half of total municipal expenditures. General management accounts for an additional 10 per cent. These costs reflect the fact that the 102 municipalities employ approximately 4,000 full-time and 2,000 part-time employees. In comparison, there are 12,000 provincial employees, plus 16,000 employees who work for the eight health authorities and the fourteen school boards. Saint John, Moncton, and Fredericton account for approximately half of the municipal employees in New Brunswick.

Since the province reduced its equalization grants, especially after the federal budget cuts of the mid-1990s, municipalities have had to reorganize their services and the employees who deliver them on a daily basis. In addition to revenues garnered through user fees, for instance, municipalities have implemented a variety of new public management (NPM) techniques. The vast majority of the province's 102 municipalities offer continuous training opportunities to their employees (72 per cent), provide their services online (63 per cent), and collaborate with other levels of government (58 per cent). A significant portion subcontract the provision of their services (48 per cent), regularly evaluate employee performance (45 per cent), assess citizen satisfaction (40 per cent), and give greater discretion to employees (40 per cent). A fair number charge user fees (33 per cent), have privatized services (31 per cent), have adopted mission or value statements (28 per cent), provide flexible work hours for employees (27 per cent), have downsized the number of employees (25 per cent), have modified their hours of operation (25 per cent), and have adopted a municipal-service improvement plan such as ISO 9000 (24 per cent). More have entered into public-private partnerships, established one-stop service centres for all municipal services, and set up performance-bonus systems for employees. Only 7.5 per cent of New Brunswick municipalities provide services in competition with private firms. This is probably because no private firm provides police protection, the only compulsory municipal service, and also because most municipalities are too small to afford many other services, public or private.

According to our survey data, only one of the eighteen NPM techniques did not improve the quality of municipal services: downsizing the number of employees or positions. The canvassed municipalities indicated at a rate higher than 60 per cent that the seventeen other techniques improved service quality. In fact, 98 per cent of them even stated that providing municipal services online improved service quality. However, only half of the NPM techniques implemented reduced service costs. The most cost-efficient NPM technique was the privatization of municipal services (81 per cent claimed that this reduced costs), followed by subcontracting municipal services (70 per cent). At the other end, few municipalities concluded that assessing citizen satisfaction (22 per cent), adopting mission or value statements (26 per cent), regularly evaluating employee performance (27 per cent), and providing online services (29 per cent) reduced costs. Less than two-thirds of municipalities that charged user fees claimed that this NPM technique reduced costs. Finally, most respondents (62 per cent) credited municipal managers for initiating the NPM techniques, followed by members of council, including the mayor (42 per cent), employees (36 per cent), citizens (20 per cent), and community groups (16 per cent). Mayors and councillors got their ideas mostly from attending conferences, while managers and other municipal staff got theirs from their own imagination and daily practice.

Provincial Government Oversight

The Department of Local Government is responsible for municipal governance, though many other departments, notably Finance, are also involved. Between June 1999 and March 2006, the department was divided into two divisions: one for environmental concerns and the other for municipal affairs. This was done to enhance the connection between environmental and community issues, but many municipal officials lamented the inferior status of their institutions within government. The Progressive Conservative government of Bernard Lord left municipalities alone after a tumultuous decade of municipal amalgamations and reconfigurations under Frank McKenna's Liberals, but subsequently the Liberals under Shawn Graham (2006–) established a distinct Department of Local Government.

The department has a staff of forty-five officials responsible for municipal affairs. The highest rank is deputy minister. Eighteen officials are consultants, advisers, or officers who are responsible for both LSDs and municipalities, nine of whom work out of regional offices that mostly serve LSDs. Many of the consultants are political/partisan appointments. Fourteen employees are administrative assistants, nine of whom serve the regional offices. The main task of regional officers is to facilitate the allocation of local services in LSDs since they have no legal status. For instance, they will tender out snow and solid-waste removal contracts for all of the LSDs in their region. Four employees are engineers providing technical and professional support. Four others work for the new Federal/Provincial/Municipal Relations Branch. Three employees work for the Assessment and Planning Appeal Board. The other employees are upper management: four directors and one manager. The total annual budget for the department is $110,365,000 (2006–7), but this includes unconditional grants ($65,632,000 or 59.5 per cent) and LSD expenditures ($35,736,000 or 32.4 per cent). Departmental administrative services cost $6,647,000 and represent 6.0 per cent. Finally, the provincial Assessment and Planning Appeal Board costs $350,000 (0.3 per cent).

The primary function of the department is to oversee local governance in New Brunswick. This is done mostly by ensuring the implementation of provincial statutes and regulations governing municipalities and LSDs, but also by advising municipalities and training their elected and administrative officials. Staff plays both proactive and reactive roles, but the latter dominates the workload. Also, as noted, the regional officers tackle issues involving primarily LSDs, though much of this work also involves partnership and agreements with neighbouring municipalities.

Municipal officials are generally satisfied with their collaboration with the department. They appreciate the fact that they are consulted often, notably through provincial-municipal meetings held at least twice a year. The three municipal associations participate, but they complain that the department sets the agenda and that their concerns are not always addressed. Collaboration with other departments is also satisfactory, with the exception of the Department of Finance. On the one hand, most municipalities have expressed concern that Finance waits until the last minute (December) before announcing the yearly unconditional grants. On the other, they complain that Finance overrules the Department of Local Government when cabinet takes decisions on municipal affairs. In their opinion, Finance's preoccupation with the bottom line is not conducive to good relations between municipalities and the provincial government. Some even argue that the province treats municipalities as the federal government treated provinces during its budget cuts of the 1990s. Thus, the provincial budget seems to determine the importance of municipal issues.

Many other departments and agencies deal with municipalities, notably Transportation (road construction and maintenance), Public Safety (police services), Health (ambulance services), Service New Brunswick (bill payments), Business New Brunswick (regional economic-development agencies), as well as Finance (tax collection and assessments).[14] Municipalities also deal on a daily basis with numerous provincial bodies like the Municipal Capital Borrowing Board and regional bodies like health authorities (snow removal for hospitals) and school boards (sharing and maintenance of sports facilities). Nineteen main statutes govern how municipalities operate, but nine stand out: the Municipalities Act, the Municipal Elections Act, the Control of Municipalities Act, the Municipal Assistance Act, the Municipal

Capital Borrowing Act, the Municipal Debentures Act, the Municipal Thoroughfare Easements Act, the New Brunswick Municipal Finance Corporation Act, and the Municipal Heritage Preservation Act.

Municipalities are very satisfied with the present borrowing scheme, whereby the province borrows on their behalf, since they obtain preferential rates on bulk borrowing. Administrative inconveniences and intermediaries do not bother municipal leaders. Municipal borrowing is governed by the Municipal Capital Borrowing Act. Municipalities must obtain authorization from the Municipal Capital Borrowing Board prior to borrowing or entering into a capital-leasing agreement in excess of $20,000. Municipalities do not issue and sell municipal bonds but instead are restricted to borrowing from governments (federal and provincial), the New Brunswick Municipal Capital Corporation, and municipal reserve funds. It is the corporation that, upon approval from the board, gives municipalities access to funds at the preferential provincial rate. Thus, all municipalities get the same interest rate and a reduced risk premium.

Demography

New Brunswick is the only known jurisdiction to have lost its urban status, though it subsequently regained it. In 1971, for the first time, the majority of New Brunswickers lived in urban areas, but in 1981 the majority again lived in rural areas. In 2001 most New Brunswickers lived in urban areas once again. The significant rural exodus of the present decade should increase that rate to 60 per cent by 2021, thereby confirming New Brunswick's status as a urban province. However, since urban dwellers do not all live in municipalities and most of New Brunswick's municipalities are rural, the demographic challenges ahead pit not urban areas against rural ones[15] but municipalities against LSDs. This has been most obvious during provincial-federal negotiations on the federal gas-tax rebate. The provincial government insisted that the rebate be split between municipalities (63 per cent) and LSDs (37 per cent), according to the province's demographic composition. Municipalities insisted on more, arguing that the formula would subsidize LSDs and the provincial government (which collects property taxes and allocates local services at a loss in LSDs), instead of improving urban infrastructure. The federal government delayed negotiations until the province and its municipalities agreed.[16]

In addition to conflicts between municipalities and LSDs, especially those bordering the eight cities, there is tension brewing between larger and smaller municipalities. The vast majority of municipalities (88 out of 102, or 86 per cent) have less than 5,000 inhabitants. In total, they serve 135,583 New Brunswickers or 19 per cent of the provincial population. By comparison, the ten largest municipalities have a total population of 284,295 or 39 per cent of the provincial population. In fact, the 'big three' urban areas (Saint John, Moncton, and Fredericton) contain approximately 250,000 New Brunswickers, or more than a third of the provincial population. Tensions between larger and smaller municipalities revolve in part around the inequities of the provincial electoral map, where rural areas and small municipalities, mostly located in the north, have a higher number of seats in the legislature than the urban cities in the south.[17] They also appear, for instance, when the cities, through their provincial association, seek permission to collect hotel taxes, while the municipal associations representing, respectively, small anglophone and francophone municipalities, oppose the idea.[18] Redefining and equalizing legislative boundaries will tilt the legislature in favour of urban areas.[19] Such changes may be only a question of time.

New Brunswick municipalities, finally, have seen slow growth in their demographic diversity. Immigration is on the rise, but the increase is marginal and is only felt in the southern cities. The number of immigrants to New Brunswick between 1991 and 2001 totalled 4,400, half of whom settled in the 'big three' urban areas. Immigration is low and cannot be expected to offset the predicted population decline. Between 1988 and 2004, only 12,270 (0.3 per cent) of almost 3.7 million people immigrating to Canada settled in New Brunswick, and a significant fraction of these eventually left for other parts of the country. Although increasing immigration is an important objective of the provincial government,[20] it is difficult to imagine a marked departure from trends established over the past twenty-five years. Indeed, if immigrants settle primarily in communities where kin and friends have already settled, as research shows, the lack of immigration in New Brunswick municipalities over the past generation does not bode well for the province, even in economically prosperous Moncton. Migration from other provinces and rural areas to cities will mean increased urbanization, but the rural exodus and the out-migration witnessed over the past will mean a reduced number of residents in

Table 1
Municipal characteristics[21]

	Total number of Municipalities	Total Number of Residents (2001)	Mean Tax Base Per Capita (2000)
Less than 1,000	38	23,894	$35,128
1,000 to 1,999	33	47,214	$33,542
2,000 to 4,999	17	64,475	$40,661
5,000 to 9,999	5	33,038	$49,681
10,000–19,999	7	106,028	$47,352
20,000 and more	3	178,267	$53,999
Total	103	452,936	$47,075

the province, especially in the northern half. This will shift the demographic balance in favour of the southern urban areas, whether incorporated or not, notably in the legislature, and this should alter existing municipal-provincial relations.

Almost all forecasts of future population in New Brunswick suggest a declining population for the province as a whole and a marked shift in the age profile, with significant increases in the number of people over the age of sixty-five. Indeed, by 2026 the population of New Brunswick is expected to be 3 per cent lower than current levels. Also, the elderly population will rise from its current level of about 16 per cent to approximately 30 per cent in 2026. Unlike many parts of Canada, New Brunswick did not experience a baby-boom echo and its population is aging at a faster rate than in most provinces. The declining and aging population poses significant challenges for local governments in New Brunswick. Between 1988 and 2004, the value of real property increased at about the same rate as incomes. With a decline in population, especially with the decline in the younger age groups, the growth in real-property values may diverge from growth in incomes owing to lower demands for property. The provincial government may also face increased financial pressures. As some economists have noted, 'the fiscal system of [the Government of] New Brunswick is structurally unbalanced as the average annual growth rate of total expenditures exceeds the rate of growth of revenues, in the absence of discretionary policies.'[22] If the provincial government reacts, as it has in the past, by reducing transfers to local government, local governments will be adversely affected. An aging population will increase demands for public services, notably health and recreation. Increases in health-care costs will probably result in reductions elsewhere, notably in unconditional grants to municipalities, while recreation costs are borne by municipalities that will increasingly have to rely on their own sources of revenues.

Within New Brunswick, there are a number of demographic trends that will exacerbate problems facing individual local governments. Between 1983 and 2004, many municipalities experienced population declines even though overall population was growing, albeit marginally. Most of these municipalities are concentrated in the north of the province. This region relies on natural resources, and markets for softwood and minerals have suffered over the past ten years. Also, recent growth in population has been concentrated in unincorporated areas. Reflecting an ongoing phenomenon since the 1960s, over 80 per cent of the population increase in New Brunswick between 1991 and 1996 was in the LSDs. Most of these LSDs border the seven urban areas, notably Moncton, Saint John, and Fredericton, and the vast majority of their residents work, shop, and play in the neighbouring cities. In other words, the LSDs have become bedroom communities; indeed, the seven urban areas have a combined daytime population of 304,061 residents. Moreover, 26 per cent of New Brunswickers live within twenty kilometres of the seven urban cores. If included in the 'urban' population, this would increase the urban share of the province's total population from 52 per cent to 78 per cent. The free-rider problem was identified in a government white paper in December 1992,[23] but, except for a handful of amalgamations in the 1990s, nothing has been done to solve it. And, given the public backlash against these amalgamations, that option has been set aside for many years.

The conclusion reached in *The Report of the Minister's Round Table on Local Governance* is worth noting: 'The fact that a large portion of the population resides in the unincorporated areas and that growth is occurring in these areas with no local government has a number of very significant implications. Development, except in a few cases is not being controlled, planned, and managed effectively and this inevitably leads to a variety of land use conflicts (eg. farming vs residential and commercial development), impacts on water supply and quality, and causes the loss of natural resources and wildlife habitats.'[24] One could add that provincial and municipal institutions also suffer financial consequences from urban sprawl and uncontrolled development along highways.

Political Culture

Municipalities are generally regarded as a level of government in New Brunswick. This has been so since 1785, when Saint John became the colony's first body corporate. The myth endures, even after the EOP reforms reduced municipalities to local service providers and the provincial government amalgamated numerous municipalities in the 1990s. Indeed, mobilizations in Moncton following the provincial government's unilateral imposition of a regional RCMP detachment, to replace the three municipal police forces, in 1998 led to a surprising change of provincial government the following year. The provincial government can thus do what it pleases with its municipal institutions, but at a price. Although New Brunswick municipalities no longer participate in education, health, justice, and welfare services, they have maintained a strong presence within the province.

That said, as noted above, municipalities rarely join to make a common front against the provincial government. An unusual exception was the unanimous support for increased unconditional grants that the province steadily reduced in the 1990s and froze in the 2000s. Another example was the request for a new Municipalities Act. On most significant issues, however, there is discord between the three municipal associations. The creation of the Association francophone des municipalités du Nouveau-Brunswick split municipalities along linguistic lines, but those tensions have since dissipated. Indeed, the small and rural Acadian municipalities that make up the vast majority of its forty-seven members usually agree with the fifty small and rural anglophone municipalities that make up the Union of Municipalities of New Brunswick, for or against the Cities Association of New Brunswick's eight members. It is worth noting that Dieppe and Edmundston are members of both the Association francophone and the Cities Association.

The high number and small size of the vast majority of New Brunswick municipalities make collaboration a necessity. Otherwise, they would not be able to afford some services on their own. As noted, numerous regional commissions help municipalities share services like land-use planning and economic development. These two are actually imposed by the province.[25] To be precise, all municipalities currently belong to a solid-waste commission but some municipalities do not participate in economic development or land-use commissions. Provincial regulations prescribe the format used in service-sharing agreements. In addition, the province names some of the members to the regional board to represent LSDs. A regional commission to share recreational services between Saint John-area municipalities was also imposed by the province as an alternative to amalgamation in the 1990s. Nevertheless, by establishing their own collaborative mechanisms, municipalities have learned to fill the regional void left when the government eliminated multifunctional county councils in 1966. For instance, Beresford, Nigadoo, Pointe-Verte, and Petit-Rocher established a joint police force, and Moncton, Dieppe, and Riverview share ten regional commissions or boards. Each of these regional mechanisms deals with a single function.

There are growing tensions between municipalities, especially those located in the north and south. This stems in great part from recent urbanization trends, involving the movement of increasing numbers of residents of the natural-resources-dependent north to the more prosperous and diversified economies of Moncton and, to a lesser degree, Saint John and Fredericton. The manifestations of these tensions do not appear as municipal issues, since all municipalities are treated equally, but the opening of new schools and the expansion of health-care facilities in Moncton as similar facilities are closed or down-scaled in northern areas raises serious concerns in the northern areas. On the other hand, there are also tensions between the 'big three' urban areas and even within these areas. Moncton is now the province's economic and demographic hub, displacing Saint John. But there has been discord between Moncton and the contiguous suburbs of Dieppe and, to a lesser extent, Riverview. Following the provincial government's refusal to amalgamate the urban-area municipalities in 1994, in favour of greater collaboration, Dieppe decided to go its own way on numerous issues, establishing its own economic-development corporation and seeking its own land-use planning commission, water system, and federal riding. It is not clear whether tensions will increase or dissipate.

The Political Dimension

The 637 municipal councillors are elected for four years. There are no limits on the number of mandates. Most councillors stay for two mandates, but some stay for more than twenty years. On average, since 1966, over 75 per cent of incumbent councillors have been re-elected if they ran again.[26]

The municipal electoral turnout hovers around 45 per cent (42 per cent in May 2008, down from 46 per cent in May 2004) but ranges from 28 per cent to 77 percent (May 2004 elections). (In comparison, the turnout rate for provincial elections reached 69 per cent in 2003 and 67 per cent in 2006.) Turnout has decreased steadily since the 1960s. This is because municipalities garner less media coverage than the provincial legislature and because 'hard services' are seldom conducive to popular interest. In fact, hard services more often than not stir up NIMBY (not-in-my-backyard) movements related to zoning. As the chief electoral officer put it: 'Local elections are very much about local issues, and "hot" issues in a particular municipality in one year may lead to a very high turnout, of both candidates and voters, while three years before or three years after, with no big issues pending, turnout in the same place may be very low, or candidates may even be elected by acclamation.'[27] There is no correlation between the size of the municipality and the voter turnout. Increases are usually attributed to controversies while low turnouts usually occur when a high number of candidates are elected by acclamation. However, acclamations are infrequent occurrences in the bigger municipalities, and voter turnout is not significantly higher there than in the smaller ones.

It is nevertheless noteworthy that the provincial government faced significant opposition when it sought to amalgamate municipalities in the 1990s. By comparison, it faced no serious opposition when it sought to amalgamate, at the same time, the fifty-one regional health corporations into eight regional corporations and the twenty-seven school boards into fifteen. And, as indicated earlier, the Liberal government also faced a serious electoral backlash when it imposed a regional RCMP detachment on the Moncton area, thereby disbanding the three local police forces. If the separation between hard and soft services has become a sacred cow in New Brunswick, the province often pays a hefty price when it intervenes in issues that are perceived to be municipal in nature. However, there was no significant popular upheaval when the province reduced and then froze its unconditional grants to municipalities. This suggests that the province can fiddle with finances, but it cannot easily tamper with functions.

The province imposes no controls over electoral behaviour and spending. Generally, the more electors, the more money candidates invest in their electoral campaign. For example, the winning mayoral candidate in Moncton spent over $40,000 in May 2004, and the two winning councillors-at-large invested over $20,000, while victorious ward councillors spent less than $5,000. Stipends for Moncton councillors are less than $17,000 per year while the mayor earns less than $40,000 per year. Candidates in smaller municipalities spend less on their campaigns than those in larger municipalities. Their stipends are also smaller, but they are rarely proportional to size. Indeed, there is only a minimal correlation between the size of municipalities and the annual stipend allocated to councillors. Many municipalities of less than 5,000 residents pay stipends approaching a dollar per resident, while the 'big three' cities pay stipends at a per capita rate that is three to four times lower. Also, since there are no political parties at the municipal level – formally, at any rate – candidates cannot give out receipts for tax deductions, as their provincial and federal counterparts are able to do. Otherwise, municipal electoral spending might increase significantly. Municipal candidates finance their own campaigns, but most receive donations and many receive in-kind support from parties. This opens the possibility for political corruption and conflicts of interest, but there have been very few cases in recent memory.

As noted, the formal absence of partisanship at the municipal level does not mean that political parties are not involved. All parties informally support their candidates. Some candidates seek party support during election campaigns in exchange for favourable votes once elected, though the number of times a councillor would actually be called upon to support policies of the party in power in Fredericton are few and far between. Conversely, parties put their candidates on the electoral list and help get them elected to obtain the pulse of municipalities and prepare future provincial and federal candidates. Numerous councillors have used the municipal forum to try their luck with a seat in the provincial legislature or the federal House of Commons. In some very rare cases, partisan endeavours become public. During the 2004 municipal elections, Conservative Premier Bernard Lord lent some of his aides to one of Moncton's mayoral candidates who was facing a prominent Liberal. This did not sit well with many citizens or the local influential newspaper.[28] Between elections, however, councils and the province do not hesitate to play the political game: councillors who share the same partisan colour as the government in Fredericton or Ottawa will act as lobbyists for the municipality, while those on the other side will be used to inform the respective official oppositions; conversely, the province uses its 'spies' on council to obtain valuable information.

Women do not seek seats on councils proportional to their demographic weight. Over the past four elections (1998, 2001, 2004, 2008), on average, only 15 per cent of the mayoral candidates and only 22 per cent of the other council candidates were women. However, the rate of electoral success for women exceeds the rate for men, with one exception: 52 per cent of female mayoral candidates won their election compared to 60 per cent of male candidates. By comparison, the rate for women elected as councillors is just below 70 per cent, while the rate for men is below 64 per cent, and the overall success rate for election to council (mayors + councillors) is 67.3 per cent for women and 62.8 per cent for men. Nevertheless, women are underrepresented on New Brunswick's municipal councils. There was no significant variation between the elections, although it is worth noting that one municipality in 2001 and another in 2008 elected only female councillors.

Visible minorities seem to fare better, but that conclusion is anecdotal since there are no statistics on the matter. In any event, since visible minorities only represent 1.3 per cent of New Brunswickers, any municipal representation would represent a bonus. Aboriginal people, Mik Ma'k and Malecite, increasingly populate municipalities, but few ever seek seats on council and even fewer get elected.

Municipal Finances

If there is one thing the Byrne commission and the EOP contributed to municipal governance, it was fiscal equalization, at least in principle. In essence, the province allocates unconditional grants to poorer municipalities to offset insufficient wealth and critical mass in order to ensure that basic local services are provided at a reasonable tax rate. The various grant formulae established since 1966 contain three basic criteria: demography, tax base, and kilometres of road. Since the formula has been changed many times over the years, one can conclude that it has inherent flaws. To complicate matters further, the province unilaterally and significantly reduced and then froze its total grant budget in recent years. As costs for basic services increased, especially in municipalities with diminishing population, revenues from the province and own sources decreased. The Byrne recommendations and the ensuing EOP frameworks are recreating the dire problems they were supposed to resolve.

One could add that, since the unconditional grants have been significantly reduced over the past decade and since they provide a relatively equal amount per capita (even the 'big three' cities receive unconditional grants in spite of significant advantages in wealth and demography), the grants may be of limited use and could be replaced by an increase in municipal tax rates. Unconditional grants to municipalities may not be the right tool to ensure equal services.

Municipalities are responsible for financing most of their activities. As indicated in the appendix, New Brunswick's total revenues are low relative to the Canadian average. This reflects the more limited range of services offered in New Brunswick (which is due in part to provincial assumption of many responsibilities). Despite accounting for only 9.1 per cent of municipal revenue in 2004, the value of unconditional transfers per capita from the provincial government was 67 per cent above the national average. New Brunswick municipalities are more dependent on unconditional transfers from the provincial government than in most parts of the country. Specific purpose transfers, on the other hand, are small in size relative to the national average.

Although municipal structure or functions have mostly remained the same over the past forty years, municipal financing in New Brunswick has changed significantly. As calculated from numbers in the appendix, own-source revenues have increased significantly, from 72 per cent of total revenues to 85 per cent between 1995 and 2004, while unconditional grants have declined dramatically, from 17.3 per cent of total revenues to only 9.1 per cent, over the same period. Again, significant differences exist among municipalities. Also, total revenues per capita in New Brunswick have grown at a faster rate than for Canada as a whole, real property taxes and especially user charges have increased at rate higher than in the rest of Canada, and transfers from the provincial government have fallen faster than experienced on average in Canada.

The declining importance of the unconditional transfer since the late 1980s is the single most important development in New Brunswick municipal finance over the past forty years. The recent history of unconditional transfers from the provincial to municipal governments can be broken into three periods. From 1988 to 1997, the unconditional transfer was basically a block grant with adjustments to account for differences in fiscal needs and tax capacity. During this period (particularly between 1993 and 1996), the transfer was subject to caps that were intended to reduce provincial government budgetary difficulties. In 1997 the province decided to abandon the adjusted-block-grant approach and to base the transfer only on equalization principles. The 1997 changes were to be phased in over a five-year period.[29] The transition was supposed to give municipalities the greater of (1) the grant determined under the 1997 formula or (2) 90 per cent of the grant received in the previous year. But in 2001 unconditional grants were frozen, and this effectively transformed the unconditional transfer from an equalization transfer back to a block grant. The freeze was maintained in nominal terms in 2002, and in 2003 grants were cut by 10 per cent. In 2004 revisions to the Municipal Assistance Act introduced a new formula which returned to the block-grant model with a temporary equalizing adjustment.[30] It is still in place.

The recent evolution of the unconditional grant in New Brunswick represents a significant move away from the principles of the EOP. Since 2006, the size of grant has been based on past, not current, disparities in fiscal capacities and fiscal needs. The grant is not responsive to the changing fortunes of municipalities nor is it consistent with the basic principles typically suggested as a foundation for equalizing transfers: efficiency and horizontal fiscal equity.[31]

The changes appear to be motivated by two considerations. First, the provincial government wants to attain financial control and stability. The block grant certainly achieves this objective since the total outlay is fixed by the block-grant formula. Ironically, the province has been very vocal in its resistance to changes to the national equalization program introduced by the federal government to achieve the same objectives. Secondly, the block grant reduces the political costs associated with the 1997 formula since wealthier municipalities lose less than they would have under an equalization approach to unconditional financing.

Reductions in the unconditional grant over time and then a move to block funding should have two effects on municipal activities: increased reliance on own-source revenue, especially the property tax, and increased disparities across municipalities. This is exactly what we observe. Analysis of changes in New Brunswick municipal finance shows that the property-tax base in New Brunswick has grown at approximately the rate of growth in income but that growth has been uneven across municipalities. And tax rates have been increasing and dispersing.

The assessment of the property-tax base and collection of the property tax are both provincial responsibilities. Municipalities and the province levy taxes (mill rate) on this base. Assessment is based on estimated market value and the province remits to municipalities the full value of levied taxes not just taxes collected. A recent report by the auditor general on assessments performed by Service New Brunswick concluded that assessments were generally accurate. However, the report did note that assessments of 'superior homes' (residential properties with a value of $250,000 or more) and of industrial and commercial property were generally below true market value by more than 10 per cent. Corrective action was recommended, but little has been done.

The province's current base property-tax rate is set at $1.50 per $100 on the assessed value of residential property. Non-residential properties pay one and a half times this rate ($2.25 per $100). The funds collected go to general revenues and are not designated for municipal or any other specific purpose.[32] Some argue that the province has managed to fund the equalization grants to smaller municipalities by using surpluses collected from wealthier municipalities rather than the provincial property taxes imposed on non-residential property, as the Byrne report and the EOP measures recommended, but this claim is difficult to assess because data are not available.

Municipalities have the power to tax the property base and they set their own rates to achieve a balanced budget. Indeed, budgets must be balanced. If a municipality fails to balance the books by year-end, any deficit must be covered from revenues received in the next two years.

There are significant disparities between municipal property-tax rates, contrary to what one would assume by reading government claims relating to EOP measures. In fact, the disparities are similar to the ones noted in the Byrne report. Currently, municipal property-tax rates on residential property range from $0.8951 to $1.7250 per $100 of assessment. Non-residential properties must, by provincial legislation, be taxed at a rate which is 1.5 times the residential rate. Owner-occupied residences in municipalities receive a provincial property-tax credit of $1.50 per $100 of assessed value and thus do not pay provincial property taxes, but non-residential property owners in municipalities can face a rate as high as $4.8375 per $100.

In addition, municipalities have increasingly resorted to user fees over the past generation. The most important user fees are for water and sewer services, but fees for recreation facilities in urban municipalities and for culverts and garbage collection in LSDs have also appeared. Such fees vary significantly across municipalities based on cost, which in turn is based on critical mass and wealth.

An additional tax called the Business Improvement Area Levy can be imposed under the provisions of the Business Improvement Areas Act. Non-residential property owners may ask (through presentation of formal petition) a municipality to designate, by by-law, an area as a business-improvement area (BIA) to promote and enhance its appeal as a business and shopping zone. Downtowns are the most popular areas. Once designated, the non-residential property owners create a Business Improvement Corporation to develop a plan and a budget which is submitted to municipal council for approval. The council can then set a BIA levy on the non-residential property owners in the zone at a rate not to exceed $0.20 per $100 of assessed property value.

Finance is complex in the 268 unincorporated areas. The province supplies all services provided to property in unincorporated areas and there are no conventional local government institutions. However, the provincial government constructs budgets for each LSD, sets tax rates on property to cover costs of service provision in each LSD, and runs a shadow unconditional grant program which covers part of the costs of service provision in LSDs from general revenues and which contains an element of equalization to assure that residents of poor LSDs do not face relatively high tax rates because they do not have access to the average tax base.

Residents in unincorporated areas face a number of tax claims. Owner-occupied residential property owners pay a provincial property tax of $0.65 per $100 to cover the cost of basic services (police, roads, dog control, and general administration) provided by the province. This tax rate is set in the Real Property Tax Act and applies in all unincorporated areas. The minister also sets an additional local property-tax rate for each individual LSD and rural community to cover the cost of a set of services designated by legislation – solid-waste management, land-use planning, property assessment – and to cover any additional elective services (for example, street lights) that the residents recommend through a consultative process.

The calculation of the local tax rate proceeds in three steps. First, the province prepares an expenditure budget for each LSD based on the cost of designated and elective services to be provided. Next, the unconditional grant is determined (discussed in detail below) and subtracted from planned expenditures remaining in the net budget. Finally, the tax rate per $100 of assessed value required to finance expenditures is found by dividing net expenditures by the total property base divided by 100.

Calculation of the unconditional grant also involves three steps. First, a fiscal capacity (FC) measure is constructed for each LSD and rural community.[33] To implement this unconditional grant scheme fully, the province would have to budget to cover about half of all costs incurred in the LSDs. But the government does not do this. Instead, it determines a fixed pot and the actual unconditional transfer for a LSD is found by using a scale-back factor.[34] The factor currently in use is approximately 0.2; thus, the implicit cost-sharing rate is about 10 per cent rather than 50 per cent. This levy is not charged to residential non-owner-occupied properties (for example, cottages and apartment buildings) or to non-residential properties (for example, businesses).[35] On the other hand, the Real Property Tax Act specifies that all residential property (which includes cottages, apartments, and so on) in LSDs shall be taxed and that non-residential property in LSDs shall be taxed at a rate one and one half time the residential rate.

The local tax rates in LSDs, including the basic $0.65 per $100 of assessment, vary widely from a high of $1.70 per $100 to a low of $0.7755 per $100. The range of rates on owner-occupied property in the LSDs is remarkably close to the range of rates found across municipalities (where the high is $1.7250 per $100 and the low is $0.8951 per $100). In general, however, local taxes are low in the LSDs: the average local rate for a residential owner-occupied property in the LSDs is $0.9515 per $100 total while average rate in incorporated municipalities is $1.4791 per $100. Two factors explain this difference between municipalities and LSDs. First, there is a variation in the number and level of services, with municipalities generally providing more and better services. Secondly, there is a significant gap between the amount of property taxes collected by the province from the LSDs based on the $0.65 rate, and the amount it spends on the services it provides to LSDs. In fact, the gap is estimated at $39.6 million and would be eliminated if the LSD tax rate rose from the current $0.65 to $0.8327.[36] The current rate has remained unchanged since 1984 and bears no relation to actual costs, but the province has been wary of increasing the rate because of electoral backlash. Indeed, almost half of the seats in the legislature are controlled by residents of LSDs.

Given that the population in unincorporated areas is concentrated around the eight New Brunswick cities (26 per cent of the population in LSDs live within a twenty-kilometre radius and 69 per cent live within a fifty-kilometre radius), the tax-rate differential is a major concern for city governments, which believe that many residents of LSDs enjoy a free ride by consuming services provided by the cities without bearing a share of the cost. Cities are also very concerned that the differential provides an incentive for business to locate in surrounding LSDs to take advantage of lower tax rates. A combination of local responsibility and province-wide municipal equalization could allow service variation in response to changes in local preferences without abandoning the ideals of equal opportunity and horizontal equity. One of the main rationales for local government is the possibility of tailoring public policy to reflect the preferences of the local population.

Analysis

Our data identify seven flaws in the present system of municipal governance in New Brunswick. First, many small municipalities are unable to provide the quantity and the quality of local services requested by their residents. They are either too small or too poor to afford them. Alternatively, their staff is too small to provide the appropriate level of service. To paraphrase former Premier Frank McKenna, there are too many small municipalities in the province to ensure equal local opportunities and services to all New Brunswickers. Second, the province interferes in municipal governance by determining equalization grants on the basis not of local need but of its own provincial budget. Third, it refuses to eliminate inequities between municipalities and LSDs, notably the 1984 rural property tax rate of $0.65, because of political expediency. Fourth, the functional distribution between provincial and municipal institutions left a regional void that has been haphazardly and only partially resolved over the years. Fifth, there is a growing gap between the quantity and quality of services provided by the bigger and smaller municipalities. Sixth, there is a growing gap between the tax rates charged in different municipalities. There is a logical correlation between the size of municipalities (the bigger the municipality, the more services it provides) and the tax rate it charges to provide such services, but the correlation is not linear. Thus, small municipalities have to pay significantly more for the same services than cities. The most cost-efficient municipalities are in the middle range, though their tax rates would probably be higher than those of the big cities if they had to provide the same services at the same level. Finally, equalization grants no longer reduce inequities between municipalities. In sum, if all of the above flaws do not warrant a new royal commission on municipal finance and taxation, they at least appear to justify thorough and significant changes.

During our interviews, many provincial and municipal officials voiced the same sentiment. But most of them also fear that significant changes to municipal governance will rescind the egalitarian principles of the EOP. Although most state that municipalities have a vital role to play and that their councils are necessary to respect local preferences for 'hard' services, many suggest that standardization of municipal services has reduced the councils' legitimacy and usefulness. The progressive reduction in the municipal electoral turnout rate is an indication. In addition, numerous municipalities complain that they lack the critical mass or wealth to meet more stringent provincial standards. In short, the EOP principles are under stress because inequities persist in local governance in spite of the EOP initiatives of 1966.

Elected and administrative officials within both the provincial and municipal spheres identify five key solutions. First, update the 1966 Municipalities Act to meet many of the present-day needs of municipalities. The act imposes obligations on municipalities and is restrictive concerning what municipalities can do and how they can finance their activities. It should be significantly more permissive, according to most of our respondents.

Second, there should be fewer municipal and regional bodies. Many suggested, independently of each other and off the cuff, the same number of municipal units: about 50 instead of 371. In addition, many suggested a significant reduction in the number of regional bodies, though no specific numbers were provided. Some added that a reduced number of municipalities (and their corresponding increase in size and mass) could replace the nearly 500 regional bodies in the province, with the exception of school boards and health authorities, which should remain. Premier McKenna's vision is thus shared, at least in part, by many elected and administrative officials involved in municipal governance. But it is not simply a question of the number of local institutions; the bigger municipalities thus created must assume additional functions and have access to more financial sources.

Third, increase municipal participation in major policy decisions, notably federal-provincial negotiations on issues pertinent to municipalities like the gas-tax rebate and the infrastructure programs. Many municipalities complain that the province treats all things municipal as a provincial jurisdiction according to section 92 of the constitution. That does not mean the province should consult municipalities only when it sees fit and only on issues it deems pertinent, they argue, or that Ottawa must play a more significant role in municipal affairs. But it does mean, in their opinion, that municipalities should participate in multilevel policy making instead of implementing policies adopted on their behalf without their valuable input beforehand.

The federal-provincial-municipal infrastructure program has been successful in generating improvements in local environmental infrastructure. A similar program for rural areas exists and has also had some success. Nevertheless, municipalities complain that the province identifies municipal infrastructure needs, then secretly negotiates amounts with the federal government and unilaterally allocates the infrastructure funds according to provincial preferences. In the 2004 federal budget, Ottawa proposed giving municipalities a share of gas-tax revenues to assist them in making infrastructure improvements. While federal-provincial discussions of the gas-tax rebate arrangements were proceeding, the provincial government introduced An Act respecting a Fair Deal for Cities and Communities in New Brunswick which states: 'The Government of New Brunswick is committed to ensuring equity between incorporated areas and unincorporated areas in the allocation of gas tax funding when an agreement is entered into between the Governments of Canada and New Brunswick under the New Deal for Cities and Communities.' The legislation's purpose was to add strength to the provincial government's negotiating position: it wanted the federal transfers to be split between municipalities and LSDs according to demographic proportions of 63–37 per cent. Since infrastructure costs in LSDs are significantly subsidized by the province, much of the 37 per cent of federal funds would flow into general provincial government coffers. The federal government knew this, but it was unable or unwilling to intervene in an area of provincial jurisdiction. It simply stated that it would wait until the province and its municipalities came to an agreement. Municipalities stood to lose 40 per cent of the federal transfer under the province's preferred arrangement. The cost to New Brunswick would be $116 million. The issue was resolved in November 2005 when the province and the municipal associations agreed to a deal whereby municipalities receive 63 per cent of the gas-tax rebate.[37]

It is worth noting that municipalities have found an indirect way through the provincial stranglehold on all things municipal in the province – the Federation of Canadian Municipalities (FCM). Many municipal officials claim that the FCM, notably its research and lobbying on municipal issues in Ottawa, has opened the door for New Brunswick municipalities. They believe that the province can no longer control municipal issues in this age of multilevel governance and, especially, of client/citizen-focused policy making and implementation wherein the average client/citizen does not care about jurisdictional feuds so much as about service quality and costs.

Fourth, the province should reconsider the functional and financial aspects of municipal governance. Municipalities, many claim, should be able to tackle any function they deem appropriate, save for some functions like education, health, and justice, and they should also have the ability to pay for these functions. As it now stands, the province allows municipalities to tackle most functions but severely limits their ability to cover their costs. For instance, cities recently asked the province to let them impose a hotel levy to obtain revenues to promote tourism, but the province refused on the pretext that it had promised no additional taxes.[38]

Finally, LSDs must be eliminated in favour of elected municipalities in rural areas. In the opinion of most officials interviewed, it is not logical that in unincorporated areas citizens have no real say in their local services (though the contrary argument would state that they have more democratic power than citizens living in municipalities who only vote for candidates and rarely, if ever, decide on local services and taxes, as residents in LSDs are able to do through compulsory referenda). More convincing is their argument that it is illogical to have local services in LSDs, notably those bordering municipalities, provided by the province at a reduced and provincially subsidized property-tax rate. Moreover, cities have been arguing for more than a decade that people in surrounding LSDs are free riders and are not paying their fair share for local services, and that low tax rates in many LSDs are affecting residential and commercial location decisions to the detriment of municipalities. In addition, recent problems in water safety have demonstrated the vulnerability of LSDs and their citizens in solving complex local problems.[39] Assuming environmental issues continue to dominate local governance in the near future, the lack of formal decision-making structures in LSDs will exacerbate the inequities between New Brunswickers.

A call for more democracy in the LSDs began with Commission on Land Use and the Rural Environment (1993), and was then strengthened by a series of studies including the report of the Municipalities Act Review Panel (September 1999), the Report of the Minister's Round Table on Local Governance (June 2001), and the Final Report of the Select Committee on Local Governance and Regional Collaboration (January 2003). The legislature recently adopted a bill enabling villages and LSDs to become rural communities provided they have sufficient population (2,000) and property-tax base ($100 million) to sustain a local government.[40] If an area opts to become a rural community, an elected council will govern the affairs of that community through the same process used in municipal elections and by-elections. The council will ensure that the provision of local services is in keeping with the community's needs, wants, and ability to pay. Only one service is mandated – the provision of community-planning services (for example, development approvals, subdivision approvals, building permits and inspections) – and the council can take on the responsibility for additional local services (for example, fire protection, street lighting, recreational facilities) when it is ready to do so. Such a decision will be made through the making of a by-law, which will provide an opportunity for all community members to have a say. The rural community will have financial powers in keeping with its responsibilities: it will establish a budget and set the tax rate required for its administration and the community-planning services it is mandated to provide, as well as for any other services it assumes responsibility for. But it is not clear why rural dwellers would want such an institution, especially since it will increase their property taxes and such taxes will be primarily allocated to pay for the management of existing services.

Conclusion

The province of New Brunswick, with a population of 730,000, is much smaller than several Canadian cities. But despite this small size and the growing inequities it generates, New Brunswick's municipal experience offers unique and important insights into problems of governance. First, as home to a population which is divided on linguistic lines – approximately one-third of the population declares French as their mother tongue – the evolution of governance structures has been shaped by the aspirations of two linguistic groups, one of which is in a minority position. Second, there are significant regional differences in economic activities and income, with francophone areas experiencing, on average, lower average incomes.[41] Finally, and most significantly, New Brunswick was the site of a revolutionary change in governance structures in the mid-1960s, a change that radically reassigned government responsibilities and was designed to achieve equal opportunities across regions and linguistic groups.

However, the EOP has become a sacred cow that opponents to any municipal reforms use to their advantage. Notably, the province controls its municipalities and LSDs in such a stringent manner that multilevel governance, in particular, could be considered a misnomer in the province. Indeed, the province considers its municipalities as 'children,' as one interviewee claimed. Yet a thorough study of the Byrne report leads to different conclusions. In fact, the commission adamantly recommended that municipal governance, as well as education and health services, be governed by technocratic provincial commissions free from the politically driven provincial government. Instead, provincial departments run the show out of Fredericton. This may be a more democratic endeavour, but it does not seem to have been effective in eliminating the municipal inequities which led to the Byrne commission being established. The province modified municipal governance in 1966 and significantly reduced inequities between rural and urban, rich and poor, and francophone and anglophone areas in the fields of education, health, justice, and social services. However, inequities in the municipal sector remain.

In fact, as our research shows, the egalitarian principles outlined by the Byrne report will be significantly modified in the next decade. For one thing, the principles set out in the report cannot resolve the inherent inequities between municipalities. In fact, the commission conceded this point, but few provincial officials have bothered with such details. Nor have they bothered with the fact that the commission's recommendations have never been fully implemented. Indeed, some of the most significant recommendations were neglected altogether. Nevertheless, the Byrne report and its selective interpretation rule the roost. Consequently, those involved with municipal governance in New Brunswick both praise and question the egalitarian principles that frame municipal governance in the province. Furthermore, there are too many small municipalities and unincorporated areas, and local governance and service allocation needs an exhaustive overhaul in light of present and predicted conditions. A thorough reconsideration of the Byrne principles is thus warranted. However, reducing the number of municipalities, moving from the prescriptive to the permissive approach, and tampering with sacrosanct egalitarian principles may need much more political courage than recent provincial governments have been able to muster.[42]

NOTES

1 Premier McKenna made the comment during a meeting with francophone school board officials in January 1995 to explain why his government
   was going to reduce the number of school boards from 42 to 15. During
   its ten years in office, the McKenna government reduced the number of
   school boards from 42 to 2 (one for anglophones and one for francopho-
   nes), health corporations from 51 to 8, and municipalities from 112 to 103.
2 Daniel Bourgeois, 'Municipal Reforms in New Brunswick: To Decentralize or Not to Decentralize?', in Edward C. LeSage, Jr and Joseph Garcea,
   eds., *Municipal Reforms in Canada: Municipal Governance for the 21st
   Century* (Don Mills, Ont.: Oxford University Press, 2005). A 'free rider' in
   this context is someone who uses a municipality's public services but is
   not required to pay for them.
3 We base our study on the following kinds of data: government reports,
   documents, and press releases; media reports; financial and demographic
   data taken from municipal and provincial sources and Statistics Canada;
   and interviews. We surveyed the 103 municipalities on a number of
   issues. Sixty-nine responded, including all eight cities, 16 of the 25 towns,
   and 45 of the 70 villages. This represents a highly reliable sample. We
   also conducted interviews with 18 experienced elected and administrative officials from both the provincial and municipal spheres of governance. The purpose of these interviews was to identify what worked well
   and what improvements, if any, were needed in the province's municipal
   system. The interviews were conducted between December 2004 and
   June 2005.
4 For a more detailed presentation of the Byrne report and the EOP, see
   Robert Young, 'Remembering Equal Opportunity: Clearing the Under-
   growth in New Brunswick,' *Canadian Public Administration*, vol. 30, no. 1
   (1987): 88–102.
5 Here is one example of the commission's disdain for politicians: 'Mandatory joint provision is recommended to save municipalities from their
   own folly – a type of folly founded in human nature itself.' Report of the
   Royal Commission on Finance and Municipal Taxation in New Brunswick
   (Fredericton, November 1963), 188. Similar comments are found in the
   report arguing against the control of provincial politicians.
6 For a positive assessment, see Roger Ouellette, *The Robichaud Era, 1960–70*
   (Moncton: Canadian Institute for Research on Regional Development,
   2001). For a nuanced assessment, see Bourgeois, 'Municipal Reforms in
   New Brunswick'; and Geoffrey Martin 'Municipal Reform in New

Brunswick: Minor Tinkering in Light of Major Problems,' *Journal of Canadian Studies*, vol. 41, no. 1 (2007): 75–99.

7 Legislation passed in 1995 and 2004 introduced the possibility for citizens in an unincorporated LSD to become a rural community and elect via universal suffrage a rural community committee. This community would have decision-making authority in only one area: land-use planning. But, if formed, the committee would also assume responsibility for organizing any public meetings of residents to address elective service provision and associated tax changes and for communicating with the minister. Only one unincorporated LSD has chosen to become a rural community.

8 The number of LSD advisory council members at any given time varies for two reasons. First, approximately 30 per cent of LSDs have no advisory council, and that rate changes on a yearly basis. Second, advisory councils are not always complete. So, even though they number from three to five members, they range from 810 to 1,350 members in total at any point in time.

9 New Brunswick, Foreword, *Strengthening Municipal Government in New Brunswick's Urban Centres* (Fredericton: Ministry of Municipalities, Culture and Housing, December 1992).

10 Daniel Bourgeois, 'La décentralisation administrative de 1992 au Nouveau-Brunswick et le contrôle du territoire,' *Égalité*, no. 38 (autumn 1995): 59–97, 87.

11 Daniel Bourgeois and Yves Bourgeois, 'Territory, Institutions and National Identity: The Case of Acadians in Greater Moncton, Canada,' *Urban Studies*, vol. 42, no. 7 (2005): 1123–38.

12 Revised Statutes of New Brunswick, Municipalities Act (1966) c. M-22.

13 Municipalities are not obligated to have a municipal plan, but, if they have one, it must be reviewed every five years.

14 Until March 2006, unconditional grants were administered by the Department of Finance rather than the Department of Local Government, which led many municipal and provincial officials to complain that 'the tail is wagging the dog,' meaning: the provincial budget took precedence over municipal finances and the Department of Local Government needed permission from the Finance Department to tackle issues pertaining to municipal finances. The transfer of responsibilities has been greeted positively by these officials, but the fact remains that Finance determines total expenditures in unconditional grants.

15 In fact, only one of the 103 municipalities in New Brunswick meets Statistics Canada's criteria for urban status. Riverview (population: 17,010) is the only municipality with a demographic density (502

hab/km^2) that is greater than Statistics Canada's 400 habitants per km threshold.[2]

16 'Government Introduces Legislation to Guarantee Rural N.B. Fair Share of Gas Tax,' Fredericton, Environment and Local Government News Release, 5 October 2005, http://www.gnb.ca/cnb/news/fin/2005e0559fn.htm. See also Bill 45 (An Act respecting a Fair Deal for Cities and Communities in New Brunswick), http://www1.gnb.ca/legis/bill/editform-e.asp?ID=351&legi=55&num.

17 New Brunswick, *A New Electoral Map for New Brunswick – Final Report of the Electoral Boundaries and Representation Commission*, Fredericton, February 2006, http://www.gnb.ca/0101/AmendedFinal/PDF/finalreport-e.pdf, 9.

18 'Premier Seeks Public Thoughts on 2005 Provincial Budget,' Moncton *Times and Transcript*, 7 February 2005, A3.

19 *A New Electoral Map for New Brunswick*, 58–67.

20 New Brunswick, Immigration and Repatriation Secretariat: http://www.gnb.ca/immigration/english/index.htm.

21 New Brunswick, *A Vision for Local Governance in New Brunswick*, the Report of the Minister's Round Table on Local Governance (June 2001), 20, and Statistics Canada 2001 census data. Note that the dissolution of the village of Saint-André in 2006 has slightly altered these data.

22 Joe Ruggeri, David Goodwin, and Yang Zou, 'Fiscal Balances and Fiscal Sustainability,' in Joe Ruggeri, ed., *Government Budgeting and Fiscal Sustainability in New Brunswick* (Fredericton: Policy Studies Centre, University of New Brunswick, 2004), 112.

23 New Brunswick, *Strengthening Municipal Government in New Brunswick's Urban Centres* (Fredericton: Municipalities, Culture, and Housing, December 1992).

24 New Brunswick, *The Report of the Minister's Round Table on Local Governance* (Department of Environment and Local Government, Fredericton, 2002), 10.

25 The Greater Saint John area also has a Regional Facilities Commission, but this body was established in 1998 by the province as an alternative to amalgamation.

26 Electoral data were compiled from media and government documents.

27 New Brunswick, *Report of the Municipal Electoral Officer on the Triennial Municipal Elections – May 10, 2004* (Fredericton, n.d.). The reference to the three-year mandates, instead of four, should not confuse the fact that, until May 2004, the mandates lasted three years. See 'Amendments to Lengthen Terms of Office,' Fredericton, Environment and Local Govern-

ment News Release, 20 April 2004,
http://www.gnb.ca/cnb/news/gl/2004e0467el.htm.

28 'Lord Backers Rally behind Moncton Mayoral Hopeful,' Moncton *Times and Transcript*, 16 March 2004, A1. See also the newspaper's negative editorial on the subject: "'Moncton PCs Are Interfering,' Moncton *Times and Transcript*, 17 March 2004.

29 The 1997 unconditional-grant formula followed a tradition of dividing municipalities into groups (see Table 4 for current groupings) and 'equalizing' relative to the group average. For example, the granting formula introduced in 1997 involved a subtle variation on the following formula:
$$UCT_i/P_i = E/P - t^*B_i/P_i$$
where UTC_i/P_i is the unconditional grant per capita; E/P is the average per capita expenditure in the group; t is the average property tax rate in the group; and B_i/P_i is the per capita property tax base as assessed by the province. E/P can be thought of as the expenditure needs (or standard) for the municipality, and, since rearrangement of the formula yields $E/P = t^*B_i/P_i + UCT_i/P_i$, the grant is set to allow municipality i to achieve the average per capita expenditure in its group by levying the group-average tax rate on its own base.

30 The temporary equalizing adjustment involved constructing an index of tax capacity where the index for municipality i was:
$$Ii = [(B_i/P_i)/B/P]^*100$$
where B_i/P_i is the per capita property-tax base in municipality i and B/P is the per capita base of the group to which the municipality belongs. If the index is 100 or more (i.e., if the municipality's tax base per capita is larger than its group average), the municipality receives the unconditional grant it received in 2004. If the index is less than 100, the municipality receives an equalizing supplement. The supplement exists for two years only, and beginning in 2007 the unconditional transfer becomes a pure block grant based on 2006 payment levels escalated at 2 per cent per year.

31 For a review of the normative rationales for equalizing transfers, see Robin W. Boadway, 'The Economics of Equalization: An Overview,' in Robin Boadway and Paul Hobson, eds., *Equalization: Its Contribution to Canada's Economic and Fiscal Progress* (Kingston, Ont.: John Deutsch Institute, 1998), 27–82.

32 The provincial property-tax rate was established in 1966, following the Byrne report, to assist the province with the provision of standard social services (especially education) across the province.

33 For LSD i, this is defined as:
$$FC_i = B/P/(B/P + B_i/P_i)$$

where B is the tax base in all unincorporated areas, P is the population in all unincorporated areas, Bi is the tax base in LSDi, and P_i is the population in LSD_i. This fiscal-capacity measure is then applied to the previous year's expenditures in LSD i to yield the unconditional grant UCT_i;

$$UCT_i = FC_i * E_i t\text{-}1$$

where $E_i t\text{-}1$ is the previous year's expenditures in LSD i. Note that, if the per capita base in LSD i equals the per capita base across all LSDs , $FC_i = 0.5$ and the unconditional transfer is equal to one-half the previous year's expenditures and can be interpreted as a cost-sharing rate Also note that, if LSD i has a smaller per capita base than the average of all incorporated LSDs, the unconditional transfer covers a larger share of expenditures.

34 Scale-back factor = $G/(0.5*E_{t\text{-}1})$ where G is the provincial government budget for unconditional transfers to the LSDs and $E_{t\text{-}1}$ is the previous year's expenditures in the LSDs.

35 New Brunswick, *The Report of the Ministers Round Table on Local Governance.*

36 New Brunswick, *Review of the Provision of Government Services to Local Service Districts and Property Taxation Levels* (Fredericton: Audit and Consulting Services, Office of the Comptroller, October 2002).

37 See http://www.gnb.ca/cnb/news/gl/2006e0839gl.htm.

38 'Premier Seeks Public Thoughts on 2005 Provincial Budget,' Moncton, *Times and Transcript*, 7 February 2005.

39 'Environment Is Main Focus of Investment in Rural Infrastructure,' Fredericton, Regional Development Corporation, News Release, 12 April 2003, http://www.gnb.ca/cnb/news/env/2004e1391pr.htm.

40 Statutes of New Brunswick, An Act Respecting Rural Communities (2005), c. 7, http://www.gnb.ca/0062/acts/BBA-2005/Chap-7.pdf.

41 An examination of 2003 data on average household income and the proportion of the population indicating French as mother tongue for New Brunswick municipal governments produces a simple correlation coefficient of -0.28.

42 Between the completion of this chapter, in March 2007, and its publication, New Brunswick Premier Shawn Graham appointed a commissioner to examine 'the structure and organization of local governance in the province, regional co-operation, property taxation, and local government funding arrangements, as well as the legislative framework required to implement an action plan he is to submit to government in the fall of 2008. 'Commissioner on the Future of Local Governance Appointed,' Fredericton, Office of the Premier, 19 September 2007, http://www.gnb.ca/cnb/news/pre/2007e1183pr.htm). We rest our case.

5 Manitoba

TOM CARTER

Local government in Manitoba has evolved over a period of 130 years. Its origins (since the arrival of European settlers) date to the granting of municipal status to and the creation of the city of Winnipeg in 1873.[1]Despite considerable opposition from the Hudson Bay Company, a major landowner within the new city boundaries that feared increased taxation on its land, the provincial legislature granted the city of Winnipeg a charter. This was followed closely by the incorporation of other municipalities, both urban and rural, in the immediate vicinity of Winnipeg.

Since these early beginnings, the evolution of municipal government in Manitoba has been affected by a number of trends and circumstances, including the dominance of Winnipeg within the province and the absence of mid-sized cities; changing demographics; the changing nature of the agricultural economy; fiscal poverty; and the province's geographic diversity, spanning, as it does, areas of prairie, parkland, boreal forest, and tundra with their varied resources. Provincial governments – which at times have taken bold (some would suggest creative) steps while at other times showing a reluctance to act – have also influenced evolution. So have the dynamic personalities of certain politicians and the changing relationships, roles, and responsibilities of the various levels of government, including the First Nations.

Existing provincial-municipal relationships are rooted in legislative models developed during the late nineteenth and early twentieth centuries in Manitoba when the province was still largely a rural society with small urban service centres. Many argue that those early models have not evolved sufficiently to provide the necessary legal, fiscal, and governance relationships between the province and municipalities to allow municipalities to address current and future challenges. It is argued generally that a new partnership and new approaches to planning are needed: a model that revolves around consultation and consensus building; increased local autonomy and accountability for that autonomy; and a new fiscal partnership.[2]

These arguments have spawned a recent revival of discussion on intergovernmental relationships in Canada. This discussion has focused on the federal-municipal relationship, driven initially by the initiatives of the 'Big City Mayors' and the debate around the 'New Deal' and the distribution of gas-tax revenue. More recently, the work of the External Committee on Cities and Communities has raised the question of devolution of additional authorities and responsibilities to local government. With the election of a new federal Conservative government in January 2006, the discussion has lost some of its urgency, but, all the same, it has highlighted many areas where federal-municipal connections could be strengthened and has marginalized the issue of provincial-municipal relationships in the province of Manitoba.[3] This chapter attempts to redress the balance by focusing mainly on the provincial-municipal connection. Municipalities after all, are creatures of the provinces and provinces have responsibility for municipalities under sections 92 (8) and (16) of the Constitution Act, 1982. Nevertheless, given the nature of many past and present initiatives in the province, municipal relationships with the federal government will not be ignored.

More specifically, the purpose of this chapter is to provide a general overview of the municipal system in Manitoba with a particular emphasis on the changes that have occurred in municipal structure, functions, and authority, in the relationship with the provincial and federal governments, and in the municipal framework in general. Specific attention will be focused on the city of Winnipeg, the primate (largest) city and economic engine of the province. Given the size and importance of Winnipeg, the chapter will examine the city's special status and the additional powers this status provides, and explore whether these powers are adequate to deal with the challenges facing a city that is part of a larger metropolitan area. The chapter will also analyse current trends and issues within the province that are affecting the role of municipal governments and resulting in changes to the municipal system. Finally, the chapter will discuss the need for a new municipal framework that will allow municipalities to operate effectively in a rapidly changing environment.

The chapter has been prepared on the basis of a thorough assessment of the relevant literature and legislation. The literature review encompassed both academic and non-academic sources. Census data have been used to profile certain characteristics and features of the province and the municipal system. Semi-structured interviews were also conducted with key informants at the municipal and provincial levels.

Demographic and Economic Circumstances: Diversity and Change

General Population Trends

Changing demographics have played, and continue to play, an important role in shaping the municipal system in Manitoba. The province has experienced relatively slow population growth in recent decades. The 2006 population of 1,148,401 residents has increased only 16.2 per cent since 1971 while the population of Canada has increased 46.6 per cent over the same period. Saskatchewan, Manitoba's neighbour to the west, increased 4.5 per cent and Ontario to the east increased 57.9 per cent.[4] Seventy-two per cent of Manitoba's population is urban (living in centres of 1,000 people or more), with the other 28 per cent living in smaller communities or rural areas. The urban-rural split has changed little since 1971, when the ratio was 69 per cent to 31 per cent. Significant growth in Manitoba's urban centres occurred during the 1941 to 1961 period when the urban proportion of total population increased from 44 to 64 per cent.[5] Since then, however, growth has been much more modest.

Winnipeg's Dominance

A unique demographic feature of the province is the dominance of the city of Winnipeg. With a metropolitan-area population of 694,668 in 2006, it accounts for just over 60 per cent of the total provincial population.[6] If all people in the commutershed are included, this figure rises to approximately 70 per cent.[7] Furthermore, just over 96 per cent of the growth that has occurred in Manitoba since 1971 has been in the Winnipeg metropolitan area.[8] Immigration is reinforcing the uneven growth in the province, since new arrivals are very concentrated in Winnipeg. In the period from 1999 to 2006, 80 per cent of new arrivals settled there. Most of the remainder have settled in the south-central area of the province – Steinbach, Morden, Winkler, Altona, and Carman.[9]

Despite the prominence of Winnipeg, since 1951 the metropolitan area has had the lowest rate of population growth of the ten largest metropolitan areas in Canada. Between 1976 and 2001, Winnipeg experienced a growth rate of 5.2 per cent, while the average for the top ten metropolitan areas was 21.6 per cent.[10] In 1951 Winnipeg was the fourth-largest urban area, behind Montreal, Toronto, and Vancouver. In 1976 Winnipeg ranked fifth, surpassed by Ottawa-Hull. Currently, Winnipeg has dropped to eighth place, overtaken by Calgary, Edmonton, and Quebec City. If current trends continue, Winnipeg will soon fall from the ranks of the top ten metropolitan areas, surpassed by Hamilton, Kitchener, and London.[11]

Local Government Administrative Units in Manitoba

The Municipal Officials Directory indicates that in 2006 there were 81 urban and 120 rural municipalities in Manitoba, as displayed in Table 1.[12] The 81 urban municipalities are composed of 9 cities, 52 towns, and 20 villages and constitute 72.6 per cent of the provincial population. In addition to rural and urban municipalities, there are a number of other organizational and administrative units of local government within the province. Some rural municipalities encompass local urban districts which generally contain a minimum of 250 residents with a population density of at least 400 residents per square kilometre. Although they are not politically independent, they generally develop service plans for the urbanized areas they represent. They also have limited borrowing power under the auspices of the municipality of which they are part, and may be in charge of activities such as local improvements and garbage collection. In most cases, they form an advisory group that works with the council of the surrounding rural municipality.

Part of northern Manitoba is not municipally organized and falls under the jurisdiction of the Northern Affairs Act as opposed to the Municipal Act. The Northern Affairs Act provides for formation of community councils, and there are fifty such communities, forty-seven of which are unincorporated and three incorporated. The part of Manitoba covered by this act includes 82 per cent of the geographical area of Manitoba but contains only about 82,000 people or 7 per cent of the population. Indian reserves comprise half of this population.[13] There are also Local Government Districts (LGDs) in areas of the province that are not organized into municipalities. LGDs have many of the same responsibilities of a municipality but they do not have an elected council. Instead, a resident administrator and a chief administrative officer work directly with the province, since, under the Local Government Districts Act, LGDs are administered by the province. LGDs generally establish an advisory body to work with the resident administrator and chief administrative officer. There are only two LGDs left in the province: Pinawa and Mystery Lake.

There are also a number of other administrative units that represent collections of municipalities organized to undertake specific functions: Conservation Districts and Watershed Management Areas with environmental responsibilities; Planning Districts to facilitate regional planning; and Regional Development Districts to promote community development, to name a few. These administrative units are discussed in greater detail below.

Municipal Population Trends:
Decline More Common Than Growth

As mentioned earlier, just over 60 per cent of the total population lives in metropolitan Winnipeg, 55 per cent in the city of Winnipeg alone (Table 1). Viewed from another perspective, 76 per cent of the population living in urban municipalities in Manitoba live in the city of Winnipeg and 83 per cent in the metropolitan area.

In terms of population size, the vast majority of both urban and rural municipalities are small. In 2006, 78 per cent of the urban municipalities in Manitoba had a population of less than 2,500. For rural municipalities, the proportion was 77 per cent, and 45 per cent have a population under 1,000. Rural municipalities, as a group, grew by just over 11,000 people during the 1991–2006 period. Growth was generally concentrated in those municipalities in the vicinity of Winnipeg. Overall growth in urban municipalities amounted to 25,499 people during the same period. As shown in Table 2, many small urban centres experienced significant decline while others grew.

Population changes in urban municipalities by population-size category are very confusing. The largest population increase of 32.2 per cent occurred in urban municipalities with populations between 10,000 and 14,999. The smallest municipalities with populations in the

Table 1
Manitoba municipalities by population size, 2006[14]

Population Ranges	Municipalities		Population by Size Group		% Provincial Population
	#	%	#	%	
Urban Municipalities					
500,000–700,000	1	1.2	633,451	76.0	55.2
25,000–50,000	1	1.2	41,511	5.0	3.6
10,000–15,000	3	3.7	37,240	4.5	3.2
5,000–9,999	6	7.4	44,281	5.3	3.9
2,500–4,999	7	8.6	23,955	2.9	2.1
1,500–2,499	8	9.9	15,260	1.8	1.3
1,000–1,499	10	12.3	11,843	1.4	1.0
500–999	28	34.6	20,086	2.4	1.7
0–499	17	21.0	6,386	0.8	0.6
TOTAL	81	100.0	834,013	100.0	72.6
Rural Municipalities					
10,000–15,000	3	2.5	36,225	14.6	3.2
5,000–9,999	9	7.5	64,875	26.2	5.6
2,500–4,999	16	13.3	54,397	22.0	4.7
1,500–2,499	15	12.5	28,681	11.6	2.5
1,000–1,499	23	19.2	29,243	11.8	2.5
500–999	39	32.5	28,358	11.5	2.5
0–499	15	12.5	5,887	2.4	0.5
TOTAL	120	100.0	247,661	100.0	21.6

0–499 and 500–999 range experienced more modest increases of 9.6 per cent and 9.3 per cent respectively. Most of the growth in these size categories can be attributed to growth in small urban communities around Winnipeg or in small centres that have become popular recreational retreats to which many people are moving to live when they retire. The most significant population decreases were experienced by urban municipalities with populations between 2,500 and 4,999, which recorded a 14 per cent population decrease. This is generally accounted for by centres moving out of their population-size category to another as they grow or decline. The highest absolute growth occurred in the city of Winnipeg. The absolute numbers provided in

Table 2
Population changes within population-classification ranges: Manitoba municipalities[15]

| Population Ranges | Year | | Population Change 1991 to 2006 | |
	2006	1991	(%) Change	Absolute Change
Urban Municipalities				
500,000–700,000	633,451	615,215	3.0	18,236
25,000–50,000	41,511	38,575	7.6	2,936
10,000–15,000	37,240	28,163	32.2	9,077
5,000–9,999	44,281	51,436	-13.9	-7,155
2,500–4,999	23,955	23,888	0.3	67
1,500–2,499	15,260	15,217	0.3	43
1,000–1,499	11,843	11,848	0.0	-5
500–999	20,086	18,332	9.6	1,754
0–499	6,386	5,840	9.3	546
TOTAL	834,013	808,514	3.2	25,499
Rural Municipalities				
10,000–15,000	36,225	11,102	226.3	25,123
5,000–9,999	64,875	58,869	10.2	6,006
2,500–4,999	54,397	54,073	0.6	324
1,500–2,499	28,681	49,071	-41.6	-20,390
1,000–1,499	29,243	26,394	10.8	2,849
500–999	28,358	34,000	-16.6	-5,642
0–499	5,887	2,850	106.6	3,037
TOTAL	247,661	236,359	4.8	11,302

Table 2 illustrate that the percentage increases and decreases are based on very modest numbers. Overall, there have been relatively modest changes in population numbers.

Changes in population by size category are equally confusing in rural municipalities. The most noticeable population trend in the 1991 to 2006 period was the 226 per cent increase experienced in municipalities with a population ranging between 10,000 and 15,000. This is largely explained by the shift of Springfield (population 12,602) from a lower to higher population-size group. Rural residential development in rural municipalities around Winnipeg (including Springfield) and growth in selected rural municipalities where there has been cottage development also contribute to increases in certain population-size categories. An example of this is the 107 per cent population increase (3,037 people) in rural municipalities with populations under 499. Rural municipalities with a population in the 1,000–1,499 range experienced an 11 per cent increase, while those in the 1,500–2,499 range had a 42 per cent reduction.

Overall, there has been rural depopulation and, at the same time, greater concentration in the Winnipeg region. By 1986, 78 per cent of the provincial population lived within 150 kilometres of Winnipeg's city centre.[16] This trend towards concentration has continued for a number of reasons. First, the city of Winnipeg is increasingly the employment hub of Manitoba, and people move to the city for jobs, particularly with uncertainty and decline in the farm economy. The amalgamation of small farms into larger commercial ones has reduced both the number of family farms and the number of farm employees, strengthening decline in rural areas. And, as the number of farms decline, their supporting industries decline as well. The 'increased diversification' of the non-agricultural economy in centres around Winnipeg also pulls people nearer to the city. More recently, increased international immigration to Winnipeg and the surrounding communities has added to this concentration in Winnipeg and vicinity.

Taking overall population trends into consideration, it would be hard to argue that growth pressures are a significant force in municipal change in Manitoba outside the Winnipeg metropolitan area. A few selected communities, most within the Winnipeg commutershed, certain small centres, and some rural municipalities in 'cottage country' are the exception. Most smaller urban centres and nearly all rural municipalities face population decline and the loss in services and revenue associated with it. Downsizing, as opposed to growth, is often the basis for future planning and development strategies in Manitoba municipalities.

The Aboriginal Population: A Challenge for Local Government

Manitoba possesses two other important demographic characteristics that pose challenges for municipal governments: a sizeable aboriginal population, with many aboriginal people living in urban communities; and an increasingly aging population. Focusing first on the aboriginal population, the 2006 census notes that 175,395 people, or nearly 16 per cent of the Manitoba total, identified themselves as aboriginal.[17] The aboriginal population increased 36 per cent between 1996 and 2006, making it the fourth-largest in the country, behind the aboriginal populations of Ontario, British Columbia, and Alberta.[18] By the year 2016, the aboriginal population in Manitoba is expected to represent 20 per cent of the provincial population, and the aboriginal population growth rate is expected to be six times that of the non-aboriginal population.[19] These significant growth rates mean that aboriginals will comprise a large part of the future economy as both workers and consumers.[20]

Winnipeg, with approximately 68,385 aboriginal people in 2006, was home to more than one-third of all Aboriginal people in the province and over half of those living off-reserve.[21] They represented 9.8 per cent of the Winnipeg population, up from 6.9 per cent in 1996. The aboriginal population was, and is, most concentrated in Winnipeg's inner city, where approximately one in five people identified themselves as aboriginal. This proportion was three to four times higher than in other areas of the city.[22]

Aboriginal people living in Manitoba and in Winnipeg have higher rates of poverty, lower levels of education and skills development, lower labour-force participation rates, and a much higher need for a range of educational, health care, and social services. Within ten years, it is estimated that aboriginal people will make up a quarter of the workforce in Winnipeg.[23] However, unemployment among aboriginal people is currently three times that of the rest of the population,[24] and, to compound the problem, approximately 40 per cent of the aboriginal population is under sixteen years of age. These factors will pose significant challenges for the city of Winnipeg and other municipalities in the province, which will have to respond to the need for a wide variety of aboriginal services and to initiate and engage in partnerships and activities with aboriginal governments that are mutually beneficial, even though it can be argued that, from a jurisdictional perspective, responsibility lies with senior levels of government, particularly the federal government.[25] The development of aboriginal reserves – though it has not yet occurred in Winnipeg – also raises a host of jurisdictional and service-needs issues. In its report *First Steps: Municipal Aboriginal Pathways*, the city of Winnipeg outlines its policy platform regarding its urban aboriginal population.[26] Specifically, it details actions it will take in the following five areas: employment, economic development, safety, quality of life, outreach, and education. Activity stemming from this policy document has been relatively modest to date, but, with growing numbers of aboriginals and with their increasing need for services, municipalities are facing mounting pressures to respond with program initiatives.

An Aging Population: Service Implications for Local Government

The most significant demographic cohort in Manitoba is the 'baby boomers' born between 1947 and 1966. They account for 29 per cent of the province's total population. The front end of the boomers turned fifty-eight in 2005, and the end of this generation, born in 1961, turned forty-four in 2005.[27] Because of the significance of this cohort, the Manitoba population is characterized by significant aging, although the median age of 38.1 years is the third-youngest in Canada.[28] In 2006, 14 per cent, or 161,890 Manitobans, were over the age of sixty-five. The national proportion is 13.7 per cent.[29] Despite a very young aboriginal population and a growing number of new arrivals that have a younger age profile than the general population, the proportion of the population over the age of sixty-five has been increasing for the past couple of decades and is projected to continue to increase, reaching 21.3 per cent in 2026. In addition to an increasing number of seniors, there will be more older seniors: the 65–74 age group will increase from 7 per cent in 2001 to 11 per cent of the total population in 2026; those aged 75–84 from 5.1 per cent to 6.8 per cent; and those 85-plus from 1.9 per cent to 2.6 per cent.[30]

The proportion of seniors varies between urban and rural areas. In the four largest urban centres in 2006, 13.7 per cent of the population was sixty-five or over, while in rural areas this rose to 14.6 per cent. Winnipeg's 65-plus population represents 14.1 per cent of its total, and this rises to 14.6 per cent in Brandon and 15 per cent in Portage la Prairie. In some smaller urban centres, the proportion is even higher. In Minnedosa (a centre of 2,475 people) the proportion is 26 per cent, in Neepawa (3,300 people) it is 27 per cent, and in Hamiota (820 people) it is 35 per cent. Rural municipalities generally have much lower proportions of seniors. In Landsdowne, in central Manitoba, 13 per cent of the population is over sixty-five, and in Minto it is only 11 per cent.[31] Over the past decades there has been a significant movement of seniors from farms and very small communities to larger centres, in search of housing, medical care, and other support services.

In 2006, 59 per cent of all seniors in Manitoba lived in the metropolitan area of Winnipeg.[32] Demographics reveal that Winnipeg's population is aging at a faster rate than that of Canada as a whole, and Winnipeg has a higher percentage of population over the age of sixty-five than many metropolitan areas. At the same time, it has a lower percentage of population in the 20–34 age range, largely because of young people leaving the province in search of better employment opportunities.[33] The number of seniors living in the Metropolitan Area is also increasing because of the arrival of migrants from smaller communities searching for services and better housing options.

In Winnipeg, the number of elderly living in suburbia is significantly higher than the number of seniors living in the older residential areas of the inner city (65,100 compared to 14,165). In 2001, 80 per cent of seniors aged sixty-five and over and 77 per cent of those seventy-five and over lived outside the inner city. 'Near seniors,' aged 45–65, are even more suburbanized.[34] The rising number and proportion of elderly in suburbia has been compounded by the tendency of people to age in place (the young people who moved into new suburban homes have stayed in suburbia), which is causing suburban locations in metropolitan areas to rapidly become gray.[35]

For municipalities, the aging of the population has major implications for the workforce, housing, health, social policy, infrastructure, and planning. Older populations use more medical and health services, make less use of the education system than younger populations, and need different types of recreational facilities. They need public transit and expanded and affordable housing options.[36] The design of suburbs may not be compatible with an aging population. Further, the impact of this population is unevenly distributed across the province, and throughout urban areas. Those communities with the most rapidly aging population are sometimes those that are growing most slowly yet have the highest demand for services coupled with the weakest tax base.[37] As the level of specialization of services needed increases, the trend will be for those services to be concentrated in larger urban areas. Changing service and planning needs will have both direct and indirect effects on municipalities and are certain to have spending implications.

The City of Winnipeg and the Capital Region:
Competition or Cooperation?

The Capital Region comprises the City of Winnipeg and fifteen municipalities surrounding the city. In 2006 the region was home to 730,305 people or 64 per cent of the Manitoba population.[38] Almost 87 per cent of the Capital Region's population resided within the city of Winnipeg. The 96,850 non-Winnipeg residents were distributed among the fifteen municipalities, whose populations ranged in size from just over 1,000 (St François Xavier) to 12,990 (Springfield), as laid out in Table 3.

Between 2001 and 2006, the Capital Region's population grew by 18,853 people, a five-year growth rate of 2.6 per cent. Close to 14,000 or 74 per cent of this increase occurred in the city of Winnipeg.[39] The stronger growth in Winnipeg represents a reversal of the trend during the previous decade, during which growth occurred in the surrounding municipalities. Over the 1991 to 2006 period, 50 per cent of the growth in the region was in surrounding municipalities.

Employing approximately 65 per cent of the provincial labour force and accounting for approximately 65 per cent of Manitoba's GDP,[40] the Capital Region is the economic engine of Manitoba. However, the dominance of the region, as well as the uneven growth within it, creates a number of problems for the province and the municipal jurisdictions that the region contains. With slower growth in the city over the longer term, and an inner city characterized by urban decline, taxing to help upgrade infrastructure and combat social problems and physical decline has resulted in Winnipeg residents paying higher property taxes than residents in surrounding municipalities. The lower taxes in these municipalities are one reason for higher long-term growth rates and the spreading of urban development beyond city of Winnipeg boundaries. Several municipalities in the Capital Region also successfully compete with Winnipeg for new investment in industrial and commercial development, and the result again is further population growth outside city boundaries. People also move to surrounding municipalities to access large 'two to five acre lots' where they can enjoy a more 'rural' type of lifestyle. It is still too early to tell what effect increasing energy and transportation costs will have on people's willingness to live in these centres and commute to Winnipeg.

The province has struggled to control intermunicipal competition and the fragmented and often sprawling development outside city boundaries that it produces. Given the emerging importance of cities and city regions as economic drivers, the province wants to have a Capital Region that is well planned and administered effectively. It wants the region to be competitive on a national and international basis, as opposed to having the various jurisdictions jockeying for position. To date, however, the province has been largely unsuccessful in introducing effective regional growth-management strategies.

Table 3
Population of municipal jurisdictions in the Manitoba Capital Region[41]

Municipality	2006			2001		
	2006 population	% of total population outside Winnipeg	% of total population in the Region	2001 population	% of total population outside Winnipeg	% of total population in the Region
Cartier (R)	3,162	3.3	0.4	3,120	3.4	0.4
East St Paul (R)	8,733	9.0	1.2	7,677	8.4	1.1
Headingley (R)	2,726	2.8	0.4	1,907	2.1	0.3
Macdonald (R)	5,653	5.8	0.8	5,320	5.8	0.7
Ritchot (R)	5,051	5.2	0.7	4,958	5.4	0.6
Rockwood (R)	7,692	7.9	1.1	7,654	8.3	1.1
Rosser (R)	1,364	1.4	0.2	1,412	1.5	0.2
Selkirk (C)	9,515	9.8	1.3	9,752	10.6	1.4
Springfield (R)	12,990	13.4	1.8	12,602	13.7	1.8
St Andrews (R)	11,359	11.7	1.6	10,695	11.6	1.5
St Clements (R)	9,706	10.0	1.3	9,115	9.9	1.3
St Francois Xavier (R)	1,087	1.1	0.1	1,024	1.1	0.1
Stonewall (T)	4,376	4.5	0.6	4,012	4.4	0.5
Tache (R)	9,083	9.4	1.2	8,578	9.3	1.2
West St Paul (R)	4,357	4.5	0.6	4,082	4.4	0.5
Total Population Outside Winnipeg	96,854	100.0	13.3	91,908	100.0	12.9
Winnipeg (C)	633,451	–	86.7	619,544	–	87.1
Total Population In Region	730,305	–	100.0	711,452	–	100.0

Finally, the dominance of Winnipeg within the region and the province presents a political dilemma in that support for urban initiatives often carries the stigma of the province appearing biased towards the city.

The Manitoba Economy: Diversified, Slow Steady Growth

Initially Manitoba's economy had a strong focus on natural resources, including agriculture, forestry, and mining. These sectors remain important. Agriculture is still the backbone of rural Manitoba, with cash receipts evenly balanced between livestock and crop production. Wheat, barley, and oilseeds are major crops and Manitoba is the leading Canadian producer of flaxseed, sunflower seeds, buckwheat, and field peas. The hog industry has become the dominant source of revenue in the livestock sector.[42] Mining has also gained strength, with near-record-high prices for base metals because of increasing global demand. Combined, agriculture and mining account for 6 per cent of GDP. Manufacturing is Manitoba's single largest industry, providing 12 per cent of GDP in 2007. Service industries account for 72 per cent of the economy. This is larger than the 68 per cent share for Canada as a whole. Important components of this sector include transportation, wholesale and retail trade, finance, insurance, real estate, and information and cultural activities.[43]

Winnipeg is a diversified manufacturing centre, with a strong presence in industries such as aerospace and with research and development in the health-care field (for example, the Level Four Disease Control Laboratory).[44] Manitoba's central location and Winnipeg's position as a transportation gateway to western Canada and to the American Mid-West make the province an ideal base for a variety of services including transportation, wholesale distribution, and telemarketing centres. The trucking and transportation industry is a major contributor to employment. Other factors that sustain the economy include a highly skilled workforce, an abundance of natural resources, and low business costs (particularly affordable housing and commercial and industrial rents).[45]

Although the economies of both Manitoba and Winnipeg are well diversified, the province and the city have been able to attract only limited numbers of businesses in the 'new economy,' that is, information technology, research and development, and other high-technology industries.[46] Winnipeg is also home to very few corporate head offices. In addition, the province does not have any significant amount of oil revenue, and so has missed the windfall of revenues that Alberta and, to a lesser extent, Saskatchewan have received in recent years. Hydroelectric power, however, provides a renewable and lasting source of revenue and, with markets south of the border hungry for energy, there is no difficulty in marketing electricity. Hydroelectric sales exceeded $1.5 billion in 2007.[47] A good characterization of Manitoba's economy would be balanced, diversified, and slow growing, with no single source of significant revenue windfalls. Despite the continued appreciation of the Canadian dollar, Manitoba's real GDP grew by 3 per cent in 2007, exceeding the growth rate in Canada as a whole. Growth for 2008 and 2009 is projected at 2.7 per cent, above the national average in both years.[48]

Total expenditures for the province of Manitoba during the 2008/2009 fiscal year were projected at $12,227 million, representing an increase of $745 million over 2007/2008. Health spending accounts for 35.8 per cent of total expenditures; education for 26.6 per cent; community economic and resource development for 12.1 per cent; and family services (social assistance) and housing for 10.9 per cent.[49]

Total revenues for the 2008/2009 fiscal year are projected at $12,324 million, an increase of $667 million from the previous year. The projected surplus for 2008/2009, therefore, is $97 million. Approximately 68 per cent ($8,417 million) of 2008/2009 revenue will be own-source revenue, mainly personal income tax and retail sales taxes.[50] Federal transfers will account for $3,905 million or 32 per cent. This is an increase of 5.9 per cent from the previous year because of steps taken by Ottawa to address the 'fiscal imbalance' between the federal and provincial governments.

This brief overview of the Manitoba economy and the financial position of the province shows that, under the current system, there is no wealth of funds to be tapped without raising taxes – retail and/or personal. Without significant sources of revenue from growth sectors, and highly dependent on revenue from personal income and retail sales taxes, the province is not in a position to increase funding to municipalities by any substantial amount. This forces municipalities to rely on their own funding sources – principally the property tax. Rural municipalities and many of the smaller urban municipalities cannot collect as much revenue from sales of services and regulatory fees as large cities such as Winnipeg, which leaves them even more dependent on property taxes. As has been noted in countless studies, new sources of revenue, or different approaches to revenue sharing between municipalities and other levels of government, are needed. The financial situation of local governments is explained in more detail in a subsequent section.

Evolution and Change in Municipal Governance in Manitoba

Early Developmental Legislation

The Manitoba government introduced legislation to allow for the creation of municipalities in 1873. This initial legislation began the process of setting rules under which municipalities were to operate, and a provincial cabinet minister was appointed as municipal commissioner to oversee the operations of municipalities. The city of Winnipeg was incorporated as the first municipality and was granted a special charter in 1873. Between 1873 and 1880, several municipalities around Winnipeg were incorporated. In 1877 the province imposed the county system on Manitoba: Selkirk County, for example, included the municipal units of Winnipeg, Springfield, the town of St Boniface, and what would become the rural municipalities of St Boniface, Assiniboia, St Paul, and Kildonan. This could be considered the first provincial effort to impose a regional framework on municipal units. The Municipalities Act (later the Municipal Act) of 1880 divided the province into twenty-six counties. In 1886, however, the 'rural municipality' was introduced by the province to replace the counties since the latter were considered too large to ensure effective local administration.

The City of Winnipeg Charter and the Municipalities Act of 1880 represent the initial legislative building blocks that defined the early roles and responsibilities of municipalities. The specific powers of municipalities included passing by-laws concerning nuisances, safety, sanitation, fire, police, and regulation of markets. Revenue was to be raised in two ways: a tax upon real and personal property, and licensing fees for certain business activities.[51] After this initial legislation, subsequent changes to the Municipal Act and the introduction of new pieces of legislation continued to change the responsibilities and authority of municipalities and their relationship to the province. In 1911 the City of Winnipeg Charter was amended to provide for a City Planning Commission to ensure a more organized approach to planning. This was followed, in 1916, by the passage of the Town Planning Act and changes to the Municipal Act that gave municipalities clear authority to regulate land use by adopting town-planning schemes that were essentially what we know today as zoning by-laws. (Prior to this, municipal authority to regulate land had not been clearly defined under the Municipalities Act.) The Town Planning Act had the general objective of making suitable provision for traffic control, sanitation, street layout, use of land, and amenities like parks and recreation areas. These plans still required the approval of the provincial minister. The changes of 1916 also gave the municipalities the power to appoint a planning commission that would become the local authority responsible for planning and for establishing specific provisions relating to the locations of buildings on their sites. Further, the new Town Planning Act allowed the minister to appoint a comptroller for town planning who would be the executive officer responsible to the minister. The act was further strengthened in 1921, when the province set out specific procedures for the preparation of town-planning schemes. There was very little other activity until the late 1940s.

The period 1873–1921, then, laid the basis for municipal governance in Manitoba. Several trends were evident during these years. There was identification of a growing number of responsibilities for municipalities – as urban centres grew and agriculture and other activities occurring in rural municipalities diversified – prompting a greater need for planning and development controls. At the same time, it was clear that the granting of more authority and responsibility was done within guidelines and procedures that established provincial control. Municipalities were certainly creatures of the province. It was also clear at this early stage that Winnipeg, with its special charter, occupied a place of unique status in the municipal hierarchy.

Planning for Urban Regions

From the late 1940s forward, an increasing number of pieces of legislation continued to add to the responsibilities of municipalities, providing them with increased authority in several areas but always within continually changing provincial regulations. However, a new trend appeared in planning and governance legislation with efforts by the province to introduce planning on a broader regional basis – first in the area of Winnipeg but later throughout the province in the many rural municipalities. The fragmentation of the Winnipeg urban area into a number of municipal units made it difficult to provide services and administer community affairs. The introduction of legislation and initiatives to develop broader frameworks for regional planning and cooperation between municipalities has been marked by infrequent 'great leaps forward,' some backward steps, and a great deal of running hard on the spot but going nowhere.

This era, characterized by provincial initiatives emphasizing planning on a broader regional basis, began in 1947 when the province created the Metropolitan Planning Committee, made up of representatives of the provincial government and twelve municipalities in the Winnipeg region (including Winnipeg). This committee combined with the Town Planning Commission, created by Winnipeg city council in 1944, to form a Joint Executive Committee on Metropolitan Planning for Greater Winnipeg. Background studies for a Greater Winnipeg master plan were quickly followed by provincial legislation creating a Metropolitan Planning Act, which set up a Metropolitan Planning Commission to replace the Joint Executive Committee. A Metropolitan Plan for Greater Winnipeg was adopted in 1950.

The Metropolitan Plan led to little action. Concerned with the lack of any regional cooperation on planning and development, the province created the Manitoba Provincial/Municipal Committee (MPMC) to advise the government on matters involving municipalities. The 1953 report of the MPMC recommended a form of metropolitan government for the Greater Winnipeg Region and the surrounding fifteen municipalities. Nothing happened.

Nevertheless, these initiatives did herald a new role by the province in local government, and a new relationship between the province and municipalities. In particular, they signalled a concerted effort on the part of the province to try to influence municipal action in the planning field by encouraging municipalities to plan on a broader basis, to consider the nature of their relationship with other municipalities, and to assess the impact of their actions on other jurisdictions.

Two-Tier Metropolitan Government

These early initiatives were followed by another major study by the provincially appointed Greater Winnipeg Investigating Commission in the period 1955–9, which again recommended a form of metropolitan government for the Greater Winnipeg Region. Following this study, there was progress. In 1960 the Metropolitan Corporation of Winnipeg was created and, in 1961, the Metropolitan Winnipeg Act created a two-tier system of local government for seven cities including the city of Winnipeg, five suburban municipalities, and one town.

Individual municipalities maintained control over libraries, fire service, police, and other things deemed local. The Metropolitan Corporation looked after and coordinated services deemed regional: sewer, water, arterial streets and bridges, transit, land-use control and planning, assessment, municipal golf courses, flood control, and regional parks. Many of the municipalities were unhappy with the format and the loss of control over key aspects of development. They were particularly concerned over the loss of control over assessment.

The act also created an 'Additional Zone,' giving the Metropolitan Corporation land-use control over an eight- to eleven-kilometre radius around the city's north, east, and south boundaries so that it could control the nature and direction of future development. In 1968 the Metropolitan Development Plan was adopted for Winnipeg and the surrounding municipalities to provide long-term direction for urban growth. The plan also applied to the Additional Zone. This development plan differed from the old town planning schemes, which were essentially zoning by-laws, in that it was intended to provide medium- to long-term policy direction for land-development decisions. The plan was forward-looking as opposed to static. The provincial legislature sent a clear message that regional planning strategies should replace individual municipal plans, particularly for services deemed regional in nature.

Unicity: A Bold Step Forward?

Because of the opposition of constituent municipalities, the two-tier government did not seem to be a satisfactory and final solution. The level of cooperation between the participant municipalities was not sufficient to provide any significant influence on the pattern and nature of growth and development. In 1970 the province released a White Paper entitled *Proposals for Urban Reorganization in the Greater Winnipeg Area.*[52] There followed a 'great leap forward' (depending on one's perspective on the effectiveness of amalgamation). On 1 January 1972 the City of Winnipeg Act came into effect. Local governance and planning moved from the individual municipal level to a broader regional jurisdiction, largely as a result of direct provincial intervention. Twelve municipalities making up Metropolitan Winnipeg were amalgamated into one municipal corporation (Unicity) and the Additional Zone remained in place. With Unicity thus formed, Winnipeg became the first large city in North America to move beyond the stage of split-level metropolitan government to a single administration. The area municipalities were replaced with a fifty-member city council that controlled an urban territory with a population of 550,000. Subsequent changes reduced the number of councillors to twenty-nine in 1977, and then to fifteen in 1992. The city is currently divided into fifteen wards and five community committees. Councillors play a dual role. As members of council they are concerned with decisions that affect the entire city. As members of community committees, their concern is more with local issues.

Was Single-Tier Government Successful?

The creation of this single-tier government was supposed to overcome jurisdictional fragmentation, enhance administrative and financial centralization, and presumably promote efficiencies. Another key objective of the Unicity was to promote planning on a broader regional basis to deal more effectively with issues such as transportation, water supply, tax equalization, economic development, and other services that need to be planned regionally as opposed to being left to the indi-vidual – and often competitive – activity of municipalities. At the same time, with the introduction of the community committees, there was an intent to foster increased involvement between urban residents and local government and incorporate some decentralization of political power.[53] A community committee was established for every three to six wards to supervise local planning and services. Resident advisor groups (RAGs) composed of private citizens were attached to each committee to advise councillors. The RAGs were a legislative frame-work that sparked citizen involvement but they were given virtually no money and could only advise councillors, who in turn could ignore them, so effective citizen involvement remained a challenge.[54]

The driving force behind Unicity amalgamation was the provincial New Democratic Party (NDP) and the 'central-city business interests' who felt that the fragmented municipal system was not serving the interest of development. The NDP White Paper on Unicity had ini-tially brought this issue to the fore of the political arena.[55]

Thereafter, all remained quiet on the regional planning framework until 1986 when *Plan Winnipeg*, approved by the province, contained an urban-limit line to try to prevent development in surrounding municipalities. Urban growth had reached a point where it was occur-ring beyond the boundaries of Unicity. This growth prompted the City of Winnipeg Act Review Committee to wade back into the issue of regional government. Its final report recommended the abolition of the Additional Zone, and also that parts of surrounding rural municipalities adjacent or close to the city's boundaries which were urban in nature be annexed to the city, reaffirming the Unicity principle that urban development in the Winnipeg metropolitan area should remain under one jurisdiction for planning purposes.

Initially, it was believed that the Unicity amalgamation would provide a stable and coherent local government system that would facilitate tax and service equalization throughout the Winnipeg metropolitan area. Many also felt that tax revenue from the more affluent suburbs would support the revitalization of the inner city.[56] Others have argued that the Unicity served as the catalyst for further urban deterioration and poor inner-city representation, which has facilitated the domination of suburban interests.[57] Since Unicity was created, suburban residents have been unable to separate themselves from the problems of the central city through municipal boundaries. They have, however, been able to elect councillors who have leaned towards capital investment in the suburbs rather than inner-city and downtown revitalization.

Andrew Sancton suggests that 'Unicity can best be described as Canada's most massive and significant municipal consolidation until 1998.'[58] Since Unicity, development and population have increased significantly more in the periphery than in the city of Winnipeg.[59] The dynamics in the region have also produced a rare Canadian example of deconsolidation. In 1992 the province allowed Headingley, at the extreme western end of the city, to secede from Unicity following a local referendum in which 87 per cent of residents supported secession. The residents successfully argued that the city had ample land for new development because it was not growing as quickly as the founders of Unicity had predicted.[60] They also maintained that the creation of Unicity facilitated suburban growth, in part by spreading the costs throughout the metropolitan area rather than concentrating them on the new residents and their immediate neighbours within relatively small suburban municipalities.[61] Several revisions have been made to the original structure of Unicity but the basic thrust of the reform has remained in place. While the province did eliminate the Additional Zone in 1991, urban areas of adjacent rural municipalities have never been annexed as was suggested in 1986. The concept of a regional planning framework seemed to have suffered a blow and taken a step backwards.

The Capital Region:
New Efforts to Organize Local Government on a Regional Basis

Since 1986, numerous committees and commissions have been formed, and studies conducted, to deal with development and population growth beyond the city of Winnipeg. The focus has been the Capital Region. The Winnipeg Capital Region is composed of the rural municipalities of Cartier, East St Paul, Headingley, Macdonald, Ritchot, Rockwood, Rosser, Springfield, St Andrews, St Clement, St François Xavier, Taché, and West St Paul; the town of Stonewall; and the cities of Selkirk and Winnipeg (see Table 3). The stated purpose of the Capital Region is to create a regional planning framework for the city of Winnipeg and the fifteen surrounding municipalities.

In 1989 the province formed the Capital Region Committee consisting of the mayors and reeves of thirteen rural municipalities, three provincial ministers, and later elected officials of the town of Stonewall, the city of Selkirk, and the rural municipality of Headingley. Its purpose was to consult and plan for the Capital Region, but little progress was made in developing a regional planning framework. In 1996 the province released a Capital Region Strategy, which identified five key policy areas (partnerships, settlement, economy, environment and resources, and human resources) as the focus for planning in the region. The document contained 30 subpolicies within these five areas and 200 actions to guide decision making in the region. None of the recommendations was implemented in any significant way.

In 1998 the province agreed to a recommendation from the Capital Region Committee to establish an independent panel to undertake a review and make recommendations to government respecting the effectiveness of the existing legislation, a policy and procedural framework to guide land-use planning and development, and provision of services in the municipalities in the Capital Region. The panel's report the following year (*Final Report of the Capital Region Review Panel*) concluded that the solution to the region's problems lay largely in enacting a statute which would allow municipalities to join together to solve problems. The panel's view was that such an association should be voluntary and the province should play a largely supportive role. Yet voluntary cooperation had not been effective in the past and there was considerable scepticism that it could lead to effective regional planning. The province's response – in a 2001 report entitled *Planning*

Manitoba's Capital Region: Next Steps – outlined a much more forceful provincial position. The report indicated that the province would:

- take the lead in developing planning policies that better address growth-management issues facing the Capital Region;
- appoint a Regional Planning Advisory Committee;
- dedicate professional planning staff with responsibilities to deal specifically with the Capital Region;
- diligently apply Provincial Land Use Policies;
- undertake a review of the statutes governing planning in Manitoba;
- develop and maintain common databases on the Capital Region and undertake research to provide additional data;
- give priority to maximizing the use of existing infrastructure;
- work with municipalities to develop tax-sharing models;
- use the existing Capital Region boundaries in initiating the regional-planning process; and
- develop strategies to resolve intermunicipal disputes.[62]

The provincial government then appointed a Regional Planning Advisory Committee (RPAC) for the Capital Region to consult and report back on policies for a regional plan with the ten actions listed above in mind. After consulting with stakeholders,[63] the RPAC presented its findings to the provincial government in a report entitled *A Partnership for the Future: Putting the Pieces Together in the Manitoba Capital Region*.[64]

In the spring of 2005, acting on this report, the Manitoba government adopted the Capital Region Partnership Act to support the government's direction in the Capital Region. The intent of the act is to nudge the sixteen constituent municipalities towards a partnership that would enable regional solutions to be found on such issues as land-use planning, infrastructure development, environmental protection, and water quality and supply – in essence a regional plan.[65] In fact, the act goes even further, suggesting that the cabinet could make regulations to force the creation of an organizational and governance structure for the capital region.

Planning to Compete versus Planning to Cooperate

Currently, all sixteen municipalities in the Capital Region have adopted development plans that outline medium- to long-term goals and policies. These plans guide land development in each of the region's municipalities. As it now stands, each of the plans is conceived largely in isolation from what is happening in surrounding communities though many issues are intermunicipal in nature, and often development in one municipality affects another.

Municipalities tend to be competing as opposed to cooperating. Although competition is modest to date, further competition among municipalities and duplication of services will contribute to socially and economically unsustainable development.[66] In the long term, competition will have negative and costly effects on development decisions.

Many argue that Winnipeg, because of its size, has an unfair advantage in that it is able to offer incentives that other municipalities cannot match, such as financial assistance to businesses willing to relocate to the city. The city sells land at reduced rates to businesses and provides other forms of assistance as well. Occasionally, the city and the province jointly provide this assistance.[67] However, the city is at a disadvantage in terms of land prices and property taxes, both of which tend to be lower outside the city limits. Regional planning would facilitate the most efficient use of existing infrastructure and resources. Accordingly, a long-term goal of the province is to ensure that development plans of municipalities and planning districts conform to a Capital Region Policy Plan. The Capital Region exists by the grace of the provincial government, and, accordingly, it holds the ultimate decision-making power about planning and development within the region.

Tax Equalization and Service Sharing in the Capital Region

The RPAC, in an attempt to remove jurisdictional differences in taxes and development costs, also recommended tax and service sharing to 'foster regional advantages and benefits.'[68] Ultimately, one of the most appealing aspects of tax- and service-sharing agreements is the potential for reduced fiscal disparities and service levels among the various municipalities. Currently, successful tax-sharing agreements exist between the five Pelly Trail Municipalities (the rural municipalities of Russell, Silver Creek, and Shellmouth-Boulton; the town of Russell; and the village of Binscarth); between the city and rural municipality of Portage la Prairie and the municipalities of Hanover and Niverville; and between the rural municipality of Brokenhead and the town of

Beausejour.[69] Yet, despite these examples of successful tax and service sharing, Winnipeg and adjacent municipalities have not pursued such options to any extent. Currently there exists a significant degree of resistance to this approach because there is a lack of regional under-standing, limited knowledge and acceptance of regional problem solving, and a mistrust of those who propose the agreements. In order for municipalities to embrace regional problem solving, the provincial government will have to take the lead role.

The city of Winnipeg has been hesitant to engage in service-sharing agreements because it feels that, with its planning requirements differ-ing from those of municipalities outside the city, service sharing may lead to urban sprawl. Before entering into such agreements, the city would want to see changes in other areas. For example, the province provides subsidies for sewer and water services in municipalities outside Winnipeg but not in the city and the current method of prop-erty-tax assessment encourages residential construction beyond city limits. Until such 'inequities,' as they are perceived by the city, are addressed, Winnipeg city council is reluctant to move forward on any extensive tax and service sharing.

This reluctance notwithstanding, the issue of tax and service sharing could provide Winnipeg and the surrounding municipalities with the opportunity to fund mutually beneficial regional services and/or capital projects. This would serve to decrease competition among municipalities and perhaps make it easier to address decline in Win-nipeg's inner city and environmental problems in the region as a whole.

The Changing Environment for Small Urban and Rural Municipalities

Although there has been less legislation concerning smaller urban and rural municipalities, and fewer studies and commissions focused on them, changes have occurred. After the passage of the initial Town Planning Act and the Municipal Act in the early part of the century, little happened to affect smaller urban and rural municipalities until the 1950s. Recognizing the need for greater planning expertise in these areas, the province created the Municipal Planning Board within the Department of Municipal Affairs in 1959. The mandate of the board's staff was to provide professional land-use planning services to munic-ipalities outside Greater Winnipeg. A new Planning Act in 1964 introduced relatively few new concepts and regulations but did require the government to add even more staff to provide planning advice and services to rural municipalities and to other government departments working with these municipalities.

In 1972 the provincial government created a new Department of Urban Affairs to deal with city of Winnipeg issues of provincial interest, while the Department of Municipal Affairs remained to deal with municipalities outside Winnipeg. Planning authority in Manitoba was now divided – Winnipeg under the city of Winnipeg Act and the rest of the province under the 1964 Planning Act. In 1975 a new Planning Act was introduced again, applying to all areas outside Winnipeg. The new legislation:

- allowed for creation of planning districts (two or more municipalities formally joining for land-use planning purposes);
- adopted Provincial Land Use Policies;
- created an interdepartmental planning board;
- implemented interim land-use control;
- adopted a system of municipal/district development plans and zoning by-laws to replace old planning schemes;
- implemented a subdivision approval system; and
- allowed the provincial minister to delegate the approving-authority function to planning districts with adopted development plans.[70]

The act signalled a new provincial direction in relationships with small urban and rural municipalities. It attempted to move these smaller municipalities towards greater involvement in planning and control of development and it encouraged planning on a regional basis.

Following passage of the act, an Interdepartmental Planning Board was established in 1976. It consisted of a Committee of Deputy Ministers who met regularly to discuss items of mutual interest in the various municipalities outside the city of Winnipeg. This resulted in a better level of coordination and consultation at the departmental level. Also in 1976, the Provincial Planning Branch was created within the Department of Municipal Affairs to provide a review role in planning matters. The branch reviewed development and subdivision plans and monitored the application of Provincial Land Use Policies. These policies, which do not apply to the city of Winnipeg, were revised and again adopted as a regulation under the Planning Act in 1980. They were further amended and updated in 1994 and again in 2001 – generally to reflect sustainable-development principles and create more effective guidelines for large feedlot and hog operations.

In 1997 the province launched a Consultation on Sustainable Development Implementation (COSDI) to incorporate environmental issues and management into land-use planning and decision making. The Sustainable Development Act was adopted in 1998. In 1999 the provincial government recombined the departments of Rural Development (formerly Municipal Affairs) and Urban Affairs under a new name: Intergovernmental Affairs. In 2000 a Community and Land Use Planning Services Division was created in Intergovernmental Affairs with expanded planning services for municipalities outside Winnipeg.

This summary of legislative and administrative changes affecting municipalities outside Winnipeg suggests that the province has been continually demanding a more sophisticated level of planning but that, because of limited expertise in the smaller municipalities, it has had to provide more resources through the Provincial Planning Branch. The province has also encouraged the development of planning districts under which municipalities plan on a regional, as opposed to an isolated municipal, basis, particularly as the population and tax base of individual municipalities decline. Changes that have been made to the Planning Act encourage the development of plans that are forward-looking and that fit into planning-district objectives, as opposed to the traditional static zoning-based planning schemes. Provincial Land Use Policies, which recognize sustainable-development principles, provide guidelines for land-use planning and control. Over the last several decades, the province has certainly provided smaller municipalities with more authority within broad legislative frameworks, but it has also provided more expertise from the provincial bureaucracy. Several of the people interviewed indicated that, in their opinion, Manitoba provided more planning staff per capita to assist municipalities than any other jurisdiction in Canada.

Local Government Involvement in Multilevel Governance Initiatives

Discussion to this point has focused almost entirely on provincial-municipal relationships, but local municipalities also work closely with the federal government on many initiatives. Loleen Berdahl[71]

suggests that it is impossible to look at urban issues without considering the role of the federal government because there is a federal
dimension to urban-policy issues. There are obvious and compelling
reasons for federal involvement in urban issues such as immigration,
regional economic development, transportation, taxation, building
basic infrastructure, and the role of cities in the national and international economy. Many of these factors involve a set of circumstances
and impacts that are beyond the scope of any one level of government.

Municipalities complain that Ottawa does not adequately consider
the effect of its policies on the urban areas, despite the fact that many
of them have significant urban attributes and challenges. They
contend that there is an inadequate municipal voice in the federal government's urban policies and programs.[72] Local governments are in
the best position to identify their key urban-policy priorities but need
a formal mechanism for communicating these priorities to the federal
government. Currently, no mechanism for regular consultation among
all three levels of government exists. Communication tends to be ad
hoc, and this limits the ability of governments to work together to
address urban issues.

Tripartite Agreements

Tripartite agreements appear to be a good vehicle to encourage intergovernmental cooperation.[73] Manitoba and its cities, principally Winnipeg, have a long history of engaging in successful tripartite agreements with the federal government. The best examples of multilevel
governance initiatives under such agreements in the province have
involved efforts to revitalize decaying central business districts and
surrounding inner-city residential areas. Although the focus has been
largely on Winnipeg, attempts at inner-city revitalization have
extended to other urban centres such as Brandon and Thompson and,
when initiatives directed at municipal main streets are included, to
even smaller centres.

Activity in this theme area was initiated in Winnipeg in 1969 with
the adoption of a Metro Downtown Plan to assist with the development and redevelopment of downtown Winnipeg. In 1981 *Plan Winnipeg*, a comprehensive planning document outlining policy and
development directions for the city, was released. A major focus of the
plan was redevelopment and revitalization of the inner-city business
and residential areas. In 1981 the Winnipeg Core Area Initiative (CAI)

was introduced. Funded by the three levels of government, the initiative directed approximately $100 million, shared equally, at social, economic, and physical renewal of Winnipeg's downtown. The CAI was renewed in 1986 with similar levels of funding shared in the same fashion. Among other things, the CAI provided support for industrial development, housing incentives, and funding for training and employment and for strategic capital projects such as The Forks and the North Portage Avenue Redevelopment.

The CAI was followed by the Winnipeg Development Agreement: a tripartite agreement (ended in 2001) that resulted in the three levels of government pooling $75 million for a number of projects in the areas of community development and security, labour-force development, and strategic and sectoral investments. Western Economic Diversification (WED) coordinated federal participation in this agreement, including the departments of Human Resources Development Canada (HRDC) and Canadian Heritage.

On 20 May 2004 a new agreement was signed by all three parties, again with pooled funds of $75 million. This new Canada-Manitoba-Winnipeg Agreement for Community and Economic Development funds four strategic programs: Aboriginal Participation, enhancing opportunities for aboriginal people; Building Sustainable Neighbourhoods, focused on neighbourhood renewal and capacity building; Downtown Renewal, to revitalize Winnipeg's downtown; and Supporting Innovation and Technology, to build a knowledge-based economy and improve Winnipeg's economic competitiveness.[74]

Tripartite agreements facilitate cooperation among all three levels of government with respect to making decisions that affect the quality of life of municipalities. Failing to include all three orders of government reduces the opportunity for governments to work together cooperatively and to address urban issues holistically.[75] Tripartite agreements allow municipal governments to sit as equal decision-making partners, and should allow for flexibility in the funding requirements for cities and enhance the funds available to them. Municipalities have to work in partnership with the federal government to address common policy issues despite the fact that, in a strict constitutional sense, municipal governments are a provincial responsibility.

To date, tripartite agreements have had a number of shortcomings. Often, they have a limited shelf life and a narrow focus, are sporadic and episodic in nature, and fail to incorporate a principled strategy for engaging municipal governments. Moreover, they impose inconsistent financial demands on municipalities, and deliver inconsistent financial resources. Further, they may not always be part of long-term municipal strategies.

The funding structure of tripartite agreements can also present problems since municipal governments have significantly less fiscal capacity than federal or provincial governments. They may experience considerable financial strain if required to provide a full third of the project's funds. At times there is also the question of whether federal and provincial contributions to tripartite agreements represent additional funding or are simply money siphoned from one project to another. Nevertheless, the overall experience with tripartite agreements has been positive in Manitoba.

Municipal Functions and Authority

The most recent Municipal Act of 1 January 1997 gave Manitoba municipalities powers to pass by-laws to spend, provide services, regulate, license, and take enforcement actions in more general terms than in the past. At the same time, the courts were instructed to interpret these powers more broadly.[76] Local government responsibilities, however, are never black and white. There are so many variations among municipalities – different program mechanisms, cost-sharing arrangements, and partnership agreements – that definitive statements on many functions are difficult, if not impossible.[77] In general, however, local government is responsible for the protection of the health and safety of its citizens. This can range from fire protection to animal and pest control, food inspection to ambulance services and emergency planning and preparedness.

Ambulance services are a good example of the variation that can exist in local government responsibilities. Ambulance services are a responsibility of the province and operate within a larger provincial health-care delivery system as a core service under Regional Health Authorities. However, the service can also be delivered by municipalities with funding from the province. Rural municipalities often partner to deliver ambulance services. Winnipeg has combined firefighters and paramedics into one service and contracts with the provincial Winnipeg Regional Health Authority to deliver ambulance services, but receives funding under a range of provincial programs. Policing is a municipal responsibility, and Winnipeg and several other major urban centres have their own police force, but most municipali-

ties in the province contract the services of the RCMP. Very few municipalities are involved in the delivery of such utilities as electricity. Winnipeg recently sold Winnipeg Hydro to Manitoba Hydro, the provincial utility. A few northern communities have generating facilities, but
electricity is generally provided by the provincial agency.

Planning and development falls within the local government
sphere, including the development of zoning by-laws. Outside the
city of Winnipeg, the Provincial Land Use Policies provide direction
to municipalities, while the city of Winnipeg has greater flexibility to
establish land-use plans. Municipalities also have authority to regulate and license building construction, site requirements such as
density and setbacks, occupancy standards, and other aspects of the
development and redevelopment of homes and commercial structures. Larger urban municipalities – particularly Winnipeg, Brandon,
and Portage – also assume considerable responsibility for long-term
strategic planning for downtown and neighbourhood revitalization
and for strengthening community groups, particularly in declining
neighbourhoods.

Generally, municipalities are responsible for basic infrastructure,
which includes but is not limited to roads, water (purification and distribution), drains and drainage, and sewage and waste-water collection and treatment and solid-waste management. Local governments
are responsible for road construction and maintenance, but many
major roads have been designated as provincial roads and fall under
provincial jurisdiction. For smaller centres and rural municipalities,
the situation is more beneficial since the province is responsible for all
provincial highways as well as for main transportation routes through
municipalities, including those that are often main thoroughfares
within a town. Steinbach's Main Street renewal project is an example
of a provincial-municipal partnership. The province covered the costs
to rebuild the roadway, while the city paid for the sidewalks and
boulevard enhancements through frontage levies and general taxation.[78] Traffic control is the responsibility of local government, as is
public transit, but the latter is provided only in a few major urban
centres.

Provision of public services such as libraries, parks, recreational
facilities, cemeteries, and airports (except those operated by the federal
government) are also a local government responsibility. Public-works
projects, often linked to these general areas, are also a local government responsibility, although much of the funding may come from

other levels of government. Local governments also become involved in promoting economic development, tourism, and cultural events but generally in partnership with the province or the federal government. They also regulate and provide security, and sometimes funding, for cultural events.

Local government manages and collects a range of fees: business licensing, amusement taxes on entertainment events, inspection fees, and building-permit fees, for example. They also have the authority to establish these fees and the terms of payment. Property assessment is a provincial responsibility in all municipalities except the city of Winnipeg, but property-tax collection is a local government responsibility. This includes the collection of school taxes that are then turned over to the respective school divisions. Municipalities also have authority to provide tax credits for initiatives such as home renovation and development of heritage sites, but few municipalities outside Winnipeg provide such credits.

Finally, in Manitoba the provincial government has assumed responsibility, from the city of Winnipeg, for what used to be municipal functions, such as public health and social assistance.[79] Larger urban municipalities, particularly Winnipeg, still take some responsibility in the area of social housing, providing grants for home renovation and construction of affordable housing, and in the area of inner-city revitalization, with grants to local organizations. The municipal share of social or affordable housing is generally less than a quarter of the cost, depending on the program: home-renovation grants are approximately $1,000 per unit in Winnipeg and capacity-building grants to community organizations generally cover the costs of one or two key staff positions.

Within this general context, however, in the province of Manitoba there is no laundry list of specific responsibilities for municipalities. The Municipal Act (1997) states in a very general way that municipalities should provide good government, services that are necessary and desirable for residents and businesses, and sound management of assets; develop a safe and viable community; and foster economic and social development. There is certainly a list of functions that municipalities perform, but these functions vary considerably from one municipality to another. Often the functions differ by size and capacity of the municipality. Small town and rural municipalities often deliver only basic infrastructure services such as water and waste management. Larger municipalities may add recreational and cultural services and protective services such as fire and police, land-use planning, and economic-development activities. It is in the large cities like Winnipeg that the widest range of services, including support for housing programs, revitalization initiatives, and special cultural groups and events, is provided.

As Chris Leo points out, with a revised and amended Municipal Act (1997), all municipalities in Manitoba have greater ability to govern.[80] They also have been freed to enter into contracts with other municipalities or agencies for the delivery of services and to undertake joint ventures in partnership with other municipalities and non-profit or private agencies. Several municipalities in the province have moved to a market model for service delivery.[81] They enter into contracts with other municipalities or private firms to provide specific services – snow clearing, garbage removal, waste management, pest and weed control, and a host of other services. Many municipalities work together on a regional basis to address areas of common concern, and planning districts introduced by the province enable municipalities to coordinate regional development plans.[82]

City of Winnipeg Charter

Winnipeg clearly has more authority than other municipalities in the province, as well as many more responsibilities. The city charter lays out the jurisdictional framework for the city of Winnipeg, while the Municipal Act does the same for the other municipalities in Manitoba, including those in the Capital Region. The most recent City of Winnipeg Charter came into force on 1 January 2003. It essentially granted the city broader authority in an attempt to provide it with increased autonomy and financial flexibility. The charter combines municipal powers into fourteen broad categories (Table 4).

Granting the city powers in the fourteen spheres allows it to act in the manner most appropriate to the situation, and eliminates the need for constant approval by the province or for legislative amendments as new issues present themselves. Overall, the charter grants the city of Winnipeg greater powers and flexibility, new tools to address community priorities, the ability to raise money, and enhanced public accountability. Some specific issues addressed by the charter and the enhanced flexibility are noted in Table 5.

Table 4
City of Winnipeg Charter – spheres of jurisdiction

1 Health, safety, and well-being	8 Waterways
2 Activities in public places	9 Water
3 Streets	10 Waste
4 Activities of businesses	11 Public transportation
5 Floodway and floodway,fringe areas	12 Ambulance services
6 Buildings, equipment, and materials	13 Fire protection
7 Public convenience	14 Police

Municipal Fiscal Resources, Responsibilities, and Issues

Municipal Sources of Revenue

As 'creatures of the province,' Canadian municipalities have limited authority to generate and spend money. What authority they have is derived directly from provincial legislation and regulation. The main municipal revenue sources are property taxes, user fees, grants, and transfer payments. In comparison to their American and European counterparts, Canadian transfer payments are low.[83] Payments in lieu of taxes, investment income, and miscellaneous fees from licences, amusement taxes, permits, and fines are also included as sources of revenue.[84] Other sources of municipal revenue include development charges and special capital levies, such as local improvements. It should be noted that, in Manitoba, sewer and water rates are used as a source of general revenues for the municipalities as well.[85]

The following is a brief description of the main municipal revenue sources and funding mechanisms that apply to Manitoba:

- *General financing*: generated through property-tax revenues and may include borrowing for tax-supported capital expenditures.
- *Reserves*: money transferred from current operations of the municipality to funds set aside for specific capital projects and spent at a future date.
- *Debt issuance*: funds borrowed for infrastructure or other major projects, generally in accordance with borrowing limits set by the province.
- *Development charges*: charges collected from land developers to

Table 5
City of Winnipeg Act vs. City of Winnipeg Charter

Issue	City of Winnipeg Act	City of Winnipeg Charter
Spheres of jurisdiction	City can act only if it has the specific powers to do so, and even then it can act only in the manner outlined by the province.	The city's powers have been consolidated into fourteen broad categories. The city can act in the most appropriate manner in these areas without the need for ongoing legislative amendments.
Natural person powers	City can exercise standard corporate powers only if it has the specific power to do so. Current corporate powers are highly detailed.	City is able to carry out standard administrative corporate activities without the need for express legislative authority.
Outdated process requirements	The act is prescriptive in nature, laying out specifically how city powers must be exercised and limiting the city's powers unnecessarily in some cases.	Provides the city with broad authority to regulate, license, and take enforcement action within its spheres of jurisdiction.
Provincial approvals	City must obtain the province's approval for various matters, such as the creation of sinking funds or the appointment of special constables.	City can undertake a number of activities without the need for the provincial approval previously required.
Neighbourhood rejuvenation and growth	Council cannot specifically direct new property-tax revenue raised in a community to be used to revitalize that community.	City can implement Tax Increment Financing to target selected communities for investment to support council initiatives for rejuvenation.
Derelict properties	Limited power to force owners of derelict properties to repair those properties, which can cause entire neighbourhoods to deteriorate over time.	If, after a notice and an appeal period, the owner still fails to repair or otherwise deal with the vacant and derelict property, the city can take title to the property and repair or demolish it.
Planning process	Up to seven different planning hearings are required throughout the planning process.	City can establish a Planning Commission with panels focused on the whole or parts of the city, and city council retains responsibility for critical decisions. Council can also delegate certain decisions to appropriate personnel or committees.

offset some infrastructure expenditures incurred in servicing new developments.

- *Developer funding*: Capital expenditures funded by private-sector developers, usually in cost-shared arrangements with the municipality.
- *User fees*: monies collected as services are consumed and usually applied to services such as transit, recreation programs, and water usage. Funding derived from this typically does not cover the total costs of operating and maintaining the service.
- *Hotel Liquor, Meal, and Land Tax*: under the Municipal Revenue Act, municipalities have the authority to impose the liquor, meal, and hotel tax on accommodation and a land tax on property transfers; however, in Manitoba no municipalities have opted to impose such taxes since they are concerned about the negative impact on business, particularly the tourist business.
- *Local improvements and surcharges*: funds collected directly from users and targeted towards specific local community projects or improvements to existing infrastructure.
- *Transfer payments*: transfers of money from the province and/or federal government. Transfer payments may be of two types: general transfers that may be spent as the local government decides; and specific transfers or grants for specific projects or purposes.
- *Building Manitoba Fund*: provides Manitoba municipalities with a share of provincial income tax and fuel-tax revenues in support of municipal roads, recreation facilities, public transit, public safety, and other municipal infrastructure and services. The fund is equal to two cents per litre of the provincial gasoline tax, one cent per litre of the provincial diesel fuel tax, and 4.15 per cent of provincial income taxes. In 2008 Manitoba municipalities received $143 million, an increase of 5.5 per cent over the 2007 level.[86]
- *Video Lottery Terminals (VLTs)*: Manitoba municipalities also get an unconditional payment from VLT revenues. The provincial government provides all local governments with 10 per cent of net proceeds from VLTs within their territory (excluding those in casinos). Funds are distributed on a per-capita basis, plus a base grant of $5,000 per municipality. Winnipeg also receives a share of casino revenue.[87]
- *Tax Increment Financing (TIF)*: Granted to the city of Winnipeg, it offers the city more flexibility in financing its operations. Within

this mechanism there are two streams of revenue. The first stream represents the tax on the original property value before redevelopment, and continues to go to the city's general revenue. The second stream consists of the projected increase in tax revenue resulting from new development and higher property values. This allows the city to borrow against the projected revenue stream, on the understanding that future tax revenue will permit it to pay off the loan. This tax increment is funnelled into a special fund to subsidize the redevelopment of the TIF district. The city of Winnipeg is the first local government to have the ability to reinvest local taxes into specific areas.[88] This financing mechanism is a problem in two significant ways. There is no guarantee that property values will increase as projected, resulting in the city's inability to pay off the loan. As well, this financing tool commits future city councils to certain future expenditures that they may not support.

It can be argued that the Manitoba provincial government has been relatively generous when compared to other provinces in terms of transferring both powers and money to local governments. The province offers its municipalities a number of distinct funding mechanisms not common in other provinces. It is the only province that shares income tax, and the TIF is not extensively used in other provincial jurisdictions.

There are significant flows of funds from the provincial to the local level under a number of other program mechanisms. For example, under the general rubric of 'community economic development,' provincial funding to local communities includes:

- The Neighbourhoods Alive! Program: helps community organizations strengthen local capacity and revitalize designated urban neighbourhoods through locally planned and supported initiatives. In the five years since the program was launched, the province has committed over $26.5 million – $16.6 million to support nearly 400 community projects and $9.9 million for the repair, rehabilitation, or construction of 1,700 units of housing in Winnipeg, Brandon, and Thompson.[89]
- The Building Infrastructure initiative: provides funds under Hometown Manitoba for physical upgrades to main streets and public spaces in rural and northern communities. Under Community Places, it provides funds to not-for-profit community organizations

for facility construction and upgrades which furnish recreation
benefits to communities.[90]
- The Winnipeg Partnership Agreement: provides one-third of the
  $75 million that will be spent in Winnipeg over the five-year life of
  the program on aboriginal participation, building sustainable
  neighbourhoods, downtown renewal, and supporting the introduction of innovation and technology.[91]
- The Municipal Rural Infrastructure Program: invests funds in
  upgrading and constructing leisure and recreation centres in communities across the province.[92]

These and other similar examples illustrate the significant level of
provincial funding that flows to local governments.

Dependence on Own-Source Revenue

A more detailed look at local government revenues and expenditures
(see the appendix) also shows that Manitoba municipalities are significantly dependent on own-source revenue, although slightly less so
than Canadian municipalities as a whole (78 per cent vs. 83 per cent in
2004). As data in the appendix demonstrate, transfers from the
province are divided according to specific and general purposes. Specific-purpose operating revenue amounted to $105,563,000 in 2004,
down 61 per cent since 1995. General-purpose provincial transfers
amounted to $193,524,000, an increase of 146 per cent since 1995. The
decrease in specific and increase in general provincial transfers may
signal greater flexibility for local governments. Total provincial operating transfers, however, have declined 15 per cent since 1995. Federal
transfers of revenue to local governments amounted to $16,524,000 in
2004, a significant drop of 57 per cent since 1995. Total transfers from
all levels of government were $315,611,000 in 2004, a decline of 19 per
cent over the ten-year period.

Local government own-source revenue also illustrates some interesting trends. Property tax accounted for $478,698,000 – an increase of
23 per cent over 1995 and accounting for 34 per cent of total revenue
available to local governments in Manitoba in 2004. Other taxes that
are property-related amounted to $149,258,000 – down about 1 per
cent since 1995 and accounting for 10 per cent of total revenue. Total
tax revenue collected within the municipalities in 2004 was
$664,537,000 – up close to 18 per cent since 1995 and accounting for 47

per cent of total revenue. The sale of goods and services netted $356,442,000 for local governments in 2004, up 41 per cent since 1995 and accounting for 25 per cent of total revenue.

These figures illustrate that, over the decade 1995–2004, local governments have generated more of their revenue from own sources, particularly property tax and the sale of goods and services. Transfers from other orders of government have declined as a proportion of total revenue. The rate of decline has been greater than for Canada as a whole.

Revenue was up 8 per cent overall between 1995 and 2004 while the increase in the inflation rate during this time frame was approximately 22 per cent.[93] Regardless of how one approaches the analysis, over the decade local governments had to depend more and more on own-source revenue to finance operations and development activities and were losing the battle of increases in costs versus increases in revenue.

On the expenditure side, local government operating expenditures rose in most categories over the decade. They were down in social services (97 per cent) and debt charges (35 per cent). The significant decline in social-services spending reflects the transfer of responsibility for social services (social assistance) from local government to the province. The most significant increases occurred in general government services, environment, protection of persons and property, and transportation and communication. Large percentage increases in operating spending occurred in housing and regional planning and development but the dollar amounts in these categories are small. Total operating expenditures in 2004 were $1,175,107,000 – up 10 per cent since 1995. The equivalent figure for Canada as a whole was 33 per cent.

On the capital-expenditure side, local government expenditures over the decade were down 32 per cent overall, most of which is accounted for by decreases in capital spending on transportation and communication and on the environment. However, figures for 2006 suggest that capital spending by Manitoba municipalities has increased dramatically since 2004.

Combining operating and capital, the most significant increases in expenditures occurred in general government services, regional planning and development, and protection of persons and property. Local governments are meeting expenditures but only by increasing revenue from their own sources.

According to Berdahl, Canada's municipalities are powerless to address financial issues in an effective manner because they rely too much on limited own-source revenues.[94] Municipal governments are highly dependent on property tax, and, because this is a revenue tool that does not respond quickly to economic growth, their revenues are not able to keep pace with population growth and inflation. Further, many municipalities in Manitoba are not growing but are rather in decline, and municipal governments everywhere in the province must address growing demands in a context of scarce resources. As a consequence, municipalities are being increasingly forced to 'plan by assessment.'

This reliance on property tax is exemplified by the position of the city of Winnipeg. Just over 50 per cent of all revenue comes from the property tax.[95] Approximately 43 per cent of property-tax revenue comes from commercial property taxes, with 58 per cent from residential property taxes.[96] Sales of service and regulatory fees account for another 33 per cent, government grants and transfers contribute approximately 11 per cent, and other lesser amounts are raised from land sales, interest, and other minor revenue sources. Government grants and transfers include money from tax sharing (48 per cent), funds for ambulance, libraries, and other services (28 per cent), unconditional grants (20 per cent), funds for transit (18 per cent), and money for a variety of other projects (8 per cent).[97]

In a study of the six large prairie cities, Casey Vander Ploeg[98] provides a good assessment of where Winnipeg spends its money. The largest area of expenditure in 2004 was in protective services (police, fire, and emergency medical services), which consumed $0.22 of every dollar. The second was capital and municipal infrastructure, which consumed about $0.17 of every dollar. The third-largest spending area was transit, roads, traffic control, street lighting, and other transportation-related expenditures. Winnipeg spent about $0.07 of every dollar on transit, while road-related spending and general public works consumed $0.14 of every dollar. Parks, recreation, and culture consumed $0.09, utilities such as sewer, water, storm drainage, and solid-waste removal $0.08, and general administration $0.07. Winnipeg, one of the most indebted cities in the west, spent $0.09 on interest on the debt. With the exception of spending on debt retirement, expenditures in Winnipeg were not significantly different from those of other cities in the prairies.

Despite the difficult fiscal situation, a new deal on fiscal relations between the province and municipalities is unlikely. The province is in dialogue with the federal government (as are other provinces) to try to resolve what it perceives as fiscal imbalances between the federal and provincial levels. The province is of the opinion that 'there are both economic justification and public expectation that the federal government play some role in areas of provincial jurisdiction. The current fiscal advantage that the federal government enjoys relative to most provinces has given it the capacity to act – to cut taxes, to pay off debt and to increase program spending in areas of both federal and provincial jurisdiction – in a way that is simply not available to most provinces.'[99] The province feels that increased funding from the federal government must focus on these areas: plugging the leaks in the Equalization Program; addressing the funding shortfall with respect to major social programs such as health and education; and funding the unique issues of provinces, such as the circumstances of Manitoba's aboriginal population.[100]

The province is also of the opinion that 'the provinces have the practical experience and administrative expertise when it comes to managing the vast and complex range of major social programs that Canadians rely on.'[101] The implication of this fiscal situation and provincial stance is that municipalities can expect little in the way of increased revenue from the province until the fiscal imbalance is addressed. The province is not contemplating any new major fiscal arrangement with municipalities at this time, and there is no mention in the province's current thinking on fiscal matters of a new arrangement between the federal and local orders of government.

Local Governments and the Issue of Tax Shifting

In September 2003 the then mayor of Winnipeg, Glen Murray, unveiled a 'New Deal' for the city. The main scope of the New Deal was to bring the plight of cities onto the national stage and, more important, provide them with the autonomy and fiscal mechanisms necessary to fulfil their municipal responsibilities. Cities across Canada have been increasingly demanding federal-municipal tax-sharing agreements, most notably with respect to the federal fuel tax.[102] Winnipeg was the first city in Canada to investigate the possibility of tax shifting, an option that has also been explored in the United States and Europe. The equation proposed by Murray was: *New Revenues* (to invest in Winnipeg) + *Tax Shifts* (away from property value taxes and to consumption taxes and user fees) = *New Deal*.[103]

For taxpayers, the New Deal translated into reduced property tax and a decrease in transit fares. However, consumption taxes, such as fuel, hotel, liquor, and sales taxes, and user fees, such as for garbage collection, would increase. Other taxes, such as the business and amusement taxes, would be dropped. These measures would allow the city to reduce its reliance on property taxes, and residents would pay for the goods and services they consume.[104] In October and November 2003, a number of town hall meetings were held in order to gauge public response and answer questions. Public sentiment was mixed. The province essentially unravelled the New Deal by refusing to allow the city to implement a 1 per cent municipal sales tax, which represented the largest source of revenue under the plan.[105]

In response to the New Deal's defeat, Murray proposed a 'Newer Deal' in April 2004. Billed as 'simpler,' it asked for less from the citizens. For taxpayers, the Newer Deal translated into a 4 per cent property-tax cut in its first year, followed by a five-year tax-freeze. The city was seeking two-thirds of 1 per cent of the Goods and Services Tax (GST) collected in Winnipeg to assist with the cost of improving deteriorating infrastructure. It was estimated that this would result in $15 million of additional income. The city also requested that all provincial grants be converted to formula-based income-tax sharing, allowing it to capitalize on progressive taxation that can be funnelled directly towards a host of social services. Last, the city asked for a portion of the provincial fuel tax collected in Winnipeg. Fuel-tax funding would be directly tied to road infrastructure and would result in approximately $66 million in additional funding.[106] The Newer Deal was constructed in isolation, without input from the provincial or federal governments.

It can be argued that the city of Winnipeg and other municipalities already possess a number of flexible and unique financial mechanisms. The province has already made numerous exceptions in order to provide them with some of the tools necessary for financial viability. Even in an era of fiscal restraint across all levels of government, the city of Winnipeg has been granted more financial flexibility than most large urban centres in Canada. From a political standpoint, if a New Deal were to be offered to the city of Winnipeg, it would only be fair that the same offer be extended to all other municipalities within the province. Had the New Deal been the result of a cooperative effort between all three levels of government, perhaps the outcome would have been more positive, but, in any case, these 'Deals' did stimulate thought on a new funding mechanism for municipalities. Despite the failure of the 'New Deal' and the 'Newer Deal,' the Association of

Manitoba Municipalities (AMM) continues to strongly advocate tax shifting to other sources of revenue, with less reliance on property taxes.[107]

Education Funding in Manitoba

Manitoba is one of those provinces that continue to rely heavily on property taxes as the main source of education funding. Over the past twenty years, the proportion of revenue generated from property for public schools has increased, while the proportion directly funded by the provincial government has significantly decreased, although this is starting to change. Most of the recent property-tax increases can be directly attributed to the rising costs of education.[108]

Manitoba has employed two different types of school-based property tax. The first, the Education Support Levy (ESL), was in effect until 2006; it was imposed and collected by the provincial government utilized a uniform mill rate across the province, and was included in the provincial share of education funding.[109] The second type of school-based property tax is the special levy, which is imposed by local school boards and collected by municipalities. Special levy rates vary across the province and have risen substantially over the past few years.[110] The AMM's Task Force on Education Funding indicated that, when the ESL was in effect, one-half of the funding for public education came from property tax.[111] However, Dennis Owens now contends that the provincial government currently funds 56.7 per cent of education costs while 38.1 per cent is covered by property taxes set by the local school boards.[112]

Owens suggests that there are a number of problems associated with the current system of education funding. Most significant is that property taxes imposed by local school boards have steadily increased and in some communities represent more than half of the total property-tax bill. Farmers are particularly disadvantaged in this regard because, in addition to residential property taxes, they must also incur the cost of a special levy on their farmland. Owens suggests that farmers comprise only 3 per cent of the Manitoba population but, owing to the special levy, are responsible for approximately 9 per cent of the total cost of education. However, in the 2006 budget, the province increased the rebate on farmland education tax to 60 per cent.[113] Finally, because of varying property values across the province, mill rates differ accordingly as school boards endeavour to provide a uniform level of education. Therefore, residents in communities with little commercial property and/or low property values shoulder a greater proportion of property taxes than residents in wealthier communities.

Although the province has made changes, the AMM is advocating the development and employment of alternative provincial revenue sources to fund the portion of education costs currently financed by taxes on property. In its view, the province should move away from the current model to a higher level of support from provincial general revenues, and a corresponding decrease in property-tax revenues. Specifically, the AMM suggests that 80 per cent of education costs be funded through provincial general revenues, and 20 per cent through property taxation imposed by the local school division/district authorities.[114]

Provincial Government Regulation and Control

The various pieces of legislation used by the province in regulation and control of municipal activities have been highlighted in a number of areas of this chapter. The Planning Act, the Municipal Act, and the City of Winnipeg Act are all key pieces of legislation. But there are others: the Water Protection and Conservation Districts Act and the Provincial Land Use Policies are among many other examples of provincial control.

The previous Planning Act (1964) had encouraged municipalities to amalgamate or cooperate to form planning districts to develop land-use plans for regions as opposed to individual municipalities.[115] The new Planning Act (2005) went even further, authorizing planning districts and municipalities to develop regional strategies. These strategies would coordinate development, promote cooperation in service delivery, and develop plans and strategies to share infrastructure. Municipal development plans would have to fit in, and conform to, regional strategies once these regional strategies were in place.[116]

All this is very similar to the Conservation Districts Act (1987) and the more recent Water Protection Act (2004), which also introduce the concept of broader regional approaches to watershed planning and water-management areas. The primary goals of conservation districts are the sustainable use of water and soil resources and maintaining and improving the environmental economics of agricultural Manitoba. In each district an organization of local people (usually representatives of municipal councils or reeves of municipalities) cooperate to manage natural resources and solve resource-management problems. Districts, generally based on a drainage basin or watershed incorporating several municipalities, are the unit of planning. These districts have an impact on municipal governance and put in place another set of legislation that promotes, encourages, and authorizes municipalities to coordinate their activities and plans on a broader regional basis.

The Provincial Land Use Policies do not apply to the city of Winnipeg, although amendments to *Plan Winnipeg* are reviewed with these policies in mind. They do apply to all the remaining Manitoba municipalities, including those in the Capital Region. Developed in the late 1970s, the policies have been modified on many occasions. They cover nine specific areas: general development; renewable resources; agriculture; water and shore land; recreational resources; natural features and heritage resources; flooding and erosion; provincial highways; and mineral resources. They touch on almost every area of development. Intended to promote sustainable development, they serve as a guide for provincial and local authorities undertaking and reviewing land-use plans. New land-use plans, amendments to existing plans, and the development of individual projects that could have an environmental impact are all reviewed and approved or rejected on the basis of these policies. Although they are applied with commonsense and sensitivity to local circumstances, plans and projects are unlikely to be approved if they do not meet the policies' guidelines.

These measures illustrate that provincial oversight, although respectful of local circumstances, still requires municipalities to meet broad criteria that protect the environment and to provide for orderly and integrated development that takes into consideration many different sectors and issues. They also illustrate that the provincial government is strengthening legislation to encourage ('force' might be too strong a term) municipalities to amalgamate or cooperate to plan on a broader regional basis.

Municipal Governance

Each municipality in Manitoba is governed by an elected council consisting of a head of council (mayor or reeve) and at least four councillors. Municipal elections are held every four years on the fourth Wednesday in October. The author's survey of municipal and provincial officials (eleven provincial and nine municipal), exploring responsibilities, funding issues, provincial oversight, and other issues important to local government, suggests that municipal elections are well

Table 6
Municipal government positions held by women in Manitoba (2008)[117]

Description of Position	# of Positions in Manitoba	# of Positions Held by Women	% of Positions Held by Women
Mayor or Reeve	195	19	9.7
Chief Administrative Officer	190	110	57.9
Councillor	966	167	17.3

run and that, in most municipalities, political parties do not overtly contest elections. In larger centres there are informal, or even formal, partisan slates of candidates, for both council and mayor.

One of the biggest problems many municipalities face is getting local people interested. Often it is hard to get anyone to run, particularly in smaller municipalities. It is an even greater challenge to get more women involved.[118] Table 6 illustrates the insignificant involvement of women in political positions: women account for only 10 per cent of mayors and reeves and only 17 per cent of councillors. Women are much more prominent in administrative positions. Municipal politics, the author was told, certainly are a stepping stone to provincial or federal office.

There was a general consensus that municipalities had sufficient power to provide the services that citizens expect. It was noted that the amended City of Winnipeg Charter provided the city with more flexibility and authority to plan and finance development, and that Winnipeg was probably better positioned than other urban municipalities to set long-term policy directions. Several people indicated that it was not a problem of power but rather of inadequate boundaries that limited effective planning in many municipalities. The municipalities were often too small or did not encompass all areas of related development in a region. In smaller municipalities, it was not the absence of power that was a concern but the lack of capacity and expertise to plan and administer effectively – a major reason the province has provided staff to assist municipalities outside Winnipeg.

People noted a few functions they felt municipalities should be carrying out but were not. There was a consensus that large urban municipalities such as Winnipeg should play a more direct role in housing and urban-revitalization programs including the provision of more funding. A number of functions that people felt all municipalities should not undertake fell in the area of social services and public health.

There was general agreement that municipal employees were becoming more professional and competent. However, this was not a general trend throughout the entire province. Small municipalities were less likely to have professional staff. The recent numerous and rapid changes to legislation were creating a problem for the small and less skilled staff of smaller municipalities, as was the complexity associated with new environment, land-use, and water-management legislation. It was noted that the University of Manitoba provided excellent training for municipal administrators but smaller municipalities often could not afford to hire people with this expertise. Many of those interviewed suggested that small municipalities should join forces and hire staff to work for them jointly.

The Association of Manitoba Municipalities was given high marks for its role in the province. The AMM was created in 1999 as a result of the merger of the Union of Manitoba Municipalities and the Manitoba Association of Urban Municipalities. All municipalities in Manitoba are current members of the AMM. The organization is divided into seven districts: Northern, Parklands, Interlake, Mid-Western, Western, Central, and East. Each district is represented by two board members, one rural and one urban. The exception to this is the city of Winnipeg, which is represented by one director.

One of the main functions of the AMM is to lobby the provincial and federal governments on issues affecting Manitoba municipalities. Most of the issues tackled are raised directly by members through resolution or correspondence. The AMM also monitors and responds to new legislation affecting the municipal governments. The people interviewed said that the AMM is a strong and excellent advocate, particularly for small municipalities.

Interviewees all agreed that more and more municipalities are contracting out services – principally on the basis of reduced costs because contractors generally have non-unionized labour. People were divided on the long-term benefits of contracting out. Some were concerned about quality of service and reduced ability to control costs over the long term.

The principal limitations faced by municipalities, it was suggested, were financial limitations and lack of expertise to carry out initiatives. People were quick to point out that Manitoba does provide certain financial mechanisms to facilitate revenue flow, borrowing, and the ability to finance projects at the municipal level (Tax Increment Financing, for example), but these mechanisms were far more effective for large, as opposed to small, municipalities. Funding disparities, it was claimed, were greater in small municipalities despite the more complex nature of problems in larger centres.

The majority of those interviewed felt that provincial oversight of municipal activities was adequate but not overbearing. There was general agreement that legislation provided more flexibility than in the past. Some felt that there should be greater control and more oversight of small municipalities where there was less expertise. Others felt that the province provided these smaller jurisdictions with sufficient support for planning.

The most significant challenges facing municipalities identified by those interviewed included lack of adequate funding, deterioration of infrastructure, developing downsizing strategies in rural and small town municipalities, and devising a philosophy that would facilitate their participation in broader regional planning initiatives. It was agreed that provincial legislation was encouraging (if not forcing) municipalities to amalgamate or cooperate in the development of regional plans.

Nearly all of those interviewed believed that increased flows of money from Ottawa would be beneficial, but people were divided on whether the federal government should be directly involved in the municipal scene. It was pointed out that tripartite agreements had worked well in Manitoba and that this should be the vehicle for increased federal involvement in municipal affairs. But it was also suggested that there were a number of barriers to improved federal-municipal collaboration: constitutional responsibility and jurisdictional issues; lack of federal knowledge about municipal/urban issues; the short-term involvement of most federal programs; and the federal cookie-cutter approach that does not always suit local circumstances. But the money would be great!

The Adequacy of the Municipal Framework

Although growth overall is modest in municipalities in Manitoba, there are still the two solitudes: in one, population growth is matched by economic growth and revenue increases; in the other, there is population stagnation or decrease, job losses, economic deterioration, and falling revenues relative to expenses. Immigration is reinforcing the uneven growth in Manitoba, with its concentration in the Winnipeg metropolitan area.

These two solitudes present two sets of challenges. Where growth is occurring, municipalities play a catch-up-game of providing and repairing infrastructure and delivering social and community services. In a politically fragmented urban landscape, spillover almost always guarantees intermunicipal competition for growth and scarce resources to support growth. This has happened, albeit at a modest level, in the Winnipeg Capital Region. Potential solutions can be found only where the governance framework is the entire urbanized area or city-region, not individual local municipalities.

By definition, municipalities must have legally defined boundaries that encompass the territory within which they can enforce their legal authority. For Winnipeg, the actual urbanized area extends far beyond its legal boundaries, making a case for regional or metropolitan governance. Sancton[119] argues that the central problem of metropolitan and regional governance is that existing legal boundaries do not necessarily define the most efficient areas for carrying out assigned municipal functions. In particular, large-scale infrastructure projects, such as sewage-treatment plants and water services, are ideal candidates for regional planning since they would result in cost savings and reduce service and infrastructure duplication. The Regional Planning Advisory Committee further suggests the following services as potential sharing areas: drainage, water supply, flooding, transport, landfills, policing, fire protection, libraries, and recreational and cultural facilities.[120]

Municipalities that are characterized by stagnation face a different set of challenges – how to maintain adequate infrastructure and services while downsizing. Declining places need strategies that recognize their vulnerability and limited resources and the inevitability of a decreasing population and employment base. They need strategies for systematic downsizing which ensure that the process is both efficient and equitable: Can they maintain an appropriate level of services for those left behind? Is there a strategy for making them both smaller and more sustainable? In some areas of the province where population decline and stagnation is widespread, developing strategies on an individual municipal basis may not be the best approach to solving these challenges. Regional approaches are necessary in rural areas but for a different reason than in the Winnipeg Capital Region.

As a result of these circumstances, a constant theme for a number of years in the evolution of provincial-municipal relationships in Manitoba has been the struggle by the province to strengthen regional planning, either by dissolving and amalgamating municipalities into larger municipal units or by trying to develop partnership approaches to planning on a regional basis. However, despite facilitative legislation and the encouragement of the province, many municipalities operate as separate entities, divorced from each other, trying to solve the same problems as neighbouring municipalities on their own, and often detached from, though not unaffected by, national and global forces that they cannot hope to challenge on their own. By and large, municipalities have been competing as opposed to cooperating entities.

Individual, small municipalities do not have the most suitable framework for dealing with today's demographic, economic, and social realities, particularly in a policy world that purports to achieve urban sustainability.[121] Municipalities in Manitoba vary immensely in their size, income sources, social capital, planning expertise, fiscal capacity, and the range of services they offer to residents. There are too many governments.

Because of the risk of stepping on provincial toes and interfering in provincial jurisdictions, the federal government has had minimal involvement in municipal affairs in Manitoba. Ottawa must be mindful of its interaction with municipalities so as to avoid being perceived as excessively interfering with provincial matters.[122] In addition, the relationship between the federal and municipal governments has been erratic because the federal government lacks a sustained policy on urban issues.[123] Accordingly, federal involvement in municipal issues in Manitoba has been limited to indirect intervention and arrangements such as tripartite agreements.

Though municipalities do not fall under federal jurisdiction, there is nothing that prevents the federal government from spending in municipal spheres. This presents an opportunity to strengthen the federal-municipal relationship. It is also important to recognize the difference between 'urban' and 'municipal.' According to Berdahl,[124] 'municipal institutions are indeed solely within provincial jurisdiction, but urban issues simply refer to policy issues of importance in urban areas. The federal government is prohibited from interfering with the structure and operation of municipal institutions, but it faces no such constitutional constraint when it comes to urban issues.' Considerable funds have flowed to Manitoba municipalities, particularly Winnipeg, through tripartite agreements.

The federal government can influence the direction, character, and development of local economies through a number of policies and programs. Housing initiatives, aboriginal initiatives, infrastructure spending, and health-care endeavours all affect municipal-service provision. Despite the highly urban nature of many of its programs, the federal government has not yet coordinated a formal, permanent urban strategy or institutional structure to engage with municipal governments.[125] Any new municipal framework must include federal involvement and more federal funding. Successful tripartite initiatives in Winnipeg suggest that this may be an appropriate framework, because of municipal involvement. As the Canadian Institute of Planners has argued, 'Canada's municipalities can play a crucial role in helping the federal government meet its national priorities – for the integration of immigrants, for opportunities for Aboriginals living in urban centres, for tackling homelessness, and for emergency preparedness and response. Municipalities need a real seat at the table of national change.'[126]

Recent discussion on a new framework for local government has focused on the concept of 'double devolution.' It has been promoted most recently in the final report of the External Advisory Committee on Cities and Communities, and the concept has attracted considerable attention in Manitoba – particularly at the provincial level.[127] The report contends that Canada has experienced a long period of devolution of responsibilities from federal to provincial and territorial governments and from provincial and territorial to municipal governments. The report basically supports this process of devolution, suggesting that 'government roles and resource bases should move to the most local levels at which they can operate effectively. Decisions are best made as close to service consumers and tax payers as is possible.'[128] Hence, 'the Committee recommends a double devolution, shifting some responsibilities and resources from the federal government to the provincial and territorial governments, and then from the provincial and territorial governments to the local level; the double devolution should ensure that choices about how to raise and use resources, including tax choices, move to the most appropriate local levels, where accountability to citizens is most direct.'[129] This devolution, it is argued, should be preceded and accompanied by:

• development of a municipal taxation structure that gives local governments access to revenues, some of which grow with the

economy while others provide a stabilizing influence – in essence new sources of predictable, long-term funding;
- provision of funding (by federal and provincial governments) to renew aging infrastructure and close the municipal infrastructure gap;
- development of integrated and sustainable strategies that provide capacity-building measures for community leaders, as well as the introduction and sharing of best practices; and
- development of a process that ensures all levels of government will harmonize their policies and programs to support community efforts to pursue long-term visions and goals.

Although double devolution may be a feasible approach for some of Canada's larger cities, and perhaps for the city of Winnipeg within the Manitoba context, it seems unlikely that it would be a realistic approach for smaller urban and rural municipalities. Interviews with provincial and municipal officials suggest that:

- smaller local governments have too big a capacity deficit to be able to handle the transfer of responsibilities.
- many smaller municipal jurisdictions have such small and limited tax bases, and so few taxable areas that grow with the economy, that providing an improved taxation structure is next to impossible. The challenge in many local jurisdictions in Manitoba is to build a better tax base in environments of decline, not growth.
- some local government jurisdictions are so small geographically and demographically that development of integrated, sustainable strategies within the jurisdiction is very unrealistic. Even the city of Winnipeg would find this difficult without working with other municipalities in the region.
- in areas outside Winnipeg, some services are provided on a regional, as opposed to municipal, basis, so regional, as opposed to municipal, strategies make more sense.

Without moving towards a broader form of regional government, which would include amalgamation of smaller municipalities into larger regional units, it is difficult to understand how double devolution could work effectively. For double devolution to be a viable strategy in Manitoba, this would have to be a necessary first step.

Conclusion

Municipalities in Manitoba are generally effective administrative units, but many face the challenge of a declining population and tax base while others struggle with modest growth pressures and urban development that is overlapping areas of fragmented jurisdiction. Relationships with the province and with the federal government are, in general, positive and facilitated (particularly in the case of Winnipeg) by tripartite agreements that have been reasonably effective vehicles for program funding.

Provincial municipal governance has been dominated in recent years by a couple of key themes. The province has been granting greater authority to municipalities within broad facilitating legislation. At the same time, it has been encouraging municipalities to amalgamate or cooperate to plan on a wider regional scale. To date, legislation has encouraged this to happen on a voluntary basis, but recently it has contained stronger language. Forcing the issue would certainly create winners and losers because small municipal entities in a regional framework will never be able to compete effectively with large ones. Perhaps it is time for boundary changes. Perhaps there are too many local governments in Manitoba.

NOTES

I would like to thank Leah Ross of City Planning at the University of Manitoba, Chesya Polevychok, my research associate, and John Osborne, my research assistant, for their contributions to the literature and data search for this chapter.

1 Alan F.J. Artibise, *Winnipeg: An Illustrated History* (Toronto: J. Lorimer, 1977).
2 Casey Vander Ploeg, *Rationale for Renewal: The Imperatives behind a New Big City Provincial Partnership*, Western Cities Project Report no. 34. (Calgary: Canada West Foundation, 2005).
3 Ibid.
4 Statistics Canada, *Population of Census Divisions and Census Metropolitan Areas* (Ottawa: Government of Canada, 2007).
5 Statistics Canada, *Population Urban and Rural by Province and Territory: Manitoba* (Ottawa: Government of Canada, 2005a).

6 Statistics Canada, *Population of Census Divisions*, 2007.
7 Destination Winnipeg, *Winnipeg Fast Facts* (Winnipeg: Destination Winnipeg, 2006).
8 Statistics Canada, *Population of Census Divisions*, 2007.
9 Manitoba Department of Labour and Immigration, *Manitoba Immigration Facts: 2005 Statistical Report* (Winnipeg: Government of Manitoba, 2006).
10 Statistics Canada, *Population of Census Divisions*, 2007.
11 Peter Holle, *Winnipeg Population Ranking Plummeting: Out of Top Ten Cities* (Winnipeg: Frontier Centre for Public Policy, 2002).
12 Intergovernmental Affairs and Trade, *Municipal Officials Directory* (Winnipeg: Province of Manitoba, 2007).
13 Province of Manitoba, *Manitoba Community Profiles* (Winnipeg: Government of Manitoba, 2006).
14 Source: Statistics Canada, *Population Counts by Census Subdivisions*, 2006 Census. Note: There are no urban municipalities with populations between 50,000 and 499,000. The Statistics Canada definition of 'urban' is centres with more than 1,000 people. There are some urban municipalities in the province with less than 1,000 people: historically these centres had 1,000 or more people, and, while their population has declined, their designation has not. The 120 rural municipalities include Local Government Districts.
15 Source: Statistics Canada: *Population Counts by Census Subdivisions*, 2002a and 2006. Note: because there are no centres in them, some size categories are excluded. Aboriginal reserves are not included in Table 2.
16 Emhad C. Haque, 'Population of Manitoba: Patterns and Trends,' in John Welsted, John Everitt, and Christopher Stadel, eds., *The Geography of Manitoba: The Land and Its People* (Winnipeg: University of Manitoba Press, 1996), 108–24.
17 Statistics Canada, *Aboriginal Identity by Province and Territory* (Ottawa: Government of Canada, 2008).
18 Ibid.
19 Province of Manitoba, *Manitoba in Profile* (Winnipeg: Province of Manitoba, 2004).
20 Oscar Lathlin, 'Strengthening Aboriginal Participation in the Economy.' Presentation to the Manitoba Chamber of Commerce, 16 March 2004.
21 Statistics Canada, *Aboriginal Identity*, 2008.
22 Tom Carter and C. Polevychok, 'Is Winnipeg's Aboriginal Population Ghettoized?' Research Highlight no. 3 (Winnipeg: University of Winnipeg, 2003).
23 Tom Carter and C. Polevychok, *Scoping Research on Issues for Municipal*

Government and Aboriginal People Living within Their Boundaries (Ottawa: Federation of Canadian Municipalities, 2004).

24 Carter and Polevychok, 'Is Winnipeg's Aboriginal Population Ghettoized?'

25 Lathlin, *Strengthening Aboriginal Participation.*

26 City of Winnipeg, *First Steps: Municipal Aboriginal Pathways* (Winnipeg: City of Winnipeg, 2003).

27 Manitoba Finance, *2006 Manitoba Budget: Budget Paper A – The Economy* (Winnipeg: Manitoba Provincial Government, 2006a).

28 Statistics Canada, *Population of Census Divisions and Census Metropolitan Areas*, 2007.

29 Ibid.

30 Statistics Canada, *Population Projections for Canada, Provinces and Territories, 2005–2031*, Catalogue #91-520-XWE (Ottawa: Government of Canada., 2005).

31 Statistics Canada, *Population of Census Divisions and Census Metropolitan Areas*, 2007.

32 Ibid.

33 Ibid.

34 Tom Carter, 'Seniors' Squalor: A Housing and Socio-Economic Overview.' Presentation to the Centre on Aging – Spring Symposium, University of Manitoba, Winnipeg, 2005.

35 Gerald Hodge, *The Graying of Canadian Suburbs: Patterns, Pace and Prospects* (Ottawa: Canada Mortgage and Housing Corporation, 1994).

36 Ibid.

37 Ibid.

38 Statistics Canada, *Population of Census Divisions and Census Metropolitan Areas*, 2007.

39 Ibid.

40 Western Economic Diversification Canada, *Guidelines for Federal Policy Priorities in Urban Areas* (Winnipeg: Government of Canada, 2004).

41 Source: Statistics Canada, *Population Counts by Census Subdivisions*, 2002a and 2006, Census of Population. Note: C = City; T = Town; R = Rural.

42 Manitoba Finance, *2008 Manitoba Budget: Budget Paper A – The Economy* (Winnipeg: Manitoba Provincial Government, 2008a).

43 Ibid.

44 Manitoba Finance, *2008 Manitoba Budget: Budget Paper D – The Manitoba Advantage* (Winnipeg: Manitoba Provincial Government, 2008).

45 Ibid.

46 C. Polevychok and T. Carter, *Economic Restructuring in Winnipeg: Attract-*

ing Creative Workers and Capturing Investment in the New Growth Sectors.
Research Highlight no. 7 (Winnipeg: University of Winnipeg, 2006).

47 Manitoba Finance, *Manitoba Budget Paper A*, 2008.

48 Ibid.

49 Manitoba Finance, *Manitoba Budget Paper D* (Winnipeg: Manitoba Provincial Government, 2008).

50 Ibid.

51 Artibise, *Winnipeg*, 1977.

52 Province of Manitoba, *Proposals for Reorganization in the Greater Winnipeg Area* (Winnipeg: Department of Municipal Affairs, 1970).

53 Tom Carter, 'Winnipeg: Heartbeat of the Province,' in Welsted, Everitt, and Stadel, eds., *The Geography of Manitoba*, 148.

54 Alan Artibise and Tom Carter, 'Winnipeg: Canada,' in *Encyclopedia of Urban Cultures* (Danbury, Conn.: Grolier Publishing, 2002), 413.

55 Andrew Sancton, *Merger Mania: The Assault on Local Government* (Montreal and Kingston, Ont.: McGill-Queen's University Press, 2000).

56 Ibid.

57 Susan McFarlane, *Building Better Cities: Regional Cooperation in Western Canada* (Calgary: Canada West Foundation, 2001).

58 Andrew Sancton, 'Metropolitan and Regional Governance,' in Edmund P. Fowler and David Siegel, eds., *Urban Policy Issues* (Don Mills, Ont.: Oxford University Press, 2002), 63.

59 P. Diamant and T. Carter, *Canadian Response to Urban Governance Survey: OECD Group on Urban Affairs* (Ottawa: Canada Mortgage and Housing Corporation, 1997).

60 Andrew Sancton, 'Canadian Cites and the New Regionalism,' *Journal of Urban Affairs*, vol. 23, no. 5 (2001): 543–55.

61 Sancton, 'Metropolitan and Regional Governance,' 2002.

62 Manitoba Intergovernmental Affairs, *Planning Manitoba's Capital Region: Next Steps* (Winnipeg: Manitoba Intergovernmental Affairs, 2001).

63 Regional Planning Advisory Committee, *Strengthening Manitoba's Capital Region: General Principles and Policy Directions – A Public Discussion Paper* (Winnipeg: Manitoba Intergovernmental Affairs, 2002).

64 Regional Planning Advisory Committee, *A Partnership for the Future: Putting the Pieces Together in the Manitoba Capital Region* (Winnipeg: Manitoba Intergovernmental Affairs, 2003).

65 Elizabeth Fleming, 'The Capital Region Partnership Act,' *Fast Facts July 26, 2005* (Winnipeg: Canadian Centre for Policy Alternatives-MB, 2005).

66 Regional Planning Advisory Committee, *A Partnership for the Future.*

67 Diamant and Carter, *Canadian Response to Urban Governance Survey.*

68 Regional Planning Advisory Committee, *A Partnership for the Future.*
69 Ibid.
70 Manitoba Intergovernmental Affairs, *The Planning Framework in Manitoba's Capital Region: A Brief Historical Perspective.* Background Reports published under Manitoba's Capital Region Initiative (Winnipeg: Provincial Planning Services Branch, Manitoba Intergovernmental Affairs, 2002).
71 Loleen Berdahl, *Structuring Federal Urban Engagement: A Principled Approach* (Calgary: Canada West Foundation, 2002).
72 Denis Wong, *Cities at the Crossroads: Addressing Intergovernmental Structures for Western Canada's Cities* (Calgary: Canada West Foundation, 2002).
73 Loleen Berdahl, *Looking West 2007: Urban Policy Priorities and Assessing Governments* (Calgary: Canada West Foundation, 2007)
74 Government of Manitoba, 'Urban Development Agreement for Winnipeg: A Framework,' http://www.gov.mb.ca/ia/tripartite/Framework %20May%2020.2004.pdf; Government of Manitoba, 'Urban Development Agreements,' http://www.wd.gc.ca/ced/urban/default_e.asp?printVersion=1. Both accessed 3 August 2004.
75 Berdahl, *Structuring Federal Urban Engagement.*
76 Regional Planning Advisory Committee, *A Partnership for the Future.*
77 Karin Treff and D.B. Perry, *Finances of the Nation* (Toronto: Canadian Tax Foundation, 2005).
78 Editorial, 'Steinbach a Huge Contributor,' *The Carillon,* 20 May 2004, http://www.thecarillon.com/editorialsmay20_04.html.
79 Regional Planning Advisory Committee, *A Partnership for the Future.*
80 Chris Leo, 'Municipal Reform in Manitoba: Homogenizing, Empowering, and Marketing Municipal Government,' in Joseph Garcea and Edward C. LeSage, Jr, eds., *Municipal Reform in Canada: Reconfigurations, Re-empowerment and Rebalancing* (Don Mills, Ont.: Oxford University Press, 2005).
81 Ibid.
82 Treff and Perry, *Finances of the Nation.*
83 Sancton, 'Canadian Cites and the New Regionalism.'
84 Western Economic Diversification Canada, *Guidelines for Federal Policy Priorities in Urban Areas.*
85 Diamant and Carter, *Canadian Response to Urban Governance Survey.*
86 Manitoba Finance, *Budget Paper A,* 2008.
87 Manitoba Finance, *Provincial Municipal Tax Sharing* (Winnipeg: Government of Manitoba, 2004).
88 Ibid.
89 Manitoba Finance, *2006 Manitoba Budget: Budget Paper F – Community Economic Development* (Winnipeg: Manitoba Provincial Government, 2006).

90 Ibid.
91 Ibid.
92 Ibid.
93 Manitoba Bureau of Statistics, *Economy: Inflation, Manitoba vs. Canada* (Winnipeg: Government of Manitoba, 2006).
94 Berdahl, *Structuring Federal Urban Engagement*.
95 City of Winnipeg, *2003 New Times. New Ideas. New Deal. Questions and Answers*, http://www.winnipeg.ca/interhom/pdfs/NewDeal/NewDeal_Q_and_A.pdf (accessed 3 August 2004).
96 B. Gartner, *Western Cities Report Card* (Calgary: Canadian Federation of Independent Business, 2004).
97 City of Winnipeg, *Consolidated Financial Statement 2003*, http://www.winnipeg.ca/interhom/pdfs/departments/cfo/2003arfinancial.pdf (accessed 3 August 2004).
98 Casey Vander Ploeg, *Big Spenders? An Expenditure Profile of Western Canada's Big Six*, Western Cities Project (Calgary: Canada West Foundation, 2004).
99 Manitoba Finance, *2006 Manitoba Budget: Budget Paper C – A New Focus on Fiscal Relations* (Winnipeg: Manitoba Provincial Government, 2006), 2.
100 Ibid.
101 Ibid.
102 City of Winnipeg, *First Steps: Municipal Aboriginal Pathways*.
103 Ibid.
104 Ibid.
105 N. Ternette, 'Glen Murray's Failed New Deal,' *Canadian Dimension*, vol. 38, no. 5 (2004): 28–32.
106 Berdahl, *Structuring Federal Urban Engagement*.
107 Association of Manitoba Municipalities, *Budget Consultation Submission* (Winnipeg: Association of Manitoba Municipalities, 2006).
108 Dennis Owens, *Eliminating School Property Taxes in Manitoba* (Winnipeg: Frontier Centre for Public Policy, 2005).
109 Ibid.
110 Ibid.
111 Association of Manitoba Municipalities Task Force on Education Funding, *Rethinking Education Funding: Challenges and Opportunities* (Winnipeg: Association of Manitoba Municipalities, 2001).
112 Ibid.
113 Association of Manitoba Municipalities, *Roles, Responsibilities and*

Resources of Municipal Government in Manitoba (Winnipeg: Association of Manitoba Municipalities, 2006).

114 Ibid.
115 Fleming, 'The Capital Region Partnership Act.'
116 Ibid.
117 Source: Manitoba Municipal Directory, Intergovernmental Affairs, 2008.
118 *The Municipal Leader: Increasing Diversity in Municipal Politics* (Association of Manitoba Municipalities, 2005).
119 Sancton, 'Metropolitan and Regional Governance.'
120 Regional Planning Advisory Committee, *A Partnership for the Future.*
121 Larry S. Bourne, 'Beyond the New Deal for Cities: Confronting the Challenges of Uneven Urban Growth,' Research Bulletin no. 21 (Toronto: Centre for Urban and Community Studies, University of Toronto, 2004).
122 Wong, *Cities at the Crossroads.*
123 Ibid.
124 Berdahl, *Structuring Federal Urban Engagement*, 44.
125 Ibid.
126 Canadian Institute of Planners, *Framework for an Urban Strategy for Canada*. Submission to the Prime Minister's Caucus Task Force on Urban Issues, 12 March 2002.
127 External Advisory Committee on Cities and Communities, *From Restless Communities to Resilient Places: Building a Stronger Future for all Canadians* (Ottawa: Infrastructure Canada, 2006).
128 Ibid., 20.
129 Ibid., 25.

6 British Columbia

PATRICK J. SMITH AND KENNEDY STEWART

Successful multilevel governance in Canada requires federal, provincial, and municipal governments cooperating to achieve goals of benefit to those residing in areas where the jurisdictions of these three governmental tiers geographically overlap. Such cooperation means not just municipal governments doing the bidding of more senior governments, but also policy sometimes being directed from the bottom up. This chapter offers an appraisal of the multilevel-governance readiness of municipal governments in British Columbia by providing an overview of local institutions, processes, and players, along with some brief case examples. We argue that, while current governance arrangements and processes have created conditions apparently conducive to multilevel governance, there are still key flaws that undermine success in this area.

On the positive side, whereas governments in other provinces can often be heavy-handed when dealing with their local governments, especially when it comes to municipal restructuring, British Columbian governments tend to deal with local governments through a process of 'gentle imposition,' a distinction that dates back at least to the early 1950s.[1] K. Grant Crawford described the attitude of the province towards its municipalities during this initial post-war era as one of 'leniency' that included an 'effort to stimulate their growth and keep them solvent.'[2] In the same spirit, Community Services Minister Ida Chong recently described the provincial response to the formation of a new municipality, Queen Charlotte Village, as reflecting the B.C. government's 'commitment to helping communities decide for themselves what type of local government best meets their needs.'[3]

This 'lenient' approach usually means that provincial-municipal relations are relatively cordial and conducive to multilevel governance at the provincial-municipal/regional levels. In addition, recent legislative changes, especially the Community Charter, allow local governments more freedom to enact policies with limited provincial interference.[4] These changes not only enhance the goodwill between the province and municipalities but also give local governments more autonomy to participate as multilevel-governance partners.

On the negative side, the relative lack of provincial government toughness has left municipal institutions distinctly underdeveloped when it comes to local accountability measures. British Columbians probably are less empowered to hold their councils accountable for their actions than Canadians living in any other province.[5] This lack of accountability is apparent during local elections, and it is also marked at the regional-district level where mainly indirectly elected officials make major policy decisions. Flawed democratic institutions undermine the ability of local officials to claim that they speak for local citizens, and weaken their legitimacy in driving multilevel policy initiatives.[6] As British Columbia moves towards the close of the first decade of the twenty-first century, there is also evidence of the province reasserting a more traditional top-down provincial position vis-à-vis local democracy. Nowhere is this more evident than in the creation of the South Coast British Columbia Transportation Authority.[7]

In this overview, both the positives and negatives of the gentle-imposition approach (and more recent reassertions of provincial ascendancy) in its relation to multilevel governance are explored. The first section provides a historical background of the development of local government in British Columbia. We next review structural and functional aspects of B.C. local government before turning our attention to the issues of finance and provincial oversight. Following this, demographics, organizations, and politics are addressed in separate sections, and final remarks are offered in a Conclusion.

History

The roles, powers, and responsibilities of B.C. municipalities began to develop even before Confederation. In the colony of British Columbia, New Westminster was first incorporated as a city in 1860, and the city of Victoria was incorporated in 1862 in the colony of Vancouver Island. The skeletal frame of municipal governance was first set out in a general ordinance in 1865 in the colony of British Columbia. This allowed municipalities a form of 'home rule,' whereby they could essentially do anything not otherwise forbidden by law. The arrange-ment lasted until 1873, when British Columbia, now a Canadian province, passed legislation granting municipalities a fairly broad range of powers (notably excluding debt exposure).

A major legislative overhaul occurred in 1896 with the Municipal Incorporation Act, the Municipal Clauses Act, and the Elections Act. These acts created a system roughly similar to contemporary Canadian practice, establishing two types of municipalities (cities and towns for high-density populations, and districts for low-density areas) with powers to borrow, to tax persons and properties, and to collect licens-ing fees.[8] Under these new arrangements, municipalities were allowed to possess only the powers clearly outlined in the legislation, instead of the earlier home-rule authority. Local governmental responses to these early pieces of municipal legislation were generally hostile, for they were seen as containing a significant downloading of major responsibilities onto local governments. Under these acts, municipali-ties lost autonomy and were expected to use mostly property taxes to finance services such as roads, water, sewage, parks and recreation, policing, fire services, schools, and hospitals.[9]

The new laws prompted the creation, in 1905, of the Union of British Columbia Municipalities (UBCM), an organization that has subse-quently played a significant role representing municipalities to the provincial government. For example, an early UBCM president, New Westminster Mayor William Keary, was appointed to a 1912 Royal Commission on Municipal Government which held hearings across British Columbia and studied thirty-two North American cities. The commission recommended granting more municipal autonomy and establishing a Department of Municipal Affairs, boards of control, and a Public Utilities Commission. But the 1914 Municipal Act that formed the basis of local governing in the province until 1957 ignored most of the commission's recommendations.[10]

In 1957 Premier W.A.C. Bennett and his Social Credit government enacted a new consolidated Municipal Act, most of which was based on provisions contained in Ontario's Municipal Corporations Act of 1849. Despite its antiquated foundation, the act formed the basis of municipal law and jurisdiction in the province for most of the subse-quent four decades. Little new municipal legislation of consequence – other than amendments in the mid-1960s to create regional districts – was enacted until the New Democratic Party (NDP) ended Social Credit dominance in 1991.[11] Between 1991 and 2001, NDP premiers, especially former Vancouver mayor Michael Harcourt, attempted to simplify and clarify municipal legislation, beginning with allowing local political party names on municipal ballots (under Harcourt) and culminating in the Local Government Act, 2000 (at the end of the Glen Clark administration). Here, the changes were essentially focused on efficiency, leaving accountability dilemmas for local and regional institutions outstanding. The B.C. Liberals, led by another former Vancouver mayor, Gordon Campbell, replaced the New Democrats in 2001. The Liberals' 2001 election manifesto included a promise to undertake a major overhaul of municipal legislation. Campbell and his government did subsequently enact a new BC Community Charter in 2004 as an addition to the Local Government Act, but this most recent provincial overview legislation has been more symbolism than substance.[12]

Between 1896 and 2000, British Columbian municipalities operated under three important principles: 1) they had to follow rules set out by the province; 2) they were mandated by the provincial government to perform certain administrative activities; and 3) any actions undertaken by municipalities had to be authorized by provincial legislation.[13] Although the Local Government Act and the Community Charter increased the power held by municipalities after 2000, these three basic tenets of municipal government remain important, since municipal powers are legislatively, not constitutionally, entrenched. Other recent B.C. legislation, such as the Significant Projects Streamlining Act (2004), serves as a continuing reminder of British Columbia's more traditional provincial-municipal relationship. This act grants provincial ministers the authority to override local governments on specific projects about which the province and any local government cannot reach agreement. Similarly, the province's 'right to farm' legislation can override municipal by-laws – another reminder of the fundamental jurisdictional order.[14]

Structure

The 948,600 square kilometres of British Columbia are divided into twenty-nine regional districts (including the Islands Trust), which are further subdivided into 160 municipalities of various types. There are forty village municipalities (normally with populations less than 2,500), seventeen towns (populations of 2,500–5,000), forty-eight district municipalities (generally large geographic areas with low population density), and forty-nine cities (populations generally over

5,000). There are also three townships (Langley, Esquimalt, and Spallumcheen), one island municipality (Bowen), one resort municipality (Whistler), and one Indian government district (Sechelt). In addition, there are 164 unincorporated electoral areas where direct elections are held to choose representatives on regional district councils. Beyond these structures there are also fifty-nine school districts and five regional health authorities comprising sixteen health-service delivery areas. Once a municipality is designated as a specific type, this designation is altered only by local request. As a result, there are cities with fewer than 5,000 inhabitants, towns with populations over 5,000, and very populous district municipalities, such as Delta which has over 100,000 residents.[15]

Prior to 1965, British Columbians found it difficult to attain economies of scale for municipal service delivery for those living outside formally delineated municipalities or in densely populated areas containing many municipal governments. These conditions prompted the province to create regional districts in 1965. While regional districts' responsibilities vary, they have three traits in common: 1) regional districts provide a forum through which region-wide decisions can be taken by representatives selected from elected municipal councils or by direct election from non-incorporated electoral areas; 2) regional districts provide services of a regional nature, such as water supply, waste management, and sewage services, individual municipalities remaining free to opt-in as it suits their needs; and 3) they allow for considerable flexibility in form and function – though opting back out is more difficult once a municipality 'signs on' to a regional function.

Improvement districts in British Columbia are similar to regional districts in terms of purpose and services offered but operate on much smaller geographical areas and are more limited in their power and role. Unlike municipal or regional governments, improvement districts tend to provide specific services: 80 per cent of the 260 improvement districts provide a single service to their residents. The most common services provided by improvement districts are water services, fire protection, street lighting, and drainage. Improvement districts have a fairly wide mandate to tax, toll, or otherwise collect from residents for services provided.[16] There is also the Islands Trust, created in 1974, with a regional mandate to preserve and protect the environment of the southern Gulf Islands (lying between Vancouver

Island and the mainland). The Islands Trust Act created a trust council that may create by-laws, acquire and dispose of land, develop land-use policies, assist in the preservation of the environment on the islands, and work in other areas outlined within the act.[17] Environmental issues on the Gulf Islands render the trust's activities controversial.[18]

In addition to the standard types of local government created through the Local Government Act and the Community Charter, certain municipalities are governed by separate provisions and legislation. The most significant example of a separately constituted municipal body is the city of Vancouver, which is governed by its own charter. This contains provisions regarding elections, voting and elections financing, city council and mayoral duties, council powers and responsibilities, licensing, fire prevention, street traffic, health, property taxes, parks, planning and development, and heritage conservation. The city of Vancouver has some responsibilities not assigned to other municipalities, such as those pertaining to business taxation, public works, airports, and policing. As well, Vancouver possesses additional property and planning powers.[19] The municipality of Whistler is also covered by its own legislation, the Resort Municipality of Whistler Act, which establishes distinctive features of the municipality, such as the size of council, limits on borrowing and liabilities, development of local service areas, and service provision and charges. In 2007 the B.C. government also passed the Community Services Statutes Amendment Act, which allows existing municipalities to be redesignated as resort municipalities.[20] Under an accompanying B.C. Resort Municipality Revenue Sharing Program, an additional twelve municipalities (including seven mountain resort municipalities) are eligible for this designation, which will allow them a share of $10 million in provincial funding and the power to add 2 per cent to a hotel rental tax if they undertake a 'results-based' five-year tourism-development plan with the province.[21] As with many provincial initiatives in British Columbia, this is another example of 'gentle imposition' by the province.

Finally, with respect to First Nations, the beginnings of a modern treaty process in British Columbia suggest the growing development of relations between local/regional governments and aboriginal governments in more formal ways. The Greater Vancouver Regional District (GVRD), for example, is engaged in such discussions with the Tsawwassen First Nation regarding regional services.[22]

Functions

With few exceptions, the general list of functions of B.C. municipalities is not significantly different from the common list for local governments across the rest of Canada. In addition, the range of 'local' functions has not changed significantly in British Columbia over the past decade, with the exception of the GVRD, which until January 2008 had a degree of authority over regional transportation.[23] (British Columbia's new South Coast British Columbia Transportation Authority – still calling itself Translink – offers a new public management structure where local controls are reduced significantly.[24]) For the most part, regional districts still predominate in terms of 'hard' service delivery such as water, sewage, and drainage, while municipalities are more oriented towards protective, recreational, cultural, and other 'soft' services. Planning represents a joint exercise, with local governments responsible for zoning and Official Community Plans that must conform through Regional Context Statements to Regional District Plans.[25]

Until 2004, most of the legal basis for local powers was derived from the Local Government Act, completed in 2000 and replacing the long-standing B.C. Municipal Act. The Local Government Act clearly sets out the powers and responsibilities vested by the province in the municipal level of government. In addition, it describes how the powers of regional districts differ from municipal powers. The Local Government Act remains the primary legislative document for regional governments, and, though there is recognition that the forty-year-old, uniform regional district template needs some adjustment to accommodate major metropolitan areas, the province has largely been content to await some consensus on the issue among regional districts and the Union of British Columbia Municipalities.[26] At mid-2008, discussion between the UBCM and the province continues, with no legislative action anticipated prior to the May 2009 B.C. provincial general election.[27]

Recently, however, there have been signs of what may become a different approach. The ministerial decision to split the Vancouver Island Regional District of Comox-Strathcona (a regional district of only 100,000 population) represents new provincial thinking about the potential of customizing regional district solutions for particular circumstances. The 2008 decision to create the new regional districts of Comox Valley and of Strathcona was intended to deal with local political differences resulting from the fact that one part of the region was under considerable growth pressures.[28] A similar thrust aims to improve the performance of the Okanagan region.[29] This 'region' comprises three regional districts centred on Vernon, Kelowna, and Penticton and twelve other municipalities. Here the challenge is to encourage greater regional cooperation, particularly on economic development, perhaps through a process like Frankfurt's Regional Dialogue Forum.[30]

As noted above, the Local Government Act remains the primary legislative document for regional districts and also still defines important characteristics and functions of municipalities, such as elections, land-use planning, improvement districts, heritage conservation, and regional-growth strategies.[31] However, the 2004 Community Charter has become a significant provincial legislative document for municipal governments. This charter provides municipalities with a more flexible legal framework which, it is hoped, will increase the level of authority and autonomy of the municipal level of government.[32] Under the charter, municipal governments are defined as a 'democratically elected, autonomous, responsible and accountable order of government,' which is a distinct departure from past legislation that merely recognized the local level of government as a creature of the province.[33] The charter also confirms that municipal governments require adequate powers to deal with the present and future needs of their residents, to access the resources necessary to provide services, and to determine the public interest of their municipality. In addition, it stipulates that provincial and municipal governments respect each other's authority and jurisdiction, that consultation between the two levels is necessary in matters of mutual interest, and, perhaps most important, that the provincial government 'must not assign responsibilities to municipalities unless there is provision for resources required to fulfill the responsibilities.'[34]

Despite the increased autonomy of municipalities, provincial precedence is ultimately maintained. As the charter states, 'the authority of municipalities is balanced by the responsibility of the Provincial government to consider the interests of the citizens of British Columbia generally.'[35] This was clearly shown when the UBCM objected to the Significant Projects Streamlining Act, and the premier replied that 'what we were saying quite clearly is "We're not going to allow one municipality to hold up the provincial interest."'[36] Similarly, the legislative proposals contained in Bill 36, creating the new South Coast

British Columbia Regional Transportation Authority, seem to have brought much greater provincial control, a mere a decade after Greater Vancouver was made responsible for transportation and transit planning and development.[37]

Further functional changes may follow the GVRD decision of August 2007 to change the name of the regional district to 'Metro Vancouver.'[38] By mid-2008, the minister of community services had not 'allowed' the name change, preferring 'Metro Vancouver Regional District' to 'Metro Vancouver.' Use of the new name continues despite this lack of formal provincial recognition. Another area of contention concerns regional policing. Whereas some have called for a regional force, others, including key provincial ministers, seem to prefer the current mix of municipal forces and municipally contracted RCMP detachments.[39] With little likelihood of legislative changes for regional districts before the 2009 election, not much will happen on this file before Vancouver's 2010 Olympics.

Finance

While municipal governments in British Columbia historically relied on funds from senior governments, the province's municipalities are now almost entirely self-supporting. Local governments generate almost 85 per cent of their revenue from the property tax (45 per cent), property-related taxes (9 per cent), and sales of goods and services to residents (29 per cent). Only 7 per cent of revenue comes from provincial or federal transfers.

The shift from senior-government support to local self-reliance can be seen in the financial data in the appendix. There we see that total local tax revenue increased by 38 per cent between 1995 and 2004, while total transfers from federal and provincial governments dropped by 51 per cent. The most dramatic reduction has been in specific-purpose (or conditional) grants from the province, which have dropped by 62 per cent since 1995. Despite these provincial and federal cuts, overall local government revenue in British Columbia has risen by 26 per cent over the last decade. These same data show that the average B.C. municipality makes do with $386 per capita less than the average Canadian municipality, with about half of this representing lower senior-government transfers and half attributable to lower local taxes.

In 2004 total operating expenditures of B.C. municipalities amounted to $4.4 billion, with police, fire, and other protective services making up a quarter of this figure. Municipalities spent almost 20 per cent of operating expenditures on recreation and culture, 15 per cent on environmental services, and 14 per cent on transportation and communication. Lowest-priority operational expenditures include education, housing, social services, and health, all receiving less than 1 per cent of overall operational expenditure. Since 1995, general government, transportation/communication, and protection services, along with the environment and recreation and culture, have had the greatest operational expenditure increases, while health, debt charges, and other expenditures have seen the greatest decreases. In short, increases have been sharpest in the core areas of municipal activity. Reinforcing their low priority for municipal governments, housing and social services have also seen mild decreases in funding since 1995. This at a time when homelessness and related social-service challenges had a negative impact on B.C. municipalities, especially in metropolitan Vancouver and Victoria where in 2007, for example, there was a 14,000-person waiting list for social housing, with 9,000 from Greater Vancouver.[40]

Municipalities in British Columbia collectively spent $1.6 billion on capital projects in 2004. Of this amount, 17 per cent was spent on recreation and culture, 19 per cent on transportation/communication, and 37 per cent on the environment. Low-priority items – again – include social services and housing. The category with the biggest increase in capital expenditures between 1995 and 2004 was general government services (110 per cent).

Per capita combined operating and capital expenditure in B.C. municipalities in 2004 is remarkably similar to that in all other Canadian municipalities. The only major differences are in the areas of social services, where B.C. municipalities spent only 1 per cent of the Canadian average (a difference explained by the weight of Ontario municipalities, which are required to spend heavily on social services), and in recreation and culture, where they spent 25 per cent more than the Canadian average. Whereas municipal per capita spending on housing has increased since 1995 by more than 200 per cent across Canada (mainly accounted for by Ontario), the equivalent figure for British Columbia is only 7 per cent.

In sum, major challenges in the area of homelessness, housing, and social services continue to confront B.C. municipalities, especially in the larger urban centres. Yet local governments on their own show little capacity to resolve these issues without more horizontal policy making.[41] As Anne Golden and her fellow commissioners on Toronto

Mayor's Task Force concluded, the problems confront local governments but the solutions require multilevel governance.[42]

Provincial Oversight

The first Department of Municipal Affairs in British Columbia was established in 1934.[43] With three staff and a small budget, the department was responsible for administration, review, and processing of local by-laws, evaluation of administrative practices and procedures including financial management, special programs respecting building regulations, and regional planning processes for municipalities. After the mid-1960s, the department was also responsible for regional districts.[44] The department's name and purview remained constant for over four decades.

In 1976 the Department of Housing and the Department of Municipal Affairs were merged. In 1978 the housing function was transferred to the Ministry of Lands, Parks and Housing.[45] Following the election of Social Credit premier Bill Vander Zalm in 1986, a government-wide restructuring saw the creation of the Ministry of Municipal Affairs and Transit, and then two years later the Ministry of Municipal Affairs, Recreation and Culture absorbed all functions relating to culture, recreation, and historic resources.

The 1991 election of Michael Harcourt and his New Democratic Party produced more changes. All functions relating to culture were transferred to the Ministry of Tourism, while the housing functions were absorbed into the new Ministry of Municipal Affairs, Recreation and Housing. Two years later, recreation and housing were stripped away, only to be transferred back under the Glen Clark NDP government elected in 1996. With the election of Gordon Campbell and his Liberal government in 2001, the ministry responsible for municipal affairs was renamed the Ministry of Community, Aboriginal and Women's Services – or MCAWS. The B.C. media immediately referred to it as the 'Ministry of Lost Causes.'

Currently, provincial responsibility for municipal affairs falls under the control of the Ministry of Community Services. The ministry provides the legislative, policy, and regulatory framework for local government, as well as a number of advisory services. The ministry also partners with local governments, other ministries, and the federal government in coordinating resources to solve pressing issues such as those of the inner city.[46] Ministerial oversight is, in part, provided by an inspector of municipalities, a position that has existed in British Columbia since 1914. The inspector may intervene in municipal business if he or she 'believes it expedient to make an inquiry into or concerning a matter connected with a municipality or the conduct of a part of its business' or if 'a complaint is made to the inspector about a matter of municipal business, actual or projected.' If the inquiry finds that municipal actions are not in the public interest, the provincial government may compel the municipality to act in the manner the province sees fit.[47] This is a fairly rare occurrence.

The threat of ministerial intervention into municipal affairs has been tempered because the Community Charter now requires provincial ministers to consult with the Union of British Columbia Municipalities before reducing revenue transfers or repealing or amending the Community Charter, the Local Government Act, or the Local Government Grants Act. Ministers must also consult the UBCM before enacting, amending, or repealing regulations regarding property taxes or mandatory binding arbitration as set out in the Community Charter. However, the charter does not require the provincial government to involve the municipal level in the decision-making process. If a dispute arises between provincial and municipal governments, either party may request assistance to resolve the dispute. Yet arbitration is binding only if both parties agree to make it so, which effectively maintains provincial paramountcy.[48] The language of the Community Charter continues to underscore the theme of 'gentle imposition' in local-intergovernmental relations, but other laws, such as the Significant Projects Streamlining Act and the Farm Practices Protection (Right to Farm) Act, suggest that a degree of more traditional provincial-municipal thinking continues in the provincial capital.[49]

The Municipal Finance Authority (MFA) is an important municipal organization created in 1970 by Social Credit Minister of Municipal Affairs Dan Campbell, who was also the architect of the regional district system. Formed at the behest of the province, the MFA stands as another example of various provincial governments' supportive approach to municipal affairs in British Columbia. The MFA operates much like a credit union by pooling the borrowing needs of local governments, providing financing and investment management, and leasing financial services to local communities.[50] It is owned by the municipalities, with each municipality having one share and the province – other than enacting the legislation – playing no other role. It is run by a board of thirty-five members – all elected officials from the now twenty-eight regional districts along with additional members for the Capital Region District (two) and the Greater ('Metro') Vancouver Regional District (eight).[51] At present the credit rating of the MFA is set at AAA by Moody's Investors Service and at AA+ by Standard & Poor's Rating Service. This rating is actually higher than that of the province, and borrowing rates are lower than those of the province of Ontario. The MFA's success is such that since 1994 it has returned $250,000 to each member municipality annually.[52]

For the past couple of decades, the provincial government in British Columbia has described its oversight role with respect to the municipalities as 'rowing not steering.' While there is some truth in this image, an alternative view, and a more accurate one, is that the province's oversight can be best portrayed as 'rowing *and* steering.' The provincial government in British Columbia in therefore less different from its counterparts in the other Canadian provinces than its self-depiction might suggest.

Demographics

British Columbia is Canada's third most populous province, with its 4.3 million residents representing approximately 13 per cent of the total Canadian population.[53] Eighty-three per cent of the provincial population (or just under 3.5 million of its residents) resides in approximately 1 per cent of the overall provincial territory. Over half (54.4 per cent) live in the Vancouver-centred 'Lower Mainland,' which is described as the economic engine of the province.[54]

As shown in Figure 1, annual population growth rates fluctuated dramatically between Confederation and the First World War. However, these rates slowed and stabilized somewhat between 1914 and 2006, although there were some periods of higher growth during and after the Second World War. Later spikes can be attributed to various federal government immigration policies and events such as the 1986 World Exposition, hosted by British Columbia and Vancouver. The 2010 Olympics may have a similar impact.

Sixty-four per cent of those living in British Columbia reside in cities, 20 per cent in district municipalities (many of these highly urbanized), 3 per cent in towns and villages, and the remaining 13 per cent in unincorporated areas. These percentage figures have stayed constant for over a decade.[55] Just over half of the provincial population lives in municipalities located within the GVRD, which includes the

Figure 1: B.C. population and population growth (1867–2006)[56]

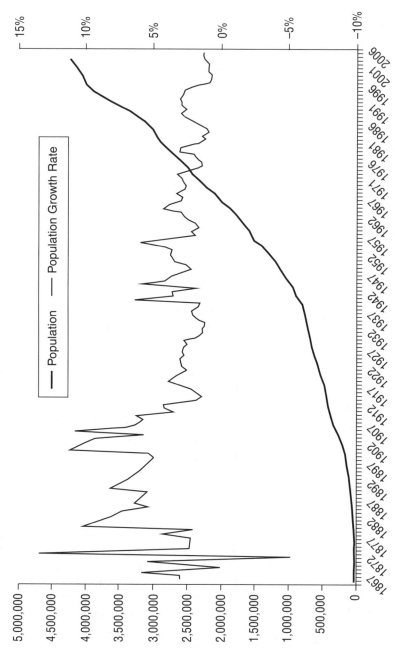

almost 600,000 residents of the city of Vancouver. Since 1986, the annual growth rate for the GVRD has been 2.1 per cent, with the region growing from 1,475,542 in 1986 to its 2006 size of 2,181,882.

British Columbia is now Canada's most ethnically diverse province: 25 per cent of the 2006 census population is from a visible minority (in Canada as a whole the figure is 16 per cent). One in ten residents is Chinese.[57] While those with some British ancestry continue to make up over one-third of the Vancouver's Census Metropolitan Area (CMA) population, South Asians and Chinese dominate among the region's 'more than 200 ethnic groups,' with 86.8 per cent of the province's visible minorities living in Greater Vancouver.[58] In 2005, of the 44,676 new permanent residents coming to British Columbia, 39,434 (88 per cent) chose to live in Greater Vancouver.[59] Of those immigrants, 73 per cent had Asian and Pacific origins, 11 per cent were from Europe, 9 per cent came from Africa and the Middle East, and the remaining 7 per cent were from other source areas.[60]

As a result of immigration, the ethnic make-up of Greater Vancouver makes it Canada's second-highest visible-minority CMA.[61] Some 41.7 per cent of the region's total 2006 population self-identified as a visible minority, which was just behind Toronto (42.9 per cent). The largest ethnic group is of Chinese origin – 18.2 per cent of the total population – with almost three-quarters born abroad.[62] Reflecting these immigration patterns, 61 per cent of the public-school population of the city of Vancouver has English as a second language.[63] These shifting demographics increasingly translate into political conflicts about who represents these communities and how political institutions might be adapted to be more reflective of the changing demographic, social, and cultural make-up of a region that has been affected strongly by globalization.[64]

No understanding of local governing in British Columbia can exclude the First Nations. Fifty-four per cent of Canada's aboriginal peoples now live in urban Canada.[65] There are 487 First Nation reserves in British Columbia, three Indian settlements, and the Nisga'a Indian Government District, which contains five Nisga'a villages. Aboriginals make up 4.4 per cent of the total population, with 123,785 identifying themselves as North American Indian and 44,265 as Métis.[66] Of British Columbia's urban population, 3.4 per cent are identified as aboriginal, while 10.4 per cent of the province's rural population is aboriginal. Most of the Indian reserves have very small populations, and 73 per cent of the aboriginal population live off-reserve.

Vancouver is second only to Winnipeg in off-reserve aboriginal people, and the Vancouver CMA has 40,310 aboriginals, representing 2 per cent of the population.[67]

Two elements underpinning the relations of B.C. municipalities with First Nations are noteworthy. The first concerns social differences. In Greater Vancouver, for example, 60 per cent of the 372 members of the Tsawwassen First Nation are under twenty-five years of age, whereas only 35 per cent of the population of the adjacent municipality of Delta fit this description. In Tsawwassen First Nation, average income is $20,065. In Delta it is $67,844. Unemployment in Delta stands at 7.4 per cent while it is 38 per cent in the Tsawwassen First Nation, where 40 per cent of the population lives on social assistance.[68] These stark differences have added to the tension between Delta residents and reserve residents, most of which involves land use and service provision. Even with the 2007 Tsawwassen vote in favour of the first modern urban treaty in British Columbia, this municipal-First Nation tension continues.[69]

The second element is that virtually all provincial lands in British Columbia are unceded by aboriginal peoples. The requirements of various Supreme Court decisions are pushing senior governments to settle outstanding claims.[70] The slow and largely unsuccessful treaty process (estimated to have cost $14 billion over the fourteen years of its existence) certainly adds to the complexity of local governing in British Columbia. For example, the Tsawwassen treaty cedes municipal, regional district, and provincial lands to the First Nation as well as requiring these authorities to negotiate further cooperative agreements on land use and service delivery. It also ensures First Nation representation on the GVRD board.[71]

Municipal and local levels of government already work with aboriginal groups and First Nations in a number of policy areas in the province. The Union of British Columbia Municipalities has drafted a number of agreements with the Lower Mainland Treaty Advisory Committee, including agreements on parks and recreation development, economic development and land use, capacity development, and resource management.[72] In terms of treaty negotiations, the provincial government and the UBCM signed two memoranda of understanding giving local governments a more important role in treaty negotiations than that of most third parties, but without granting negotiation power to local governments. In other words, local governments are 'in the room' but not 'at the table' at these meetings.[73]

Earlier attempts to accommodate the self-government requirements of the treaty process include the Sechelt Indian Government District and the Nisga'a District. In 1986 the Sechelt First Nation was given an array of self-government powers allowing it to operate much like a B.C. municipality.[74] While the 1999 Nisga'a agreement was much more comprehensive and extended greater powers,[75] few First Nations see either the Sechelt or the Nisga'a arrangement as a model for their self-governing aspirations. That a single model will accommodate aboriginal governance in the province is unlikely. But, as British Columbia's first 'urban treaty,' the Tsawwassen Treaty may offer a glimpse of the kind of municipal-First Nation regime that might emerge in urban British Columbia.

Organizations

There exist several important public organizations for municipalities in British Columbia. The Union of British Columbia Municipalities is the main representative of the collective rights and interests of local governments in the province. This organization has operated since 1905 and has significant input in provincial matters of municipal concern. It maintains offices and staff in both metropolitan Vancouver (Richmond) and Victoria. Through its executive, meetings, and conventions, the UBCM produces publications on numerous issues affecting municipalities, consults with the province on proposed policy changes affecting municipalities, and generally acts as the collective municipal representative at the provincial level. UBCM meetings normally include a full slate of provincial ministers and the premier along with opposition leaders and backbenchers, even during periods of fiscal stress and policy battles with the province.

While the capacity of the UBCM to influence matters provincial has ebbed and flowed over its first century, it has been a consistent player in local government policy making, perhaps most particularly over recent decades. Under the Glen Clark government (1996–9), the municipal affairs minister insisted on formal dialogue with the UBCM on legislative matters.[76] The UBCM significantly influenced the content of the NDP's Local Government Act(s) and the Community Charter. In addition, while the UBCM was not able to prevent passage of the Significant Projects Streamlining Act, its resistance may have dissuaded the province from resorting to the measure. In comparative terms, it could be argued that the UBCM represents one of Canada's most effective municipal organizations.[77]

Aside from the Municipal Finance Authority (discussed above), there are other municipal organizations in the province. For example, the Local Government Management Association represents local officials. It strives to promote professional management and leadership excellence in local government, and to create awareness of the local government officers' role in the community.[78] Canada's Institute of Public Administration also has Vancouver, Victoria, and northern B.C. chapters with many local officials participating.[79] The Municipal Insurance Association pools the resources of all provincial municipalities in order to achieve more favourable insurance rates.[80] The Municipal Information Systems Association is a specialized organization that promotes greater coordination between information-technology services in various municipalities.[81] Finally, there exist many regional municipal groups, such as the Lower Mainland Municipal Association, the North Central Municipal Association, the Association of Vancouver Island and Coastal Communities, the Okanagan Mainline Municipal Association, and the Association of Kootenay and Boundary Municipalities.[82]

Politics

Municipal elections in British Columbia are held every third November as stipulated by the Local Government Act and the Vancouver Charter. All mayors and councillors are elected at-large through multi-member plurality voting systems where the municipality is treated as a single constituency from which up to ten councillors are elected. In large municipalities, voters may be sometimes faced with a single ballot listing over 150 candidates from which to choose, with little information about these contestants or their policies. While council may, by by-law, allow some or all councillors to be elected from neighbourhood constituencies, no municipality has moved to implement a 'ward system' despite years of bitter debate on this issue in Vancouver and elsewhere.[83] At-large elections remain the norm in the province, even though they have been widely rejected in the rest of Canada.[84] Elections for regional district board members representing unincorporated areas are held on the same day as other municipal elections. (All other regional district directors are indirectly elected from municipal councils.) Costs for the elections are borne by the municipality or regional district unless other arrangements are made with the provincial government.

Candidates running in municipal elections are required to disclose only campaign contributions and expenses and there are no election-expense limits. Contributions must be made through the candidate's financial agent. Anonymous contributions cannot exceed $50 from any individual or corporation, and individuals, corporations, unincorporated commercial or business organizations, trade unions, non-profit organizations, and other contributors who donate more than $100 must be identified and classified as such.[85] Beyond this, there are no limits on contributions, and contribution records may be destroyed by individual municipalities after seven years.[86] Campaign financing is of particular concern in large municipalities such as Vancouver, where in 2005 the candidates together spent approximately $4 million campaigning to win council positions that pay salaries of just over $50,000.[87]

The complexities of distributing information to voters in at-large elections has spurred the growth of local political parties, especially in the largest municipalities such as Vancouver, Surrey, Victoria, and Burnaby. Smaller municipalities tend to be free of organized partisan activity or inclined towards more temporary slates of candidates. Vancouver has had a 'party' system of sorts in place since the 1930s when the right-leaning Non-Partisan Association (NPA) formed to counter candidates backed by the Co-operative Commonwealth Federation (CCF). While other parties have come and gone, the NPA has been a juggernaut, controlling majorities on council for most of the twentieth and early twenty-first centuries. NPA dominance was broken in the 1970s by the centrist Electors' Action Movement (TEAM), but it was not until 2002 that a left-leaning party gained control of Vancouver city council: in that election year, the Coalition of Progressive Electors (COPE) elected a mayor and eight (of ten) councillors. The Vancouver Green Party and the Vancouver Civic Action Team have also been involved in municipal politics in the city, and numerous other smaller parties have participated. The November 2005 civic election saw the return to Vancouver's natural ruling party – with the NPA winning five council seats and the mayoralty owing in no small part to the split of the left in the city.[88]

One of the most significant legislative changes undertaken by the province to foster the development of local political parties was a simple addition to the Municipal Act under NDP Premier Mike Harcourt in 1992. Harcourt, a former mayor of Vancouver, provided for the inclusion of local party names on municipal ballots. Most other jurisdictions do not have such a provision. In a province with at-large local elections, this change has become a reform of some significance, especially in British Columbia's larger centres.[89]

Other municipalities in the Lower Mainland also now have organized or semi-organized political associations and parties. Some of these also predate the Harcourt reform, as in Burnaby, British Columbia's third-largest city. There, the Burnaby Citizens Association (BCA) won the mayoralty and seven of the eight councillor positions in 2002, and maintained a majority in the 2005 elections. This leftist party has controlled Burnaby council since 1988.[90] Surrey also has major parties including the left-leaning Surrey Civic Electors and the right-of centre Surrey Electors Team. When Surrey's current mayor broke with Surrey's main party, she and three other women councillors formed an all-woman council grouping, and British Columbia's second-largest city now has a female majority on council.[91] Richmond has a significant party structure, with the Richmond First Voters Society, the Richmond Green Party, the Richmond Independent Team of Electors, the Richmond Non-Partisan Association, and Team Richmond all playing a part in civic politics. West Vancouver, Delta, Langley City, and Langley Township also have identifiable organized or semi-organized political parties. Victoria, too, has a party system of sorts, including the left-leaning Victoria Civic Electors.[92]

Voter turnout rates greatly vary for civic elections in British Columbia. Unlike provinces such as Quebec and New Brunswick where the provincial chief electoral officers collect and compile elections statistics, British Columbia has no official record-keeping system for municipal-election results, finance, or related matters. According to self-reported turnout rates of 108 of 157 municipalities published by the UBCM, the median turnout of registered voters in 2005 was 40 per cent. The village of Tahsis reported the highest turnout of 2005, with 94 per cent of those registered to vote casting ballots. The town of Sidney had the lowest turnout rate, just 9 per cent. Median voter turnout rates of different classifications of municipalities are as follows: district municipalities, 44 per cent; villages, 60 per cent; towns, 37 per cent; and cities, 30 per cent. Other types of municipalities (such as townships and resort municipalities) have a median turnout of 24 per cent.[93] In general, in British Columbia, the larger the municipality is, the lower the average turnout.[94] Kennedy Stewart has described this phenomenon as an understandable reaction on the part of voters in big cities where, under the at-large system, as many as 100-plus candidates may appear on the ballot.[95]

With respect to gender, women do not find anything approximating equality in political representation. The local-government profile shows that males dominate as both mayors and councillors across the province.[96] Before the most recent municipal elections, of all (but 2) municipalities, 125 mayors were male and only thirty female. Municipal councils were not as skewed, but there were still twice as many males on council as females, with 547 males and 270 females. Women tend to be better represented in smaller municipalities. On regional district boards (indirectly elected from municipal councils, except for unincorporated areas, which elect their own representatives directly), there were 296 men and 96 women, and chairs of the boards were also predominantly male, with almost 3 male chairs for every female (19 men, 7 women). In the Lower Mainland, women's representation is just slightly higher than for the province as a whole. There is a long way to travel before gender equality is achieved in British Columbia's local authorities.[97]

One of the main links between British Columbia municipal and provincial politics comes through the flow of locally elected officials to provincial office. For example, British Columbia premiers have increasingly come from the municipal pool of politicians. Since 1986, four of the seven premiers of the province have had their political start in municipal politics, each from Greater Vancouver. William Vander Zalm was mayor of Surrey before becoming premier, Rita Johnston served on Surrey city council, and Mike Harcourt and Gordon Campbell were both previously mayors of Vancouver. All were former GVRD directors. Former Liberal Deputy Premier Christy Clark moved in the other direction in her unsuccessful bid to become the NPA mayoral candidate in 2005, and so did Bill Vander Zalm, after his provincial failure in 1990, when he ran unsuccessfully for Vancouver mayor. The flow of GVRD-based municipal politicians to provincial office sometimes leads to tensions between this part of the province and 'the rest.' However, the tension is somewhat balanced by a more diverse UBCM leadership. For example, the recent presidents of that organization include politicians from Castlegar and Kelowna, and only two of the seventeen executive members hail from GVRD municipalities – a pattern with some history in the UBCM.

Conclusion

Taking effect in January 2004, the Community Charter offered the potential to usher in a new period in B.C. local governance and provincial-local relations. In replacing aspects of the Local Government Act (which remains in force), the charter grants several specific and important powers to municipal governments. First, and arguably most critically, municipal governments are now recognized as a separate and autonomous order of government, no longer simply a creature of the provincial government. Secondly, the Community Charter grants municipal governments all the powers, rights, privileges, and capacity of a natural person. This power – as with similar recent changes in several other Canadian provinces – enables local governments to act more freely in those areas in which they have jurisdiction without being limited to specifically prescribed corporate powers. Related to this, the number of municipal decisions subject to provincial approval has been reduced, though by no means eliminated. Finally, the provincial government must now consult with municipal governments if it plans to change the funding or responsibilities of municipalities (though it is difficult to see how this requirement would bind when services delivered to municipal residents by the province are merely abandoned and not passed to municipal governments).

Taken together, these changes have created an environment in which the local level of government is potentially more powerful and independent than used to be the case. In terms of process, these changes have generally followed the long-standing B.C. precedent of gentle imposition, with the province waiting for a degree of local, or regional, consensus before proceeding with legislative reform. At times, through this process, as with the creation of the Municipal Finance Authority, the province has 'encouraged' such local thinking – and then largely stepped back while local action emerges. In other instances, the province has positively responded to clearly expressed local wishes, such as when regional districts were created.[98]

With this new legislation, the province has not only accorded more autonomy to local governments but has also bound its hands to some extent regarding future legislative change. For example, the charter contains extensive requirements about provincial-municipal relations. The provincial government is now required to consult with the Union of British Columbia Municipalities regarding any proposed changes to legislation affecting municipalities, including reducing the amount of financial transfers, amending the Community Charter or the Local Government Act, changing property-tax rates or mandatory binding arbitration, and amending regulations under the Local Government Grants Act. The minister must not only provide information to the

UBCM and allow time for review, but must also respond to any concerns raised by the union. Despite all this, the actions of British Columbia's transportation minister regarding the building of the RAV (Richmond-Airport-Vancouver) transit line and the Sea to Sky highway to Whistler (the major highway-building proposals of the Pacific Gateway project), and the legislation significantly shifting powers away from the GVRD and Greater Vancouver Transportation Authority, support the conclusion that not all has changed in the province. More traditional Canadian provincial 'imposition' is evident in British Columbia when provincial interests are clear.[99]

Perhaps the worst shortcoming in the current legislation pertains to the accountability of the newly empowered local councils. In Peter Self's terms, the province facilitated the expansion of the efficiency side of the efficiency-accountability equation but has not ensured that council policy follows local public will.[100] We have argued elsewhere that democratic accountability is not addressed in the Community Charter – just as it was not in the Local Government Act.[101] That accountability deficit – a particular problem in British Columbia's larger municipalities and metropolitan regional districts – remains the major item on any 'what's left to do' list in British Columbia. The failure of the province – and of local and regional authorities – to address this, other than through the sort of window-dressing accountability frameworks set up for local school districts, continues to be significant. As suggested by the 2004 Vancouver Electoral Reform (Berger) Commission, elections in the city of Vancouver – and by extension other B.C. municipalities – should have electoral-finance controls, ward systems, proper result reporting, and oversight.[102] This would begin to improve local accountability in the province. Reforms to the Local Government Act in 2008 extended disclosure conditions to cover nomination periods but did nothing to set limits on contributions and spending. They also 'allowed' municipalities to post such information online but did not require it. Finally, they did nothing with regard to accurate and ongoing public record keeping.

In addition to changes to legislation governing municipalities, there has long been discussion of overhauling regional-government legislation. Not all agree on the need for this. For example, Robert Bish has noted that British Columbia local governance is effective for several reasons. First, municipalities and regional districts create a two-tiered local system that allows for services to be delivered at an acceptable scale. Highly localized issues, such as business licensing, can be undertaken by the municipal level, while services that would work better on a larger scale, such as sewage management, can be dealt with at a regional level. Secondly, these arrangements are flexible, allowing local governments to tailor service delivery and scale according to specific needs. Services can be delivered by the municipality or the regional district, but they can also be delivered by several municipalities without involving the entire region if the members so choose.[103] Andrew Sancton also supports the more flexible GVRD-like arrangements rather than more rigid forms of regional government such as one-tier mega-cities.[104] However, like their lower-tier municipal counterparts, regional districts also suffer from low accountability. Most regional district representatives are indirectly elected from local councils, and this makes it extremely difficult for voters to decide who is ultimately responsible for regional policy decisions.[105] Given the 2007 legislation that dismantled and reassembled the Greater Vancouver Transportation Authority, it seems that this view might be shared by the current B.C. government. Yet these legislative changes will do nothing to improve regional political accountability to citizens; instead, the South Coast British Columbia Transportation Authority will embody a much more corporate, new public management model, with far more potential for ministerial direction.

Many of the B.C. reforms of the past decade suggest a clear willingness on the part of provincial governments to consider the needs of municipal governments and generally to work collaboratively with the local level. Importantly, the local governmental reform process had a gestation period stretching over both NDP and Liberal governments, indicating that this collaborative streak is not simply a partisan characteristic. The municipalities have generally welcomed the collaborative approach and seem generally satisfied with those reforms based on it. These changes provide the potential for stronger, more cooperative intergovernmental relations, including general parameters for governments to follow and new dispute-resolution mechanisms. As an example, in April 2005, all three levels of government (with the UBCM representing the municipal level as a whole) signed an agreement to transfer federal gas taxes to local levels of government.[106] While there would likely be more resistance to any tri-level issue more contentious than this, the agreement indicated that there is some room for multilevel cooperation and collaboration in British Columbia. The province has since let the UBCM act as distributor of these funds to British Columbia's municipalities. That, and examples such as Vancouver's Safe/Supervised Injection Site (SIS), suggest some ongoing recognition that many of the major 'city' issues will require such multilevel cooperation.

The need for multilevel solutions to major city issues and its recognition by governments would seem to be a necessary condition for achieving good public policy in Canada's municipalities. In this respect, British Columbia and its local governments are not different from most municipalities and provinces in Canada. The worrying bit for advocates of local autonomy in this more multi-governing world (whether in municipal or regional form) is that in British Columbia the province still uses its heavy hand often enough to allow the conclusion that more traditional thinking about local-senior government relations continues to find significant expression.

NOTES

Primary research assistance was provided by Dion Curry, MA, political science, Simon Fraser University (SFU), and PhD candidate, Sheffield University, with additional research assistance by Matt Bourke, MPP, SFU, and Kevin Ginnell, PhD candidate, SFU. The authors also thank the editors for their contribution to this chapter.

1 Paul Tennant and David Zirnhelt, 'Metropolitan Government in Vancouver: The Politics of Gentle Imposition,' *Canadian Public Administration*, vol. 16 (spring 1973): 124–38.
2 Kenneth Grant Crawford, *Canadian Municipal Government* (Toronto: University of Toronto Press, 1954), 47.
3 The Honourable Ida Chong, 'Queen Charlotte Becomes B.C.'s Newest Municipality' [press release], 8 July 2005, Ministry of Community Services, http://www2.news.gov.bc.ca/news_releases_2005-2009/2005 CS0061-000662.htm.
4 Patrick Smith and Kennedy Stewart, 'Local Government Reform in British Columbia, 1991–2005: One Oar in the Water,' in Joseph Garcea and Edward C. LeSage, Jr, eds., *Municipal Reform in Canada: Reconfigurations, Re-Empowerment and Rebalancing* (Don Mills, Ont.: Oxford University Press, 2005), 25–56.
5 Patrick J. Smith and Kennedy Stewart, *Making Local Accountability Work in British Columbia* (Vancouver: Institute of Governance Studies, Simon Fraser University, 1996), government-commissioned report for B.C. Ministry of Municipal Affairs and Housing.

6 As a B.C. example, Vancouver ranks lowest among eight major Canadian cities on a range of indices of effective political control by councils. See Patrick Smith and Kennedy Stewart, 'Immature Policy Analysis: Building Capacity in Eight Major Canadian Cities,' in L. Dobuzinskis, M. Howlett, and D. Laycock, eds., *Policy Analysis in Canada: The State of the Art* (Toronto: University of Toronto Press/IPAC Series in Public Management and Governance, 2007), 265–87.

7 On this, see, for example, Patrick Smith, 'British Columbia Changes Metro Vancouver's Transportation Governance – A Re-Examination of Peter Self's "Dilemma Thesis": Efficiency vs. Accountability?' *Local Matters*, Institute of Public Policy, Auckland University of Technology, New Zealand, vol. 2, http://www.ip.pnz..org, April 2008, 2–5.

8 Robert L. Bish and Eric G. Clemens, *Local Government in British Columbia*, 3rd ed. (Richmond, B.C.: Union of British Columbia Municipalities, 2007).

9 Union of British Columbia Municipalities (UBCM), *UBCM: The First Century* (Richmond, B. C.: Union of British Columbia Municipalities, 2005), 3–4.

10 Ibid., 24–6, 39–60.

11 The NDP was first in office in British Columbia during 1972–5 but did little on the municipal front other than to create the Islands Trust and the Agricultural Land Reserve and Commission. See Neil Swainson, 'The Provincial-Municipal Relationship,' in T. Morley et al., eds., *The Reins of Power: Governing British Columbia* (Vancouver: Douglas and McIntyre, 1983), 237–69.

12 Smith and Stewart, 'Local Government Reform in British Columbia.'

13 Robert L. Bish, *Local Government in British Columbia* (Richmond, B.C.: Union of British Columbia Municipalities, 1990), 9. This was also a point made by then Municipal Affairs Minister Mike Farnworth (a former Port Coquitlam city councillor) as part of his rationale for initiating the Local Government Act as a replacement for British Columbia's prior Municipal Act. (Interview with the authors, Vancouver, 1998.)

14 P.J. Smith and Kennedy Stewart, 'Local Whole of Government Policymaking in Vancouver: Beavers, Cats, and the Mushy Middle Thesis,' in Robert Young and Christian Leuprecht, eds., *Municipal-Federal-Provincial Relations in Canada* (Series: Canada: The State of the Federation, 2004) (Montreal and Kingston: McGill-Queen's University Press, 2006), 251–72.

15 UBCM, 'Fact Sheet 22: Municipal Facts and Figures' (2002), http://ubcm.ihostez.com/content/pdfstorage/207616182526200331721PM60421.pdf.

16 UBCM, 'Fact Sheet 17: Municipal Facts and Figures' (2002), http://ubcm
.ihostez.com/content/pdfstorage/207616182526200330233PM7864.pdf.

17 Patrick Smith, 'Regional Governance in BC,' *Planning and Administration*,
vol. 13 (1987): 7–20; and David Jones, 'The Islands Trust on the Local
Government Continuum: Administrative Agency or Local Self Government,' MA thesis, Department of Political Science, SFU, 1994.

18 Terry Glavin, 'Islanders Lose Grip on Forests,' 25 May 2006, *Georgia
Straight*, http://www.straight.com/article/islanders-lose-grip-on-forests-0.

19 See Vancouver Charter, Revised Statutes of British Columbia (RSBC),
http://www.qp.gov.bc.ca/statreg/stat/v/vanch_21.htm.

20 The Honourable Ida Chong, 'New Amendments Mean Vibrant, Sustainable Communities' [press release and backgrounder], 13 March 2007,
Ministry of Community Services,
http://www2.news.gov.bc.ca/news_releases_2005-2009/2007CS0014-
000223.htm.

21 http//www.cserv.gov.bc.ca/gov_structure/resort_mum_program/eligi-
ble_muns.htm.

22 http//www.tsawwassenfirstnation.com and the Lower Mainland Treaty
Advisory Committee (www.lmtac.com).

23 Smith, 'British Columbia Changes Metro Vancouver's Transportation
Governance.'

24 Interview with Derek Corrigan, mayor of Burnaby, and GVRD land use
and transportation chair, 14 May 2008.

25 Bill Lane, 'Ensuring Sustainable Land Use,' Bob Bose, 'Metropolitan Governance and Strategic Planning in Greater Vancouver,' and Patrick Smith,
'Urban Governance and Growth Management: Greater Vancouver and
British Columbia,' in P. Smith, T. Hutton, and H.P. Oberlander, eds.,
Urban Solutions to Global Problems: Vancouver-Canada-Habitat II (Vancouver: UBC Centre for Human Settlements/SFU-IGS, 1996), 27–33, 143–51,
and 156–68 respectively.

26 Gary Paget, executive director and deputy inspector of municipalities,
Governance and Structure Division, Local Government Department, Ministry of Community Services, Victoria, telephone interview, 8 October
2006; Brian Walisser, executive director, Policy and Research Division,
Local Government Department, Ministry of Community Services, Victoria, telephone interview, 8 October 2006.

27 Interview with Marie Crawford, associate executive director, UBCM, 13
May 2008.

28 See http://www.rdcs.bc.ca/notices. As of 15 February 2008, the two new
regional districts had had their inaugural meetings.

29 Conversation with B.C. Ministry of Community Services staff, 21 August 2007.

30 Regional Dialogue Forum, Frankfurt, Germany, www.dialogforum-flughafen.de.

31 Minister of State for Community Charter, 'The Community Charter: A Discussion Paper,' http://www.civicinfo.bc.ca/Local_Content/Briefs-Backgrounders/3343.PDF.

32 Ministry of Community Services, 'Highlights of the Community Charter,' http://www.mcaws.gov.bc.ca/charter/legislation/highlights.htm.

33 Community Charter, Statutes of British Columbia (SBC), 2003, c. 26, s. 1(1).

34 Ibid.

35 Ibid.

36 *UBCM: The First Century*, 222.

37 Bill 36, The Greater Vancouver Transportation Authority Amendment Act, 2007, http://www.leg.bc.ca/38th3rd/1st_read/gov36-1.htm. This change followed the report of the Translink Governance Review Panel. See http://www.th.gov.bc.ca/translinkreview/documents/TranslinkReport_070126.pdf.

38 See Chad Skelton, 'Goodbye GVRD, Hello Metro Vancouver: Changing Times, Changing Names,' Vancouver *Sun*, 3 August 2007, and interview with Derek Corrigan (mayor of Burnaby), 14 May 2008.

39 Matthew Ramsey, 'Merge Police Forces, Says Senior Officer: One Department Best Way to Suppress Violence,' *The Province*, 25 March 2007. For a fuller discussion of Metropolitan Vancouver governance, see P.J. Smith, 'Even Greater Vancouver: 21st Century Reforms in Canada's Third Largest City Region,' in Don Phares, ed., *Who Will Govern Metropolitan Regions in the 21st Century?* (Armond, N.Y.: M.E. Sharpe, 2008).

40 See Miro Cernetig, 'BC Targets Homeless with Riverview Project,' Vancouver *Sun*, 27 July 2007.

41 Kennedy Stewart and Patrick Smith, 'Building Provincial Capacity to Solve Urban Aboriginal Homelessness in Vancouver,' paper for the British Columbia Political Studies Association, Abbotsford, B.C., 3 May 2008; and Kennedy Stewart and Patrick Smith, 'Sins of Omission: Multi-level Policy Disasters and Community Responses – Vancouver's Aboriginal Peoples,' paper for the Canadian Political Science Association, Vancouver, June 2008.

42 *Taking Responsibility for Homelessness*, Report of the Mayor's Homelessness Action Task Force (Toronto: City of Toronto, January 1999).

43 Department of Municipal Affairs Act, SBC 1934, c. 52.

44 British Columbia Archival Information Network, Ministry of Municipal Affairs fonds, 1936–81, http://aabc.bc.ca/access/aabc/archbc/display/BCA-2042.

45 Ibid.

46 Ministry of Community Services, *2005/06 Annual Service Plan Report* (Victoria: Ministry of Community Services, 2006). For an example of the complexities of partnership, see Francis Bula, 'Addict Programs Get $10 Million: Ottawa Allocates Funds to Treat Downtown Eastside Users but Remains Silent on Insite,' Vancouver *Sun*, 5 May 2008.

47 Local Government Act, RSBC, 1996, c. 323, pt. 29.

48 Community Charter, c. 26, s. 285.

49 Significant Projects Streamlining Act, SBC, 2003, c. 100; Farm Practices Protection (Right to Farm) Act, RSBC, 1996, c. 131.

50 Municipal Finance Authority (MFA) of British Columbia, 'About the MFA,' n.d., http://www.mfa.bc.ca/about.htm.

51 Municipal Finance Authority Act, RSBC, 1996, c. 325.

52 MFA, 'About the MFA.'

53 Statistics Canada, 'Canada's Population,' *The Daily*, 28 September 2007, http://www.statcan.ca/Daily/English/060927/d060927a.htm.

54 David Bond, 'Sustaining the Metropolitan Economy,' in Smith, Oberlander, and Hutton, eds., *Urban Solutions to Global Problems*, 68–71. See also Craig Davis and Thomas Hutton, 'The Two Economies of British Columbia,' *BC Studies*, vol. 82 (1989): 3–15.

55 Ibid.

56 All figures from British Columbia Statistics, 'Population and Demographics,' 2007, http://www.bcstats.gov.bc.ca/DATA/pop/popstart.

57 Ibid, 22. Some 73 per cent of British Columbia's ethnically Chinese population is also 'foreign-born.'

58 See *Canada's Ethnocultural Mosaic, 2006 Census, Catalogue 97-562-X* (Ottawa: Statistics Canada: April 2008), 22.

59 Citizenship and Immigration Canada, 'Facts and Figures 2005, Immigration Overview: Permanent and Temporary Residents,' http://www.cic.gc.ca/english/resources/statistics/facts2005/overview/index.asp.

60 Ibid.

61 Ibid, 32.

62 Ibid., 32–3.

63 Figures from Catherine Eddy, manager, Vancouver School Board (VSB) Reception Centre, Vancouver, 27 September 2006. The VSB uses two definitions in describing students belonging to the ESL (English as a second language) category. Its 'broad' definition includes any student who has

learned a first language other than English or whose mother tongue home language is neither English nor French. The narrower definition includes students actually needing ESL assistance for low English-language skills. In 2005–6 the latter definition applied to 25.2 per cent of the public-school student population in Vancouver.

64 Patrick Smith, 'The Making of a Global City: Fifty Years of Constituent Diplomacy – The Case of Vancouver,' *Canadian Journal of Urban Research*, vol. 1 no. 1 (1992): 90–112. Caroline Andrew and Patrick Smith, 'World Class Cities: Can or Should Canada Play?' in Caroline Andrew, Pat Armstrong, and André Lapierre, eds., *World Class Cities: Can Canada Play?* (Ottawa: University of Ottawa Press, 1999), 5–26.

65 Statistics Canada, *Aboriginal Peoples in Canada in 2006: Inuit, Metis and First Nations, 2006 Census, Catalogue # 97-558-XIE* (Ottawa: Statistics Canada, 2008), 13.

66 British Columbia Statistics, 'British Columbia Statistical Profile of Aboriginal Peoples 2001,'
http://www.bcstats.gov.bc.ca/data/cen01/abor/tot_abo.pdf.

67 Statistics Canada, *Aboriginal Peoples in Canada in 2006*, 42, 13.

68 Tsawwassen First Nation, 'Who We Are,' 2007, http://www.tsawwassen-firstnation.com/whoweare.php.

69 See 'Treaty Still Needs Provincial and Federal Legislative Approval,' Vancouver *Sun*, 27 July 2007.

70 *Delgamuukw v. British Columbia* [1997] 3 S.C.R. 1010.

71 See Tsawwassen First Nation, 'Who We Are.'

72 UBCM, 'Regional District and First Nation Governments: Building Effective Relations,' 2005, http://ubcm.fileprosite.com/content/pdfstorage/440241417119200530422PM62174.pdf.

73 UBCM, 'Negotiating Modern Day Treaties,' 2007,
http://www.civicnet.bc.ca/siteengine/activepage.asp?PageID=7.

74 Sechelt Indian Government District Enabling Act, RSBC, 1996, c. 416.

75 Nisga'a Final Agreement Act, SBC, 1999, c 2.

76 Interview with Mike Farnworth, October 1997.

77 Interview with Marie Crawford, associate executive director, UBCM, 13 May 2008.

78 Local Government Management Association of British Columbia, 'About the Local Government Management Association,' http://www.lgma.ca/about.php.

79 Institute of Public Administration of Canada, 'Regional Groups,' 2006, http://www.ipac.ca/regional/index.html.

80 Municipal Insurance Association, 'Home,' 2007, http://www.miabc.org/.

81 Municipal Information Systems Association, 'MISA BC,' 2007,
    http://www.misa.bc.ca/.
82 A full listing of links can be found on the UBCM's civicnet website,
    under 'BC Associations,'
    http://www.civicnet.bc.ca/siteengine/ActivePage.asp?PageID=104.
83 Kennedy Stewart, 'Measuring Local Democracy: The Case of Vancouver,'
    Canadian Journal of Urban Research, vol. 6, no. 2 (1997): 60–83.
84 Kennedy Stewart, *Think Democracy: Local Options for Democracy Reform in
    Vancouver* (Vancouver: Institute of Governance Studies Press, Simon
    Fraser University, 2003).
85 Local Government Act, c. 323, s. 90(4)(b); Vancouver Charter, SBC 1953, c.
    55, pt. 1(8).
86 Denisa Gavan-Koop, Stephanie Vieille, and Patrick Smith, 'A Tale of 27
    Cities: Questions on Accountability, Right to Know and Local Governing
    in British Columbia,' paper for the British Columbia Political Studies
    Association, North Vancouver, B.C., May 2007.
87 Frances Bula, 'Civic Parties Spent Record $4 Million on Election,' Vancou-
    ver *Sun*, 21 March 2006.
88 Kennedy Stewart and Patrick Smith, 'The COPE Interlude. The (Pre-
    dictable) Rise & Fall of Vancouver's Radical Civic Left 2002–2005.' Paper
    for the Canadian Political Science Association, York University, Toronto,
    June 2006.
89 Smith and Stewart, 'Local Government Reform in British Columbia.'
90 Interview, Derek Corrigan, mayor of Burnaby, 14 May 2008.
91 Denisa Gavan and Patrick Smith, 'Gendering Governing in British
    Columbia: Local vs. Federal and Provincial Experiences in Metropolitan
    Vancouver,' paper for the B.C. Political Studies Association, North Van-
    couver, May 2006.
92 Smith and Stewart, *Making Local Accountability Work.*
93 UBCM, 'Civic Election Results,' 2007,
    http://www.civicnet.bc.ca/siteengine/ActivePage.asp?PageID=34.
94 Smith and Stewart, *Making Local Accountability Work.*
95 See Stewart, 'Measuring Local Democracy.'
96 These numbers were developed through searching municipal websites
    and Civicinfo resources.
97 Gavan and Smith, 'Gendering Local Government in British Columbia.'
98 H. Peter Oberlander and Patrick J. Smith, 'Governing Metropolitan Van-
    couver: Regional Intergovernmental Relations in British Columbia,' in
    Donald N. Rothblatt and Andrew Sancton, eds., *Metropolitan Governance:
    American/Canadian Intergovernmental Perspectives* (Berkeley, Calif., and

Kingston, Ont.: Institute of Governmental Studies Press, University of California, Berkeley, and Institute of Intergovernmental Relations, Queen's University, 1993), 329–73.

99 Interview, Dr Nancy Olewiler, B.C. Transit Board member, 14 May 2008.

100 Peter Self, *Administrative Theories and Politics* (London: Allen and Unwin, 1977), chapter 8.

101 Smith and Stewart, 'Local Government Reform in British Columbia.'

102 Thomas H. Berger, *A City of Neighbourhoods: Report of the 2004 Vancouver Electoral Reform Commission* (Vancouver: City of Vancouver, 2004), http://www.city.vancouver.bc.ca/erc/.

103 Robert L. Bish, 'Accommodating Multiple Boundaries for Local Services: British Columbia's Local Governance System,' paper presented at a colloquium at the Workshop in Political Theory and Policy Analysis, Indiana University, Bloomington, 21 October 2002.

104 Andrew Sancton, *Merger Mania: The Assault on Local Government* (Westmount, Que.: Price/Paterson, 2000).

105 Smith and Stewart, *Making Local Accountability Work in British Columbia.*

106 Canada, British Columbia, and the UBCM, *Agreement on the Transfer of Federal Gas Tax Revenue under the New Deal for Cities and Communities 2005–2015*, 19 September 2005.

7 Prince Edward Island

DAVID BULGER AND JAMES SENTANCE

Prince Edward Island is a small place. It is small in land area and small in population. Size accounts for a number of anomalies, not the least of which is the fact that, while it has the smallest population, the Island also has the highest population density of any province in Canada.[1] It is this high density that sometimes perplexes outside observers, especially when it is put into the perspective of community incorporation. Few places in Prince Edward Island that are identifiable 'localities' have undergone the incorporation provided for by the Municipalities Act, occasioning mystification, if not consternation, on the part of at least one federal minister.[2]

Over against this high population density must be placed one salient fact: the population of the entire province, slightly in excess of 135,000, would barely clear the threshold necessary for the designation of a municipality as a Census Metropolitan Area (CMA). The Island population is smaller than the smallest of the twenty-five largest CMAs. The twenty-seven members of the Legislative Assembly represent, on average, 5,000 people. In some CMAs, municipal councillors represent up to ten times this number.[3] As a result, a great many people on the Island will tend to look to the provincial government rather than some other level for the provision of services. This fact may go some distance towards explaining at least two things: the provincial involvement in services that would be municipal in other jurisdictions, and the reluctance of people in many localities to interpose another level of government, incorporated municipal government, between themselves and the province.

It has always been this way. St John's Island was a prize of war, part of the French North American possessions ceded to the British crown by the Treaty of Paris in 1763. One year later, Captain Samuel Holland was dispatched to undertake a complete survey of the king's new property. He started his survey with St John's Island. 'The Island was to be divided into three counties of roughly 500,000 acres each, the counties in turn to be divided into "parishes." Each parish was to be surveyed into "townships" of 20,000 acres.'[4] The western county was called Prince, the central one Queens, and the eastern county Kings. Holland also laid out a county seat for each county, namely George-town (King's), Charlottetown (Queen's), and Princetown (Prince), a never realized settlement on the shores of Malpeque Bay.

Like Princetown, the vague physical outlines of which may still be seen near the community of Malpeque, these governmental divisions remained vague. The counties never functioned as counties (and, cur-rently, so little meaning attaches to county divisions that the incorpo-rated community of Malpeque lies partly in Prince County and partly in Queens). Indeed, for a century, with the exception of the creation of the city of Charlottetown in 1855, the only 'municipal' government was the province itself, which regularly administered, through legisla-tion, the affairs of what today are incorporated municipalities. Coun-ties, parishes, and townships remained lines on the map, the only def-erence to counties being the holding of quarter sessions at Georgetown, Charlottetown, and Summerside (which supplanted the ghostly Princetown). Indeed, it was not until 1982 that one of the town-ships, 'Lot'[5] 11, incorporated itself as the 'Community of Lot 11,' that is, a municipality (and even then, the incorporation did not include all of the lot).

The size of the population, coupled with the small land mass, has tended to dictate that intervening levels of government be regarded as superfluous. For much of the Island, the province suffices. Otherwise, incorporated municipalities represent the limit to which any further subdivision of government need extend. Counties are meaningless, parishes forgotten, and regions non-existent. And, as we will see, the number of identifiable localities that are not incorporated far exceeds the number that are. Seemingly, in a very real sense, the provincial government is also, in large measure, a municipal one.

The Province as Municipality: A Brief History

The General Assembly of St John's Island began legislating in 'munic-ipal' matters early in its existence. Not all early legislation is extant, so there may have been acts as early as 1773, when the Assembly first met. However, setting aside a 1780 act preventing 'the running at large of Stone Horses or Stallions,' which had municipal implications, the first recorded piece of legislation is the 1781 act 'to prevent disorderly riding of Horses, and driving of Carts, Trucks and Sleds, or any other Carriage whatsoever within *Charlotte Town*.'[6]

While the original does not survive, legislation in 1786 amended a 1781 act 'for raising a Fund to make and keep in repair the Streets and Wells of *Charlotte Town*.' This was the first municipal-assessment legislation in the province, providing for a tax on real property in the town. On the other hand, it did not establish a municipal system of government but rather appointed overseers who were responsible for the quality of the well water and for removing nuisances from the streets. They reported directly to the governor. Only later, with further amendment to this piece of legislation, was there provision for assembling the inhabitants in a sort of 'town meeting,' but this was not yet a municipal council.

Between 1781 and 1832, legislation that was specifically municipal was directed only to the town of Charlottetown. Other acts dealing with land use, highways, fences, and so forth might well affect other communities, but Charlottetown alone was specifically regulated by acts of the Assembly. Thus, the firing off of 'Guns and other Fire-Arms' was regulated 'in the town and suburbs of *Charlotte Town*' (1790), the running at large of 'Geese' was prohibited (1795), fire prevention was addressed and 'fire-wards' created, trespasses by unruly 'Horses, Cattle and Sheep' and the 'running at large of Hogs' were prohibited, 'Hog Reeves' were appointed (1825), and provision was made for the establishment of a 'Fire Engine Company' (1827).

In 1832 the Assembly acted to prevent the running at large of swine in Princetown and legislated an 'Act to Provide for the Better Preservation of Public and Private Property at Georgetown against Accidents by Fire.' While Charlottetown continued to dominate the Assembly's attention, both Georgetown and Princetown were often the subjects of legislation. Summerside joined them in 1858 (running at large of swine). Provincial care continued until Charlottetown was incorporated by an act of the Assembly in 1855[7] and Summerside twenty-two years later, in 1877.[8]

However, between the incorporation of Charlottetown and the incorporation of Summerside, probably owing to the growth of communities throughout the Island, in 1870 the government brought in what may be termed its first real municipal act, 'An Act for the Better

Government of Certain Rising Towns and Villages in this Island.'⁹ This
act contained many elements that are continued in the current Municipalities Act, including the voluntary nature of municipality formation
by petition, or, more strictly, by a 'memorial' to the lieutenant-governor-in-council from a number of inhabitants 'deemed sufficient.' In
addition, the act provided for the election of wardens, required the
wardens to be residents of the community, and empowered them to
appoint their chair – all like the current legislation. Again, as in the
Municipalities Act, the lieutenant-governor-in-council could change
the boundaries of the community, and the municipality was a corporate body with the power to make by-laws and to appoint a secretary-
treasurer, who could not be a warden. Finally, in language that is actually more clear than the current act, a warden who missed meetings for
three months lost his seat.

The Rising Towns and Villages Act was continued with revisions
until 1948, when it was repealed and replaced by 'An Act to Provide
Uniform Legislation for the Towns of Prince Edward Island,' known
by its shorter title, the Town Act.[10] The Town Act, in turn, was replaced
by the current legislation, the Municipalities Act, in 1988, at the time of
a general revision and consolidation of the PEI statutes.

There is one more piece of legislation that must be noted, and that is
the Act Respecting Public Schools, enacted in 1877,[11] which replaced
earlier acts from 1825 and 1852. While public schools then, as now, fell
under provincial jurisdiction not municipal, there is a provision in this
piece of legislation that, in a curious way, has an effect upon the
current municipal situation in Prince Edward Island.

Section 5 of the act empowered the provincial Board of Education to
divide the province into school districts, no district containing 'less
than forty resident children between the ages of five and sixteen years.'
In 1877 farm families tended to be large, and so it is not inconceivable
that four or five families would easily provide the requisite forty 'resident children.' Thus, the number of school districts was large as well.

The districts had to be identified by name. Such an identification,
while not a municipal one, was still *official* and recorded. Consequently, these school districts became places that, while falling far
short of any real municipal character, appeared on maps. For example,
in Township 11, Foxley River, Freeland, Murray Road, Conway, and
Inverness appear on current highway maps (whereas 'Frederick Cove,'
never a school district, does not). A visitor passing through would not
see much 'municipal' character to these places. On the contrary, each

is a sparse scattering of houses and farms. They are villages in name only. But each appears on the 2005 highway map because each was a named school district.

The significance of this lies in the current concern that there are a large number of unincorporated communities on Prince Edward Island. Since the vast number of these places would probably not have been officially identified had they not been school districts, PEI may be said to have more 'official' places than other provinces. What would otherwise be simply a spot along the highway has the official character of a village – but only because of the Act Respecting Public Schools. Thus, the apparent imbalance in incorporation may be largely a chimera.

Legislation

Municipalities on Prince Edward Island are governed by a number of provincial statutes. In some instances, the inclusion is 'consequential,' an effect of legislation that has a broader object but necessarily touches on municipal governments. In other instances, acts are more specifically directed to municipalities, and the Planning Act in particular will be dealt with later in this chapter.

As far as the specific organization of municipalities is concerned, there are three enabling statutes. The two cities have their own constitutive legislation, the Charlottetown Area Municipalities Act[12] and the City of Summerside Act,[13] respectively. Partially this stems from the fact that both cities were originally incorporated by separate acts of the legislature, but mainly it is because the current legislation also achieves the effect of amalgamating a number of former municipalities into expanded communities. The Charlottetown Area Municipalities Act creates two adjoining towns as well, Cornwall to the west and Stratford across the Hillsborough River to the south. Both Cornwall and Stratford are the result of amalgamations too.[14] The third piece of legislation is a general Municipalities Act[15] for the province as a whole. While certain provisions apply to Charlottetown and Summerside, this act is concerned with other incorporated communities in the province, both in their constitution and in their governance.

All three pieces of legislation have clear similarities. In each instance, the municipality is constituted a 'corporation,' as that word is understood under the terms of section 16 of the Interpretation Act.[16] That section vests the familiar corporate powers, namely, to sue and be sued, to enter into contracts, to hold real property, to regulate proceedings and business, and so on. Municipalities, under the law of Prince Edward Island, are 'legal persons' and their powers are limited to the functions set out in law. Those powers, in general terms, are found in 'shopping lists' included in each of the three acts. Though there are five different lists (since the Charlottetown Area Municipalities Act is divided into three parts, one for the city of Charlottetown, one for the town of Stratford, and one for the town of Cornwall, each with its list of powers), they are virtually identical and include those functions that would typically be regarded as 'municipal,' for example, sewer and water and solid-waste collection.

On the other hand, these shopping lists are precisely that: an expression of a broad range of *possible* municipal powers. In reality, a number of functions are either not realized at all – in the case of smaller municipalities – or are actually performed by the provincial government. While this will be discussed shortly, when municipal services are addressed, one significant example may suffice: only the cities of Charlottetown and Summerside have responsibility for their streets. In all the other seventy-three incorporated communities, the care and maintenance of the roads falls to the provincial Department of Transportation and Public Works.[17]

In the case of communities, there is one significant check on municipal powers. Section 36 of the Municipalities Act requires the council of a community to prepare estimates for the cost of services to be voted on by the community at large at the annual meeting provided for by section 55 of the act. In addition, section 55 provides that 'matters of concern' may be discussed at the annual meeting. This constraint does not apply to towns or cities, however, and two recent high-profile controversies, both surrounding the construction of town halls in Stratford (constructed) and Cornwall (initially deferred in response to community complaints but eventually constructed), may prompt a move to extend the provisions of section 55 to towns at least.

Those persons who responded to interviews during this study thought, by and large, that the legislated powers were sufficient.[18] This positive reaction was equally divided between 'government' respondents and 'others.' Since 28 per cent of respondents either misunderstood the question, interpreting 'powers' as financial power, or did not actually address the question, the nearly 94 per cent of the rest who thought that powers were sufficient, either across the board or at least in cities, is significant. Development Minister Mike Currie said that 'generally speaking, municipalities have sufficient powers to provide services that citizens expect of them,' and this was echoed by Summerside's mayor, Basil Stewart. Charlottetown Mayor Clifford Lee thought that municipalities ought to have broader powers of taxation, while opposition MLA Richard Brown was of the view that 'towns do not have sufficient powers, and rural areas do not have sufficient powers at all.' Finally, even though he himself was one of those responding positively, Stan Campbell is president of the Federation of Prince Edward Island Municipalities, which, in a comprehensive proposal[19] submitted in conjunction with a current review of the Municipalities Act, has suggested that municipalities be given 'natural person' status.

Respondents were more equally divided on the question of whether there were additional things that municipalities ought to be doing. Forty-seven per cent of those who answered the question thought that there were additional things that municipalities ought to be doing, but there was no clear agreement on what that ought to be. Suggestions ranged from public transit (Shawn Murphy, MP for Charlottetown) to roads (Mitch Murphy, provincial treasurer). Forty-two per cent believed there was nothing additional that should be done (for example, Premier Pat Binns: 'overall, functions and responsibilities of municipalities are pretty appropriate'), and the remaining 10 per cent found it hard to identify anything. Again, both 'government' and 'other' respondents were pretty equally divided on this point.

Sixty per cent of respondents felt that there was nothing that municipalities were currently doing that they ought not to be. In this instance, twice as many 'other' respondents as opposed to 'government' respondents fell into this category, possibly reflecting a sense on the municipal side that current activities are entirely appropriate, while on the 'government' side this may reflect a 'watchdog' mentality. Premier Binns maintained that waste management should be handled at the provincial level, while Treasurer Murphy pointed to both health and education as functions beyond municipal scope. Minister of Community and Cultural Affairs Elmer MacFadyen was of the view that the city of Charlottetown should not have taken over responsibility for the harbour, a belief shared by Charlottetown's deputy mayor, Stu MacFadyen.[20]

Councils

Incorporated municipalities have councils made up of a mayor (in towns or the two cities) or a chairman (in incorporated communities) and at least three councillors. Under the Municipalities Act, the maximum number of councillors is set at six. According to the terms of their own legislation, Summerside and Charlottetown exceed this number with a maximum of eight in Summerside and ten in Charlottetown. From among the councillors, a chairman may appoint a vice-chair and a mayor may appoint a deputy mayor.

Council terms are three years, the starting points for which were made uniform on 1 January 2000. Elections are non-partisan in practice. While persons running for office may belong to political parties – two former mayors of Charlottetown have run as candidates provincially and one Charlottetown councillor was a candidate for the federal Conservatives – parties do not participate in elections. A majority of interviewees (62 per cent) thought that municipal politics was, or might be, a stepping stone to provincial and/or federal office, but it was observed that municipal politicians, including those referenced just above, have not generally been successful in moving from the municipal to the provincial or federal levels. Summerside Mayor Basil Stewart noted succinctly: 'Sometimes local municipal politicians move to another order of politics, but the majority do not – at least not here in PEI.' Premier Binns was even more categorical in his response: 'Municipal politics can be detrimental to provincial or federal office.'

Members of council must be eighteen years of age, Canadian citizens, and ordinarily resident in the community to be eligible for election. The exception is the resort municipality made up of Cavendish and its neighbours. Section 8.1(1) defines a 'temporary resident' as 'a landowner in a resort area who is a seasonal resident or the operator of a business enterprise in the area or a farmer who lives outside the area but owns and farms land in the area.' Temporary residents who live on Prince Edward Island may be elected to council and, if so, are disqualified from holding office in any other municipality. At least two councillors in the resort municipality must be permanent residents.

Mayors, chairmen, and councillors in other municipalities can lose their seats by ceasing to be residents. Failure to attend meetings can also result in the vacating of a seat. However, the legislation is badly drafted in this respect. While section 21(7) provides that any office 'shall be declared vacant upon a resolution of council to that effect if the holder ... has missed three consecutive meetings,' section 15(4.2) stipulates that a vacancy may be declared where the holder has been 'absent from the regularly scheduled meetings of the council for more than three successive months.' Since, by section 21(1), councils may hold 'special meetings,' it would be possible for a member of council to miss 'three consecutive meetings' without missing 'regularly scheduled meetings ... for more than three successive months.' Arguably, these provisions are in conflict and should be harmonized.

Councils are required to hold one meeting each year and to fix the date, place, and time of regular meetings. Though this provision appears to be mandatory, twenty of the incorporated communities, as of the 2005 Municipal Directory, did not appear to have regular meetings but instead met only at the 'call of the chairman' or had no fixed meeting time. When meetings are held, they are 'open' and require a quorum of the mayor or chairman, and not less than half of the sitting members.

Provision is made for committees of council. The mayor or chairman may appoint standing committees, whereas special committees are appointed by resolution of council. The city of Charlottetown has fourteen standing committees and in 2005 it had eleven special committees. The town of Cornwall, by comparison, has five standing committees and no special committees.

The mayor or chairman is the chief executive officer of the council. As in many Canadian municipalities, this means that the office does not include active administrative responsibility. On the contrary, all municipalities in Prince Edward Island must have a chief administrative officer (CAO), appointed by the council. The person appointed cannot be a member of council, and the minister of community and cultural affairs must be notified of the name and business address of the appointee. The CAO is required to attend all meetings and record resolutions, decisions, and proceedings. He or she keeps the minutes of council, together with the books, documents, and financial records. The CAO issues notification of meetings, is the custodian of the municipality's corporate seal, and handles the finances, including countersigning all cheques. In addition to the CAO, each council may appoint such other municipal officers as required. Clearly, the size of the staff will vary with the size of the municipality and the municipal functions that are undertaken.

To Incorporate or Not to Incorporate

Anyone who consults a map of incorporated municipalities on PEI will be struck by the large areas where there are few incorporated communities. These would include the northwestern section of the province from West Point to North Cape, an area north and east of Borden-Carleton, and a huge expanse starting at the eastern border of Charlottetown and running north to Tracadie Bay and then eastward along the Gulf shore as far as the western borders of the community of Eastern Kings. This area also extends southward as far as Orwell Bay and then eastward until it meets the western borders of the community of Central Kings. Finally, there is an area along the Northumberland Strait shore, from just east of Wood Islands around to St Mary's Bay, in which there are only two incorporated communities.

A current highway map of Prince Edward Island lists something in excess of five hundred named places of settlement. Of these five hundred places, there are two cities, seven towns, and sixty-six incorporated communities, for a total of seventy-five incorporated municipalities. However, this disparity must be approached with caution. A number of incorporated communities include 'localities' which are identified on the highway map. For example, the incorporated community of Kingston includes the locality of Kingston, from which it gets its name, but also the localities of Elmwood, Emyvale, and Green Bay. When included localities are taken into account, 123 places fall within incorporated communities.

Still, that leaves a large number of places unincorporated, a fact that, as already noted, has drawn the attention of one federal cabinet minister. When this is juxtaposed with the already mentioned highest population density in Canada, it may appear a considerable conundrum as viewed from the Olympian heights of Parliament Hill. Certainly, there is no technical obstacle to incorporation. Section 5 of the Municipalities Act provides as follows:

Upon receipt of a petition signed by at least twenty-five residents of an area indicating
(a) their desire to have a municipality established for the area;
(b) in general terms, the geographical boundaries of the municipality;
(c) whether the municipality is to be a town or community; and
(d) the services to be provided by the municipality,
the Minister shall call a public meeting of the residents of the area to discuss the matters contained in the petition and to determine if there is public support therefor.[21]

The minister is also empowered to conduct a plebiscite and a feasibility study (section 7), but is not required to do so. After considering the petition and the recommendation of the minister, the lieutenant governor may incorporate by order published in the *Gazette* (section 8[1]).

Obviously, this process is voluntary and self-directed, at least as far as initiating the petition is concerned. Clearly, if there are not at least twenty-five residents interested in seeking incorporation, the area will remain unincorporated. One of the more striking features of a map showing incorporated areas, other than the large spaces in which there are few incorporated communities, is the 'cluster' aspect of municipal incorporation. A total of fourteen communities exist in what may be termed 'isolation.' All the rest connect with at least one other incorporated community. Not surprisingly, the area around Charlottetown is heavily incorporated, possibly because proximity is the 'mother' of the petitioning initiative, possibly because these are largely bedroom communities for the city, and possibly because incorporation allows these communities to fend off the city's dominance in their region. Where, as in the West Point area, there is no significant urban presence, there is little incorporation.

On the other hand, in many of the unincorporated areas of the province, the population is simply too small to support municipal organization. The community of Belfast (incorporated 1972), for example, has a population of 1,839. This makes it larger than the town of Georgetown, possibly giving rise to a puzzle as to why Georgetown should be a town and Belfast only a community. The answer of course is that Belfast achieves its larger population only by including within its boundaries sixteen other localities. It covers the largest geographical area of any community in the province, occupying a bight of land from Orwell Cove south to the Northumberland Strait and eastward to a line drawn roughly north from Wood Islands.

It might be thought that the old township or 'lot' system could be employed to produce incorporated communities. Indeed, as already mentioned, one incorporated community is called 'Lot 11 and Area' (but this title is misleading, since it does not include all the places in Lot 11, a number of which lie in the adjoining municipality of Lady Slipper). But this expedient may simply produce communities with small population bases. For example, in 2006 the population of Lot 9, which lies in that unincorporated northwestern sector noted above, was 362, while the population of Lot 42, which lies in the unincorporated area east of Charlottetown, was 299.

The Federation of Prince Edward Island Municipalities has recently recommended that no municipality be incorporated without a significant population base.[22] While it has not formally set a number, the position of the federation is that a municipality ought to be able to hire a chief administrative officer and that a population base of 1,000 minimum is necessary to provide a sufficient tax base for a full-time CAO. (It is worth noting, in this regard, that only twelve municipalities on the Island have a population of 1,000 or more, namely, the two cities, six of the seven towns, and five communities. Forty-four of the sixty-six communities have populations of fewer than 500 persons, Tignish Shore having the fewest at 72.)

In addition to the lack of a model provided by neighbouring incorporated communities, and the small populations in many areas, there is one other factor that has already been mentioned and that helps to explain the relative dearth of incorporated entities: the size of constituencies in the provincial legislature. Since these are, on average, slightly in excess of 5,000 people, the provincial MLA is as accessible as municipal councillors in some cities, and more accessible than councillors in many others. Again, since there must be an initiative for incorporation, people must see some value in the idea. When services are provided by the province, when the provincial representative is as accessible as a municipal councillor, the idea of another layer of government is a very difficult sell.

In the order that the lieutenant governor makes under section 8 of the Municipalities Act, there is a discretion to determine whether the incorporated community will be a 'town' or a 'community.' But, as far as determining whether the new municipality will be a 'town' or a 'community,' the act provides no criteria. Sheer size of population does not seem to be a determining factor. While Cornwall (4,412) and Stratford (5,869) are larger in population than any 'community' under what may be termed 'usual' circumstances – the resort community's population of 280 swells to 7,000 seasonally – the aforementioned community of Belfast (1,839) exceeds the towns of Alberton (1,115), Georgetown (721), Kensington (1,385), and Souris (1,248) in size of population. Other 'large' communities include Eastern Kings (1,272), Lady Slipper (1,076), Malpeque Bay (1,238), and Miltonvale Park (1,185).

On the other hand, all the towns, with the exceptions of Cornwall and Stratford which are the results of amalgamations, are single entities with long histories as municipal units. The large communities are, if not formal amalgamations, cobbled together out of a number of pre-existing localities, covering, with the exception of Miltonvale Park, considerable territory. Presumably, then, the primary criterion for designating a place a 'town' is the fact that the place is geographically and historically a town (particularly in the case of Georgetown), or is sufficiently concentrated in area, like Cornwall and Stratford, to function as a town. This, coupled with a population that ordinarily exceeds 1,000, will apparently influence the exercise of discretion.

Services

The provincial government completely undertakes two service functions which may be municipal responsibilities elsewhere. The first of these is solid-waste removal. Following a localized trial in the eastern part of Prince County, the provincial government established a crown corporation, Island Waste Management Corporation, which collects and disposes of solid household waste throughout the entire province. Householders must separate waste into recyclables, compost, and other solid waste. Industrial waste is collected and disposed of by private companies. The cost of waste collection is assessed as a surcharge on top of the property tax.

The other area is education. The Island is divided into three school boards, namely, the Western Board, which supervises schools in Prince County and western Queen's County, the Eastern Board, which has the responsibility for eastern Queen's County and King's County, and the Commission scolaire de langue francais, which administers French-language schools in Abrams Village, Dublois, Charlottetown, South Rustico, Souris, and Summerside. The province appropriates a portion of the property taxes, which it collects on its own behalf and on behalf of both incorporated and unincorporated communities, to pay the cost of education.

Municipalities have no formal role in medical care, including the establishment and maintenance of hospitals. This service area is entirely provincial. The provincial control extends also to ambulance services, which are provided by private companies under contract to the province. Each company has a zone of coverage which encompasses a number of incorporated municipalities.

As already observed, only Charlottetown and Summerside have responsibility for the maintenance of their streets. While many communities are simply settlements along provincial highways, even places with networks of streets, such as Kensington, Georgetown, and Cornwall, are served by the provincial Department of Transportation and Public Works. Again, the province makes the necessary appropriation to provide for this, as will be discussed further below.

Four communities, Charlottetown, Summerside, Borden-Carleton, and Kensington, have municipal police departments. All other communities are policed by the Royal Canadian Mounted Police on contract to the province. Municipal police department members are sworn as provincial police constables, providing them with jurisdiction throughout the province. While the normal jurisdictional boundaries are observed, this breadth of jurisdiction can be useful when municipal constables are called in to assist the RCMP in their areas of patrol. There are six RCMP detachments. One of these, the Stratford detachment, serves only the town of Stratford. Otherwise, the detachments police a combination of highways, rural areas, and incorporated communities. The Montague detachment, for example, is responsible for ten incorporated communities in the southern part, while the Souris detachment polices eight incorporated communities in the northeastern sector.

Discounting the Charlottetown Airport Fire Service and the Cavendish Farms Industrial Fire Department, there are thirty-seven fire departments on Prince Edward Island. Of these, two, the West Point Fire Department and the East River Fire Department, are not based in any particular community but rather are specifically set up to serve areas of the province. Given that the other departments have community bases, only one, the Lennox Island Department, has a fire-coverage area contiguous with the boundaries of its community, namely, the Lennox Island First Nations Reserve. All other community-based departments cover areas that are larger than their municipalities. As an example, the North River Fire Department covers the territory from Rice Point on the south shore almost to Rustico Bay on the north shore and from Brookvale in the west to Brackley in the east, an area that includes fourteen incorporated communities other than the department's home base of the town of Cornwall.

With respect to services in general, 60 per cent of those interviewed, including Minister of Community and Cultural Affairs Elmer Mac-Fadyen, believed that municipalities were providing adequate levels of service, while an additional 10 per cent thought that some municipalities were and others were not. Half of the respondents believed that municipalities were performing well in the delivery of basic services – fire, policing, recreation, water, sewer, and so on. There was no significant consensus as to those policy areas in which municipalities were performing badly, though 28 per cent did focus on planning. Summerside Mayor Basil Stewart observed that Summerside maintains a Policy Review Committee which 'meets regularly to review policies, by-laws, regulations. They review policies periodically to ensure they are adequate and current for the community, and the committee also reviews policies, by-laws, etc., at the request of community individuals.' Summerside appears to be unique in this respect.

Finance

Revenues

The appendix shows revenues for the Prince Edward Island municipal sector, using 2004–5 and (for comparative purposes) 1995 as reference points. While the figures are for Prince Edward Island as a whole, the two urban poles of Summerside and Charlottetown account for the bulk of the funds presented there.

The provincial profile of revenue sources is fairly close to the norm. Property taxes are the single largest element of own-source revenue, the rest made up primarily of user charges on services provided – water, sewer, parking, recreational facilities, and so on. Compared to Canadian averages, however, there is more of an emphasis on taxes for own revenues and less reliance overall on transfers. Per capita revenue from all sources is also well below Canadian averages on a per capita basis, about 30 per cent of the Canadian average. This would be partly a function of the reduced list of functions taken on by municipalities in Prince Edward Island, and partly a reflection of the more rural character of the Island and its population.

The trends shown reveal modest change in the pattern of revenue sources over ten years, with revenues from transfers from all sources growing at about half the rate of own-source revenues. Somewhat more dramatic change would be apparent if the time period under consideration went back a year further, since tax revenues grew significantly that year, offset by a cut in transfers. This corresponded to municipal reforms that consolidated an assortment of communities into enlarged cities of Charlottetown and Summerside and created expanded towns of Stratford and Cornwall. Property-tax rates were raised in a number of the previously outlying areas, to balance the extension of new services to these areas.

In Canada generally, the ten-year trend in revenue sources is towards stronger growth in own-source revenues than is the case for PEI, with shrinking transfers, in particular specific-purpose transfers from the provincial level of government, accounting for much of the divergence. But the Canadian numbers also show some growth in general-purpose transfers, in contrast to PEI's decline. Overall, although the divergence in ten-year trends has thus led to some convergence in the distribution of revenue sources, it has still left Island municipalities towards the low end of provinces in terms of the relative importance of revenue from transfers (and at the high end in terms of own revenues).

In real terms, there has been a modest increase in revenues over the ten years, almost all of that attributable to property-tax revenue increases, driven primarily by increases in property assessments. Most other categories of revenue, with the exception of federal transfers, have seen either declines or increases that have largely just reflected inflation and the modest growth of population.

Transfers from the senior levels of government include both conditional and unconditional grants. Unconditional grants, which currently make up about 40 per cent of provincial grants, have declined from two-thirds a decade ago. Specific-purpose transfers from the federal government fluctuate quite a bit and appear to be linked to specific projects of the infrastructure type, notably roads and sewers, recreation, and the like. These grew considerably in the mid-1990s, declined by the end of the decade, and have risen again in recent years. Provincial specific-purpose transfers have been much more stable but again tend to emphasize road, sewer, and recreation infrastructure and maintenance.

New federal funds for municipalities – Goods and Services Tax (GST) rebates and gas-tax rebates – have been implemented since the period reported in the appendix, but some comment on them seems appropriate. The GST rebate did not find its way to municipalities on PEI. It was effectively clawed back by the imposition of new charges on the collection of property taxes that matched the amounts of the rebate. The gas tax, on the other hand, has reached the municipal level, the 2008 federal budget directing $7.5 million to PEI municipalities in 2008, with $15 million to come the next year.

Of those respondents who professed any knowledge of finance (14 per cent of those asked did not know), there was general agreement (84 per cent) that municipal finances are not adequate. Still, Basil Stewart believed that Summerside's finances were sufficient. This probably reflects the 'success story' that Summerside, in many respects, has become. Faced with a massive loss of municipal revenue when the Summerside Air Force base was closed, the city dug in, attracted businesses, and, indeed, provided itself with a solid financial base.

Likewise, better than half of the respondents (62 per cent) believed that provincial government support was inadequate. When this is broken down along 'government' and 'others' lines, however, it is clear that more than half of the 'government' respondents (60 per cent) believed that provincial government support is adequate. Intergovernmental Affairs Deputy Minister Leo Walsh was definite that support is adequate. Likewise, Minister MacFadyen observed: 'Municipalities tend to say no, but I say it is.' On the other hand, opposition MLAs were of the view that support was inadequate.

Again, better than half of 'government' respondents (70 per cent) believed that the current grant structure is appropriate. On the other hand, of the total who professed to know about grants, slightly more than half (56 per cent) believed that the grant structure is inappropriate. Not surprisingly, 89 per cent of those individuals come from the 'other' grouping. Robert Ghiz, then leader of the Opposition, pointed to problems in equalization, while Stan Campbell, president of the Federation of Prince Edward Island Municipalities, was categorical in saying that the grant structure was inappropriate.

There are fairly significant disparities in assessment levels per capita across the province. These have been addressed by an equalization program, the intent of which is to bring revenue levels up to the provincial average. The disparities tend to be greatest in the two less well-developed counties of the province, Kings and Prince. Summerside, the second-largest urban area in the province, is included on the 'have not' list. Since 1995, however, the province has apparently engaged in a practice of systematically underfunding the equalization pool, so that transfers have fallen well below what the formula would suggest. In its 2005 budget for example, Summerside estimated that, based on the 1986 Equalization Program formula, it should have received $1.8 million in equalization rather than the $370,000 it actually did.[23] This probably accounts for a good bit of the fall in provincial general-purpose transfers since the 1990s that was noted above. It is probably worth pointing out that, since the property-tax system is administered by the province, disparities in assessment levels are largely due to differences in the actual value of property, not differences in assessment practices as is sometimes the case. Acknowledging the problem, the government of Robert Ghiz, elected in 2007, promised to review the formula, and in its first budget increased transfers to the municipalities, including an increase of $300,000 for equalization.

Most of the respondents believed there to be disparities, but less than half, 48 per cent, thought the disparities to be serious. One respondent felt that actual budgetary disparities (as opposed to assessment levels) would be difficult to measure across the province. Harry Gaudet, CAO of Charlottetown, remarked: 'It is difficult to measure the disparities between municipalities because there is such a quantum difference between full-service municipalities, and rural municipalities that do not provide full services.' On the other hand, Summerside's mayor, Basil Stewart, maintained that, notwithstanding the difficulties in measuring them, 'disparities in revenue are related to the disparities in equalization payments; some communities are getting equalization monies when they do not need them and other communities are not getting an appropriate amount of money because they do not have the population to warrant such funds. So yes, the disparities in revenue are quite serious.'

Education on PEI is entirely a provincial responsibility, completely divorced from municipal government. Property taxes could be deemed to play a significant role in funding the system, though there is no specific link between property-tax revenues and education expenditures. However, assuming there was a link, in 2003 the province retained for its own purposes $51.7 million in property-tax revenue, about 55 per cent of the total property tax collected. In that year it made grants to school boards of about $130 million, 40 per cent of which could be argued to be property-tax revenues. Attributing all of those revenues to education, however, is probably inappropriate, since the province provides a variety of services in areas across the province which could be thought of as funded by property taxes, the best (and largest) current example being waste management, which is now run and funded on a province-wide basis through the Island Waste Management program.

The fact that the province collects property taxes for its own purposes is not without some controversy in municipal circles. The submission of the Federation of Prince Edward Island Municipalities in the context of the 2004–5 provincial budget, for example, clearly presented this as a core problem, noting that it limits the ability of municipalities to raise property-tax revenues, out of a concern for the overall burden on property taxpayers.[24]

Expenditures

Expenditures for the municipal sector on PEI are broken down by function in the appendix, again providing 1995 and 2004/5 as reference points over the past decade. Here there are more notable departures from the norm, corresponding to the differences in functions performed at the municipal level in PEI discussed elsewhere. Education, social services, and housing are largely not present. Patterns of expenditure are reasonably consistent over time once allowance is made for the distorting effect of irregular levels of infrastructure spending. As noted regarding revenues, the levels of expenditure found in PEI on a per capita basis are well below national averages. Again, much of that is due to fewer functions being assumed by the Island's municipalities.

As the presence of a deficit makes clear, PEI municipalities can run a deficit, and they can borrow to finance operations on an interim basis. They are required, however, to transfer that deficit to the next year's budget.[25] On the capital side, municipalities are allowed to borrow for capital expenditure if approved by residents. There is a limit on overall debt of 10 per cent of the current assessed value of real property in the municipality.[26] Current debt-charge levels (about 1.5 per cent of total expenditures) would suggest that system-wide there is little danger of this limit being met. In fact, one could cite a number of examples of some reluctance, either by residents or by municipal leaders, to use debt financing extensively. The two new expanded towns of Stratford and Cornwall, for instance, have both met with resident resistance to plans for new municipal buildings. In Cornwall, plans for a new town hall were scaled back significantly and pressure existed for further scaling back.[27] The city of Charlottetown has also proceeded with significantly higher levels of debt in recent years, and the current administration has come under fire as well.

Recent Changes

The situation depicted here (based on 2005 data) has seen a few changes in the past few years. Some events relate to federal initiatives – the GST rebate, the Municipal Rural Infrastructure Program, and the gas-tax rebate. As noted above, the GST rebate was offset by the imposition of new charges for the collection of property taxes by the province. The gas-tax rebate would seem to be proceeding, with Charlottetown receiving $1.5 million in 2008 and Summerside $700,000, despite earlier concerns that the province might divert a significant amount of that funding as well.

Functional reallocations and changes will probably have a more lasting impact, though, interestingly, the trend on PEI reverses that found in many other provinces where responsibilities and their attached expenses have been offloaded onto municipalities. Over the past few years, responsibility for waste disposal has been taken away from municipalities and handed over to the provincially funded Island Waste Management Corporation. On the other hand, on its own initiative, the city of Charlottetown has finally taken it upon itself to implement a public-transit system, which was up and running in the summer of 2005.

Of more interest over the next few years will be the fallout from the provincial government's freeze on owner-occupied residential property-tax assessments until 2010. This was in response to a perception that taxes were rising too quickly because of increases in market-based assessment levels, though increases in service charges for waste disposal, added to the property-tax bill, were partly to blame. Once the fairness of the system has been evaluated, some reforms are projected to be implemented. In the meantime, this has had a significant impact on municipal revenues, which cannot be expected to rise as quickly as in the recent past. In their 2008 budgets most municipalities, including Charlottetown and Summerside, resisted the urge to raise property-tax rates but did increase service fees.

The other significant development to come will be the outcome of the provinces review of equalization and municipal funding, which the premier has suggested will be addressed in the 2008 sitting of the Legislative Assembly.

Demography

The Island's population reached 135,851 in the 2006 census, easily the smallest of the provinces. Unlike most of the other small provinces, however, it is still growing, with a 12.1 per cent growth rate over twenty-five years to 2001 – similar to Manitoba's and higher than Newfoundland, Nova Scotia, New Brunswick, or Saskatchewan.

Like most provinces, PEI faces an increasingly aged population, though overall population projections point to a levelling out over the next few decades (at about 140,000) rather than the absolute decline projected for many of the smaller provinces. The major difference here, as with the growth rates, is that PEI actually enjoys net in-migration from other provinces in most years. International immigration, on the other hand, is at very low levels, though rising in the past few years, which is what separates PEI's population growth rates from those of the larger provinces.

Although there is a steady continued fall in farm-based population (down to under 5 per cent in 2001 from over 10 per cent in 1981), and a drift in Island population towards Queen's County (the most urbanized of the three counties), the urban population as defined by Statistics Canada is still the lowest of the ten provinces, below 50 per cent in 2001 (Canada as a whole was 79.7 per cent urban), despite PEI being Canada's most densely populated province. Indeed, with the exception of newly amalgamated urban areas around Charlottetown (Stratford and Cornwall), there is no real trend towards greater urbanization in the past decade or so. Charlottetown in fact saw its population decline modestly in the last two censuses. Although increasingly oriented towards the cities and towns, many Islanders are moving to or staying in rural areas, smaller towns, and villages. The drift to Queen's County shows up as much in 'ribbon' development in the countryside as in growth in the Charlottetown area.

Planning

It will probably come as no surprise that Prince Edward Island provides for planning on both a province-wide basis and a local municipal one. The Planning Act[28] furnishes the provincial government with two sets of powers. First, it is given an overriding supervisory power over all planning in the province. As part of this function, it supplies planning-advisory services to municipalities, promotes cooperation between municipalities with respect to intermunicipal or regional planning issues, requires that municipal plans impose requirements that are not less stringent than province-wide requirements, and provides the avenue for appeal of planning decisions of councils or the minister.

The second power is one to make planning regulations 'applicable to any area except a municipality with an official plan and bylaws.' Since fewer than half (thirty) of the incorporated municipalities had official plans as of December 2004, and since incorporated municipalities occupy only a small part of the land area, the provincial regulatory power must be regarded as extensive on PEI. That power extends to land use, definition of areas to be regulated, the creation of land-use zones, the subdivision of land, the servicing of land, building standards, permits, roads, mobile-home courts, parking, summer cottages, and, of course, fees.

The minister may, under a land-identification program, prevent commercial or industrial development or the subdivision of land. The minister is given powers of enforcement, including remedial actions. The minister may enter into subdivision agreements with developers, though these agreements may be altered or cancelled in certain circumstances. In addition, the lieutenant-governor-in-council is empowered to make regulations with respect to special planning areas, defining their purpose and objectives and regulating development in them. Those regulations may supersede or suspend the by-laws of a municipality in whole or in part, and substitute in their place by-laws regulations made under the act.

It should be noted that, from the provincial perspective, the Planning Act is not the only piece of legislation that regulates land use. The Prince Edward Island Lands Protection Act[29] sets up limits for land ownership, citing as reasons the difficult history of absentee landownership on the Island, the high population density, and the fragile nature of the Island's ecology. The absolute maxima are 1,000 acres for a natural person and 3,000 acres for a corporation, but these are reduced by sections 4 and 5 of the act, which limit non-resident persons (section 4) and corporations (section 5) to a maximum of five acres or 165 feet of shore frontage, unless permission to exceed has been granted by the lieutenant-governor-in-council. In addition, the government may attach conditions to permits issued pursuant to sections 4 and 5 limiting subdivision of the land, identifying the land under the land-identification program, consolidating the land with adjoining parcels, and/or requiring the applicant to become a resident of the Island (section 9[1]).

The fact that land use and regulation may be subject to separate pieces of legislation and their accompanying regulations might be a source of considerable confusion were it not for the existence of the Island Regulatory and Appeals Commission (IRAC).[30] This multifaceted board has functions ranging from regulating the price of gas at the pumps to settling disputes between landlords and tenants in residential tenancies. In addition, it is empowered, under section 5 of the act

(b) to hear and decide matters relating to land use, to decide upon the disposition of applications respecting the acquisition of land by non-residents and corporations where so required by any Act;

(c) to hear and decide appeals from decisions of

(i)   the Director under the *Rental of Residential Property Act* R.S.P.E.I. 1988, Cap. R-13.1,

(ii) the Provincial Treasurer under the *Real Property Assessment Act* R.S.P.E.I. 1988, Cap. R-4 or the *Real Property Tax Act* R.S.P.E.I. 1988, Cap. R-5,

(iii) the Provincial Tax Commissioner under the *Revenue Tax Act* R.S.P.E.I. 1988, Cap. R-14;

(d) to perform such other functions as may be conferred on the Commission under any enactment.[31]

Thus, notwithstanding the powers vested in the lieutenant governor-in-council under the Prince Edward Island Lands Protection Act, applications for permits to exceed the maxima must be filed with IRAC, which then considers the applications and makes a binding recommendation to the lieutenant-governor-in-council.

Likewise, under the Planning Act, IRAC has a role to play in the land-identification program discussed above, most particularly in reviewing, altering, or cancelling land-identification agreements between the minister and developers. But over and above this function, it is IRAC that functions as the board of appeal in planning matters, whether the decision is made at the provincial or municipal level.[32]

Part III of the Planning Act is directed to those cases where, as provided for in section 9, the council has adopted an official plan. As of December 2004, thirty municipalities had adopted official plans. Both cities and all seven towns, not surprisingly, had official plans. As to the twenty-one incorporated communities, by and large it is the larger places, having populations of 500 or more, which have plans. Where smaller communities have produced plans, they are either close to an urban area like Sherbrooke (the smallest, with a population of 178, near Summerside) or they have special reasons, notably sizeable seasonal resident populations (like the resort municipality and Brackley). In the instance of one recent addition to the group, Hazelbrook, a dispute between residents and the owner of an industrial-waste site may have prompted the development of an official plan. Where an official plan is in place, the municipality is responsible for administration of the plan within its boundaries. Its land-use policy and by-laws must be consistent with provincial policy, plans, and regulations.

Where a plan is contemplated, the council may appoint a planning board to prepare the plan. The board has powers to conduct a survey of physical, social, and economic conditions, to recommend an interim planning policy, to propose an official plan together with by-laws, and to hold public meetings associated with all aspects of the plan. This last power is crucial. The planning board is required to give residents and other interested persons an opportunity to make representations. There must be at least one public meeting, advertised, together with the content of the plan, on at least two occasions in a newspaper circulating in the area. Records of meetings are to be kept by the planning board.

The official plan, including a statement of economic, physical, social, and environmental objectives, a statement of policies for future land use, and proposals for periodic review, is recommended to council on majority approval of the members of the board present. The council then submits the plan to the minister, upon whose approval the plan becomes the official plan. The council may then implement the plan through by-laws, which, again require an opportunity for public input. Councils may appoint development officers to administer the by-laws. Not surprisingly, in a province with a number of small incorporated communities, the act provides for the possibility of joint planning boards, but at present no joint planning board exists in the province.

It may well be asked whether these various planning provisions have any 'teeth.' We have already noted that ribbon development continues apace around Charlottetown. At the time of writing, two new subdivisions are being cleared in the town of Cornwall, and developers, ranging from the large APM Group (which has real estate holdings all over the world) to more modest builders, are busily turning farmland into suburbia in what used to be the communities of West Royalty and Winsloe (now amalgamated into Charlottetown).

It has been observed that the entire Island is 'sprawl.' But appearances may belie. If 'sprawl' is defined as a movement of people from the urban core to the periphery, there is no question that developments in suburban Charlottetown and the bedroom communities of Cornwall and Stratford can be considered 'sprawl.' But it must be borne in mind that Prince Edward Island is not an 'urban' place. On the contrary, the population is essentially rural, with roots in, and ties to, small communities and localities. While rural depopulation was identified by some respondents as a demographic problem, in fact, where possible, individuals will attempt to live close to home and travel to work. It is not uncommon for people living near Souris to work in Charlottetown or for someone who lives in Conway to travel to a job in Summerside. These are not urbanites who have fled the city. On the contrary, they are rural people who see no reason to leave home.

Ribbon or strip development can be viewed in the same light. Travelling the Island's roads one often comes upon 'strips' of houses. But there is an observable pattern. Often there is an older house, though well renovated, together with one or two newer ones. A study of mailboxes will tend to show that the surnames are the same. And the explanation is obvious: the older house belongs to the older generation, the others belong to the children who have built on plots given to them by their parents. This is not uncommon and cannot be put into the same category as thoroughgoing strip development in other places. All this is not to say that planning should not be strengthened, but merely to advance the caveat that, when it is, it must be placed in a context appropriate to PEI and not imported holus-bolus from highly urbanized places such as the Greater Toronto Area.

Organizations, Issues, and Proposals

Those persons interviewed mainly identified the Federation of Prince Edward Island Municipalities as the most influential organization in municipal matters. Indeed, most were hard-pressed to identify any other organization which had influence. One-third of respondents stated flatly that they knew of no other organizations. Just under a quarter identified 'business' or, more specifically, the Chamber of Commerce as influential. Other responses included ad hoc groups, the transit lobby, the Tourist Industry Association of PEI, seniors and farmers, and maybe environmental groups.

Equally, there was no clear agreement about what are 'big' municipal issues. Twenty-nine per cent identified infrastructure as the 'big' issue, followed closely by finances (24 per cent). Next in order came delivery and/or equality of services (19 per cent) and economic development (14 per cent). On the other hand, there was a clear consensus about demographic issues, with two-thirds identifying PEI's aging population as a significant demographic challenge. This was followed by immigration (19 per cent) and rural depopulation (14 per cent).

One issue that may be about to wake from its slumber is taxation. Property-tax rates on PEI are high. This has been masked by the fact that real estate values are low, and further by the fact that, until recently, market-value assessment was not used. However, the shift to market-value assessment, coupled with a rise in house prices, has increased taxes across the board. Added to this is the cost of the provincial government's expensive experiment in solid-waste collection, which is a tax surcharge and which shot up by 40 per cent in the first three years that the program was in operation Island-wide. The high rate of taxation was a major complaint put forward by those residents who attempted, without success, to derail the construction of the aforementioned new town hall in Cornwall.[33] That complaint may well be heard again.

It will probably come as no surprise that, with a relatively small number of organizations actually involved in municipal matters, proposals for municipal change and/or reform have been few and far between. Setting aside ad hoc groups formed around single issues, the only identifiable proposals have emanated from the Federation of Prince Edward Island Municipalities. On the other hand, those proposals have the virtue of being comprehensive and were submitted to the provincial government in conjunction with a review of the Municipalities Act.

Chief among these are recommendations that the act recognize municipalities as a distinct order of government, detail its purposes and those of municipalities, provide a basis for a strong relationship between the municipal and provincial governments, and make provision for provincial government consultation with both the federation and municipalities before any changes are made 'to programs that have direct and substantial implications for municipalities.'[34] Mention has already been made of the key recommendation that creation of new municipalities rest on a minimum population size and a demonstration that the proposed entity will be viable. Another key recommendation already alluded to is the according of 'natural person' powers. However, the federation does not appear to see this as an alternative to corporate powers, but rather as a tool for greater flexibility in implementing those corporate powers, though this is coupled with a recommendation to define municipal powers more broadly. In addition, the federation advances a large number of 'housekeeping' recommendations about the functioning of councils, the maintaining of budgets, and the creation and implementation of by-laws.

Whether these proposals will be implemented is another question. Seventy per cent of respondents either thought that there were no significant changes coming at the municipal level of government or were not sure. Clearly, the president of the federation wanted to see change, especially in the area of dialogue with the province, but otherwise the general consensus seemed to be that there would not be much change.

Provincial Mediation and Multilevel Governance

Provincial oversight of municipalities was generally regarded as good or adequate (71 per cent of respondents). On the issue of whether the province was likely to tighten or loosen its supervision, slightly over half of those who responded to the question (53 per cent) thought that the situation was going to remain the same. Both Premier Binns and the provincial treasurer, Mitch Murphy, held the position that more autonomy could be available if municipalities wanted it. On the other hand, Harry Gaudet, the Charlottetown CAO, observed that the province had already tightened its supervision over the planning process.

The constancy of the situation was echoed in the response to the question of whether the interviewees saw any changes in the relations between the various levels of government. Seventy per cent did not foresee any significant change. While all of those who answered the question about the benefits of a flow of federal monies to municipalities thought it was a good thing, 24 per cent of respondents held that there should be no unmediated direct payments. Not surprisingly, this group included the premier, three cabinet ministers, and a deputy minister. A slightly larger percentage (29 per cent) were adamant that the money should flow directly and that the province should not be involved.

Probably not surprisingly, all members of the 'other' grouping thought that increased federal collaboration with municipalities was a good thing. Not surprisingly, too, the naysayers (24 per cent) came from the 'government' ranks. Again, on the government side, a caveat against direct dealing was raised, enunciated as follows by Premier Binns: 'It is important that the province is part of the process since municipalities are created under provincial law. Federal government should not deal directly with municipalities.' The federal government should be negotiating with the province first. There was a fairly equal split on whether or not federal collaboration would improve or worsen policies. One-third of respondents, all from the 'government' side, were clear that it would worsen policies, with the remainder of the 'government' interviewees – except one person – expressing only a cautious 'maybe.' Twenty-nine per cent thought that it would improve policies, while the remainder expressed various degrees of uncertainty. Possibly the most perceptive response was that of Harry Gaudet, the Charlottetown CAO. He observed that 'we need to improve policies first in order to make the federal-municipal relationship work effectively.'

Respondents found it difficult to identify specific aspects of the system in PEI that would be conducive to greater municipal-federal collaboration. Again, on the 'government' side there was near unanimity that there should be no direct collaboration. Leo Walsh, deputy minister of intergovernmental affairs, who did not rule out direct collaboration, was of the opinion that the federal government would experience 'inadequacies or difficulties' in working with small municipalities, since its focus would tend to be the Greater Toronto Area. Of those who thought that there were aspects of the PEI system that would be conducive to collaboration, the responses showed no clear patterns. Once more, possibly the most perceptive reply came from the Charlottetown CAO, Harry Gaudet, namely, that, contrary to Leo Walsh's opinion, the 'smallness' of PEI was its greatest strength. 'Everyone knows the politicians and the politicians know their constituents. This makes it easier to work on projects because there are mutual interests.'

Having said this, though, Gaudet then observed that the greatest obstacle to federal-municipal collaboration would be the provincial government. Apparently, given the responses of those 'government' persons interviewed, this observation is borne out. Even Stan Campbell, president of the Federation of Prince Edward Island Municipalities, was of the opinion that 'we have to go through the province' and that municipalities are creatures of the province. On the other hand, Mitchell Tweel, Charlottetown councillor and vice-president of the federation, has authored a resolution calling upon the federal and provincial governments to amend the Constitution Act, 1867 to recognize municipalities as a distinct order of government. Given the current amending formula, the likelihood of that succeeding is very small.

NOTES

1 There are 23.8 persons per square kilometre according to the 2001 census.
2 John Godfrey, 'What is Good Public Policy in Canadian Municipalities,' Luncheon Address, 28–29 October 2004, Ottawa.
3 Toronto, with a population of 2,431,494, has forty-four councillors representing an average of 56,397 people; Winnipeg, population of 619,544, has fifteen councillors representing an average of 41,302 people. Even Moncton, which is not a CMA, has ten councillors representing an average of 6,100 each.
4 Douglas Boylan, 'Rule Britannia,' in F.W.P. Bolger, ed., *Canada's Smallest Province* (Halifax: Nimbus Publishing, 1991), 33–6, 35.
5 So-called because each of the townships was awarded to creditors of the crown in 1767 in lieu of payment of debts. The distribution of the townships was determined by a 'lottery,' hence the common usage 'lot.'
6 Unless otherwise indicated, all legislation cited is found in *The Acts of the General Assembly from the Establishment of the Legislature in the Thirteenth Year of His Late Majesty King George the Third, A.D. 1773, to the Fourth Year of the Reign of His Present Majesty King William the Fourth, A.D. 1834.*
7 Statutes of Prince Edward Island (SPEI), 1855, 18th Victoria, c. 34.
8 SPEI, 1877, 40th Victoria, c. 15.
9 Report of the commissioners appointed to consolidate and revise the statues of Prince Edward Island, 1890, no. 120 (33 Vic. c. 20).
10 SPEI, 1948, c. 39.
11 Report of the commissioners appointed to consolidate and revise the statues of Prince Edward Island, 1890, no. 103 (40 Vic. c. 1).
12 SPEI, 1994, c. 6.
13 SPEI, 1994, c. 59.
14 The amalgamation exercise has been extensively discussed by John Crossley. See Crossley, 'Municipal Reform in Prince Edward Island: Uneven Capacity and Reforms,' chapter 10 of Joseph Garcea and Edward C. LeSage, Jr., eds., *Municipal Reform in Canada: Reconfiguration, Re-Empowerment, and Rebalancing* (Don Mills, Ont.: Oxford University Press, 2005), 218–41.
15 Revised Statutes of Prince Edward Island (RSPEI), 1988, c. M-13.
16 RSPEI, 1988, c. I-8.
17 The provincial treasurer, Mitch Murphy, responding to the question about whether there were things which municipalities could do that they were not currently doing, suggested that they might take over responsibility for roads within their boundaries.

18 Interviewees were grouped into those associated with the provincial government, the 'government' group (ministers, 'government' MLAs, deputy
ministers, and provincial bureaucrats), and 'others' (one MP, members of
the opposition, two mayors, a deputy mayor, municipal councillors,
municipal bureaucrats, and the president of the Federation of Prince
Edward Island Municipalities). In some instances, the distinction
between the responses of these two groups will be significant. It should
also be realized that, between the time of the interviews in 2005 and 2006
and the publication of this volume, there has been a change of government in Prince Edward Island. Short of interviewing the new incumbents, which is not possible, the views attributed to government
members must be seen in their appropriate time context.

19 Federation of Prince Edward Island Municipalities, *An Act for the Future*,
submission to the Municipalities Act Review Committee, September
2004, 3.7.

20 This may go beyond coincidence. The MacFadyens are brothers.

21 RSPEI, 1983, c. 33, s. 5.

22 *An Act for the Future.*

23 City of Summerside, *2005 Budget*, 6.

24 Federation of Prince Edward Island Municipalities, *A Partnership for the
Future*, 2004–5 provincial budget submission, February 2004.

25 Municipalities Act, 41(b).

26 Ibid, 44.

27 The proposed town hall construction was first 'postponed' as the result
of residents' complaints and was then constructed in a 'scaled-back'
version which was, nonetheless, almost as expensive as the first proposal.

28 RSPEI, 1988, c. P-8.

29 RSPEI, 1988, c. L-5.

30 RSPEI, 1988, c. I-11.

31 RSPEI, 1991, c. 18, s. 5; 1993, c. 29, s. 4; 1994, c. 25, s. 30 (effective 4 July
1994); 1994, c. 29, s. 1.

32 Even though IRAC has these powers, it may be described as timid in
exercising them. A study of appeals demonstrates that the board normally upholds the status quo.

33 The concern regarding taxation was considerable. A petition was served
on the town council which had over 1,800 names on it. There were flaws
in the petition. The wording was ambiguous, and those who circulated it
were not careful to ascertain whether or not the person signing was a resident of the community. However, setting aside names that provided
addresses outside the community, names that provided no address at all,

and names that appeared bogus, the total number of people opposing the town hall could be safely set at 1,665. The electors of Cornwall total 3,257, according to Elections PEI. In a remarkable failure of representative democracy, council defied the popular will.

34 *An Act for the Future.*

8 Saskatchewan

JOSEPH GARCEA AND DONALD GILCHRIST

In Saskatchewan, as in other provinces, the configuration of the municipal system is important not only for the nature and scope of local governance but also for multilevel governance. Ultimately, of course, it is also important for economic and social development within the local, regional, and provincial communities. This chapter is an overview of the municipal system in the province of Saskatchewan, of the debates regarding the effects of the system both for local municipal governance and for multilevel governance, and of the prospects for reforms. The chapter consists of four sections discussing: 1) the origins and evolution of the municipal system; 2) its contemporary structural, statutory, institutional, decision-making, functional, and financial frameworks; 3) some key debates about the implications of the existing municipal system for local municipal and multilevel governance and the need for reforms to it; and 4) some observations regarding the prospects for substantial reform.

Origins and Evolution of the Municipal System

The roots of Saskatchewan's municipal system are traceable to 1883, when a few fledgling municipal entities, including fire and local improvement districts, were established through ordinances of the territorial governor which provided guidelines regarding such matters as geographic boundaries, elections, functions, and finances. However, it was not until after Saskatchewan became a province in 1905 that the major structural and statutory foundations for the existing municipal system were laid. That occurred in 1908 when a special commission that was appointed in 1906 submitted its report on the design of a municipal system to the provincial government. The commission, which was heavily influenced by existing municipal governance systems in the older provinces, recommended that the province establish a system consisting of cities, towns, villages, and rural municipalities. That same year, the provincial government created a department to deal with municipal affairs and one year later the legislature enacted separate legislation to govern cities, towns, villages, and rural municipalities. To this day, those remain the major categories of municipalities throughout most of the province, save for the Northern Administrative District where there are no cities or rural municipalities. (Another type of municipal organization is the hamlet; they are very small quasi-municipalities with limited decision-making and advisory powers within the rural municipalities and the Northern Administrative District.) The rural municipal system was established by subdividing the southern half of the province, between the American border and the Northern Administrative District, into municipalities. The original rural municipalities are approximately 1,000 square kilometres, but the handful of those established in 1977 along the southern border of the Northern Administrative District – products of the conversion of improvement districts to rural municipalities – are up to twelve times larger than the original ones.

Saskatchewan's municipal system has evolved over the past one hundred years, but neither its constitutional and political status nor its statutory, functional, financial, and institutional foundations have been altered in a fundamental or transformative manner. Indeed, the history of the municipal government system in Saskatchewan is largely one of stasis, with only minor incremental adjustments from time to time.[1] The area in which the adjustments have been particularly limited during the past century has been the basic structure of the municipal system. This is so despite repeated recommendations of provincially appointed commissions and task forces to restructure the system to create regional municipal governments. The most significant factors influencing the system have been the strong conservative dimension of Saskatchewan's political culture, the entrenched municipal autonomy tradition, and the significant political power that municipal officials wield within the province, both individually and collectively.[2]

Features of the Existing Municipal System

There are some distinct and notable features of Saskatchewan's political system that have important implications for both local and multi-level governance. This is particularly true of the structural framework.

Structural Framework

The general structure of the municipal system was established during the first few decades following the creation of the province. In 1905 there were 146 municipalities (4 cities, 43 towns, 97 villages, 2 rural municipalities), and 359 municipal districts. By 1908, the number of rural municipalities had jumped to 200 through the consolidation and conversion of most municipal districts into rural municipalities. Neither the types nor the number of municipalities has changed much since. Unlike some other provinces where consolidation has reduced the number of municipalities, in Saskatchewan such a major reduction has not occurred. Consequently, the number of municipalities has remained relatively high for most of the past century (see Table 1). In 2006 the 985 municipalities (and quasi-municipalities) included 13 cities, 147 towns (two of which are northern), 296 villages (13 of which are northern), and 296 rural municipalities.

Saskatchewan has the second-highest number of municipalities and quasi-municipalities and the lowest population per municipality ratio (approximately 1,209 per municipality) in Canada. Most of the population in Saskatchewan is concentrated in a relatively small number of municipalities. At the turn of the twenty-first century, approximately 40 per cent of the population resided in Regina and Saskatoon (44 per cent in their Census Metropolitan Areas [CMAs]), the two largest cities, and approximately 55 per cent in the thirteen cities. Of the remaining population, approximately 20 per cent resided in towns and other small urban municipalities, 18 per cent in rural municipalities, 2 per cent in northern municipalities, and 5 percent on Indian reservations. Most of the municipalities have very small populations: 97 per cent have less than 2,000 people, 65 per cent less than 500, and 20 per cent less than 100 (see Table 2). Current demographic trends suggest that a continuing migration of the population to the major urban centres will mean that many small communities will get even smaller over time. There are only three exceptions to this trend: those resort villages that attract retirees from inside and outside Saskatchewan; small urban and rural communities with lower-priced housing and lower taxes that are within relatively close commuting distance to Regina and Saskatoon; and the communities that are fortunate to enjoy the benefits of the expansion of existing industries or the location of new industry in their region. If a dramatic increase in population were to occur in Saskatchewan, all indications are that it would be concentrated in these particular types of urban, rural, and resort communities.

Table 1
Saskatchewan municipalities by type in 2006

	Number of municipalities and quasi-municipalities	Minimum population
Urban Municipalities		
Cities	13	5,000
Towns	145	500
Villages	283	100
Resort Villages	40	100
Subtotal	481	
Rural Municipalities	296	None
Organized Hamlets	173	45 Voters
Subtotal	469	
Northern Municipalities		
Northern Towns	2	500
Northern Villages	13	100
Northern Hamlets	9	50
Northern Settlements	11	None
Subtotal	35	
Total[3]	985	

Saskatchewan does not have either two-tier municipalities or any multifunctional regional special-purpose authorities. Instead, in addition to the local municipalities, it has a wide array of single-function special-purpose authorities. This includes, for example, regional authorities for education, health, economic development, transportation planning, land use, watersheds, emergency planning, parks, and libraries. Indeed, one of Saskatchewan's challenges is that there is a plethora of such regional authorities which invariably do not share common boundaries.

In addition to these special-purpose bodies, Saskatchewan's municipal system interfaces extensively with First Nations and Métis communities and governmental systems. The data from the 2001 national census reveals that 130,190 people self-identified as aboriginal in the province, with approximately two-thirds indicating First Nation ancestry and one-third indicating Métis ancestry.[4] Collectively, persons of aboriginal ancestry constitute approximately 14 per cent of the province's total population, and approximately 13 per cent of the

Table 2
Distribution of population by community type[5]

	1981	1986	1991	1996	2001	2006
Population						
Cities	467,536	511,687	520,496	529,771	528,134	533,246
Regina	162,984	175,064	179,178	180,400	178,225	179,246
Saskatoon	154,210	177,641	186,058	193,647	196,811	202,340
Towns	159,087	164,457	156,818	155,095	153,090	148,484
Villages	58,947	60,063	55,431	52,510	49,309	43,985
Resort Villages	873	1,285	2,331	2,657	3,227	4,492
Rural Municipalities	240,472	231,119	209,923	197,131	187,825	175,659
Indian Reservations	26,255	28,016	31,260	39,139	43,340	48,141
Northern Villages & Hamlets		11,107	11,010	12,380	12,376	12,576
Unorganized & Crown Colonies	15,125	1,879	1,659	1,556	1,632	1,574
Saskatchewan	968,313	1,009,613	988,928	990,237	978,933	968,157
Share of population (%)						
Cities	48.3	50.7	52.6	53.5	53.9	55.1
Regina	16.8	17.3	18.1	18.2	18.2	18.5
Saskatoon	15.9	17.6	18.8	19.6	20.1	20.9
Towns	16.4	16.3	15.9	15.7	15.6	15.3
Villages	6.1	5.9	5.6	5.3	5.0	4.5
Resort Villages	0.1	0.1	0.2	0.3	0.3	0.5
Rural Municipalities	24.8	22.9	21.2	19.9	19.2	18.1
Indian Reservations	2.7	2.8	3.2	4.0	4.4	5.0
Northern Villages & Hamlets		1.1	1.1	1.3	1.3	1.3
Unorganized & Crown Colonies	1.6	0.2	0.2	0.2	0.2	0.2

total self-identified aboriginal population in Canada. The fact that the self-identified aboriginal population for the province is 14 per cent is quite significant when compared to the demographic make-up of the rest of Canada, where only 3.3 per cent of the population self-identified as aboriginal. Self-identification and under-reporting suggest that the number and percentage of people with some aboriginal ancestry are likely higher. There are almost two hundred Indian reserve band councils and eleven regional tribal councils in Saskatchewan. In the case of the Métis Nation, there are both local and regional councils which represent Métis living in their respective communities. Furthermore, these aboriginal governments all have several authorities which deal with planning and delivering an array of programs and services to their respective members. The aboriginal communities in Saskatchewan have achieved a remarkably high degree of what has been referred to as 'institutional completeness' and continue to achieve even more with each passing year.[6] This development has very important implications both for the need and for the ability of municipal governments to deal with existing and emerging aboriginal governments and agencies on an array of governance, programming, service, and financial matters.

Saskatchewan, then, has one of the most highly fragmented municipal systems in Canada upon which is superimposed an equally highly fragmented system of regional authorities, all of which interface with an array of aboriginal local, regional, and provincial governments and authorities. The fragmented nature of the system has significant consequences both for local governance and for multilevel governance.

Statutory Framework

Saskatchewan's statutory framework for municipal governance has also been fragmented. Separate statutes have existed for the major categories of municipalities from the inception of the municipal system.[7] During the past quarter-century, the original statutory framework was subjected to two rounds of reforms. The first occurred between 1983 and 1989 when major reforms entailed the enactment of the following statutes: the Northern Municipalities Act, 1983 for municipalities in the northern half of the province; the Urban Municipality Act, 1984 for cities, towns, and villages in the southern half of the province; and the Rural Municipality Act, 1989 for rural municipalities in the southern half of the province.

The second round of reforms has occurred since the turn of the twenty-first century. During this round, two new major municipal statutes were enacted, two were repealed, and two are being reviewed for potential reforms. The first statute to be enacted was the Cities Act, 2002, which was designed to apply only to cities. The statute was enacted at the request of cities to provide them with a greater degree of authority and autonomy to govern their respective municipalities. They made it very clear that they were seeking a statutory framework which embodied the general framework and principles contained in the modernized municipal statutes of Alberta and Ontario. Towards that end, the statute embodied the principles of 'natural person powers' and 'areas of jurisdiction.' When the Cities Act came into force in January 2003, all cities were granted the option of operating under the Cities Act or the Urban Municipality Act. Just before the Cities Act came into force, all cities passed resolutions indicating that they would operate under its aegis.

The second statute to be enacted was the Municipalities Act, 2005, which repealed and replaced both the Urban Municipalities Act, 1983 and the Rural Municipality Act, 1989. The statute was enacted largely as a result of the interest generated by the enactment of the Cities Act. That interest generated extensive consultations and negotiations between provincial and municipal representatives from 2003 to 2005 on whether to produce one statute for all urban municipalities other than cities and one for rural municipalities, or whether to produce a single integrated statute for both of those particular types of municipalities. Ultimately, they agreed to produce a single statute for both types. The result was the enactment of the Municipalities Act, 2005, which came into force on 1 January 2006. The decision to enact this measure was rooted in the preferences of provincial and municipal officials. For their part, urban and rural municipal officials, and to some extent also their provincial counterparts, wanted all such municipalities to operate under a statutory framework that was comparable, though not necessarily identical, to the one that had been enacted for cities. Municipal officials felt that this would provide them with greater jurisdictional authority and autonomy with which to operate their municipalities. Provincial officials believed that it would result in a statutory framework that would not only be more responsive to the needs, preferences, and capacities of these particular municipalities but would also be more consonant with the so-called 'provincial interests.' The provincial government took the position that a single municipal act for urban and rural municipalities would be conducive to intermunicipal collaboration and coordination and also to voluntary municipal restructuring.[8]

The Cities Act, 2002 and the Municipalities Act, 2005 are very similar and resemble the municipal statutes of Alberta and Ontario. Both are rooted in the philosophy that replacing what traditionally had been relatively prescriptive legislation with permissive legislation would contribute to the achievement of two key goals. The first was to provide municipalities with greater authority and autonomy to deal with their own internal affairs and their relations with each other as well as with other orders of government and non-governmental for-profit and not-for-profit organizations. The second goal was to increase the level of accountability of municipal governments to the ratepayers and residents. In effect, it was designed as a quid pro quo which entailed greater authority in exchange for greater accountability. In keeping with the goal of increased authority and autonomy, the statutes included provisions such as those regarding 'spheres of jurisdiction' and 'natural person powers.' In keeping with the goal of increased accountability, four different sets of provisions were included. The first creates opportunities for residents and ratepayers to place important issues on the public-policy agenda through petitions and to vote on them through plebiscites and referenda; the second requires more extensive access to municipal documents; the third compels municipal councils to hold almost all council and committee meetings in public; and the fourth requires cities to establish an administrative review officer who is essentially the municipal ombudsman. That officer operates independently of the city administration and reports directly to council regarding administrative problems and the need for improvements to the administrative systems. The mandate of such officers is limited to any decision, recommendation, act, or omission of any of the following: the city council; a standing, advisory, or other committee established by city council; the board of a controlled corporation of the city; and a person acting as a lawyer for the city. Evidently, fledgling efforts to institutionalize and utilize the position of administrative review officer have been challenging. The existence of such officers is not well known among residents in the various cities and the future of the post is uncertain. An alternative for the province is to create a municipal ombudsman's office, either as a division of the provincial ombudsman's office or as a separate and distinct position.[9]

The two municipal statutes that are being reviewed for potential reforms are the Northern Municipalities Act, 1983, under which northern municipalities are governed, and the Lloydminster Charter, under which the border city of Lloydminster is governed. The Northern Municipalities Act is being reviewed to determine whether it should be reformed to render it more like the Municipalities Act, 2005, or whether to integrate it into that particular statute. Deliberations on reforming the statute have been relatively slow because the municipal and provincial governments are monitoring the implementation of the Cities Act and the Municipalities Act to determine how well they work for southern municipalities and how well suited some of their principles and provisions are for northern municipalities.

Similarly, the Lloydminster Charter is being reviewed to determine whether and how to include the key principles and provisions contained within both the Cities Act of Saskatchewan and the Municipal Government Act of Alberta. Towards that end, in 2004 and 2005, the Saskatchewan and Alberta legislatures repealed the Lloydminster Municipal Amalgamation Act, 1930, which created a single integrated municipal corporate entity for the neighbouring border communities, and replaced it with the City of Lloydminster Act, which was enacted by both provincial legislatures. This is the first step in their joint efforts to produce and enact a new Lloydminster Charter which will embody the innovative principles and provisions contained in the Cities Act and in the Municipalities Act of Saskatchewan and the Municipal Government Act of Alberta.[10] The existing Lloydminster Charter gives both the Saskatchewan and Alberta governments the authority to deal with various matters, but, for general purposes of the statute, Saskatchewan's minister is designated as the lead minister. However, for some important matters which have a potentially significant effect on the provincial interest of either province (for example, municipal financing), ratification by the ministers and/or the cabinet of both provinces is required.[11] The reason that Saskatchewan's minister was given a prominent role in the existing Lloydminster Charter was that, when it was enacted, the majority of the population lived on the Saskatchewan side of the border. During the past thirty years, however, the population on the Alberta side has grown much more rapidly, to the point where it is more than twice the size of the population on the Saskatchewan side. It will be interesting to see how ministerial and cabinet responsibilities of the two provincial governments will be aligned when this statute is reformed in the future.

In addition to the major municipal acts discussed above, municipalities are governed by dozens of other statutes related to an array of governance matters ranging from elections, municipal financing, and public health to policing, pest control, and cemeteries.[12] Although the aforementioned reforms to the statutory framework resulted in the reduction of the number of core municipal statutes by one, they did not result in any notable reduction in the multitude of other statutes which impinge on municipal governance. Two such statutes of some importance are the Rural Administrators Act and the Urban Administrators Act, the core function of which is to sanction the creation of two

professional associations of administrators having delegated responsibility for regulating the qualifications and behaviour of specified
municipal administrators.[13]

Institutional Framework

Saskatchewan's municipal sector consists of three sets of institutional
frameworks – the municipal, the provincial, and the intergovernmental. Each is discussed in turn below.

MUNICIPAL INSTITUTIONAL FRAMEWORK
The municipal institutional framework consists of associations of
municipalities and associations of municipal professional staff. The
former includes the Saskatchewan Association of Rural Municipalities
(SARM), the Saskatchewan Urban Municipalities Association (SUMA),
the Saskatchewan Association of Northern Communities (SANC),
which is also known as the 'New North,' and the Provincial Association of Resort Communities of Saskatchewan (PARCS). PARCS represents cottage owners and resort communities in Saskatchewan. Its goal
is to ensure that senior levels of government are aware of its members'
concerns. PARCS advocates for, and develops, policy positions on
resort-community issues.

Although these four organizations may appear similar, there are
some significant differences in their organizational capacity and political power. This is especially true when the associations of urban and
rural municipalities are compared to the associations for the northern
communities and the resort communities. Whereas the first two have
several hundred municipalities as members, the latter two have only
three to four dozen members. Moreover, unlike the first two, which
have substantial financial and human resources, the latter have only
very limited resources. Finally, whereas the first two have province-
wide and regional conventions which are among the largest gatherings
of associations in the province, the conventions of the latter are much
smaller. The annual conventions of the SARM and SUMA tend to be
highly political events that produce resolutions that are forwarded to
the various provincial government departments for their consideration and response. One of the most significant parts of those conventions tends to be the sessions in which the resolutions submitted by
various municipalities are debated. Also important are the so-called
'cabinet bear-pit sessions' where most, if not all, provincial cabinet

ministers are present to listen to, and field questions from, individual members of those associations regarding any matter of interest to them. These sessions are institutionalized to the point where attendance by the premier and cabinet ministers is expected, rather than something that is negotiated.

SANC and PARCS have not achieved the same level of organizational and political capacity as SARM and SUMA. For its part, SANC has always faced substantial challenges in acquiring the requisite financial and human resources. The decision by the Northern Revenue Sharing Trust Account committee to provide it with stable annual operating grants starting in 1999 has helped to make SANC more viable. However, it has not provided SANC with all the resources that it needs to operate more effectively in representing and serving its members. Although it does not have many of the organizational attributes that would render it as self-sufficient and as politically powerful as its southern counterparts, SANC can be politically influential within the northern part of the province when two conditions exist. The first is when the two northern seats for the provincial legislature become important for any of the major parties in holding the balance of power. The second is when SANC is able to maintain a high degree of legitimacy in the eyes of its membership and voters within northern communities. One of the significant characteristics of SANC is that its executive, like most if not all of its member communities, consists of Métis people. It is not an exaggeration to say that municipal governance in northern Saskatchewan is essentially Métis governance of communities with a relatively high concentration of Métis people.

There are at least three major staff associations with direct interest in the municipal sector. The first two are the associations of municipal administrators. One is the Urban Municipal Administrators Association of Saskatchewan (UMAAS), which includes members who work for the urban and the northern municipalities, and the other is the Rural Municipal Administrators Association of Saskatchewan (RMAAS), which includes only members who work for the rural municipalities. These associations perform three core functions: certification of municipal officials, advancing the knowledge and understanding of their members regarding policy and administrative matters, and representing and protecting the interests of their members vis-à-vis the employers (that is, the individual municipalities and the municipal associations). Notwithstanding the fact that these staff associations have been established to advance the employment interests of their members vis-à-vis the municipalities, there is a very close alliance between them and their corresponding associations of municipalities. This alliance usually sees them on the same side of the table in negotiations with the provincial government about jurisdictional, regulatory, and financial matters.

The other two relatively important staff associations are the Association of Professional Community Planners of Saskatchewan (APCPS) and the Saskatchewan Economic Developers Association (SEDA). ACPS is an association open to all planners, planning students, and persons interested in planning. The most interesting aspect of this organization, in terms of multilevel governance, is that its membership includes planners who work either full time or on a contract basis for the municipal and provincial governments and various other local authorities (for example, economic-development authorities). SEDA is an association of economic-development officers in the province, most of whom work for regional economic-development authorities and who, by virtue of the nature of their jobs, are actively involved in discussions and negotiations involving various orders of government. Both APCPS and SEDA are much smaller than the staff associations of municipal administrators and tend to be less politically active within the municipal sector.

Collectively, the various types of associations are prominent and influential stakeholders within the political system and they exercise considerable political power in advancing the interests of their respective organizations and the municipal corporations and communities for which they work.

PROVINCIAL INSTITUTIONAL FRAMEWORK

The two most important provincial institutions involved in dealing with municipalities and municipal issues are the department responsible for municipal affairs and the Saskatchewan Municipal Board. The most significant branch within the Department of Municipal Affairs is Provincial-Municipal Relations and Municipal Advisory Services. As its name suggests, that agency consists of two major units. The first is Provincial-Municipal Relations, which facilitates department interaction with the municipal sector in Saskatchewan as well as some of the department's liaison on municipal matters nationally. It coordinates the department's participation in various fora, which include the following:

- meetings with representatives of the three major municipal associations, some involving both SUMA and SARM, and the others
  involving only SANC;
- meetings with representatives of the City Mayors Caucus;
- meetings of the Municipal Programs and Services Steering Committee with executive directors of SUMA, SARM, SANC, RMAAS,
  and UMAAS; and
- meetings of the provincial/territorial ministers responsible for
  local government.

The second unit is Municipal Advisory Services, which provides the
following services to municipal governments:

- administrative and technical advice to administrators and councillors;
- educational programs for municipal officials such as the Municipal
  Leadership Development Program, which is offered in partnership
  with SUMA, SARM, SANC, UMAAS, and RMAA;
- educational seminars at annual conventions of the associations;
  and
- preparation of municipal information manuals, technical bulletins,
  and online documents.

The provincial government maintains two relatively distinct municipal advisory services units – one located in Regina to provide such
services to urban and rural municipalities in southern Saskatchewan,
and the other located in LaRonge to serve municipalities in northern
Saskatchewan. Although these units are at the service of all municipalities, the bulk of the advice that they dispense is for smaller urban
municipalities, rural municipalities, and northern municipalities,
which generally do not have the financial resources to hire the requisite number of persons with the planning and management expertise
needed by a municipal corporation. The cities are not very dependent
on such services because they have an array of planning and management specialists on staff.

There are at least two other major agencies which operate under the
aegis of the provincial government and deal with important facets of
municipal governance. The first is the Saskatchewan Municipal Board
(SMB), which is a quasi-judicial body responsible primarily for the fol-

lowing matters: ensuring sound financial borrowing practices by all municipalities; hearing and deciding on appeals regarding planning, assessment, fire prevention, and development matters; and reviewing challenges to applications for alteration of municipal boundaries or amalgamation of municipalities. The second is the Saskatchewan Assessment Management Agency (SAMA), which was originally created in 1987 by statute to provide property-assessment services for municipalities and school divisions. Pursuant to the act, which came into force on 1 January 2005, SAMA is governed by a board consisting of eleven members appointed by the lieutenant-governor-in-council.[14] SAMA is jointly funded by the province, municipalities, and school boards. Whereas the province's funding is provided through a combination of an operating grant and some fees for service related to special programs, the municipal funding is provided through a levy on the municipalities that use its assessment services, and the school boards' share of the funding is provided by an allocation directly to SAMA from the department responsible for K-12 education.[15]

INTERGOVERNMENTAL INSTITUTIONAL FRAMEWORKS

Saskatchewan's municipal sector consists of several intergovernmental consultative and coordinative mechanisms which have been institutionalized to varying degrees. This includes provincial-municipal, intermunicipal, municipal-educational, and municipal-aboriginal mechanisms.[16] The most important institutions are discussed below.

To facilitate provincial-municipal consultations and coordination, several intergovernmental mechanisms have been established. The first is the trilateral Municipal-Provincial Forum, consisting of representatives of SARM, SUMA, and the provincial government. The second is the bilateral Municipal-Provincial Roundtable, consisting of representatives of SANC and the provincial government. The third is the multilateral forum in which the provincial Municipal Programs and Services Steering Committee meets on a quarterly basis with the executive directors of SUMA, SARM, SANC, RMAA, and UMAAS.

Another provincial-municipal coordinating mechanism which has been established recently is the steering committee for the Municipal Capacity Development Program. The committee, consisting of representatives of the provincial government and the three main municipal associations (that is, SARM, SUMA, and SANC), devised the Municipal Capacity Development Program, which aims to assist neighbouring municipalities to engage in collaborative efforts to enhance capacity for dealing with infrastructure and community-development needs and, by extension, to enhance their sustainability. Staffing for the program was made possible by a $781,000 grant from the national Municipal Rural Infrastructure Fund.[17] This grant was instrumental in the decision of the three municipal associations to enter into the partnership to develop and deliver the program. Without such funding, it is highly doubtful that the program would have attracted the municipal associations' participation.

During the past fifteen years, some coordinating mechanisms have also been established to facilitate consultations and coordination between representatives of municipal and First Nations governments. The notable ones were the 'roundtables,' which involved representatives of the SARM, SUMA, and the Federation of Saskatchewan Indian Nations (FSIN), established to deal with two major issues stemming from the Treaty Land Entitlement (TLE) process – tax-loss compensation for municipalities when land is converted to reserve status, and the reserve-creation processes. The roundtables proved to be a very valuable forum to resolve those issues. One of the significant products of one of the roundtables was the report, produced jointly by the FSIN and SUMA, which outlined the principles and procedures for the creation of reserves in urban areas.[18] Unfortunately, the roundtables ceased meeting after those two matters were resolved and they have not been institutionalized to deal with the broad range of issues requiring coordination between municipal and aboriginal governments.

A notable intergovernmental coordinating mechanism involving municipalities in northern Saskatchewan is the Northern Development Board Corporation. In addition to SANC's representative, the board consists of representatives of the Métis Nation – Saskatchewan, the Prince Albert Grand Council and the Meadow Lake Tribal Council, representing northern First Nations, and the Athabasca Economic Development and Training Corporation. The board is one of the mechanisms established as part of Saskatchewan's Northern Strategy, the goal of which is to foster social and economic development in northern Saskatchewan.[19]

In recent years tri-level intergovernmental coordinating mechanisms involving representatives of the municipal, provincial, and federal governments have been established to deal with specific policy issues, programs, and projects. Notable examples of such mechanisms are those created for the implementation of the programs and projects resulting from some of the federal government's gas-tax revenue sharing under the 'New Deal' for all municipalities, as well as project funding under the Canada-Agriculture Infrastructure Program (CAIP) and the Prairie Grain Roads Program (PGRP) for rural municipalities. The principal functions of such tri-level coordinating committees have been one or more of the following: to establish the principles and parameters of such programs, to devise processes and priorities for their implementation, and to make decisions regarding the specific projects which will be funded.[20]

Decision-Making Framework

Every fully incorporated municipality has a council headed by a mayor (in the case of cities, urban municipalities, and northern municipalities) or by a reeve (in the case of rural municipalities). The size of municipal councils varies from as few as four to as many as eleven members. At the lower end of that range are the councils for northern, small urban, and rural municipalities, and at the upper end are the councils for large urban municipalities and cities.

The municipal statutes stipulate the ranges for the size of councils but provide municipalities with substantial discretion in determining the precise size within those ranges. The minimum for cities is a mayor and six councillors; for urban and northern municipalities, a mayor and at least two councillors; and for rural municipalities, a reeve and at least one councillor for each division, which generally means six. Cities and urban and northern municipalities are all allowed to increase the number of councillors according to the regulations specified in the statutes.

The municipal statutes stipulate the configuration, functions, and powers of the chief elected officials (mayors and reeves) and chief administrative officers (managers, administrators, and clerks). In the new statutes, special efforts were made to ensure that the functions and powers of these officials were distinguished from those of municipal councils so as to eliminate some of the confusing overlap which existed in previous statutes. Municipalities in Saskatchewan have substantial freedom in determining the types and number of managers and administrators for their operation. Indeed, the only statutory requirement for most municipalities is that they appoint a chief administrator and an auditor.[21] In the case of northern municipalities with a population over 500, there is the additional requirement for them to appoint a solicitor. The total number of full-time and part-time municipal employees in Saskatchewan is approximately 20,000.[22] When the employees are combined with the elected officials, the total number of personnel involved in the municipal sector is about 24,000.

The term of office for councils in cities, urban municipalities, and northern municipalities is three years, but it is two years for rural municipalities. Moreover, whereas all candidates for the mayor and councillor positions in cities, urban municipalities, and northern municipalities stand for election at the same time, candidates for the reeve and councillor positions for rural municipalities do not. Instead, they have staggered electoral terms. Elections for reeves and councillors of odd-numbered municipal divisions are held in even-numbered years, and those for councillors in even-numbered divisions are held in odd-numbered years. Consequently, at least half of the voters in rural municipalities are engaged in choosing representatives annually.

One of the major changes resulting from the recent reforms to the statutory frameworks for cities pursuant to the Cities Act, and for urban and rural municipalities pursuant to the Municipalities Act, is that the province has devolved to municipalities the responsibility for municipal-election finances. Consequently, at least sixty days before an election, the municipal councils may establish, through a by-law, the regulations related to either or both of the following: disclosure requirements regarding campaign contributions and expenses, and election-campaign spending limits. This proved to be of little interest to most municipalities. Indeed, only the two largest cities devoted much attention to this matter and to date only Saskatoon's municipal council has adopted such regulations. Regina did not and it became one of the election issues as one of the mayoral candidates criticized the incumbent mayor and council for not having produced such regulations prior to the 2006 election. The key elements of Saskatoon's regulations are the election-expense limits of $100,000 for mayoral candidates and $10,000 for council candidates, and the requirement that all candidates disclose the names of everyone making a contribution greater than $250 to their campaigns.[23]

Voter turnout in municipal elections is generally very low, ranging from 20 per cent to 50 per cent. Higher voter turnout tends to occur in smaller municipalities. However, more important than the size of municipalities for voter turnout is whether there are high-profile and contentious issues either in the election campaigns or in campaigns relating to plebiscites and referenda, which are usually held on the same day as the municipal elections. The general pattern tends to be that the higher the profile and degree of controversy, the higher the voter turnout.

Saskatchewan, like other western provinces, has a history of extensively using plebiscites and referenda as mechanisms for registering the preferences of voters on various types of issues related to municipal governance (for example, ward versus at-large electoral systems), regulation (store hours, smoking in public places, and casinos), and service provisions (such as facilities and infrastructure). Generally, plebiscites and referenda are initiated by the municipal councils rather than ratepayers.

One of the interesting aspects of the election campaigns in these municipalities is that they tend to focus largely on local community issues related to planning, provision of 'hard' and 'soft' municipal services, taxation levels, and, increasingly, safety and quality of life. Rarely is much attention devoted to broader issues related either to the general aspects of municipal governance in the province or to multilevel governance. Candidates and voters tend to leave it to the elected officials at the provincial and federal levels to deal with those types of issues. Similarly, municipal elections in Saskatchewan are rarely, if ever, contested on platforms that are either critical or supportive of any provincial or federal policy or program initiatives that impinge on the municipal sector. Similarly, purely municipal issues do not become so-called 'hot-button' or 'cleavage' issues in provincial or federal elections.

Functional Framework

The functions of Saskatchewan's municipalities are highly varied. The reason is that, although all municipalities have the authority, and in some cases the duty, to perform a range of functions, there are considerable differences in the functions that they choose to perform. The differences are linked to the type and size of municipalities. Rural municipalities and small municipalities with populations of less than approximately 500 tend to perform very limited functions related to the provision of basic infrastructure services (roads, water, waste management, and so on). The medium-sized and larger municipalities tend to perform a broader set of functions which, in addition to basic infrastructure services, include protective services (police and fire), community services (recreational and cultural services), land-use planning and development, and economic development. Not surprisingly, the most diverse and extensive panoply of functions is found in the cities, and particularly the largest cities.

Although the functions performed by Saskatchewan municipalities are similar to those performed by their counterparts in other provinces, they are not identical. Indeed, in some cases they are not even identical among all municipalities within the province. There are at least three functions in which notable differences exist. The first is a tax-collection function. Saskatchewan municipalities are required to collect the school portion of local property taxes and then transfer it to the provincial government for allocation to school boards. The mill rate on the education tax is set by the school divisions; the municipalities merely collect it. Historically, the municipalities collected and transferred those taxes without notable incidents, but in recent years some rural municipalities have delayed the transfers as a protest over what they perceived to be the unduly high level of property tax on agricultural land. Their demand was, and remains, that the provincial government reduce the level of their school boards' dependency on the property tax by providing them with more funding from other revenue bases. More generally, the municipalities regard the education property tax as a significant impingement on the municipal revenue base.

The second relatively unique function is property assessment. This is generally the responsibility of the Saskatchewan Assessment Management Agency. SAMA has both a governance function – which requires it to regulate the rules of assessment through the Saskatchewan Assessment Manual, to audit assessments, and to confirm municipal assessment rolls – as well as a non-governance function – which requires it to provide assessment services to municipalities. SAMA performs the assessment-services function for most municipalities and quasi-municipalities. But the four largest cities (Saskatoon, Regina, Moose Jaw, and Prince Albert) are authorized to conduct their own assessments within their respective corporate boundaries.[24]

The other idiosyncratic function is in the utilities sector. During the early years after the creation of the province, many municipalities were involved in the provision of some of the utility services. Today only Saskatoon and Swift Current perform a major role in providing a utility service other than water and sewage. They have retained their power utilities and continue to provide power, purchased from the provincial power utility, to approximately half of the homes within the pre-1958 corporate boundaries.

Unlike some other provinces, in recent years Saskatchewan has not undertaken a major realignment of functions either between the provincial and municipal governments or between the municipal governments and any other local governing authority. The only realignments have occurred in minor roles and responsibilities related to the certification of administrators, the training of firefighters for some communities, and the provision of building inspectors for some small urban and rural municipalities. The major reason for the limited scope of such reforms is that the municipal associations have not been willing to enter into discussions regarding any functional realignment for fear that it would lead to downloading of some roles or responsibilities to them from the provincial government.[25] At most there have been some adjustments to the level of financial responsibility either between the provincial and municipal governments or among municipal governments related to the performance of such functions as property assessments and policing. The rationale for adjustments to the level of financial responsibility has been either that the beneficiaries of certain services should assume their fair share of the costs or that it is desirable to achieve more equitable cost-sharing arrangements among municipalities.[26] The only other notable functional adjustment in recent years was in the financial responsibility for health, which occurred when the provincial government eliminated the health levy it had been imposing on municipalities.

Financial Framework

This section reviews the structure of local government finances in Saskatchewan. Local government is understood as services provided by municipalities, excluding education, although some attention will be given to education since it shares the local property-tax base with municipalities. As shown in the appendix, Saskatchewan's local governments, compared to all Canadian local governments, are relatively more reliant on own-source revenues and on property taxes, with provincial transfers per capita significantly smaller than in the other provinces. Per capita federal transfers, all of which were for specific purposes, were significantly below the national average. The reasons for this are unclear.

The remainder of this section is concerned with Saskatchewan's experience over the period 1988–2004, for which Statistics Canada has produced consistent data series. The provincial budget was in crisis in the first half of the 1990s and the consequences were shared with local

Figure 1: Trends in local general government finance[27]

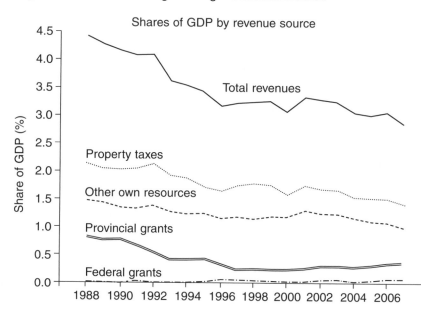

governments and school boards (which share the property-tax base).
Figure 1 shows that, as a share of GDP, municipal expenditures
declined significantly throughout the period from 1988 through 1996
and were roughly a constant share thereafter. Provincial grants, as a
share of GDP, declined over the same period, sharply in the early
1990s, and have been a stable and small share since 1997. The province
has recognized this and recently increased some grants, albeit on a
temporary basis.

Figure 2 shows that real expenditures per capita declined into the
early 1990s and recovered thereafter to attain the levels of the late
1980s by 2001 (current expenditures) and 2004 (capital expenditures).
The latter is reflected in the now widely discussed infrastructure
deficit, the remedy of which will require real increases in the near
future. Over the whole period, then, the falling share of municipal government in GDP is a result of GDP growing relative to municipal governments, combined with declining real per capita expenditures
through the early 1990s. It reflects a dependence on a relatively inelas-
tic revenue base and reductions in provincial grants.

Figure 2: Trends in current and capital expenditure[28]

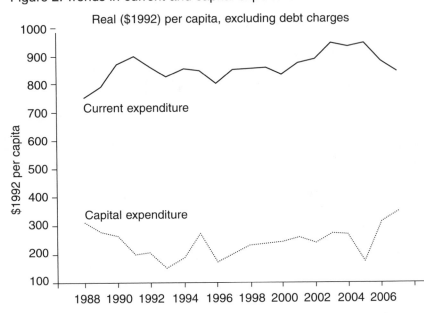

Real ($1992) per capita, excluding debt charges

Figure 3 shows the impact on own-source local finance. Property taxes and other own-source revenues increased sharply relative to provincial transfers but the balance between the two remained stable. Figure 4 shows that school boards steadily increased their reliance on the property base until 2000. The combined effect on local ratepayers resulted in a commission on education finance (the Commission on Financing K-12 Education) which was charged with finding the appropriate balance between provincial and school board contributions, the appropriate balance between the use of the property tax and other sources of taxation, and the best way of achieving fairness in financing education among the existing classes of property taxpayers (agricultural, business, and residential). The commission recommended an increase in provincial grants and reduced education property taxes, to be financed with an increase in the provincial sales tax and an extension of the base to include restaurant meals (which proved contentious) and province-wide education taxes on commercial property at a uniform rate. The recommendations have not been implemented.

Figure 3: Relative composition of local municipal finances[29]

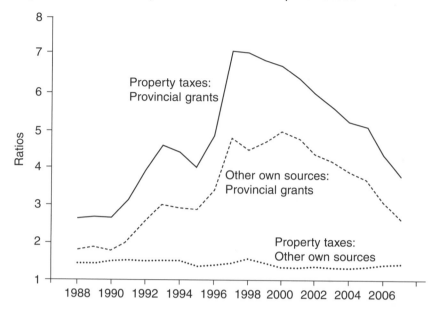

Figure 5 breaks down local government expenditures. Administration expenditures tracked the decline and recovery in overall expenditures while the major categories of transportation, protection, recreation, and environment remained roughly constant. The brunt of the cuts was absorbed in the category of other expenditures, here an aggregate that includes health, social services, housing, tourism and industrial promotion, planning, and other services.

PROPERTY TAX
A new property tax structure was implemented in 1997 motivated by tax assessments that deviated significantly from market values across and within classes of seemingly comparable properties. The prospective tax shifts made the reassessment contentious however, and a variety of remedial measures were designed in response. The result is surprisingly complex, perpetuates historic anomalies, is vulnerable to political action at both the local and provincial levels, and interacts with the structure of municipal and education grants.

Figure 4: School property tax relative to provincial education grants[30]

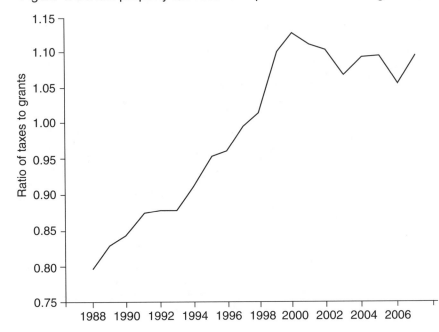

Property assessment. Under the new structure, all property in Saskatchewan is assessed at 'fair value' following rules and procedures in the Saskatchewan Assessment Manual as determined by the Saskatchewan Assessment Management Agency under the authority of the Assessment Management Agency Act. A fair value is the sum of the land value and the depreciated replacement cost of buildings, with a market-adjustment factor applied to buildings to ensure that fair values in a relevant market area approximate the average selling price of comparable properties. The result is intended to be close to market value and, in the discussion below, fair values are treated as market values. (One distinction between a market and a fair value is that a fair-value assessment cannot be appealed on the basis that it does not reflect market value but only on the basis of an incorrect application of the rules.)

Assessments are updated every four years, with the current 2005 valuation based on 2002 market conditions; the 2009 revaluation will

Figure 5: Expenditures by responsibility[31]

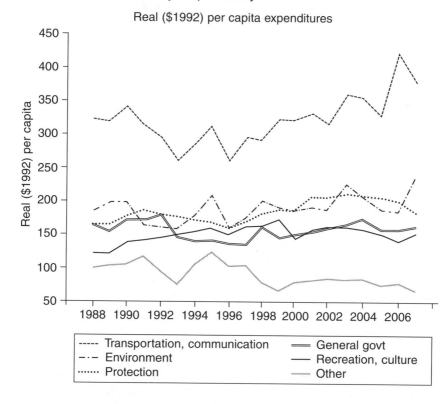

Real ($1992) per capita expenditures

Legend:
- - - - - Transportation, communication
- –·– Environment
- ······ Protection
- ═══ General govt
- ─── Recreation, culture
- ─── Other

use 2006 conditions. Reassessment has been contentious and both agricultural and other non-residential property owners have sought non-market measures based on productivity and income approaches, with the objective of obtaining fair values below market values. However, the 2009 revaluation will use market value for residential and commercial properties for consistency with other Canadian jurisdictions (though heavy-industry property, linear property, and resource-production equipment will continue to use a regulated system). The 2005 revaluation utilized a productivity method for agricultural land rather than a local market index factor that would take into account local sales values. Market-value assessment of agricultural property remains contentious and this property will continue to be assessed using the current regulated system based on productive value. One consequence is the valuing of agricultural land proximate to urban areas as equivalent to distant, but equally productive, land.

Not all properties are assessed in rural municipalities. Agricultural assessments apply only to land (agricultural improvements are exempt) and exempt the residential property if the land assessment exceeds the residential assessment. Since the residential property is not normally assessed if it is apparent that the limitation will not bind, assessment data understate agricultural values on a province-wide basis.

Assessed values (to which local mill rates are applied) are fair-value assessments weighted by a percentage of value established by the province for each class of property to enable the province to limit tax shifts between property types. The 2001 percentages were: 50 per cent for non-arable (range) land, 55 per cent for other agricultural land, 70 per cent for residential property, 100 per cent for commercial and industrial property, and 75 per cent for other industrial land and improvements (such as elevators, railways, and pipelines). In 2005 the provincial percentage of value for non-arable land was reduced from 50 per cent to 40 per cent to limit a province-wide property-tax shift to pasture land. The provincial percentages feed into needs-based provincial grants. Percentages of value remain unchanged for all other types of property.

Rate structure. The 1997 implementation of the new property-tax structure created a range of tax tools to enable municipalities to manage tax shifts locally, for example, between residential and commercial property as well as within the residential and commercial property types. These tools included the authority to establish property subclasses, mill rate factors (effectively creating class-specific mill rates), base taxes, and phase-ins of tax changes resulting from revaluations. The 2001 revaluation introduced a minimum-tax option. Following a recent review, some tax tools were removed, including a never-used authority of municipalities to phase in assessments, a seldom-used authority of towns, villages, resort villages, rural municipalities, and northern municipalities to phase in property taxes (cities retain this authority), and the authority of towns, villages, and resort villages to create a residential condominium subclass for the purposes of applying local property-tax tools (cities retain this authority). Thus, the rate structure as well as the assessment principles continue to evolve.

In its simplest form, property tax payable in Saskatchewan is the product of a fair-value assessment determined by the assessing authority, a provincially determined percentage of value for the property class, a locally determined mill rate, and a local mill rate factor for the property class. Local mill rate factors enable municipalities to scale a uniform mill rate by property type and thereby to set different mill rates for each class. Municipalities have the option of distinguishing property subclasses with differing mill rate factors, and the identification of subclasses with distinct mill rate factors is quite extensive. For example, among Saskatchewan cities in 2004, subclasses distinguished within residential properties included single-family, condominium, and multi-unit dwellings by number of units (for instance, under four units, three to eleven units, more than twelve units) and by value (less or greater than $100,000). Among non-residential properties, there were subclasses for halls (profit and non-profit), motels, new hotels and motels, exterior hotels, golf courses, shopping centres, and special commercial properties, with some properties identified quite specifically. The utilization of subclasses has varied across communities and over time.

Municipalities may, and several do, impose a base tax (a fixed-dollar levy per residential unit, for example) or a minimum tax for particular property classes. (The larger cities – Saskatoon, Regina, Moose Jaw, Prince Albert, Lloydminster, and Weyburn – do not; others such as Melfort and Swift Current do.) Tax payable is then the sum of the base tax and the computation outlined above or the minimum tax. The use of base taxes and minimum taxes contrasts with the property-tax relief policies observed in other provinces and with general views on equitable property taxation. The base tax and minimum tax do not increase levies by their nominal amount since the required uniform mill rate is reduced, but, where utilized, their effect is to increase the levy on lower-valued properties and reduce it on higher-valued ones; if other tax tools are unchanged, a residential base tax shifts burdens from non-residential to residential properties. Weyburn, which does not impose a base tax, provided an illustration in which a residential base tax of $400 would reduce the municipal mill rate from 16.5 to 8.4 mills and increase taxes on properties with a fair-value assessment below $70,608. Moose Jaw, which also does not impose a base tax, provided an analysis showing that a $400 base tax would increase levies on 55.6 per cent of properties; levies on properties with fair values between $25,000 and $50,000 (22.2 per cent of all properties) would increase by an average of 49.2 per cent. These analyses are consistent with experience in cities that do impose base tax. For example, 48 per cent of residential revenues in Melfort, 66 per cent in Yorkton, and 51 per cent in Swift Current were collected as base tax in 2004. It is interesting that local governments are able to enact policies that senior governments would not dare to consider.

The government has a stated goal of reducing education property taxes to a level that finances 40 per cent of education costs, with the remainder financed from the provincial tax base.[32] This is a long-term goal towards which the government has moved selectively, with relief targeted to agricultural land. From 2006, the government will reduce farmland education taxes by $53.8 million, a 38 per cent reduction, which results in a 40 per cent share for farmland. Thirty per cent of a one-time adjustment in the 2004 federal Equalization Program payment provided education property-tax relief for all classes of property in 2005 and 2006, with the province funding an 8 per cent credit (capped at $2,500 for apartments and commercial and industrial properties) against the education portion of property taxes. However, continuation of this relief is contingent upon provincial revenues and perhaps the outcome of Saskatchewan's efforts to obtain a more favourable Equalization Program arrangement.

GRANT PROGRAMS

Saskatchewan municipalities receive grants under several programs which can be loosely divided into unconditional transfers for general purposes to be determined locally and conditional transfers in support of specific purposes. (Education grants are not covered here, though, as noted, they provide tax relief for local ratepayers and thereby also create tax room for municipalities. Also not covered are the benefits of expenditure programs managed directly through provincial and federal departments.) The programs are as follows.

Grants in Lieu of Taxes. The federal government has long paid grants-in-lieu of taxes. Partly in response to many years of lobbying by the municipalities, the province introduced a four-year phase-in of grants-in-lieu of municipal, library, and school taxes in 1998 for most provincial property owned or managed by Saskatchewan Property Management. Most health and education facilities (including the two universities) owned by the province are excluded. The 2005 grants totalled about $11 million.

Urban Revenue Sharing Grants. Urban Revenue Sharing Grants totalled $44.1 million in 2005–6. There are three components to the grants: a basic grant, a per capita grant, and an equalizing foundation grant. The equalization component adjusts for the excess of recognized expenditures over recognized revenues, if positive. Recognized revenues include property taxes, grants in lieu of taxes, licences and fees, electrical surcharges, utility surpluses, and other own-source revenues. Thus, for example, the surplus from a locally owned utility (as in Saskatoon) is partially recaptured by the province; more generally, the prospect of recapture is a disincentive to developing non-property-tax revenue options. Recognized expenditures include the costs of normal municipal services (protective services, transportation, environmental health, public health and welfare, environmental development, and culture and recreation) and policing costs. Whether the recognized rates accurately reflect costs of services is unclear; for example, the recognized rates embedded in education grants do not reflect costs accurately.[33] However, all of this detail is somewhat moot, because between 1997 and 2001 the grants were frozen at the 1997–8 levels, and since 2001 the grants have been increased only in the per capita component using 1996 populations until 2004–5 and 2001 populations thereafter. Thus, the equalization formula has not been applied between 1998–9 and 2005–6 inclusive and the effect of freezing at the 1997–8 levels has been to embed the equalization adjustments based on the pre-property-tax-reform assessments. The use of lagged populations understates the needs of growing relative to declining communities. For example, the 2001 census populations for Regina and Saskatoon were 178,225 and 196,811 while the 2004 city populations, based on census and health records, were 191,400 and 205,900, respectively. The understatements in the grant formula were 7.4 per cent and 4.6 per cent.

Rural Revenue Sharing Grants. There are two components to the unconditional rural revenue sharing grants – an unconditional grant and an organized hamlet grant, both of which are paid to the municipality. In 2005–6 the organized hamlet grants totalled $0.5 million, comprised of a base amount plus a per capita amount. The unconditional grants totalled $29.95 million based on a formula that includes the road system and other service expenditures. The transportation component is based on the taxable assessment per kilometre and the relative cost of road construction to provide equalization of fiscal capacity among rural municipalities. The component for other services uses net operating expenditures in each rural municipality with an adjustment for the taxable assessment per capita; thus, assessment practices and provincial percentages of value feed into the grant structure as well as affecting tax levies. (This observation also holds for education grants; in fact, the ability of local governments to undo, partially or completely, the effects of the provincial percentages of value means that the primary effect of the percentages is through the grant structure.) The transportation and other services components are then added together to determine the unconditional grant for each rural municipality.

Canada-Saskatchewan Municipal Rural Infrastructure Agreement. This agreement is intended to support infrastructure renewal in smaller communities, directing money to projects that benefit municipalities with populations of less than 250,000. Since this definition includes all Saskatchewan communities, the Saskatchewan implementation imposes a restriction that directs at least 80 per cent of the support to projects outside the cities of Regina and Saskatoon and up to 5.3 per cent to projects in northern Saskatchewan. At least 45 per cent will be directed to 'green' projects. The amounts involved are substantial, with matching notional totals of $38 million from each of the provincial and the federal governments distributed over 2005–6 through 2008–9. The qualifying project categories are wide-ranging: drinking and waste water, solid waste, public transit, local roads, culture (including museums, local heritage, performing arts, cultural and community centres, and libraries), recreation facilities, tourism enhancement (including convention and trade centres), environmental energy improvements (such as energy-efficiency retrofits), and connectivity (that is, broadband services).

Canada-Saskatchewan Infrastructure Program. The Canada Saskatchewan Infrastructure Program implemented a five-year (2001–6) commitment announced by the federal government in the 2000 budget. The funding is a grant for approved projects, with a maximum federal investment (over five years) of $56.71 million, matching Saskatchewan funding, and with recipients contributing at least a one-third share of the total. The project criteria are similar to those of the Canada-Saskatchewan Municipal Rural Infrastructure Agreement.

Northern Saskatchewan Grant Programs. The Northern Water and Sewer Programs support water and sewer systems in the communities of northern Saskatchewan. The Northern New Facilities Assistance Program covers 100 per cent of the cost of new works, and the Northern Water and Sewer Upgrading Grant Program covers up to 85 per cent of the costs of expanding and upgrading existing facilities. The Northern Capital Grants Program provides financial and technical assistance to northern communities for up to 90 per cent of the costs of constructing or upgrading municipal facilities and for the acquisition of municipal equipment.

Canada Strategic Infrastructure Fund. The federal Canada Strategic Infrastructure Fund is a program designed to fund major strategic infrastructure projects in large cities. Regina and Saskatoon are the only Saskatchewan municipalities that qualify for support under this program. Although the province is not required to contribute, it has agreed to support portions of projects in each city. The 2005–6 budget is $5.9 million with a total provincial contribution of $9 million over two years.

New Deal-Federal Gas Tax Program. Saskatchewan municipalities have been receiving funds through the New Deal-Federal Gas Tax Program. The province administers payments through the New Deal Secretariat, which reviews municipal-infrastructure investment plans outlining how municipalities propose to spend their gas-tax allocations.

Debates regarding the Need for, and Nature of, Reform

The extant literature and interviews with knowledgeable observers reveal that Saskatchewan debates regarding reform to the municipal system have been, and continue to be, pervasive.[34] Debates on the need for, and nature of, reform have focused primarily on the effects that the current configuration of the structural, statutory, institutional, decision-making, functional, and financial frameworks have both for local municipal governance and for multilevel governance. Invariably such debates have revolved around questions related to the effects of the configuration of the municipal system not only for efficient, effective, and equitable governance but also for democratic, responsive, and accountable governance.[35]

During the past decade, the most substantial and significant debates have mainly concerned reform to three key elements of the municipal system, namely, the statutory framework, the structural framework, and the financial framework. The debates regarding the functional and decision-making frameworks have been less significant. The basic points made by protagonists in the debates about the statutory, structural, and financial frameworks are outlined below.

Questions about the statutory framework appear to have been resolved, at least for the time being. These questions concerned reforms that would not only provide municipalities with greater clarity regarding their precise powers and duties but also increase the autonomy of municipalities in exercising their powers and performing their duties. Proponents argued that such reforms would contribute to improved local municipal governance and also improved multilevel governance because they would minimize confusion and maximize the autonomy of municipalities to deal with various matters as they saw fit, with fewer statutory and regulatory constraints. The reforms discussed in a previous section of this chapter seem to have satisfied the key municipal and provincial stakeholders. Nevertheless, the jury is still out on whether the reforms have actually improved either local municipal governance or multilevel governance. The only part of the province where this particular debate still persists is in northern Saskatchewan, where the municipal stakeholders are considering reforms to the statute that applies to northern municipalities. They are now focusing on whether the new statutory framework for municipalities in southern Saskatchewan has produced, or will produce, substantial benefits both for local municipal governance and for multilevel governance.

The second major debate has focused on the financial framework. The issue is whether the sources and volume of financial resources that accrue to the municipal governments are appropriate and sufficient. The principal protagonists in this debate tend to be representatives of the municipal and provincial governments. Unlike their provincial counterparts, who tend to argue that the current composition and volume of financial resources are appropriate and sufficient, municipal representatives tend to argue that there is a fiscal imbalance which disadvantages them in comparison to the provincial government. To reduce that imbalance, municipal representatives have maintained that there is a need to consider at least two major reform options – reducing the reliance of school boards on the property-tax base, and increasing the amount of money transferred to municipalities through revenue-sharing arrangements. The municipal representatives argue that both local municipal governance and multilevel governance will be adversely affected until the fiscal imbalance is addressed.

The most pronounced debate about the configuration of the municipal system is focused on its fragmentation. Three kinds of problems are usually cited. First, fragmentation impedes efforts among municipalities to achieve a higher level of coordination and collaboration among themselves in developing and implementing various policies, programs, and projects.[36] Secondly, it creates problems of communication, coordination, and collaboration between municipalities and the other orders of government and governing authorities. This is because municipal governments are required to deal with a relatively large number of municipal stakeholders who often have diverse needs, preferences, and capacities. Thirdly, fragmentation creates problems in generating the right policies, programs, and projects within the context of multilevel governance. The highly fragmented and variegated nature of the municipal system gives rise to major challenges for representatives of municipal governments to produce and to implement policies that are fully consonant with the needs and preferences of all municipal governments and their respective communities.[37] These particular challenges can and do lead to frustration on the part of all governmental representatives involved in multilevel governance. In turn, this leads either to inaction, nominal action, or delayed action by the various orders of government, both individually and collectively, on important matters that require substantial and immediate action.

Prospects for Reform

Notwithstanding a widespread consensus that several of the frameworks within the municipal system should be reconfigured to improve both local governance and multilevel governance for the benefit of the local, regional, and provincial communities and economies, the likelihood that reform will occur in the very near future is not very high. In the realm of municipal-governance reform, Saskatchewan has been, and continues to be, a model of timidity and stasis. This is a paradoxical situation for a province that, for several decades in the post-Second World War era, prided itself on being a bold and courageous leader in designing and implementing leading-edge reforms to governmental institutions, policies, and programs at the provincial level.[38]

At the municipal level, however, Saskatchewan has never been a very bold or courageous leader or even a bold and courageous follower.[39] The obstacle is what can be described as a missionary zeal by local communities to control their political and economic affairs and to resist any proposals for reforms that they believe would affect that control. The value of local democratic control has trumped managerial values of effectiveness and efficiency in planning and development since the inception of the municipal system. All efforts to restructure the system during the past half-century have been met with very strong resistance comparable to that which almost threatened to halt the final implementation of publicly funded health care in the province in the early 1960s.

A recent analysis of Saskatchewan political culture and public policy has raised questions regarding some persistent myths, including the one suggesting that the province has a relatively unique or distinct form of socialist or communitarian ethos.[40] The response to proposals for restructuring the municipal system in the province suggests that the agrarian socialism for which Saskatchewan is renowned[41] seems to be rooted in what might be termed 'bounded communitarianism' or 'parochial communitarianism,' in which the local interest takes precedence over both the regional public interest and the provincial interest.

Unless this changes, the configuration of Saskatchewan's municipal system will remain much as it is now. Hence, the structure of the municipal system will continue to be an impediment not only to efficacious multilevel governance but also to good governance at the local and provincial levels. In their search for improved governance and development in this province, municipal and provincial officials should launch another substantial effort to assess and correct the problems posed by the current structural configuration of the municipal system. However, it should not be assumed that either the reconfiguration of the structural frameworks of the municipal system or the reconfiguration of the functional, financial, and jurisdictional frameworks will automatically result in better local or multilevel governance. The success of reform everywhere, including Saskatchewan, is highly contingent on the will and ability of elected and appointed officials and their communities to recognize problems and deal with them in a highly strategic and competent manner, with the public interest squarely in sight.[42]

Despite that caveat, improvements to the municipal system in Saskatchewan are essential to achieve improvements in local municipal and multilevel governance and ultimately for economic and social development at the local, regional, and provincial levels. Financial and political interests and nostalgia should not be allowed to continue standing in the way of producing a municipal system that would permit municipal governments as well as other orders of government and specialized governing authorities to perform their core functions in a more efficient and effective manner. The development of Saskatchewan's local, regional, and provincial communities and economies depends on it.

Although the prospects for substantial reform in the very near future are not very good, there is some cause for optimism that some reforms will be implemented. The reason for this is a growing recognition among the various governmental stakeholders of the importance of the configuration of the municipal system for the efficacy of both local municipal governance and multilevel governance. More specifically, there is a sense among them that the changes in the statutory and jurisdictional frameworks that have been accomplished in recent years have to be matched by substantial reforms to the structural, institutional, decision-making, functional, and financial frameworks. In the case of the structural framework, the emerging consensus is that there is a need to move towards 'regional governance' by creating either regional municipalities or regional municipal services authorities. In the case of the institutional framework, the emerging view is that a framework of intergovernmental coordinating mechanisms is needed, one that involves municipal, provincial, federal, and aboriginal governments. In the case of the functional framework, the sense is that attention must be devoted to the alignment of functions, not only between provincial and municipal governments but also among the regional planning and development authorities that currently exist or may emerge in the future. Finally, in the case of the financial framework, the emerging consensus is that efforts have to be made to address the interrelated issues of the differences in fiscal capacity of various municipalities and the so-called fiscal imbalances between the various orders of government in light of their respective functional loads.

Both the need for reform and the general parameters of a reform agenda are relatively clear. What remains unclear is whether the political and administrative will and capacity exists to articulate and implement the reform agenda. The fact that terms such as 'eliminating obstacles' and 'clearing the path'[43] are being used more extensively today by representatives of the provincial and municipal organizations provides for a modicum of optimism that substantial reforms might be developed and implemented in the near future.

NOTES

1 See: Saskatchewan, Saskatchewan Royal Commission on Agriculture and Rural Life, *History of Rural Local Government in Saskatchewan* (Regina: Queen's Printer, 1955); Saskatchewan, *Report of the Royal Commission on Agriculture and Rural Life: Rural Roads and Local Government. A Summary* (Regina: Queen's Printer, 1956); Jenni Morton, *The Building of a Province: The Saskatchewan Association of Rural Municipalities* (Regina: PrintWest, 1995); F. Colligan-Yano and Mervyn Norton, *The Urban Age: Building a Place for Urban Government in Saskatchewan*, Saskatchewan Urban Municipalities Association (Regina: Century Archive Publishing, 1996); Mervyn Norton, *The New Urban Age: Bridging to Our Future as Urban Government in Saskatchewan*, Saskatchewan Urban Municipalities Association (Regina: Century Archive Publishing, 2004); Joseph Garcea, 'Saskatchewan's Municipal Reform Agenda: Plethora of Processes and Proposals but Paucity of Products,' in Joseph Garcea and Edward C. LeSage, Jr, eds., *Municipal Reform in Canada: Reconfigurations, Re-Empowerment and Rebalancing* (Don Mills, Ont.: Oxford University Press, 2005), 83–105.
2 Garcea, 'Saskatchewan's Municipal Reform Agenda.'
3 The total of 985 municipalities comprises 801 municipalities and 184 quasi-municipalities.
4 Statistics Canada, 'Aboriginal Population Profiles,' 2001 Census of Canada, Cat. no. 94F0043XIE (Ottawa, 2002), http://www12.statcan.ca /english/Profil01/AP01/Index.cfm?Lang=E.
5 CMA populations in 2001 and 2006 were: Regina, 192,800 and 194,971; Saskatoon, 225,927 and 233,923. Source: Statistics Canada, Census of Canada; and authors' calculations based on tables prepared by Saskatchewan Bureau of Statistics, Department of Finance.
6 Raymond Breton, 'Institutional Completeness of Ethnic Communities and the Personal Relations of Immigrants,' *American Journal of Sociology*, vol. 70, no. 2 (1964): 193–205.
7 Colligan-Yano and Norton, *The Urban Age*; Norton, *The New Urban Age*.
8 Saskatchewan, 'Overview of New Legislation for Urban & Rural Municipalities,' *Proposed Municipalities Act* (Regina, 2004), 4, http://www.municipal.gov.sk.ca/pdf/overview_new_leg_munact.pdf.

9 Saskatchewan, Task Force on Municipal Legislative Renewal, *Municipal Governance for Saskatchewan in the 21st Century: A Framework for Renewal, Summary of Final Reports* (Regina, 2000), http://www.municipal.gov.sk.ca /publications/publication_atoz.html#m.

10 Saskatchewan, 'The City of Lloydminster Act Introduced in the Legislature Today,' News Release 340, Government Relations and Aboriginal Affairs (Regina, 2004), http://www.gov.sk.ca/newsrel/releases/2004/06 /07-340.html; Alberta, *City of Lloydminster Act* (Edmonton, 2005), http://www.canlii.org/ab/laws/sta/c-13.5/20050801/whole.html.

11 Saskatchewan, Lloydminster Charter (Regina, 1979).

12 Saskatchewan, Task Force on Municipal Legislative Renewal, *Final Report on the Urban and Rural Municipal Sectors* (Regina, 2000), 43.

13 Saskatchewan, *Overview of New Legislation.*

14 Two members nominated by SARM, one by SUMA representing urban and northern municipalities with populations under 30,000, one by SUMA representing cities with populations exceeding 30,000, two nominated by the Saskatchewan School Boards Association (SSBA), three by the minister responsible for municipalities, one by the minister responsible for municipalities based on the recommendation of the minister responsible for K-12 education, and one who serves as the chairperson of the board, nominated by the provincial minister responsible for municipalities in consultation with the SARM, SUMA, and SSBA executives. Source: Saskatchewan, *Saskatchewan Assessment Management Agency. Annual Report 2004* (Regina, 2005), http://www.sama.sk.ca/pdfs.

15 Ibid.

16 Colligan-Yano and Norton, *The Urban Age*, 140–1.

17 Saskatchewan, 'Federal and Provincial Government Investment Improves Long-term Municipal Planning.' News Release, 21 December 2006, http://www.gov.sk.ca/news?newsId=3348254d-9065-4ea5-8e10-63a4f9e68f1.

18 Joseph Garcea, 'The FSIN and the FSIN/SUMA Task Force Reports on Urban Reserves: Purposes, Processes, and Provisions,' in L. Barron and J. Garcea, eds., *Indian Urban Reserves in Saskatchewan* (Saskatoon: Purich Publishing, 1999), 132–58.

19 Canada, Western Economic Development Corporation, 'Projects Approved under Northern Development Agreement' (Ottawa, 2006), http://www.wd.gc.ca/mediacentre/2006/apr21-01a_e.asp.

20 Saskatchewan. Government Relations, '$147 Million for Saskatchewan Municipalities under the New Deal for Cities and Communities,' News

Release 776, 2005, http://www.gov.sk.ca/newsrel/releases/2005/08/23-776.html.

21 Saskatchewan, *Overview of New Legislation.*

22 Statistics Canada, 'Public Sector Employees, Wages and Salaries,' CANSIM, Table 183–0002 (Ottawa, 2006).

23 Saskatoon, Bylaw No.8491 – The Campaign Disclosure and Spending Limits Bylaw, 2006, http://www.saskatoon.ca/org/clerks_office/elections/disclosure/index.asp.

24 Saskatchewan, *Saskatchewan Assessment Management Agency Act,* http://www.qp.gov.sk.ca/documents/English/Statutes/Statutes/A28-1.pdf; Saskatchewan. Saskatchewan Assessment Management Agency, *Annual Report 2006,* http://www.sama.sk.ca/pdfs/SUMA 2006 Report SAMA.pdf.

25 Garcea, 'Saskatchewan's Municipal Reform Agenda,' 87–90.

26 Saskatchewan, *Updating Municipal-Provincial Roles and Responsibilities: Review of Municipal Functions* (Regina, 2000).

27 Statistics Canada, CANSIM tables 385–0024 and 384–0013.

28 Ibid.

29 Statistics Canada, CANSIM table 385–0024.

30 Statistics Canada, CANSIM table 385–0009.

31 Statistics Canada, CANSIM tables 385–0024 and 384–0013.

32 Saskatchewan, *Final Report of the Action Committee on the Rural Economy: Phase 1* (Regina, 2002), http://www.rd.gov.sk.ca/acre/FinalReport02.pdf.

33 Saskatchewan, Commission on the Financing of Kindergarten to Grade 12 Education, *Finding the Balance (Final Report)* (Regina, 2004), http://www.cfe.gov.sk.ca.

34 Saskatchewan, Task Force on Municipal Legislative Renewal, *Final Report on the Urban and Rural Municipal Sectors* (Regina, 2000); idem, *Municipal Governance for Saskatchewan in the 21st Century: Final Report on the Northern Municipal Sector* (Regina, 2000); and idem, *A Framework for Renewal, Summary of Final Reports* (Regina, 2000).

35 Garcea, 'Saskatchewan's Municipal Reform Agenda,' 83–5.

36 Saskatchewan, Task Force on Municipal Legislative Renewal, *Final Report on the Urban and Rural Municipal Sectors.*

37 Ibid.; Task Force on Municipal Legislative Renewal, *Final Report on the Northern Municipal Sector; Saskatchewan Assessment Management Agency. Annual Report, 2005;* Jack Stabler and Rose Olfert, *Functional Economic Areas in Saskatchewan: A Framework for Municipal Restructuring,* prepared for Saskatchewan Government Relations (2000), http://www.municipal.gov.sk.ca/publications/pdf%5Ccpb%5Cfunctionaleconareas.pdf; Rose

Olfert, Mark Partridge, and Murray Fulton, 'Growing Saskatchewan in an Urban Age' (2006), http://crerl.usask.ca/policy.php.

38 A.W. Johnston, *Dream No Little Dreams: A Biography of the Douglas Government of Saskatchewan, 1944–1961* (Toronto: University of Toronto Press, 2004).

39 Garcea, 'Saskatchewan's Municipal Reform Agenda,' 103.

40 Dale Eisler, *False Expectations: Politics and the Pursuit of the Saskatchewan Myth* (Regina: Canadian Plains Research Centre, 2006).

41 Seymour Martin Lipset, *Agrarian Socialism: The Cooperative Commonwealth Federation in Saskatchewan. A Study in Political Sociology*, rev. ed. (Garden City, N.Y.: Doubleday Anchor, 1968); Mildred A. Schwartz, 'Democracy and Agrarian Socialism,' in 'Extensions: A Journal of the Carl Albert Congressional Research and Studies Centre' (1998), www.ou.edu/special/albertctr/extensions/sp98/schwartz.html.

42 Saskatchewan, Task Force on Municipal Legislative Renewal, *A Framework for Renewal, Summary of Final Reports* (2000).

43 Saskatchewan, *Final Report of the Action Committee on the Rural Economy: Phase: 8* (2005), http://www.rd.gov.sk.ca/acre/ACREFinalReport-May2005.pdf.

9 Alberta

EDWARD C. LESAGE, JR AND MELVILLE L. MCMILLAN

This chapter provides an overview of the municipal government system in Alberta with reference to select significant developments that have affected this system over the past three decades. We begin with an introduction to system organization which focuses on the types and nature of the principal and auxiliary authorities that comprise it. A review of the powers and functions of Alberta municipal government follows, with attention to the more or less unique functions of Alberta municipalities. Municipal finances are examined next. Democratic institutions and processes (for example, elections, public participation) are subsequently considered, with provincial-local relations the next focus. Municipal administration is the final subject reviewed. In the concluding section, we offer reflections on selected system components, with assessments of the performance and vitality of each. Issues that receive our consideration are jurisdiction and functions, municipal finances, local democracy and the democracy deficit, provincial-municipal relations, and the special challenges of regional governance. Our selection is admittedly eclectic, based on our perception of important developments and issues and our particular interests and expertise.

As we state in greater detail at the onset of the final section of the chapter, we believe that the Alberta municipal system functions reasonably well. This does not mean that it operates without difficulties or that reform of select aspects is unnecessary or ill-advised. Elements of the system certainly can be reformed. In recent years, pressures induced by Alberta's economic boom have revealed weaknesses in existing municipal finance arrangements, institutional arrangements relating to land-use planning and growth management, and intermunicipal collaboration. Intergovernmental relations between the province and municipalities have been strained by this same headlong economic activity, and aspects of these invite reform. Other extant institutional arrangements, perhaps less affected by the immediate pressures of a boom economy, fall short of what we and others might wish; for example, following each triennial round of municipal elections, there is much talk of a democratic deficit owing to persistently low participation in municipal elections. Still, all considered, the Alberta municipal system 'works,' and we believe that this is the result of its generally sound structure and organization, certain prudent reforms that have been carried out over the years, energetic sector representation offered by the province's municipal associations, the contribution of dedicated and honest players, and the generally good quality of municipal and provincial administration.

Alberta's Municipal System

Structural Components

The present Alberta municipal system comprises a limited number of municipality types. These are formally divided into four urban classifications (cities, towns, villages, and summer villages), one rural classification (municipal districts), and an extraordinary form (the specialized municipality).[1] Additionally, there are three quasi-municipal forms (improvement districts, special areas, hamlets) and an allied form (Métis settlements) which is not formally part of the municipal system. The Alberta municipal system also features various agencies, boards, committees, and commissions including statutorily flexible regional services commissions (RSCs). Recently, as something of a parallel development to the RSCs, new voluntary partnerships have appeared in the major metropolitan areas that are akin to U.S. councils of governments (COGs). A number of other voluntary economic-development partnerships also have appeared in the province's smaller urban regions.

Under the Municipal Government Act (MGA) of 1994, the distinction between urban and rural jurisdictions is defined by a simple criterion: urban authorities are municipalities that may be formed for an area in which a majority of the buildings used as dwellings are on parcels of land with an area of less than 1,850 square metres. Rural authorities are those in which a majority of buildings used as dwellings are located on parcels of land of at least 1,850 square metres.[2] The 'specialized municipality' is exempt from this scheme.

Municipalities and Quasi-Municipal Authorities

The MGA specifies that a city may be formed for an area in which there is a population of 10,000 or more. No formal definition of a 'city' exists as such under Alberta's municipal legislation, and indeed it is possible for a municipality to exceed the population number and not hold city status. There are sixteen Alberta cities ranging in population from Calgary (1,019,942) to Wetaskiwin (11,673).[3] The total city population is 2,273,525 or nearly 68 per cent of Alberta's 'official' 2007 municipal population of 3,354,304.[4] To put these figures in perspective, and to underscore the pressures of growth that are a leitmotif of this chapter, we note that while the number of cities has stayed constant over the past twenty years,[5] at sixteen, population in these jurisdictions has grown significantly; in 1987 there were 1,565,811 city residents.[6]

There are 110 towns in Alberta.[7] An Alberta town can be formed with a population of 1,000 or more while also meeting the density criterion for an urban authority. A municipality can exist as a town with a population greater than 10,000 (the threshold for city status); in 2007 nine of the 110 towns exceeded this figure, with one being more populated than seven municipalities possessing city status. The number of towns has increased only marginally over the past twenty years (there were 108 towns in 1987). By contrast, the population of towns has grown noticeably. In 1987 the total town population was 306,794; in 2007 it was 431,932, or 13 per cent of the official population total.

Villages are small urban municipalities with a population of 300 or more. There were 100 of them, with a total population of 39,881, in 2007. In 1987 there were 124 villages, indicating a modest amount of dissolution between decades ago and recently. The village population of 1987 was also larger than today (45,037). Although the current minimum population number for a village is 300, roughly 40 per cent of the existing 100 villages report populations under this minimum. The least populated village has a mere thirty-five residents, while the most highly populated have 1,000. With the proclamation of the Municipal Government Act, the ability to establish new summer villages was eliminated, although summer villages remain recognized as a category in the legislation.[8] There are fifty-one summer villages with a total population of 6,164, or a mere fraction of the total official population. In 1987 summer villages totalled forty-eight, with a total population of 3,477.

The specialized municipality is a new and unique classification introduced in 1994. The classification is, as the name implies, special.

Section 83 of the MGA allows the minister to establish a specialized municipality when no other classification appears to meet the needs of the local population. This can be done without resorting to a special act of the legislature. The specialized municipality can be applied to hybrid urban-rural arrangements, such as Strathcona County and the regional municipality of Wood Buffalo. On 31 December 2007 there were four specialized municipalities which together had an official population of 185,287 or 5.5 per cent of the total population. Specialized municipalities vary considerably in their population cohorts: the regional municipality of Wood Buffalo (88,131) and Strathcona County (82,511) are among the largest municipalities in the province, while Mackenzie County (10,002) and the municipality of Jasper (4,643) are notably less populated. On 1 January 2008 the municipality of Crowsnest Pass became a specialized municipality; previously it was a town.

Alberta has only one formal classification of rural municipality – the municipal district (MD). Another form, the Alberta 'county,' was established in the early 1950s and abolished with the school and municipal reforms of 1994.[9] There are sixty-four municipal districts, up from the 1987 tally, which stood at fifty. During the interval, the numbers were expanded by the provincial government's efforts to eliminate as many improvement districts (IDs) as possible. The bulk of these authorities became municipal districts. The total population of municipal districts in 2007 was 440,836 or 13 per cent of the official population. There is significant variance in municipal district populations. The MD of Rocky View No. 44 has a population of 34,597, while the MD of Ranchland sports a miniscule population of 86. In 1987 the total rural municipality population was 367,148.[10]

Hamlets are, strictly speaking, not municipalities since they are not incorporated, but they deserve mention since they are mentioned in the MGA. A municipal district or a specialized municipality can designate a hamlet. The minister of municipal affairs is the designating authority in IDs. The hamlet designation has proven useful in recent years to provide some means of local representation and, also, some modicum of urban services to the few villages that opt for dissolution. Prior to the Strathcona County's designation as a specialized municipality, the large suburban settlement of Sherwood Park existed as a hamlet within the county structure. This improbable arrangement was rationalized with the grant of specialized municipality status, wherein Sherwood Park was redefined as an urban service area (USA) within the specialized municipality. There are over 340 hamlets in Alberta.

Alberta's local system also comprises three categories of quasi-municipal jurisdictions (improvement districts, special areas, and Métis settlements) and a range of agencies, boards, and commissions. Improvement Districts are unincorporated rural administrative units. They are the responsibility of the provincial government, which, through Alberta Municipal Affairs, levies and collects taxes and oversees local service provision, including the creation and maintenance of road systems and also the establishment of community infrastructure where urban-like agglomerations exist. Today there are only seven IDs. Of these, five exist with boundaries that are coterminous with national parks and two with boundaries coterminous with a provincial park. The 2007 official population of IDs was 1,994. By comparison, in 1987 there were nineteen IDs with an official population of 74,357. The decrease in the number of authorities and the total population reflects a concerted effort by the province to reduce the number of these authorities. The provincial government argued that local residents should pay for a larger portion of the municipal-like services that it was supplying in these jurisdictions, and that they should do so under municipal status.

Special areas are another form of quasi-municipal rural government. Three exist, and are all situated in southeast Alberta. The authorities were established under the Special Areas Act of 1938 in the face of depression and draught that ravaged these vast dry lands (2,067,274 hectares). The hard-learned fact that these lands are not suitable for intensive agriculture has perpetuated their continuing provincial administration. The Special Areas Act remains largely unaltered from its inception. By last official count, the special areas population stands at 4,729. In 1987 the population was 6,010, reflecting continuing (albeit gradual) depopulation.

Métis settlements are a unique form of quasi-municipal entity defined under the Métis Settlement Act. Seven Métis colonies were established in 1938 and 1939.[11] There are presently eight settlements, although this figure obscures the history of settlement formation, amalgamation, and dissolution. The Métis settlement population stands at 5,956. The Alberta Legislative Assembly passed 'Accord legislation' in 1990. This legislation established the present eight Métis settlement corporations, which are 'governed by elected councils with extensive powers to control their own destinies and finances.'[12] It is a codification of a negotiated finale to a long legal and political fight between the Federation of Métis Settlements of Alberta (FMSA) and the government of Alberta – in which subsurface rights to minerals under settlement lands, and royalties flowing from these minerals, were disputed. In exchange for self-administration of the Métis settlement lands through the settlement councils, the FMSA relinquished claims to mineral ownership and royalty shares. At present, the minister for aboriginal affairs and northern development is responsible for the Métis Settlement Act and that part of the provincial administration dedicated to regulating and providing services to the Métis settlement population.

We offer three observations to conclude this survey. First, it is clear that Alberta is an urbanized province. Roughly two-thirds of the province's municipal population resides in municipalities categorized as cities (2,237,525), and a little over half the population lives within the corporate boundaries of the two largest cities. Contrary to the common perception, for Alberta frequently portrays itself as a land of wide-open spaces and country living, the province is one of Canada's most urbanized.[13] Secondly, as revealed in the 1987 and 2007 population comparisons, population growth is occurring in smaller authorities. This growth is admittedly uneven, with some towns and other non-city jurisdictions growing at great rates while others in the same categories are declining despite buoyant economic times; nevertheless, the overall direction is one of growth. Thirdly, this growth has led to inevitable stresses on the system, including requirements for new infrastructure and services, the need to repair or upgrade existing infrastructure and to deliver more effectively a host of services, and intensified intermunicipal conflicts between core, suburban, and ex-urban municipalities in the metropolitan areas and urban and rural municipalities elsewhere. Provincial-municipal relationships are also strained.

Agencies, Boards, Commissions, and Committees

Many agencies, boards, commissions, and committees (ABCs) are found in the Alberta municipal system. Because they are so numerous, and because so many are established by local initiative under broad permissive powers within the Municipal Government Act, it is well beyond the scope of this overview to offer a full catalogue. However, a rough exposition is possible if the ABCs are considered within three frameworks: provincially mandated or prescribed municipal ABCs, municipally commissioned ABCs, and regional ABCs. There are also select independent authorities that deserve mention in passing.

Several ABCs are either provincially mandated or must be established if a municipality wishes to provide services or regulate activities in a functional area. Under the Police Act, urban municipalities must establish and appoint members to a police commission if the municipality has a municipal police force. A council must create an arm's length public library board under the Libraries Act if it wishes to establish a municipal public library. Establishment of an assessment review board is necessary under the Municipal Government Act if a complaint is received on an assessment matter. Alternatively, councils can establish one or more assessment review boards in anticipation of complaints. A municipality must create a subdivision authority under the MGA, and a subdivision and development appeal board is mandated under the Municipal Government Act. Under the Residential Tenancies Act, a city may establish a Landlord and Tenant Advisory Board (LTAB). Edmonton, for example, has an LTAB to advise council on residential tenancy issues and other matters relating to the plan, programs, and services delivered by the board. Further, general powers of the MGA provide councils with wide-ranging powers to establish regulatory commissions such as boxing and wrestling commissions, taxi commissions, and a presumably unlimited number of advisory or deliberative ABCs. Concerning the latter, Edmonton has established, for example, the Advisory Board on Services for Persons with Disabilities, the Animal Control Advisory Board, the Community Services Advisory Board, the Edmonton Aboriginal Urban Affairs Committee, the Edmonton Design Committee, the Edmonton Historical Board, and several associations dedicated to the revitalization of business zones.

Alberta municipal legislation has special provisions on regional administration, although some of the most significant local regional institutions were eliminated through the 1994 and 1995 revisions to the Municipal Government Act. Present assessment legislation permits the establishment of joint assessment review boards.[14] Planning legislation permits (and it would be fair to say that the Ministry of Municipal Affairs encourages) the creation of intermunicipal subdivision and development appeal boards.[15]

Regional services commissions are special authorities that can be established by regulation under the Municipal Government Act for purposes of producing intermunicipal services. The legislation permits these bodies to be multifunctional, even though to date almost all focus on a single function. Prior to 1994, the functional domain of RSCs was restricted to 'hard' utilities such as water, sewer, and waste management. Since then, it has expanded to cover a range of joint municipal services including regional services relating to airports, emergency-response services, municipal planning services, and real property assessment services. There are now over fifty RSCs.[16]

Although it is possible for RSC legislation to be used to form a regional airport authority, most regional airport authorities that have developed in Alberta have been enabled under the Regional Airports Authorities Act. Other specialized regional authorities include regional health authorities, regional school authorities,[17] irrigation districts,[18] and drainage authorities.[19] While not formally part of the municipal system, these authorities are often intertwined with municipal authorities in the broad enterprise of producing good local governance.

Some of the most significant local regional institutions – regional and metropolitan planning commissions, which placed most of the province under an orderly regional planning regime – were completely eliminated as a result of 1995 reforms to the Municipal Government Act. These commissions exercised considerable authority over land use and development control, and in ways that rural authorities often complained were to their disadvantage.[20] In the Edmonton region, tensions between urban and rural authorities were especially pronounced, but there were other cleavages as well, including those between the central city and the suburbs. Other regions experienced similar conflicts and, for these reasons and others that were putatively defensible during the Klein government's spasm of neo-conservative re-engineering and downsizing in the mid-1990s, the commissions were abandoned. Alberta was left with what amounted to a voluntary regional planning regime. This arrangement, which included requirements for intermunicipal consultation and elective provisions for establishing intermunicipal development plans, was serviceable to greater or lesser degrees across the province during the remainder of the 1990s and the first years of the new millennium. However, these voluntary provisions quickly became strained in several regions with the dramatic economic growth of the new century.

Early in 2007, a high-level consultative body (the Minister's Council on Municipal Sustainability [MCMS]) recommended the creation of some form of new regional planning agency in the province's metropolitan and high-growth areas, a proposal that a new premier and his cabinet accepted. This was one of several recommendations emanating from the council (others are addressed in following sections), and it was of particular urgency given mounting urban-rural and core city-suburb conflicts over land use, growth management, and the equitable sharing of investments and costs associated with a hot economy's pressure on services and infrastructure. The MCMS eschewed recommending the creation of regional planning authorities in areas of the province where municipalities continued to demonstrate the ability to manage intermunicipal relationships effectively, or where the intractable planning issues affected a small number of municipalities. In these instances, the recommended strategy was to require municipalities to negotiate an intermunicipal development plan that addresses key issues (regional planning, land use, cost-sharing and/or revenue sharing) and to use final-offer arbitration where the negotiating municipalities reach an impasse. The province accepted these recommendations, but with the caveat that its ongoing Land Use Framework consultation may affect their implementation. Thus, while the province is clearly placing greater emphasis on regional planning and development control, it appears willing to forgo the creation of entities similar to the old regional planning commissions in regions where it can avoid doing so.

Following on the heels of the MCMS report was C.D. Radke's *Working Together*.[21] The government had commissioned Radke, a retired deputy minister of municipal affairs, to take direct aim at vexing problems of regional planning and growth management in the Edmonton metropolitan region and, somewhat secondarily, at regional service-delivery issues. Radke's final report recommended a new provincially mandated regional board for the Capital Region (the Capital Region Board [CRB]), effective January 2008. The government accepted this recommendation and almost all others contained in *Working Together*. Requiring membership and participation of the twenty-five municipalities defined by the province as comprising the Capital Region's complement, the board is charged with developing an integrated land-use plan for the region, reviewing and approving amendments to (or new) municipal development plans, intermunicipal development plans, and area structure plans, and approving a ten-year intermunicipal transit plan. Further, the board is charged with delivery of regional information services and intermunicipal public transit. Additional monitoring and reporting responsibilities extend to housing and several other major functions. In the future, with provincial approval, functions such as the delivery of potable water, waste water, solid-waste management, recreation, and economic development will fall under the board's authority – although it is far from certain that the board will pursue these responsibilities. Board governance is achieved through binding votes using a double-majority system that recognizes Edmonton's dominance of the region (71 per cent of the population and something in the range of 60 per cent of total property assessment)[22] while giving voice to the multitude of small municipalities in the region and extending some influence to the largest municipalities surrounding the city.[23]

Partnerships, Alliances, and Liaisons

A great number of special intermunicipal arrangements exist either through principal-agent relationships fashioned between or among municipalities or through the creation of non-profit companies under part 9 of the Alberta's Companies Act. Regional partnerships of local governments have developed over the past decade in the Edmonton and Calgary metropolitan areas. Somewhat analogously, economic-development collaborations have appeared in several of the province's other urban regions. The recently disbanded Alberta Capital Region Alliance (ACRA) and the still operating Calgary Regional Partnership (CRP) were established under the part 9 device and were similar to American councils of governments and Australian regional organizations of councils.

The newly established Capital Region Board is better understood with a nod to ACRA, which was the first municipal partnership in the province. Its lineage is traced directly back to the Edmonton Metropolitan Region Planning Council (EMRPC), which the province killed fiscally in 1993 and legislatively in 1995. First named the Capital Region Forum, ACRA was to 'promote and improve harmony and cooperation amongst' the region's municipalities and 'promote and encourage cooperation and collaboration.'[24] The forum's founders also envisioned a service-delivery role that included provision of planning services and a role in fashioning a broad regional growth-management plan. However, these ambitions were quickly confounded by regional political dynamics. In 1997 the forum moniker was dropped, and the newly named ACRA emerged as a more modest collaboration that was defined to serve as a venue in which municipalities and other regional organizations (and organizations with regional concerns and interests) would share information and ideas. ACRA strove to facilitate the aggregation of regional interests and the articulation of regional issues and initiatives that were collectively advanced to the provincial and (sometimes) federal government. When its membership reached a high-water mark in 2006, ACRA possessed twenty-three member municipalities. However, in October 2006, Edmonton city council formally voted to withdraw from the alliance, citing a number of concerns but most particularly the failure of the organization to address regional land-use management issues and (what the council deemed as) a chronic lack of equity in the distribution of local tax revenues. Other urban municipalities in the region demonstrated some measure of sympathy with the city's case, and ACRA's membership dropped. With provincial creation of the Capital Region Board, ACRA was consigned to history.

The Calgary Regional Partnership is of more recent vintage than ACRA. Members have met regularly and published annual reports since 2001, with articles of association and incorporation documents finalized in May 2004. Its functions are essentially the same as ACRA's. The CRP comprises nineteen members. Unlike ACRA, not all its members are municipal since the partnership includes the townsite of Redwood Meadows, a private development, and the Tsuu T'ina First Nation (the Sarcee Indian reserve), which is located on the outskirts of Calgary. Since the Minister's Council on Municipal Sustainability pointedly recommended that regional-planning administrations should be reconstituted in both of the province's principal metropolitan regions, it is likely that the CRP also will be replaced by some form of regional-planning and service-delivery entity.

Calgary and Edmonton's one-time energetic rivalry appears to have metamorphosised in recent years to something of a new and successful partnership. Whereas in the 1980s and 1990s the two cities were often competitive in their efforts to acquire provincial funding, of late this competition has been replaced by a willingness to collaborate in efforts to score more funds.[25] This is not to suggest that competition has been eliminated – both cities certainly eye one another with attention to the equitable division of provincial funds, and in this Edmonton is especially sensitive to real or apparent slights. Nonetheless, beginning with negotiations resulting in the province pledging a five-cent-a litre-transfer of fuel-tax revenues for both cities, the value and potential of collaboration began to dawn on the one-time competitors. Calgary and Edmonton mayors and senior administrators participated actively on the Minister's Provincial/Municipal Council on Roles and Responsibilities in the 21st Century (or, as it would become known, the 3Rs Council – a largely invisible precursor to the MCMS), and were both at the table in the framing of the Canada-Alberta 'New Deal' gas-tax agreement. They provided common fronts in these forums. The mayors were back at the table with the newly formed Minister's Council on Municipal Sustainability, and senior administrators from both organizations participated in the short-lived federal Liberal government's Alberta Federal, Provincial, Municipal Trilateral Table on Community Sustainability.[26] City officials also collaborate on various administrative matters including joint-purchasing arrangements, and they apparently share policy and administrative information freely.

First Nation municipal issues are important to provincial and municipal governments (and presumably, to First Nation governments). The Alberta Association of Municipal Districts and Counties (AAMD&C) and the Alberta Urban Municipalities Association (AUMA) formally studied municipal-aboriginal issues within a joint advisory committee, producing a report in April 2005.[27] This review was conducted to study, from the municipal perspective, existing or potential issues in First Nation-municipal relations. Among the issues identified were ones concerning the ability of First Nations to purchase fee-simple lands with few restrictions as to which land is added to reserve land, the deleterious effect on municipal property-tax bases resulting from assessable asset transfer to reserves, and the absence of mechanisms requiring First Nations to negotiate for ambulance, waste management, and road maintenance and other municipal services. The committee further flagged the growing numbers of 'urban Aboriginal peoples' and the challenges posed as a result to social and physical infrastructure planning.[28] Municipalities also expressed concern over unilateral senior government-First Nation-related policy initiatives that affect municipal governments. Of particular concern here is the consistent failure of federal, provincial, and First Nation governments to engage municipalities early on in these efforts. Presumably the failure to invite municipalities to the policy table results in proposals that do not reflect municipal requirements and preferences; those then require considerable municipal representation before they can be altered, if indeed this is possible, to accommodate municipal concerns.

Municipal Jurisdiction

Powers

The powers of Alberta municipalities have long been defined in the Municipal Government Act.[29] This legislation was substantially revised in 1993 (proclaimed in 1994), and a separate instalment to it was added in 1994 (proclaimed in 1995), following lengthy consultations through the Municipal Statutes Review Committee (MSRC) and an intensive review of planning legislation. Under the MGA, municipalities are charged with providing good government, services, facilities, or other things that are necessary or desirable in the council's opinion, and with maintaining safe communities.[30] This legislation is of note in that it recognizes municipal government as an order of government without specifically saying so. Further, the MGA provides that municipalities should legislate freely within broadly defined 'spheres of jurisdiction' and operate with many of the corporate freedoms enjoyed by businesses.[31] These core elements of the legislation represent a significant departure from previous municipal legislation that permitted municipalities to do only what the province narrowly permitted. Indeed, variations on the legislation have been adopted in nine provinces and territories.

There are many highly specified aspects of municipal power and responsibility, notwithstanding the liberal construction of the MGA. A section of the act (part 3, division 8) is dedicated to setting limits on municipal powers, specifically on the disposal of land and mines and minerals, acquisition of land outside municipal boundaries, control of profit corporations, firearms, and, oddly, the Forest and Prairie Protection Act. Elsewhere in the MGA there is detailed prescription concerning the establishment of municipalities, councils, municipal organization and administration, public participation, financial administration, property assessment, taxation, assessment review, the Municipal Government Board (MGB) (a provincial oversight body), various legal matters, and land-use planning. As the architects of the act explain, sections relating to matters such as governance are necessarily precisely defined since the MGA is the municipal 'constitution' and the high level of definition both protects the public interest and educates the citizenry on matters of local governance. Many other provincial acts qualify municipal prerogative. The MGA makes clear that, in the event of 'inconsistencies' between a local by-law and the act, or between a local by-law and other provincial legislation, 'the bylaw has no effect to the extent of the inconsistency.'[32] All the same, the change in the jurisdictional rules is regarded as important, and the ability for municipalities to operate within broadly legislative parameters has survived a telling test before the Supreme Court of Canada.[33]

Functions

The Municipal Government Act defines most functions performed by Alberta municipalities under nine general local law-making spheres. For example, in the area of promoting the safety, health, and welfare of people, Alberta municipalities provide or assist in the delivery of fire protection, ambulance services, disaster response, water, waste-water treatment, solid-waste removal, storm sewers and drainage, other environmental services (e.g., weed control), land-use planning, zoning and development controls, subdivision and land development, public housing, building rentals, family and community social services, daycare, recreation boards, parks and recreation facilities (e.g., swimming pools, ski facilities, trails), cultural institutions (e.g., libraries, museums, exhibition halls), convention and trade centres, and cemeteries. A range of activities related to the public peace is conducted by the police and other law-enforcement and regulation officials; these officials enable municipalities to regulate the behaviour of people, activities, and things in, on, or near a public place or place that is open to the public. Similarly, municipal law enforcement and other officials regulate nuisances, including unsightly property and, in rural areas, fence maintenance.

Municipal provision of transport and transportation systems includes the regulation and provision of roads, streets, walks, lighting, airports, bridges, and public transit. Functions concerning business, business activities, and persons engaged in business involve a plethora of regulatory activities and supports. The former include licensing and zoning, while the latter involve economic-development initiatives of various sorts ranging from business attraction and retention initiatives to convention centre and trade-centre development, redevelopment projects and initiatives, and public-private investments including, of late, either promoting or providing the development of high-speed Internet and Wi-Fi services.

Alberta's two largest municipalities remain involved in the production and delivery of power and water through wholly owned corporations. ENMAX is a subsidiary of the city of Calgary, which operates and competes in Alberta's restructured electricity industry. EPCOR is a private company formed in 1996 and owned by the city of Edmonton that builds, owns, and operates power plants, electrical transmission and distribution networks, water and waste-water treatment facilities, and infrastructure. Edmonton's municipally operated telephone service was privatized in 1990 to form the Edmonton Telephones Corporation (ED TEL), which the city sold to TELUS Corporation in 1995. Elsewhere, some municipal utilities continue to operate as part of municipal administration, including Medicine Hat's municipal gas works.

Much has been made of Alberta's extension of 'natural person powers' to municipalities under section 6 of the MGA. 'Natural person powers' are almost endless – a municipality can enter into contracts, purchase or sell goods and services, borrow money, provide loans and guarantees, make investments, set up a company, hire employees, construct or lease buildings, set up non-profit organizations, purchase shares in a company, enter into partnerships or joint ventures, and more. The innovation's significance is that it permits municipalities to perform corporate activities more freely than under the traditional and picayune corporate-power provisions of municipal legislation.

There are some functions for which Alberta municipalities do not possess legislative responsibility, although this does not necessarily mean they are barred from contributing to the financing or production of these services. Hospitals and clinics are of note. These functions are either provincially or regionally administered, and have been since the early days of Tory rule, when the province assumed all municipal responsibility in an effort to place municipalities on better financial footing. Food and restaurant inspections fall to the province's regional health authorities. We hasten to add that in the real world things are less sharply defined than in legislation. For example, under the MGA, municipalities can make arrangements to attract physicians (a matter of extraordinary importance to the province's rural and lightly populated regions). Presumably this qualifies as making provision for, if not actually supplying, health-related services. Moreover, the MGA stipulates that one of the purposes of a municipality is to provide for the health of its citizens without specifically stating what this entails.

While municipalities do not provide direct income security per se, they provide or otherwise support various forms of non-taxable income support including a range of services for children, youth, and seniors, discounted fares for senior citizens at various public venues, subsidized social housing, and senior citizen lodges. The province heavily subsidizes municipal family and community support services (FCSS) under the Family and Community Support Services Act. Municipalities provide support to senior lodges by underwriting their budgeted operating deficits.

Municipal Finance

This section first outlines the scope and functions of municipal finance and then explores the patterns and trends of expenditures and revenues, which reveal some significant adjustments over the past decade and a half. We also highlight major variations among the classes of municipalities, note recent changes in federal and provincial fiscal relations with Alberta municipalities, and, finally, sketch ongoing initiatives in the municipal-provincial fiscal arena.

An Overview of Scope and Functions

Identifying municipal governments' powers and responsibilities is valuable but it does not indicate their relative importance. One perspective on this issue comes from looking at the level and pattern of municipal expenditures. This perspective may understate the importance of certain activities – the importance of a safe water supply or the benefits of zoning, for example – but it has the advantage of using a common denominator and is particularly amenable for a public-finance analysis. The Alberta table in the appendix provides information on the levels and allocations of the expenditures of Alberta's municipalities in selected years. Here, we take a somewhat more detailed perspective, focusing on 2005. Note initially that municipal expenditures amount to $1,982 per capita. This amount represents 5.1 per cent of the average per capita personal income of Albertans and 6.7 per cent of their personal disposable income (PDI). Neither amount is especially large. However, municipal expenditures account for about one-fifth (19.6 per cent in 2005) of consolidated provincial and local expenditures in Alberta.[34]

The distribution of municipal expenditures reveals much about what municipal government does and, in particular, where it spends public money. Transportation (at 24.9 per cent of total outlays) is the single largest area of expenditure. About 85 per cent of that outlay is for streets and roads and 11 per cent goes to public transit. Three functional areas each represent about 15 per cent of total outlays: environment, recreation and culture, and protection. Within the environmental area, water and sewerage services are of roughly similar magnitude and solid-waste services take a somewhat smaller share of that budget. At 13.3 per cent of total outlay, recreation dominates the recreation and culture category. Policing and fire account for over 90 per cent of expenditures for protection, with policing, at over 8 per cent of total expenditures, the dominant area. The general government category is next largest, at 12.1 per cent of the total expenditure budget. Because municipalities often borrow to finance at least part of their capital investments, debt-service costs can be important. In 2005 they were 5.1 per cent of total outlays. Regional planning and resource conservation came next, at about 3 per cent each. A number of categories individually account for less than 2 per cent of expenditures – health, social services, education, housing, and other. In total, they amounted to only 5 per cent of total expenditures in 2005.

Although about 25 per cent larger in per capita terms than the average of expenditures in the other provinces excluding Ontario, the distribution of municipal expenditures in Alberta parallels that nine-province average. The unusually large responsibility of Ontario municipalities for social services results in the Canadian average expenditure distribution not being representative of either Ontario or other provinces.[35]

Patterns and Trends: Expenditures

With the exception of a dip in 1996, real per capita municipal expenditures in Alberta have been essentially constant, averaging $1,629 over the sixteen years 1988–2004.[36] The increase to $1,787 in 2005 is a notable upward move reflecting the adjustment to Alberta's current economic boom. Among functions, however, expenditures have varied. Most notable has been the declining importance of debt-servicing costs – from 17.4 per cent of municipal expenditures in 1988 to only 5.1 per cent in 2005 because of declining interest rates and declining liabilities. This reduction in debt-service costs afforded room in budgets for tax relief and/or greater program spending.[37] As a share of program spending, some activities (environmental services and recreation and culture) remained constant while others increased somewhat (general government and protection), but most notable was the decline in transportation's share. Transportation expenditures fell from 35.3 per cent to 26.2 per cent of program spending and from 29.1 per cent to 24.5 per cent of total outlays. The 'bottom line' is also noteworthy. Alberta municipalities went from running a modest deficit in 1988 to significant surpluses.

Patterns and Trends: Revenues

Like expenditures, the real dollar per capita revenues of Alberta municipalities have been quite stable from 1988 to 2004, increasing notably only in 2005. Municipal governments obtain most of their revenue from sources that they control themselves, that is, own-source revenues. In 2005 such revenues provided 87.8 per cent of municipal revenues. Property and related taxes account for half of these revenues. Real property taxes are the major source of taxes and provided 28.8 per cent of total revenue. Property-related taxes (lot levies, special assessments, grants in lieu of taxes for public property, business taxes, and other) account for the rest of the property and related taxes. Revenue from sales of goods and services represents one-third of own-source revenues and investment income is most of the remainder.

Transfers from other governments account for the rest of municipal revenue (that is, the non-own-revenue portion). Transfers were 12.2 per cent of revenues in 2005. With provincial transfers providing 11.6 of the 12.2 per cent, the federal share is a tiny 0.6 per cent. Provincial transfers are almost entirely (over 95 per cent) for specific purposes (that is, are conditional) as opposed to general or unconditional grants.

While the revenues of Alberta municipalities are absolutely larger than the Canada-wide average, the distribution of municipal revenue sources in Alberta is similar to that average. Transfers account for a somewhat smaller share of revenues in Alberta (12.2 per cent versus 17.1 per cent) so own-source revenues are larger. Within own-source revenues, sales (29 per cent versus 22 per cent) and investment income (9.3 per cent versus 4.9 per cent) are above the Canadian average (reflecting a significant investment in utilities) while property and related taxes are a rather lower share (at 42 per cent versus 52.7 per cent) of total revenues.

A declining trend in transfers was the defining factor in Alberta municipal finance from 1988 to 2004. Prior to 1992, transfers provided almost 22 per cent of revenue. By 1996, they had dropped to 12.6 per cent and, by 2004, they were only 10.4 per cent. General-purpose grants were essentially wiped out and specific-purpose grants cut. This reduction in provincial funding put a significant extra financial burden on the municipalities (effectively shifting about 10 per cent of municipal funding from the province to the municipalities).[38] The transfer cut resulted from the provincial efforts at deficit reduction and elimination that began in 1993 and 1994.[39] Thus, part of the burden of eliminating the provincial deficit was borne by the municipal governments.[40] Despite the end of the deficit and the emergence of provincial surpluses, provincial grants showed a relative recovery only in 2005. That recovery marks a turnaround in provincial policy.

How did municipalities respond to the cut in transfers? How did they manage to maintain real per capita expenditures? Although the decline in debt-service charges gradually softened the blow, the municipal response was to control spending and to raise property taxes. Few other categories of own-source revenue show any increase from 1988 to 2004. While the percentage of total revenue from sales did increase, it is really no greater a share of own-source revenues. More specifically, the increase in own-source revenues came from higher real property taxes, which went from 21.3 per cent to about 30.5 per cent of total revenue (or from about 27 per cent to about 33 per cent of own-source revenue). Property taxpayers most directly felt the burden of efforts to maintain municipal spending and services.

Trends and Fiscal Indicators

Recent years have seen considerable attention directed to the fiscal condition of Canadian municipalities.[41] As part of that, much concern has been expressed about municipalities, and cities especially, being squeezed fiscally between downloaded responsibilities, rising expectations, and a slowly growing tax and revenue base. Various fiscal indicators of Alberta municipalities will now be examined to obtain further insight into the basis for this concern.

The cut in provincial transfers and the more gradual decline in debt-servicing costs have been noted but deserve further discussion in this context. Debt charges fell from 17.4 per cent of total expenditures in 1988 to 5.1 per cent in 2005, a reduction that gradually released over 12 per cent of funds for other purposes. The cut in transfers came more abruptly, with transfers falling from 21.4 per cent to 11.3 per cent of revenues between 1992 and 1996 and then remaining at about that lower level through 2004. Thus, any 'fiscal dividend' that municipalities might have realized from lower debt-servicing costs was essentially captured by or negated by the provincial government's grant reductions, leaving municipalities no better off.

Table 1 shows municipal expenditures in real dollars per capita and as a share of PDI. Data for both 2004 and 2005 are reported because 2005 appears to be a turnaround year for Alberta municipalities. Although more relevant for revenues, we refer to PDI because property taxes and charges for municipal services are paid from disposable income (income after provincial and federal income taxes are paid).

Despite the uneven economic conditions from 1988 to 2004, real per capita municipal expenditures were surprisingly uniform (aside from a dip in 1996), at $1,629 to $1,698 per capita.[42] Program expenditures provide a better indicator of the level of services. Per capita real program expenditures fell sharply between 1992 and 1996 but recovered by 2001 and, by 2004, at $1,575 per capita, were 12 per cent over the 1988 level. With an improved economy, the burden of municipal total expenditures relative to PDI declined markedly (for example, from 8.55 per cent in 1988 to 6.43 per cent in 2004) while program spending slipped from 7.06 per cent to 6.06 per cent. Thus, because of rising incomes, the relative burden of municipal expenditures declined over the study period.

Has municipal government expenditure grown relative to that of the provincial and other local governments in Alberta, perhaps owing to added responsibilities? The data in Table 1 suggest no trend. Municipal government is, at 17 per cent in 2004 and 2005, only one percentage point larger relative to consolidated provincial-local government in 1988 and 1992.

While the aggregates have been relatively stable, there has been a notable shift between operating (or current) and capital outlays. Per capita constant dollar capital spending was sharply higher in 2001 and 2004, increasing from about 19.6 per cent to 27 per cent of municipal budgets.[43] Meanwhile, current expenditures declined by about $170 real dollars per capita from 1992 levels (a reduction of about 13 per cent). Interestingly, transfers supporting capital spending remained relatively constant while those in support of operations fell from $295 to $79 per capita (or from 21.68 per cent to 6.45 per cent of operating budgets). Thus, both unconditional grants and operating grants were severely reduced by provincial cutbacks.

The data for 2005 portend a change. The move to $1,787 real dollar per capita expenditures, an increase of $116 over 2004, represents a

Table 1
Trends in municipal expenditure, Alberta, selected years, 1988–2005[44]

	1988	1992	1996	2001	2004	2005
Total Expenditure						
Per Capita Constant (2001) Dollar[a]	1697	1698	1445	1629	1671	1787
As a Percentage of PDI[b]	8.55	8.42	7.28	6.61	6.43	6.58
Program Expenditure						
Per Capita Constant (2001) Dollar[a]	1401	1454	1265	1519	1575	1696
As a Percentage of PDI	7.06	7.21	6.35	6.16	6.06	6.24
Municipal Program Expenditure as a Percentage of Consolidated Provincial and Local Program Expenditure	16.21	16.10	19.05	15.79	17.34	17.14
Capital Expenditure						
Percentage of Total Expenditure	19.35	19.95	19.66	27.86	26.73	28.82
Constant (2001) Dollars Per Capita[a]	328	339	294	454	447	515
Percentage Transfer Funded	31.06	24.37	29.47	31.09	23.08	27.11
Constant (2001) Dollar Transfers Per Capita[a]	102	83	84	141	103	139
Current Expenditure						
Percentage of Total Expenditure	80.65	80.05	80.34	72.14	73.27	71.18
Constant (2001) Dollars Per Capita[a]	1369	1359	1161	1175	1224	1272
Percentage Transfer Funded	19.11	21.68	10.41	8.07	6.45	8.03
Constant (2001) Dollar Transfers Per Capita[a]	263	295	121	95	79	102
Per Capita Personal Disposable Income ($)						
Constant (2001) Dollars[c]	21,046	20,436	20,343	24,658	26,003	27,172

notable shift. Also notable is that the change was fuelled largely by an increase in grants. With a one-third increase to $241 real dollars per capita, grants are moving back towards 1988 and 1992 levels. The strong growth in constant-dollar disposable income in 2004 continued in 2005, resulting in the expenditure growth having limited impact on PDI.

Table 2
Absolute and relative levels of own-source municipal revenues, real property taxes, and consolidated property taxes, Alberta, selected years, 1988–2005[45]

	1988	1992	1996	2001	2004	2005
Own-Source Revenue						
Per Capita Constant (2001) Dollar[a]	1378	1377	1461	1579	1552	1705
As a Percentage of PDI	6.51	6.66	7.14	6.41	6.07	6.28
Real Property Tax						
Per Capita Constant (2001) Dollar[a]	377	410	516	497	528	560
As a Percentage of Total Revenue	21.35	23.25	31.02	27.27	30.46	28.83
As a Percentage of PDI	1.78	1.98	2.53	2.01	2.03	2.06
Consolidated Property Taxes						
Per Capita Constant (2001) Dollar[a]	959	1037	1129	1021	1026	1045
Portion Municipal	0.39	0.39	0.46	0.49	0.51	0.53
As a Percentage of PDI	4.53	5.02	5.54	4.14	3.95	3.85

The own-source revenue side of the picture is reported in Table 2. Own-source revenue increased from 78 per cent to almost 90 per cent of municipal budgets, with the bulk of that adjustment coming between 1992 and 1996. Real per capita own-source revenue increased between 1996 and 2001 from $1,377 to over $1,550.[46] The growth in own-source revenues almost matched the growth of PDI, leaving the own-source revenue share at 6.28 per cent in 2005, almost the same as the 6.51 per cent level in 1988. Thus, own-source revenue, although larger absolutely and a larger component of municipal budgets, is not a greater burden as a share of income.

Property taxes, the major source of municipal own-source revenue, have become more burdensome. Real property taxes, the portion of property and related taxes most obvious to taxpayers, rose sharply in 1996 and have been relatively stable since then. Between 1988 and 1996, real property taxes increased (mostly between 1992 and 1996) in constant dollar per capita terms from $377 to $516 (a 37 per cent increase), increased as a percentage of municipal revenues from 21.35 per cent to 31.02 per cent (a 45 per cent increase), and increased relative to PDI from 1.78 per cent to 2.53 per cent (a 42 per cent increase). Although subsequently moderated by relatively stable property taxes, rising real incomes, and reduced federal and provincial income taxes, the real property-tax burden relative to disposable incomes in 2005 was, at 2.06 per cent, still 15.7 per cent above the 1988 level. Thus, both the absolute and relative municipal property-tax burden has increased for the Alberta taxpayer.

Concern about the property-tax burden is not exclusively with respect to municipal property taxes. Over the period from 1988 to 2005, there were also local (school board) and then provincial property taxes to support schooling. It is thus useful to examine also the overall property-tax burden. Per capita constant dollar consolidated provincial and local property taxes were $959 in 1988 and $1,045 in 2005. Other than for an upward blip in 1996, the real per capita amount has essentially been constant since 1992. The burden relative to disposable incomes, however, has been lower since 2001 than in any of the earlier years reported. Consolidated property taxes in 1980 and 1985 amounted to only 4.0 per cent and 3.9 per cent of disposable income, about the same as the levels (only again) realized in 2004 and 2005. Hence, the 5 per cent to 5.5 per cent levels experienced during the early and mid-1990s were relatively high and probably helped to promote the concern within Alberta about the property-tax burden and to pressure the provincial government to constrain the school tax. Since the province assumed responsibility for school finance, the school portion of the property-tax burden has diminished while the municipal share has increased – from about 39 per cent to 53 per cent of the consolidated property tax. Therefore, total property taxes have remained relatively stable but the municipal portion has increased.

In summary, municipalities managed to maintain real per capita spending across the 1988–2004 period and even realize some increase in real per capita program spending despite the cut in provincial transfers. In both real per capita and in relative terms, capital spending has become more important and operating expenditures have fallen. The cut in provincial transfers, concentrated between 1992 and 1996, was a shock to Alberta's municipalities. Unconditional transfers essentially disappeared and transfers supporting operations fell to almost one-quarter of earlier levels. While there was concern about provincial offloading of expenditure responsibilities to municipalities, the evidence suggests that the overall economic magnitudes were small. The real offloading was on the revenue side, with the cut in transfers that required municipalities to rely more on own-source revenues. Municipalities responded to the 10 per cent loss of revenues by raising property taxes. But raising taxes was a challenge given the economic doldrums of the time and the fiscal-restraint stance of the provincial government. Relief came mostly from economic recovery in the late 1990s and the strong economy after 2000. Personal disposable income rose sharply and, with it, real municipal expenditures and own-source revenues. Despite those increases, expenditures and municipal own-source revenues have diminished as a share of PDI. Municipal real property taxes, however, were still a larger (though moderated) share of disposable income in 2005 than in 1988 or 1992.

While municipal governments have experienced difficult times, especially during the 1990s, there are some positive signs. Data from Alberta municipal statistics show municipal long-term debt in 2004 at 57 per cent of what it was in 1990.[47] Per capita debt declined from $1,689 to $755. In real per capita terms, municipal long-term debt decreased to one-third the 1990 level. Furthermore, financial assets increased. Notably, 2004 reserves were almost four times those in 1990 and, at $949 per capita, exceeded long-term debt by a healthy margin.[48] This dramatic turnaround in financial position suggests that (collectively) municipal governments are less fiscally disadvantaged than sometimes claimed and are better positioned to address municipal operating and (especially) capital needs than is often suggested.[49]

Municipal Finances by Municipal Class[50]

Municipal finance and recent changes to it vary in significant ways among types of municipalities. Certainly, per capita spending has recently been greatest in the largest cities and in the rural municipalities. Rural municipalities spend primarily on roads, which represent about 60 per cent of their outlays in contrast to less than one-quarter in urban municipalities. The urban municipalities spend more heavily on protection, recreation, and environment. From 1988 to 2001, real per capita spending declined or was constant in the urban municipalities but increased by about 30 per cent in the rural areas. Nor did the substantial reduction in (primarily provincial) transfers occur uniformly. The relative amounts and the timing varied. Rural municipalities got the smallest reduction and it came later while the smaller cities took the more serious cuts and those began earlier. While all municipalities were called upon to rely more heavily upon own-source revenues, real per capita own-source revenues increased notably only in the villages and, especially so, in the rural municipalities. Real property taxes, particularly, and revenue from sales, less so, had to increase to offset the reduction in grants.[51] Rural municipalities obtain, on average, over 80 per cent of their property-tax revenue from non-residential and non-farm sources, much of that related to the energy industry. The contribution of energy property to tax revenues affords a fiscal advantage to fortunate municipalities. In urban municipalities, 54 per cent of property taxes are from residential properties and 40 per cent from other land and improvements (that is, largely commercial and industrial).[52]

The Evolving Transfers

It is useful to reflect somewhat further on federal and provincial transfers to local governments. The federal transfers are small relative to municipal budgets and highly variable in amount and allocation. Those to Alberta municipalities have ranged from \$8.28 to \$22 per capita (real dollars); the share of federal transfers devoted to specific programs has varied from 8 per cent to 58 per cent (transportation) and 8 per cent to 39 per cent (housing), and their contribution to expenditures by function has fluctuated from as much as 70 per cent to as little as 6.5 per cent (housing). In 2004, except for housing (6.5 per cent), federal grants accounted for no more than 3.3 per cent of expenditures in any functional category. The variation may reflect local choices as well as federal priorities. Federal funds may make significant and important contributions to small specialized programs, but, in general, federal transfers in the 1988–2004 period have not been a sustained source of funding for municipal programs (and perhaps have even been an unreliable one).

Provincial transfers to municipalities are larger but they, too, have proven to be highly variable in recent years. Unconditional grants that had provided about 9 per cent of municipal funds virtually disappeared, while conditional funds fell from 14.7 per cent to 8.7 per cent (mostly as a result of cuts to transfers supporting current, as opposed to capital, outlays). The functional allocation of the grants, however, is relatively stable. Transportation receives the largest share, ranging from 40 per cent to 60 per cent between 1988 and 2004, with its share expanding as grants were reduced. Environmental services and recreation and culture are the other two major functional categories regularly receiving large shares. Transportation grants represent about one-fifth of municipal transportation expenditures, while environmental and recreation grants account for about one-tenth of those types of outlays. Provincial transfers tend to represent larger shares of some typically smaller expenditure categories (for example, social services, housing, and resource conservation and development).

New Developments in Municipal Finance

Just as the reduction in transfers was the defining feature of municipal finance in the 1990s, transfer growth can be expected to be the defining feature of municipal finance in Alberta during the first decade of this century. First, we witnessed a substantial turnaround in federal transfers to all Canadian municipalities as a result of the Martin government's 'New Deal' for municipalities. The initial move came with the 2004 federal budget, which provided municipalities with full (versus the partial 57 per cent) relief from the federal Goods and Services Tax (GST). This measure was estimated to provide Canadian municipalities with $580 million in sales-tax relief in its first year. That amount translated to just over $18 per capita but the benefit will continue and will grow annually with expenditures.[53] Although $18 per capita represented only 1 per cent of per capita municipal expenditures, it was naturally welcomed. While a continuing legacy, because the benefit is not an explicit transfer, it will soon be lost from sight and go unrecognized.

The second phase of the federal initiative came with the announcement of the 'New Deal for Cities and Communities' program in the 2005 federal budget. It was to provide $5 billion in funds for municipalities over the next five years, starting with $600 million in 2005–6 (which translates to about $18.75 per capita). Combined, these two new sources of federal funds represented about 2 per cent of municipal expenditures for Alberta municipalities and a slightly higher percentage for municipalities in most other provinces. That percentage may increase somewhat over the five-year term. This new money, which the Harper government committed to making permanent (in addition to adding further support for infrastructure), is a huge increase from past levels of federal support (for example, $6.50 per capita for Canada and $8.28 for Alberta in 2001) and it is to be in addition to existing federal funds. Also, it has the potential to be much more sustained and reliable than past federal transfers. That new federal money offsets a notable portion, perhaps one-third, of the collective percentage reduction in provincial transfers during the 1990s. The warm response of the provinces to this significant (economic and political) initiative in an area of provincial jurisdiction very likely reflected the fact that most provinces saw the federal funds as providing important benefits to the provincial governments by easing municipal demands for expanded provincial grants. Even Alberta was quick to sign the new agreement.

At the time of writing, the economic situation in Alberta is quite different from the way it was when the cuts in transfers were introduced. For several years, the energy sector and the economy generally have been vibrant (and recently booming). Increasing energy prices have fuelled provincial surpluses, and the provincial government has been declared debt free. Given the new provincial bounty, and faced with demands for provincial assistance in dealing with a municipal infrastructure deficit and the infrastructure demands of a rapidly growing economy plus a rather disgruntled electorate, the Klein government promised to embark on a five-year program to transfer $600 million annually to Alberta's municipalities for infrastructure development. That program was implemented with the 2005 budget, the funds being largely allocated to municipalities on the basis of population. The transfer converts to about $185 per capita in 2005. That addition would approximately double the level of recent per capita provincial transfers. The commitment represented a striking shift in provincial policy. Alberta municipal finance statistics show provincial transfers increasing to $1,068.5 million in 2006 from $575.5 million in 2004; that is, from $180 to $318 per capita in two years. The provincial government also assumed responsibility for police services in communities with up to 5,000 persons, double the previous threshold of 2,500. However, the province's plans to shift responsibilities for ambulance services from municipalities to the provincial government's regional health authorities was aborted in 2005 at the last minute (and at considerable inconvenience to the municipalities) when initial costs to the province were predicted to balloon beyond the expected $55 million to $128 million. The province decided to re-examine that shift in responsibility.

The province's economy and the provincial finances continue to excel. Under the new leadership of Premier Ed Stelmach, the province introduced major new grants for municipalities in its 2007–8 budget. Foremost was the ten-year Municipal Sustainability Initiative (MSI), which is to provide $400 million in 2007–8 primarily for core and community sustainability infrastructure.[54] That program is to expand to $500 million in 2008–9 and $600 million in 2009–10. These funds are in addition to the Klein government's five-year Alberta Municipal Infrastructure Program, allocating $600 million per year. At the end of that program, the Stelmach government's MSI is to increase to $1.4 billion per year in 2010–11. (These projections assume that provincial revenues permit the anticipated levels of funding.) In addition, more provincial funding was announced for municipal water and wastewater investments. Clearly, if provincial revenues continue to be at least maintained, Alberta municipalities will realize a massive transfer program to support municipal infrastructure that will, in turn, indirectly assist other areas of municipal spending.

Recent Developments in Alberta Municipal-Provincial
Fiscal Relations

In November 2001 the then minister of municipal affairs, Guy Boutilier, established the Minister's Provincial/Municipal Council on Roles and Responsibilities in the 21st Century. Members consisted of the minister, the mayors of Calgary and Edmonton, the presidents of the AUMA and the AAMD&C, a representative from the Alberta Economic Development Authority, and three members of the Legislative Assembly. The council's mandate was largely to clarify roles and responsibilities, resolve issues, and recommend improvements in the provincial-municipal partnership. With some effort, the municipal representatives soon succeeded in having the council's scope expanded to include resources as well as roles and responsibilities. Thereafter, it was known as the 3Rs Council.

One might have thought that the council had the potential for making significant improvements in the provincial-municipal system given the reduced transfers, emerging infrastructure deficit, and other fiscal problems facing municipal governments over the previous decade. In a notable move in the spring of 2002, the AUMA advocated extending to municipalities the right to tax in provincial areas (for example, fuel, income) or develop a new tax. As a further result of its own 3Rs exercise, it made other recommendations including ones about which functions should be allocated to the province, which to the municipalities, and which should be joint.[55] To garner greater internal support, the new tax-room proposal was diluted to seeking a defined share of provincial and federal taxes. Regardless, the municipal participants were prepared and anxious to pursue meaningful changes. Despite this potentially ambitious start, the 3Rs Council was notable mostly for its invisibility. It had no website and reference to it at the Municipal Affairs website was limited to the initial announcements. What little public attention it received came mostly from the municipal participants' public complaints about its slow pace and the provincial unwillingness to discuss resources.

Perhaps reflecting the internal diversity of views, the 3Rs Council engaged the Canada West Foundation to come up with a closing document. In its resulting *Foundations for Prosperity* paper,[56] the foundation recommended: a) that municipalities and the province make a mutual commitment to eliminating the municipal infrastructure debt and its causes by 2015; b) that a Municipal Infrastructure Council be established, with the task of defining (by June 2005) a mix of infrastructure-financing instruments from new municipal tax tools,[57] legislated provincial revenue sharing, and phased provincial withdrawal from the education property tax that would be in place by December 2005; and c) that the province lead in engaging the federal government in municipal-infrastructure finance. While the 3Rs Council acknowledged that it had supported the paper's preparation, it noted that the document did not necessarily reflect a consensus on the part of its membership. Notably, of the broad scope of issues brought to the table, only the infrastructure problem emerged in the closing document.

The 3Rs initiative may have contributed to Premier Klein's infrastructure transfers, but the initiative lapsed with a change of ministers. Late in 2005, the new minister of municipal affairs, Rob Renner, inaugurated the Minister's Council on Municipal Sustainability. The effort represented another attempt to address enduring provincial-municipal relationship themes. There were three foci: relationships, revenue sources, and roles and responsibilities. This time, besides the minister, only the mayors of Calgary and Edmonton and the presidents of the rural and urban municipalities associations were invited to participate. The parties divided the preparation of background materials, with the AUMA examining who might do what under roles and responsibilities, the city of Edmonton and the AAMD&C looking at regional relationships, and the city of Calgary attending to prospective new revenue sources and arrangements for municipalities. As with the 3Rs Council, the discussions were again held in camera and without public record.

Although many matters were to be on the table when addressing local revenues and finances, the players in this rejuvenated provincial-municipal dialogue were highly attentive to provincial musings concerning the province 'getting out of' the education property tax and leaving the property tax solely to the municipalities. As part of that, there was the suggestion that the province would offset part of its cost of relinquishing the property tax by reducing or eliminating transfers to the municipalities. Meanwhile, the council suggested that the province provide municipalities with additional annual funding equivalent to the amount collected through the education property tax. In the end, the provincial education property tax continued and the province introduced major new grants for municipalities in its 2007–8 budget, primarily in the form of the new MSI. Beginning in 2008–9, these monies are being distributed, with a first call being per-community base amounts but with the 'large majority' to be allocated on the basis of 48 per cent per capita, 48 per cent according to education property tax requisitions, and 4 per cent according to local road kilometres. In addition, more provincial funding was announced for municipal water and waste-water investments.

The MCMS also recommended that the province enact legislation that permits municipalities, at their discretion, to levy and collect additional own-source revenues,[58] and that the province redefine the notion of economic rent or permit municipalities to assess directly 'resource utilizers' for municipal costs relating to resource development. None of these recommendations was accepted by the province, which asserted its sole role in determining economic rent and resource-royalty rates and reserved decision on new own-source revenue sources. Similarly, the province reserved decision on establishing a permanent program providing financial assistance to municipalities that lack sufficient assets and revenues to remain financially viable.

Provincial-municipal fiscal relations in Alberta are rapidly reverting towards the earlier grants model with minimal other changes. In fact, in this round, there is a strikingly heavy reliance on conditional grants and minimal provision for tax-base-disadvantaged municipalities. Grants can be expected to depend upon the fortunes of the Alberta government, so municipal fiscal well-being will continue to be closely tied to the province's volatile economic cycle. Unfortunately, it is largely that problem that motivated the recent sequence of initiatives examining provincial-municipal fiscal relations. The grants are welcome relief for municipalities and many, certainly from outside the province, would see them as generous. However, they do not address the issues of local control or predictability. The large and cyclic nature of resource revenues in provincial finances poses a dual problem in the municipal context: How much of that abundance should be shared with municipalities and their taxpayers and how should a sharing arrangement be implemented? Those issues have really not been addressed and they deserve further investigation.

Local Democratic Institutions and Processes

Organization of Representative Structures

Alberta's municipal councils are defined squarely within the Canadian norm for council organization. All Alberta municipalities must possess a CEO – either a mayor or reeve. By legislation, the electors of towns and cities must elect a mayor at large unless the council passes a by-law permitting appointment by councillors.[59] Councils appoint CEOs of villages, summer villages, and municipal districts unless they pass a by-law providing for election at large.[60] CEOs of specialized municipalities are selected through the process defined by the provincial regulation establishing the authority.

In most Alberta cities, council members are elected at large. The larger cities (Calgary, Edmonton, Red Deer, Lethbridge, and Medicine Hat) all have ward elections. Edmonton is unique in having two-member wards – the other ward-represented cities have single-member wards. Calgary has fifteen council members in toto, with fourteen ward representatives and a mayor. Edmonton has thirteen council members in toto, with a mayor and twelve ward representatives. Red Deer, Lethbridge, and Medicine Hat each have councils of nine – eight councillors and a mayor. The norm in the other cities is seven council members, which is the 'default' membership defined by legislation. Importantly, under section 143 of the Municipal Government Act, cities and towns can pass by-laws that raise or lower the number of council members by an even number from the norm of seven so long as the number is no fewer than three. There are 136 elected city officials.

Town mayors and councillors are elected at large, and there appear to be no instances in which a town council has established a ward system. At present, the number of town council members ranges from five to seven. Village and summer village councils nominally consist of three councillors, one of whom is the mayor. However, villages can pass a by-law to increase the number of councillors to a higher odd number, and roughly half of Alberta's village councils have used this provision.

Representational structures of specialized municipalities differ. For example, the regional municipality of Wood Buffalo is divided into four wards with a different number of councillors elected within each ward. Strathcona County contains seven one-member wards. Four of the wards are within the Sherwood Park urban service area (USA) and three within the rural service area (RSA). The mayor is elected at large. Under each of these specialized municipality arrangements, the RSA populations enjoy larger per capita representation but the USA representatives are in the majority and the urban population effectively elects the mayor.

The representational organization of rural municipalities is broadly uniform, with large single-member wards or, in common rural parlance, electoral divisions. The number of divisions varies from three (MD of Ranchland No. 66) to 11 (MD of Opportunity No. 17), with the most common number being seven. Under the traditional arrangement, the council selects a reeve. However, recent changes to legislation permit the election of a mayor-at-large, and this innovation has appeared in the Capital Region with the election of mayors in Sturgeon County and Parkland County.

Different governance arrangements exist across the province's improvement districts. Three of the seven IDs possess advisory councils that are composed of chairpersons and councillors who are either elected locally or appointed by the minister of municipal affairs. These committees guide the activities of the IDs' chief administration officer, a provincial official. The minister of municipal affairs is legally the municipal authority for the ID but in practice most power and responsibility has been delegated to the councils where they exist. Where councils do not exist, an ID manager, who is a provincial employee housed within the Department of Municipal Affairs' Municipal Advisory Services branch, supervises administration. Métis settlement councils are composed of five elected members who choose a chair from their number. Alberta municipalities are given wide freedom to define the legislative, executive, and administrative machinery of government. Over the past century, municipalities experimented with various forms. Variations of council-manager government are found across the province. Strong city-manager systems are found in the largest municipalities, including Calgary, Edmonton, Red Deer, Lethbridge, and Wood Buffalo. All these municipalities have administrations headed by a single official bearing the title of city manager and, importantly, constituting the administrative principal at the nexus of the political-administrative interface. The same model exists in Strathcona County and in many of the large rural municipalities, although the title of the official can be that of county manager, chief administrative officer (CAO), and commissioner or chief commissioner.

Despite the mandatory appointment of CAOs, many of the province's smaller municipalities operate within a time-tested council-committee arrangement in which the CAO exists in a relatively weak position relative to committee chairs and the portfolio-focused committees. Reputedly, in some authorities, the committees administratively supervise staff, thereby rendering moot the intent of the MGA and the functionality of the council-manager regime.

The power of the elected CEOs varies, and in recent years, with the movement to manager-styled governments, offices of the mayor have gained power and influence. This transition, which has occurred roughly over the past two decades, speaks to the development of more powerful and more strategically capable mayoral-support administrations in these authorities. CEOs of medium-sized cities are not as fully bolstered, but they too have garnered additional influence during a period when municipal issues and municipal government have become more fashionable.

Elections

Municipal elections are held every three years in Alberta on the third Monday in October and are administered under the Local Authorities Election Act. This legislation also guides elections of school authorities and was used as a basis for the unique 2001 election of a portion of regional health authority board members.

Alberta municipal elections draw fewer voters than provincial or federal elections. Since there are no systematically collected province-wide municipal election statistics on record, it is not possible to comment on whether there is a negative correlation between municipality size and voter turnout as reported in British Columbia.[61] Given the very large number of acclamations in rural municipalities and villages, it is likely that less of a correlation exists in Alberta than in British Columbia.[62]

Regardless, Calgary and Edmonton consistently have meagre voter turnouts. Consider the Edmonton data: in only four elections of thirty-six held since the end of the Second World War has Edmonton's voter turnout exceeded 50 per cent and in no instance has the percentage exceeded 60 per cent.[63] Further, six elections saw turnouts of less than 15 per cent although none has been under 23 per cent since 1963, the year in which reforms were introduced to promote vitality in municipal elections. Edmontonians posted an abysmal 27 per cent turnout in 2007,[64] which contrasts starkly with a 42 per cent turnout in 2004. Thirty-three per cent of eligible voters turned out for Calgary's 2007 municipal election, prompting some Calgarians to boast of bettering Edmonton's turnout. This braggadocio may have been inadvisable given that a mere 20 per cent of eligible Calgary voters had bothered to vote in 2004.[65] Low voter turnouts have not been restricted to the largest cities; only 27 per cent of eligible Red Deer voters participated in the 2004 municipal election, and that city's 2007 participation sagged to 21.5 per cent.[66] Airdrie, a suburban city to the north of Calgary, posted a truly appalling 12.5 per cent turnout in 2007.[67]

Incumbency clearly has its advantages in Calgary. Only one Calgary mayor and eight aldermen were unseated in the twenty-five years prior to the 2004 municipal vote,[68] although in 2007 three incumbent councillors lost their seats. In 2004 incumbent mayor David Bronconnier received 79 per cent of all votes cast for mayor, and in 2007 a still overwhelming 61 per cent.[69] By contrast, Edmonton electors defeated no less than four sitting mayors during the same period, including incumbent Bill Smith in 2004. On occasion, voters will sweep out a whole council, such as in 2001 when the whole of the St Albert city council was unseated. However, such radical turnovers are as rare as they are newsworthy.

Under the Local Authorities Election Act, there are no spending limits and no limits to personal donations to municipal campaigns. The campaign expenditures of those running for office in the two largest cities have been escalating, especially in contests for mayor. Mayoral contests have become well oiled and media-tailored, and thus costly. The cost of Edmonton's competitive 2004 mayoral election doubled that of the 2001 contest, and was the most expensive ever, with candidates spending $1.6 million, while the cost of ward contests was up by a third for the same election.[70] Calgary's 2007 mayoral contest was still more expensive, even given the differences in the population sizes of the two cities. Mayoral candidates spent over $2.3 million on the contest. Incumbent mayor David Bronconnier spent lavishly enough ($731,430), but his principal competitor, Alnoor Kassam, spent an astounding $1,545,021. This largely self-financed campaign garnered Kassam only 17 per cent of the mayoral vote – a distant second-place finish.[71] Collectively, Calgary mayoral and councillor candidates spent almost $3.5 million seeking office in 2007.[72]

Alberta municipal election contests are putatively non-partisan. In many smaller centres, they well may be wholly non-partisan. However, in the largest cities, and even in many smaller centres, the political affiliations of candidates are more or less known. One reason that a fiction of non-partisanship is often maintained in Alberta is that municipal politicians wish to avoid Tory wrath or, more particularly, avoid bringing it down on the municipality if not on themselves.[73] However, an anti-local partisan bias well may be part of the Alberta political culture, as well as a Canadian norm.

No province-wide demographic data exist on municipal candidates, making it difficult to comment on who, in terms of sex, ethnic origin, occupation, or socio-economic status, gets elected and who does not. Data are available, however, on female representation in municipal office. Federation of Canadian Municipalities (FCM) research reveals that women comprised 16 per cent of Alberta's mayors and 24 per cent of Alberta municipal councils in 2004.[74] Greater representation of women seems to be something of a trend. Following the 2007 province-wide municipal elections, women comprise a quarter of all council members and hold 21 per cent of CEO positions (mayoral and reeve) and 26 per cent of councillor positions.

Female representation among the municipal-status categories (that is, city, town, village, summer village, specialized municipality, rural municipality) is not uniformly distributed. For example, only one in sixteen city CEOs (6 per cent) is a woman, while two of the province's five specialized municipalities are led by women. Female representation as CEOs and councillors within Alberta's other urban municipal status categories (for example, towns, villages, summer villages) is slightly above the province-wide norm: 24 per cent of town, 30 per cent of village, and 24 per cent of summer village CEOs are women; 27 per cent of town, 27 per cent of village, and 30 per cent of summer village council members are women. By contrast, in rural municipalities, women account for only 11 per cent of CEOs and 18 per cent of councillors.

A prominent concern voiced during the Municipal Affairs consultations that preceded the recent reforms to the Local Authorities Election Act was that local returning officers should be given powers to police elections; however, the provincial legislature chose to reaffirm the returning officer's role as an administrator, though the role would be more sharply defined. Still, voter-identification procedures now can be set out under local law, and persons convicted of offences under specific provincial and federal acts are prohibited from running for office or serving as official agents or scrutineers. Elected authorities with populations or 10,000 or greater can set the number of signatures required for nomination up to 100 (up from 25), and require a deposit of up to $1,000 (up from $500). Elected authorities are now permitted to challenge an election before the courts, whereas previously only candidates and citizens could do so.

The same Municipal Affairs consultations produced proposals to place limits on campaign expenditures (with contributions by any person, corporation, trade union, or employee organization not to exceed $2,000), to require disclosure of all contributions received by a candidate over $375, and to increase the term of municipal office to four years.[75] None of these proposals was written into the legislation. Moreover, though the provincial government stated that the amended local election legislation was developed to address the widely observed problem of low voter participation in elections, it is difficult to see how this has been accomplished – a point made by the Opposition in the Legislative Assembly during debate, and a matter that we will revisit in our concluding considerations.[76]

Plebiscites, Petitions, Transparency, and Public-Input Mechanisms

Alberta has long had provisions for public participation through petition and plebiscite in its municipal government legislation.[77] Although provincial legislators have, from time to time, either given or taken away grass-roots elements of democracy, the ability of citizens to quash or force councils to alter local legislation has been, and continues to be, an important feature of Alberta democratic local government. With the 1994 reforms to the MGA, the Legislative Assembly bolstered the public-participation provisions in the act. The act now has a full 'part' dedicated to public participation,[78] with provisions (some of which existed in the previous version) on the right to petition a public meeting (section 229), to force public votes on new by-laws and resolutions, and to force the amendment or repeal of existing by-laws and resolutions (section 232), among others. Interestingly, many by-laws that are passed or defeated though public votes are protected for specified periods of time from council initiatives.

The architects of the 1994 act bolstered plebiscite provisions as a countervailing measure to the liberalized law-making powers vested in councils. That is, citizens were given greater powers to check and balance the enhanced powers of councils. Citizen powers were also bolstered with the addition of revised planning legislation to the act in 1995. The public gained opportunities for input into the formation of local planning policy and administration through new legislated requirements for public hearings and appeal mechanisms. Further, greater transparency and disclosure provisions were built into the act to better enable citizens to hold councils accountable. The ability of councils to hold in camera meetings was restricted and, albeit a little later, municipalities were put under the investigative authority of the provincial information access and privacy commissioner.

Stories from local newspapers reveal that the petitioning and plebiscite provisions of the MGA are indeed used, though in many instances it is not clear whether plebiscites have been initiated by citizen petition or by councils. In recent years there have been plebiscites on smoking-ban by-laws, the construction of new municipal buildings and recreation facilities, municipal budget by-laws, the election of reeves, casino location within municipalities, borrowing, and RCMP supplementary budget requisitions. Petitions cover the same issues and more and are clearly initiated by citizens.[79]

Edmonton and Calgary have special submunicipal institutions in the form of community leagues/associations that, among other things, provide vehicles for citizen input. These bodies are organized within community boundaries that are initially defined by the city. There are roughly 150 community leagues in Edmonton and 130 community associations in Calgary. In both cities, these neighbourhood organizations are represented on a city-wide basis through federations. The Federation of Calgary Communities also includes community associations from select neighbouring towns and residential agglomerations. Edmonton's planning, parks and recreation, and engineering departments use the leagues as avenues through which to consult on proposed neighbourhood improvements.[80] The leagues and associations periodically also raise issues with city departments and agencies. In rare cases, the leagues and associations provide the venues or volunteer machinery to mount protests or establish counter-policy forums in opposition to city actions or those of private interests.[81]

Interest Groups and Lobbying

Alberta's municipal governments are subject to representation from organized interests that lobby councils and administrations and otherwise seek to influence local government decisions.[72] Business groups are arguably the most effective, if not the most pervasive municipal government lobbyists. Within the business community, business associations affiliated with land development (the Urban Development Institute [UDI]), housing (the Alberta Home Builders Association), and road building (the Alberta Roadbuilders and Heavy Construction Association) are reputedly the most successful and the most engaged. A decade ago in Edmonton, special and perpetuating relationships were observed between the planning department and the UDI, and between the transportation department of the day and the Roadbuilders Association.[73] The special relationship with the business community obviously continues: when those interviewed for this chapter were asked to name province-wide organizations that pressured municipalities, the UDI was mentioned above all.[74]

Other groups lobby municipal governments. These include environmental and social-advocacy groups, recreation and related associations, and ratepayer associations. When asked about non-business advocates, our interviewees mentioned the Sierra Club most frequently, although we were informed that this organization has little effect and can generate considerable hostility in the province's rural precincts. This view does not seem to be shared within some of the urban municipalities, where environmental concerns about suburbanization, pesticide use, and efforts to promote smart growth are either entertained or encouraged. The Sierra Club has mounted campaigns addressing these matters and recently published 'The Alberta Smart Growth Report,' authored by a former Edmonton municipal councillor.[75] Representations by the Sierra Club and other environment groups to municipal councils reflect an active and growing environmental politics at the local level. The sympathetic hearing given these organizations by urban councils speaks, in part, to AUMA and FCM support of the Kyoto Accord and to broader environmental and sustainability initiatives mounted by both organizations.

Ratepayer associations remain active in many Alberta communities although their memberships tend to grow or diminish in light of budget controversies, and particularly in light of prospects for increased local taxes. These groups were especially active in the early 1990s. Anti-smoking lobby groups have had significant influence on local smoking by-law initiatives. Less successful, although not less active, have been anti-gambling lobbies, which focused their efforts at the local level. These groups were highly visible during the 1998 municipal elections when local plebiscites were held in thirty-seven communities giving guidance to the provincial government concerning video-lottery terminals, specifically their retention in or removal from commercial establishments.[76]

Provincial-Municipal Relations

A Thumbnail History of Tory Rule with Attention to Recent Developments

Over the long term of the Lougheed premiership (1971–85), the provincial government made wide-ranging and concerted efforts to build up Alberta's institutional structure and capacity by creating new institutions and renovating old ones in the name of modernity. The municipal system was subject to this reformist program. Lougheed's governments paid considerable attention to the development of the provincial administration's capacity to control, guide, and aid the local authorities. Where largesse was possible, the province exercised it. Periodic efforts were made to lighten the financial burden of municipalities, and there was a comprehensive review of municipal finances that resulted in a grant regime that sustained many small municipalities. By contrast, little in the way of structural change was introduced to the system. The absence of structural reform was owing, in part, to reforms of the post-war Social Credit era in which the rural municipal system was significantly consolidated and some success was achieved in consolidating the municipal structures of the two largest urban CMAs.[87] However, this was clearly only part of the story since the Tories were loath to initiate sweeping structural reforms to municipal government. Whether this penchant was attributable to some philosophic preference or to pragmatic politics is not clear.

With a decline in international energy prices that gained momentum in the mid-1980s, the Getty premiership (1985–93) began what would be a gradual and sustained provincial disengagement from the municipal sector. While not abandoning municipalities, the government did not sustain its level of guidance and assistance to them and ceased to build its bureaucratic capacity in the municipal area. During this period, initiatives such as eliminating most of the remaining improvement districts were on the front burner. The Getty government's principal commitment to municipalities, and its legacy, was an extensive review of the Municipal Government Act which was intended to establish a new type of municipal legislation and, putatively, a new provincial-municipal relationship. Time ran out for the Getty premiership before this could be accomplished, but detailed draft legislation did emerge from an extended consultation with citizens and the municipal-policy community through the Municipal Statutes Review Committee. As described above, the new legislation represented an effort to 'free' municipalities from the all-embracing regulatory grip of the provincial government. Some provincial officials, speaking off the record, acknowledged the 'adolescence' of the municipal system – a child of the province no more. However, it is important to note that the metaphor refers to adolescence and not adulthood, which quite accurately reflects the province's intent to grant some freedoms but by no means full jurisdictional freedom to municipalities.

The premiership of Ralph Klein, a former popular Calgary mayor, took Don Getty's disengagement program considerably further. Klein won his first province-wide mandate on promises of fiscal stringency that were supported by an undeclared ideological commitment to deflate the state.[88] The Klein program of 'fiscal responsibility' and smaller government resulted in the revision and passage of the groundbreaking, Getty-era draft legislation while the government concomitantly slashed its administrative and financial support to the municipal sector. Municipalities were freer in a de jure sense but also poorer and saddled with additional responsibilities either downloaded or offloaded by the province.

During the first years of the new millennium, and with the arrival of a new economic boom, the provincial government's engagement with the municipal sector increased. However, the foundation of this relationship and the contents of its political discourse and policy initiatives were, nonetheless, influenced by the legacy of the Getty and Klein disengagement model. For some time, the Klein government showed a lack of imagination and energy as it grappled with the problems that prosperity brought, as was certainly reflected in the 3Rs exercise. Policy innovations, desperately needed to address urban and many other issues exacerbated by the booming economy, went unaddressed. Admittedly, the government was finally moved to begin to reinvest in municipal infrastructure and other underfunded aspects of municipal government, and in amounts that were significant, but, again, policy-wise, Klein and many of his cabinet seemed oblivious, or simply unconcerned. In 2006 the party faithful rebuked the premier, prompting his quick exit.[89]

With the Conservatives' surprise selection of dark-horse candidate, Ed Stelmach, (a former Klein cabinet minister and rural county councillor) as their new leader in November 2006, and his assumption of the premiership in December, the next chapter of Alberta provincial-municipal relations opened. Premier Stelmach and his minister of municipal affairs and housing inherited the Minister's Council on Municipal Sustainability. As has already been noted, the MCMS exercise distinguished itself from the lackluster 3Rs initiative. It submitted its report to the minister in March 2007, with twelve major recommendations focusing on provincial and municipal roles and responsibilities, new municipal revenues, and intermunicipal relationships including issues concerning land-use planning and growth management, dispute resolution, and regional services delivery.[90] In its official response, the government agreed in principle to seven of the recommendations, rejected two, and reserved judgment on others.[91] The MCMS recommendations accepted by the government included the previously discussed land-use planning and growth-management proposals, the tackling of several difficult issues involving shared roles and responsibilities, more provincial money to combat the so-called infrastructure deficit, and the challenges presented by the robust economy. The Municipal Sustainability Initiative emanated from the last commitment.

These provincial government initiatives suggest a new era in provincial-municipal relations in which the province is more attentive to, and engaged in, municipal policy issues. However, the new government's agenda is only beginning to emerge. Indeed, the MCMS recommendations rejected or held in reserve by the government may say as much about future municipal policy direction as those that have been accepted. The government did not accept the MCMS recommendation that the current alignment of current municipal and provincial roles and responsibilities not be changed. This recommendation represented a reversal of the 'classic' positions of municipal-policy community actors, since the norm has been for the province to reject municipal demands for realignment of roles and responsibilities. The government did not accept the recommendation that the concept of 'economic rent' and resource-royalty rates should include prospective costs incurred by municipal governments in supporting resource development. The government also did not accept the MCMS proposal that municipalities should be provided with powers to raise revenues directly from resource developers, nor did it take up the suggestion (not a recommendation) that a long-term agreement should be signed between the province and municipalities to ensure a stable funding and policy framework. Still, on the strength of its efforts to provide significant new infrastructure funding, its acceptance of several significant MCMS proposals, and its comparatively energetic efforts to subdue the tempests of Capital Region land-use planning and inter-municipal relations, the Stelmach government has already distinguished itself from the desultory Klein years.

The Minister of Municipal Affairs

Although the minister of municipal affairs has many prerogatives under the MGA that relate to specific matters of approval or regulation of municipal activity, part 14 of the act specifies general ministerial powers and is therefore of particular interest. The minister can intervene in intermunicipal disputes, provide municipalities with 'information' on the assessment of property, and inspect matters connected with the management, administration, or operation of a municipality. The minister can order inquiries into the affairs of a municipality, the conduct of elected and appointed officials, and the conduct of persons involved in agreements with municipalities. Upon the request of the minister, a bank or financial institution must provide financial information relating to a municipality's accounts. More significant yet, the minister possesses powers under section 574 to order a municipal council or its officials to take actions to remedy improprieties, irregularities, and improvidence of any sort. The minister can dismiss councils and CAOs and has the power to appoint an official administrator as supervisor of the municipality and its council. Finally, the minister, upon holding a dissolution study, may recommend to the lieutenant-governor-in-council that a municipality be dissolved.[92] Needless to say, provincial-municipal relations are defined within these sweeping, and arguably draconian, powers.

The current Ministry of Municipal Affairs encompasses several entities that formally exist apart from the department, although these may use departmental corporate and administrative services. The entities include the Municipal Government Board and the Alberta Emergency Management Agency. The MGB is located within the Department of Municipal Affairs. The board is a quasi-judicial tribunal that has responsibility for a number of matters previously handled by either the Local Authorities Board or the Alberta Planning Board. These bodies were eliminated with the introduction of the 1994 MGA and its 1995 amendment act. The MGB hears appeals on property assessment, equalized assessment, linear property assessment, and subdivision approval (or rejections) that it deems to have a provincial interest. The board also hears intermunicipal disputes, including annexation initiatives not solved at the mediation stage, conflicts between local housing authorities and municipalities, and matters that may be directed to the board by the minister or the lieutenant-governor-in-council.

The Department of Municipal Affairs

Since May 2007, the Department of Municipal Affairs has been organized in three principal divisions: the Local Government Services Division, the Public Safety Division, and the Corporate Strategic Services Division. The Local Government Services Division is composed of two branches (Municipal Services, Assessment Services) and an administrative unit that serves the Special Areas Board. The Municipal Services Branch contains many elements of what might be described as the traditional core of Municipal Affairs. The branch provides policy-related services pertinent to the department's responsibilities in areas of land-use planning, municipal planning, and property taxation. It also supplies support services and advice to municipalities on governance and administration matters. The administration of improvement districts is also accommodated within the branch. Assessment Services oversees the policies and procedures for property assessment and the annual determination of each municipality's share of the education property tax. The branch is also responsible for linear property assessment (for example, electric power generation, telecommunication systems, petroleum and gas wells, pipelines). The Special Areas Board provides municipal services and long-term land management in the special areas. The municipal services include taxation, licences, permits, leases, local works, and improvements.[93]

Municipal Affairs' Public Safety Division is responsible for providing a framework for safety codes and standards to ensure that buildings, facilities, and associated equipment are built, operated, and maintained safely. The Corporate Strategic Services Division provides internal departmental administrative services and is also home to several ongoing provincial initiatives that are perhaps best described as only partially relevant to the traditional focus of the ministry. These include public library services, community services, and the Alberta Nonprofit/Voluntary Sector initiative.

The foregoing description of the Department of Municipal Affairs is a necessarily temporal one insofar as the structure of the department is subject to periodic spasms of re-engineering. With Ed Stelmach's assumption of the premiership in December 2006, a new ministry of Municipal Affairs and Housing was created by the government's grafting on elements of the former ministry of Seniors and Community Supports. In March 2008, however, the premier again reorganized the ministry, hiving off the housing portfolio and creating a new Ministry of Housing and Urban Affairs and the Alberta Municipal Affairs briefly described above.

Other Provincial Boards and Agencies of Note

Although the MGB is the principal tribunal that addresses municipal matters, other provincial tribunals also have regulatory authority over some aspects of municipal activity, or activities of significance that occur within the boundaries of municipalities. These include the Natural Resource Conservation Board, the Alberta Energy and Utilities Board, and the Police Review Board. Of the province's five officers of the legislature, only the information and access commissioner possesses powers to investigate municipalities. The ombudsman, ethics commissioner, and auditor general have no investigative or oversight responsibilities that touch on municipal jurisdiction. The Office of the Chief Electoral Officer consults with Municipal Affairs on election matters but has no direct role in the administration of municipal elections.

Municipal Associations and Related Associations

Alberta has two principal municipal associations: the Alberta Urban Municipalities Association and the Alberta Association of Municipal Districts and Counties. The AUMA is the accepted voice for the province's urban municipalities although, as noted previously, the two largest cities often work separately in the promotion or defence of their interests. All the same, Calgary and Edmonton are well represented in the governing councils of the association. Four board members (two each from the principal cities) are appointed and not elected by the membership, and there is a regular, if not frequent, rotation of big city candidates into the presidential nomination pool. The AUMA Board of Directors is also organized to provide representation and voice to each classification of urban municipality. Geographical representation is built into the AUMA board structure, too. Elections for the board are held annually at its fall convention.

The AAMD&C is the voice of rural municipalities. Its Board of Directors is elected annually at the association's fall convention. The board is composed of seven members, with the president and the vice-president elected at large each year and five district directors who are elected to staggered two-year terms by municipalities within the district they represent.

The member services and advocacy focus of both associations are similar. There are three separate components to the AUMA's membership services: the Alberta Municipal Services Corporation (AMSC), a broadly conceived services administration that, among other things, operates a program to purchase electricity collectively and is developing strategies and services that relate to Alberta SuperNet, designed to provide high-speed Internet and telecommunications services in Alberta municipalities; MUNIX, which provides general insurance services to member municipalities; and a pensions and benefits administration unit. In 2005 each of the three entities was assigned separate boards that relate to the AUMA board through an Executive Committee and an Audit and Finance Committee. The membership-services operations are businesses and therefore not all urban municipalities purchase or enrol in the services. The volume of the AUMA business services stood at $107 million in 2006. The AUMA's permanent staff complement is roughly thirty-five.

The AAMD&C provides insurance services to its membership and other organizations through Jubilee Insurance, an insurance agency wholly owned by the AAMD&C. Originally extending coverage only to AAMD&C members, the service grew to serve school jurisdictions and occasionally towns, villages, seniors' foundations, recreation centres, and other local government-related entities. Recently, however, in light of representations from the AUMA, urban subscribers are no longer actively recruited although some remain with the plan. Between 1974 and 2005, the Jubilee Insurance Board had representation from the Alberta School Boards Association (ASBA);

however, in 2005, the ASBA withdrew from the business and established a discrete service for its school authority members.

The AAMD&C also operates a trade division that offers bulk-purchasing opportunities to rural municipalities and, since 1970, to a long list of 'Associate' members that include the range of urban municipalities, school authorities, and various other community organizations. The AAMD&C full-time staff complement is roughly twenty.

Both associations actively lobby the provincial government. They also work with government ministries in the formulation of legislation and government programs. Annual or semi-annual conventions have traditionally provided the venues in which both associations have drafted representations to the province. These gatherings remain significant and democratic insofar as there are relatively open processes whereby member municipalities bring resolutions for provincial action to the floor for approval of the membership. In recent years, the associations have attempted to provide more focus to their governmental advocacy through establishing policy priorities and striking internal committees, or task forces, to address what their boards believe to be large pressing issues confronting the memberships. The AUMA has been especially active in developing formal policy-review machinery and processes to address strategic issues, formulate policy options, and press its membership, the provincial government, and others to effect reforms.

There are a number of minor associations that take interest in specific municipal-related issues. These include the Community Planning Association of Alberta, the Economic Developers Association, and the Alberta Culture and Recreation Association, all of which include municipal council members and are often dominated by them. They articulate province-wide issues in their respective areas of concern and lobby the government of Alberta through channels other than those afforded by Alberta Municipal Affairs.

Municipal Administration

Employment Numbers and Unionization

Alberta municipal administration is remarkably diverse, which is not surprising given the range of municipality types and populations and the contexts in which it is practised. All the same, certain generalizations can be offered about the organization of municipal administrations and the issues and trends in this area.

Alberta Municipal Affairs statistics on workforce complements – self-reported by municipalities – provide a rough estimate of the permanent municipal workforce.[94] In 2006 Alberta municipalities reported employing a little below 32,000 full-time employees. Cities employed 24,000 of these, and Calgary and Edmonton accounted for 20,000. Specialized municipalities employed 1,350 full-time staff, the province's towns employed 2,900 full-time employees, and villages and summer villages accounted for fewer than 400 full-time employees. Coincidentally, municipal districts and counties employed the same aggregate number of full-time employees as towns – 2,900. However, whereas the average number of full-time employees in the rural authorities is forty-five, the full-time town complements average a more modest twenty-nine employees. Villages and summer villages have very few full-time staff, averaging only two employees. A fairly large percentage of summer villages share a CAO, but these arrangements appear to occur as a result of the CAO's initiative. Importantly, these statistics do not include large complements of part-time municipal workers and the large cohort of contracted workers who produce municipal services. Thus, the employment statistics are understated.

Although Alberta has the reputation of being a province in which unions do not flourish, slightly over 19,600 municipal employees operated under 112 union agreements in 2005.[95] The cities and the largest specialized municipalities are all unionized in some fashion, but the reach of unionization also extends to towns, villages, municipal districts, and counties. Employees of 26 of the province's 109 towns are unionized (24 per cent) and, perhaps improbably, two villages are unionized. Thirteen of sixty-four counties and municipal districts (20 per cent) are unionized. Most of this unionization covers outside workers though many office workers are also union members.

Women comprise 46 per cent of the municipal CAO cohort, something that on the face of things looks like an admirable accomplishment of male/female representational parity. Alas, the Alberta municipal system has quite a way to go before achieving anything resembling gender equality. There are no female CAOs employed by specialized municipalities, improvement districts, or the special areas, and only 20 per cent of rural municipality CAOs are female.[96] Of these, rural municipalities with the smallest populations disproportionately employ women CAOs. Towns employ women as CAOs by a percentage that is higher than that registered by rural municipalities; 36 per cent of town CAOs are female. Yet women are again more heavily represented within the less populated half of the town category. Females constitute a hefty majority of village CAOs (74 per cent) and a significant majority of summer village CAOs (59 per cent). While these statistics may cheer those who seek gender parity in the municipal arena, they also underscore the system-wide reality that sees woman underrepresented in the big administrative jobs. This point is driven home when considering the city category data: women head two of sixteen city administrations, but there are no women CAOs in any of the eight most populated authorities. Provincially, in fact, the sixteen largest municipalities employ male CAOs.

Municipal Administrators and Professional Associations

Alberta's municipal CAOs, and those in their senior executive teams, are represented by a number of professional associations. A number belong to two or even three of these associations. CAOs employed in the larger urban municipalities, and in a small number of the larger and 'urbanized' rural authorities, are members of the Canadian Association of Municipal Administrators.[97] Greater numbers of CAOs are members of the Society of Local Government Managers of Alberta (SLGM). The SLGM was established in 1988 under Alberta's Societies Act and was granted recognition under Alberta's Professional and Occupational Associations Registration Act (POARA) in 1991. The significance of POARA status is that the society possesses the exclusive right to award the title of Certified Local Government Manager (CLGM), and the province places requirements and strictures on the occupational organization to codify practice, prescribe member-qualifying educational requirements, and investigate member practices in the light of complaints or on its own volition. The regular membership of the SLGM is skewed towards rural and town administrations, with small representation from cities, specialized municipalities, villages, provincial employees, and others.[98]

The Local Government Administrators of Alberta (LGAA) is older and its membership larger than that of the SLGM. Cities are not represented in the LGAA but towns and village administrations are well represented.[99] The Alberta Rural Municipal Administrators Association (ARMAA) represents rural municipal officials and, unlike the LGAA, which competes in some fashion with the SLGM, functions as a fraternal society, thereby leaving professional qualification, practice definition, and practice oversight to the SLGM. Almost all, if not all, CAOs of rural municipalities belong to ARMAA, but senior rural administrators are also heavily (and concomitantly) represented within the regular membership of the SLGM.[100]

Municipal Alberta Considered

Alberta's municipal governments are successful if the accepted purpose of municipal government is to provide good government, maintain safe communities and services, and provide facilities that are either necessary, or reasonably desired, by most of the public. Albertans' municipal water, streets and roads, recreation and cultural amenities, local law enforcement agencies, and many other services are reasonably well provided for, even if there exist infrastructure deficits and municipalities are challenged by the rapid growth of the boom economy.[101] There are certainly many reasons for this apparent success. The system is mature and stable. Alberta's municipalities are democratic notwithstanding such enduring realities as low voter turnout, differential power between citizens and special interests, and the statistical under-representation of women in elected office, to mention a few. There are legislated opportunities for citizen participation and many municipalities routinely provide opportunities for citizen input of some sort, although how much of this informs council decision making is a matter of debate. Local elections are routinely well administered, and many council seats are contested although the number of acclamations might give one pause, and mounting campaign costs are a matter of concern for some. There is little evidence of systematic corruption at the local level.[102] The civic administrations of the largest municipalities are professional and competent. Smaller local authorities may be less 'sophisticated' insofar as they do not possess professional depth in their operating divisions, but many CAOs and other officials have received formal training in public and business administration, and the vast majority effectively advise their councils and lead their staff. Competence and professionalism bolster Alberta local democracy and unquestionably contribute to the general success of Alberta municipal government.

The provincial government plays an important role in fostering the adequacy of the system. Granted, municipal politicians have their complaints, some of which may be well founded, but the government of Alberta has been prudent in its reforms and continues to consult municipalities and the public on most matters of significance prior to bringing forward reform. The extent to which the province embraces municipal and citizen representations is a matter of dispute among members of the Alberta municipal-policy community. Suffice it to say that in many instances policy choices are complex and zero-sum, and the province necessarily has its own interests and requirements to serve that do not always conform to those of municipal government. Credit must be extended to the province for recent financial contributions to municipal government that are the envy of other provinces. Although some suggest that the provincial government, once more oil-rich, finds it easy simply to write large cheques and consider its responsibilities to the municipal community covered, none would have the province keep the funds. Indeed, complaints that the province is disinterested in the crucial problems of the municipal sector have become more muted since the Stelmach government has directed its attention towards such tough-to-crack policy issues as intermunicipal relations, regional land-use planning and development management, provincial and municipal roles and responsibilities, municipal finance, and its own leadership responsibilities in the municipal arena.

The general health of the Alberta municipal system is also promoted by the activities of its two principal municipal associations and the host of smaller associations and other organized interests that pay attention to municipal matters. Perhaps indicating the maturation of Alberta local government generally, the principal associations have developed greater policy-advocacy capabilities and have also become more disciplined, expert, and assertive in bringing focused attention to select issues of concern to their memberships.

There is, of course, room for reform and an extra dollop of enlightened leadership. What follows are comments on five areas. In each, problematic particulars are discussed and selected reforms contemplated. Some of this commentary is offered as a reflection on observations and opinions provided by individuals in positions of authority who were interviewed by the authors in the summer of 2005.[103] Although the sample is clearly not scientifically drawn or technically representative, those interviewed are regarded as leaders in the Alberta municipal field and collectively possess many scores of years of experience.

Jurisdiction and Functions

Within municipal Canada, the division of jurisdiction and functions between provinces and municipalities is a perennial matter of contention. Historically, municipalities have chafed against restrictive provincial regulation and legislation, and both municipalities and provincial governments have desired clearer definitions of functional divisions of responsibility. In the ideal provincial-municipal world, there would be ample allotments of jurisdictional powers between the orders of government, and functional clarity. Within recent Alberta policy discourses (that is, the 3Rs and the MCMS), jurisdictional and functional concerns have been important, although little by way of reform has been implemented.

Perhaps one reason that little reform has taken place is that, despite the rhetoric, little reform is required – at least in terms of the jurisdictional powers granted municipalities. We asked municipal and provincial officials whether they thought Alberta municipalities possessed sufficient powers under legislation. Our respondents were nearly unanimous in stating that they believed that most Alberta municipalities possessed sufficient powers owing to the permissive powers of the MGA. This point was later echoed in the final report of the Minister's Council on Municipal Sustainability, which recommended that the present alignment of roles and responsibilities remain.

If there is an exception to the general view that municipalities possess adequate powers, it is that the largest municipalities, especially Calgary and Edmonton, might benefit from receiving additional powers to carry out certain activities that are currently limited or restrained by provincial legislation. Precisely what those powers might be is not clear, at least in the responses from our interviews. Additional powers to tackle affordable housing was suggested by our city of Edmonton interviewees, but, even among them, there was understanding that the solution to the problem of affordable housing would involve the provincial and federal government. Indeed, the multilevel-governance complexity of policy problems in the metropolitan centres seemed to resonate in discussions. Although alignment of roles and responsibilities may make sense in certain circumstances, the greater challenge is to fashion working arrangements in which governments can coordinate their policies, regulation, and service provision. This point is not lost on Alberta governments, but the challenges of such coordination are considerable.

Policy questions involving roles and responsibilities also logically concern municipal shedding or uploading of responsibilities (if not jurisdictional powers). We asked our interviewees if municipalities should be relieved of certain functions or, somewhat differently, if certain functions should be supported to a greater extent by the province. Several respondents (municipal ones) mentioned ground ambulance services as a candidate, undoubtedly owing to the province's unkept 2004 promise to transfer ambulance responsibilities to regional health authorities. Safety-code inspections were also mentioned as a candidate for uploading – this function was downloaded to municipalities in the 1990s. Most recently, regional-transportation funding and allocation issues have come to the fore. The MCMS called for study of the realignment of responsibility and funding sources for municipal transportation services, a realignment that might include establishing some form of regional entity to address regional transportation requirements. Whether regionalization involves a change in jurisdictional responsibilities within the system is not clear. The newly established Capital Region Board is charged with delivery of intermunicipal public transit, but, while it will operate with a board composed of municipal leaders, the organization itself is a provincial entity.

Respondents stated that municipalities could do more within their legislatively defined spheres of jurisdiction if they possessed more stable revenues and additional revenue sources. This is undoubtedly true; however, many municipalities are able to access at least some additional revenues through existing own sources but are apparently politically limited in doing so. Additional revenue is not the whole remedy – a point made by several of our interviewees. A significant difficulty in carrying out present functions – and most certainly relating to taking on new functions – turns on working closely and harmoniously with the provincial and federal governments, and with other municipalities and local governments within a region. Greater capacity is needed for this, as are, perhaps, new institutional forms to facilitate such interjurisdictional cooperation.

Municipal Finances

Municipal financing will continue to be a significant issue for Alberta municipalities. Our analysis demonstrated the ebb and flow of provincial assistance and some of the consequences. Post-2004, both the federal and Alberta governments have enhanced their support to municipalities – the federal government with its GST relief and 'New Deal' funds, and, most notably, the province with its new infrastructure grants. The province's infrastructure program is striking in that the Klein government's 2005 transfer of $3 billion over five years essentially doubled the level of provincial grants to municipalities and made a significant move back towards pre-1993 levels. The Stelmach government's 2007 program supplements and extends that funding. Some might argue that such a restoration of funding sets right the fiscal downloading since the mid-1990s, but that would imply contentment with 'rough justice' and ignore the havoc of the wild ride over the previous decade. While the massive infusions of infrastructure manna and other targeted grants and fiscal transfers are welcome, they do not address the 'structural' finance problem that is said to challenge municipalities. Municipalities argue that they need stable and elastic financial sources and would appreciate some control over those sources, or at least greater predictability. While there is some logic to this position, it is difficult to separate need, rhetoric, and strategic behaviour. The real test would be to provide municipalities a significant alternative (elastic) revenue source and see who is willing to utilize it. The viable options are relatively few and they have their pros and cons.[104] Thus far, no Canadian province has been willing to extend municipalities significant tax powers beyond the property tax. In Alberta, the problem is made significantly more complicated by the role and volatility of natural-resource revenues in the provincial budget.

Despite the recent municipal-provincial councils, the province does not appear to accept that there may be serious structural problems with the financial means of municipal authorities. Perhaps additional municipal tax bases are desirable. Perhaps some reallocation of responsibilities should be introduced. Certainly, provincial transfers to municipalities need review. The province has not taken a comprehensive look at municipal finances for a long time and a new, expert review is long overdue.[105] We wonder why, if unwilling to extend tax authority, the province continues to be so reluctant to establish a reliable revenue sharing program, why there is a continuing (though seemingly undeclared) provincial policy of providing transfers only through conditional grants, why certain grant schemes appear so arbitrary, and why the province has failed to provide sufficient aid to the poorest and the highest-growth authorities. Much may be right with the system, but it is in need of comprehensive in-depth public analysis, public discussion, and provincial leadership directed towards long-term solutions.

Local Democracy and the Democracy Deficit

Several reviews of Alberta local government have noted the need to bolster local democracy. The Getty-era Municipal Statutes Review Committee emphasized the importance of greater public participation, and the 'new' MGA that eventually emanated from that extended effort included new provisions for citizen involvement and greater transparency and accountability in the conduct of council and municipal business. Theoretically at least, the provisions of part 7 of the act served as the basis for a democratic counterweight to empowered councils, and there is some evidence that these designs have worked in practice.

Recommendations made in 2005 by the Alberta Tory caucus MLA committee reviewing the Local Authorities Election Act (the Prins Committee) addressed the low levels of municipal election voter turnout, observing that this was the overarching topic heard by the committee at virtually every public meeting.[106] The MLA committee provided plausible explanations for low voter turnout in municipal elections, some undoubtedly derived from the academic literature. However, the committee's prescriptions for remedying the problem, while commendable, are not without challenge and are, on occasion, seemingly impracticable. Suggesting that more effort be placed on educating the young about local government and promoting youth involvement in the political process is laudable because 'civics' education is not addressed comprehensively in the education of Alberta's youth. The rub is that, while governmental and citizenship education, in general, is deficient in Alberta primary and secondary school curriculums, any expansion of what exists must compete with a multitude of other subjects that are also, arguably, under-taught. The practicability of adopting an 'innovative alternative voting mechanism' is even more questionable, though the proposal has certain significant appeal on its face. If this means proportional representation (PR), we say that municipal Alberta's unique, and long, experience with such systems has not demonstrated any sanguine effect on turnout; to the contrary, the public seems to have been confused by the details of the PR approach.[107] Committee suggestions that urban political parties might foster voter turnout and participation are probably valid, but the notion of local political parties is not likely even to be placed on the reform agenda unless a political leader emerges who focuses on electoral and political participation as a prime issue (the emergence of a significant issue might have the same result). Even at this, the establishment of local political parties (much less political parties with provincial party affiliations) is a difficult sell in Alberta.

We do not hold great hope that the province or the municipalities associations will take great interest in actively addressing the local democratic deficit. The province, while providing some citizen empowerment within the reformed MGA to counterbalance broader powers of councils, has not addressed such problems as local campaign financing, demonstrated much concern over low municipal voter turnouts (the Prins Committee recommendations went unanswered), or even made a stab at the relative dearth of civics education in the public-school curriculum. To its merit, Alberta Municipal Affairs has recently published a *Public Input Toolkit for Municipalities* that provides useful advice and guidance on planning and delivering public-participation processes and opportunities.[108] A complementary document, *Citizen's Guide to Participation in Municipal Decision-making*, is available too. The AUMA has also recently published a *Citizen Engagement Toolkit*, which borrows from the province's publication. This effort reflects the association's commitment to citizen participation, contained in its most recent business plan (2007–9). The AUMA envisions active local democracies that incorporate 'meaningful citizen participation' and citizens knowledgeable about municipalities who engage their leaders in the development of positive community strategies. How much more the province or the municipalities' associations will invest in fostering public participation and citizen engagement is a matter for conjecture. Suffice it to say that many municipal officials view citizen participation as something to be managed and contained. One is struck, when viewing the mechanisms discussed in province's *Public Input Toolkit*, by the extent to which control over the input process remains with the municipality. Indeed, while the *Guide* lists several sections of the MGA that apply to communicating with the public and to soliciting public input, it fails to mention directly some of the most potent citizen-input sections of the act that pertain to petitions and plebiscites. Thus, while acknowledging the value of these efforts to prompt citizen participation, and while granting that success in municipal attempts to foster greater public input will go some way towards remedying the democratic deficit, we believe that other local political actors must be active if public apathy is to be overcome. What constitutes 'meaningful' input for the public may not always square with what municipal officials define as meaningful. But, then, democracy is a contest of ideas and values.

Provincial-Municipal Relations

The 1994 Municipal Government Act proposed a new relationship between the province and municipalities in which the local authorities would be freer to act as independent governments for their communities. To date, almost a decade and a half after passage of the legislation, this envisioned liberty is only partially evident, and the potential provided by the act is far from being realized. Both the province and municipalities must behave differently to realize the act's potential. The province must continue to discipline itself to prevent slipping back into a legislative and administrative paternalism in which picayune matters are inserted into municipal legislation to excise a political irritation or bureaucratic inconvenience. Ministers of municipal affairs, in particular, must understand the intent and the possibilities of the 'new' MGA and turn their department towards realizing both. Such discipline may be difficult, as is evident in ministerial actions taken in 2005 that sought to rectify admittedly serious governance and administration problems in the Town of Lac La Biche.[109] One wonders how liberated local government is achieved when it is the minister – not the local electorate through its plebiscite or electoral powers – who fires the CAO and authoritatively mandates council harmony. While we fully admit that the minister holds power under the MGA to fire CAOs and direct councils, the spirit of the act implores the ministry to use the bully pulpit of government to remind the citizenry of its responsibilities and opportunities.

Municipalities also have a role in realizing the potential of the MGA. To be sure, many municipalities have little need to act much differently than they have traditionally, given the stable requirements of governance in their jurisdictions or the conservative preferences of their electorates. However, energetic municipalities are certain to find that the province's municipal legislation provides them considerable room for independent, even imaginative action. What this means in practical terms for provincial-municipal relations is that municipalities might best relate to the provincial government as partners in the governance enterprise. Some do this as a matter of course, but many do not. There is a paradox of freedom here in which municipalities are theoretically free (or, at least, freer than they were before 1995), but many are timid with these freedoms and often rely heavily on the province for guidance perhaps better found within the general municipal community.

Regionalism

Regional government ranks with the sales tax (and perhaps local political parties) as a political non-starter in Alberta. Any mention of regional government is guaranteed to produce an immediate and negative reaction within most of the municipal community. Provincial government officials (elected and appointed), too, have little taste for the concept. Regional cooperation is a more widely accepted approach to addressing regional issues, and from research that we have conducted in the Edmonton area, as well as from our other work with respect to regional service commissions, it is clear that municipalities are prepared to cooperate when the advantages are obvious to them.[110] All the same, provincial acceptance of the proposal of the Minister's Council for Sustainable Communities that Alberta's two metropolitan regions be placed under some form of regional-planning and service-delivery regime reveals that some forms of regional administration are necessary and generally acceptable in contemporary Alberta. In this regard, the Stelmach government's emerging philosophy on regional planning and service delivery is perhaps best described (with apologies to William Lyon Mackenzie King) as one of regional administration when necessary but not regional government. It remains to be seen whether this formula works. The tough question concerns the criteria for deciding whether provincially sponsored regional administration is indeed 'necessary.' Conflict over growth management and land use has grown significantly in recent years, and this has placed considerable strain on existing land-use planning structures. This shift in regional policy is a striking move and the new Capital Region Board will be a major test.

Alberta Municipal Affairs has provided grants over the last several years through the Regional Partnership Programme for establishing partnerships. Although welcome, these grants are small and provincial policies generally do little to address winner-loser situations in which there is inequitable distribution of revenues or the sharing of costs for the production of certain services that affect a region or significant subregions of one. Furthermore, there appears to be an uneven (and perhaps unfair) distribution of responsibilities for what might be considered regional services. In a number of regions, some form of general regional service-delivery entity would appear appropriate, most likely through the creation of special-purpose agencies or, perhaps, general-purpose agencies collectively 'owned' by the municipalities of the region. Regional services commissions exist as a structural form that can facilitate regional service production. However, to date, despite a steady increase in the number of RSCs over the past decade, these bodies have not been used to the extent they might be. RSCs would appear to have potential for promoting regional economic development and providing regional emergency-response services as well as regional recreational and cultural facilities and services, to mention some of the most salient examples. One need only look to British Columbia's regional district system to gain a full appreciation of what fully fledged Alberta RSCs might look like.[111] It will be of interest to see if the provincial funding promised under the Municipal Sustainability Initiative, with its incentives for partnering and collaborative action, will stimulate such new and expanded uses of the RSCs.

NOTES

The authors thank Annamarie Senkiw and Sheela Subramanian for their research assistance, and Judith Garber, the publisher's two anonymous reviewers, and the editors for their helpful comments and suggestions.

1 A point of confusion for the observer of the Alberta municipal system is the distinction between the legislatively defined classification of an authority and the legal name of the incorporation. While most urban authorities display their classification in the authority's legal corporate name, there are exceptions: Alberta Beach is a village; the municipality of Crow's Nest Pass is a town; and the municipality of Jasper is a specialized municipality, as are the regional municipalities of Wood Buffalo, Strathcona County, and (to emphasize the point) the Municipal District of McKenzie, No. 23. Perhaps the greatest point of confusion rests with the 'county' nomenclature that is found in forty-three of the sixty-four rural municipalities' legal corporate names. Alberta counties were eliminated as a municipal classification with the passage of the 1994 Municipal Government Act; however, almost all rural authorities possessing 'county' in

their corporate names retained the excised word even though the legislation made them municipal districts.

2 Alberta, Municipal Government Act, M-26, s. 78, Revised Statutes of Alberta (RSA), 2000.

3 Municipal population statistics are drawn from the 2007 Municipal Affairs Official Population List. This document provides official population figures as of 1 September 2007, in compliance with the Determination of Population Regulation 63/2001 under section 604 of the Municipal Government Act. See http://www.municipalaffairs.gov.ab.ca/ mc_official_populations.cfm (accessed 13 May 2008).

4 The official 2007 population residing in the six categories of true municipalities is 3,341,624. An additional 1,994 persons reside in improvement districts, 4,729 reside in the special areas, and 5,956 reside in Métis settlements. Thus, the total official Alberta municipal population tallied by Municipal Affairs is 3,354,304. In addition to these residents, 60,037 comprise the Indian Register Population, and another 1,150 live in the Townsite of Redwood Meadow (which is not a municipality). With these populations added to the total official population, the total unofficial population of Alberta is 3,416,391. See Municipal Affairs' '2007 Official Population List.'

5 Our use of a twenty-year (1987) metric for population and municipal-class number comparisons is largely a convenience.

6 This statistic should be lower for comparative purposes because the city of Fort McMurray, Alberta's fastest growing municipality, was included in the 1987 city list but not in the 2007 list since today it is a specialized municipality.

7 This number requires qualification since, as of 1 January 2008, the municipality of Crowsnest Pass, formerly a town, became a specialized municipality. There is a companion inaccuracy with the count of four specialized municipalities; the number should be five in 2008. Similarly, one village, Sangudo, reverted to hamlet status within Lac Ste Anne County in 2007, thereby creating a discrepancy between the number of villages shown on the most recent official population list and the most up-to-date count of municipalities in the village category.

8 Municipal Government Act, s. 89(1).

9 The Alberta county form of government was created in an effort to establish coterminous boundaries among municipal, school, and hospital authorities. Efforts to bring hospitals into this arrangement were never achieved, but in many instances reformers succeeded in effecting a loose consolidation of rural municipal and school administrations. County

government was also designed to extend to urban areas but this innovation did not take root. For additional discussion, see Edward C. LeSage, Jr, 'Municipal Reform in Alberta: Breaking Ground in the New Millennium,' in Joseph Garcea and Edward C. LeSage, Jr, eds., *Municipal Reform in Canada: Reconfiguration, Re-Empowerment, and Rebalancing* (Don Mills, Ont.: Oxford University Press, 2005), 57–82.

10 The 2007 and 1987 population statistics are not entirely comparable since the then named Strathcona County, which in 1987 held a population of 49,800, does not appear in the 2007 official population statistics (it is now classified as a specialized municipality). However, against this deficit, the rural municipality population has been bolstered by the addition of the populations of several former improvement districts following the establishment of these bodies as true local democratic rural governments.

11 Jack Masson with Edward C. LeSage, Jr, *Alberta's Local Governments: Politics and Democracy* (Edmonton: University of Alberta Press, 1994), 129.

12 Ibid., 130.

13 See http://www.ccsd.ca/factsheets/demographics/ (p.2) for a summary of the percentage of provincial populations living in urban areas calculated using Statistics Canada 2001 census data. Alberta is third, behind Ontario and British Columbia, in the percentage of the provincial population living in urban areas.

14 Municipal Government Act, s. 456.

15 Ibid., s. 627(1)(b).

16 One RSC of interest is the Oldman River Regional Services Commission (ORRSC). This is the only RSC that provides regional planning services to a region. The fact that there is just one RSC that provides such services is something of a surprise, for one of the envisioned purposes of the functionally strengthened RSCs was to assume programs of regional and metropolitan planning commissions which the government effectively killed in 1993 and eliminated outright in 1995. The ORRSC provides a range of planning, mapping, and library services, much as was done through the regional planning commissions. The big difference is that the ORRSC does not possess the regulatory clout possessed by the old regional and metropolitan commissions – clout that made them very unpopular among rural authorities. A more conventional regional service commission is the Capital Region Wastewater Commission, established under regulation (AR 129/85), which joined thirteen regional municipalities but not Edmonton. The commission is a service consortium devoted to supplying sewage transmission and treatment services to commission members.

17 Christopher Bruce, Ronald Kneebone, and Kenneth McKenzie, eds., *Government Reinvented: A Study of Alberta's Deficit Elimination Program* (Toronto: Oxford University Press, 1997), 383–416.
18 Masson, *Alberta's Local Governments*, 121–4.
19 Ibid., 125–6.
20 See ibid., chapter 12, with particular attention to 421–5, for a complete discussion of municipal land-use and regional planning in Alberta to 1994.
21 Douglas Radke, 'Working Together: Report of the Capital Region Integrated Growth Management Plan Project Team' (Edmonton: Alberta Municipal Affairs and Housing, November 2007).
22 See ibid., tables 13 and 14, pp.79–80.
23 Board approval of policy and plans requires seventeen of the region's twenty-five municipalities representing at least 75 per cent of the population to vote affirmatively. Thus, any Edmonton vote in the negative effectively vetoes a motion owing to the 75 per cent threshold. At the same time, Edmonton must work to ally itself with sixteen other area municipalities to pass a board motion, and the sixteen others must comprise an additional 4 per cent of the global regional population.
24 Capital Region Forum, 'The Capital Region Forum Business Plan: A Proposal for a New Era of Inter-municipal Cooperation' (Edmonton: Capital Region Forum, 2005), 8.
25 It is important not to overstate the competition since, even during the 1990s, the mayors of Edmonton and Calgary pursued joint lobbying initiatives and occasionally met together. See Mike Sadava, 'Duerr and Reimer "Bury Hatchet" to Get Cities Working Together,' Edmonton *Journal*, 22 April 1991, B1.
26 See s. 2.4 of the 'Canada-Alberta Agreement on the Transfer of Federal Gas Tax Revenues under the New Deal for Cities and Communities 2005–2015,' signed 14 May 2005.
27 See Alberta Association of Municipal Districts and Counties and Alberta Urban Municipalities Association Advisory Committee on Aboriginal Issues, 'Building Relationships: The Final Report of the AAMD&C-AUMA Advisory Committee on Aboriginal Issues' (Edmonton: AAMD&C and AUMA, 15 April 2005).
28 For additional background on municipal-First Nation relations, see Temera Consulting Services, 'Report concerning Relations between Local Governments and First Nation Governments: Submitted to the Provincial/Territorial Senior Officials Local Government Committee by Alberta Municipal Affairs, in Cooperation with British Columbia's Ministry of

Community, Aboriginal and Women's Services and Manitoba Intergovernmental Affairs' (Edmonton: Alberta Municipal Affairs, 31 May 2002).

29 See LeSage, 'Municipal Reform in Alberta,' 57–82, for a complete discussion of jurisdictional and functional reforms. The content of this subsection is drawn largely from it.

30 Municipal Government Act, s. 3.

31 Under section 6 of the Municipal Government Act, Alberta municipalities possess general by-law-making authority in nine spheres:

- safety, health, and welfare of people and the protection of people and property;
- people, activities, and things in, on, or near a public place or place that is open to the public;
- nuisances, including unsightly property;
- transport and transportation systems;
- business, business activities, and persons engaged in business;
- services provided by or on behalf of the municipality;
- public utilities;
- wild and domestic animals and activities in relation to them; and
- enforcement of all by-laws.

32 Municipal Government Act, s. 13.

33 See LeSage, 'Municipal Reform in Alberta,' 77–8, for discussion of the United Taxi Drivers of Southern Alberta v. Calgary case.

34 School authorities are the other component of local (i.e., subprovincial) government in Alberta. As a share of local expenditures, the school-municipal split is 45–55. Alberta's school authorities have recently experienced important changes in their powers and financing. Prior to the mid-1990s, school boards received support from the province and levied local property taxes to make up the remainder of the revenue (from 15 to 40 per cent over the preceding thirty years) to finance local schooling. Following some other provinces, the system was reformed to (in effect) remove taxing powers from the school boards and to make the province responsible for providing essentially all the boards' funding. The province basically took over the local school taxes and now levies a uniform property tax for school purposes. Growth of provincial school taxes has been constrained by provincial government policy. As a result, they are gradually becoming less important relative to provincial school expenditures and municipal property taxes.

35 For further discussion of Canada-wide patterns and interprovincial com-

parisons, see M.L. McMillan, 'Municipal Relations with the Federal and Provincial Governments: A Fiscal Perspective,' in R. Young and C. Leuprecht, eds., *Municipal-Federal-Provincial Relations in Canada* (Series: Canada: The State of the Federation, 2004) (Montreal and Kingston, Ont.: McGill-Queen's University Press, 2006), 45–81; and idem, 'Canada: Local Government Organization and Finance,' in A. Shah, ed., *Local Governance in Industrial Countries* (Washington, D.C.: World Bank Institute, 2006).

36 Nominal amounts are adjusted to 2001 dollars using the national GDP Implicit Price Index.

37 Program spending is expenditure excluding debt-service costs.

38 Federal grants increased in importance briefly in the mid-1990s and were then as quickly reduced. Federal transfers remain highly variable.

39 Municipalities in other provinces experienced similar reductions during the 1990s for similar reasons. See McMillan, 'Municipal Relations.'

40 McKenzie demonstrates that the bulk of the reduction in federal transfers to the provinces was passed on as reductions in provincial transfers to local (i.e., school and municipal) governments. See H. McKenzie, *The Art of the Impossible: Fiscal Federalism and the Fiscal Balance in Canada* (Ottawa: Canadian Centre for Policy Alternatives, July 2006).

41 Much of the expression of these concerns has come from the provincial and national municipal associations. More independent views are found in numerous publications. Popular sources include H.M. Kitchen, *Municipal Finance in a New Fiscal Environment* (Toronto: C.D. Howe Institute, 2000); R. Gibbins, L. Berdahl, and C. Vander Ploeg, *Foundations for Prosperity: Creating a Sustainable Municipal-Provincial Partnership to Meet the Infrastructure Challenge of Alberta's 2nd Century* (Calgary: Canada West Foundation, 2004); C. Vander Ploeg, *Dollars and Sense: Big City Finances in the West, 1990–2000* (Calgary: Canada West Foundation, 2001); idem, *Big City Revenue Sources: A Canada-U.S. Comparison of Municipal Tax Tools and Revenue Levers* (Calgary: Canada West Foundation, 2002); TD Bank Financial Group, *A Choice between Investing in Canada's Cities or Disinvesting in Canada's Future* (Toronto: TD Economics, April 2002), Special Report; idem, *Mind the Gap: Finding the Money to Upgrade Canada's Aging Public Infrastructure* (Toronto: TD Economics, May 2004), Special Report. For a broader discussion, see P. Boothe, ed., *Paying for Cities: The Search for Sustainable Municipal Revenues* (Edmonton: Institute for Public Economics, University of Alberta, 2003); Canadian Tax Foundation, 'Municipal Finance and Governance Reform Symposium,' *Canadian Tax Journal*, vol. 50, nos. 1, 2, and 3 (2002): 145, 550, 968; H.M. Kitchen and E. Slack, 'New

Finance Options for Municipal Governments,' *Canadian Tax Journal*, vol. 51, no. 6 (2003): 2215–75; and McMillan, 'Municipal Relations.'

42 High unemployment (7 to 9.5 per cent) and stagnant per capita PDI characterized the years from 1988 to 1996 and low unemployment (4.7 per cent) and 20 per cent higher per capita PDI characterized the 2001–4 period.

43 The increase in capital outlays does not appear to be due to more rapid population growth. For example, comparing 1991–8 to 1998–2005, the population-growth rates in the two periods were essentially the same but the GDP growth was twice as high in the second.

44 a) Deflated using the Canada GDP Implicit Price Index; b) PDI is Personal Disposal Income; c) Deflated using the Canadian CPI.

45 a) Deflated using the Canadian CPI.

46 Municipal revenues are deflated using the Canada CPI (Consumer Price Index) because municipal taxes and prices of municipal sales reflect forgone consumer products. Using the Alberta CPI results in small differences (at most) for these years.

47 See appendix C of Alberta Urban Municipalities Association, *Municipal Financial Analyses in Support of the 3R's Project* (Edmonton: Alberta Urban Municipalities Association, June 2006).

48 This data is consistent with Statistics Canada data on the financial assets and liabilities of local governments in Alberta.

49 For example, see the references in n.35.

50 Statistics Canada does not provide data by type of municipality. The data supporting this section come from the Municipal Information System maintained by Alberta Municipal Affairs.

51 Revenues from sales are chiefly an option for urban areas since sales contribute only 7 per cent of revenues in rural areas. The expansion in sales revenues occurred primarily in the villages, towns, and smaller cities.

52 Other land and improvements is the source of only 12.6 per cent of rural property-tax revenues.

53 The benefits to the municipalities of the full GST relief have been diminished somewhat as a result of the reductions in the GST rate from 7 per cent to 6 per cent (as of July 2006) and more recently to 5 per cent. However, the total benefits increase with spending and, currently, Alberta municipalities are spending more than previously.

54 The complication that arises from playing infrastructure catch-up this late in the cycle is that municipalities are already losing value to inflated construction costs and the added infrastructure demands are further aggravating the pressures on the economy.

55 See Alberta Urban Municipalities Association, 'Submission to the Alberta Financial Management Commission' (Edmonton: AUMA, May 2002).

56 Gibbins, et al., *Foundations for Prosperity.*

57 Reflecting the focus on infrastructure, the Canada West Foundation discussed a rather narrow list of new tax tools: for example, taxes on hotel occupancy, vehicle registration, parking places, fuel consumption, land transfers, and vehicle rentals.

58 Proposed new taxes included: an amusement tax; a tourism tax; a property-transfer tax; a vehicle-registration tax; expanded scope for development levies in support of directly related local services; and limited split mill rates within the non-residential property class. Alberta municipalities possess the ability to legislate split mill rates between the residential and non-residential property classes. The proposal for a 'limited' mill-rate enactment reflects council concerns that municipalities might be over-enthusiastic in applying the provision.

59 Municipal Government Act, s. 150(1).

60 Municipal Government Act, s. 150(2).

61 See Figure 2.1 in P. Smith and K. Stewart, 'Local Government Reform in British Columbia, 1991–2005: One Oar in the Water,' in Garcea and LeSage, eds., *Municipal Reform in Canada*, 23.

62 By our calculations, using 2004 election data available from Alberta Municipal Affairs, 47 per cent of rural municipal council members and 38 per cent of village council members are acclaimed. Twenty per cent of town council members sit by acclamation. Seven per cent of city council members are acclaimed. These figures provide only part of the acclamation picture. Seventeen (16 per cent) of the 109 town councils are wholly composed of acclaimed members, and 38 per cent of town mayors are acclaimed. Somewhat surprisingly, given the high percentage of councillor acclamations, only six (9 per cent) of sixty-four rural councils are fully acclaimed. Acclamations are not restricted to the province's smaller municipalities; four of Calgary's fifteen council members were acclaimed in 2004.

63 See Edmonton Public Library, Election Turnouts 1892–2004, http://www.epl.ca/Elections/info/EPLTurnouts.cfm.

64 See 2007 Election Results, http://www.edmonton.ca/portal/server.pt /gateway/PTARGS_0_0_265_210_0_43/httpper cent3B/CMSServer/ COEWeb/city+government/municipal+elections/2007+Voter +Turnout.htm.

65 Paula Arab, 'There's No Excuse for Voter Apathy,' Calgary *Herald*, 19 October 2007, final edition, A26.

66 See Red Deer 2007 Municipal election results: http://www.city.red-deer.ab.ca/Connecting+with+Your+City/City+Services+and+Departments/Legislative+a nd+Administrative+Services/Election+2007/2007+Election+Results.htm. 2004. Election results for earlier years are no longer accessible on the city of Red Deer website.

67 Arab, 'No Excuse for Apathy.'

68 Jason Feteke, 'Odds in Incumbents Favour Come Oct. 18: Experience an Asset Heading into Fall Vote,' *Calgary Herald*, 22 September 2005, B4.

69 See official 2007 Calgary municipal election results: http://www.gov.calgary.ab.ca/election/.

70 Gordon Kent, 'Mayoral Election Most Expensive Ever,' Edmonton *Journal*, 9 February 2005, final edition, B1.

71 Campaign expenditure data acquired through 'Statutory Declaration of Candidates for Municipal Office with Campaign Expenses and Campaign Contributions filed for 2007 election.' Available online from the Calgary City Clerk's Office, http://www.content.calgary.ca/CAA/City+Hall/Business+Units/City+Clerks+Department /index.htm.

72 Colotte Derworiz and Kim Guttormson, 'Record Spending in Civic Election: Campaign Expenses Reach Almost $3.5M,' *Calgary Herald*, 21 February 2008, final edition, B1.

73 'Tone Down the Rhetoric: Calgary Not Well-served by Partisan Squabbling,' *Calgary Herald*, 4 August 2004, final edition, A10.

74 Federation of Canadian Municipalities, *Increasing Women's Participation in Municipal Decision Making: Strategies for More Inclusive Canadian Communities* (Ottawa: Federation of Canadian Municipalities, 2004), 63, FCM 1047E.

75 Alberta Municipal Affairs, 'Local Authorities Election Review Consultation Paper' (Edmonton: Alberta Municipal Affairs, Municipal Services Branch, September 2005).

76 See *Alberta Hansard* for debates on Bill 28: Local Authorities Election Amendment Act, 2006. First Reading: 23 March aft. (H.617). Second Reading: 11 April eve. (H.876–8) – passed. Committee of the Whole: 2 May eve. (J.1232–5) – passed. Third Reading: 16 May eve. (H.1622–3) – passed. The legislation came into force on 24 May 2006; Statutes of Alberta (SA), 2006, c. 22.

77 Masson, *Alberta's Local Governments*, 301–6.

78 Municipal Government Act, pt. 7.

79 The authors searched the MuniMall newsletter backfiles using the descriptors 'plebiscite' and 'petition.' See http://www.munimall.net/newsletter/index.nclk.

80 Ron Kuban, *Edmonton's Urban Villages: The Community League Movement* (Edmonton: University of Alberta Press, 2005), 125.

81 Masson, *Alberta's Local Governments*, 260–1; Kuban, *Edmonton's Urban Villages*, 182–3.

82 For an extended discussion of local interest politics, see Masson, *Alberta's Local Governments*, 247–71.

83 E.C. LeSage, Jr, 'Public Participation in the Budgeting Process: Edmonton's Ongoing Experiment,' in K. Graham and S. Phillips, eds., *Citizen Engagement: Lessons in Participation from Local Government* (Toronto: Institute of Public Administration of Canada, 1998). Also see C. Leo, 'Global Change and Local Politics: Economic Decline and the Local Regime in Edmonton,' *Journal of Urban Affairs*, vol. 17, no. 3 (1995): 277–99.

84 Interviewees included a Municipal Affairs assistant deputy minister and two other highly placed departmental officials, the president and executive director of the AAMD&C, the executive director of the AUMA, two urban mayors of Edmonton region municipalities, an Edmonton-area CAO, and a city of Edmonton general manager.

85 See Allan Bolstad, 'The Alberta Smart Growth Report' (Edmonton: Sierra Club of Canada, June 2005).

86 G. Smith and H. Wynne, *VLT Gambling in Alberta: A Preliminary Analysis* (Edmonton: Alberta Gaming Research Institute, 2004), 18–20.

87 See Masson *Alberta's Local Governments*, and Eric J. Hanson, *Local Government in Alberta* (Toronto: McClelland and Stewart, 1956), for discussions of the Alberta local government system in the Social Credit era.

88 See Bruce et al., *Government Reinvented*, and Trevor Harrison and Gordon Laxer, eds., *Alberta and the Future of Canada* (Montreal: Black Rose Books, 1995), for essays providing detailed examinations of this period.

89 Jason Fekete and Tony Seskus, 'Tories Desert Klein: Premier "Shocked" Party Turned against Him,' Calgary *Herald*, final edition, 1 April 2006, A1.

90 Minister's Council on Municipal Sustainability, 'Report to the Minister of Municipal Affairs; Presented by the Minister's Council on Municipal Sustainability' (Edmonton: Alberta Municipal Affairs and Housing, 5 March 2007).

91 Alberta Municipal Affairs and Housing, 'Backgrounder: Government Response to Report of the Minister's Council on Municipal Sustainability' (Edmonton: Author, 17 July 2007).

92 Municipal Government Act, div.7, pt.4.

93 Provincial Archives of Alberta, *An Administrative History of the Government of Alberta* (Edmonton: Author, 2006), 479.

94 Statistics represent full-time municipal employees as reported by munici

palities in 2006. These are self-reported in annual reports to Alberta Municipal Affairs. See http://www.municipalaffairs.gov.ab.ca/cfml/profiles/index.cfm.

95 These statistics were made available by the Mediation Branch of Alberta Human Resources and Employment, 1 June 2005.

96 Derived from 2007 chief administrative officers list. Accessed at AMA's 'Municipal Officials Search': http://www.municipalaffairs.gov.ab.ca/mc_municipal_officials_search.cfm.

97 The 2004 Municipal Affairs CAO Survey reports that 13 per cent of respondents belonged to CAMA. Other professional organizations and societies with small percentages of members among the CAOs surveyed were: Government Finance Officers Association (7 per cent), International City/County Management Association (2 per cent), Certified Management Accountants (1 per cent), and the Institute of Public Administration of Canada (15 per cent). See Alberta Municipal Affairs, *CAO Survey 2004*, 15.

98 The *CAO Survey 2004* reports that 21 per cent of the CAOs responding to the survey had SLGM membership. Survey findings further reveal that 16 per cent of all urban CAOs respondents, and 39 per cent of all rural respondents, were SLGM members.

99 The *CAO Survey 2004* survey found that 56 per cent of all CAO respondents were members of the LGAA. This number comprised 68 per cent of all urban respondents and 25 per cent of all rural respondents.

100 Some 88 per cent of rural CAO respondents to the AMA study report ARMAA membership, and the percentage of rural CAOs belonging to the SLGM is twice that of urban CAOs. See ibid., 15.

101 Calgary ranks with Montreal, Ottawa, Toronto, and Vancouver as the cities with the highest quality of life in North America according to Mercer Consulting. All these Canadian cities are within the top fifty in the world ranked according to quality of life. See http://www.citymayors.com/features/quality_survey.html, 3 April 2008 (accessed 7 May 2008).

102 There are, however, certainly instances of shenanigans, as evidenced in a special inspector's report on election irregularities in Calgary's Ward 10 during the 2004 municipal election. See Clark, 'Inspectors Report.'

103 See n.84.

104 For a discussion, see, for example, M.L. McMillan, 'Municipal Relations with the Federal and Provincial Governments' and 'Local Government Organization and Finance.'

105 The last comprehensive review of municipal finances was through the

Provincial-Municipal Finance Council, which tendered its final report in 1979. See Provincial-Municipal Finance Council, *Report of the Provincial-Municipal Finance Council on Responsibilities and Financing of Local Government in Alberta* (Edmonton: Government of Alberta, Provincial Municipal Finance Council, 1979). Also see McMillan, 'Local Fiscal Reform in Alberta?: A Review and Assessment of the Report of Alberta's Provincial-Municipal Finance Council,' *Canadian Tax Journal*, vol. 28 (March-April 1980): 164–80.

106 R.L. Prins, L. Snelgrove, and R. Liepert, 'Report on the Local Authorities Election Act Review' (Edmonton: Alberta Municipal Affairs, November 2005).

107 See Masson, *Alberta's Local Governments*, 286–92.

108 See Policy Coordination Unit, 'Public Input Toolkit for Municipalities,' Alberta Municipal Affairs, September 2005, www.municipalaffairs.gov.ab.ca.

109 See Ministerial Order L: 171/05, and attending correspondence from Rob Renner, minister of municipal affairs, to Ron Lett, mayor, Town of Lac La Biche, 23 December 2005.

110 N. Hepburn, E.C. Lesage, Jr, and M. McMillan, 'Shared Service Arrangements: Determinants of Success – A Study of Economic Development and Recreation and Culture Shared Service Arrangements among Municipalities of the Alberta Capital Region' (Edmonton: Western Centre for Economic Research, Information Bulletin no. 78, June 2004).

111 See Robert Bish, 'Inter-municipal Cooperation in British Columbia,' *Public Manager*, vol. 35, no. 4 (2006–7): 34–9, for a recent discussion of British Columbia's regional districts.

10 Newfoundland and Labrador

JAMES P. FEEHAN, JEFFERY BRAUN-JACKSON,
RONALD PENNEY, AND STEPHEN G. TOMBLIN

The purpose of this chapter is to outline and examine critical features of municipal governance in the province of Newfoundland and Labrador. It will review the development of municipal governance, paying close attention to St John's, the capital city and the longest-standing municipality. This chapter will also review several other topics, including the historical context and evolution of municipal government, functions performed by municipalities, municipal finance, oversight functions performed by the provincial government, demographics, political culture, key policy actors, electoral systems, and trends in local governance.

Historical Background

In 1949 Newfoundland became part of Canada. At the time, supporters of Confederation expected this to result in rapid modernization to the Canadian standard. Presumably, one facet of the modernization would be the establishment of local government, which would provide residents an opportunity to voice their concerns at the community level. The problem was that local government had little foundation in the former dominion despite the fact that early permanent English settlements had been established there as far back as 1610. The idea of local government arrived late because most communities were very small and lacked an infrastructure that required maintenance and servicing by a municipal council or board.

During the development of Newfoundland in the eighteenth and nineteenth centuries, several factors mitigated against the establishment of a strong tradition of local government, including the isolation of outport communities,[1] the lack of support for paying direct taxes to support municipal institutions, and the absence of a tradition of locally managed services. These factors are captured in broad observations made by S.J.R. Noel.[2] First, Noel points out, outside St John's, there were few communities that had sufficient populations to support any form of local government. For example, at the turn of the twentieth century, of 1,300 communities across Newfoundland, only 18 had populations exceeding 1,000 people. Noel's second observation is that the use of direct taxation to support municipal services was opposed by local communities because the need simply did not exist and residents preferred to work cooperatively. Finally, Noel notes that the people who settled Newfoundland in the seventeenth and eighteenth centuries (the Irish and the West Country English) had come from places that had no strong and deeply rooted traditions of local government. As a consequence, they did not bring with them any desire to create the necessary institutional framework to support local government.

It was not until 1890 that Newfoundland's legislature, the House of Assembly, enacted the Local Affairs Act, which permitted outport communities to elect district boards responsible for such services as roads, bridges, sanitation, and lighting. These district boards generally coincided with existing electoral districts for the House of Assembly. The problem with this system was that all funds were provided to the boards directly by the central government in St John's; the boards were not permitted to raise their own funds.[3] The legislature allocated funds to the boards for specific purposes and Assembly politicians had much say in how and where the monies would be spent. The district boards were forbidden from running deficits without authorization. As Noel notes, the vast majority of people living in Newfoundland did not have any first-hand experience with local government until well into the twentieth century.[4]

Moreover, much of Newfoundland's history since 1800 has involved the struggle to obtain greater degrees of sovereignty from Britain for the territory as a whole, rather than devolution of government to the community level. In 1832 representative government was permitted for the first time.[5] Responsible government came in 1855 and, at various stages, further advances in self-government were made. In 1907 Newfoundland was recognized as a dominion within the British Empire. Thus, the historical evolution was one of shifting decision making from London to St John's. Throughout that period, there was little agitation for community-level government.

St John's was the exception. Individuals and groups permanently settled there petitioned the British governor to provide basic services for residents including police and fire protection. The governor and other officials generally ignored the calls for the provision of local government because of its potential to interfere with the fishery: 'The settlers were not consulted and they had no voice. The only question to be answered was whether civil government "will or will not be for the benefit and advantage of the fishery and navigation of this kingdom."'[6] The need for municipal government in St John's had been identified as early as 1816 when local administrators had noted that 'in this filthy overcrowded and unsanitary town, nearly 10,000 people had their homes. Yet St. John's possessed not the slightest vestige of municipal control, the few magistrates there exercising but a tardy and ill-recognized authority.'[7] Even with the obvious need to establish local government in St John's, it did not arrive until 1888.[8] That was some 250 years or more since the first permanent settlement there. Part of the reason for the delay was that the British had stuck to their principle that Newfoundland was 'a great ship to be moored off the banks.'[9]

Unlike Newfoundland, other British possessions across North America had the full support of the British in the establishment of their colonies, with the mother country investing substantially more in physical infrastructure and local transportation services. Newfoundland's infrastructure was underdeveloped. Communication with outlying communities occurred mostly through shipping and was sporadic at best, especially for the more isolated communities and those located on the Labrador coast. The fact that so much of the population lived in numerous small fishing communities scattered along the coasts of the island and Labrador added to the challenges of building the kind of transportation and communication linkages normally associated with municipal government.

During the Great Depression of the 1930s, Newfoundland suffered severely. A 1933 royal commission (the Amulree Commission) that examined the situation recommended that the government be managed by an appointed commission until such time as the dominion's fiscal position improved sufficiently. In 1934 the Newfoundland legislature accepted this arrangement as the condition of financial assistance from Britain. In response, Britain suspended the legislature and the electoral process and established a Commission of Government, consisting of the governor and six appointed commissioners.

The commission's mandate was to administer the dominion until such time as it was again self-supporting. Under the auspices of the Dominions Office in London, the commission governed until 1949.

Several commissioners noted that the absence of a local government tradition in the country was a 'great retarding factor in the development of a public spirit and a sense of civic responsibility.'[10] In 1937 the Commission of Government enacted a Local Administration Act which gave the governor-in-commission the power to organize any municipality. The act, however, provided the proposed new councils with only one source of taxation: property taxes. Because property taxes were vehemently opposed by residents, no outport community took advantage of the act. By 1942, the Commission of Government had adopted another strategy whereby special legislation would be passed for each community wishing incorporation. The community would then be free to decide what mode of taxation would be most appropriate.[11] Thereafter, municipal incorporation remained slow, but there was some success. In 1942 the central Newfoundland town of Windsor incorporated and nineteen other communities did so prior to Confederation with Canada.[12]

Before 1949, the void in municipal governance outside St John's was filled in a few instances by 'company towns.' These alternate forms of 'government' were created in new communities that developed as a result of industrialization and economic expansion during the late 1890s and early 1900s. The communities are generally described as company towns because the services provided to residents were paid for by the major employer located in the area, typically a newsprint mill or mining operation. As the interior of the country was developed in the late 1890s, the government gave its support to corporations wishing to own and develop land with the object of creating new communities. These communities differed from outports in that they were larger in population and employment was not related to the fisheries. Residents in company towns were paid an hourly wage for work and there was no credit system of the kind that existed between the fishers and merchants. Incomes were higher in company towns than in outports and trade-union activity was strong.

Yet the companies that built these towns exercised significant control over the residents.[13] In Buchans, a mining town, the company-owned railroad provided the only way in and out of town for residents. People lived in housing built by the company and privately constructed homes were forbidden. In Grand Falls, only those employed by the paper mill were permitted to live in company-owned houses. A separate community, Grand Falls Station, was established on the opposite side of that railroad line as a place where non-millworkers could live. Those not working at the mill were prohibited from socializing with millworkers and social life in the town was organized on the basis of one's employment at the mill.[14] Grand Falls Station continued to grow but lacked basic municipal services such as sewer and water. Grand Falls, conversely, had these services provided by the paper company. In 1938 a local group incorporated Grand Falls Station into the new town of Windsor and it eventually amalgamated with Grand Falls in the 1980s. Most of the larger and better-known company towns (Grand Falls, Buchans, Corner Brook, Deer Lake, Labrador City, Wabana, and Wabush) have long since stopped being owned by the companies that created them, and are now part of municipalities. At present, only the community of Churchill Falls is a company town; it is administered by the company that created it in the 1960s.[15]

Support at the community level for local government was particularly weak; most people simply did not want it. Critics felt that municipal government was unnecessary and even threatened established community practices. Interestingly, this attitude was reflected in the 1997 Task Force on Municipal Regionalization.[16] Historically, there had never been a clear consensus on the need for municipal government since most communities had clean water, sewage ran into the ocean, crime was not a problem, and either a local company or the Newfoundland government met most of the community's other needs. People felt that the only things they owned were their houses and because of this they developed a fear of municipal government taxing their property.[17] Opposition to the idea of municipal government was powerful and at times violent.

Against this backdrop of weak infrastructure and a culture that did not value municipal governance, there were few opportunities to push municipal reforms. Nevertheless, the post-Confederation provincial government of Premier J.R. Smallwood encouraged municipal government because it felt this was necessary to facilitate economic development.

In 1949 the provincial government introduced the Local Government Act, which applied to all communities outside St John's.[18] It allowed municipalities to establish themselves but maintained overarching control, providing for uniform powers throughout the province. Municipalities were all subject to the same standards as far as zoning, garbage, engineering, and other local functions were concerned. The provincial government put mechanisms in place to ensure that there were 'tight financial and administrative controls over town and rural district councils.'[19]

This overarching control, combined with communities being uninterested and generally opposed to municipal government, meant that most communities were slow to incorporate.[20] In order to encourage incorporation outside the St John's area during the 1950s and 1960s, the provincial government provided incentives, including cash benefits. The number of municipalities rose dramatically to 300 by 1974.[21] But with the rise in the number of municipalities came new problems. During the expansion, many small towns with limited resources and declining populations were merged. Resources were often stretched too thinly and many municipalities were unable to provide reasonable levels of service.

By 1974, it had become clear to observers that there was a crisis with respect to municipal governance. Implementing the Local Government Act had not led to the success that the province had hoped to achieve. Many municipalities, particularly rural ones, were in horrible condition with severe infrastructure gaps. In response, the provincial government established a royal commission to study the problem and propose solutions.

The Royal Commission on Municipal Government in Newfoundland and Labrador (the Whelan Commission)[22] was established in 1974. One of its main findings was that municipalities needed more authority to conduct their own affairs. The government acknowledged this point, noting: 'Municipal leaders feel their authority may be placed in jeopardy unless they can point to statutory rules and be legitimized by officials in St. John's.'[23] The commission felt that, with too much power in the minister's hands, there was no responsibility at the local level, particularly in areas such as finance. Municipalities also had no incentives to achieve service goals.

Most of the commission's recommendations were implemented, including additional powers and more self-reliance for local governments. The commission further determined that it was not in the best interests of the public to continue incorporating small municipalities. The communities were also given proper access to property taxes and their financial situation was greatly improved. Another important recommendation, that of implementing regional service boards, was given legislative approval. However, regional service boards never became popular; there are currently only a few in existence and they deal with either water supply or waste management.

Current State of Municipal Governance

The body that oversees the municipalities in Newfoundland and Labrador is the Department of Municipal Affairs (DMA), formerly the Department of Municipal and Provincial Affairs. It was established in 1952 to handle the large number of municipalities that were established after 1949.[24] The DMA has the authority to assume responsibilities from municipalities as necessary, including those for planning and engineering. The provincial government can also create regional councils and force amalgamations.

The provincial government has relaxed the tight control that it had prior to 1974, but the DMA still oversees municipalities and can initiate changes to legislation governing municipalities as appropriate. Thus, the chain of command remains more top-down than bottom-up.

Establishment of a municipality begins with a feasibility report that is issued by the minister to determine the needs of the community.[25] Subject to ministerial approval of the report, the minister establishes the number of councillors required, the size of the wards, whether or not there should be a ward-based system of election, and the date of the first election, thereby shaping the municipality from its inception.[26] The minister also has the power to dissolve a council if he or she feels it is unable to carry out its responsibilities. The minister may decide whether the mayor should be directly elected, and can install an administrator to manage the municipality if its council cannot manage its own finances. The minister also has substantial power over municipalities' financial concerns.

Once a municipality is established, its council has ninety days to develop a budget.[27] The budget is subject to ministerial approval. The minister has the discretion to alter, refuse, or accept that budget.[28] Yet, even though the minister has power over the budget, the municipalities have the power to tax, as determined by legislation.[29] Council collects taxes from property and businesses, service charges, and water and sewer fees.

The powers that are given to a municipal council are much more limited when it comes to borrowing. The minister must approve borrowing and it must be under 20 per cent of the amount of the next municipal budget.[30] To make borrowing more difficult, the amount borrowed must be repaid within one year. In special cases, long-term borrowing can occur, but the regulations are much stricter in the process. When a municipality engages in long-term borrowing, the application to the minister must be accompanied by a financial fore-cast for the next five years.[31]

The Urban and Rural Planning Act was amended in 2001 to devolve powers to the municipalities from the provincial government. Before the updated act, municipalities would propose an amendment and the DMA would appoint a commissioner to study it and make a recommendation. After the commissioner made a recommendation, the minister would decide whether or not to approve it. Often, municipalities would contest amendments by the minister's office and council had to be cognizant of the minister's reaction. Currently, the process is smoother and less time-consuming. The council appoints a commissioner, who reports to it. Once the commissioner has made a recommendation, council will decide on whether or not to approve it. After a council has approved a plan amend-ment, it is submitted to the minister of municipal affairs, who must reg-ister it unless it conflicts with a provincial law or policy.

The Municipalities Act governs most of the municipalities in the province, but there are separate acts for each of the three cities – St John's, Corner Brook, and Mount Pearl. It is important to note that the City of St John's Act gives it more powers than any other community to make decisions on separate matters. Like other municipalities, St John's has the power to tax and borrow, but, because of its size, it may borrow small amounts (under one and a half million dollars) without the minister's approval.[32] The city does its own property assessments, unlike the other municipalities, which rely on a provincial assessment agency. The city is also responsible for bus services. Still, while the city of St John's does have additional powers, the final authority for the majority of functions rests with the provincial government.

There are also a few striking differences between municipal services in Newfoundland and Labrador and those in the other provinces. Municipalities have no role in education. The funding of education is entirely a provincial government responsibility. Moreover, it is financed from provincial government general revenues, not property taxes.[33] Policing is entirely a provincial responsibility as well.

Regional Entities

An interesting and unique development in municipal governance has been the move to establish Inuit community governments. Under the

Labrador Inuit Lands Claims Agreement, which was signed in January 2005, there is an Inuit regional government for the area of Nunatsiavut. As part of that agreement, there are Inuit community governments for Nain, Hopedale, Makkovik, Postville, and Rigolet, which are small coastal communities within the region covered by the agreement. Each community government consists of a number of councillors and a chief executive officer called an AngajukKâK,[34] who also serves as a constituency representative in the Nunatsiavut Assembly of the regional Inuit government.

Other than in Nunatsiavut, there are no regional governments in the province, nor a history of them. Yet there can be regional government. The lieutenant-governor-in-council has the ability to implement regional councils and in so doing may 'amalgamate regions and annex areas to regions; establish and alter boundaries of regions; and disestablish a region.'[35] A regional council so established assumes financial responsibility for the services it will provide and receives its revenue from direct user fees or assessments on municipalities. The potential powers of the regional council include the ability to take control of the municipalities' finances and all that this entails, including such things as engineering services, emergency services, animal control, lighting, and solid-waste collection. The advantage of regional councils is that they can allow services to be shared and paid for by several different communities, thereby reducing costs. Any regional council created is to assume financial responsibility for all of the cities and towns within the region, although it still requires budgetary approval by the minister. A council would let those cities and towns know what their budgets will be and ensure that they adapt accordingly.

The Whalen Commission strongly recommended that the provincial government implement regional boards, since they were better able to manage multiple municipalities at much less cost.[36] In 1977 the Henley Commission, which was established to study regional government for St John's and adjacent communities, suggested using the legislation for regional boards to create a two-tiered system of government, believing that it was necessary for the St John's region.[37] The Henley Commission's recommendations were introduced twice in the House of Assembly but were defeated both times.[38]

In 1990 the provincial government did raise the idea of regional government but this time in the form of regional service boards. Peter Boswell suggests there was no need for such a proposal since the Municipalities Act already in place could have simply been amended to create regional service boards.[39] The idea of a regional services board has not been embraced. The opposition to such bodies is rooted in fear of a loss of community autonomy. The city of St John's, in particular, was opposed to both regional governments and regional service boards because it felt that it could lose control of its finances and that such boards would unnecessarily complicate the delivery of services. To be sure, there are a number of regional boards in the St John's urban region: for fire protection, water, and sewage treatment. However, their day-to-day administration is actually handled by the city of St John's.

Regional boards of other types that have actually been established in Newfoundland and Labrador are not regional governments per se and have no revenue-raising authority. They include regional health boards, regional school boards, and regional economic-development boards. The first regional health boards were established in 1995. Regional school boards have a long history in the province. The abolition of the province's system of denominational education in 1997 and the pressure of declining enrolment has led the provincial government to amalgamate many school boards in recent years. Regional economic-development boards were implemented in 1992 as part of the provincial government's Strategic Economic Plan.[40] Originally there were seventeen economic zones, later twenty, with the goal of 'facilitating the development of economic plans by the people in each zone; facilitating joint initiatives by communities within the zone; promoting economic opportunities and strengths of each zone and region; and facilitating more regionalization of Government administration.'[41] The plan has been somewhat successful for, under it, municipalities have been able to cooperate on economic strategies.

One example of regional cooperation is the Avalon Waste project. This ambitious effort aims to merge forty-three disposal sites into one location, which will be at Robin Hood Bay, the existing St John's landfill. The enhanced site will service the Avalon peninsula as well as other areas of eastern Newfoundland. This facility will also meet much higher environmental standards. The need for the project is demonstrated by the fact that there are 240 landfill sites in the province, ten times more than in the other Atlantic provinces combined.

The Greater Avalon Waste Management Committee acknowledges that municipal governments have legislative authority for solid-waste management and represent the focal point of impacts caused by the introduction of modern waste-management practices. The committee involves fifteen individuals from entities such as Municipalities Newfoundland and Labrador (MNL), formerly known as the Newfoundland and Labrador Federation of Municipalities, the provincial government, and various municipalities throughout the region. The plan is to have the system implemented by 2010.

The difficulty with respect to implementation is cost, which is expected to be around $200 million. The committee also needs to ascertain what kind of waste is going into the dumps. As it stands, waste facilities in the province are generally in terrible condition. They do not meet environmental standards and many of them are located adjacent to small communities. The 'teepee' incinerators are particularly environmentally destructive and have exceeded their recommended lifespan. To help on the financial side, the province is considering increasing tipping fees, which are much lower than in the rest of Atlantic Canada.

The issue of dumps is a concern for the expanding tourism industry because many are near small towns and hiking trails. The large number of rodents at the uncontrolled dumps is also a health concern. A 2001 public consultation found that people would support an increase in fees or taxes to help increase 'green' initiatives. It also discovered that people are very supportive of regional cooperation in this field as a means to cut costs and increase the effectiveness of waste management.

Finally, while not a regional governing entity or municipal service, the MNL is an important institution. This body, which acts on behalf of the municipalities, was created in 1951 as an organization to 'correlate the views of municipalities on matters of common interest, and to present a united front in relations with the provincial government.'[42] The MNL has made major strides in representing municipalities, to the point where it plays a significant role in policy decisions. Before the DMA implements new policies, it meets with the MNL to determine the effects of such policies. This helps ensure that municipalities throughout the province have a counterbalance in place. If a policy were likely to have serious consequences for the municipalities, the MNL could warn the department of these consequences in order to avoid them. The MNL also reports to the provincial government annually and makes recommendations, of which about half are implemented.[43]

Until 2000, the MNL received some funding from the provincial government. That is no longer the case. Nevertheless, the MNL has evolved into an institution with significant influence. Currently, it has a yearly operating budget of around $750,000, which gives it the ability to consider policy options independently of the provincial government. The MNL has branched into multiple areas to accomplish its policy goals. It recently started publishing a newsletter called *Municipal News – The Voice of Municipal Government*, which covers most of its new initiatives. As Christopher Dunn reports, the MNL has also been engaged with federal agencies, notably the Atlantic Canada Development Agency, on issues related to local economic development.[44]

Finance

The appendix provides a snapshot of per capita municipal expenditures in 2004 by major spending category for Newfoundland and Labrador compared to Canada as a whole. This data shows that total per capita expenditure in Newfoundland and Labrador in 2004 was $805.59, compared to the Canadian total of $1,734.67. In Newfoundland and Labrador, 69 per cent of municipal expenditures went to general government services, transportation and communication, and environment (which includes water, sewage, and garbage collection). Other than recreation and culture, and debt charges, the other smaller categories accounted for tiny shares of overall spending. In particular, municipal expenditures on health, social services, and education were very close to nothing. In Newfoundland and Labrador, the provincial government provides these services and municipalities' involvement is largely peripheral.

It is interesting to observe that spending is not uniformly lower across all the major categories, that is, each is not equal to 46 per cent of the national figure. In addition to health, social services, and education, per capita expenditures in 2004 are also low for housing and for protection of persons and property, only 6.9 per cent and 16.8 per cent, respectively, of the national values. Spending in all these areas is dominated by the provincial government. Other than St John's, municipalities have not had any substantive involvement in housing. With regard to the significantly lower expenditure on protection of persons and property, many fire departments are staffed by volunteers, and, unlike in other provinces, police services are provided by the provincial government.

The only categories where the Newfoundland and Labrador per capita expenditure figures are roughly comparable to the national ones are general government services, at 82 per cent, and debt charges, at

106 per cent. Thus, only debt charges faced by municipalities were actually higher than the national average for 2004, although the initial figures for 2006 indicate that they are now below the national average.

The greater debt charges deserve more comment because the higher province-wide figure does not capture the great disparity in the debt situations of municipalities across the province. A great many small rural municipalities are in severe difficulties.

Although municipalities must by law maintain balanced budgets, many receive assistance from the provincial government (mostly for capital expenditures) and have gradually accumulated significant debts. Unlike in the rest of Canada, the provincial government does not pay grants in lieu of taxes. The situation has been further worsened by the fact that there was an unofficial policy over the last decade in which rural municipalities knew they would be approved for assistance projects and felt they could deal with the financial implications at a later date. These small communities also need financial assistance to survive because most face extreme out-migration, a shutdown of economic activity and employment, and rapidly aging populations. As a result, many small municipalities can barely cope with their debt burdens.

Turning to the revenue side of the fiscal picture, we see that the scale of municipal revenues in the province is much lower than across the country. In 2004 per capita municipal revenue was just 51.0 per cent of the national figure.

In Newfoundland and Labrador, property taxes are the main source of tax revenue for municipalities. In 2004 real property and other property-related tax revenues per capita totalled $485.93 (i.e., $325.15 + $160.78). That is 98.0 per cent of tax revenue. The corresponding proportion for the national figures is 97.2 per cent, which illustrates a crucial common characteristic, namely, property-related taxes are close to being the sole source of municipalities' tax revenue. At the same time, both nationally and in Newfoundland and Labrador, municipalities are dependent on transfers from higher levels of government, primarily the provincial level. On this point, in Newfoundland and Labrador, transfers accounted for 23.80 per cent of total per capita municipal revenue ($209.37 out of $879.04) while the comparable national figure was16.8 per cent ($289.80 out of $1,723.19). Most other revenues come from the sale of goods and services, which includes water.

Thus, other than for scale, the per capita figures show a general similarity between municipal revenues in Newfoundland and Labrador

Table 1
Residential and property tax rates for Newfoundland and Labrador's three cities: 2003[45]

City	Residential Property: Mill Rate	Business Property: Mill Rate
Corner Brook	11.75	14.00
Mount Pearl	11.50	13.50
St John's	12.70	18.70

and across Canada. That similarity is captured by two factors. First, property taxation overwhelmingly dominates as the main tax-revenue source. Secondly, transfers from provincial governments are important sources of municipal revenues. On the other hand, there is one difference that is worth highlighting: in Newfoundland and Labrador, as already indicated, the provincial government does not provide municipalities with grants in lieu of property taxes. (It should be noted that, in the appendix, grants from government in lieu of taxes are not considered as transfers and are included in 'Other Taxes, Property Related.')

Given the importance of property taxes, it is worthwhile to elaborate on their use in Newfoundland and Labrador. There is a fair degree of variation in property-tax rates across the province's municipalities. Perhaps not surprisingly, given their status, tax rates in the three incorporated cities are among the highest. These are given in Table 1, above. It shows the standard tax rates on residences and business properties in those localities. For each, the tax rate is expressed as a mill rate, which is the annual amount of tax per $1,000 of assessed value of the properties.

The vast majority of other municipalities employ such property taxes as well, but the majority of them use somewhat lower mill rates. According to information provided by the DMA, of those municipalities employing property taxes, most use a property tax on residential property of between 7 and 11 mills; for business property taxes, municipalities tend to use either the same mill rate as used on residential property or a higher rate. Also, business-occupancy taxes are sometimes employed.

With assessed values being typically lower for comparable properties outside the cities, most other municipalities have limited scope for raising substantial revenues from property taxes. In fact, the majority of municipalities supplement their property tax with poll taxes, most of which range from $100 to $300 per year. A very few of the small rural municipalities use only the poll tax and no property tax.

At the national level, many municipalities have been arguing for more access to tax instruments beyond property taxation. This is happening in Newfoundland and Labrador as well. In 2002 a consultant's report for the Newfoundland and Labrador Federation of Municipalities came to the conclusion that municipalities in general do not have access to tax bases sufficient to provide for themselves.[46] Many have had to attempt to find new money to increase their own revenues but have had great difficulty in doing so. Part of the reason is that the municipalities feel that they have to keep their taxes low because they are competing with bigger, more successful cities and with unincorporated areas where tax rates are non-existent. There are also problems with collection of taxes. A 2002 study found that 86.1 per cent of municipalities had a problem with delinquent taxpayers.[47] With the differences in financial power between the municipalities being so great, the provincial government has been implementing programs to help reduce the inequality.

To help with the drastic differences in the economic positions of different municipalities, the provincial government established Municipal Operating Grants (MOGs) in 1991 to help communities with their operating expenses.[48] MOGs are based on need. They have four components:

- An equalization component whereby municipalities that collect property taxes at a lower rate than the provincial average are funded so they reach the provincial average. The values of the property taxes are based on the preceding year's assessments. Municipalities that do not impose property taxes are provided $40 per house.
- A local revenue incentive based on local revenues in the community. If a municipality is below the provincial average, its finances are raised.
- A household-living component that is calculated at $85 a house.
- A road component that is based on $500 per kilometre in the municipality.

Even though the fiscal scale of municipal government in New-foundland and Labrador is low relative to the Canadian average, its municipalities still face the difficulty that, as operating expenses increase, revenue sources often do not keep pace. Property and business owners can bear only so much of the tax burden; otherwise, economic activity will relocate to where costs are less expensive, people will not pay, or, in some cases, businesses may simply close down. Municipalities are dependent on the provincial government for important sources of income in order to provide services to residents and business owners. With the amount provided by the provincial government through the DMA for debt servicing on a downward trend, many, if not most, of the smaller municipalities need long-term government assistance for survival. Municipal Operating Grants are provided to municipalities that are not able to raise enough in local revenue to provide for their services and debts.

To help compensate for reductions in MOGs, the provincial government initiated a debt-relief program in 1997–8 for municipalities with large amounts of debt.[49] This program is aimed at municipalities that spend more than 30 per cent of their revenue on financing their debts and are in arrears. These municipalities are required to raise their tax rates to the provincial average and in return they receive financial assistance. The program has helped ninety-four municipalities address their financial predicaments.[50] In addition to a debt-relief program targeted at municipalities with high amounts of debt, the provincial government has also been helping with debt incurred from loans for infrastructure development.

The provincial government has been involved in assisting municipalities with infrastructure development. Under these initiatives, the province provides financing in areas such as water, sewer, and other engineering services. The water and sewer program was initiated in 1991 and has provided major assistance to communities in an expensive area of infrastructure.[51] The province has also provided assistance in developing capital infrastructure through the Municipal Capital Works Program and the Multi-Year Capital Works Program. These programs are established under variable cost sharing with the provincial government; in 2007 the provincial share was set to range from 70 per cent to 90 per cent. The provincial government also works with the federal government on programs such as the Canada-Newfoundland Initiative Program (CNIP). These programs are important and provide assistance to those municipalities that lack the fiscal capacity to participate.

A long-standing provincial mechanism for assisting municipalities is the Municipal Financing Corporation. It was established in 1964 by the provincial government with the goal of assisting communities to finance development through bonds and loans. The corporation has extended financial assistance to all communities except St John's. Providing long-term financing for infrastructure programs, the corporation borrows money for short-term and long-term loans by the issue of debentures, and then uses this money to finance projects for the municipalities. It also uses the purchase and sale of assets such as property or other securities to accomplish its goals.

Section 4 of the Municipal Financing Corporation Act enables the corporation to draw up contracts and agreements dealing with real and personal property rights of all kinds. The corporation also has powers to hire its own staff (subject to the approval of the lieutenant-governor-in-council), appoint its own board members, and make its own by-laws directing how the corporation will act and function. It has the power to borrow in a manner the corporation feels is appropriate, pay and receive interest, enter into agreements with municipalities and governments, invest property or money, be recognized in foreign countries and assign staff to foreign countries, issue promissory notes, lend money to municipalities and other municipal corporations, and create sinking funds.

The financial positions of the corporation and the DMA were thoroughly reviewed and audited in 1999. Debt owed to the corporation from municipalities had increased in the six years prior to 1994. Arrears on debt were such that many municipalities could not pay their bills yet were still taking on new projects. The DMA was not strictly monitoring municipalities, since many were handing in their budgets late and incomplete. Many municipalities' roads and other infrastructure were in a state of disrepair, making future debt more likely. There was also inadequate information on the finances of the Municipal Financing Corporation. The DMA could not provide an accurate account of the municipal debt burden, which was estimated to be more than $497 million in 1998.

The auditors found that the amount of debt owed to the corporation from the municipalities had decreased from $445 million in 1994 to $330 million in 1998. The primary reason for this decrease was that municipalities were taking fewer loans from the corporation and more from chartered banks. The auditors were unable to estimate how much debt the chartered banks had accumulated. They estimated that, even though municipal debt to the corporation had decreased, arrears owed had increased from $10.8 million in 1993 to $19.2 million in 1998.[52]

Although the DMA has powers to override municipal control, this in fact rarely happens. The DMA tries to provide the municipalities with as much decision-making autonomy as possible.[53] The department usually consults with officials from the MNL to discuss what the implications will be for municipalities before implementing a policy.[54] Finance is one area where the department has had to be vigilant. Municipalities throughout the 1990s were considered lax with their accounting. Many municipalities would submit budgets late and there was a low compliance rate. The department, however, was able to change this and raise the compliance rate from an estimated 50 per cent to 90 per cent.[55] This was accomplished with incentives for compliance and punishments for non-compliance. Municipalities that handed in their budgets late could be excluded from MOGs or other financial benefits, whereas those that returned their budgets on time were able to apply for additional grants and assistance.

Much of the reason for the Department of Municipal Affairs' effectiveness is that its budget has been adequate. Over the last ten years, the department's operating budget has actually increased, allowing it to function properly.[56] Currently, the department has a staff of around 126, of which an estimated 60 work on policy and planning issues.

Federal involvement in municipal financing over the last ten years has primarily been on the capital side of expenditures. Ottawa regularly provides infrastructure assistance to the municipalities through the DMA. Federal involvement varies by year and project. However, Ottawa regularly contributes to several major cost-shared programs such as Canada National Infrastructure Program and the Coastal Labrador Program. There has been an average contribution to the CNIP of approximately $14.4 million since 1999, with a high of $30 million in 1995, and an average contribution to the Coastal Labrador Program of $3.2 million since 1994.[57] The federal government also provides direct investment to municipalities throughout Newfoundland and Labrador. The amounts averaged $6.4 million from 1993 to 2003, with a high of $11.2 million in 1997 and a low of $2.6 million in 2002.[58]

Municipalities have increasingly become federal clients insofar as they interact through channels that do not much involve the provincial government. These interactions are usually, but not always, small in scale, have few implications for policy, and relieve the pressure on the provincial treasury.[59] For example, the city of St John's has initiated

Table 2
Change in population: 2006 compared to 1992[60]

Canada	15.0%
Newfoundland and Labrador	-12.1%
Prince Edward Island	5.9%
Nova Scotia	1.6%
New Brunswick	0.1%
Quebec	7.6%
Ontario	20.0%
Manitoba	5.8%
Saskatchewan	-1.8%
Alberta	28.2%
British Columbia	24.3%

several projects that have accessed federal services. The St John's Civic Centre received $4 million from the Atlantic Canada Opportunities Agency (ACOA) as well as a further grant to construct a sky walk connecting the Civic Centre to other facilities. Also, the St John's Harbour Clean-up has received support from the federal government for one-third of the (under-) estimated capital cost of $93 million. The city works with the St John's Board of Trade to develop and distribute economic-development information and applies to ACOA for funding to subsidize costs. The Grand Concourse Authority, a partnership with the city and the Johnson Family Foundation, has received ACOA and Human Resources and Development (HRD) Canada funding. ACOA even has an urban file as a result of the importance given to municipal issues by the federal government.[61]

The Demographic Challenge

Demographics have played a major role in the weakening of municipalities in Newfoundland and Labrador. The population has fallen significantly, declining every year since 1992 up to the end of 2006. Table 2 indicates the percentage change in population for Canada and each of the provinces between 1992 and 2006.

As shown, over the period from 1992 to 2006, the Canadian population increased by approximately 15 per cent. During this same period, Newfoundland and Labrador experienced a loss of 12.1 per cent of its population. Most other provinces had increasing populations over those years. The two exceptions were New Brunswick, whose popula-

Figure 1: Natural population change in Newfoundland and Labrador, 1949–2006[62]

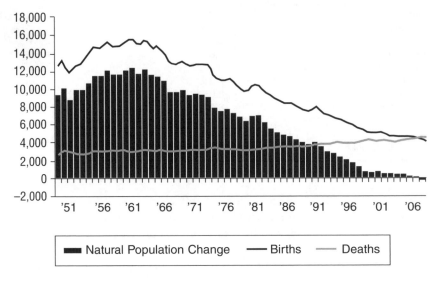

tion remained stable, and Saskatchewan, which had a modest decline of 1.8 per cent. Yet no province has experienced anything like the reduction that Newfoundland and Labrador did.

Moreover, that population loss occurred despite the fact that the number of births in Newfoundland and Labrador exceeded the number of deaths over this time period. As shown in Figure 1, there has been a natural population increase each year since 1949, with the possible exception of 2006, which appears to be the first year when the number of deaths and births matched one another. The figure also shows that, since the 1960s, the natural increase in population has been getting smaller: a common phenomenon in more and more places, largely reflecting a downward trend in birth rates.

Thus, the substantial population loss that has occurred since 1993 is due to large-scale out-migration. We use the term 'large-scale' in the sense that the out-migration exceeded the natural increase in population by a wide enough margin to cause a 12.1 per cent reduction since 1993. That out-migration is a reflection of substantial economic dislocation.

It is no coincidence that, when the Economics and Statistics Branch of the Department of Finance asked young people why they were leaving, 76 per cent said that the main reason was 'job related.'[63] During the mid-1990s, out-migration was highest following the federal government's closure of the groundfisheries, the mainstay of employment in many rural areas. Given that unemployment rates already had been in the double digits for some time, the economic future for youth looked quite dim. Large numbers of younger workers left for better opportunities outside the province, though many in rural areas relocated to the northeast Avalon, which encompasses St John's, Mount Pearl, and a number of nearby towns and communities. Even with the northeast Avalon gaining people from rural Newfoundland and Labrador, the population still decreased 1.2 per cent from 1991 to 2001.[64] The decrease in the northeast Avalon was small in comparison to rural areas of the island; for example, the west coast of the island lost an average of 17.5 per cent of its population from 1991 to 2001.[65]

What has made the demographic situation even worse is that out-migration has primarily been by youth. That has caused a significant change in the median age of the population relative to the national trend. In 1992 the province's median age was 31.2 years, almost two and a half years younger than the national median age of 33.6. By 2006, the situation was reversed, with the median age in the province being 41.3 while the Canadian median age was 38.8.[66]

The loss of population, particularly youth, has resulted in severe problems for municipalities, especially rural ones, which lose people not only to out-migration from the province but also to internal migration to larger centres with greater employment opportunities. Small municipalities with limited resources and budgets are left to care for an elderly population. One major consequence is that rural municipalities can no longer look to skilled youth to help develop their communities. Additionally, certain areas that need young people for survival, such as volunteer fire departments, no longer function properly. The financial strain created by this demographic trend is apparent as the municipalities' tax bases continue to decrease. The municipalities also lose many government funds such as MOGs because these are partially based on the size of the community. With a loss of funding, providing services, especially to older people who require additional assistance, becomes difficult. Finally, as municipalities lose their funding and their young, the infrastructure also collapses. This demographic trend is rapidly leading to the decline of many rural Newfoundland and Labrador communities.[67]

The long-term projections appear to be an increased urban population in the northeast Avalon along with an overall decrease in the provincial population and a continued decline in rural Newfoundland and Labrador.[68] This will create even more difficulties for the provincial government in balancing the interests between rural Newfoundland and Labrador and the northeast Avalon, which is expected to continue to grow.

In the coming years, growth in the province's oil and gas sector as well as other resource and economic developments are likely to counter out-migration and even allow Newfoundlanders and Labradorians who have left to return. That would most likely be to the benefit of larger centres. Many rural communities would continue experiencing the severe complications of population loss and aging. Thus, while out-migration may be coming to an end, the internal dynamics of population movements will continue to pose problems for rural areas.

Governance Structure

Newfoundland and Labrador's political culture affects the evolution of municipal governments almost as significantly as demographic change. The distinctiveness of the province's political culture derives from its long history, especially its struggles to gain control over its territory and natural resources, and an identity that has its own linguistic distinctiveness, myths, heroes, music, art, literature, poetry, and the like. The culture reflects feelings of toughness, sacrifice, and resilience in the face of tremendous geographic, economic, and physical barriers to settlement and communication. The challenges inherent in living on the island and in Labrador have bred an intense 'sense of place.' Yet this has not translated into support for municipal government. That is a critical historical feature of the political culture.

The fact that there has not been a strong tradition of local government in Newfoundland is significant. For example, the Newfoundland royal commission established in 1933 to determine whether the dominion could remain fiscally solvent noted the following with respect to municipal government:

The absence of any form of municipal government and the conduct of the entire administration of the country from St. John's, which is itself to a large extent out of touch with the outports, have had an unfortunate effect upon the people in retarding the development of a public spirit and

a sense of civic responsibility ... The formation of municipal Governments in the more important outports, under proper control and with the
proper safeguards, would do much to induce a sense of responsibility in
those called upon to contribute towards the expenses of such governments ... If such steps in the field of municipal government could
proceed hand in hand with the gradual suppression of the credit system,
we would look forward with confidence to the development of a new corporate spirit, which would not only ease the problems of administration
and carry with it all the advantages of team-work as opposed to individual effort, but would also result in the general advancement of the people
to a level far removed from the conditions of the past.[69]

The lack of municipal government has meant that, historically, few
people have had opportunities to participate in governance and
administration. The key intermediary between the interests of local
residents and the central government apparatus in St John's was the
member of the House of Assembly (MHA). To quote Noel: 'In the legislature he [the MHA] was the guardian and spokesman of local interests, the sole liaison between the governors and the governed. In addition, he was customarily expected to perform a multitude of local
duties that made him, for practical purposes, an unofficial mayor and
councillors rolled into one; and at the same time he was looked upon
by his constituents as the provider of free legal advice and other
welfare services of every kind.'[70] Indeed, one may argue that the challenges facing Newfoundland and Labrador were, prior to more recent
times, broad-based rather than local, for example, the state of the
fishery, education, health, transportation between communities, trade
agreements, and economic development.

While attitudes to municipal government have changed, and the
need for strengthening such institutions has grown as communities
have become larger and the demands for municipal services have
increased, there is still a lingering weakness in some municipal institutions. As indicated below, surveys of municipal councillors reveal
that significant numbers of these individuals lack the knowledge and
educational levels required for large-scale municipal management.

With respect to voter turnout, Newfoundland and Labrador has one of
the lowest levels for federal elections in Canada.[71] And voter turnout is
quite low for municipal elections too. The centre of politics in the
province continues to be the House of Assembly. One explanation for low
municipal election turnout is that not enough people put themselves

forward as candidates. There are anecdotal reports of people waiting until ten minutes before the nomination closes before handing in their forms to be a candidate. Province-wide election statistics were kept during the 1985 and 1993 municipal elections. In both elections, voter turnout was 53 per cent. In the 1985 election the highest turnout was in Hawke's Bay, at 96 per cent, and the lowest was in St Phillips, at 13 per cent. In 1993 the highest turnout remained in Hawke's Bay, at 86 per cent, while the lowest was in Happy Valley-Goose Bay, at 21 per cent.

Municipalities in the province vary greatly in size and financial power. As a result, the challenges that the provincial government faces in managing such a diverse group of municipalities usually ensure that the 'lowest common denominator is achieved.'[72] Many municipalities are excluded from effective participation because of a lack of human resources and money.

In 2002 the MNL conducted a poll on the situation for municipalities and in particular for municipal councillors. Key findings included:

- most municipalities had very limited support staff;
- most councillors worked very few hours;
- the pay for councillors was minimal;
- the education level of councillors was low;
- there was little interest in municipal affairs within the community;
- the turnover rate for councillors was high;
- most councillors had not received training in their positions; and
- many councillors were frustrated by the lack of resources.

The poll further found, for example, that 44 per cent of municipalities had two staff members or less.[73] In 2002 a majority of councillors were paid but received less than $1,000 a year, with a mere 5 per cent receiving more than $10,000 per year.[74] Part of the reason for the low pay was the low number of hours worked, with approximately 70 per cent of councillors working less than ten hours per week. To make the situation worse, of the councillors surveyed in 2002, only 30.6 per cent had received training related to either the Municipalities Act or the Urban and Rural Planning Act.[75] The formal education level achieved was also quite low: about 21 per cent had not finished high school and 29 per cent had not gone further than high school. The lack of resources for training coupled with a general lack of resources has created a high turnover rate (42.6 per cent of councillors having served between one and four years).[76]

There are organizations that are trying to improve training for councillors and staff, most notably the Newfoundland and Labrador Association of Municipal Administrators (NLAMA) and the Municipal Training and Development Corporation.[77] Both organizations are committed to improving training in the province. The NLAMA has also been particularly effective at creating salary guidelines for municipal administrators and helping to establish a training program through Memorial University that provides certificates in municipal administration.[78]

Another important element in municipal government is the position of 'town manager.' The town manager is to act as 'the chief executive and administrative officer of the council and head of its administrative branch.'[79] While in charge of administrative duties, including the execution of proper planning and the decisions of council, the town manager receives his or her directions from council. The town manager may advise council but council is not required to accept the town manager's advice. Council is in charge of policy and may replace the town manager if it sees fit.

Notwithstanding the problems enumerated above, there is considerable interest in seeking election to municipal office in Newfoundland and Labrador. The main reason given for running by those surveyed was 'being unhappy with the current council' (65 per cent), and 56.9 per cent of councillors polled said that they continue to serve because they want to support and create more opportunities for their communities.[80] Those surveyed felt that they were able to make a difference, with 46.5 per cent of councillors saying that their community will be either 'much better off' or 'better off' in one year.[81] Unfortunately, this statistic decreases with time; in five years, only 39.2 per cent feel their community will be 'much better off' or 'better off.'[82]

Many councillors are also constrained when running for office by considerations of campaign finance. In many small communities, running for office simply means knocking on a few doors so costs are not a concern. However, in the medium-sized and larger cities, where mounting a campaign is essential, running for office may be an expensive proposition. In order to gain funds, candidates must rely on donations. Provincial legislation (the Municipal Elections Act) governs donations and their reporting.[83] There is also the question of ethics, for candidates must be wary of donations from developers and others who may expect favours in return for contributions.

The Municipal Elections Act sets out the basics of the electoral process. If a candidate is elected, the length of term is four years. Elections are held on the last Tuesday of September. The minister may delay the election for up to one year if he or she so desires. By-elections are held only if a seat is vacated more than one year before the general election. The minister also has the discretion to hold an election if he or she thinks that one is necessary.

Under the Municipal Elections Act, the minister establishes whether or not the municipality will have a ward system.[84] Interestingly, this can also be altered by council, with a two-thirds vote allowing individual municipalities the option of determining which system would work best for them.[85] The majority of municipalities employ an at-large voting system. Two municipalities that use the ward system, or a variation of it, are St John's and the town of Conception Bay South.[86] St John's uses a mixed system, whereby five councillors are elected by ward and four are elected at large.[87]

Once councillors have been elected, they can decide how the election of the mayor will occur, unless the minister has directed that there be a separate election for that position or a council by a two-thirds majority opts to have a direct election for the post. This is a situation unique to Newfoundland and Labrador.[88] Having indirect elections, whereby councillors choose the mayor, has the advantage of producing a mayor whose leadership is accepted by his or her peers. Additionally, in indirect elections for mayor, council is not required to pick the individual who receives the most votes as mayor.[89] In Newfoundland and Labrador, the person chosen as mayor 40 per cent of the time was not the councillor with the most votes.[90] In contrast, it has been a long-standing practice for the mayor of St John's to be directly elected. Interestingly, since 1997, that practice has been extended to the position of deputy mayor of St John's; prior to that time, the deputy mayor was elected by the elected councillors from among themselves, which is the practice still followed by all other municipalities in the province.

Scope for Amalgamation and Cooperative Arrangements

Given that Newfoundland and Labrador has a small, highly dispersed population, it is not surprising that that the amalgamation debate has surfaced there just as it has in other provinces. In 1997 there was a major report on the need for regionalization and the sharing of services. The Task Force on Regionalization conducted interviews and seminars with municipal officials and the public throughout the province.[91] It came to the conclusion that regionalization was a necessary step that would benefit the province. The sharing of services between rural municipalities was suggested as a potential solution to their problems. However, the public was not very supportive. The task force found that the 'overwhelming response was one of "go away, leave us alone, we're already doing the best we can to share with our neighbours."'[92] This attitude may be changing, however, since very recently some municipalities approached the DMA requesting amalgamation.

Amalgamation has occurred on the northeast Avalon. Between 1985 and 1991, and not without opposition, the communities of Airport Heights, Kilbride, Shea Heights, Torbay/Logy Bay, and the Town of Goulds, all adjacent to St John's, were incorporated into the city.[93] However, the amalgamation of some of these areas, particularly Goulds and Airport Heights, was quite costly for the municipality. Bringing the newly amalgamated areas up to standard with the rest of the city was not easy, since all required upgrades for engineering, water, and sewer services.[94]

Fierce debate about amalgamation continues to focus on St John's desire to expand, with the inclusion of the adjacent city of Mount Pearl as well as the urban area of the town of Paradise. The municipal council of Mount Pearl has strongly opposed amalgamation with St John's. Mount Pearl has a successful economy and a population that is committed to maintaining its independence. The proponents of amalgamating Mount Pearl with St John's (one of whom was the leader of St John's from 1997 until 2008, Andy Wells) suggest that a united area would decrease harmful competition between the two municipalities and reduce costs by the sharing of services, and they further argue that the reason for Mount Pearl's success is that it uses all of the services of St John's without bearing its share of the costs. The opponents of amalgamation counter that the competition is good, since it makes both municipalities more competitive, that the two cities already share services, and that, in any event, the residents of Mount Pearl are determined to preserve their autonomy. The amalgamation debate in St John's is one that has vocal supporters on both sides who are committed to their positions. Indeed, not only is Mount Pearl wary of suggestions of amalgamation, but it and St John's are often in conflict. For example, in 1997 Mount Pearl convinced the provincial government to conduct a feasibility study into transferring Southlands, a major residential development in St John's, to it. While no such transfer took place, this is illustrative of the rivalry between the two cities.

Many other communities are also reluctant to consider amalgamation, though one such exercise has occurred recently: the municipalities of Catalina, Port Union, and Melrose have voluntarily amalgamated. Others might follow suit. Grand Falls-Windsor and Bishop's Falls have done an exploratory study on amalgamating but there has been no action. A couple of other municipalities have had talks but there have been no studies on the issue yet.

While the scope for horizontal cooperation among municipalities is limited because of rivalry between adjacent communities as well as by the physical distance between them, there is also limited potential for vertical cooperation. The potential for tri-level governance projects in Newfoundland and Labrador is low because of past failures. Thus, 'any further tri-level initiatives are most unlikely' in Newfoundland and Labrador.[95] With a small and dispersed population, drastic population decline, heavy municipal debt burdens, decaying infrastructure, and limited resources, the obstacles to successful tri-level projects are indeed many. Nonetheless, tri-level projects could provide much needed infrastructure development, economic assistance, and human-resource development for the province.

The only tri-level project currently in existence in Newfoundland and Labrador is the harbour clean-up project in St John's. The reason St John's has been able to undertake this project is that it is the one municipality with sufficient capacity. Although other municipalities would be interested in engaging in infrastructure development, human-resource development, and financial projects, they are not in the position to do so. In small isolated communities where most councillors work few hours for little pay, municipal governments are unlikely to have the ability to engage in tri-level projects.

The system of municipal governance in Newfoundland and Labrador has flaws and there are mixed views as to whether it is performing adequately. Officials in the Department of Municipal Affairs believe that that they meet regularly with enough people to give them a sense of what local communities need. The MNL argues that this is inadequate and that there should be meetings with all of the municipalities represented, as occurs in other provinces and parts of the world. The DMA also uses a very top-down approach, retaining the ultimate authority over decision making. Many municipalities feel that the provincial government does not trust them and give them enough leeway in decision making, although recent trends suggest that this is beginning to change. People in the province are not wholly satisfied. The MNL recently asked for another royal commission to investigate an alleged crisis in rural municipalities. The provincial government responded by saying that it was unnecessary.

Conclusion

Local government came late to Newfoundland and Labrador. Beyond St John's, it is largely a post-1950 phenomenon. In part, that was the result of population distribution and historical development. Even today, the scale of municipal government is relatively low by Canadian norms and the provincial government is more dominant in a number of service areas, notably policing, social services, education, and housing. As elsewhere in Canada, property taxes are the main source of municipal tax revenue and significant transfers come from the provincial government. However, in Newfoundland and Labrador, the provincial government does not pay any grants in lieu of property tax.

Rather than the pressures of population growth and congestion, the main challenge for most municipalities in the province is the loss of population, which in turn is caused by economy-related out-migration. Some of the larger municipalities with stable economic bases are able to cope. However, most rural municipalities have suffered severe losses of people and the weight of the debt burden has fallen on those who remain. Thus, even providing the most basic of services is a challenge. Amalgamations of adjacent rural municipalities may ease but not eliminate the difficulties. Without provincial government assistance for debt burdens and economic revitalization of rural areas, a significant number of rural municipalities may not be sustainable. Even as the prospects for the province as a whole improve, it is unlikely that the demographic challenges in those areas will ease because return migrants and younger people are drawn to other parts of the province where employment prospects are greater.

On the other hand, in the northeast Avalon, the population density is relatively high, the population has been more stable, and the economic base has been strong in recent years. This region contains the cities of St John's and Mount Pearl, which border one another, and several other municipalities in close proximity. Capitalizing on rising economic growth, realizing more benefits associated with offshore oil and gas developments, and dealing with regional services, such as waste management, water, and transportation, will probably induce greater municipal cooperation, either through actual amalgamations, regional government, or, more likely, intermunicipal agreements.

NOTES

The authors are grateful to Andrew Sancton and an anonymous reader for their advice. Also, thanks are due to Dan Mussel for able research assistance. Errors and omissions remain the sole responsibility of the authors.

1 The term outport refers to any small coastal community in Newfoundland and Labrador.
2 S.J.R. Noel, *Politics in Newfoundland* (Toronto: University of Toronto Press, 1971), 17–18.
3 Melvin Baker, *Local Government in Newfoundland and Labrador before 1982.* Originally published in *The Encyclopaedia of Newfoundland and Labrador*, vol. 2 (St John's: ISER, 1984).
4 Ibid., 18.
5 Melvin Baker, *Aspects of Nineteenth Century St. John's Municipal History* (St John's: Harry Cuff Publications, 1982), iv.
6 Paul O'Neill, *The Oldest City: The Story of St. John's, Newfoundland* (Portugal Cove-St Phillip's, Nlfd. and Labrador: Boulder Publications, 2003), 313–14.
7 *Report of the Newfoundland Royal Commission for the Preparation of the Case of the Government of Newfoundland for the Revision of the Financial Terms of the Union* (St John's, 1957), 16.
8 Baker, *Aspects of Nineteenth Century St. John's Municipal History*, 48.
9 Ibid., 25.
10 Baker, *Local Government in Newfoundland and Labrador before 1982.*
11 Ibid.
12 Christopher Dunn, 'Urban Asymmetry and Provincial Mediation of Federal-Municipal Relations in Newfoundland and Labrador,' in Robert Young and Christian Leuprecht, eds., *Municipal-Federal-Provincial Relations in Canada* (Series: Canada: The State of the Federation, 2004) (Montreal and Kingston, Ont.: McGill-Queen's University Press, 2006).
13 Jeff Webb, *Company Towns: Newfoundland and Labrador Heritage* (St John's: Memorial University of Newfoundland), www.heritage.nf.ca/society/company_towns.html.

14 Ibid.

15 Ibid.

16 *Task Force on Municipal Regionalization Final Report* (St John's: Department of Municipal and Provincial Affairs, 1997), 9.

17 *Report of the Royal Commission on Municipal Government in Newfoundland and Labrador* (St John's, 1975), 25–6.

18 Ibid., 32.

19 Ibid.

20 Ibid., 31.

21 Peter Boswell, *Municipal Administration 1702 by Distance Education: Introduction to Local Government* (St John's: Memorial University of Newfoundland, School of General and Continuing Studies, 1991), 3–8.

22 *Report of the Royal Commission on Municipal Government in Newfoundland and Labrador*, 1.

23 Ibid., 15.

24 *Report of the Royal Commission on Municipal Government in Newfoundland and Labrador*, 28.

25 Municipalities Act, 1999, s. 14, http://www.gov.nf.ca/hoa/statutes/m24.htm, 10 June 2004.

26 Ibid., s. 12.

27 Ibid., s. 77.

28 Ibid.

29 Katherine Graham and Susan D. Phillips, 'Emerging Solitudes: The New Era in Provincial-Municipal Relations,' in Martin Westmacott and Hugh P. Mellon, eds., *Public Administration and Policy: Governing in Challenging Times* (Scarborough, Ont.: Prentice Hall Allyn and Bacon Canada, 1999), 75.

30 Municipalities Act, s. 93.

31 Ibid.

32 Department of Municipal Affairs, City of St John's Act, 1990, s. 310, http://www.gov.nf.ca/hoa/statutes/c17.htm, 10 June 2004.

33 Until 1992, there were school tax authorities. These institutions were regional entities, established under provincial legislation, with the power to impose poll taxes and property taxes in their respective areas in order to raise funds for school boards also within the area. They were separate from municipal governments. They were abolished by the provincial government in 1992, with all funding thereafter provided by the province.

34 See www.nunatsiavut.com.

35 Municipalities Act, pt.II.

36 Boswell, *Municipal Administration*, 3–15.
37 Richard Tindal and Susan Nobes Tindal, *Local Government in Canada*, 5th ed. (Scarborough, Ont.: Nelson Thompson Learning, 2000), 136.
38 Ibid.
39 Boswell, *Municipal Administration*, 3–21.
40 Government of Newfoundland and Labrador, *Change and Challenge: A Strategic Economic Plan for Newfoundland and Labrador* (St John's: Queen's Printer, 1992).
41 Government of Newfoundland and Labrador, *Report of the Auditor General to the House of Assembly on Reviews of Departments and Crown Agencies* (St John's: Auditor General, Government of Newfoundland and Labrador, 2003), 379.
42 *Report of the* Royal Commission on Municipal Government in Newfoundland and Labrador, 34.
43 Boswell, *Municipal Administration*, 4–6.
44 Dunn, 'Urban Asymmetry.'
45 Department of Municipal Affairs, unpublished data supplied to the authors, 2006.
46 Institute for the Advancement of Public Policy, *The Need for a Change in Mind-Set: A Report on Alternative Sources of Municipal Revenues* (St John's,: 2002), 7.
47 Li Feng. *Newfoundland and Labrador Federation of Municipalities Municipal Survey 2003* (St John's: Newfoundland and Labrador Federation of Municipalities, 2003).
48 Department of Municipal and Provincial Affairs, *Annual Report 2003*, 13, http://www.gov.nf.ca/mpa/pdf/2002_2003Annreport.pdf, 8 July 2004.
49 Ibid., 14.
50 Ibid.
51 Ibid.
52 Municipal Financing Corporation Act, http://www.canlii.org/nl/laws/sta/m-21/20050819/whole.htm. The 1999 auditor's review can be found at: http://www.gov.nl.ca/ag/1999_Annual_Report/Municipal-Debt.pdf#xml=http://search.gov.nl.ca/texis/search/xml.txt?query =municipal+finance+corporation&pr=provincial&prox=page&rorder =500&rprox=750&rdfreq=250&rwfreq=500&rlead=500&sufs=2&order =r&cq=&id=4125ac2b22.
53 Boswell, *Municipal Administration*, 4–5.
54 *Report of the Royal Commission on Municipal Government in Newfoundland and Labrador*, 28.
55 Ibid.

56 Budgeting Division of the Treasury Board, *Budget Estimates, 1994–2004* (St John's: Department of Finance).

57 Ibid.

58 Statistics Canada, *Local General Government Revenue and Expenditure 1993–2003 – Dollars; Newfoundland; Federal Government* (Toronto: CHASS, 2004), http://dc2.chass.utoronto.ca/cansim2/English/ArrayA.html, 23 July 2004.

59 Dunn, 'Urban Asymmetry.'

60 Source: Statistics Canada, Table 051–0001.

61 Dunn, 'Urban Asymmetry.'

62 Government of Newfoundland and Labrador, Department of Finance, Economics and Statistics Branch, *Demographic Change: Issues and Implications* (St John's, October 2006), 3.

63 Government of Newfoundland and Labrador, Department of Finance, Economics and Statistics Branch; Labrador and Planning and Coordination Branch; and Atlantic Canada Opportunities Agency, Government of Canada, *Long Term Projections for Newfoundland and Labrador: A Consultative Approach* (St John's: Government of Newfoundland and Labrador, 2001), appendix 3, 7.

64 *Demographic Change: Newfoundland and Labrador Issues and Implications,* 9.

65 Ibid.

66 Statistics Canada, 051–0001.

67 Royal Commission on Renewing and Strengthening Our Place in Canada, *Our Place in Canada: Main Report* (St John's, 2003), 39.

68 These are the overall projections based on a medium-case scenario as presented by the consultants on the project *Long Term Population Projections for Newfoundland and Labrador: A Consultative Approach.*

69 Newfoundland Royal Commission, 1933, *Chapter X: Subsidiary Recommendations. Municipal Government,* http://www.heritage.nf.ca/law/amulree/chap10_6.html. The credit system referred to in the quotation was widely used in outport Newfoundland until Confederation. The system was highly exploitative in that merchants would extend credit to fishermen to allow them purchase supplies, food, and clothing for their families in return for their expected catch. The system created a cashless economy in rural Newfoundland.

70 Noel, *Politics in Newfoundland,* 20.

71 Rand Dyck, *Provincial Politics in Canada,* 3rd ed. (Scarborough, Ont.: Prentice-Hall Canada, 1996), 46–7.

72 Ibid.

73 Li Feng, *Preliminary Analysis: Newfoundland and Labrador Federation of Municipalities Municipal Survey 2003*, 5.
74 Li Feng. *Preliminary Analysis: Newfoundland and Labrador Federation of Municipalities General Survey of Municipal Councillors* (St John's, 2003).
75 Ibid., 12.
76 Ibid., 4.
77 Peter Boswell, *Municipal Councillors Handbook*, 5th ed. (St John's: Municipal Training and Development Corporation c/o Department of Municipal and Provincial Affairs, 2001), 17.
78 Boswell, *Municipal Administration*, 4–7.
79 Ibid., s. 54.
80 Li Feng. *Preliminary Analysis: Newfoundland and Labrador Federation of Municipalities General Survey of Municipal Councillors*, 1, 7.
81 Ibid., 3.
82 Ibid.
83 Municipal Elections Act,s. 67(1–2), http://www.gov.nf.ca/hoa/statutes/m20-2.htm, 10 June 2004.
84 Ibid., s. 14(1).
85 Ibid., s.14(2–3).
86 Boswell, *Municipal Administration*, 5–6.
87 City of St John's, 'Mayor and Council Members' (St John's, 2004), http://www.stjohns.ca/cityhall/council.jsp.
88 Boswell, *Municipal Administration*, 5–3.
89 Ibid.
90 Ibid.
91 *Task Force on Municipal Regionalization Final Report*, 1–5.
92 Ibid., 5–6.
93 John Heseltine and John Jozsa, *St. John's Amalgamation Review* (St John's: ATi Consulting Corporation, 2001), 21.
94 Ibid.
95 Boswell, *Municipal Administration*, 4–5.

Conclusion

ROBERT YOUNG

The chapters collected here present a remarkable survey of municipal government in Canada's provinces. They have truly described the foundations of our governance. We do not use 'foundations' to imply that other governments and governance systems are built on or depend in some way on municipal governments, because of course the reverse is true: the federal and provincial governments are constitutionally primordial, and municipal governments and other local authorities emanate from provincial jurisdiction. Nor do we mean that municipal governments are foundational in that they are 'closer to the people,' as the commonly heard phrasing has it. This may be true in rural and small-town Canada, but not in cities of any substance and certainly not in the big metropoles. Instead, what is foundational here are the provincial-municipal systems of governance. In every province, these partnerships, however asymmetrical, are very important. Within parameters set by the provincial governments, municipalities deliver services that are vital to citizens: these can include policing, fire protection, local roads, recreation facilities, waste and sewage disposal, water supply, libraries and cultural facilities, and public transit. But other important services have been progressively provincialized. In some respects, the big policy story of the past several decades has been the shift in responsibility for education, health, and social services to the provincial level from local authorities more or less closely associated with municipal governments. On the other hand, as the scope of provincial governments' activities has broadened, municipal governments increasingly have become agents of provincial policy. Municipal governments must respond not only to the main provincial ministry that supervises their administration and finances but also to other provincial departments that regulate economic and social activity. Many provincial policies about the environment, water quality, policing, land use, agriculture, building standards, emergency planning, and other areas are implemented through municipal action. So, bearing in mind the largely autonomous provincial role in health, education, and social services, but especially in comparison to the increasingly distant federal government, it is correct to think of local government activity, in partnership with the provinces, as foundational to governance in Canada.

Diversity

Surveying the ten systems treated here, we can draw out certain central themes. But it is remarkable how the authors of these chapters, despite working from a common template, have focused on particular aspects of their own provincial-municipal system. We find Ontario still settling down from the tremendous shocks to municipal form and function of a decade ago. Quebec underwent similar changes, especially the spectacular mergers and subsequent de-mergers in its metropolitan areas, and now has a peculiarly complex system, such that a resident of downtown Montreal enjoys (!) no fewer than six levels of Canadian government. Reform in Nova Scotia has been halting, and we find a reason in the intricate problems of funding roads and other services. In New Brunswick the focus is on rising intermunicipal inequality and the inadequacies of funding formulae – appropriate for a province that once rationalized functions more systematically and thoroughly than any other, in the name of Equal Opportunity. Manitoba, a macrocephalous province, is focused on the primate city, Winnipeg, and its struggles with suburbs. British Columbia's stance towards its municipal governments is permissive and supportive, but the pattern of 'gentle imposition' is punctuated by sharp assertions of the overall provincial interest. The account provided of Prince Edward Island is infused with a characteristically deep sense of history and place (incorporated or not). Saskatchewan is revealed as a province manifesting an almost Cartesian preoccupation with design and mechanism, and possessing a multiplicity of municipalities of different categories along with agencies and authorities and liaison devices, all interwoven through deeply consultative and consensual processes. We have Alberta, a system described in great detail, where the provincially imposed financial pressures are being alleviated and municipalities have been given freer rein to govern: it is all working pretty well, except around the capital region. In Newfoundland and Labrador, finally, a supportive provincial government deals with municipalities on the far periphery of the province that are in serious decline while those on the near periphery of the capital city can be non-cooperative to the point that amalgamation is suggested – but who would want to see expunged from the map the charmingly named Mount Pearl, let alone Paradise?

The chapters collected here also testify to the enormous diversity and intricacy of local government. Newfoundland mayors, for example, are not directly elected but are chosen by the councillors (with the perennial exception of St John's). Language issues envelop municipal government in the Moncton area. Quebec's regional county municipalities seem to bridge the urban-rural divide rather effectively. Alberta's Métis settlements and its specialized municipalities are ingenious solutions to very particular situations, as is the fantastic system of governing Lloydminster. The Ontario Municipal Board is another wondrous device, the deep functions of which are mysterious – or perhaps contestable. The residue of the original lot divisions still linger in PEI. For some reason, half of the rural municipalities in Saskatchewan hold elections one year and the other half the next year.

Surely even the most experienced observers of the local government scene in Canada have encountered new information here. And all readers can appreciate that the authors convey an unparalleled feel for the places and provinces they describe. Despite the complexity and the diversity, however, several themes pervade the chapters, and it is to these that we turn.

Provincial Control

It is commonly understood that provincial governments control their local 'creatures' rather closely. There is much evidence of this in the chapters collected here. For instance, under the Newfoundland Municipal Act, the minister has the power to decide on the number of councillors a municipality will have and to determine its system of wards. The Nova Scotia chapter presents the list of areas in which municipal governments are allowed to spend money, and it is a detailed and precise list (including 'lighting' and 'school crossing guards'). In several provinces, there is also close supervision of finances, especially borrowing, as in Saskatchewan, where municipal defaults occurred in the 1930s. Land-use policy is sometimes a matter of great provincial interest, as is currently the case in Ontario. Restructuring of municipal governments is determined by provincial administrations, as shown in several chapters, particularly those covering Nova Scotia, Quebec, Manitoba, and Ontario. The reallocation of responsibilities, which is sometimes quite radical, is a matter of provincial initiative, as in Ontario's notorious Local Services Realignment exercise. So the structure, functioning, and financial affairs of local governments are subject to provincial dictates, and the lead ministry and other departments prescribe certain behaviours and proscribe others.

But close, routine supervision is slackening. Beginning in Alberta in 1994, a trend has developed towards increasing the autonomy of municipal governments. The Alberta Municipal Government Act laid out general spheres of jurisdiction within which municipalities could operate, instead of listing a set of narrow functions, and it also attributed broader corporate powers to municipalities. These changes have been echoed in British Columbia, Quebec, Manitoba, Ontario, Saskatchewan, and Nova Scotia.[1] The result, as David Cameron puts it, 'is that municipalities have been given a broader brush with which to paint.'

As the various chapters show, however, provincial governments will intervene when vital interests are at stake or where local solutions cannot be devised. One cannot expect local governments to change policy willingly when their interests cannot be reconciled with those of the province. So, for example, the government of British Columbia took the lead in driving through the infrastructure required for the 2010 Olympic Games. Provinces do rule. Sometimes coordination problems cannot be overcome when too many municipalities are involved or when relations between them are too fractious. Hence the Ontario government is leading the planning for the Greater Golden Horseshoe, including the Greenbelt it imposed, and it was the provincial government of Nova Scotia which directed that a referendum question about Sunday shopping be included on all municipal election ballots. Just as only Manitoba and the province of Newfoundland and Labrador can deal with the issues about their capital cities' suburbs, so Alberta finally imposed a Capital Region Board on Edmonton and its quarrelsome neighbours in early 2008.

Yet the municipal-provincial relationship is not just about control and autonomy. It is more subtle. The provinces are indeed 'responsible' for their municipalities, but this is a two-edged term. Provincial governments do not just control municipalities. They need to take the municipal system into account, since they are responsible for it. They cannot neglect the well-being of municipalities, especially the larger ones that anchor their economies. If there are systemic problems or acute crises, provincial governments do take action. In some provinces, the lead provincial departments are remarkably benevolent and even solicitous, as in British Columbia and Newfoundland and Labrador, and municipalities in all provinces have this department as an established interlocutor (which is not the case when they wish to approach the federal government). As David Siegel points out, the lead minister generally acts as an advocate for municipal interests within the cabinet (and caucus). Moreover, at the provincial level, understanding and sympathy are often at hand because of the large proportion of politicians who have experience at the municipal level.

As all the chapters show, an important cog in the system consists of the associations of municipalities. Andrew Sancton notes in the Introduction that municipalities are members of 'interest groups,' which is true, and, like some interest groups in other policy areas, the municipal associations are often partners in running the system. They aggregate member municipalities' interests and convey them to government, and they can deploy considerable expertise, research capacity, and analytic skill in the search for solutions to problems. They are most influential when not fragmented, which they are in Quebec, Saskatchewan, New Brunswick, and Alberta (where the urban-rural divide is very difficult to manage). Manitoba has recently experienced a union of its rural and urban associations, an interesting development. The associations are very strong in British Columbia and Ontario, despite the noteworthy withdrawal of Toronto from the Association of Municipalities of Ontario. In these two provinces, the ritualistic representations to provincial authorities overlie continuing and generally productive consultations and negotiations about evolving issues of structure, function, and policy.

A major shift in most provincial-municipal systems is the allocation of greater power to the major cities. In most places, this breaks a long-standing norm of equal treatment for all municipalities. St John's has always had a special act, as have Charlottetown and Summerside in PEI. But the Vancouver Charter conveyed special power. More recently, so did amendments to the Saskatchewan Cities Act. Winnipeg has received special legislative consideration. Montreal has a charter and has benefitted from the Contrat de Ville, which spelled out various activities that provincial government departments would do in the city and also costed them. And Toronto is now not only armed with special powers and access to revenue sources but is also a formal partner of the Ontario government, as proclaimed in the portentous Stronger City of Toronto for a Stronger Ontario Act of 2006.

So there is more autonomy for local governments in most provincial-municipal systems, and the larger centres generally enjoy more jurisdictional latitude. It will take some years before judgments can be formed about how and where municipalities are using their new autonomy. Two experienced observers have argued that, at least in Ontario, many municipal governments, despite constant complaining, have existed for a long time in a state of 'comfortable subordination' to provincial desires; if they are to exercise their new powers with 'assertive maturity,' a deep attitudinal change will be required.[2]

Finances

The financial capacity of municipalities is an issue running throughout the chapters collected here. Across the country, fiscal pressures have driven municipal pleas for more money, especially for investment in infrastructure. These have been amplified by other interests, particularly business, and also conveyed to the federal government through a powerful campaign mounted by the Federation of Canadian Municipalities, the municipal voice in Ottawa.[3] The analysis of finances in most of our chapters shows a major reason for this angst – a significant drop in provincial-municipal transfers. Overall, general-purpose transfers from provincial governments to municipalities fell from a peak of $1.92 billion in 1992 to $1.17 billion in 2000, a drop of 39 per cent (in current dollars), while specific-purpose transfers fell over the same period from $7.57 billion to $5.87 billion.[4] The general trend was more or less sharp in different provinces. As Daniel Bourgeois notes in his analysis of fiscal matters in New Brunswick, 'the declining importance of the unconditional transfer since the late 1980s is the single most important development in New Brunswick municipal finance over the past 40 years.' The Alberta chapter discusses in some detail how municipalities responded by raising their own-source revenues. Across Canada, income from sales of goods and services – essentially user fees – almost doubled over the 1992–2004 period, from $6.90 billion to $12.43 billion; at the same time, property-tax revenue rose from $12.77 billion to $23.91 billion. Obviously, it is politically painful to enact such increases. In any case, own-source revenue accounted for

74.0 per cent of total municipal revenues in 1992 and for 83.2 per cent in 2004, a very substantial shift. This self-reliance conveyed more autonomy, in principle, but it had costs. One was that capital spending was essentially flat over the whole decade between 1990 and 2000, amounting to about $8 billion per year in current dollars: this was a steady decline in inflation-adjusted terms, and a large drop when population increase is considered as well.

The system was under real strain, manifested in both political tensions and crumbling infrastructure. But there has been a gradual re-equilibration, and this is a most noteworthy development in the municipal world. Municipalities in most provinces have been less fortunate than those in Alberta, where large provincial grants for investments in infrastructure have been forthcoming in recent years. But, in the country as a whole, all provincial transfers to municipalities rose by an average of 7.4 per cent per year over the 2003–7 period. The federal government has also played a role in restoring equilibrium. Under the 'New Deal for Cities and Communities' of the Paul Martin government (2004–6), municipalities became fully exempt from paying the Goods and Service Tax, and agreements to share the federal gasoline tax with municipal governments were signed with every province and territory. Both Martin and his successor, Stephen Harper, also substantially increased federal grants for infrastructure, through a series of programs, and the Harper Conservatives also established a separate envelope for spending on public transit. Federal government specific-purpose transfers to municipalities rose from about 0.6 per cent of all municipal revenues in the early 1990s to 1.67 per cent in 2005. This is a small proportion, but these transfers represented 7.2 per cent of all capital expenditures by municipalities.

Still on the financial front, there are some fundamental issues within the various provincial-municipal systems. One is the disparities between the tax bases of different municipalities, and the basic fact that similar rates of taxation can produce greater revenues (and better services) in relatively rich areas. Provincial governments operate equalization and grant schemes which more or less offset the effects of disparities, but there is much variation in the degree of equality attained. Of course, this is one dimension of the perennial local government problem: there are trade-offs to be made between equality and autonomy. Matters of cross-subsidization also underlie debates about amalgamation, as is shown in the Nova Scotia chapter.

Another financial issue is the use of the property tax. This tax base is generally shared with primary and secondary education, though the authority to make levies, conduct assessments, and collect the tax varies widely across the provinces. But, in most provinces, municipal purposes and education needs compete for access to the base: this is clearly shown in Figure 3 in the Ontario chapter, which shows a major 1998 shift in favour of the municipalities. In Quebec, there was a similar reduction in the proportion of education expenditures that were paid off the property tax (a decrease that was made up by higher provincial grants to school boards), and this left room for the municipalities to occupy more fully the tax base (which the provincial government neutralized by cutting its transfers to municipal governments). Our chapters show that there is considerable tension about this matter in Nova Scotia, Manitoba, PEI, and Alberta – despite a movement that has extended the municipal proportion of property tax revenues from 39 per cent to 53 per cent – and especially in Saskatchewan, where discontent simmers about the taxation of agricultural land. Since there are large social benefits from education expenditures, there certainly is an argument that more costs should be funded from general provincial revenues, leaving the municipalities a greater share of the property tax. But then, of course, intermunicipal inequalities might escalate.

Demography

Demographic challenges pervade the treatments of Canada's provincial-municipal systems. Rapid growth in the bigger centres is one aspect of this. Our chapters make it clear that in-migration from rural areas continues to create growth in places like St John's, Halifax, Winnipeg, and Saskatoon. This raises the problem of accommodating new inhabitants in a sustainable manner, and also issues of equity and cooperation when settlement occurs in municipalities on the suburban fringe. Provincial and municipal governments have used a variety of mechanisms to deal with these matters. A particular demographic phenomenon is the very rapid growth in the largest metropolitan regions – Vancouver, Toronto, and Montreal. Almost all of the population increase there is caused by immigration into Canada, as large proportions of new immigrants cluster in the major centres. Issues of immigrant settlement have drawn much attention, but growth rates in the big cities are actually far lower now than they were in the immediate post-Second World War period and in the 1901–31 era, when urban population growth rates were more than double the current ones. However, the new pressures involve coping not just with developmental and infrastructural needs but also with social exclusion, because recent flows of immigrants to Canada overwhelmingly come from non-European origins. Movements of aboriginal people into the cities, especially in the western provinces, raise similar challenges (and opportunities), ones that uncertainties about jurisdiction and responsibility render even more complex.

From the viewpoint of municipal government, a problem that is unprecedented in its current scale is population decline in rural and small-town Canada. This is an issue identified in almost every chapter here. In Newfoundland and Labrador there are serious questions about municipal sustainability: beyond the Avalon peninsula, as the administrative fabric and social infrastructure decline, many municipalities have become indebted, and though the provincial government is supportive, the future seems grim for municipal government. In Nova Scotia, population attrition was an important reason for creating the Cape Breton Regional Municipality, while population decreases and rural poverty in northern New Brunswick have led to the inequalities of the 1950s and 1960s reasserting themselves. In Ontario, comparing the situation of the rural areas and the north of the province with that of the dynamic cities, David Siegel writes about 'two solitudes.' There is a real problem in the periphery – 'maintaining the existing quality of public services as the number of residents and taxpayers declines.' The Quebec chapter notes a substantial population decline in the northerly regions. The chapters about the prairie provinces present similar findings. In Manitoba, Tom Carter emphasizes as well the factor of age distribution: an aging rural population is inclined to move to larger centres where there are better health services and more housing alternatives. This demographic problem is a tremendous challenge with no easy solutions. Amalgamation along the lines of Cape Breton is not always advisable or efficient. British Columbia's regional-district model is a possibility, as is direct provincial administration, with advisory committees, such as we find in some sparsely settled areas of the country. Very large functionally specialized authorities might be appropriate in some instances. In any case, all the systems must cope in some way with the tough issues arising from the combination of meagre populations with plentiful geography.

Democracy

The quality of local democracy is a perennial concern that has several facets. One is the simple issue of probity. Money is always an issue in politics, and a lot of money is at stake in municipal decisions, notably about procurement and land use. We find a great deal of variation across the country in rules about candidates' spending limits and campaign contributions and reporting. But there is very little research into the effects of these rules, nor is there much on the source of campaign donations.[5] Accountability is a related issue. One theme of our British Columbia chapter is that the accountability of elected representatives to the public is weak. In the Saskatchewan chapter is an account of changes that could serve as a model for other places – opportunities for petitions and plebiscites, access to documents, open meetings, and an ombudsperson. But our Saskatchewan authors also strongly warn about local democracy confounding broader interests and leading to stasis: 'The value of local democratic control has trumped managerial values of effectiveness and efficiency in planning and development since the inception of the municipal system.' When it comes to local democratic control, the perspectives of our experts differ a great deal!

There is, however, broad agreement that municipal politicians should be representative of their publics. It is important to have diverse interests and perspectives represented at the decision-making table. This is especially needed, perhaps, at the municipal level, where, with few exceptions, there are no political party organizations capable of taking into account the views of under-represented groups. The chapters here show that women are not proportionally represented on municipal councils or among mayors. Visible minorities are not systematically addressed in the chapters, but they are under-represented as well. And there is a very weak aboriginal presence among elected decision makers, even in the west.

Voting turnout at elections is always a matter of interest. The verdict arising from the chapters is that electoral participation is low, so much so in Alberta that the authors write of a 'democratic deficit.' Depending on the nature and goals of a municipality, citizen participation can be important in building a consensus and legitimizing decisions. But turnout rates in most municipalities are well below those characteristic of provincial and federal elections. Turnout appears to be higher in smaller centres; on the other hand, incumbents in such places are generally successful, and, as is stressed in the Quebec chapter, a great many elections are uncontested. Turnout also seems to be higher where parties exist at the municipal level, though proper tests cannot be made. It is a curious feature of the Canadian system that municipal politics is generally non-partisan, and that where parties exist they do not overlap closely with federal or provincial parties. As described in the New Brunswick chapter, there are sometimes 'shadow' party slates at the municipal level, and individual candidates often are known by many voters to have party connections. But only in the larger centres of British Columbia and Quebec are there functioning municipal parties. Apart from the apparent effect on turnout, none of our contributors was prepared to evaluate the larger impact of these organizations on municipal policy making.

The state of local democracy bears on two other issues. One concerns the very essence of municipal governments, which can be understood as simple providers of services to people living in geographical proximity or instead as political bodies, 'the means by which a local community can express and address its collective objectives.'[6] This is a tension that runs through the whole study and practice of local government, and it is reflected in many of our chapters. As David Cameron puts it, 'are municipalities essentially administrative units carrying out largely mundane, if important, service functions, or are they also political institutions seeking to chart the future shape and style of human communities?' Whichever view is taken, the quality of local democracy is vital. In the first view, it is essential that citizens receive the mix of goods and services that they want, and have them supplied in an efficient manner. This requires democratic mechanisms that accurately send signals about service preferences and that provide for close political oversight of municipal administrations. In the second view, it is obvious that vigorous debate and broad participation are required in order to ensure that important collective decisions are representative and legitimate.

The second related issue was raised in the Introduction. It concerns whether municipal governments in Canada possess 'the capacity to act autonomously, purposefully, and collaboratively in the intergovernmental arena.' Here, democratic vitality is not always necessary. If municipal governance is mainly about service provision, then the governments require strong, expert administrations. Effective intergovernmental performance is largely a bureaucratic matter of helping to design and implement programs that are created in partnership with the relevant departments and agencies, primarily provincial ones. It is hard to see how strong local democracy advances this cooperation very much. On the other hand, if municipal governments are about collective choices that represent the will of the community about its future direction, then a solid democratic foundation for these decisions is essential. A municipality with a vision of its place in the province and the country, and an appreciation of its policy needs, must have strong public support to enter intergovernmental policy arenas and negotiate successfully to achieve its objectives. These municipal governments need the legitimacy that comes through democratic processes.

Further Matters

The contributions collected here describe provincial-municipal systems that are complex and idiosyncratic, but they reveal general issues that are intriguing and of much practical importance to Canadians. They also illuminate problems worthy of investigation, and demonstrate that local government is a rich field of study with many questions that deserve further research.

The problem of population decline on the periphery certainly needs a lot of work, preferably on a comparative basis across the provincial systems. Immigrant settlement in the big cities demands much more study, especially of how municipalities could play a stronger role in attracting immigrants and helping them settle, and also of the sense of identification of recent immigrants with their municipality, province, and Canada. The many agencies, boards, and commissions that are associated with individual municipalities or that operate on a regional basis are largely unmapped, and they raise intriguing questions about accountability and democratic control. There is a lot of interesting work to be done on how policy is shaped in particular issue-areas, especially focusing on the intergovernmental mechanisms that increasingly determine policy and on the sometimes uneasy relationship of these structures with the demands and policy proposals of local organizations.

All in all, municipal government in Canada has come through a period of significant change. In many provinces there are new opportunities. We trust that the work of the scholars presented here will help our understanding of how challenges can be met and opportunities seized, and that it has pointed the way to further fruitful research into the foundations of governance in Canada.

NOTES

1 See also Joseph Garcea and Edward C. LeSage, Jr, *Municipal Reform in Canada: Reconfiguration, Re-empowerment, and Rebalancing* (Don Mills, Ont.: Oxford University Press, 2005).

2 David Siegel and C. Richard Tindal, 'Changing the Municipal Culture: From Comfortable Subordination to Assertive Maturity,' parts I and II, *Municipal World*, March and April 2006, 37–40 and 13–17.

3 TD Bank Financial Group, *A Choice between Investing in Canada's Cities or Disinvesting in Canada's Future*, TD Economics Special Report, April 2002; Conference Board of Canada, *Mission Possible: Successful Canadian Cities*, the Canada Project, Final Report, vol. III, February 2007; Federation of Canadian Municipalities, *Building Prosperity from the Ground up: Restoring Municipal Fiscal Balance*, June 2006.

4 These data and subsequent ones are from Statistics Canada, CANSIM, Table 3850024, http://dc1.chass.utoronto.ca/cgi-bin/cansimdim/c2_getArray.pl.

5 See Robert MacDermid, 'Campaign Finance and Campaign Success in Municipal Elections in the Toronto Region,' presented to the Canadian Political Science Association, Saskatoon, June 2007.

6 C. Richard Tindal and Susan Nobes Tindal, *Local Government in Canada*, 7th ed. (Toronto: Nelson, 2009), 7.

Appendix:
Municipal Financial Data for Canada and by Province

CANADA
LOCAL GENERAL GOVERNMENT REVENUE AND EXPENDITURES

1995, 2004, and 2006 (Dollars x 1,000)

REVENUE	2004 Revenue	% Change Since 1995	2006 Revenue	2004 Per Capita	% Change Since 1995	2006 Per Capita
Own source revenue						
Real property taxes	23911097	72.13	26692369	745.14	57.68	815.53
Other Taxes, Property Related	5242578	-0.46	5542508	163.38	-8.82	169.34
Other Tax Revenue	815615	94.21	880216	25.42	77.92	26.89
Total Tax Revenue	29969290	53.07	33115093	933.94	40.23	1011.76
Sales of Goods and Services	12432849	57.63	14218944	387.45	44.40	434.43
Other Income from Own Sources	3594460	15.34	4349208	112.01	5.66	132.88
Transfers, general and specific						
From Province: Specific Purpose	6909121	-19.97	8993031	215.31	-26.68	274.76
From Province: General	1657222	22.00	1842702	51.64	11.76	56.30
From Province: Total	8566343	-14.26	10835733	266.95	-21.46	331.06
From Federal: Specific	733045	30.90	1363025	22.84	19.91	41.64
Total Transfers	9299388	-11.87	12198758	289.80	-19.26	372.71
Total Own Source Revenue	45996599	50.40	51683245	1433.40	37.78	1579.07
Total Revenue	55295987	34.43	63882003	1723.19	23.15	1951.77
Total Revenue as % of GDP	4.28		4.44			

EXPENDITURES	2004 Operating	% Change Since 1995	2006 Operating	2004 Capital	% Change Since 1995	2006 Capital	2004 Total	% Change Since 1995	2006 Total	2004 Per Capita	% Change Since 1995	2006 Per Capita
General government services	4846841	40.68	5537274	1007285	79.48	877241	5854126	46.11	6414515	182.43	33.85	195.98
Protection of persons and property	8681601	53.09	9654851	551044	45.54	703915	9232645	52.62	10358766	287.72	39.81	316.49
Transportation and communication	6686801	23.08	7283817	4112483	37.90	5401669	10799284	28.33	12685486	336.54	17.56	387.58
Health	1370315	117.94	1550825	101347	-44.69	119460	1471662	81.24	1670285	45.86	66.03	51.03
Social services	5458351	6.89	6030401	319081	300.83	149260	5777432	11.40	6179661	180.04	2.05	188.81
Education	194163	35.00	218479	15802	247.22	10506	209965	41.51	228985	6.54	29.64	7.00
Resource conservation and industrial development	811721	50.20	879254	343668	28.36	507615	1155389	42.97	1386869	36.01	30.97	42.37
Environment	5161198	46.35	6081027	3851050	33.14	5054709	9012248	40.39	11135736	280.85	28.61	340.23
Recreation and culture	5131447	40.58	5819762	1643257	40.31	2094910	6774704	40.51	7914672	211.12	28.72	241.82
Housing	1737177	272.94	1996539	272195	148.00	405890	2009372	249.12	2402429	62.62	219.82	73.40
Regional planning and development	849999	62.19	1028675	163087	-3.81	166650	1012986	46.06	1195225	31.57	33.80	36.52
Debt charges	2234220	-30.14	2270912	9557	-55.15	9786	2243777	-30.30	2280698	69.92	-36.15	69.68
Other expenditures	35041	-74.92	22073	75672	-40.56	51146	110713	-58.54	73219	3.45	-62.02	2.24
Total Expenditures	43198775	33.03	48373789	12465528	39.30	15552757	55664303	34.38	63926546	1734.67	23.11	1953.14

Sources: Revenue and Expenditure: Statistics Canada. CANSIM, table 385–0024, Local general government revenue and expenditures, current and capital accounts, year ending 31 December, annual.

Population: Statistics Canada. CANSIM, table 051–0005, Estimates of population, Canada, provinces and territories, quarterly (persons) – third quarter.

GDP: Statistics Canada. CANSIM, table 384–0001, Gross Domestic Product (GDP), income-based, provincial economic accounts, annual.

ALBERTA
LOCAL GENERAL GOVERNMENT REVENUE AND EXPENDITURES
1995, 2004, and 2006 (Dollars x 1,000)

REVENUE	2004 Revenue	% Change Since 1995	2006 Revenue	2004 Per Capita	% Change Since 1995	2006 Per Capita
Own source revenue						
Real property taxes	1963691	70.60	2384403	609.20	45.29	698.53
Other Taxes, Property Related	917882	69.36	1203339	284.76	44.24	352.53
Other Tax Revenue	118324	151.82	176233	36.71	114.46	51.63
Total Tax Revenue	2999897	72.40	3763975	930.66	46.83	1102.68
Sales of Goods and Services	1854082	74.25	2249006	575.20	48.40	658.86
Other Income from Own Sources	1033114	-2.99	1361259	320.51	-17.38	398.79
Transfers, general and specific						
From Province: Specific Purpose	621349	50.37	1108355	192.76	28.06	324.70
From Province: General	36230	-66.79	46670	11.24	-71.72	13.67
From Province: Total	657579	25.90	1155025	204.00	7.22	338.37
From Federal: Specific	52179	-23.35	103209	16.19	-34.72	30.24
Total Transfers	709758	20.22	1258234	220.19	2.38	368.61
Total Own Source Revenue	5887093	52.16	7374240	1826.37	29.59	2160.34
Total Revenue	6596851	47.93	8632474	2046.55	25.99	2528.95
Total Revenue as % of GDP	3.49		3.66			

EXPENDITURES	2004 Operating	% Change Since 1995	2006 Operating	2004 Capital	% Change Since 1995	2006 Capital	2004 Total	% Change Since 1995	2006 Total	2004 Per Capita	% Change Since 1995	2006 Per Capita
General government services	569086	56.34	691568	82779	21.82	77655	651865	50.91	769223	202.23	28.52	225.35
Protection of persons and property	825838	65.48	956858	70931	92.00	86632	896769	67.31	1043490	278.21	42.49	305.70
Transportation and communication	960906	37.04	1120811	637550	83.06	1019099	1598456	52.31	2139910	495.89	29.72	626.90
Health	103843	103.58	129200	3330	-63.32	5665	107173	78.36	134865	33.25	51.90	39.51
Social services	102734	38.47	116591	352	375.68	2989	103086	38.81	119580	31.98	18.22	35.03
Education	8517		15278	655		6238	9172		21516	2.85		6.30
Resource conservation and industrial development	87530	49.49	113229	43776	9.76	54372	131306	33.39	167601	40.74	13.60	49.10
Environment	462905	62.28	605316	385745	73.70	729325	848650	67.28	1334641	263.28	42.46	390.99
Recreation and culture	722483	75.04	853020	195334	69.80	310816	917817	73.90	1163836	284.74	48.10	340.95
Housing	39067	182.99	62460	23763	741.76	18543	62830	277.86	81003	19.49	221.80	23.73
Regional planning and development	156091	109.39	208201	37847	143.62	77132	193938	115.30	285333	60.17	83.36	83.59
Debt charges	328687	-34.37	320978				328687	-34.37	320978	101.97	-44.11	94.03
Other expenditures												
Total Expenditures	4367687	43.90	5193510	1482062	72.80	2388466	5849749	50.26	7581976	1814.78	27.97	2221.20

Sources: Revenue and Expenditure: Statistics Canada. CANSIM, table 385–0024, Local general government revenue and expenditures, current and capital accounts, year ending 31 December, annual.
Population: Statistics Canada. CANSIM, table 051–0005, Estimates of population, Canada, provinces and territories, quarterly (persons) – third quarter.
GDP: Statistics Canada. CANSIM, table 384–0001, Gross Domestic Product (GDP), income-based, provincial economic accounts, annual.

BRITISH COLUMBIA
LOCAL GENERAL GOVERNMENT REVENUE AND EXPENDITURES
1995, 2004, and 2006 (Dollars x 1,000)

REVENUE	2004 Revenue	% Change Since 1995	2006 Revenue	2004 Per Capita	% Change Since 1995	2006 Per Capita
Own source revenue						
Real property taxes	2472555	37.75	2580616	586.17	24.26	596.34
Other Taxes, Property Related	527694	65.40	629583	125.10	49.20	145.49
Other Tax Revenue	180639	46.43	189635	42.82	32.09	43.82
Total Tax Revenue	3180888	42.17	3399834	754.10	28.25	785.65
Sales of Goods and Services	1720857	55.53	1930396	407.97	40.30	446.08
Other Income from Own Sources	396679	-7.54	489723	94.04	-16.59	113.17
Transfers, general and specific						
From Province: Specific Purpose	177454	-62.09	227262	42.07	-65.80	52.52
From Province: General	113733	-20.52	146797	26.96	-28.30	33.92
From Province: Total	291187	-52.36	374059	69.03	-57.02	86.44
From Federal: Specific	48356	-40.44	76288	11.46	-46.27	17.63
Total Transfers	339543	-50.96	450347	80.50	-55.76	104.07
Total Own Source Revenue	5298424	40.44	5819953	1256.11	26.68	1344.90
Total Revenue	5637967	26.27	6270300	1336.60	13.90	1448.97
Total Revenue as % of GDP	3.58		3.49			

EXPENDITURES	2004 Operating	% Change Since 1995	2006 Operating	2004 Capital	% Change Since 1995	2006 Capital	2004 Total	% Change Since 1995	2006 Total	2004 Per Capita	% Change Since 1995	2006 Per Capita
General government services	531834	67.31	626390	316006	266.01	159016	847840	109.75	785406	201.00	89.21	181.49
Protection of persons and property	1147633	46.18	1282735	57009	0.77	80151	1204642	43.13	1362886	285.59	29.11	314.94
Transportation and communication	616196	76.28	692369	307428	14.56	465700	923624	49.48	1158069	218.97	34.84	267.61
Health	19811	-82.98	28337	25459	-80.16	32125	45270	-81.50	60462	10.73	-83.31	13.97
Social services	7384	-5.33	2184	2377	12.33	2104	9761	-1.56	4288	2.31	-11.20	0.99
Education	842		1390	10			852		1390	0.20		0.32
Resource conservation and industrial development	49185	13.37	57461	6040	-55.31	90172	55225	-2.94	147633	13.09	-12.45	34.12
Environment	674311	22.78	783257	532754	22.33	705424	1207065	22.58	1488681	286.16	10.58	344.01
Recreation and culture	854694	41.00	959880	262703	-6.32	423260	1117397	26.03	1383140	264.90	13.69	319.62
Housing	19367	-7.48	24857	8756	119.94	8776	28123	12.88	33633	6.67	1.83	7.77
Regional planning and development	88547	15.48	116069	18839	2.79	10585	107386	13.03	126654	25.46	1.96	29.27
Debt charges	352150	-29.21	354513	567	19.87	64	352717	-29.16	354577	83.62	-36.10	81.94
Other expenditures	12923	-63.84	11403	44537	422.86	30964	57460	29.84	42367	13.62	17.13	9.79
Total Expenditures	4374877	28.44	4940845	1582485	21.50	2008341	5957362	26.52	6949186	1412.32	14.13	1605.85

Sources: Revenue and Expenditure: Statistics Canada. CANSIM, table 385–0024, Local general government revenue and expenditures, current and capital accounts, year ending 31 December, annual.
Population: Statistics Canada. CANSIM, table 051–0005, Estimates of population, Canada, provinces and territories, quarterly (persons) – third quarter.
GDP: Statistics Canada. CANSIM, table 384–0001, Gross Domestic Product (GDP), income-based, provincial economic accounts, annual.

MANITOBA
LOCAL GENERAL GOVERNMENT REVENUE AND EXPENDITURES
1995, 2004, and 2006 (Dollars x 1,000)

REVENUE	2004 Revenue	% Change Since 1995	2006 Revenue	2004 Per Capita	% Change Since 1995	2006 Per Capita
Own source revenue						
Real property taxes	478698	22.70	511458	408.27	18.20	433.99
Other Taxes, Property Related	149258	-0.75	151621	127.30	-4.39	128.66
Other Tax Revenue	36581	56.18	40670	31.20	50.46	34.51
Total Tax Revenue	664537	17.83	703749	566.76	13.52	597.16
Sales of Goods and Services	356442	40.87	400493	304.00	35.71	339.84
Other Income from Own Sources	90102	-20.33	100369	76.85	-23.25	85.17
Transfers, general and specific						
From Province: Specific Purpose	105563	-61.14	125856	90.03	-62.56	106.79
From Province: General	193524	146.32	200273	165.05	137.30	169.94
From Province: Total	299087	-14.59	326129	255.08	-17.72	276.73
From Federal: Specific	16524	-57.17	81347	14.09	-58.74	69.03
Total Transfers	315611	-18.82	407476	269.18	-21.79	345.76
Total Own Source Revenue	1111081	19.46	1204611	947.61	15.08	1022.16
Total Revenue	1426692	8.18	1612087	1216.78	4.21	1367.92
Total Revenue as % of GDP	3.58		3.60			

EXPENDITURES	2004 Operating	% Change Since 1995	2006 Operating	2004 Capital	% Change Since 1995	2006 Capital	2004 Total	% Change Since 1995	2006 Total	2004 Per Capita	% Change Since 1995	2006 Per Capita
General government services	191498	60.35	203801	25654	25.37	13057	217152	55.23	216858	185.20	49.54	184.01
Protection of persons and property	274623	38.99	304273	9310	14.18	6920	283933	38.01	311193	242.16	32.95	264.06
Transportation and communication	235542	30.77	258285	95749	-42.29	134421	331291	-4.26	392706	282.55	-7.77	333.23
Health	31898	32.03	13556	634	-70.25	252	32532	23.74	13808	27.75	19.20	11.72
Social services	3727	-97.33	2968			14	3727	-97.33	2982	3.18	-97.43	2.53
Education			12						12	0.01		0.01
Resource conservation and industrial development	32464	28.56	36398	2257	-33.09	2658	34721	21.30	39056	29.61	16.85	33.14
Environment	174254	36.55	187658	48964	-43.03	110158	223218	4.52	297816	190.38	0.69	252.71
Recreation and culture	126353	0.91	125948	21077	21.76	23903	147430	3.44	149851	125.74	-0.35	127.15
Housing	2892	99.17	2673	1999	-50.59	1673	4891	-11.04	4346	4.17	-14.30	3.69
Regional planning and development	21907	106.01	33802	1942	476.26	776	23849	117.38	34578	20.34	109.42	29.34
Debt charges	79294	-34.72	67688	1008	1300.00	10	80302	-33.93	67698	68.49	-36.35	57.44
Other expenditures	643	1268.09	37	1012	965.26	152	1655	1065.49	189	1.41	1022.78	0.16
Total Expenditures	1175107	9.56	1237099	209606	-31.91	293994	1384713	0.32	1531093	1180.98	-3.36	1299.20

Sources: Revenue and Expenditure: Statistics Canada. CANSIM, table 385–0024, Local general government revenue and expenditures, current and capital accounts, year ending 31 December, annual.
Population: Statistics Canada. CANSIM, table 051–0005, Estimates of population, Canada, provinces and territories, quarterly (persons) – third quarter.
GDP: Statistics Canada. CANSIM, table 384–0001, Gross Domestic Product (GDP), income-based, provincial economic accounts, annual.

NEW BRUNSWICK
LOCAL GENERAL GOVERNMENT REVENUE AND EXPENDITURES
1995, 2004, and 2006 (Dollars x 1,000)

REVENUE	2004 Revenue	% Change Since 1995	2006 Revenue	2004 Per Capita	% Change Since 1995	2006 Per Capita
Own source revenue						
Real property taxes	356757	61.12	405426	474.29	60.91	541.70
Other Taxes, Property Related	44784	-6.93	54757	59.54	-7.06	73.16
Other Tax Revenue	4336	69.77	5915	5.76	69.55	7.90
Total Tax Revenue	405877	49.17	466098	539.59	48.97	622.76
Sales of Goods and Services	197350	64.60	216897	262.37	64.39	289.80
Other Income from Own Sources	6992	-25.99	8931	9.30	-26.08	11.93
Transfers, general and specific						
From Province: Specific Purpose	33386	-29.73	37816	44.39	-29.83	50.53
From Province: General	65045	-32.87	71416	86.47	-32.96	95.42
From Province: Total	98431	-31.84	109232	130.86	-31.93	145.95
From Federal: Specific	8831	-37.17	24169	11.74	-37.25	32.29
Total Transfers	107262	-32.31	133401	142.60	-32.40	178.24
Total Own Source Revenue	610219	52.01	691926	811.26	51.81	924.49
Total Revenue	717481	28.14	825327	953.85	27.98	1102.73
Total Revenue as % of GDP	3.05		3.27			

EXPENDITURES	2004 Operating	% Change Since 1995	2006 Operating	2004 Capital	% Change Since 1995	2006 Capital	2004 Total	% Change Since 1995	2006 Total	2004 Per Capita	% Change Since 1995	2006 Per Capita
General government services	61818	37.25	76805	6247	8817	8088	68065	37.88	84893	90.49	37.70	113.43
Protection of persons and property	149039	26.69	166838	10819	3842	4842	159858	27.49	171680	212.52	27.33	229.38
Transportation and communication	96104	18.00	111098	55064	39011	83037	151168	23.98	194135	200.97	23.81	259.39
Health	1986	25.70	2466	3	70	31	1989	-0.60	2497	2.64	-0.73	3.34
Social services												
Education	26		27	90			116		27	0.15		0.04
Resource conservation and industrial development	16105	70.60	17748	1954	2045	5239	18059	69.65	22987	24.01	69.43	30.71
Environment	129749	79.58	145118	88056	55274	69448	217805	61.73	214566	289.56	61.52	286.68
Recreation and culture	73512	27.94	85346	14774	10668	33200	88286	12.77	118546	117.37	12.62	158.39
Housing	880	29.99	989	963	73	865	1843	68.16	1854	2.45	67.94	2.48
Regional planning and development	14172	79.64	18012	6952	5368	1295	21124	37.22	19307	28.08	37.04	25.80
Debt charges	29508	-12.66	32210	25	1		29533	-12.88	32210	39.26	-12.99	43.04
Other expenditures	233	23200.00	929	1370	1583	1744	1603	78.71	2673	2.13	78.48	3.57
Total Expenditures	573132	34.16	657586	186317	126752	207789	759449	32.40	865375	1009.65	32.23	1156.24

Sources: Revenue and Expenditure: Statistics Canada. CANSIM, table 385–0024, Local general government revenue and expenditures, current and capital accounts, year ending 31 December, annual.
Population: Statistics Canada. CANSIM, table 051–0005, Estimates of population, Canada, provinces and territories, quarterly (persons) – third quarter.
GDP: Statistics Canada. CANSIM, table 384–0001, Gross Domestic Product (GDP), income-based, provincial economic accounts, annual.

NEWFOUNDLAND AND LABRADOR
LOCAL GENERAL GOVERNMENT REVENUE AND EXPENDITURES
1995, 2004, and 2006 (Dollars x 1,000)

REVENUE	2004	% Change	2006	2004	% Change	2006
	Revenue	Since 1995	Revenue	Per Capita	Since 1995	Per Capita
Own source revenue						
Real property taxes	167932	37.85	180627	325.15	50.82	354.90
Other Taxes, Property Related	83041	37.94	84793	160.78	50.92	166.60
Other Tax Revenue	4984	-21.08	5268	9.65	-13.65	10.35
Total Tax Revenue	255957	35.90	270688	495.58	48.69	531.85
Sales of Goods and Services	80146	51.63	91335	155.18	65.90	179.46
Other Income from Own Sources	9767	14.76	9888	18.91	25.55	19.43
Transfers, general and specific						
From Province: Specific Purpose	77830	-4.24	75306	150.69	4.77	147.96
From Province: General	22492	-48.68	19497	43.55	-43.85	38.31
From Province: Total	100322	-19.81	94803	194.24	-12.26	186.27
From Federal: Specific	7815	63.46	3603	15.13	78.84	7.08
Total Transfers	108137	-16.74	98406	209.37	-8.91	193.35
Total Own Source Revenue	345870	38.51	371911	669.66	51.54	730.73
Total Revenue	454007	19.61	470317	879.04	30.86	924.08
Total Revenue as % of GDP	2.33		1.89			

EXPENDITURES	2004 Operating	% Change Since 1995	2006 Operating	2004 Capital	% Change Since 1995	2006 Capital	2004 Total	% Change Since 1995	2006 Total	2004 Per Capita	% Change Since 1995	2006 Per Capita
General government services	72335	56.21	81714	5158	249.69	12898	77493	62.18	94612	150.04	77.44	185.89
Protection of persons and property	21297	-29.78	23061	3608	221.28	170	24905	-20.82	23231	48.22	-13.37	45.64
Transportation and communication	74115	9.15	79931	38919	73.15	45540	113034	25.06	125471	218.85	36.83	246.53
Health	334	626.09	80				334	626.09	80	0.65	694.39	0.16
Social services	940	298.31	1006				940	298.31	1006	1.82	335.77	1.98
Education	151		151				151		151	0.29		0.30
Resource conservation and industrial development	3999	172.97	4208	1375		1014	5374	266.83	5222	10.40	301.33	10.26
Environment	44061	33.29	48810	51489	27.63	65139	95550	30.18	113949	185.00	42.43	223.89
Recreation and culture	45057	27.44	50735	8349	-12.89	9098	53406	18.84	59833	103.40	30.02	117.56
Housing	2233	31.28	2410			22	2233	31.28	2432	4.32	43.62	4.78
Regional planning and development	3847	39.74	10158	415	-56.59	84	4262	14.91	10242	8.25	25.72	20.12
Debt charges	38392	-46.29	32725				38392	-46.29	32725	74.33	-41.24	64.30
Other expenditures						59			59			0.12
Total Expenditures	306761	5.49	334989	109313	43.91	134024	416074	13.45	469013	805.59	24.12	921.52

Sources: Revenue and Expenditure: Statistics Canada. CANSIM, table 385–0024, Local general government revenue and expenditures, current and capital accounts, year ending 31 December, annual.
Population: Statistics Canada. CANSIM, table 051–0005, Estimates of population, Canada, provinces and territories, quarterly (persons) – third quarter.
GDP: Statistics Canada. CANSIM, table 384–0001, Gross Domestic Product (GDP), income-based, provincial economic accounts, annual.

NOVA SCOTIA
LOCAL GENERAL GOVERNMENT REVENUE AND EXPENDITURES
1995, 2004, and 2006 (Dollars x 1,000)

REVENUE	2004 Revenue	% Change Since 1995	2006 Revenue	2004 Per Capita	% Change Since 1995	2006 Per Capita
Own source revenue						
Real property taxes	647539	40.03	739237	689.86	38.76	791.33
Other Taxes, Property Related	188838	43.42	211062	201.18	42.12	225.93
Other Tax Revenue	7937	74.32	8693	8.46	72.74	9.31
Total Tax Revenue	844314	41.04	958992	899.50	39.76	1026.57
Sales of Goods and Services	212854	106.52	241318	226.77	104.64	258.32
Other Income from Own Sources	30912	-21.83	36943	32.93	-22.54	39.55
Transfers, general and specific						
From Province: Specific Purpose	29741	-89.04	31649	31.68	-89.14	33.88
From Province: General	36809	77.39	34764	39.21	75.78	37.21
From Province: Total	66550	-77.22	66413	70.90	-77.43	71.09
From Federal: Specific	12796	-48.92	39484	13.63	-49.39	42.27
Total Transfers	79346	-74.99	105897	84.53	-75.21	113.36
Total Own Source Revenue	1088080	46.79	1237253	1159.20	45.45	1324.44
Total Revenue	1167426	10.30	1343150	1243.73	9.29	1437.80
Total Revenue as % of GDP	3.91		4.20			

EXPENDITURES	2004 Operating	% Change Since 1995	2006 Operating	2004 Capital	% Change Since 1995	2006 Capital	2004 Total	% Change Since 1995	2006 Total	2004 Per Capita	% Change Since 1995	2006 Per Capita
General government services	122979	66.16	133849	27383	1111.10	8934	150362	97.14	142783	160.19	95.34	152.84
Protection of persons and property	222013	55.49	246471	10546	-25.09	15022	232559	48.26	261493	247.76	46.91	279.92
Transportation and communication	109180	35.89	126235	37523	6.02	72109	146703	26.75	198344	156.29	25.60	212.32
Health	1400	46.60	5174	186	-82.92	223	1586	-22.41	5397	1.69	-23.11	5.78
Social services	9612	-96.53	10385				9612	-96.53	10385	10.24	-96.56	11.12
Education	171013	23.37	185206	434			171447	23.69	185206	182.65	22.56	198.26
Resource conservation and industrial development	10510	109.95	17615	6334	276.58	1182	16844	151.85	18797	17.94	149.56	20.12
Environment	151220	114.16	216846	69306	-17.13	214856	220526	42.97	431702	234.94	41.67	462.12
Recreation and culture	96491	39.24	112198	27388	109.74	34409	123879	50.42	146607	131.98	49.05	156.94
Housing	2535	-57.89	3545			3545	2535	-85.15	3545	2.70	-85.28	3.79
Regional planning and development	18339	79.46	18424	6844	19454.29	129	25183	145.59	18553	26.83	143.36	19.86
Debt charges	37727	9.06	36188				37727	9.06	36188	40.19	8.06	38.74
Other expenditures	6312	257.42	6109 ..			25	6312	4.37	6134	6.72	3.41	6.57
Total Expenditures	959331	5.32	1118245	185944	11.62	346889	1145275	6.29	1465134	1220.13	5.32	1568.38

Sources: Revenue and Expenditure: Statistics Canada. CANSIM, table 385–0024, Local general government revenue and expenditures, current and capital accounts, year ending 31 December, annual.
Population: Statistics Canada. CANSIM, table 051–0005, Estimates of population, Canada, provinces and territories, quarterly (persons) – third quarter.
GDP: Statistics Canada. CANSIM, table 384–0001, Gross Domestic Product (GDP), income-based, provincial economic accounts, annual.

ONTARIO
LOCAL GENERAL GOVERNMENT REVENUE AND EXPENDITURES
1995, 2004, and 2006 (Dollars x 1,000)

REVENUE	2004 Revenue	% Change Since 1995	2006 Revenue	2004 Per Capita	% Change Since 1995	2006 Per Capita
Own source revenue						
Real property taxes	11561715	114.89	12898001	927.50	89.51	1013.85
Other Taxes, Property Related	1574503	-8.78	1572116	126.31	-19.55	123.58
Other Tax Revenue	329136	115.78	320501	26.40	90.30	25.19
Total Tax Revenue	13465354	85.50	14790618	1080.22	63.60	1162.62
Sales of Goods and Services	5585492	62.80	6522882	448.08	43.58	512.73
Other Income from Own Sources	1511803	64.98	1791834	121.28	45.50	140.85
Transfers, general and specific						
From Province: Specific Purpose	4564424	-21.12	6013957	366.17	-30.44	472.73
From Province: General	741152	10.66	857390	59.46	-2.41	67.40
From Province: Total	5305576	-17.83	6871347	425.62	-27.53	540.12
From Federal: Specific	540169	77.15	958915	43.33	56.23	75.38
Total Transfers	5845745	-13.54	7830262	468.96	-23.75	615.50
Total Own Source Revenue	20562649	77.17	23105334	1649.58	56.25	1816.20
Total Revenue	26408394	43.78	30935596	2118.54	26.80	2431.70
Total Revenue as % of GDP	5.10		5.56			

EXPENDITURES	2004 Operating	% Change Since 1995	2006 Operating	2004 Capital	% Change Since 1995	2006 Capital	2004 Total	% Change Since 1995	2006 Total	2004 Per Capita	% Change Since 1995	2006 Per Capita
General government services	1757712	31.62	1930766	377058	113.67	410933	2134770	41.20	2341699	171.26	24.53	184.07
Protection of persons and property	3909831	68.90	4322437	241325	36.49	301944	4151156	66.60	4624381	333.01	46.93	363.50
Transportation and communication	2445886	13.46	2497591	1912805	54.13	2424707	4358691	28.32	4922298	349.66	13.17	386.92
Health	1197519	184.32	1359799	68204	114.92	69850	1265723	179.46	1429649	101.54	146.46	112.38
Social services	5213963	15.36	5777959	316284	309.70	144119	5530247	20.30	5922078	443.65	6.10	465.51
Education	8472		10967	7625		529	16097		11496	1.29		0.90
Resource conservation and industrial development	318229	56.23	331930	175613	26.31	178315	493842	44.09	510245	39.62	27.08	40.11
Environment	2181358	53.36	2541709	1801998	73.83	2131925	3983356	61.99	4673634	319.55	42.86	367.37
Recreation and culture	1836406	36.88	2127836	688901	37.80	804312	2525307	37.13	2932148	202.59	20.94	230.48
Housing	1330851	730.11	1460881	167792	198.83	284015	1498643	592.30	1744896	120.22	510.56	137.16
Regional planning and development	212421	28.89	241193	48663	-14.91	50087	261084	17.61	291280	20.94	3.72	22.90
Debt charges	513929	-19.25	556750	7788	-61.75	9703	521717	-20.57	566453	41.85	-29.95	44.53
Other expenditures	12979	-86.90		28743	-74.61	18200	41722	-80.34	18200	3.35	-82.66	1.43
Total Expenditures	20939556	41.72	23159818	5842799	61.15	6828639	26782355	45.55	29988457	2148.54	28.36	2357.25

Sources: Revenue and Expenditure: Statistics Canada. CANSIM, table 385–0024, Local general government revenue and expenditures, current and capital accounts, year ending 31 December, annual.

Population: Statistics Canada. CANSIM, table 051–0005, Estimates of population, Canada, provinces and territories, quarterly (persons) – third quarter.

GDP: Statistics Canada. CANSIM, table 384–0001, Gross Domestic Product (GDP), income-based, provincial economic accounts, annual.

PRINCE EDWARD ISLAND
LOCAL GENERAL GOVERNMENT REVENUE AND EXPENDITURES

1995, 2004, and 2006 (Dollars x 1,000)

REVENUE	2004 Revenue	% Change Since 1995	2006 Revenue	2004 Per Capita	% Change Since 1995	2006 Per Capita
Own source revenue						
Real property taxes	44392	43.29	50500	322.10	40.32	364.37
Other Taxes, Property Related	298	108.39	342	2.16	104.07	2.47
Other Tax Revenue	510	117.95	822	3.70	113.43	5.93
Total Tax Revenue	45200	44.15	51664	327.96	41.16	372.77
Sales of Goods and Services	16685	22.85	17015	121.06	20.30	122.77
Other Income from Own Sources	1257	-45.82	1161	9.12	-46.94	8.38
Transfers, general and specific						
From Province: Specific Purpose	3885	60.67	15328	28.19	57.34	110.59
From Province: General	1834	-17.50	1827	13.31	-19.21	13.18
From Province: Total	5719	23.23	17155	41.50	20.68	123.78
From Federal: Specific	1653	2.73	7796	11.99	0.61	56.25
Total Transfers	7372	17.95	24951	53.49	15.51	180.03
Total Own Source Revenue	63142	33.61	69840	458.14	30.84	503.91
Total Revenue	70514	31.78	94791	511.63	29.05	683.94
Total Revenue as % of GDP	1.75		2.19			

EXPENDITURES	2004 Operating	% Change Since 1995	2006 Operating	2004 Capital	% Change Since 1995	2006 Capital	2004 Total	% Change Since 1995	2006 Total	2004 Per Capita	% Change Since 1995	2006 Per Capita
General government services	9268	67.56	10869	1696	319.80	1034	10964	84.73	11903	79.55	80.91	85.88
Protection of persons and property	14439	66.31	14066	663	68.27	464	15102	66.39	14530	109.58	62.95	104.84
Transportation and communication	10561	56.09	12340	7954	-9.88	8257	18515	18.75	20597	134.34	16.29	148.61
Health	210	1300.00	210				210	1300.00	210	1.52	1271.00	1.52
Social services	41	4000.00	107				41	4000.00	107	0.30	3915.07	0.77
Education	10					395	10		395	0.07		2.85
Resource conservation and industrial development	1004	281.75	1059			154	1004	281.75	1213	7.28	273.84	8.75
Environment	6328	24.47	8598	9932	70.86	21091	16260	49.22	29689	117.98	46.12	214.21
Recreation and culture	9347	77.77	9906	1376	326.01	17991	10723	92.13	27897	77.80	88.15	201.28
Housing	68	871.43	56			19	68	871.43	75	0.49	851.31	0.54
Regional planning and development	2143	289.64	2369	1438		292	3581	551.09	2661	25.98	537.60	19.20
Debt charges	1072	-53.83	1589	9	-88.46	9	1081	-54.96	1598	7.84	-55.89	11.53
Other expenditures	10						10	-96.55		0.07	-96.62	
Total Expenditures	54501	58.07	61169	23068	43.03	49706	77569	53.28	110875	562.82	50.10	799.99

Sources: Revenue and Expenditure: Statistics Canada. CANSIM, table 385–0024, Local general government revenue and expenditures, current and capital accounts, year ending 31 December, annual.
Population: Statistics Canada. CANSIM, table 051–0005, Estimates of population, Canada, provinces and territories, quarterly (persons) – third quarter.
GDP: Statistics Canada. CANSIM, table 384–0001, Gross Domestic Product (GDP), income-based, provincial economic accounts, annual.

QUEBEC
LOCAL GENERAL GOVERNMENT REVENUE AND EXPENDITURES
1995, 2004, and 2006 (Dollars x 1,000)

REVENUE	2004 Revenue	% Change Since 1995	2006 Revenue	2004 Per Capita	% Change Since 1995	2006 Per Capita
Own source revenue						
Real property taxes	5645121	43.15	6303381	746.05	36.76	821.92
Other Taxes, Property Related	1641350	-24.83	1503934	216.92	-28.18	196.10
Other Tax Revenue	49908	135.83	41947	6.60	125.30	5.47
Total Tax Revenue	7336379	19.33	7849262	969.56	14.00	1023.49
Sales of Goods and Services	1992662	35.28	2116583	263.35	29.24	275.99
Other Income from Own Sources	432721	-2.07	464763	57.19	-6.44	60.60
Transfers, general and specific						
From Province: Specific Purpose	1150900	1.28	1215173	152.10	-3.24	158.45
From Province: General	315029	166.30	304377	41.63	154.42	39.69
From Province: Total	1465929	16.84	1519550	193.73	11.63	198.14
From Federal: Specific	18847	42.22	18580	2.49	35.87	2.42
Total Transfers	1484776	17.11	1538130	196.23	11.88	200.56
Total Own Source Revenue	9761762	21.07	10430608	1290.10	15.67	1360.08
Total Revenue	11246538	20.53	11968738	1486.32	15.15	1560.64
Total Revenue as % of GDP	4.28		4.21			

EXPENDITURES	2004 Operating	% Change Since 1995	2006 Operating	2004 Capital	% Change Since 1995	2006 Capital	2004 Total	% Change Since 1995	2006 Total	2004 Per Capita	% Change Since 1995	2006 Per Capita
General government services	1330740	35.21	1577886	144260	-18.04	163448	1475000	27.13	1741334	194.93	21.46	227.06
Protection of persons and property	1888062	32.73	2093682	128899	89.94	196206	2016961	35.33	2289888	266.56	29.29	298.59
Transportation and communication	1815859	13.21	2018506	902359	21.64	939789	2718218	15.88	2958295	359.23	10.71	385.74
Health	3698	-38.38		558	-90.31	7976	4256	-63.82	7976	0.56	-65.43	1.04
Social services	104179	45.80	101998	1	-98.00	2	104180	45.70	102000	13.77	39.20	13.30
Education	4646	-10.76	5113	6988	53.55	3294	11634	19.24	8407	1.54	13.92	1.10
Resource conservation and industrial development	263656	111.02	269068	100704	55.38	167254	364360	92.02	436322	48.15	83.45	56.89
Environment	1126151	39.65	1336068	774239	-4.26	908814	1900390	17.66	2244882	251.15	12.41	292.72
Recreation and culture	1180976	37.21	1303460	351086	87.59	379790	1532062	46.20	1683250	202.47	39.68	219.48
Housing	317894	24.27	424014	68450	121.36	91395	386344	34.74	515409	51.06	28.73	67.21
Regional planning and development	305318	88.80	347934	11150	-80.67	8601	316468	44.24	356535	41.82	37.81	46.49
Debt charges	832487	-34.24	851503				832487	-34.24	851503	110.02	-37.17	111.03
Other expenditures			..			2	..		2			
Total Expenditures	9173666	21.18	10329232	2488694	16.01	2866571	11662360	20.04	13195803	1541.28	14.68	1720.65

Sources: Revenue and Expenditure: Statistics Canada. CANSIM, table 385–0024, Local general government revenue and expenditures, current and capital accounts, year ending 31 December, annual.

Population: Statistics Canada. CANSIM, table 051–0005, Estimates of population, Canada, provinces and territories, quarterly (persons) – third quarter.

GDP: Statistics Canada. CANSIM, table 384–0001, Gross Domestic Product (GDP), income-based, provincial economic accounts, annual.

SASKATCHEWAN
LOCAL GENERAL GOVERNMENT REVENUE AND EXPENDITURES
1995, 2004, and 2006 (Dollars x 1,000)

REVENUE	2004 Revenue	% Change Since 1995	2006 Revenue	2004 Per Capita	% Change Since 1995	2006 Per Capita
Own source revenue						
Real property taxes	528800	45.92	590776	531.66	48.95	599.25
Other Taxes, Property Related	100843	7.71	113970	101.39	9.95	115.60
Other Tax Revenue	80580	116.89	87857	81.02	121.39	89.12
Total Tax Revenue	710223	44.01	792603	714.06	47.00	803.97
Sales of Goods and Services	316067	51.09	331085	317.77	54.22	335.83
Other Income from Own Sources	74074	-11.85	75984	74.47	-10.02	77.07
Transfers, general and specific						
From Province: Specific Purpose	45909	-16.55	63588	46.16	-14.82	64.50
From Province: General	74522	26.46	96532	74.92	29.09	97.92
From Province: Total	120431	5.69	160120	121.08	7.89	162.42
From Federal: Specific	15073	139.63	41729	15.15	144.61	42.33
Total Transfers	135504	12.70	201849	136.24	15.04	204.74
Total Own Source Revenue	1100364	39.92	1199672	1106.31	42.83	1216.88
Total Revenue	1235868	36.31	1401521	1242.54	39.14	1421.62
Total Revenue as % of GDP	3.09		3.11			

EXPENDITURES	2004 Operating	% Change Since 1995	2006 Operating	2004 Capital	% Change Since 1995	2006 Capital	2004 Total	% Change Since 1995	2006 Total	2004 Per Capita	% Change Since 1995	2006 Per Capita
General government services	152928	29.80	148072	18212	-24.10	19437	171140	20.68	167509	172.06	23.19	169.91
Protection of persons and property	213897	50.41	228293	13005	86.10	9314	226902	52.08	237607	228.13	55.24	241.02
Transportation and communication	277164	53.14	312850	106173	10.41	191069	383337	38.31	503919	385.41	41.19	511.15
Health	5648	3.88	6924	2699	-39.71	3149	8347	-15.81	10073	8.39	-14.06	10.22
Social services	10074	32.45	10474	65	-37.50	32	10139	31.50	10506	10.19	34.24	10.66
Education	474		335			50	474		385	0.48		0.39
Resource conservation and industrial development	26136	-61.22	26979	4762	17.15	6449	30898	-56.76	33428	31.06	-55.86	33.91
Environment	148692	38.56	144605	74665	-4.90	74840	223357	20.20	219445	224.56	22.69	222.59
Recreation and culture	142993	33.86	143379	46410	150.97	44034	189403	51.14	187413	190.43	54.28	190.10
Housing	1183	111.25	1528	125	2400.00	282	1308	131.50	1810	1.32	136.31	1.84
Regional planning and development	19794	73.69	21641	22912	172.83	17515	42706	115.75	39156	42.94	120.23	39.72
Debt charges	17909	-37.49	13862	160	-24.88		18069	-37.40	13862	18.17	-36.10	14.06
Other expenditures												
Total Expenditures	1016892	30.94	1058942	289188	19.77	366171	1306080	28.29	1425113	1313.13	30.96	1445.55

Sources: Revenue and Expenditure: Statistics Canada. CANSIM, table 385–0024, Local general government revenue and expenditures, current and capital accounts, year ending 31 December, annual.

Population: Statistics Canada. CANSIM, table 051–0005, Estimates of population, Canada, provinces and territories, quarterly (persons) – third quarter.

GDP: Statistics Canada. CANSIM, table 384–0001, Gross Domestic Product (GDP), income-based, provincial economic accounts, annual.

Index

The Institute of Public Administration of Canada Series in Public Management and Governance